Generative Phonology
Description and Theory

Generative Phonology
Description and Theory

MICHAEL KENSTOWICZ
CHARLES KISSEBERTH
Department of Linguistics
University of Illinois
Urbana, Illinois

ACADEMIC PRESS, INC.
Harcourt Brace Jovanovich, Publishers
San Diego   New York   Berkeley   Boston
London   Sydney   Tokyo   Toronto

ACADEMIC PRESS, INC.
1250 Sixth Avenue, San Diego, California 92101

United Kingdom Edition published by
ACADEMIC PRESS, INC. (LONDON) LTD.
24/28 Oval Road, London NW1 7DX

Library of Congress Cataloging in Publication Data

Kenstowicz, Michael J
  Generative phonology.

  Bibliography: p.
  1. Grammar, Comparative and general--Phonology.
  2. Generative grammar. I. Kisseberth, Charles W.,
  joint author. II. Title.
  P217.K38   414   79-319
  ISBN 0-12-405160-X (cloth)
  ISBN 0-12-405161-8 (paperback)

PRINTED IN THE UNITED STATES OF AMERICA

89   9 8 7 6 5 4

To Our Students

Contents

Preface

Our goal in writing this book has been to provide a thorough and comprehensive introduction to generative phonology. It is our hope that by carefully reading the text and working through the problems at the end of each chapter, the student will acquire a basic understanding of the fundamental concepts of generative phonology and an ability to apply these concepts in further study of phonological structure. We want the student not only to be able to read and understand articles and books written within the generative framework, but also to be aware of the many unresolved questions confronting the phonologist and perhaps to join in answering some of these questions.

Our approach differs from previous treatments of the subject in several respects. First, it places considerable emphasis on language description and analysis, rather than restricting itself entirely to the underlying theory. We intend the reader not only to acquire a knowledge of the basic structure of the generative theory of phonology, but also to have a good idea of what description within that theory will look like and how that description is to be justified. Toward this end, a goodly portion of the book is devoted to the presentation of sample analyses of phonological structure from a diverse set of languages. The discussion of these analyses illustrates most of the basic principles and techniques of phonological description and the various modes of argumentation utilized to support a given analysis.

Our approach also departs from previous treatments in that we have tried to explicate the theory of generative phonology "from the bottom up" rather than "from the top down." That is, we begin, in the first six chapters, by introducing just a few key theoretical concepts, each thoroughly motivated and illustrated. Later chapters then develop and elaborate these key concepts, gradually fleshing out the theoretical model. The inclusion of each additional piece of apparatus is carefully motivated. This approach differs from previous treatments that have tended to take the entire theory as a given and then either apply it to the description of a given language or contrast it with other theoretical approaches.

The book is organized into ten chapters. The first situates phonology in the overall model of generative grammar and introduces enough phonetics to make the material in later chapters comprehensible to readers having little background in phonetics. Chapter 2 introduces the fundamental concept of a phonological rule which relates an underlying representation to a phonetic representation. In Chapter 3 it is shown how this concept is applied to the analysis of morphophonemic alternation. Chapter 4 presents phonological sketches of four diverse languages in terms of rules relating underlying and phonetic representations. In these early chapters notation and formalism are kept to a minimum, the emphasis instead being on the careful motivation of each step in the analysis. Chapter 5 summarizes and further illustrates the major corpus-internal principles and techniques of phonological analysis. We then go on to survey some of the kinds of corpus-external evidence linguists have appealed to in support of the psychological reality of phonological descriptions.

Chapter 6 initiates the theoretical discussion. We first try to clarify what is being claimed by the idea that phonetic representations are derived from more abstract underlying representations by contrasting this view with the morpheme-alternant approach of structural linguistics. We then go on to survey various degrees of abstractness and conclude with a discussion of two proposals to limit the divergence between underlying and phonetic representation—Kiparsky's alternation condition and Hooper's true generalization condition. Chapter 7 deals with some of the issues revolving around the representation of sounds. The notion of a feature system is motivated, followed by a survey of the most commonly used features. We then proceed to a brief consideration of the role of the syllable in phonology and conclude with a discussion of some of the questions involved in the representation of tone. Chapter 8 examines various hypotheses as to how phonological rules apply to convert the underlying representation to the phonetic representation. The kinds of considerations that motivate rule-ordering statements are emphasized. Chapter 9 surveys the major notational devices commonly employed in the formulation of phonological rules. Finally, in Chapter 10 we survey the role of syntactic and lexical information in controlling the application of phonological rules.

The exercises at the end of the chapters all contain bona fide data. In a few cases we were forced to construct forms in order to fill out a paradigm; all such words follow the regular patterns of alternation exhibited by data amply attested in the sources cited. We have marked these nonattested forms by an asterisk. The data in the exercises have been organized in such a way as to suggest a particular analysis. Of course, such an analysis may require modification in the light of a full description of the language. Readers wishing to draw theoretical conclusions from such data are urged to consult the published sources.

Our transcriptions in this book have for the most part followed those utilized in the original sources. For the better-known European languages we have usually transcribed words in the original orthography or the customarily accepted transliteration when such a transcription does not obscure the point under discussion. In a few cases our transcriptions have vacillated between two representations for the same sound (e.g., the Chimwi:ni dentals have been distinguished from alveolars sometimes by an underdot and sometimes by an underbar), but such inconsistencies should not lead to any confusion.

Finally, we wish to point out here that the arguments in Chapter 7 purporting to show that the syllable is the domain of emphasis in Cairo Arabic now appear to us to be questionable. Published sources indicate that the lateral in a pair of words such as *ṭawiil* versus *ṭawiil-a* alternates between emphatic and plain. We have consulted several speakers of this dialect of Arabic and have found that none of them make such a distinction between emphatic and plain *l*. For these speakers the second word is pronounced *ṭawiil-a*. Preliminary work by one of the authors suggests that for these speakers the domain of emphasis is the entire word, with some vacillation in the treatment of inflectional affixes. While these data indicate that the syllable is not the domain of emphasis in Cairo Arabic, we nevertheless believe that the claim that the syllable may function as the domain of realization of a phonetic feature can be supported by data from other languages.

Acknowledgments

In the writing of this book we have profited immensely from the comments of numerous students who have read various versions of the manuscript over a number of years. We take this opportunity to thank them all. In addition, we wish to acknowledge the generous help of the following persons in providing us with material on their native languages, various aspects of which are discussed in this book: Mohammad Abasheikh (Chimwi:ni), S.A.C. Waane (Makua), Geoffrey Rugege (Kinyarwanda), Nicola Talhami (Palestinian Arabic), Samir Mahmoud and Wafaa Wahba (Egyptian Arabic). Besides providing some data on Mandarin Chinese, our colleague C.-C. Cheng also collaborated with one of the authors in the investigation of Makua which is reported on in Chapter 4. We also want to thank the following people for assistance in constructing some of the exercises: Farid Onn (Tagalog), Yael Ziv and Ester Bentur (Hebrew), Jürgen Döllein (Okpe), David Odden (Shona), Laurie Reynolds (Catalan), Paula Rohrbach (Mandarin Chinese). Finally, we acknowledge the aid of the University of Illinois Research Board over a number of years for financial support of some of the research reported in this book.

1

Preliminaries

The Setting of Phonology within Generative Grammar

This book seeks to introduce the student to the nature of phonological structure by examining, with varying degrees of thoroughness, aspects of the phonological structure of a number of diverse languages. Our subject matter might be said to be the sounds employed in the languages of the world—not the sounds **as** sounds, but as reflections of an underlying system or pattern. For the main theme of this book, and the general theory of language it espouses, is that the noises which people make when they speak a language are the consequences of a complex set of abstract principles or rules.

The study of the full range of vocal sounds that human beings are capable of making is **phonetics**. The study of the sounds human beings employ when speaking a language is **linguistic phonetics**. **Phonology** is the study of the system underlying the selection and use of sounds in the languages of the world. Although a number of distinct approaches to the study of phonology have been developed during the present century, we will approach the study of sound systems from the standpoint of one

1

particular theory—**generative phonology**. In the course of this book we shall reconstruct the theory of generative phonology on the basis of concrete linguistic data, rather than to characterize it in terms of similarities to, and differences from, other theories.

Generative phonology is a subfield of the general theory of language known as **generative grammar**. The ultimate goal of linguists working within this framework is to answer the question: What is the nature of language? That is, What are the inherent properties of language? What are the accidental properties? For example, it is an accidental property of language that in English the verb *be* has the phonological shape *is* in *John is likely to arrive soon*, but the shape *are* in *The boys are likely to arrive soon*. It is probably not accidental, however, that it is the verbal word *be* that varies its shape according to the nature (singular versus plural) of the subject of sentences rather than, say, the adverb *soon*. One would guess that it is an inherent property of language that verbs are more likely to change their form in agreement with a subject than are adverbs.

In addition to distinguishing what is inherent from what is accidental (and thus elucidating the nature of language), generative grammar is also naturally interested in answering the question: What is English? (or French? or Turkish?) This question is generally gotten at through another question: Assuming that people have a native, or nativelike, control of a language, what do they know that enables them to speak that language? Knowledge of a language is manifested in a variety of specific linguistic abilities. For our purposes the most important of these is the native speaker's ability to produce and understand an indefinite number of sentences he has never before encountered. Given just this one ability, we can draw an important conclusion about what form one's knowledge of language must take: It cannot take the form of a memorized list of sentences that are parroted back in an appropriate situation. A list, by definition, is finite and hence cannot account for the unlimited number of different sentences that a speaker can construct and understand. Rather, one's **grammar** (the term used to designate the knowledge of language that underlies the speaker's overt linguistic behavior and that the linguist attempts to describe and, ultimately, explain in terms of the inherent properties of language) must consist of rules or principles for forming novel sentences from a stock of stored items drawn from previous linguistic experience. It must be emphasized that when we speak of what a speaker knows, we are speaking of largely unconscious knowledge of principles of sentence formation. This kind of knowledge cannot necessarily be discovered simply by asking the native speaker what he thinks the principles are. The knowledge involved is not conscious knowledge.

Thus, the essential problem confronting the linguist who seeks to answer a question like *What is English?* is to discover what sorts of information the speaker in fact memorizes from previous linguistic experience and what sorts of principles permit this finite body of memorized information to serve as the basis for the construction of indefinitely many sentences. It seems apparent that one must memorize the constituent parts of sentences—called **morphemes**, which are the minimal syntactic units in terms of which words and, ultimately, sentences are built up— whether lexical (*house, run, in*) or grammatical (*-s* in *cats*, *-ing* in *going*, *-ed* in *slapped*). In general, it cannot be predicted that a particular meaning will be lexicalized as a single morpheme or a combination of morphemes. For example, whereas English expresses the concept 'teach' by a word consisting of a single morpheme (namely, *teach*), the Bantu language Chimwi:ni expresses the same concept by a word consisting of two morphemes (namely, *-so:m-esh-*, which consists of the root *-so:m-* meaning 'read, study' and a causative morpheme). Nor can it be predicted what the pronunciation of a particular concept will be if it is lexicalized, because in general the relationship between sound and meaning is arbitrary. In generative grammar it is assumed that the morphemes of a language are stored by the speaker in a special listlike device called a **lexicon** or **dictionary**, which contains all of the truly unpredictable, idiosyncratic information about the behavior—syntactic, semantic, phonological—of each morpheme known to the speaker. Thus, for example, in the lexical entry of a verb there will be specifications for whether it is intransitive (a one-place predicate such as *sleep*), transitive (a two-place predicate such as *hit*), doubly transitive (a three-place predicate such as *give*); whether it may occur with a singular noun as subject (*sleep*, for example) or not (*be similar*, for example); whether it may have an animate subject (*hit*, for example) or not (*elapse*, for example); and so on. For the moment we will ignore the nature of the phonological information in the lexicon, since this matter will be taken up in detail in the following chapters.

It is obvious, however, that by just knowing what the morphemes of a language are, we do not automatically know how to construct sentences in that language. We must necessarily assume the existence of a set of syntactic rules specifying how the morphemes may be combined to form sentences. For the sake of convenience, we will assume that the syntactic component of a grammar is organized roughly as presented in Chomsky (1965), where it is maintained that sentence-formation rules are of two types: phrase-structure rules and transformational rules.

These two different kinds of syntactic rules are organized in the grammar in a particular fashion. The phrase-structure rules are located in the base component of the grammar. They may be viewed as rules for constructing tree diagrams, which formally and precisely represent the grammatical relationships (subject, object, predicate, modifier, and so on) between the constituent parts of the sentence. The Phrase Structure rules of English might include the following.

(1)   Sentence ⟶ Noun phrase + Verb phrase

(2)   Verb phrase ⟶ Verb + (Noun phrase)

(3)   Noun phrase ⟶ (Article) + Noun

where the material in parentheses is optionally present. These rules will construct tree diagrams.

(4)

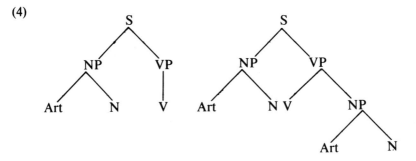

Such tree structures are then subject to a principle called lexical insertion, whereby morphemes stored in the lexicon may be inserted under the lowest matching nodes in the tree. Thus, the lexicon of English will have entries like the following.

(5)   *boy*   Noun; count; animate; . . .
                  "young," "male," "human" . . .
                  [bɔy]
          chase Verb; transitive; . . .
                  "activity," "physical"; "movement," "fast"; . . .
                  [čeys]
          kitten Noun; count; animate; . . .
                  "animal," "feline," "young" . . .
                  [kitən]

The top line of each entry is a representation of the syntactic information needed to characterize the syntactic behavior of the morpheme; the second line represents some of the semantic features characteristic of each morpheme; the final line is a representation of how the morpheme is pronounced. Needless to say, these particular entries are only schematic. Far more information is required to specify completely the linguistic behavior of each morpheme. The insertion of such lexical items into the tree structures produced by the Phrase-Structure rules yields objects like the following:[1]

(6)

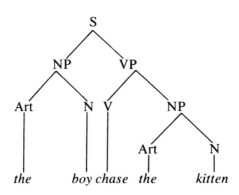

These are called deep-structure syntactic representations of a sentence, "deep" because in many cases they differ quite markedly from the surface syntactic form the sentence assumes when it is uttered or written.

Such deep-structure representations produced by the base component are then input to the transformational component of the grammar, which contains the transformational rules—grammatical rules of a formally different nature from the phrase-structure rules (which, recall, have only a "tree-building" function). The transformational rules have the power to delete material (for example, the imperative sentence *Write soon!* is assumed to derive from a deep structure containing *you* as its underlying subject), to add material (for example, many linguists assume that a sentence like *There is a man at the door* is derived from an underlying structure like *A man is at the door* via a rule inserting *there*), and to reposition material (as in *Was John here?* which is assumed to derive from a deep structure having the same basic word order as *John was here*). The transformational component gives as output the surface-structure representation of the sentence, which is analogous to the traditional notion of a parsing of a sentence, that is, a hierarchical con-

---

[1] The problem of verb tense has been ignored in this illustration.

stituent structure diagram of the morphemes composing the superficial form of the sentence as it is spoken or written.

Since knowledge of language involves the ability to understand and produce indefinitely many sentences, the syntactic component as outlined above must be supplemented by two additional components that will assign a meaning, or semantic representation, and a pronunciation, or phonetic representation, to each of the indefinitely many sentences generated by the syntactic component. The relationship between the deep structure of a sentence and its semantic representation has been highly controversial: Some writers have claimed that the deep structure is the sole input to a set of semantic interpretation rules that assign the sentence its meaning; other writers have claimed that both deep and surface structures serve as input to the rules of semantic interpretation; yet other writers have held that one cannot distinguish between deep structures and semantic representations at all, and that there are no semantic interpretation rules at all. The nature of the relationship between syntax and semantics does not impinge directly on the material dealt with in this book; thus we will ignore this very difficult problem.

In Chomsky (1965), it was assumed that the surface syntactic structure formed the input to the phonological component, whose function is to assign a phonetic representation to the sentence by modifying and supplementing the phonetic information contained in the constituent morphemes of the sentence inserted from the lexicon. Although this assumption that surface structure information is by itself an adequate basis for assigning a pronunciation to a sentence may be too strong (i.e., may prevent us from giving an adequate characterization of a speaker's knowledge of his language), it will be simpler for us to accept this position for our present purposes. By making this assumption, we can ignore highly controversial questions about the precise character of the syntactic component of the grammar. We need only ask what a surface structure must be assumed to be like, if it is to serve as the basis for determining the pronunciation of the sentences of the language. In Chapter 10 we present evidence that the constituent structure of the surface form of a sentence indeed does play a role in phonology, and will survey some of the kinds of information that must be assumed to be present in the surface structure.

All that we have said here about the overall model of grammar that we are assuming in this book is schematically illustrated in Figure 1.1. By being able to match any given deep-structure–surface-structure pairing with both a semantic and a phonetic representation, a generative grammar provides a characterization of the essence of knowledge of a language— the ability to relate particular strings of sounds with particular meanings, and vice versa.

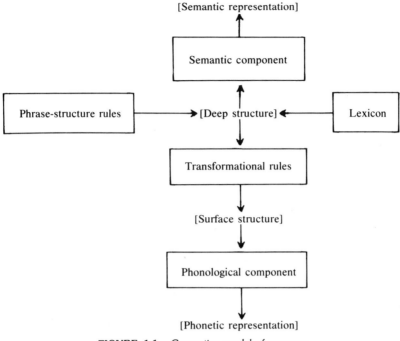

FIGURE 1.1.   *Generative model of grammar.*

Linguistic Phonetics: A Brief Survey

Traditionally, the field of linguistic phonetics is divided into two broad areas. **Acoustic phonetics** analyzes the complex sound waves of speech to determine the components that carry linguistically significant information, while **articulatory phonetics** investigates the production of speech sounds by the vocal apparatus. From a purely physical point of view any utterance is a continuum. Acoustically it is a continuously varying sound wave while from the articulatory point of view it is a continuous flow of gestures and movements. There are no obvious points of demarcation in these continua. Nevertheless, speech is perceived, and functions linguistically, as a series of discrete units called **sounds.** The general goal of linguistic phonetics is to describe accurately (both acoustically and articulatorily) all the various kinds of speech sounds that function in the languages of the world. When this goal has been attained, it will be possible to develop a universal system of notation so that any utterance in any language can be transcribed, and then, on the basis of the transcription, the utterance can be spoken to give a faithful rendering of all its linguistically significant aspects.

This of course immediately raises the question: What is linguistically significant? Or, what amounts to the same thing, How much detail must be included in the transcription so that a reading from it can be considered a satisfactory rendering of the utterance? A minimal condition is that the transcription must be narrow enough so that any two sounds that permit otherwise identical utterances to be distinguished in any language are transcribed differently. For example, the two *t*s in the English words *top* and *stop* are phonetically distinct. The one in *top* is aspirated (there is a puff of air between the release of the tongue closure and the onset of the vowel), while the *t* of *stop* is unaspirated (the vowel begins immediately after the release of the tongue closure). Although aspirated and unaspirated *t*s are never the sole distinguishing factors in any English utterance, there are many languages where this difference is distinctive. In Thai 'to do' is *t*ʰ*am* while 'to pound' is *tam*. The only difference between these two words is that the first begins with an aspirated *t* and the latter with an unaspirated *t*. Consequently, according to the position we are adopting here two distinct symbols must be provided by phonetic theory to distinguish these sounds, and in an adequate transcription of English the two *t*s in *top* and *stop* would be transcribed differently, since the difference is distinctive in some language.

There are, however, other phonetic differences that are characteristic of a given language but which, as far as is presently known, are not contrastive in any language. For example, in French stops like *p*, *t*, and *k* (sounds produced with closure) must be released at the end of a word, while in English these sounds are normally unreleased in this position. To our knowledge, the difference between a released and a nonreleased stop is not distinctive in any language. Nevertheless, an adequate phonetic description of French or English would have to indicate this difference. The minimal condition is thus insufficient. A completely adequate phonetic transcription would have to indicate all phonetic differences that may vary from one language to another, regardless of whether such differences are distinctive in any given language. Only invariant phonetic properties that arise from physiological and anatomical constants in the human vocal apparatus can be omitted from a phonetic transcription that claims to be completely accurate.

In this book we will follow the customary practice of providing phonetic transcriptions that satisfy the minimal condition. We will only indicate phonetic differences that are never distinctive in any language when those differences are specifically under discussion.

In addition to taking this position on how much detail to incorporate into a system of phonetic transcription, most phonologists have assumed that an adequate phonetic transcription can be viewed as a linear string of sound types or phones. Transcribing an utterance, then, amounts to dividing up the continuous utterance into its constituent sounds and identifying each sound as an instance of one of the distinct sound types provided for by phonetic theory.

Although in an adequate phonetic theory each sound type would be defined in both acoustic and articulatory terms, we shall present here primarily an articulatory description, since an acoustic description would require a much more technical discussion. Viewed as a product of articulation, a speech sound can be usefully characterized as air movements made audible by the vocal apparatus. Schematically, the vocal apparatus can be described as a pipe bifurcated at both ends. At the lower end of the pharynx, or throat, we find the larynx (the "Adam's apple," which visibly protrudes in the throat of many adult males), which acts as a valve determining whether or not the pharynx will open into the trachea (windpipe) and ultimately to the lungs. This valve is closed when one swallows food, so that the food may pass from the pharynx into the esophagus and ultimately to the stomach. The velum (the back portion of the roof of the mouth), located at the upper end of the pharynx, also acts as a valve. If it is raised, the nasal cavity is blocked off and air may pass only between the oral cavity, or mouth, and the pharynx. If the velum is lowered, air may pass between the nasal cavity and the pharynx.

Any speech sound can be viewed as the product of four production processes: an airstream process, a phonation process, an oral–nasal process, and an articulation process.

If speech consists of a moving body of air made audible, it follows that the vocal apparatus must move a body of air. This is called the **airstream process**. The vast majority of speech sounds in all languages are produced with the same airstream process: the expulsion of air from the lungs into the trachea. This contraction of the lungs creates a moving body of air that is then modified by the various other processes.

When the moving body of air reaches the larynx, it is subject to **phonation**. The larynx is a very complicated structure that contains the vocal cords, which are similar to two elastic lips sitting across the air passage. The vocal cords can assume a variety of positions and configurations. Two are most significant. First, the vocal cords may be brought close together (approximated) along their entire length. The air from the trachea flowing through this constriction creates a suction effect that draws the cords tightly together. But as soon as the cords come together, they block off the airflow and hence the suction effect that keeps them together. They are then blown apart by the air pressure that has built up behind this temporary closure. Air passes out between them, causing the suction effect to repeat itself, and the whole process starts over again.

Since this opening and closing of the glottis (the space between the vocal cords) is very rapid (60 to 360 times per second in normal conversation), the vocal cords can be said to be in vibration. Speech sounds thus produced are called **voiced** sounds. In consonants they are typically opposed to **voiceless** sounds, which are produced with the cords relatively far apart so that the suction cannot take place and there is no vibration of the cords. Compare the following pairs of words, arranged with initial voiced versus voiceless consonants: *zoo* versus *Sue*; *vile* versus *file*. In order to convince yourself that the vocal cords are vibrating in the production of the initial consonant of the first word in each pair, stick a finger in each ear and say *zoo* aloud (don't whisper!) prolonging the *z*; then say *Sue*, prolonging the *s*. In *zoo* you should feel a buzzing sensation, which is absent at the beginning of *Sue*. This is the vibration of the cords.

In pairs of words like *bat/pat*, *dim/Tim*, and *goal/coal* the initial consonants of the first words are (partially) voiced, while the initials of the second words are voiceless and aspirated as well. Although there is still some controversy about its precise nature, **aspiration** is commonly defined as a delay in the onset of the vibration of the cords after the release of a preceding voicelesss consonant. Thus, in a word like *pat* there is a brief period of airflow after the release of the lips and before the onset of the following vowel. On the other hand, in *spat*, where the *p* is voiceless and unaspirated, the onset of the vowel begins more or less simultaneously with the release of the lip closure for the *p*. Aspirated consonants are usually distinguished from nonaspirated ones by a superscripted *h*. Thus, the *p* in *pat* would be transcribed as p^h and the *p* of *spat* is simply *p*. It follows from this definition of aspiration that the so-called voiced aspirates of languages like Hindi and Sanskrit (as in the b^h of *bhrama*) involve a different phonation type, since the *b* is voiced. See Ladefoged (1971) for discussion.

The third process involved in the production of any speech sound is called the **oral–nasal** process. This simply describes the position of the velum and the direction of the outgoing air. If the velum is raised, the nasal passage is blocked off and the air must flow into the mouth. Sounds produced with a raised velum are called **oral** sounds. If the velum is lowered, air may pass into the nose. Such sounds are called **nasals** or **nasalized** sounds. The term nasal usually refers only to consonants like *m* and *n*, which are produced with a complete stoppage of the airflow into the mouth. Hence all of the air must flow into the nasal cavity. Compare *mat* and *bat*, where the only significant difference is that the velum is lowered in the production of the first sound in *mat* while it is raised in the production of the initial sound in *bat*. The term nasalized usually refers to sounds that do not involve a complete blockage of the oral cavity. Some of the air can flow out of the mouth as well as out of the nose. Nasalized vowels form a linguistically significant contrast with oral vowels in many languages, such as French.

There are nasalized vowels in English also. Compare the vowel of *see* with *seen* and the vowel of *cat* with *can't*. The vowels of the first member of each pair are oral; those of the second member are nasalized. Nasalized vowels are usually indicated by a tilde over the letter for the corresponding nonnasal vowel. Thus, the vowel of *seen* would be represented as *ĩ*. Sometimes nasalized vowels are transcribed by a hook under the vowel letter. Polish orthography employs this device. The first vowel in *gąska* 'goose' is nasalized.

Of the four speech production processes, the articulation process is the most complex. It involves various modifications of the sound wave produced by the previous three processes. In some ways it is easier to describe the articulation of vowels than it is of consonants, so we begin with the former.

Traditionally vowels are described in terms of two parameters—the configuration of the lips and the position of the highest point of the tongue in the mouth. For the configuration of the lips it is sufficient to recognize just two values. The lips can be relatively rounded and protruded (the round vowels) or relatively nonround and even spread (the nonround vowels). The position of the tongue varies along two dimensions. Vertically, the tongue can move from a relatively high to low position, as in the English words *beat, bait, bet, bat*. To designate the vowels in each of these words the letters *i, e, ɛ,* and *ä* (or *æ*), respectively, are usually employed. The tongue also varies its position along the horizontal dimension. When one says each of the following pairs of English words, the tongue moves from a relatively front position in the mouth to a relatively back position: *beat, boot; bait, boat; bet, bought; bat, bod(y)*. Also note that as you say each pair, the tongue gets progressively lower in the mouth. For the vowels of *boot, boat, bought,* and *body*, the symbols *u, o, ɔ,* and *a*, respectively, are most often utilized.

Since the lips are independent of the tongue, they can assume round and nonround configurations for each tongue position, potentially doubling the number of contrasts. For instance, *ü* (sometimes represented as *y*) has the same tongue position as *i* but with the lips in the rounded configuration. This vowel occurs in French *lune* 'moon' [lün]. The rounded variant of *e* is represented as *ϕ* or *ö*. It appears in the French *peu* 'a little'. The rounded variant of ɔ is represented as œ or sometimes as ɔ̈. It occurs in French *œuf* 'egg' [œf]. The unrounded lip shape for nonlow back vowels is quite a bit less common than the rounded configuration. Such unrounded vowels do occur, however. Some Slavic languages have the nonrounded counterpart to the high back round vowel *u*. It is usually transcribed as *y* and we will follow this practice in this book. The same vowel occurs in Turkish, where it is represented as *ι*. The unrounded partners of *o* and *ɔ* are normally indicated by the letters γ and ʌ, respectively. The vowel of English *cup* approximates the ʌ, except that it is articulated with a more centralized position. In this book we shall need to refer to only two central vowels: the high unrounded *i* and the mid-central schwa *ə*, which occurs as the final vowel in a word like *sofa*. The relative tongue positions of the vowels can be very approximately depicted in the following chart.

	Front		Central	Back	
	Unround	Round		Round	Unround
High	i	ü	ɨ	u	y
Mid-close	e	ö		o	γ
Mid-open	ɛ	œ	ə	ɔ	ʌ
Low	ä				a

Turning to the articulation of consonants, these can be usefully described in terms of the interaction between a passive and an active articulator. Generally, the passive articulator is located above the active in the oral cavity and the consonant is produced by bringing the active articulator up into contact or proximity with the passive one. Traditionally, consonant articulation is divided into two broad categories: place and manner of articulation.

A large number of positions of articulation can be distinguished (see Figure 1.2). In cases where the roof of the mouth is the passive articulator, it is very difficult to draw a line between one location and another, since there are no natural divisions here. In the following discussion we mention only the most common points of articulation.

Consonants formed by bringing the two lips into proximity are referred to as **bilabials**, while those that involve approximation of the lower lip and upper teeth are **labiodentals**. Thus, the *b* and *p* of *bill* and *pill* have a bilabial point of articulation, while the *v* and *f* of *vile* and *file* are labiodentals. The second consonant in Spanish *saber* 'to know' is a voiced bilabial fricative *β*, phonetically distinct from the labiodental *v*. In some

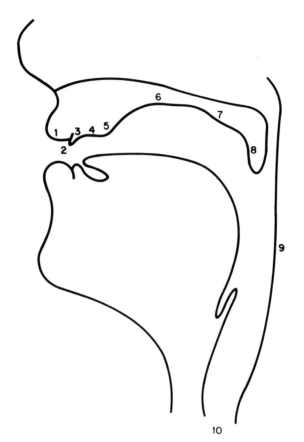

FIGURE 1.2. *Place of articulation. 1. bilabial 2. labiodental 3. dental 4. alveolar 5. alveopalatal 6. palatal 7. velar 8. uvular 9. pharyngeal 10. laryngeal.*

languages (such as the West African tongue Ewe) there is a linguistically significant contrast between these two fricatives. Sounds articulated at the back of the upper teeth are **dentals**, while those that approximate the hard gum ridge just behind the upper teeth are **alveolars**. The first sounds in English *tip* and *dip* are alveolars, while *t* and *d* in Russian are pure dentals. Many languages of Australia make a significant contrast between these two points of articulation. Sounds produced at the hard palate—the area on the roof of the mouth behind the gum ridge just before the roof begins to rise—are called **alveopalatals** (or **palatals**, for short). This is where the first sound in English *ship* is produced.

The soft palate is where the *k*s of *keep* and *coop* are articulated. This is a relatively large area with no clearly defined borders. The two *k*s of these words are actually produced at noticeably different points determined by the tongue position of the following vowel. In *keep* the *k* is relatively front; in *coop* it is farther back. This variation in position for the *k*s is always governed by the adjacent vowels in English. However, in some languages (such as Turkish) this difference is contrastive. In such cases the frontal *k* is often transcribed as *k'* and is termed a **palatal**, while the back *k* is called a **velar**. Most languages do not make a significant distinction between the two types of *k*; both are simply termed velars, and the term palatal is reserved for the alveopalatals.

The fleshy body suspended from the back of the roof of the mouth is called the uvula. This is the location at which **uvular** consonants are produced. Here we find the *q* of such languages as Arabic, Quechua, and Eskimo. The Parisian *r* is actually a trilled uvular. **Pharyngeal** consonants involve approximation between the root of the tongue and the back wall of the pharynx. Since it is difficult to make a complete closure here, only fricatives are found at this point of articulation. Arabic has voiced and voiceless pharyngeal fricatives indicated as ʕ (or 9) and ħ (or ḥ), respectively. Finally, the glottis forms the point of articulation for the **laryngeals** ʔ (the glottal stop) and *h* (a laryngeal fricative). The glottal stop, used by many English speakers in place of *t* in such words as *kitten* [kɪʔn] and *button* [bʌʔn], is formed by tightly closing the vocal cords together, thus damming up the air from behind, and then suddenly releasing this closure. For *h* the vocal cords are only slightly approximated so that a rustling sound is produced.

The second major classification of consonants is in terms of their manner of articulation. In a very rough way manner of articulation can be thought of as varying points along a dimension of proximity between the passive (usually upper) articulator and the active (usually lower) articulator. The closest degree of proximity is, of course, contact. The two articulators make contact with one another, temporarily blocking off the airflow. If the contact is released suddenly, an explosive sound is produced by the release of the air pressure built up behind the temporary closure. Sounds produced with this manner of articulation are called **stops** (or sometimes **plosives** or **noncontinuants**). The bilabial stops *p* and *b*, as in *pill* and *bill*, are produced by closing the two lips tightly together and suddenly releasing this closure. (The bilabial nasal *m* in *mill* is formed in the same way as *b* except that the velum is lowered so the air passes into the nasal cavity. Although phonetically similar to voiced stops, the nasals are traditionally isolated into a separate category of their own rather than being considered as stops.) At the dental, alveolar, and palatal regions stops are produced by a contact between the front of the tongue and the upper teeth, the gum ridge, and the hard palate, respectively. There is no commonly accepted symbolism for differentiating between the dental and alveolar points of articulation. We shall use the symbols *t* and *d* to stand indiscriminately for both dental and alveolar stops since most of the languages we shall discuss do not distinguish between these points of articulation. The corresponding nasal is represented by *n*. Alveopalatal stops are rather rare. According to Ladefoged (1971) this is to be explained by the fact that it is difficult to withdraw the blade of the tongue from this area quickly, since it makes contact with a relatively large portion of the roof of the mouth. Such stops do occur in some languages such as Serbo-Croatian. There are no commonly accepted symbols for these sounds, and we shall represent them as t^y and d^y. The alveopalatal nasal is symbolized as *ɲ* or *ñ* or *ň*. The velar stops, like the *k* and *g* of *cap* and *gap*, are formed by a closure between the back of the tongue and the soft palate. The final sound in *king* is the velar nasal. It is usually represented by *ŋ*. In the uvular stops *q* and *g̣* the contact is between the back of the tongue and the very back portion of the roof of the mouth. As we said earlier, stops do not occur at the pharyngeal point of articulation. The glottal stop is usually indicated as *ʔ* or sometimes as a raised comma.

The next class of consonants to be discussed is the **fricatives** (or **spirants**). For these the active articulator is brought into close proximity or even contact with the passive articulator, but the contact is not close enough or tight enough to block off the airflow. The airstream passes through the narrow constriction, resulting in various degrees of friction— the most characteristic feature of this class of sounds. At the bilabial point of articulation the voiced and voiceless fricatives are indicated by the letters *β* and *Φ*. The former occurs in Spanish. In labiodental fricatives like the *v* and *f* in *vile* and *file* the constriction is created by the lower lip and the upper teeth. As with the stops, one can distinguish between dental and alveolar fricatives, but once again we shall not introduce any special notation here to differentiate them, employing *z* and *s* indiscriminately for both types. The voiced and voiceless fricatives *ð* and *θ*, which occur as the initial sounds of English *them* and *thing*, respectively, differ from *z* and *s* by having the tip of the tongue extended out between the upper and lower teeth in such a way that the friction is created by the air flowing between the teeth. Hence, these fricatives are often called **interdentals**. The voiced and voiceless fricatives at the alveopalatal point of articulation are commonly indicated as *ž* and *š*. The former is to be heard in English *measure*, while *š* appears as the first sound in the word *ship*. Voiced versus voiceless fricatives at the remaining points of articulation are as follows: *γ*, *x* for velars; *γ̣*, *x̣* for uvulars; *ʕ*, *ħ* for pharyngeals; and *h* for laryngeals.

Affricates are sounds produced like stops except that the release of the closure is slow, not sudden. As a result there is a period of time after the release of the closure during which the articulators are in close approximation as in the fricatives. During this period friction results. Affricates are normally limited to the dental/alveolar and the alveopalatal regions, though bilabial and velar affricates do sometimes occur. The first sounds in English *chill* and *jail* are voiceless and voiced alveopalatal affricates, respectively. The former is usually indicated by the letter *č*, while the latter is variously represented as *ǰ* or *dž* or *ǯ*. The voiceless dental/alveolar affricate appears in German, as in the first sound in *zehn* 'ten'. It is usually represented as *c* or sometimes *ts*. The corresponding voiced affricate is represented by the symbols *dz* or *ʒ*. As we have seen, affricates share the closure property of stops and the friction property of fricatives. As such they exhibit a dual behavior. Many languages have rules that require a nasal like *n* to agree in point of articulation with a following stop. In such languages nasals are usually also required to agree with following affricates. English provides an example in which affricates pair up with fricatives as opposed to stops. The plural suffix has the shape – *iz* after fricatives like *s* and *z* (*buses, buzzes*) and affricates *č* and *ǰ* (*churches, judges*). But after a voiceless stop like *t* it appears as -*s* (*cats*) and as -*z* after a voiced stop like *d* (*maids*).

There is one major gap in the above description of the stops, fricatives, and affricates. In some languages it is necessary to determine whether the tip of the tongue or the blade of the tongue serves as the active articulator. Sounds produced with the tip of the tongue are called **apicals**, and those produced with the blade of the tongue are termed **laminals**. Although pure dentals are almost always apicals, alveolar and alveopalatal consonants may be produced with either the tip or the blade. Here we shall mention only one case in which this distinction is important (an additional example can be found in Chapter 4 in the discussion of the Australian language Lardil). The retroflex consonants found in many languages of India are apical alveopalatals—that is, the tip of the tongue is curled up and back to contact or approximate the hard palate. The alveopalatal stops t^y and d^y, on the other hand, are laminal sounds. Retroflex consonants are often symbolized with a dot under the letters for the corresponding dental/alveolar sounds.

Before proceeding to a discussion of the final two classes of consonants, we can summarize what we have said so far about the articulation of consonants in the table on page 17. The stops, affricates, and fricatives are arranged in voiceless–voiced pairs.

This leaves just two classes of consonants, the liquids and the glides. The **liquids** comprise the various kinds of *l* and *r* sounds. The *l* is called a lateral because one or both sides of the tongue are lowered while the

	Bila-bial	Labio-dental	Inter-dental	Dental/alveolar	Alveo-palatal	Retro-flex	Velar	Uvular	Pha-ryn-geal	La-ryn-geal
Stops	p b			t d	tʸ dʸ	ṭ ḍ	k g	q g		ʔ
Affricates				c dz	č dž					
Fricatives	ɸ ß	f v	θ ð	s z	š ž	ṣ ẓ	x ɣ	χ ɣ	ʕ ħ	h
Nasals	m	ɱ		n	ɲ	ṇ	ŋ			

midportion is raised, causing the air to flow out the sides of the mouth instead of through the center of the oral cavity. Here again we do not distinguish between dental and alveolar varieties, indicating both with the letter *l*. The alveopalatal lateral, as in Italian *gli*, is normally indicated by the letter λ, and the retroflexed lateral as *l*. The various kinds of *r* sounds seem to fall into three classes. In a trilled *r* the tip of the tongue is loosely positioned near the teeth or alveolar ridge and is set into vibration by the airflow. According to Ladefoged a tap *r* "is formed by a single contraction of the muscles such that one articulator is thrown against the other [1971, p. 50]." The well-known contrast between the trill of Spanish *perro* 'dog' and the tap of *pero* 'but' illustrates these two varieties of *r*. Ladefoged defines a flap *r* as "an articulation which usually involves the curling of the tip of the tongue up and back and then allowing it to hit the roof of the mouth as it returns to a position behind the lower teeth [1971, p. 50–51]." We indicate this sound by the symbol *D*. It occurs as the output of a rule found in many American English dialects that flaps *t* and *d* intervocalically after a stressed vowel: compare *writer* [rajDər] and *rider* [ra:jDər].

Glides include the *j* (often symbolized as *y*) of *yes* and the *w* of *well*. These sounds are similar to the high vowels *i* and *u*, the essential difference being that the tongue is positioned closer to the roof of the mouth for the glides than for the high vowels. For this reason the glides are sometimes called semivowels. The *j* is often called a palatal glide since the tongue approximates the palate during the articulation of this sound, while *w* is often called a labiovelar glide because in addition to a high back tongue position, the lips are rounded. A rounded version of the palatal glide, symbolized as ɥ, appears in French *lui* 'him' [lɥi]. It should be pointed out that the laryngeals *h* and ʔ are often classified as glides, but more on phonological than purely phonetic grounds.

Many languages have consonants that involve other airstream mechanisms in addition to the simple expulsion of air from the lungs. One of these is the glottalic airstream mechanism responsible for the two kinds of **glottalized** consonants. These are the **ejectives**, usually indicated by a raised comma above or after the letter for the corresponding nonglottalized consonant, and the **implosives**, often indicated by a right-falling hook attached to the letter for the corresponding nonimplosive sound (e.g., *b*, *d*, *g*). Ejectives are formed by tightly closing the glottis and then raising the larynx in the throat. This has the effect of increasing the pressure in the temporary air chamber created by the constrictions in the oral cavity and at the glottis. When the oral closure is released, the pressure in this temporary chamber is released, so that air flows out of the mouth. Ejectives are found very commonly in Amerindian and Caucasian languages, as well as in some African languages (e.g., Amharic). For implosives, the glottis is loosely closed and the larynx is lowered. This reduces the air pressure in the vocal tract relative to the outside air so that air may enter the mouth upon release of the oral closure of the consonant. Implosives can be found in many African languages (e.g., Shona).

The velaric airstream mechanism is involved in the production of the clicks. This type of sound is made by raising the back of the tongue to make contact with the soft palate. A closure is made at the lips, teeth, or alveolar ridge, creating a temporary air chamber. The body of the tongue is then moved backward and downward (the back of the tongue remaining in contact with the soft palate), creating a vacuum in the temporary chamber. When the closure in the front part of the mouth is released, air flows into the mouth. Although clicks occur in many languages as interjections (as in the English expression written either *tut-tut* or *tsk-tsk*), they occur as members of the ordinary system of speech sounds only in the Khoisan languages of South Africa and in some of the neighboring Bantu languages.

Traditionally, certain phonetic features of consonants are viewed as being superimposed on the primary articulation defined by the place and manner of articulation features just discussed. These are usually referred to as secondary articulations. One of these is labialization or rounding, formed by rounding and protruding the lips, the same gesture that is utilized in round vowels. This configuration can be superimposed on all consonants (including labials) to produce phonetic contrasts. Thus, in the West African language Nupe (Hyman 1970) there are contrasts like *e:g*^{w}*a:* 'hand' versus *e:ga:* 'stranger' and *t*^{w}*a* 'to trim' versus *ta* 'to tell'. Historically and sometimes synchronically, the labialized consonants often result from an assimilation of the rounding of an adjacent vowel. Hyman in fact argues for precisely this analysis in Nupe.

There are a number of secondary articulations implemented by the position of the body of the tongue. In labial consonants the tongue is not at all involved in the primary articulation and hence is free to assume various positions. Similarly, in the production of dentals, alveolars, and alveopalatals only the tip or the blade of the tongue is utilized for the primary articulation, leaving the rest of the tongue free. For these frontal consonants the body of the tongue can assume different positions that "color" the consonant.

The most common of these secondary articulations produced by the body of the tongue is **palatalization**, which involves raising the body of the tongue to a high front position that approximates the point it assumes in the articulation of the vowel *i*. This tongue configuration can then be superimposed on the primary articulation of a labial, dental, alveolar, or alveopalatal consonant. In many of the Slavic languages there is a significant contrast between palatalized and nonpalatalized consonants. In Russian we find minimal pairs like *brat'* 'to take' versus *brat* 'brother'; *krof'* 'blood' versus *krof* 'roof', where *C'* indicates the palatalized consonant.

Similarly, the body of the tongue can assume a high back attitude, creating the possibility of **velarization**, which is often, but not always, accompanied by labialization. In English the "clear" *l* of *leaf* is phonetically opposed to the "dark" (velarized) *l* of *feel*. The so-called emphatic consonants of the Semitic languages like Arabic involve the secondary articulation of **pharyngealization** in which the root of the tongue is retracted toward the back of the pharynx. Thus, in Egyptian Arabic we find minimal pairs like the following, where the dot under a letter stands for pharyngealization: *ṣeef* 'summer' versus *seef* 'sword'; *ḍamm* 'to annex' versus *damm* 'blood'; *ṭi:n* 'clay' versus *ti:n* 'figs'.

Certain phonetic features—the so-called prosodic features of length, stress, and pitch—are isolated into a special category because they behave differently than the other phonetic features in a number of ways. First, they often have a domain of realization that is larger than the individual speech sound or segment, especially in the case of stress and pitch. This domain is most often the syllable, but in many cases it includes larger pieces of the utterance. Second, many languages have principles that state something like: *There is only one long, or stressed, or high toned, vowel per word.* One never finds rules that state there may be only one dental, or voiceless, sound per word. For a general discussion of prosodic features the reader is referred to Lehiste (1970). In what follows we shall give a brief discussion of the contrastive role that each of the prosodic features can play.

Length refers to the duration of a sound. In many languages there is a linguistic contrast between long and short vowels. Long vowels are represented by a colon (V:), a macron (V̄), or as doubled or geminated (VV).

Short vowels are either unmarked or indicated by the breve (V̆). In Czech there is a vowel length contrast as shown by the following pairs: *mi:ti* 'to wash' versus *miti:* 'washing'; *ca:r* 'rag, shred' versus *car* 'tsar'; *dra:ha* 'road' versus *draha:* 'dear one (fem.)'.

A significant number of languages make a distinction in consonant length. For example, in Italian there are minimal pairs like *fato* 'fate' versus *fatto* 'done'. Here the long *t* of *fatto* actually spans two syllables—that is, the syllable break comes within the long *t*. As a result of this there is also a phonetic difference in the length of the preceding vowels. In *fato* the *a* is long, while in *fatto* it is short. Thus, we have phonetic transcriptions like [fa:-to] versus [fat-to], where the bar indicates the syllable break. This associated difference in vowel length is actually quite natural. In many languages vowels are long when they terminate the syllable (so-called open syllables) and short when the syllable ends in a consonant (closed syllables). Some additional examples from Italian are: *casa* 'house' versus *cassa* 'box'; *caro* 'dear' versus *carro* 'cart'; *nono* 'ninth' versus *nonno* 'grandfather'.

The precise phonetic realization of stress has not been adequately characterized. We will content ourselves with the vague definition of stress being an added component of emphasis or energy, leaving unspecified the manner in which this extra energy is produced. In many languages a stressed vowel (actually a stressed syllable) is longer in duration and has a higher pitch than an unstressed vowel. Furthermore, some languages such as English make significant contrasts in the degree of stress. For instance, compare the phrases *the White House* (where the President lives) with *the white house* (a house painted white). In both phrases the article *the* is unstressed, while the noun and adjective are stressed. But there is still a difference. In *the White House* the adjective has a stronger stress than the noun, while in *the white house* the stress on the noun is stronger than the stress on the adjective. Thus, in English there is a contrast between unstressed versus primary stress versus secondary stress.

All languages use pitch (the rate of vibration of the vocal cords) for contrastive purposes. Many languages (so-called intonation languages) use pitch differences to differentiate syntactic types such as questions, statements, commands. Thus, in English if *He came* is spoken with a rising intonation, it is normally interpreted as a question; when uttered as a statement or report, it has a falling contour. Many other languages (so-called tone languages) employ pitch differences to distinguish individual lexical items regardless of the syntactic context (such as, statement versus question) in which they are placed. For example, in Thai there are three level tones—high (V́), mid (unmarked), and low (V̀), and two contour tones—a rising tone (V̌) and a falling tone (V̂). Some minimal pairs follow.

High	Mid	Low	Rising	Falling
ná :	*na :*	*nà :*	*nǎ :*	*nâ :*
'aunt'	'filed'	'a nickname'	'thick'	'face'
kʰá :	*kʰa :*	*kʰà :*	*kʰǎ :*	*kʰâ :*
'trade'	'eaves'	'ginger'	'leg'	'me'

Finally, it should be pointed out that many regularities in phonological structure depend on two separate partitionings of the entire set of speech sounds. One of these is consonant versus vowel. **Consonant** will be understood to refer to any sound that is not a vowel, in particular both the oral (*y* and *w*) and laryngeal (ʔ and *h*) glides, as well as nasals, liquids, stops, and so on. The second partition is into sonorant versus obstruent. **Sonorants** comprise the vowels, liquids, nasals, and glides, while obstruent refers to the remaining sounds: stops, fricatives, and affricates. There are no truly satisfactory articulatory or acoustic definitions for the bases of these two different partitions. Nevertheless, they are crucial for the description of the phonological structure of practically every language.

After this brief survey of the major types of speech sounds we must briefly raise the question of how sounds are to be represented in the grammar for purposes of phonology. (For a more extensive treatment of this and related matters, see Chapter 7.) We assume that at the level of phonetic representation—the output of the phonological component of the grammar—sounds are represented as complexes of the various phonetic properties or features that define each sound type and distinguish it from all others. Each such feature is assumed to be defined in both articulatory and acoustic terms. The articulatory definition can be conceived of as the instructions the brain sends to the vocal apparatus to perform certain movements and gestures, while the acoustic definition can be thought of as information the brain looks for in order to identify a particular segment of the sound wave as an instance of a particular type of speech sound. From this point of view such symbols as *p*, *b*, *m*, and *t* are abbreviations for the complexes of phonetic properties (so-called feature matrixes) that define the sound. For example, the feature matrixes that the above symbols abbreviate might look something like the following.

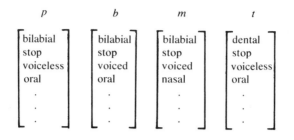

It is these feature matrixes that actually appear in phonetic representations. Such letters as *p*, *b*, and *m* never really appear in the grammar to represent sounds. They are just abbreviations for feature matrixes, used in articles and books about the grammar.

A major tenet of generative phonology has been that speech sounds are to be represented as complexes of phonetic properties in the lexicon and at all stages of the derivation of the utterance from the underlying representation to the phonetic representation. There are two main reasons for this position. First, phonological rules characteristically refer to certain restricted sets of sounds. For example, sets like [p, t, k], [m, n, ɲ, ŋ], and [i, e, ä] are classes of sounds that appear in rule after rule; sets like [e, x, n], [ʔ, r, f, w], or [a, s, b] are rarely (if ever) found in any rules in any language. If sounds are represented as complexes of properties, certain sets will be relatively simple to specify, while other sets will be relatively more complicated. Which sets turn out to be simple or complex depends, of course, on what properties we decide to define sounds in terms of in the lexicon. It happens that the classes of sounds that tend to occur in rule after rule–the so-called natural classes–are just those that require relatively little information to characterize if the sounds are represented in phonetic terms. Thus, the class [p, t, k] can be uniquely characterized as the set of sounds possessing the phonetic properties [voiceless, stop]. The set [m, n, ɲ, ŋ] is the set of all sounds having the properties [nasal, consonant], [i, e, ä] is the set of sounds characterized by the phonetic properties [vowel, front]. On the other hand, sets like [e, x, n], which rarely (if ever) occur in any phonological rule, are relatively difficult to specify if properties used to define sounds are phonetic properties. Thus, the natural groupings of sounds needed to state generalizations about the phonological structure of language are to a large extent provided by the properties which are required anyway to define the articulatory and acoustic realizations of the sounds. In order to capture this fundamental fact about the nature of language, generative phonologists have chosen to represent sounds at all levels of the grammar as complexes of phonetic properties.

Turning briefly now to phonological rules, these are operations on strings of sounds represented as feature complexes that have the effect of changing one sound into another sound. Thus, if we want to change *b* into *m*, we must change the feature matrix of *b* so that the feature oral is replaced by the feature nasal. To take another example, in many languages the class of voiced obstruents that includes the sounds [b, d, g, v, z . . .] is changed into the corresponding voiceless obstruents. The rule performing this operation would say [voiced] ⟶ [voiceless].

One further point should be made here. Many of the phonetic properties refer to a single phonetic dimension. For example, oral versus nasal can be thought of as two points along the dimension defined by the position of the velum. Round versus unround can be seen as two points along the dimension corresponding to the configuration of the lips. For most such dimensions only two points are selected by language to form a significant contrast in sounds. For instance, many languages (such as French) make a contrast between whether a vowel is oral or nasal. But no language presently known makes an underlying contrast between three degrees of nasality: fully nasal, partially nasal, and oral. Similarly, languages such as French make a distinction between whether a vowel is round (like *lune* [lün]) or nonround (like *ligne* [liɲ]). But so far as is known, no language makes a contrast between three degrees of rounding. For this reason generative phonologists have taken the position that most of the phonetic dimensions are to be represented by the same feature name with two values. Thus, on this view, the difference between an oral and a nasal vowel will be that the former is [−nasal] and the latter [+nasal]. The difference between *ü* and *i* is that the former is [+round] while the latter is [−round]. Voiced sounds are [+voice]; voiceless are [−voice]. Most phonetic dimensions can thus be represented in this **binary** fashion. Vowel height and place of articulation in consonants seem to involve more than two points along a single dimension, but some phonologists have claimed that this dimension is to be broken down into several smaller dimensions, each of which is binary. We return to this matter briefly in Chapter 7.

2

Phonological Rules and Representations

In this chapter we begin addressing the fundamental question of phonology: What mechanisms and principles must the theory of grammar contain so that the correct phonetic representation can be assigned to the utterances in any human language in such a way as to reflect the native speaker's internalized grammar as closely as possible? In Chapter 1 we observed that one's knowledge of his native language cannot take the form of a memorized list of sentences on the grounds that there are an indefinite number of well-formed sentences in any language. The speaker's internalized grammar must be assumed to contain syntactic rules or principles which enable him to construct novel sentences from a stock of stored items (morphemes, words, idiomatic phrases). But when one considers the phonological aspects of sentences, it is not nearly as obvious that rules must be invoked. Since the number of morphemes and words in a given language is finite, there is nothing incoherent about maintaining that the speaker simply memorizes the phonetic makeup of each item. After all, most aspects of pronunciation are clearly memorized in any case. There is no principle of English phonology which predicts that the word *cab* is composed of the three sounds k, $æ$, b, appearing in this particular order. In order to know how to pronounce this word, one must simply wait to hear it pronounced by someone else who already knows its pronunciation. We thus might assume that once the native speaker hears a given word pronounced, he simply memorizes what sounds make up the word and in what order those sounds are pronounced. This information would be stored in the lexicon of the speaker's grammar.

Let us see how a grammar would assign a pronunciation to sentences if we were to accept the claim that the speaker simply memorizes the pronunciation of each item he encounters. The syntactic component would generate indefinitely many surface structures, where a surface structure would be a sequence of morphemes with an associated constituent structure (i.e. the morphemes would be organized into words and words would be organized into phrases and so on). Each morpheme in the surface structure would be assigned a pronunciation simply by looking up in the lexicon the pronunciation stored there. To take a concrete instance, consider the utterance *Birds fly*. Its phonetic representation can, at the level of detail we are considering here, be given as [bɨrdz flaj]. It contains three morphemes: the noun root *bird*, the suffix indicating plurality in nouns, and the verb root *fly*. Given the view being sketched here, the speaker of English will have stored in the lexicon the information that the pronunciation of these three morphemes is /bɨrd/, /-z/, and /flaj/ respectively. By putting the pronunciations of these morphemes together in the order that the morphemes occur in the surface structure one arrives at the pronunciation of the entire sentence. Thus no phonological component of the grammar would be required: The syntactic rules, which specify the order of the morphemes in the sentence, and the lexicon, which specifies the pronunciation of each morpheme, would jointly produce a pronunciation for each sentence. Let us refer to this view of pronunciation as the **null hypothesis**.

The Null Hypothesis

On pretheoretical grounds there is nothing logically absurd or incoherent about the null hypothesis. As with all questions about the nature of grammar, it is an empirical question whether or not the null hypothesis can adequately account for the speaker's ability to pronounce the words and sentences in his language. Despite its superficial lack of implausibility, there are a number of considerations which show that the null hypothesis is incorrect. One important observation is the fact that in most languages there are morphemes or words that have more than one phonetic realization. For example, the plural suffix in English is sometimes pronounced as *-iz* (e.g., *buses*, *brushes*), sometimes as *-s* (e.g., *cats*, *lips*), and sometimes as -*z* (e.g., *birds*, *dogs*). Such a situation is called an **alternation**—that is, a given morpheme has alternant or varying pronunciations in different contexts. Each variant pronunciation is called an **alternant** or **allomorph** of that morpheme. The widespread phenomenon of alternation falsifies the null hypothesis, because even if we were to expand the lexical representation of a morpheme to include a listing of each of its alternants, it would still be necessary to include rules or statements to select the appropriate alternant in any given context. Let us call this the problem of selection. Thus, even if we were to expand the lexical representation of the plural morpheme to /-ız, -s, -z/, we still require rules to guarantee that the alternant -*s* is suffixed to *cat* and *lip* but not to *bus* or *bird*. But this additional apparatus of rules of selection is precisely what the null hypothesis denies. Hence, this hypothesis about the manner in which the grammar assigns phonetic representations must be rejected.

The preceding argument against the null hypothesis might be countered by maintaining that instead of memorizing morphemes, what the speaker does is to memorize entire words. On this view, the speaker stores in his mental lexicon both the representation [bɨrd] for *bird* and also [bɨrdz] for *birds*, [lɪp] for *lip* and also [lɪps] for *lips*, and so on. This view essentially claims that the plural morpheme is an unanalyzed portion of the entire word and that a speaker must memorize the pronunciation of the plural form of a noun just as he must memorize the pronunciation of the singular form.

The position sketched above can be argued against by demonstrating that a native speaker of English has the ability to construct plural nouns even though he has never heard these nouns (and thus could not have memorized their pronunciation), and that the pronunciation he assigns to these plural nouns follows a general principle. Thus, if a speaker of English is given the nonce forms [nɪs], [fɪp], and [mæg] and is induced to form plurals of these words, he will undoubtedly say [nɪs-ız], [fɪp-s], and [mæg-z]. The fact that the speaker will pronounce [mæg-z] rather than *[mæg-ız] or *[mæg-s], even though he has never encountered this pronunciation before, can be explained only by assuming that the distribution of the allomorphs of the plural suffix (i.e., -*ız* after sibilants, -*s* after voiceless nonsibilants, and -*z* after voiced nonsibilants) forms a part of his internalized grammar.

Consider another example making the same point in a slightly different way. In the Paleo-Siberian language Chukchee there is a vowel harmony principle whereby the vowels *i*, *u* and *e* are changed into *e*, *o*, and *a*, respectively, if the word in which they appear contains a low vowel *ɛ*, *a*, or *ɔ* (which we represent here as *o*). Thus, a locative suffix -*gjit* appears in the form -*gjet* when added to a stem containing a low vowel: *quli-gjit*

'voice', *milute-gjit* 'rabbit', but *jara-gjet* 'tent', *wopqa-gjet* 'moose'. Similarly, stems like *titi-* 'needle' and *milute-* 'rabbit' change their vowels
when the comitative suffix *-ma* is added: *tete-ma* 'with a needle',
melota-ma 'with a rabbit'.

Given the null hypothesis we must assume that the Chukchee speaker
simply memorizes the words *milute-gjit*, *wopqa-gjet*, and *melota-ma*
without any principles relating the varying pronunciations of the same
morphemes. As in the English example, this could be shown to be incorrect by exhibiting novel forms never encountered previously by the
speaker which he is nevertheless able to pronounce correctly in accord
with the harmony principle. But another way to falsify the null hypothesis
exists. Chukchee has a syntactic process of incorporation whereby an
adjective or other qualifying word may be incorporated into the noun it
modifies to form a new word. When this happens, we find that the
harmony principle operates automatically. For example, 'new gun' may
be expressed by simply placing the adjective before the noun (*nə-tur-qin
milger*) or by incorporating the adjectival root with the noun (*tur-milger*).
The following examples (from Skorik 1961) show that when the incorporation process brings together morphemes containing vowels with different
harmonic values, the harmonic changes are applied automatically.

(1)   *nə-mejəŋ-qin galgajŋ-ən*   'big bird'
        majŋə-galgajŋ-ən   'big bird'
        nə-teŋ-qin aacek   'noble youth'
        taŋ-aacek   'noble youth'
        jejvel   'orphan'
        jajval-aacek   'orphaned youth'
        n-om-qen evir?ən   'warm clothes'
        om-aver?ən   'warm clothes'

Now since, in principle, any adjective can be incorporated with any noun,
we must assume that the Chukchee speaker has a principle of harmony in
his internalized grammar to explain the harmonic changes that occur
when incorporated words are created. Since the harmonic changes that
appear in the incorporated forms are of exactly the same nature as those
which appear in words composed of a single root plus affixes (like the
locative and comitative), there is every reason to believe that these latter
alternations are also produced by the harmony principle, rather than
simply being memorized.

The above arguments against the null hypothesis involved instances
where a morpheme alternated in pronunciation depending on the nature of
the adjacent morpheme(s) in the same word. There are many instances
where a morpheme will alternate in pronunciation depending on its posi-

tion in a phrase. Such cases provide a strong argument against the null hypothesis. We will confine ourselves to a single example here. In Chimwi:ni, a Bantu language related to Swahili, vowels may be either long or short. But a long vowel is not allowed to occur (generally speaking) in any syllable preceding the antepenultimate syllable in the phrase. A vowel that is an inherently long vowel will always be pronounced as a short vowel if it is in a pre-antepenultimate position. Consider, for instance, the verb root /ɬe:t/ 'bring'. The vowel of this verb root is long in such examples as *ku-ɬe:t-a* 'to bring', *ɬe:t-a* 'bring (it)!', and *ku-wa-ɬe:t-eɬ-a* 'to bring (it) to them', but short in forms such as *ku-ɬet-eɬ-an-a* 'to bring to/for one another', *na-ku-wa-ɬet-eɬ-a-ni* 'what is he bringing to them?', and *ku-ɬet-a ma-jiwe* 'to bring stones'. Notice that the long vowel of /ɬe:t/ appears in a shortened form whenever more than two vowels follow regardless of whether those vowels are in the same word or a later word in the phrase. Given the null hypothesis, it would be necessary for the speaker to memorize and store in his lexicon all of the words and phrases that /ɬe:t/ appears in. But this is not a feasible analysis, for there are an indefinitely large number of such phrases. The speaker of Chimwi:ni knows how to pronounce /ɬe:t/ in any phrase that this morpheme happens to occur, whether he has ever heard that phrase or not. The speaker of Chimwi:mi must abstract a rule (namely, a long vowel is pronounced short if it is in a pre-antepenultimate position in the word or phrase) rather than simply memorizing the items he encounters.

Aside from its inability to deal with the phenomenon of alternations, there is another reason for rejecting the null hypothesis. Since the null hypothesis tries to list all aspects of the pronunciation of a morpheme in the lexicon, it fails to make a linguistically fundamental distinction between two types of phonetic information—namely, that some aspects of the phonetic realization of a morpheme are **idiosyncratic** properties of that particular morpheme, while others are instances of **systematic regularities** in the sound structure of the language. For example, consider the phonetic representation [kʰæ:b] of the English word *cab*. The fact that the initial sound of this word has the property of being a velar consonant (as opposed to, say, being labial or dental) is an idiosyncratic feature of this particular morpheme. If a fluent speaker of English did not happen to know this particular word *cab*, there would be no way for him to predict, on the basis of his knowledge of English, that the first sound of this morpheme would have the feature of velarity. For all he knows, the morpheme could just as well begin with a dental consonant and be pronounced *tab* or a labial consonant and be pronounced *pab*. In learning the morphemes or vocabulary of a language, most information of this sort must be simply memorized. Similarly, the fact that the initial sound in *cab* is voiceless, rather than voiced, is another idiosyncratic property of this particular morpheme. Before encountering this word, the speaker of English has no reason to expect the initial sound to be k instead of g.

But not all of the phonetic features of the first sound in *cab* are of this idiosyncratic nature. In particular, if we were to make a list of English words which begin with a voiceless stop consonant (p, t, k) and consist of just one syllable, we would find that all of them have the property of aspiration associated with their initial voiceless stop, and that there are none which do not. In English, then, there is an invariable correlation of voiceless stop consonants with the feature of aspiration in initial position in monosyllabic words. Note that there is no physiological necessity that voiceless stops be pronounced with aspiration: In English nonaspirated voiceless stops occur in noninitial position (e.g., the second sounds in *spat, stab, scab*) and in many languages nonaspirated voiceless stops occur both initially and noninitially. Thus the presence of the feature of aspiration in the initial segment of *cab* is an instance of a general regularity of English pronunciation rather than a physiological necessity: All word-initial voiceless stops in monosyllables are aspirated.

This distinction between idiosyncratic and systematic features of pronunciation reappears in the vowel of *cab*. The fact that the vowel æ: of this morpheme is pronounced with a relatively low tongue position (as opposed to i, a high vowel), and with a relatively frontal tongue position (as opposed to a, a back vowel) are idiosyncratic properties which must be memorized when learning this word. On the other hand, the fact that the vowel is long is not a peculiarity of this particular morpheme, but rather is an instance of another general regularity of English that vowels are pronounced longer before voiced consonants than before voiceless ones (compare *cab~ cap; bag~ back; pig~ pick; mad~ mat;* etc.).

To recapitulate, we can say that, from the point of view of the grammar of English, the phonetic representation [kʰæ:b] is a complex object in the sense that some of its features are properties idiosyncratic to the particular morpheme *cab*, while certain others are manifestations of general regularities in the sound pattern of English.

Why does this distinction between idiosyncratic and systematic features of pronunciation falsify the null hypothesis? Recall that the null hypothesis lists in the lexicon all of the features of the pronunciation of a morpheme. Hence it is, in principle, incapable of formally making the distinction between idiosyncratic and systematic features, since it treats all features as being of the same status. By doing so, the null hypothesis claims that this distinction should not exist; or that if it does, it is of no linguistic significance. However, anyone who has considered the matter seriously has realized that the distinction is very significant. We will discuss this matter in considerable detail in Chapters 3 and 5. Here we cite only briefly some of the kinds of evidence which can be employed to motivate it. Consider the problem a native speaker of English faces in acquiring a language like French. He will have no difficulty pronouncing certain sounds correctly, for example, the word *bas*. In general, these are sounds that occur in English. He will have varying degrees of difficulty with sounds that do not occur in English: for example, the front rounded vowel *ü* of *lune* or the uvular *r* of *roi*. But there are some sounds which occur in both English and French which present considerable difficulties nevertheless. For example, the word *pas* is phonetically [pa] with an unaspirated voiceless stop. This sound occurs in English in words like *spa*. But when trying to say *pas* the English speaker will automatically say [pʰa], aspirating the *p*. Furthermore, he will have trouble hearing the difference between his [pʰa] and the French [pa]. What explains this difficulty? Clearly it is the fact that the feature of aspiration is controlled by a rule in English speech and that this rule is projected upon his French pronunciation. On the other hand, the English speaker has no trouble in controlling the features of voicing or labiality. He has no difficulty in producing or distinguishing *pas* from *bas* or *tas*. In general, it is only the systematic features of pronunciation which cause difficulty, and then only when they appear in positions different from the ones governed by the systematic regularity.

Slips of the tongue can also be used to demonstrate the psychological reality of a systematic regularity. For example, one of the authors recently observed *tail spin* [tʰejl spɪn] pronounced as *pail stin* [pʰejl stɪn]. Notice that in this spoonerism both the *tʰ* and the *p* are changed in accordance with the systematic regularity that controls aspiration in English: The *tʰ* is deaspirated because only nonaspirated stops can stand after *s*, and the unaspirated *p* becomes aspirated because only aspirated stops can begin a word like *pail*. Once again, it would be difficult to explain why these changes should automatically occur unless it is assumed that the systematic regularity controlling the feature of aspiration forms part of the English speaker's internalized grammar.

Facts like these show that the distinction between idiosyncratic and systematic features is of linguistic significance. We must, therefore, reject the null hypothesis and develop some machinery which will enable a generative grammar to explicitly characterize the difference between these two kinds of phonetic features. In order to make this distinction, we will introduce the devices of a **list** and a **rule**. We will say that all of the idiosyncratic features of the pronunciation of a morpheme are to be listed in the lexical representation of that morpheme in the lexicon of the grammar. On the other hand, features which are instances of systematic regularities will be assigned by phonological rules in the phonological component of the grammar. Correspondingly, we will make a distinction between two levels of representation of the phonological structure of a morpheme, word, phrase, or sentence: The **underlying representation** (UR), which will contain all of the idiosyncratic information about the pronunciation of the constituent morphemes of the utterance, and the **phonetic representation** (PR), which contains the idiosyncratic information plus the predictable information about the pronunciation of the utterance.[1] For the moment, we can conceive of the UR of a sentence as being identical with the surface syntactic structure of a sentence. The phonological rules, then, make up the phonological component of the grammar, and their function is to convert the UR of any utterance into its corresponding PR by assigning predictable phonetic properties. For example, the morpheme *cab* will have included in its lexical representation the information /kæb/—all of the idiosyncratic features of pronunciation (at the level of detail we are considering here). The lexical representation of this morpheme will be inserted into each syntactic surface structure that utilizes this particular morpheme. This surface structure then forms the input to the phonological component (i.e., it is the UR), which contains the phonological rules that assign the features of aspiration to the initial voiceless stop and length to the vowel. Application of these rules then yields the PR [kʰæ:b].

Before proceeding further, let us discuss the preceding points in more detail. We have proposed to distinguish the idiosyncratic features of pronunciation from the systematic features by incorporating the former into the lexical representation of morphemes. This decision seems to accord well with the presumed psychological fact that the speaker of the language must memorize the association of these properties with one another and with the rest of the information in the lexical entry. Essentially, the lexicon of a generative grammar can be thought of as a listlike device, where each entry in the list describes an arbitrary collocation of properties in terms of which the linguistic behavior of the morpheme can be described—that is, properties which themselves are not predictable by rule. Thus the fact that *cab* contains the three sounds /k-æ-b/ is not predictable by rule. Similarly, the fact that the three sounds occur in this order rather than, say, /b-æ-k/ is also an idiosyncratic feature. Finally, the association of this phonetic information with the other syntactic and

---

[1] Actually, phonological rules will not only assign predictable features of pronunciation such as aspiration in English, they will also modify idiosyncratic features of pronunciation that fall within the scope of a phonological rule. For instance, in Chimwi:ni certain vowels must be listed in the lexicon as being long, but this underlying length will be nullified in pre-antepenultimate position due to the general rule discussed earlier in this chapter. See the following chapter for further discussion of this point.

semantic features of being a concrete, count noun denoting a certain type of vehicle is also an arbitrary connection which must be memorized. For these reasons, a listlike device such as a lexicon seems entirely appropriate.

Likewise, the concept of a grammatical rule seems entirely appropriate for characterizing those features of pronunciation which are manifestations of general and systematic regularities in the sound pattern of a language. For example, when we consider the status of the feature of vowel length in English, we find that this feature is systematically correlated with a following voiced consonant. This regularity is of an openended nature in that it holds for all combinations of a vowel plus a voiced consonant regardless of what particular morpheme they may occur in. This open-ended character of the regularity is reflected in what we might call the "projective" nature of a grammatical rule. The length rule that we formulate to account for this regularity of English states that a vowel will be pronounced long when before a voiced consonant; this rule applies regardless of the particular utterance in which this sequence of sounds occurs.

We will now begin to introduce some of the notation employed in formulating phonological rules (see Chapter 9 for more explicit discussion). We will assume that the phonetic properties of an utterance at both the underlying and phonetic representations are to be represented as a string of discrete segments, where each segment takes the form of a **feature matrix** specifying the grammatically determined operations of the vocal apparatus involved in the articulation of the corresponding speech sound. For instance, the lexical and phonetic representations of *cab*, again at the level of detail we are concerned with here, will appear as something like (2) and (3), respectively.[2]

(2)

/k	æ	b/
cons	vowel	cons
stop	low	stop
velar	back	labial
voiceless	oral	voiced
oral	stress	oral

(3)

[k^h	æ:	b]
cons	vowel	cons
stop	low	stop
velar	back	labial
voiceless	oral	voiced
oral	stress	oral
aspir	long	

[2] See Chapter 7 for discussion of the motivation for assuming that sounds are to be viewed as a complex of features.

Phonological rules are operations upon strings of feature matrixes. Each rule assigns one or more feature specifications to a matrix when that matrix appears in a certain context. In the statement of the rule, the set of segments undergoing the rule as well as the set of segments which form the context in which the rule operates are identified by mentioning all of the features necessary to uniquely indicate just those particular sets. So, for example, the vowel length rule, which specifies vowels as long before voiced consonants, takes roughly the form in (4).

$$(4) \qquad [\text{vowel}] \longrightarrow [\text{long}]/\underline{\hspace{1em}}\begin{bmatrix}\text{cons} \\ \text{voiced}\end{bmatrix}$$

In this expression, the arrow is to be read "is assigned," the slash / as "in the context of," and the environmental dash ____ indicates the segment undergoing the rule relative to its environment (in this case immediately before voiced consonants). The rule thus says "a segment having the feature [vowel] is assigned the feature [long] if that segment stands immediately before another segment having the features [voiced] and [consonant]." This rule will apply to the UR (2) above, since it possesses a segment which satisfies the requirements of the rule. The rule would not apply to the UR of a word like *cap*, because the vowel in this morpheme stands before a segment which is not characterized by the feature [voiced]. Application of the vowel length rule to the UR (2) then supplies the feature [long] appearing in the corresponding PR (3).

Turning now to the formulation of the aspiration rule, we note that the complete distribution of this feature in English is somewhat more complex than that indicated earlier. Essentially the rule is that voiceless stops are aspirated when they initiate a syllable. This not only covers cases of word-initial voiceless stops in monosyllabic words like *cab*, but also word-internal voiceless stops such as the *t* of *spitoon*, the *p* in *lampoon*, and the *k* in *racoon*. Note that this rule will correctly fail to aspirate the *p* in *spitoon*, since it does not begin the syllable. The rule will also aspirate the *p* of *applaud*, the first *t* of *attribute* (verb), and the *k* of *accrue*. Finally, in a word like *potato* [pʰətʰéyDow] the first two voiceless stops will be aspirated because they begin the syllable, while the final *t* is flapped to *D* by a rule operating in roughly the context V̇____V. Thus, the aspiration rule for English will take the form of (5).

$$(5) \qquad \begin{bmatrix}\text{stop} \\ \text{voiceless}\end{bmatrix} \longrightarrow [\text{aspirated}]/\cdot\underline{\hspace{1em}}$$

In this rule the dot stands for the syllable boundary, indicating where the syllable begins and/or ends. Thus, the segment immediately after the dot will be in syllable-initial position. This rule will now apply to the UR of *cab*, because its syllable-initial segment has the features voiceless and stop, deriving the correct PR (4).

Zoque

Let us turn to several other examples in which the distinction between idiosyncratic and systematic features of pronunciation may be expressed by the notions of a **list** and a **rule**. Examination of the data in (6) from Zoque, a language of Mexico (Wonderly 1951), permits us to set up (7) as the inventory of consonants appearing in the phonetic representations of this language.

(6)

pata	'mat'	*ŋgyunu*	'you fell'
tatah	'father'	*sis*	'meat'
tʸïtʸïy	'little'	*šohšahu*	'they cooked it'
cima	'calabash'	*kama*	'cornfield'
cehcu	'he cut it'	*nas*	'earth'
kunu	'he fell'	*ñanah*	'his mother'
kenba	'he sees'	*kaŋ*	'jaguar'
myaŋdamu	'you came'	*liŋba*	'he slashes'
ʔïŋdʸoʔpya	'he is sleepy'	*win*	'face'
ñjehcu	'you cut brush'		

(7)

Voiceless plosives	p	t,c	tʸ, č	k	
Voiced plosives	b	d,dz	dʸ, ǰ	g	
Fricatives		s	š		
Nasals	m	n	ñ	ŋ	
Liquids		l,r			
Glides	w		y		ʔ,h

A pattern is to be observed in the distribution of the stops and affricates (a class of sounds traditionally called plosives and characterized by a blockage of the air flow): Voiced plosives only appear after nasals, while voiceless plosives never appear in this position. Thus, unlike in English, where voicing is an idiosyncratic feature of stops and affricates, the voicing of Zoque plosives is predictable in terms of a rule such as (8).

(8)   [plosive] $\longrightarrow$ [voiced]/[nasal] ____

Although somewhat less obvious, the features voiced and voiceless are also predictable for all other sounds in Zoque. Just as a certain feature of a given segment may require another feature to appear in an adjacent segment (e.g., in Zoque the feature voice must appear in plosives if they follow a segment having the feature nasal), all languages have dependency relations between features contained wholly within a single segment. For example, in most languages if a segment has the feature sonorant then it must also have the feature voiced. Voiceless vowels, liquids, and nasals are distinctly less preferred than voiced ones. On the other hand, voiceless is preferred over voiced for obstruents. There are many languages which have only voiceless obstruents, while we know of no language whose obstruents are exclusively voiced. These intrasegmental relations between the features of sonorant and obstruent, on the one hand, and voiced and voiceless on the other, may be expressed by the rules in (9) and (10).

(9)   [sonorant] $\longrightarrow$ [voiced]

(10)   [obstruent] $\longrightarrow$ [voiceless]

If we accept the claim that Zoque voiced obstruents arise only as the result of phonological rule (8), then rule (10) holds true for Zoque as well.

Rules expressing intrasegmental relations are called morpheme structure rules and are commonly assumed to apply in the lexicon. If this position is accepted, then all segments in the UR will contain phonetically pronounceable sounds. The phonological rules will then simply convert one sound into another by altering its feature matrix. Thus, in Zoque, all segments will be unspecified for voicing in the lexical entry for morphemes of the language. The morpheme structure rules of (9) and (10) will then fill in the redundant features of voicing (voiced for sonorants and voiceless for obstruents). As a result, the UR of all morphemes will enter the phonological component with full fledged sounds (as opposed to segments unspecified for the position of the vocal cords). The phonological rule of (8) will then change basically voiceless plosives to voiced when they appear after a nasal. The status of morpheme structure rules in phonological theory is exceedingly unclear and, as a result, most of our discussion in this book will ignore the subject of intrasegmental relations. See Chapter 10 for brief discussion of some of the issues involved.

In the preceding paragraphs we have proposed to treat the complementary distribution of the voiced and voiceless plosives of Zoque in terms of phonological rule that changes basically voiceless plosives to voiced after a nasal. Call this the voicing analysis. Alternatively, one could posit the voiced plosives as basic and propose a rule devoicing them everywhere except after nasals. Call this the devoicing analysis. The two analyses differ with respect to which position is selected as indicating the underlying character of Zoque plosives and in which position this basic pronunciation is obscured by a phonological rule. Although on purely logical grounds the two analyses appear equivalent, we are confident that almost any linguist analyzing Zoque would propose the voicing solution. The reason is that voicing of obstruents, especially plosives, after nasals is a very natural rule found in language after language. Presumably the great frequency of this rule is to be explained on phonetic grounds (i.e., as arising naturally from the structure and dynamics of the human vocal apparatus), although we are not aware of any truly satisfying explanation along these lines. The devoicing solution, on the other hand, has very little to recommend it in the way of naturalness. Although there is a tendency for language to favor voiceless plosives in pre-consonantal and word final positions, prevocalic position, especially at the beginning of a word, is a rather stable one in which the underlying glottal position (voiced versus voiceless) usually surfaces phonetically. There is no natural tendency to devoice plosives in this position.

Papago

Papago, an Uto-Aztecan language spoken in Arizona, provides another example of the modification of underlying sounds in a particular phonetic context. Examination of the data in (11), taken from Saxton and Saxton (1969), reveals that Papago has a five-vowel system, with three high vowels and two nonhigh vowels.

(11)

tatai	'tendon'	*činig*	'to move the lips'
tatal	'mother's younger brother'	*čikpan*	'work'
tamš	'gums'	*daswua*	'to pile'
tohnto	'degenerate'	*doaǰida*	'healing'
tokih	'cotton'	*ǰɨgos*	'storm'
todsid	'to frighten'	*ǰɨwikon*	'to scrape'
čuagia	'net bag'	*ǰuni*	'dried cactus fruit'
čučul	'chicken'	*dakpon*	'to slip'
čukma	'dark'	*doʔag*	'mountain'
čɨposid	'to brand'	*ǰusukal*	'lizard sp.'
čɨlwin	'to rub'	*ǰuhki*	'rain'
čɨgitog	'to think'	*ǰiwhiadag*	'arrival'

Note also that there is a pattern to the distribution of the dental stops *t* and *d* versus the palatal affricates *č* and *ǰ*. In particular, *č* and *ǰ* only occur in position before the high vowels (cf. *čučul*, *čilwin*, *čikpan*, *doaǰida*, *ǰɨgos*, *juhki*) and *t* and *d* never occur in these positions, but they may appear in any other position: before the nonhigh vowels (*tatai*, *tokih*, *dakpon*, *doʔag*), before consonants and at the end of a word (*todsid*, *čiposid*). The situation is thus comparable to the one just examined in Zoque: A certain set of sounds appears in a particular context, while another set of phonetically similar sounds appears in a complementary class of contexts.

There are two ways in which this regularity in Papago can be expressed in terms of the concepts "list" and "rule." First, the dental stops could be set up as basic and a rule converting *t* and *d* to *č* and *ǰ*, respectively, before high vowels could be formulated. Alternatively, *č* and *ǰ* may be considered basic. This analysis would require a rule changing palatal affricates to the corresponding dental stops in three contexts: before the nonhigh vowels *a* and *o*, before consonants, and in word final position.

Several considerations favor the first alternative. First, palatalization of dentals before high vowels is a natural rule found in many languages. Second, such a rule has a rational phonetic interpretation. High vowels are produced by raising the body of the tongue: toward the hard palate for *i*, and toward the front and mid parts of the soft palate for the central and back high vowels *ɨ* and *u*. Similarly, the palatal consonants *č* and *ǰ* are articulated by raising the blade of the tongue toward the roof of the mouth, whereas dental stops do not involve such a raising of the tongue. Thus the rule shifting the dental stops to palatals before the high vowels can be viewed as a form of assimilation: The dentals are acquiring a certain feature which is employed in the articulation of the following vowel. On the other hand, a rule changing the palatals *č* and *ǰ* to *t* and *d*, respectively, before the back vowels *a* and *o*, before consonants, and in final position has no natural phonetic interpretation. Hence, all other things being equal, we are led to choose the rule which converts underlying dental stops to palatal affricates in positions before high vowels.

Universal tendencies in the pattern of underlying consonant systems also point in favor of the analysis which takes the dentals as basic. There are many languages which have plosives at the dental point of articulation and none at the palatal point. But there are few if any languages that have the palatal slot filled with *č* and *ǰ*, but lack *t* and *d*. The analysis which takes the palatals as basic would violate this universal tendency, and, all other things being equal, should thus be rejected—especially in view of the fact that the argument from phonetic plausibility points to the same conclusion.

On the basis of these considerations we can decide the matter in favor of a rule (12) shifting dental stops to the corresponding palatal affricates in position before high vowels.

(12) $\begin{bmatrix} \text{stop} \\ \text{dental} \end{bmatrix} \longrightarrow \begin{bmatrix} \text{affricate} \\ \text{palatal} \end{bmatrix} / \underline{\quad} \begin{bmatrix} \text{vowel} \\ \text{high} \end{bmatrix}$

Having examined several relatively simple examples of phonological rules, we will mention some heuristic principles which most linguists employ in phonological analysis. The first task is to isolate the sound patterns in the data by looking for gaps in the distribution of sounds or closely related sets of sounds. In the analysis of the Zoque data we noted that the voiced plosives appear only after nasals while the corresponding voiceless plosives do not, though they occur in all other positions. In Papago the set of palatal affricates appears before the high vowels but the corresponding dental stops do not, though they occur freely in other positions.

Having grouped the sounds together into sets of potential underlying segments and potential variants, the next step in the analysis is to determine which sound or set of sounds is basic and which is derived by a rule. Here two heuristic principles can be helpful. First, the conditioned variant often has a more limited distribution than the basic sound. The basic sound typically appears in a greater variety of contexts. In Zoque the voiced plosives appear only after nasals, while the corresponding voiceless plosives appear in all other positions; in Papago, the palatals *č* and *ǰ* are limited to positions immediately before high vowels, while the dentals occur before the other vowels, before consonants, and in final position. Secondly, many phonological rules involve assimilation of an underlying segment to its phonetic context. This was true of the Papago example, and also of the Zoque one, where the plosives can be viewed as taking on the voicing of the preceding nasal consonant. Hence, if we are faced with the choice between setting up some sound x as basic and deriving y by a rule, and setting up y as basic and deriving x, one criterion for deciding the issue would be to see if the rule changing x to y could be interpreted as a rule of assimilation while the converse rule changing y to x could not. If this difference in the two rules exists, then it is likely that x is the basic sound and y the conditioned variant.

As with all "rules of thumb," these criteria are not to be taken as rigid procedures which can be followed blindly. They are intended only to generate hypotheses about what principles underlie the data in the corpus. The resultant hypotheses are subject to further confirmation or disconfirmation as more and more data of the language are examined.

Chatino

Before closing this chapter, let us discuss one additional set of data from Chatino, a language of Mexico (Gleason 1955), to which the concepts of "list" and "rule" may be applied.

(13)

$k_A tá$	'you will bathe'	siyú	'juice'
$k_I sú$	'avocado'	sulá	'open!'
$k_U s_U{}^?wá$	'you will send'	tiyé	'stomach'
$s_E{}^?é$	'place'	la$^?$á	'side'
$š_I{}^?í$	'sad'	lo$^?$ó	'where'
$t_A{}^?á$	'fiesta'	ndikí	'you are burning'
$t_I hí$	'water'	nguší	'tomato'
$t_U{}^?wá$	'mouth'	kí$^?$	'fire'
kinó	'sandal'	há$^?$	'grass mat'

Examination of the data in (13) reveals the following generalizations with respect to the distribution of the voiceless vowels (indicated by upper case letters): (*a*) Voiceless vowels are limited to positions that are between voiceless consonants, (*b*) all voiceless vowels are unstressed, and (*c*) no unstressed voiced vowels appear between voiceless consonants. An additional generalization is that stress always appears on the final vowel of the word.

Since the voiced and voiceless vowels have complementary distributions, we may set up either one as basic and derive the other via a rule. The two heuristic principles discussed earlier suggest that voiced vowels are basic and voiceless ones derived, for the voiceless vowels have a more limited distribution and, furthermore, the rule producing them converts a basically unstressed voiced vowel to the corresponding voiceless vowel in position between voiceless consonants—a rule assimilating a vowel to its phonetic context. On this hypothesis, then, the rule would appear as (14).

(14)
$$\begin{bmatrix} \text{vowel} \\ \text{unstressed} \end{bmatrix} \longrightarrow [\text{voiceless}] \ / \begin{bmatrix} \text{consonant} \\ \text{voiceless} \end{bmatrix} \underline{\quad} \begin{bmatrix} \text{consonant} \\ \text{voiceless} \end{bmatrix}$$

This solution derives strong independent support from the fact that, to our knowledge, there is no language in which it has been proved necessary to postulate underlying voiceless vowels. In all those languages which have voiceless vowels phonetically, it is possible to derive them from underlying voiced vowels by phonological rule.

Recall that there is an additional regularity in the Chatino data: Stress falls predictably on the final vowel of the word. Therefore, the feature of stress must not be entered into the lexical representation of the morphemes, but rather must be assigned by rule. This rule of stress placement will differ from the rules we have considered so far in this chapter in that it will crucially depend upon the essentially grammatical information about where the word ends. Since we will be encountering in later chapters many aspects of phonological structure which depend crucially upon where a word or a morpheme begins and ends (e.g., rules which refer to the first vowel of a word, the final consonant of a word, morphemes that begin with a vowel, etc.), we will now introduce the notation that is commonly used to refer to these positions. We shall assume that the syntactic component of the grammar inserts the symbol #, called the "word boundary," immediately before the first segment in a word and immediately after the final segment in a word. In addition, we shall assume that the syntactic component inserts the symbol + (for typographical reasons a dash is perhaps used more often) between each morpheme within a word. (Of course, some words in the lexicon may be morphologically complex, thus the symbol + may be part of the lexical representation of a word.) The surface syntactic structure, which is at the same time the underlying phonological representation, of the Chimwi:ni word *kuɬe:ta* 'to bring' mentioned earlier in this chapter will be /ku + ɬe:t + a #/.

With this notation at our disposal we are now ready to formulate the Chatino stress rule. Since most of the words in (13) end in vowels, the last vowel of the word will stand in position immediately before the word boundary: For example, *kɪsú* 'avocado' will appear in the UR as /#kisu#/. For these words the stress rule can be written simply as (15).

(15)   [vowel] $\longrightarrow$ [stress]/____ #

However, for those words like *kíʔ* 'fire', which end in a glottal stop, the rule, as it is presently written, will not apply, since in the UR /#kiʔ#/ the segment which appears immediately before the word boundary is not a vowel. Rather, a glottal stop intervenes between the vowel which is to be assigned stress and the following word boundary. To handle cases like this in which certain material optionally intervenes between the segment undergoing the rule and the controlling factor in the environment of the rule (the # in this case), it has become customary in generative phonology to enclose this optionally intervening material within parentheses when stating the rule. Thus, the stress placement rule will take the form of (16).

(16)   [vowel] $\longrightarrow$ [stress]/____(C)#

In the data in (13) the only word final consonants are glottal stops. Rule (16) claims that if there are words that end with a different consonant, the preceding vowel would still be assigned stress. This seems likely to be correct.

To show how these rules work to convert the UR of 'avocado' and 'fire' into the correct phonetic representations, we provide the derivations of (17).

(17)   /#kisu#/   /#ki?#/   Underlying representation
       #kisú#   #kí?#   Stress placement
       #kɪsú#   —   Vowel devoicing

By convention, after all the phonological rules have applied the syntactic boundaries will be removed to yield the phonetic representation.

To summarize this chapter, we have seen that the phonetic representation of a sentence is determined by three distinct factors: (a) the lexical representation of the individual morphemes composing the sentence, (b) the syntactic structure in which these morphemes occur (e.g. the position of a sound relative to the word boundary), and (c) the phonological rules which specify the systematic features of pronunciation in terms of the information in (a) and (b).

Exercises

1. Georgian (Robins and Waterson 1952). *l*, a clear lateral and *ł*, a dark (velarized) lateral, are variants of the same underlying element. State the principles determining the choice of one as opposed to the other.

łamazad	'prettily'	zarali	'loss'	xeli	'hand'
leło	'goal'	kała	'tin'	xoło	'however'
saxłši	'at home'	pepeła	'butterfly'	cʰecʰxli	'fire'
łxena	'joy'	kleba	'reduce'	vxlečʰ	'I split'
kbiłs	'tooth'	ertʰxeł	'once'	cʰoli	'wife'

2. Sierra Popoluca. Aspiration is a predictable aspect of the pronunciation of consonants in Sierra Popoluca. Determine what principles underlie the distribution of this feature. In the following transcriptions, which show only as much phonetic detail as is relevant to the present problem, *t ʸ* represents an alveopalatal stop. The glottal stop *ʔ* is shown as being unaspirated in all contexts; this may be incorrect, but our source, Elson (1947), is not perfectly explicit on the matter.

petʰkuy	'broom'	hu:tʸʰ	'where'
petta:pʰ	'it is being swept'	ikapun	'his barrow'
kekʰpaʔ	'it flies'	ti:ttitʰ	'mestizo'
kekgakʰpaʔ	'it flies again'	nipʰ	'mouth'
nikʰpaʔ	'he goes'	ikkaʔ	'he killed it'
tʸu:kiʔ	'turtle'	makʰtiʔ	'ghost'
šiš	'cow'	ho:ppaʔ	'it rolls'
hos	'hole'	petʰpaʔ	'he sweeps'
ca:m	'very'	witʸʰpaʔ	'he walks'

kuy	'wood'	*ičič*	'he jerked it'
toc	'tongue'	*mičpaˀ*	'he is playing'
*mok*ʰ	'corn'	*pik*ʰ*ši*ˀ	'bow'

3. Greenlandic Eskimo (Schultz-Lorentzen 1945). There are five phonetic vowels but only three underlying vowels. What are they? What rules relate the underlying system to the phonetic? In the following transcriptions, *r* denotes a uvular trill.

ivnaq	'bluff'	*qasaloq*	'bark'
iperaq	'harpoon strap'	*ikusik*	'elbow'
imaq	'sea'	*qilaluvaq*	'white whale'
tuluvaq	'raven'	*qatigak*	'back'
itumaq	'palm of hand'	*sakiak*	'rib'
sava	'sheep'	*ugsik*	'cow'
nuna	'land'	*orpik*	'tree'
ine	'room'	*nerdloq*	'goose'
nanoq	'bear'	*marraq*	'clay'
iseraq	'ankle'	*iga*	'pot'
isse	'eye'	*igdlo*	'house'
sermeq	'glacier'	*sako*	'tool'

4. Mohawk (Postal 1968). Vowel length is not distinctive. State the rule generating long vowels.

wísk	'five'	*ké:saks*	'I look for it'
rayáthos	'he plants'	*royóˀteˀ*	'he works'
yékreks	'I push it'	*í:raks*	'he eats it'
raké:tas	'he scrapes'	*nikanúhzakeh*	'houses'
rehyá:raˀa	'he remembers'	*wahoyóˀdʌˀ*	'he worked'
rá:kʌs	'he sees her'	*ranú:weˀs*	'he likes it'

5. Sierra Miwok (Freeland 1951). Formulate a rule to predict the location of the stress in the following words.

há:naˀ	*kawá:či*
čá:mayiˀ	*watáksaˀ*
yá:ya:liˀ	*kaláŋpa:*
hánnaˀ	*paláttataˀ*
wíttapï̈ˀ	*čímteyyaˀ*
húššе:piˀ	*pátkayïˀ*

6. Margi (Hoffmann 1963). The present tense morpheme *a* sometimes appears with a high tone *á* and sometimes with a low tone *à*. The morpheme *gu̯* 'you' exhibits similar behavior. What principle determines when these morphemes have a high tone versus a low tone? The morpheme *vəl* 'fly' has a rising tone. Can the tonal shapes this morpheme induces on the *a* and *gu̯* morphemes be explained?

á dlà gú̯	'you fall'
á wì gú̯	'you run'
á ghà gú̯	'you reach'
à sá gù̯	'you go astray'
à tsú gù̯	'you beat'
à hú̯ gù̯	'you take'
á vəl gù̯	'you fly'

3

Alternations

In the preceding chapter we saw that one motivation for the postulation of phonological rules is the need to distinguish between **contrastive** and **noncontrastive** features of pronunciation. A feature is contrastive (roughly speaking) if there exist contexts in which the property in question could either appear or not appear, with no way to predict which in any given case. A noncontrastive feature, on the other hand, is one where in any given context one can predict whether the feature will occur or not. Given that speakers of a language do assign such features to words automatically, this behavior is appropriately accounted for by postulating phonological rules that assign values for noncontrastive features. Given such rules, there is no need to include noncontrastive features in the lexical representations of morphemes. Aspiration as opposed to lack of aspiration in stops and length as opposed to lack of length in vowels are phonetic properties that do not have to be included in the lexical representations of English.

In some cases a morpheme may **alternate** its pronunciation in different contexts as a consequence of the application of rules such as those in Chapter 2 that assign values for noncontrastive phonetic features. For instance, in Spanish the difference between [b], a bilabial voiced stop, and [ß], a bilabial voiced fricative, is not contrastive: The former sound occurs at the beginning of a phrase and after a nasal (whether that nasal is in the same word or not), whereas the latter sound occurs in all other contexts. The same morpheme may sometimes be pronounced with a [b] and sometimes with a [ß] depending upon the context in which that morpheme occurs; thus *el vaso* 'the glass' is pronounced [ɛl ßaso], but *un vaso* 'a glass' is pronounced [um baso]. The alternation in pronunciation between [ßaso] and [baso] is attributable to the rule that determines whether a voiced bilabial will be realized phonetically as a fricative or as a stop.

It is also very common to find alternations in the pronunciation of morphemes involving phonetic features that are contrastive in the language. Insofar as such alternations can be shown to be rule-governed rather than idiosyncratic, they provide additional evidence for the postulation of phonological rules. In this chapter we examine alternations involving contrastive features from three different languages in order to begin developing the descriptive and theoretical apparatus necessary for dealing with this important aspect of phonological structure.

Russian

Examine the following data from Russian:[1]

(1)

Nom. sg.	Dat. sg.	Nom. pl.	Gloss
xlep	xlebu	xleba	'bread'
grip	gribu	griby	'mushroom'
grop	grobu	groby	'coffin'
čerep	čerepu	čerepa	'skull'
xolop	xolopu	xolopy	'bondman'
trup	trupu	trupy	'corpse'
sat	sadu	sady	'garden'
prut	prudu	prudy	'pond'
cvet	cvetu	cveta	'color'
zakat	zakatu	zakaty	'sunset'
ras	razu	razy	'time'
zakas	zakazu	zakazy	'order'
les	lesu	lesa	'forest'
us	usu	usy	'whisker'
storoš	storožu	storoža	'guard'
duš	dušu	dušy	'shower'
rok	rogu	roga	'horn'
porok	porogu	porogy	'threshold'
rak	raku	raky	'crayfish'
porok	poroku	poroky	'vice'

[1] Our transcriptions here ignore certain variations in the pronunciation of the vowels that are dependent on stress location.

In these data the nominative singular is unsuffixed, containing just the root morpheme, while the dative singular and the nominative plural are suffixed. The dative singular suffix is always *u*, while the nominative plural suffix varies between *a* and *y* (a high, nonround, back vowel which is phonetically realized as *i* after velar consonants by a rule that we shall ignore here). Additionally, the last consonant of the noun stem exhibits a voicing alternation for some words (such as *xlep*, *xlebu*, *xleba*; *sat*, *sadu*, *sady*), while it is constant for others (such as *trup*, *trupu*, *trupy*; *cvet*, *cvetu*, *cveta*).

Now let us try to distinguish what is idiosyncratic from what is systematic about the pronunciation of these nouns. First, examination of the nominative plural and dative singular forms shows that whether or not the stem-final obstruent is voiced or voiceless is an idiosyncratic property of the final segment which must be memorized as part of the lexical representation. These data, along with many other such forms in Russian, show that we cannot predict on any phonetic, syntactic, or semantic grounds that the final consonant of the morpheme meaning 'coffin' will be voiced while that of 'corpse' will be voiceless. In fact, it is possible to find minimal pairs like *poroku*/*porogu* where the voicing quality of the stem-final consonant is the sole distinguishing feature. Hence the value (plus or minus) that a stem-final obstruent has for the phonetic property [voice] must be incorporated into the lexical representation of these stems as an idiosyncratic feature of the morpheme. The feature [voice] is contrastive in Russian for obstruents.

Second, unlike the dative singular suffix, the nominative plural suffix exhibits an alternation. Examination of the above data reveals that it is not possible to predict which alternant will appear after which noun stem solely on the basis of the phonetic character of the noun stem. Although there is some correlation between the -*a* alternant and the type of stress pattern a noun exhibits, this is not sufficient to eliminate the need for arbitrarily distinguishing stems that take the -*a* alternant from those that take the -*y* alternant. Idiosyncratic information of this sort, we claim, is properly characterized in the lexicon, where all idiosyncratic facts about the behavior of morphemes are to be stated. Thus it will be necessary to associate with each noun stem in the lexicon information as to which alternate (-*a* or -*y*) of the nominative plural suffix occurs with it. It is also an idiosyncratic fact that the nominative plural suffix occurs in the two shapes -*a* and -*y*. This variation is restricted to this particular morpheme and does not reflect a more general principle of the language. The lexical representation for the nominative plural suffix must, therefore, include the information that it has two alternants.

The situation sketched above might usefully be compared with the alternation exhibited by the English plural suffix mentioned in Chapter 2.

The alternants *-s*, *-z*, and *-iz* are determined by the **phonological** character of the final segment of the noun stem. Thus in English the distribution of the alternants *-s*, *-z*, and *-iz* can be predicted by rule. It is not necessary to associate with a noun stem any nonphonetic information in order to determine the shape that the plural suffix will assume after that stem. The distribution of *-a* and *-y* in Russian cannot be predicted in the same way; nonphonetic information must be included in the lexical entry for each noun stem indicating whether *-a* or *-y* is to be used. The exact form in which this is to be accomplished is not our concern here. The important point is that the alternation between *-a* and *-y* follows no general rule.

We have noted two respects in which the Russian data must be accounted for in terms of idiosyncratic properties of the lexical representation: the voicedness of the stem-final consonant and the selection of the alternant for the nominative plural suffix. Consider now whether the voicing alternation exhibited by the stem-final consonant of some of the stems in (1) also requires idiosyncratic lexical marking. With regard to this alternation in voicing, the following observations can be made:

(A) *There are stems with final voiced obstruents in the suffixed forms and corresponding voiceless obstruents in the unsuffixed forms. Examples are* xlep, xlebu, xleba; sat, sadu, sady.

(B) *There are stems with final voiceless obstruents in both suffixed and unsuffixed forms. Examples are* trup, trupu, trupy; cvet, cvetu, cveta.

(C) *There are no stems with a final voiced obstruent in the unsuffixed form.*

This alternation of voicing is not peculiar to masculine nouns; it occurs in a number of other morphological contexts in Russian. For example, it is also found in feminine nouns, where the underlying contrast between voiced and voiceless obstruents is preserved when the stems are followed by a case suffix, but neutralized when there is no case suffix. Thus only voiceless obstruents occur word-finally in the genitive plural (which consists of just the noun stem itself, without a case suffix) see (2) below.

How is this voicing alternation to be characterized in the grammar of Russian? One possibility is to list each alternant of the noun stem in the lexicon and to formulate rules for the selection of the appropriate alternant in the appropriate context. For example, the morpheme 'corpse' (which does not alternate in voicing) might be assigned a lexical representation such as [/trup/, noun, -y plural, etc.], while 'bread' (which does

(2)

Nom. sg.	Dat. sg.	Gen. pl.	Gloss
ryba	*rybe*	*ryp*	'fish'
tropa	*trope*	*trop*	'path'
pobeda	*pobede*	*pobet*	'victory'
sirota	*sirote*	*sirot*	'orphan'
groza	*groze*	*gros*	'storm'
krysa	*kryse*	*krys*	'rat'
lyža	*lyže*	*lyš*	'ski'
duša	*duše*	*duš*	'soul'
noga	*noge*	*nok*	'leg'
sobaka	*sobake*	*sobak*	'dog'

alternate in voicing) might be represented as [/xlep/ *or* /xleb/, noun, *-a* plural, etc.]. We would then require rules of selection like the following:

(3)   *If a morpheme has alternants that differ with respect to the voicing of a final obstruent, select the alternate with a final voiceless obstruent when the morpheme appears at the end of a word; otherwise, select the alternant with a final voiced obstruent.*

Although technically this treatment can probably be made to work, there are a number of considerations that suggest that it is fundamentally in error. The basic criticism is that this sort of analysis fails to adequately characterize the rule-governed nature of the voicing alternation in Russian. The analysis sketched above claims that it is not predictable whether a morpheme will exhibit an alternation in voicing. Since we have to list both alternants for such morphemes as 'bread' (*xleb-u*, but *xlep*), 'coffin' (*grob-u*, but *grop*), 'garden' (*sad-u*, but *sat*), and 'pond' (*prud-u*, but *prut*), this analysis claims that these alternations are an idiosyncratic peculiarity of each morpheme, an idiosyncracy which must be memorized when learning Russian. That is to say, according to this analysis it is an accident that 'bread' has two shapes (one ending in *b* and the other in *p*), and that 'coffin' has two shapes (again, one ending in *b* and the other in *p*), just as it is an accident (in the sense that it follows from nothing general about the language) that the nominative plural masculine suffix has the two shapes *-a* and *-y*. Furthermore, this analysis says that it is an accident that there are no morphemes in Russian having a nonalternating final voiced obstruent (cf., (C) above). Since there are morphemes such as 'corpse' that end in a voiceless obstruent and do not alternate, we would expect there to be morphemes that end in a voiced obstruent that do not alternate. This analysis gives no explanation for the fact that there are no words in the Russian language that end in a voiced obstruent. Not only is the absence of word-final voiced obstruents unexplained, it is not shown to be in any way connected to the rule of selection given in (3). Notice that (3) does **not** say that voiced obstruents may not occur in final position. Rather, it says that **if** a morpheme exhibits alternants differing in the voicing of the final obstruent, the alternant with the voiceless obstruent will appear when the morpheme is word final. It leaves open the question of whether there are morphemes ending in voiced obstruents that do not alternate.

It seems clear that the voicing alternation is not an idiosyncratic property of each morpheme whose stem happens to end in a voiced obstruent in suffixed forms. Rather, it is an instance of a general regularity that holds for any such morpheme having this phonetic structure, regardless of its meaning or syntactic properties. Hence the fact that 'bread' is pronounced with a final voiceless sound when at the end of a word in Russian is analogous to the fact that the initial sound of *cab* in English is aspirated. In both cases a phonetic property is determined by some general principle of pronunciation. In Russian, word-final obstruents are always voiceless, just as in English a voiceless stop is always aspirated if syllable-initial.

This suggests that the proper description of the voicing alternation in Russian is to specify the voicelessness of the stem-final obstruents of the alternating morphemes by means of a general phonological rule, just as in the preceding chapter we specified the aspiration of initial voiceless stops in English as following from the rule of aspiration. Thus, we will include in the phonological component of the grammar of Russian the following rule, called final devoicing (FD).

(4)   [obstruent] $\longrightarrow$ [voiceless]/___#

Given a rule such as (4), it is no longer necessary to include both alternants for morphemes such as 'bread', 'coffin', and 'garden' in the lexicon. If we list just the alternants ending in voiced obstruents (/xleb/, /grob/, and /sad/), then we can account for the alternants ending in a voiceless obstruent (/xlep/, /grop/, and /sat/) by means of the rule of final devoicing. Furthermore, given rule (4), it is no longer unpredictable which morphemes will show an alternation and which will not. All those morphemes that end in a voiced obstruent in their lexical representation will be pronounced with a voiceless obstruent when they appear in word-final position. To know whether a morpheme will alternate or not, all that one needs to know is whether or not it ends in a voiced obstruent.

Under the analysis we are now proposing, each stem in (1) and (2) will now have just one lexical representation, where the stem-final obstruent can be either voiced or voiceless—an idiosyncratic feature that must be memorized for each morpheme. The fact that morphemes whose lexical representations end in a voiced obstruent are sometimes pronounced with a final voiceless obstruent follows, we claim, from the general rule of FD, which applies when these consonants are syntactically at the end of a word. Thus, for example, the UR for 'coffin', when used as the plural subject of some Russian sentence, will be /#grob-y#/. No phonological rules apply to this input, and so the phonetic representation (at the level of discussion considered here) will be the same as the underlying representation. On the other hand, if the same noun is used in the nominative singular, the UR will be /#grob#/. FD will now apply, since we have an obstruent /b/ immediately before the word boundary; this rule will change the underlying voiced stop to the corresponding voiceless stop *p*.

To recapitulate briefly, we have observed that the distinction between idiosyncratic and systematic features of pronunciation is relevant to the phenomenon of alternation. This distinction can be characterized in essentially the same way that it was for examples like those in Chapter 2, which did not involve alternations. Idiosyncratic alternations are described by listing in the lexicon, while regular alternations are the result of the operation of a phonological rule that alters the underlying shape of a morpheme in some particular context.

Accounting for alternations by means of the same mechanism used to characterize the predictability of nonalternating features like aspiration in English claims, in effect, that these two phenomena are very much alike. And, indeed, they are. In both cases a property of pronunciation is determined by the context in which a segment occurs. In general, morphemic alternations occur more frequently at the edges of morphemes than in the interior, for it is the segments at the beginnings and ends of morphemes that are most likely to appear in different contexts and thus take on different phonological shapes. Segments within morphemes, however, are also affected by the context in which they appear, but since this context is often a constant one, alternations in the pronunciation of such segments are not especially frequent.

Observe that the final-devoicing rule converts underlying voiced segments into voiceless ones. In this case, a phonological rule changes underlying segments with respect to a phonetic property that plays a fundamental role in lexical representations. That is to say, in underlying representations in Russian both voiced and voiceless obstruents occur, and the choice of one over the other serves to distinguish one morpheme from another. Thus, *porok* 'threshold' has the UR /porog/, whereas *porok* 'vice' has the UR /porok/. FD has the consequence that morphemes with different URs may overlap onto the same phonetic form, as /porog/ and /porok/ do. The aspiration rule in English, as we observed earlier, does not have this property; it specifies information about an aspect of pronunciation that is irrelevant to underlying representations. The aspiration rule does not result in two distinct URs being pronounced in the same way. Clearly, however, this observed difference between the two rules is not a function of the character of the processes involved—they are both instances of context-determined pronunciation—but of the fact that the phonetic properties they assign have a different status. Henceforth we will say that a phonetic property such as voicing in Russian obstruents is lexically relevant (that is, URs of different morphemes may be distinguished by the presence or absence of such properties), whereas the property of aspiration in English is lexically irrelevant (that is, two URs cannot be distinguished solely by the presence or absence of this phonetic property).[2] We can now say that phonological rules that affect lexically relevant phonetic properties may result in identical pronunciations of lexically different morphemes; rules that affect lexically irrelevant properties do not have such side effects.

Before going any further, it is important to make clear what claims are being made by the analysis of the Russian voicing alternation that we have proposed. The basic claim has been emphasized repeatedly in the course of the discussion: The appearance of a voiceless obstruent at the end of a noun stem when unsuffixed is the consequence of a general constraint on Russian pronunciation, not an idiosyncratic feature of the individual morphemes that exhibit such an alternation. Furthermore, we have claimed that what determines the voicelessness of these obstruents is their position: namely, being at the end of a word.

What evidence is there that a general devoicing rule exists in Russian and that the conditioning factor is word-final position? First, there is the simple fact that all word-final obstruents in Russian are voiceless. The FD rule that we have postulated would account for this systematic gap; the absence of word-final voiced obstruents would be the consequence of the operation of a phonological rule. We have already argued against an analysis that lists both alternants in the lexicon on the grounds that this gap is an unexplained accident in such an analysis. But suppose it is admitted that a general rule of phonology produces such alternants as *xlep* and *sat* from underlying /#xleb#/ and /#sad#/, but instead of it being word-final position that conditions the devoicing, the rule is formulated to operate in the nominative singular form of masculine nouns and the

---

[2] Lexically relevant versus lexically irrelevant properties are more commonly referred to as distinctive versus nondistinctive or contrastive versus noncontrastive.

genitive plural form of feminine nouns. This would be done by simply listing these morphological categories as the contexts in which the devoicing rule applies. Such an analysis claims, correctly, that there is a significant connection between the voicing alternation in the different pronunciations of 'bread', 'garden', and so on (the alternation in both cases is an instance of the operation of a devoicing rule), but that it is accidental that the morphological categories of nominative singular (for masculine nouns) and genitive plural (for feminine nouns), as well as a number of other categories in other noun declensions, in adjectives, and in verbs are correlated with word-final position of the stem. That is, under this alternative analysis it is still accidental that voiced obstruents do not occur word finally, for it is purely accidental that all of the morphological environments in which the devoicing rule applies happen to match up with word-final position.

We shall show in a later chapter that it is often necessary to restrict phonological rules to apply only in certain morphological contexts. In the present case, however, the reasonableness of this analysis is diminished considerably by virtue of the facts that (1) the morphological categories to which the rule would have to refer are numerous and heterogeneous; (2) each of these categories would just happen to correlate with word-final position; (3) none of the categories correlates with nonfinal position. However, we do not have to rely on appeals to reasonableness here, for there are other relevant facts.

If devoicing is a phenomenon not governed by word-final position but by an arbitrary list of morphological categories, we have no explanation for the tendency on the part of native speakers of Russian to devoice word final obstruents when acquiring another language such as English. Notice that this same fact can also be used to argue against an analysis that claims there is no general devoicing rule at all and that the alternation must be memorized as an idiosyncratic property of each individual morpheme. If such an analysis were correct, a Russian speaker learning a language with a different stock of morphemes ought not to be inclined to devoice final obstruents at all.

Related to this point is the fact that when foreign words that end in voiced obstruents are borrowed into Russian, they are automatically adjusted to the native pattern in accord with the FD rule. For example, such words as *garaš* 'garage', *gas* 'gauze', and *klup* 'club' show a devoicing of the final consonant. The underlying voiced obstruents show up when these stems are followed by a case suffix like the dative: *garažu*, *gazu*, *klubu*.

Another piece of evidence against the claim that there is no rule of final devoicing in Russian is the fact that when new words are coined, they automatically obey the constraint that bars final voiced obstruents. For example, the first word in *Gulag Archipelago* is pronounced with a final *k*. This word is an acronym formed from the morphemes *glavnoje* 'main', *upravlenije* 'control', and *lager* 'camp'. Note that in the morpheme *lager* the *g* is followed by a vowel and hence never devoices to *k*. But when the acronym is formed, the underlying /g/, now being in final position, changes to *k*. This demonstrates the open-endedness of the final-devoicing constraint. A projective rule applying to any obstruent meeting the contextual requirements of the rule is necessary if the grammar is to predict this facet of the linguistic behavior of speakers of Russian. Without such a rule we would be claiming that it is entirely accidental that morphemes ending in invariably voiced final obstruents are never added freely to the Russian lexicon.

Related to this point is the important fact that if a Russian hears a word that he has never encountered before used in a morphological category in which the stem is followed by a case suffix, he is automatically able to use the word correctly in the nonsuffixed form, even though this form may have a different pronunciation, which he has never heard before. For instance, suppose the Russian hears someone talking about a new product: "Look at my new *rub-y!*" Our native speaker of Russian might very well ask "What's a *rup?*", but he would never say *rub*. That is, he would automatically change the voicing feature in the stem-final obstruent even though he has never, by hypothesis, heard the pronunciation *rup* before. This fact can be used to argue against another analysis that might be given to these Russian nouns. In the beginning of our discussion we observed that it is an idiosyncratic feature of each morpheme whether or not its stem-final obstruent is pronounced voiced or voiceless before a case suffix: compare *trup-y* 'corpses' with *grob-y* 'coffins'. We then selected the alternant appearing before the case suffix as the underlying form of the stem and formulated a rule to generate the nonsuffixed alternants like *grop*. On the other hand, it might be suggested that we select the nonsuffixed forms like *trup* and *grop* as basic and formulate a rule that voices obstruents before the following vowel of the case suffix. Of course, this rule would have to be prevented from applying so as to voice the final obstruents of the many morphemes like *trup* which do not show the alternation. This might be accomplished by simply including some extra, arbitrary piece of information in the lexical representations of these morphemes to indicate that they are exceptions to the voicing rule. But with this analysis it is a complete accident that there are no word-final voiced obstruents in Russian. Further, this treatment has no way of explaining why Russian speakers automatically know the correct pronunciation of a nonsuffixed morpheme when they hear it in a suffixed form. According to this analysis there is no predictable connection between the voicing character of a stem-final obstruent in the unsuffixed as opposed to the suffixed form of a stem; Russian speakers must hear each form before they can assign a correct pronunciation (voiced or voiceless) to the final obstruent.

Having provided a number of arguments for the rule of final devoicing, we will now consider how this rule interacts with several other phonological rules of Russian. Examine the verbal forms in (5).

(5)

Infinitive	Masc. past	Fem. past	Neuter past	Plural past	Gloss
pisat'	*pisal*	*pisala*	*pisalo*	*pisali*	ˈwriteˈ
viset'	*visel*	*visela*	*viselo*	*viseli*	ˈhangˈ
govorit'	*govoril*	*govorila*	*govorilo*	*govorili*	ˈspeakˈ
čitat'	*čital*	*čitala*	*čitalo*	*čitali*	ˈreadˈ
smotret'	*smortrel*	*smotrela*	*smotrelo*	*smotreli*	ˈlookˈ

1 sg. pres.	Masc. past	Fem. past	Neuter past	Plural past	Gloss
grebu	*grep*	*grebla*	*greblo*	*grebli*	ˈrowˈ
skrebu	*skrep*	*skrebla*	*skreblo*	*skrebli*	ˈscrapeˈ
nesu	*nes*	*nesla*	*neslo*	*nesli*	ˈcarryˈ
pasu	*pas*	*pasla*	*paslo*	*pasli*	ˈherdˈ
lezu	*les*	*lezla*	*lezlo*	*lezli*	ˈcrawlˈ
metu	*mel*	*mela*	*melo*	*meli*	ˈsweepˈ
pletu	*plel*	*plela*	*plelo*	*pleli*	ˈplaitˈ
obretu	*obrel*	*obrela*	*obrelo*	*obreli*	ˈfindˈ
bredu	*brel*	*brela*	*brelo*	*breli*	ˈloungeˈ
kradu	*kral*	*krala*	*kralo*	*krali*	ˈstealˈ
kladu	*klal*	*klala*	*klalo*	*klali*	ˈplaceˈ
peku	*pek*	*pekla*	*peklo*	*pekli*	ˈbakeˈ
seku	*sek*	*sekla*	*seklo*	*sekli*	ˈthrashˈ
mogu	*mok*	*mogla*	*moglo*	*mogli*	ˈbe ableˈ
beregu	*berek*	*beregla*	*bereglo*	*beregli*	ˈguardˈ

Inspection of the first group of verbs reveals several morphological properties. All the infinitive forms end in *-t'* (a palatalized dental stop), which we take to be the infinitive suffix. The material preceding the infinitive suffix is the verb stem. Hence, at the level of detail considered here, we have the URs / #pisa-t' # /, / #vise-t' # /, and so on. Examination of the past tense forms shows that the verb stem is always followed by an *-l*, which we may consider to be the past tense suffix. Furthermore, past tense verbal forms in Russian show gender and number agreement with the subject of the sentence. The agreement is in the form of a suffix that is affixed after the past tense marker -*l*-. The agreement suffix is -*a* if the subject is feminine singular, -*o* if the subject is neuter singular, and -*i* if the subject is plural. A masculine singular subject requires a form of the verb that lacks any overt suffix. Hence, we have URs like / #pisa-l# / for the masc. sg., / #pisa-l-a# / for the fem. sg., / #pisa-l-o# / for the neut. sg., and / #pisa-l-i# / for the pl.

Inspection of the second group of verbs in (5) reveals three alternations. First, some stems show a voicing alternation in their final consonant such that a voiceless obstruent shows up in the masculine past, while the corresponding voiced obstruent appears elsewhere (as in the case of *greb-/grep*, *lez-/les*, *mog-/mok*); other stems show a final voiceless obstruent in all forms (such as *nes*, *pek*). Second, there is an alternation between the presence and the absence of the past tense suffix -*l*-. In particular, this suffix is absent in some forms in the masculine past (e.g., *grep*, *les*, *nes*, *mok*,), while for others it is pronounced—all forms of the first group and *mel* through *klal* in the second. Finally, this latter group of stems shows a dental stop before the 1 sg. present suffix -*u* but not in any of the past tense forms.

Having isolated the alternations, we now proceed to determine whether they are idiosyncratic variations peculiar to individual morphemes or whether there is some generalization to account for the observed alternations by means of phonological rules. With regard to the voicing alternation, it is evident on the basis of forms like *nesu* and *lezu* that it is impossible to predict whether or not the stem-final obstruent is voiced or voiceless in the present tense form or in the feminine, neuter, and plural past tense forms. Hence, the voicing character of the stem-final obstruent is idiosyncratic information that must be memorized as part of the lexical representation of each stem. The question then is whether alternants like *grep*, *les*, and *mok* must also be memorized as idiosyncratic variants. Clearly, this is not the case, especially in view of our discussion of the voicing alternation in nouns. The fact that stems with underlying final voiced obstruents like /greb/, /lez/, and /mog/ show voiceless ones in the masculine past is automatically predicted by FD, since these obstruents stand at the end of the word. Hence, the voiceless alternants must not be listed in the lexicon since they follow from the FD rule already in the grammar.

Turning to the alternation of *l* with $\emptyset$, we once again ask whether the absence of *l* in some of the masculine past forms is an idiosyncratic property of particular stems or whether it follows from some independent property that these stems share in common. The data reveal that *l* fails to appear when both of the following conditions are satisfied: when no suffix follows and when a consonant immediately precedes. These two factors governing the absence of *l* can be captured by the following rule, which we shall call *l*-drop.[3]

(6) $l \longrightarrow \emptyset / C\_\_\_$ #

Given this rule, masculine past forms with underlying voiceless consonants such as /#nes-l#/, and /#pek-l#/ are mapped onto the correct phonetic representations *nes* and *pek* in a straightforward manner. However, observe that for underlying representations like /#greb-l#/, /#lez-l#/, and /#mog-l#/ the stem-final voiced obstruents come to stand in word-final position—the context for FD—only as a result of the application of *l*-drop. Hence, in order to devoice the stem-final consonants of these forms by FD, we must permit FD to apply not only to obstruents that appear immediately before # in the UR—as in such nouns as /#xleb#/ and /#sad#/—but also to obstruents that come to stand in word-final position as a result of the application of *l*-drop. Exactly how this is to be accomplished is the subject of much current theoretical debate. At this point we shall simply introduce the device that has traditionally been employed in generative phonology to accomplish this task. We shall say that an ordering relation may be imposed on pairs of phonological rules. This permits a given phonological rule to apply to a structure created by some other phonological rule. Hence, in the present case we shall say that there is an ordering restriction in the grammar of Russian such that FD applies only after *l*-drop has had a chance to apply. Given such an ordering restriction, we now have derivations like the following, which show how the UR is converted into the PR for the masculine past forms of 'row', 'crawl', and 'be able'.

(7)   /#greb-l#/   #lez-l#/   /#mog-l#/
          #greb#   #lez#   #mog#   *l*-drop
          #grep#   #les#   #mok#   FD

For the moment we shall assume that the device of rule ordering is made available by the theory of grammar, and we will employ it freely in the descriptions that follow. In Chapter 8 we provide an explicit discussion and justification for this device.

Turning now to the alternation of dental stops with $\emptyset$, recall that some stems show a *t* or *d* before the 1 sg. present suffix (such as *met-u* 'sweep' and *krad-u* 'steal'), but an absence of this sound in all of the past-tense forms (*mel, mela, melo, meli; kral, krala, kralo, krali*). Which

---

[3] This rule must be restricted to apply to just the past tense suffix since there is an adjectival suffix -*l* that does not delete: *kruk* 'circle', *krug-l*, *krug-l-a*, etc., 'round'.

alternant, then, is basic? If the alternant with the stop present is selected as the UR, we require a rule of deletion. But if the ∅ alternant is basic, we require a rule inserting dental stops. Examining the latter alternative first, we observe that although we could formulate a rule inserting a dental stop between vowels (the insertion of consonants to break up vowel clusters is quite common, but a dental stop is not the type of consonant that is usually inserted), there is no way to predict whether the consonant will be voiced *d* or voiceless *t*; compare the near minimal pair *bredu* with *obretu*. Hence, if the insertion analysis is to be maintained, it would be necessary to associate some extra arbitrary piece of information with each stem telling whether the inserted dental stop is to be voiced or voiceless. But this suggests that the initial hypothesis that the insertion of the dental stop is predictable was wrong. Rather, it appears that whether or not a stem ends in a *t* or a *d* before the *-u* suffix is an idiosyncratic property of the lexical representation.

There is another reason for rejecting the insertion analysis. If stems of such shapes as *me-* and *kra-* were set up as basic, we would be creating an odd gap in the inventory of basic stem shapes. There would be stems ending in labial consonants (*greb-*, *skreb-*), in velars (*mog-*, *pek-*), and dental fricatives (*nes-*, *lez-*), but none in dental stops, despite the fact that dental stops are basic sounds in Russian and occur in other positions (for example, stem initially). Furthermore, it would just happen to be the case that the consonants that get inserted before the *-u* suffix are dental stops, precisely the sounds that would be absent from stem-final position in the proposed URs. The point here is that typically the distribution of sounds is fairly symmetrical in underlying representations, and a skewed distribution in phonetic representations is characteristically the result of the application of some rule (e.g., in Russian there are no voiced obstruents at the end of a word in phonetic representation because of the rule of final devoicing).

Given that the dental stops are part of the lexical representations, we must now determine if there is any rule that will produce the ∅ alternants. Since the dental stops do not appear in the past tense, and since the past tense is marked by the suffix *-l* immediately following the verb stem, a rule deleting dental stops before *-l* suggests itself.[4] We will refer to this rule as dental stop deletion (DSD).

(8)
$$\begin{bmatrix} \text{stop} \\ \text{dental} \end{bmatrix} \longrightarrow \emptyset /\_\_l$$

[4] This rule must also be restricted to apply only in the environment of the past tense suffix *-l*, since dental stops remain before *l* internal to a morpheme (*dlato* 'chisel') as well as before other suffixes consisting of *l* (*met-l-a* 'broom'; *odut-l* 'swollen, bloated'; *pod-l* 'mean, vile'). See Lightner (1972) for discussion.

We must now determine if this rule is crucially ordered with respect to any of the other rules we have developed. Recall that *l*-drop was formulated to drop *l* in the context C_____ #. Thus, given the proposed formulations of the two rules, both are in competition with one another with respect to such URs as /#met-l#/ and /#krad-l#/. If *l*-drop applies, the conditioning factor for the deletion of the dental stops would be removed and /#met#/ and /#krad#/ (ultimately *krat* by FD) would be derived instead of the correct forms *mel* and *kral*. But if DSD applies to the UR first to obtain /#me-l#/ and /#kra-l#/, *l*-drop will no longer be applicable, resulting in the correct PRs. Thus, we shall enter into the grammar of Russian the ordering restriction that DSD precedes *l*-drop, ensuring that in any derivation DSD must be tried to be applied before *l*-drop is.

The verb 'grow' (*rostu, ros, rosla, roslo, rosli*) independently motivates the ordering of DSD before *l*-drop. As with the other verbs in (5), the correct UR is to be identified with the alternant appearing in the present tense. Given the rules and ordering restrictions already in the grammar, the derivations for *rostu, ros,* and *rosla* proceed as follows:

(9) /#rost-u#/   /#rost-l#/   /#rost-l-a#/
     ---------   *ros-l*   *ros-l-a*   DSD
     ---------   *ros*   ---------   *l*-drop
     ---------   ----   ---------   FD

Recall that DSD was ordered before *l*-drop to guarantee that in forms such as /#met-l#/ the *t* deletes instead of the *l*. But if a consonant precedes the stem-final dental stop in the UR, then upon deletion of the dental stop by DSD this consonant will come to stand immediately before the -*l*. If it is true that *l*-drop applies after DSD, the *l* should delete in the masculine past of such forms. The fact that /#ros-l#/ from /#rost-l#/ changes to /#ros#/ shows that the decision to order DSD before *l*-drop was a correct one.

All of the data in (5) are now accounted for by the three rules we have postulated (final devoicing, *l*-drop, and dental stop deletion) and the two ordering restrictions (dental stop deletion precedes *l*-drop and *l*-drop precedes final devoicing).

In the remainder of this chapter we will examine some additional analyses of various phonological alternations. In general, the goal of analysis is to distinguish idiosyncratic from regular alternations, expressing the regular ones in terms of phonological rules that, when applied to the UR, yield the various phonetic alternants. The task of analyzing an alternation can be broken down into roughly three steps.

First, a preliminary morphological analysis of the data is necessary in order to identify the various alternants of a single morpheme. Typically, this involves segmenting the words (or phrases) of the utterance into their constituent parts: roots or stems, and prefixes, suffixes, or infixes. Sometimes at this stage of analysis a sound or sound sequence may appear between two morphemes, and there is no way to tell whether it is part of the preceding or of the following morpheme. Both possibilities must be left open to be decided upon as the analysis progresses.

Second, the various alternants that a morpheme exhibits are grouped together and examined to see whether there is a pattern to the alternations; that is, are the differing shapes assumed by morpheme A paralleled by the same or similar differences for morphemes B, C, D, and so on? If so, what principle(s) underlies this pattern of alternation? Although it is impossible to state any procedures that will guarantee discovery of the principles underlying the alternations in morpheme shape, one can be guided by the fact that alternations characteristically involve natural classes of sounds (obstruents, high vowels, velar consonants, and so on). Furthermore, the contexts in which the alternations occur are usually expressible in the terms of natural classes (after a vowel, next to a labial consonant, before a high vowel, and so on) or particular positions in the word or phrase (at the end of a phrase, at the beginning of a word, in the second syllable from the end of a word, and so on).

Having determined that the sound or sound class x alternates with the sound or sound class y so that x appears in the context(s) a while y appears in the context(s) b, the third step involves setting up the UR for the alternation and stating the rule(s) that will produce the correct phonetic shapes. Here, four choices are theoretically possible: First, we may set up x as basic and formulate a rule converting x to y in the context b;[5] second, we may take y as basic and postulate a rule taking y to x in the context a; third, both phonetic variants x and y may come from some different underlying sound z by way of a rule converting z to x in the context a, and a rule taking z to y in context b; four, x and y may both be included in the UR, with rules that will delete y in environment a and x in environment b. The choice among these four alternatives is made on the basis of a number of considerations. Two of the most important are the criterion of phonological predictability and the naturalness (plausibility) of the rules.

The predictability criterion covers cases like the following: Suppose that we find some xs in context a that alternate with y in context b, but in addition there are a substantial number of other xs that do not alternate,

---

[5] We speak here only of the simplest case where a single rule derives y from a basic x. In more complex cases, two or more rules might be involved, with x being transformed into some other sound(s) before ending up, ultimately, as y.

remaining x in both of the contexts a and b. In such a situation we could not set up x as underlying and have a rule converting basic x to y in the context b, because there would be no way to distinguish the xs that alternate with y from those that do not. By the criterion of phonological predictability we are forced to see if y can be selected as underlying, with a rule taking underlying y to x in the context a. This will be possible if there are no ys that occur in both the contexts a and b. Recall the voicing alternation in Russian, for example. Some ts alternated with d (*sat/sadu*, for instance), but a significant number did not (*cvet/cvetu*, for instance). In order to predict the alternation between t and d on purely phonological grounds, we had to select the voiced sound as basic. Given an underlying voiced obstruent, it was possible to predict when devoicing would occur—namely, in final position. There are no voiced obstruents in word-final position in Russian. Had we taken the voiceless sound to be basic, it would not have been possible to predict on phonological grounds when voicing would occur: A morpheme like *sat* has a voiced consonant before a case suffix, but *cvet* does not. This difference in behavior of morphemes is not correlated with any other phonological facts.

In some cases it will not be possible to have a general rule taking basic xs to y because of the existence of nonalternating xs, or a rule taking basic ys to x because of nonalternating ys. In such situations one can sometimes motivate an underlying z for the $x \sim y$ alternation which will be converted to x and y in the appropriate environments. (Nonalternating xs and nonalternating ys would then be regarded as coming from basic xs and basic ys, respectively; only those forms where x and y alternate would be derived from z.) Often, however, such an analysis can not be motivated; in such a case, the alternation between x and y must be regarded as being the result of a rule that is restricted in its application. A speaker must learn not just the rule but also which lexical items are subject to the rule. We will refer to such rules as being lexically determined, as opposed to rules that need only refer to the phonological or syntactic environment in which a sound appears and not to the particular lexical item involved.

Many times one will find an alternation between x and y where there are no invariant xs in the contexts a and b, but no invariant ys in these contexts either. The predictability criterion is therefore inapplicable. In such cases the choice between taking x or y as basic can usually be determined by the relative naturalness of the corresponding rules x $\longrightarrow$ y versus y $\longrightarrow$ x. If changing xs to y in the environment b represents a more expected process phonetically than does changing ys to x in the environment a, then the former analysis is preferred.

In the majority of cases where the predictability criterion is applicable, the associated rule(s) will be natural as well. But it is possible to find cases where predictability considerations and naturalness considerations are in conflict. The resolution of such a conflict must be made by either weighting one of the criteria more heavily or by bringing additional factors to bear. The question of how to weight the various criteria used in selecting a phonological analysis remains one of the most important problems confronting contemporary phonological theory. Clear answers are not yet in view. For some discussion of the matter see Chapter 5 and Zwicky (1975).

After the UR has been determined and the phonological rule formulated, the final step in the analysis is to see if the rule must be ordered with respect to any other rules in the grammar. In the simplest cases this can be determined by locating a form in whose derivation two rules, A and B, interact. If the rules when applied in the order A–B produce the correct output, while the opposite order yields the wrong output, then it is necessary to place an ordering restriction on the rules to the effect that A must always have a chance to apply before B. If the same output is obtained regardless of the order in which the two rules are applied, no ordering restriction is needed and the two rules are said to be unordered.

Needless to say, these four steps are not to be interpreted as rigid procedures of analysis that must always be followed in order. In fact, this is often impossible, because a decision at one step may materially affect the choice made at another step. For instance, the way in which a particular rule is formulated often depends on its ordering relationship to the other rules. These steps are merely intended to make explicit the kinds of questions that arise in the course of the analysis of an alternation. In other words, the analysis of any phonological alternation will implicitly take a stand on the morphological structure of the words involved, on the identification of allomorphs, on the underlying and the derived forms of the morpheme, on the rule or rules relating the underlying form to the derived phonetic alternants, and on the potential interactions of these rules with other rules in the grammar.

Chamorro

The next set of data we shall discuss comes from Chamorro, a language spoken on Guam (Topping 1968). The following vowels are to be found in phonetic representations in this language.

(10)   i   u

                      I   U

                      e   o

                             ə

                      ä   a

The vowels ɪ and ʊ are described by Topping as being intermediate between *i* and *e* and between *u* and *o*, respectively. Furthermore, they only occur unstressed. As we shall see, this fact is of significance in describing the phonological structure of these vowels. But before getting to this point, let us examine the following data.

(11)

gwíhən	'fish'	*i gwíhən*	'the fish'
gúmə	'house'	*i gímə*	'the house'
túnuʔ	'to know'	*en tínuʔ*	'you know'
húluʔ	'up'	*sän híluʔ*	'upward'
pécu	'chest'	*i pécu*	'the chest'
tómu	'knee'	*i tému*	'the knee'
ótdut	'ant'	*mi étdut*	'lots of ants'
óksuʔ	'hill'	*gi éksuʔ*	'at the hill'
láhɪ	'male'	*i láhɪ*	'the male'
láguʊ	'north'	*sän lǽguʊ*	'toward north'

The forms in the left-hand column show a contrast between front and back vowels in the initial syllable of the root, while in the right-hand column this contrast is neutralized—only front vowels appear in the initial syllable of the root. By the principle of phonological predictability we are naturally led to set up as basic the vocalism appearing in the first column and have a rule that will front the root-initial vowel when preceded by various particles such as *i*, *en*, and *sän*. Furthermore, all of these particles contain front vowels, so this vowel-fronting process can be viewed as an assimilatory phenomenon. Finally, this rule must be restricted to apply only to the first vowel of the root; it does not apply to vowels in the second syllable (*pécu*, not *pécɪ*). Since we have not yet developed the notation to refer to syntactic positions like "the first vowel of a root," we shall not formalize the rule here, but merely state it in prose:

(12) Vowel fronting: Specify the first vowel of a root as having the features **front** and **nonround** when the first vowel to the left of it is a front vowel.

With the vowel-fronting process analyzed, we can now discuss the phonology of the ɪ, ʊ, and ə vowels. Toward this end, examine the following data:

(13)

dǽgɪ	'to lie'	*i dinəgíhu*	'my lie'
gódɪ	'to tie'	*i ginɪdéhu*	'my thing tied'
dágu	'yam'	*i dəgúhu*	'my yam'
pécu	'chest'	*i pɪcóhu*	'my chest'

gwíhən 'fish' *i gwɪhä̃nhu* 'my fish'
pígwə 'betel nut' *i pɪgwá*ʔhu* 'my betel nut'

Morphologically, these forms contain the definite particle *i* plus the possessive suffix *-hu* 'my'. In addition, the nominals derived from the verbs 'lie' and 'tie' contain an infix *-in-* that appears immediately after the first consonant of the root: *d-in-əgi-hu* and *g-in-ɪde-hu*. Subtracting these particles and affixes, we find the following system of alternation.

(14)   *dä̃gɪ   gódɪ   dágʊ   pécʊ   gwíhən   pígwə*
          dəgí   gɪdé   dəgú   pɪcó   gwɪhä̃n   pɪgwá

The first thing to be observed is that each of the "reduced" vowels *I*, *U*, and *ə* alternates with a pair of "full" vowels:

(15)   i   u   a
            ~ I   ~ U   ~ ə
              e   o   ä

In addition, this alternation is conditioned by stress: if the root vowel is stressed, it is a full vowel; if it is unstressed, we find a reduced vowel. Finally, notice that the stress alternates between the first and second root vowels. However, in each case it is true that the stress appears on the next-to-last (penultimate) vowel of the word. The stress is thus predictable by the following rule:

(16)   Stress assignment $V \longrightarrow \acute{V}/\_\_\_C_0VC_0\#$[6]

The problem, of course, is to decide on an analysis for the alternation between the full and reduced vowels. Clearly, if we take the reduced vowels I, U, and ə as basic, it would be impossible to predict what corresponding full vowel they will show up as when the stress is placed on them. Consequently, if this alternation is to be described in terms of a general phonological rule, we must take the unreduced vocalism that shows up under stress as basic. This step must be taken for both the first and the second root vowels because both appear as ambiguous reduced vowel when unstressed.

By this reasoning the underlying representations for the root morphemes will be /dägi/ 'lie', /gode/ 'tie', /dagu/ 'yam', /peco/ 'chest', /gwihän/ 'fish', and /pigwaʔ/ 'betel nut'. After the stress has been positioned on either one of the root vowels, the other unstressed root

---

[6] C_0 indicates zero or more consonants.

vowel will be reduced by Rule (17). (In our informal statement of this rule Ṽ is a cover symbol for unstressed vowels.)

(17)   [ῐ,ĕ] —→ ɪ, [ῠ,ŏ] —→ ʊ, [ă,ä̆] —→ ə

According to Topping the vowels of the affixes and particles carry a secondary stress. Given that the reduction rule (17) is limited to unstressed vowels, the failure of these vowels to reduce is explained. Rule (17) must be ordered after the stress rule (16) since the latter introduces the contrast between stressed and unstressed vowels. Forms like *i dəgúhu* 'my yam' indicate that reduction is ordered after vowel fronting (12). If reduction applied first to convert /i dagú-hu/ to /i dəgú-hu/, subsequent application of (12) would convert the schwa to a front vowel. Rather, we must first send *a* to *ä* by (12) and then apply reduction. The following derivations for *dǽgɪ, i dinəgíhu, dágu,* and *i dəgúhu* show how these rules work (the grave accent indicates secondary stress).

(18)   /#dägi#/   /#ì d-ìn-ägi-hù#/   /#dagu#/   /#ì dagu-hù#/
       ------   ----------------   ------   *ì dägu-hù*   Fronting
       dǽgi   *ìd-ìn-ägí-hù*   *dágu*   *ì dägú-hù*   Stress
       dǽgɪ   *ì d-ìn-əgí-hù*   *dágʊ*   *ì dəgú-hù*   Reduction

It should be noted that the underlying forms we have posited for the root morphemes in the Chamorro data are more abstract than those posited in the analysis of Russian data. In the latter case the UR of a morpheme was always identical with one of its phonetic realizations. This is not possible in Chamorro since one of the two root vowels is always unstressed and hence reduced. Nevertheless, it is necessary to posit these abstract URs to give a general account of the alternations in the language.

Tonkawa

Tonkawa, an American Indian language once spoken in Texas, presents a more striking instance of the need for relatively abstract underlying forms; additionally, it is a good illustration of how a small set of natural rules can illuminate a large degree of variation in the phonetic realization of morphemes. All of the data in the following discussion have been taken from Hoijer (1933, 1949).

To begin with, examine the data in the following four paradigms:

(19)   *picno?*   'he cuts it'   *picnano?*
         wepceno?   'he cuts them'   *wepcenano?*

	kepceno?	'he cuts me'	*kepcenano?*
	picen	'castrated one, steer'	
(20)	*notxo?*	'he hoes it'	*notxono?*
	wentoxo?	'he hoes them'	*wentoxono?*
	kentoxo?	'he hoes me'	*kentoxono?*
	notox	'hoe'	
(21)	*netlo?*	'he licks it'	*netleno?*
	wentalo?	'he licks them'	*wentaleno?*
	kentalo?	'he licks me'	*kentaleno?*
(22)	*naxco?*	'he makes it a fire'	*naxceno?*
	wenxaco?	'he makes them a fire'	*wenxaceno?*
	kenxaco?	'he makes me a fire'	*kenxaceno?*

The forms in the second column are progressive forms of the corresponding verbs in the first column. Thus, *picnano?* means 'he is cutting it'. On the basis of the above data it is possible to isolate the sequence *-o?* as suffixal material associated with third person singular present indicative verbs, though it is not possible to tell whether *-o?* consists of one morpheme or more. The 3 pl. pronominal object is indicated by the prefix *we-* and the 1 sg. object by the prefix *ke-*. The 3 sg. object is unmarked. Finally, the progressive morpheme is realized as a suffix *-n-* and appears between the verb stem and the suffix *-o?* By taking away the prefixes and suffixes, we are left with various realizations of the verb-stem morphemes.

(23)

picn	*picna*	*notx*	*notxo*
pcen	*pcena*	*ntox*	*ntoxo*
netl	*netle*	*naxc*	*naxce*
ntal	*ntale*	*nxac*	*nxace*

Examination of these alternants reveals three points: First, each stem consists of three invariant consonants and three vowels that sometimes appear and sometimes are absent. Second, it does not appear possible to predict which particular vowel will appear with which particular stem. Thus, 'cut' has *i* between the first two stem consonants in the unprefixed forms, while 'hoe' has an *o*, 'lick' an *e*, and 'make a fire' an *a*. In prefixed forms we find between the second and third stem consonants an *e* associated with 'cut', an *o* with 'hoe', and an *a* with the other two. Finally, in the progressive paradigm 'cut' exhibits an *a* before the *-n*, 'hoe' an *o*, and the remaining two an *e*. Thus, each verb stem consists of three particular consonants and three particular vowels; all of this is idiosyncratic information that must be memorized as part of the lexical representation of each verb stem. This reasoning implies the following underlying stem shapes: /picena/, /notoxo/, /netale/, and /naxace/.

What are the rules that account for the varying realizations of these stems? First observe that the progressive form of the verb shows the underlying stem-final vowel before -*n*, while this vowel is absent before the suffix -*o*ʔ. Since this suffix begins with a vowel, the alternation can be accounted for by a truncation rule that deletes the first of two successive vowels.

(24) $V \longrightarrow \emptyset / \_V$

The truncation rule permits the nonprogressive stem alternants to be derived from the stem shapes that appear before the progressive suffix. The problem now is to reduce to rule the varying realizations of the stem in the prefixed and unprefixed forms. Observe that in the unprefixed forms the second stem vowel is absent, while in the prefixed forms the first stem vowel is missing. Since the prefixes are of the shape CV, the following generalization may be extracted: in both prefixed and unprefixed forms the second vowel of the word is absent. These alternations may thus be accounted for by the rule of vowel elision stated in (25).

(25) $V \longrightarrow \emptyset / \#CVC\_$

The rules of truncation and elision thus permit all four stem shapes in (23) to be derived from a single UR.

In Tonkawa a number of verb roots function as nouns when they are unaffixed. Such is the case with the roots 'cut' and 'hoe' which appear as the nouns *picen* and *notox*. Since these roots derive from /picena/ and /notoxo/ we must invoke a rule to delete the stem final vowels in the nominal forms. Since the deletion of a vowel at the end of a word is a natural rule found in many languages, postulation of the following rule of apocope will account satisfactorily for these forms:

(26) $V \longrightarrow \emptyset / \_\#$

The nouns *picen* and *notox* pose a further problem of analysis. Recall that elision was formulated to delete the second vowel of a word. This rule must be revised so that it does not apply in the nouns. If we require that the elided vowel occupy a medial syllable in the word, the version of elision stated as (27) will produce the correct forms, provided that it is ordered after apocope.

(27) $V \longrightarrow \emptyset / \#CVC\_\_CV$

The derivations in (28) illustrate how the proposed analysis works.

(28)   / #picena-oʔ# /   / #we-picena-oʔ# /   / #picena # /

--------------	------------------	picen	Apocope
picna-oʔ	we-pcena-oʔ	---------	Elision (27)
picn-oʔ	we-pcen-oʔ	---------	Truncation

Examine the following additional data from Tonkawa:

(29)   *pilo*ʔ   'he rolls it'   *pileno*ʔ
            *weplo*ʔ   'he rolls them'   *wepleno*ʔ
            *keplo*ʔ   'he rolls me'   *kepleno*ʔ

(30)   *cano*ʔ   'he leaves it'   *caneno*ʔ
            *wecno*ʔ   'he leaves them'   *wecneno*ʔ
            *kecno*ʔ   'he leaves me'   *kecneno*ʔ

(31)   *topo*ʔ   'he cuts it'   *topono*ʔ
            *wetpo*ʔ   'he cuts them'   *wetpono*ʔ
            *ketpo*ʔ   'he cuts me'   *ketpono*ʔ

By isolating the prefixes and suffixes it is easy to see that we are dealing with stems of the basic shape /pile/, /cane/, and /topo/. These differ from the stems already examined in that they are di- instead of trisyllabic. Note that the rule of truncation correctly predicts that the stem-final vowels are not pronounced before the -*o*ʔ suffix. However, elision predicts that a UR like / #pile-n-oʔ# / should come out as the incorrect *pilno*ʔ by deletion of the *e*, since it is the second vowel of the word and not the final vowel of the word. Thus, the rule must be revised again. It will not be sufficient to limit elision to three-syllable stems, since it does apply to disyllabic stems when they appear prefixed—*weplo*ʔ, *keplo*ʔ, and so on. This suggests that the proper restriction is that the second vowel of the word elides as long as it is not the final vowel of the *stem*. With this formulation the rule will apply in the derivation of / #we-pile-oʔ# / but fail to apply in / #pile-n-oʔ# /—the desired result. But in order to ensure that in a prefixed nonprogressive form like / #we-pile-oʔ# / the *i* stem vowel is elided to give *weplo*ʔ, we must order this latest version of elision before truncation. If truncation came first, the *i* would become the last vowel of the stem and hence escape elision. Since we are replacing the restriction "not the final vowel of the word" with the restriction "not the final vowel of the stem", we must go back to the derived nominals like *picen* to see if the correct forms are produced. If we retain the restriction that elision must apply after apocope, then when / #picena # / has its final vowel deleted, the *e* becomes the final vowel of the stem and hence escapes the latest version of elision to yield the correct *picen*.

To recapitulate, we have learned two things from the disyllabic stems. First, elision must be restricted so that it elides the second vowel of the word so long as it is not the final vowel of the stem. Second, elision must be ordered before truncation. Hence, in conjunction with the earlier established ordering of apocope before elision, we have the following rule order: apocope-elision-truncation.

We shall consider a final set of Tonkawa data:

(32)	*yacxo?*	'he bakes it'	*yacxeno?*
	weicoxo?	'he bakes them'	*weicoxeno?*
	keicoxo?	'he bakes me'	*keicoxeno?*
(33)	*yaxo?*	'he eats it'	*yaxano?*
	weixo?	'he eats them'	*weixano?*
	keixo?	'he eats me'	*keixano?*
(34)	*yakwo?*	'he spurs it'	*yakwano?*
	weikawo?	'he spurs them'	*weikawano?*
	keikawo?	'he spurs me'	*keikawano?*
	yakau	'spurs'	
(35)	*yauyo?*	'he plants it'	*yauyano?*
	weiweyo?	'he plants them'	*weiweyano?*
	keiweyo?	'he plants me'	*keiweyano?*
	yawei	'field'	

Examination of the first two paradigms suggests that we are dealing with stems that have the underlying shapes /yacoxe/ or /iacoxe/ and /yaxa/ or /iaxa/. As far as the presence versus absence of their stem vowels is concerned, these stems behave exactly like the tri- and disyllabic stems examined earlier. The only difference is that the initial sound of the stem varies between *y* when a vowel follows and *i* when no vowel follows. The question is, then: Which is basic? If it is *y*, we require a rule turning *y* to *i* when a consonant follows; if *i*, then a rule taking this vowel to its corresponding glide when in position before a vowel. Both of these rules are very natural processes. Thus, without considering evidence internal to Tonkawa, there is no reason to prefer one over the other. Evidence internal to Tonkawa strongly favors choosing *y* as underlying. If *i* were basic, we would be creating underlying vowel sequences internal to a morpheme—something that otherwise does not occur in the language. Second, aside from these stems, all other stems in Tonkawa clearly begin with a consonant. Finally, if a stem shape such as /iacoxe/ were set up, we would have to drastically revise the elision rule, since it treats the *a* and *o* as if they were the first and second stem vowels.

All of these facts suggest that the glide *y* should be considered basic and that we formulate a rule to vocalize *y* to *i* when it comes to stand before a consonant as a result of elision. Inspection of the paradigms for 'plant' in (35) shows that *u* and *w* are related in the same way as *i* and *y*. The UR of the stem for 'plant' is /yaweya/, and upon elision of the medial vowel in an unprefixed form the *w* comes to stand before a consonant and is thus vocalized to *u*, as in *yauyoʔ* from /#yaweya-oʔ#/. Examination of the nominal forms *yawei* 'field' and *yakau* 'spurs' from /#yaweya#/ and /#yakawa#/ shows that the glides also vocalize when they come to stand at the end of the word as a result of apocope. All these considerations imply a vocalization rule ordered after apocope and elision.

(36) $$[y, w] \longrightarrow [i, u]/\underline{\hspace{1cm}} \left\{ \begin{matrix} \# \\ C \end{matrix} \right\}$$

To show how these rules work we give derivations of *yauyaoʔ*, *weiweyoʔ*, and *yawei*:

(37)

/#yaweya-oʔ#/	/#we-yaweya-oʔ#/	/#yaweya#/	
---------------	------------------	#yawey#	Apocope
#yawya-oʔ#	#we-yweya-oʔ#	-----------	Elision
#yawy-oʔ#	#we-ywey-oʔ#	-----------	Truncation
#yauy-oʔ#	#we-iwey-oʔ#	#yawei#	Vocalization

There are a couple of additional ordering relations with respect to vocalization that should be mentioned. First, vocalization must be ordered after truncation, since the former rule can create a sequence of vowels that are potential inputs to the latter rule. Thus, if vocalization applied first, a form like *yawei* from /#yaweya#/ would incorrectly undergo truncation and lose the *e* vowel. A possible alternative to incorporating this ordering relation—truncation precedes vocalization—into the grammar would be to restrict the truncation rule so that it only deletes a vowel before a nonhigh vowel. Vowel-truncation rules are not normally restricted in this fashion, however, and since *i* and *u* derive from underlying consonants in Tonkawa anyway, it seems more appropriate to attribute their failure to truncate a preceding vowel to their consonantal origin. Ordering truncation before vocalization claims precisely this, since at the point where truncation applies, the glides to be vocalized are consonants. Finally, imperative forms like *pileu* 'roll it!', *yakwau* 'spur it!', and *yauyeu* 'plant it!' provide an additional reason for ordering apocope before vocalization. In order to explain why the final *-u* imperative marker fails to apocopate (and also fails to truncate the preceding vowel) we must assume that it derives from underlying -*w*. But this implies that apocope must precede vocalization. If it did not, the vocalized -*u*, being a vowel, would delete in final position by apocope. Once again one could limit apocope to just nonhigh vowels, but apocopation rules are not normally restricted in this manner, and the failure of high vowels to delete word-finally is best explained by their consonantal origin in Tonkawa.

Tonkawa provides a rather striking illustration of how a complex set of alternations can be accounted for by a small set of simple phonological rules. However, this is only possible if the UR for morphemes is permitted to be rather abstract in the sense that the UR need not be identical with any of its surface phonetic alternants. Because of the elision and apocope rules, the vowels of a three-syllable stem CVCVCV- will never appear together in a single-surface alternant. If the stem is unprefixed and used as a verb, the second vowel will be elided, while in prefixed forms the first will be. If the stem is used as a noun, the final vowel will be apocopated. But as we have seen, which particular vowel appears in the stem is unpredictable, idiosyncratic information that must appear in the lexical representation. Also, the analysis we have given is possible only if the rules are permitted to interact with one another in an intricate fashion that can be described by ruling ordering. This interaction is summarized in the following diagram, where a line connecting two rules represents an ordering restriction such that a rule higher in the list must be tried before one lower in the list.

(38)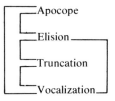

Exercises

1. Lamba (Doke 1938). Provide a phonological analysis of these data by first analyzing the words into their constituent morphemes. Identify the alternating phonetic shapes of each morpheme. Propose a unique UR for each morpheme and state the rules that will convert the UR for each word into its corresponding PR. Must an ordering restriction be placed on any of the rules? Show how your analysis works by providing derivations for *fišika*, *koseka*, and *menena*. (In these data the palatal nasal is transcribed as *ň*, and the final *a* of all words is a verbal suffix).

Past	Passive	Neuter	Applied	Reciprocal	Gloss
čita	čitwa	čitika	čitila	čitana	'do'
tula	tulwa	tulika	tulila	tulana	'dig'
četa	četwa	četeka	četela	četana	'spy'
soŋka	soŋkwa	soŋkeka	soŋkela	soŋkana	'pay tax'
pata	patwa	patika	patila	patana	'scold'
fisa	fiswa	fišika	fišila	fisana	'hide'
česa	česwa	česeka	česela	česana	'cut'
kosa	koswa	koseka	kosela	kosana	'be strong'
lasa	laswa	lašika	lašila	lasana	'wound'
masa	maswa	mašika	mašila	masana	'plaster'
šika	šikwa	šičika	šičila	šikana	'bury'
fuka	fukwa	fučika	fučila	fukana	'creep'
seka	sekwa	sekeka	sekela	sekana	'laugh at'
poka	pokwa	pokeka	pokela	pokana	'receive'
kaka	kakwa	kačika	kačila	kakana	'tie'
ima	imwa	imika	imina	imana	'rise'
puma	pumwa	pumika	pumina	pumana	'flog'
mena	menwa	meneka	menena	menana	'grow'
fweňa	fweňwa	fweňeka	fweňena	fweňana	'scratch'
pona	ponwa	poneka	ponena	ponana	'fall'
ŋaŋa	ŋaŋwa	ŋaŋika	ŋaŋina	ŋaŋana	'snigger'

2. Tagalog. Account for the alternations in the shape of the root that arise from the addition of the derivational suffixes /-in/ and /-an/.

bukas	buksin	buksan	'open'
kapit	kaptin	kaptan	'embrace'
tubos	tubsin	tubsan	'redeem'
opos	upsin	upsan	'stop'
posod	pusdin	pusdan	'tuft'
bata	bathin	bathan	'suffer'
bili	bilhin	bilhan	'buy'
dipa	diphin	diphan	'open'
polo	pulhin	pulhan	'ask for trifles'
puyo	puyhin		'saddle bag'
banig	baŋgin	baŋgan	'mat'
damit	damtin	damtan	'clothe'
ganap	gampin	gampan	'fulfill'
putol	putlin	putlan	'cut'
atip	aptin	aptan	'thatching'
talab		tablan	'penetrate'
tanim	tamnin	tamnan	'plant'
laman	lamnin	lamnan	'fill'

3. Polish. Employing the criterion of phonological predictability, formulate rules to account for the voicing alternation and the o ~ u alternation in the following data. Ignore all other alternations. Must your rules be ordered?

sg.	pl.	Gloss	1 sg.	imper. sg.	Gloss
klup	klubi	'club'	rob'e	rup	'do'
trup	trupi	'corpse'	kop'e	kop	'shuck corn'

dom	domi	'house'	vodze	vuć	'lead'
snop	snopi	'sheaf'	psoce	psoć	'frolic'
žwup	žwobi	'crib'	otvože	otvuš	'open'
trut	trudi	'labor'	stoje	stuj	'stand'
dzvon	dzvoni	'bell'	ogole	ogul	'shave'
kot	koti	'cat'	xron'e	xron'	'protect'
lut	lodi	'ice'	zwov'e	zwuf	'catch'
grus	gruzi	'rubble'			
nos	nosi	'nose'			
vus	vozi	'cart'			
koš	koše	'basket'			
nuš	nože	'knife'			
wuk	wugi	'lye'			
wuk	wuki	'bow'			
sok	soki	'juice'			
ruk	rogi	'horn'			
bur	bori	'forest'			
vuw	vowi	'ox'			
sul	soli	'salt'			
buj	boji	'fight'			
šum	šumi	'noise'			
žur	žuri	'soup'			

4. Karok (Bright 1957).

a. Segment the following words into roots and affixes and propose a rule for the $s \sim š$ alternation.

Imperative	1 sg.	3 sg.	Gloss
pasip	nipasip	ʔupasip	'shoot'
si:tva	niši:tva	ʔusi:tva	'steal'
kifnuk	nikifnuk	ʔukifnuk	'stoop'
suprih	nišuprih	ʔusuprih	'measure'
ʔifik	niʔifik	ʔuʔifik	'pick up'
ʔaktuv	niʔaktuv	ʔuʔaktuv	'pluck at'

b. Formulate rules to account for the $ʔ \sim \emptyset$ and $V \sim \emptyset$ alternations. Revise the palatalization rule to account for the following data. How must the rules be ordered? One piece of information that may help you to arrive at the correct solution is that, phonetically, no word in Karok begins with a vowel. All words begin with a consonant.

ʔaxyar	nixyar	ʔuxyar	'fill'
ʔiškak	niškak	ʔuskak	'jump'
ʔikšah	nikšah	ʔuksah	'laugh'
ʔišriv	nišriv	ʔusriv	'shoot at a target'
ʔuksup	nikšup	ʔuksup	'point'

5. Yagua (Powlison 1962). List the URs of the roots and affixes in these data and formulate an ordered set of rules to derive the correct PRs. (Long vowels are transcribed as geminates. Assume that all occurrences of e derive from underlying /a/.)

'water'	'sloth'	'pan'	'skin'	gloss
haa	pahiitu	pay	hay	noun
haahu	pahiituhu	pahyu	hahyu	to the noun
cahaa	capahiitu	capay	cahay	his noun
rahyaa	rapyahiitu	rape	rahe	my noun
cahaahu	capahiituhu	capahyu	cahahyu	to his noun
rahyaahu	rapyahiituhu	rapehyu	rahehyu	to my noun

cacaa	'he fits'	cacaay	'he gives'	caruye	'he is frying'
cacaara	'he fits it'	cacaarya	'he gives it'	caruyerya	'he is frying it'
racyaa	'I fit'	racee	'I give'	raryuye	'I am frying'
racyaara	'I fit it'	raceerya	'I give it'	raryuyerya	'I am frying it'

6. Serbo-Croatian. For purposes of this problem the data have been simplified in several respects. First, vowel length has not been indicated. Second, the accent has been simplified in the following ways: In forms that are transcribed with an accent, the location of the accent is predictable by rule; it need not be indicated in the lexicon for these words. Words which are transcribed without an accent belong to a different accentual class. For them the accent must be indicated in the lexicon. Also, for words transcribed with an accent, there is a later rule that retracts the accent one syllable to the left. Thus, a form that we transcribe as *mladá* has accent on the initial syllable phonetically. Finally, in this problem we are only concerned with the location of the accent; we do not indicate whether the accent is rising or falling in pitch.

Account for the alternations in the data with an ordered set of rules. Be sure to include a rule of accent placement for all words transcribed with an accent. Provide derivations for *múkao*, *muklá*, *kradém*, and *kráo*.

Adjectives

Masc.	Fem.	Neuter	Plural	Gloss
mlád	mladá	mladó	mladí	'young'
púst	pustá	pustó	pustí	'empty'
bogat	bogata	bogato	bogati	'rich'
béo	belá	beló	belí	'white'
mío	milá	miló	milí	'dear'
zelén	zelená	zelenó	zelení	'green'
križan	križana	križano	križani	'cross'
jásan	jasná	jasnó	jasní	'clear'
ledan	ledna	ledno	ledni	'frozen'
dóbar	dobrá	dobró	dobrí	'kind'
bodar	bodra	bodro	bodri	'alert'
veseo	vesela	veselo	veseli	'gay'
ustao	ustala	ustalo	ustali	'tired'
múkao	muklá	mukló	muklí	'hoarse'

Verbs

1 sg. pres	masc. past	fem. past	neuter past	Gloss
tepém	tépao	teplá	tepló	'wander'
skubém	skúbao	skublá	skubló	'tear'
tresém	trésao	treslá	tresló	'shake'
vezém	vézao	vezlá	vezló	'lead'

pletém	*pléo*	*plelá*	*pleló*	'plait'
kradém	*kráo*	*kralá*	*kraló*	'steal'
metém	*méo*	*melá*	*meló*	'sweep'
vedém	*véo*	*velá*	*veló*	'lead'
pečém	*pékao*	*peklá*	*pekló*	'bake'
žežém	*žégao*	*žeglá*	*žegló*	'burn'

4

Phonological Sketches

In this chapter we illustrate how the concepts and principles introduced in the previous chapters are applied to the analysis of selected aspects of the phonological structure of four widely divergent languages. Primary consideration is given to the motivation of underlying representations and the interrelationships between the rules. Details of rule formalism are largely ignored. These sketches illustrate the characteristic problems the phonologist encounters in actual descriptive practice. We shall repeatedly refer to various aspects of these analyses in later chapters which deal with more theoretical issues.

The Yawelmani Dialect of Yokuts

In this section the morphophonemics of the verbal system of the Yawelmani dialect of Yokuts (an American Indian language of California) will be examined in some detail. The phonological rules that specify the phonetic shape of Yawelmani verbal words are also operative in the nominal system, but since the nouns provide little additional insight into the workings of Yawelmani phonology, we shall ignore them in our

77

discussion. The data discussed here are taken from Stanley Newman's (1944) description. An early generative treatment is to be found in Kuroda (1967). Various theoretical aspects of Yawelmani phonology have been discussed by Kisseberth (1969, 1970). It should be pointed out that not all of the forms cited in this section, nor in previous generative analyses of Yawelmani, are actually attested in Newman's grammar, the only published source on the language. All nonattested forms are, however, completely parallel in behavior and patterns of alternation to forms that are amply attested in Newman's description. Finally, a note on the transcription is in order. The voiced stop letters (*b*, *d*, etc.) represent unaspirated voiceless lax consonants, while the voiceless stop letters (*p*, *t*, etc.) stand for tense, voiceless, aspirated consonants. A raised comma indicates glottalization, while a dot under a letter indicates an apical alveolar point of articulation. Finally, for typographical convenience, the short and long open mid vowels [ε] and [ɔ] are represented as *e* and *o*.

VOWEL HARMONY

Almost without exception, suffixes in Yawelmani have varying pronunciations involving an alternation between non-round and round vowels. To begin with, just alternations involving the short vowels *i*/*u* and *a*/*o* will be examined. Take the non-future (i.e., either past or present) suffix as an example. It appears in two forms: *-hin* and *-hun*.

(1)   *xat-hin*   'eats'   *max-hin*   'procures'
      bok'-hin 'finds'   *k'o?-hin* 'throws'
      xil-hin   'tangles'   *giy'-hin* 'touches'
      dub-hun   'leads by the hand'   *hud-hun*   'recognizes'

The examples in (1) suggest that the alternation between *-hin* and *-hun* is rule governed. If the preceding vowel is *i*, *a* or *o*, then *-hin* appears; if the preceding vowel is *u*, then *-hun* is used.

The pattern of alternation exhibited by the nonfuture suffix is in no way limited to this particular morpheme. Compare (2) and (3):

(2)   *xat-mi*   'having eaten'
                    bok'-mi 'having found'
                    xil-mi   'having tangled'
                    dub-mu   'having led by the hand'

(3)   *xat-nit* 'will be eaten'
                    bok'-nit 'will be found'
                    xil-nit 'will be tangled'
                    dub-nut 'will be led by the hand'

There are no suffixes in Yawelmani which have, invariably, *i* as their first vowel; neither are there suffixes which have, invariably, *u* as their first vowel. If a suffix has a high vowel as its first vowel, then that vowel will always appear as *i* or *u* according to the pattern stated above. Given this fact, there is no underlying contrast between suffixes with *i* as their first vowel and those with *u* (cf. the case in Russian discussed earlier, where a contrast between stems ending in voiced as opposed to voiceless obstruents could be established), and thus there is no direct evidence as to which form of these suffixes should be regarded as basic and which derived by a rule.

If we take *-hin*, *-mi*, *-nit* as the basic form of the morphemes in question, then a rule of vowel harmony can be stated as in (4):

(4)   *A high vowel is rounded (and backed) if the vowel that precedes it in the word is a high round vowel.*

(Notice that we have not restricted the above rule just to a suffixal vowel, even though all of the examples given so far have involved suffixal vowels. Evidence that other vowels undergo this harmonizing process will emerge later.) The vowel harmony rule expressed in (4) will convert the basic representation /hin/ to [hun], /mi/ to [mu], /nit/ to [nut], when an *u* vowel precedes in the word.

If, on the other hand, *u* were taken as basic, a rule such as (5) would be required to account for harmony:

(5)   *A high vowel is unrounded (and fronted) if preceded in the word by a nonround vowel or by a nonhigh vowel.*

In (5), there is no single phonetic class of segments conditioning the alternation, rather a conjunction of two separate classes (nonround vowels and nonhigh vowels). There does not seem to be any phonetic motivation for nonhigh vowels to cause *u* to shift to *i*. In (4), on the other hand, it is the high round vowel *u* that causes a following *i* to become *u*—a clear instance of assimilation. We see then that different choices of basic representations lead to different rules, and sometimes one of the rules is more reflective of a natural phonetic process.

For the reasons suggested above, an analysis that takes *i* as the basic vowel and hypothesizes the existence of a rule such as (4) seems closer to a correct characterization of these data than an analysis that takes *u* as basic and hypothesizes rule (5). Our evidence, however, is rather tenuous.

The examples in (1)–(3) illustrate suffixes containing a single vowel, where that vowel is phonetically a high vowel. Other suffixes in Yawelmani containing just one vowel vary in pronunciation between *a* and *o*. The examples in (6) illustrate such a suffix.

(6) *xat-al* 'might eat'   *max-al* 'might procure'
     dub-al 'might lead by the hand' *hud-al* 'might recognize'
     xil-al 'might tangle'   *giy'-al* 'might touch'
     k'oʔ-ol 'might throw'   *bok'-ol* 'might find'

The dubitative suffix *-al/-ol* clearly shows a pattern of alternation highly reminiscent of the alternation pattern of the high vowel suffixes in (1)–(3). Let us refer to the suffixal shapes *-hin* and *-al* as the nonround vowel alternants, and the shapes *-hun* and *-ol* as the round vowel alternants. We can then say that a nonround vowel alternant always appears if the preceding vowel is nonround (*i* or *a*). It is not possible, however, to say that the round vowel alternant always appears when the preceding vowel is round. In the case of the high round vowel alternants (*-hun*, for example), the preceding vowel must not only be round, but also high. In the case of the nonhigh round vowel alternants (*-ol*, for example), the preceding vowel must not only be round, but also nonhigh.

The pattern of alternation exhibited by the dubitative suffix is representative of a number of other suffixes in Yawelmani, as the following examples reveal.

(7)   *xat-xa*   'let us eat'
              giy'-xa   'let us touch'
              dub-xa   'let us lead by the hand'
              bok'-xo   'let us find'

(8)   *xat-taw*   'eating'
              giy'-taw 'touching'
              dub-taw   'leading by the hand'
              bok'-tow 'finding'

(*-taw/-tow* is a gerundial suffix, but we have not attempted in the glosses to indicate its precise usage). The same motivation for adopting *i* as the basic vowel of a suffix like *-hin* leads to the adoption of *a* as the basic vowel of a suffix like *-al*. In order to account for the *o* pronunciation, we require the rule given in (9).

(9) *A nonhigh vowel is pronounced round when a nonhigh round vowel precedes in the word.*

Rules (4) and (9) are highly similar; indeed, intuitively they appear to be instances of a single principle, which is given as (10).

(10)   *A vowel is pronounced round (and back) if immediately preceded by a round vowel of the same height.*

The question of whether two processes (such as the shift of *i* to *u* and of *a* to *o* in the present example) are in fact instances of a single process is often a very difficult one to answer; the question will be studied more closely in Chapter 9. For the present, we will simply assume that the extreme parallelism of (4) and (9) warrants the assumption that they are in fact instances of a general principle such as (10).

The examples considered so far have been restricted to cases where one monosyllabic suffix is attached to a monosyllabic verb root. We now turn to more complex cases. There are suffixes that may occur between the verb root and those suffixes (such as *-hin* and *-al*) which occur finally in the word, for example the indirective suffix *-sit-* 'to, into, for'.

(11)   *k'o?-sit-hin*   'throws to'
         max-sit-hin   'procures for'
         xip'wiy-sit-hin   'makes a rubbing motion for'
         t'ul-sut-hun   'burns for'

The interesting example here is *tul-sut-hun*, where it will be noted that both of the *i* vowels in the suffixes are pronounced *u*. The UR of the word is /t'ul+sit+hin/. In order for rule (10) to account for *tul-sut-hun*, we must assume that in some sense it operates twice: First, (10) rounds the *i* vowel in /sit/ since it is preceded by a round vowel; then, (10) rounds the *i* vowel in /hin/ since, as a result of the first application of (10), a high round vowel precedes. (cf., Chapter 8 for discussion of the problem posed by the multiple application of a single rule.) Another example of the same sort is *dub-wus-mu* 'having led each other by the hand', which consists of the verb root *dub-*, the reciprocal-reflexive suffix *-wis-*, and the consequent gerundial suffix *-mi*. Again, both suffixal vowels undergo the harmony rule.

Notice that (10) claims that a vowel harmonizes with the immediately preceding vowel in the word. Consequently, an *a* (or *i*) vowel in a final suffix will not harmonize with an *o* (or *u*) vowel in the verb root if another suffix intervenes containing a vowel of the opposite height. For example, the imperative suffix is *-k'a*, and it harmonizes in an example such as *bok'-k'o* 'find (it)!', but not in *bok'-sit-k'a* 'find (it) for (him)!'. The *i* vowel in /sit/ does not harmonize since the preceding round vowel is not of the same height as *i*; the *a* vowel in -*k'a* does not harmonize either, since it is not preceded by a round vowel of the same height.

Our analysis so far has been restricted to monosyllabic suffixes; examination of disyllabic suffixes confirms the analysis we have presented. (10) predicts that if a suffix has two vowels of the same height, then either both will harmonize or neither will, depending on whether the vowel preceding the suffix is a round vowel of the same height as the suffixal vowels in question. If the disyllabic suffix contains two vowels unlike in height, (10) predicts that the first will harmonize if the preceding vowel is round and of the same height, but the second vowel of the suffix will never harmonize. These predictions are indeed correct.

For instance, the suffix -*iwis*, reciprocal/reflexive, occurs in the following two verbal nouns: *ʔoyowx-iwis* 'one who feels sorry for himself' and *t'uy-uwus* 'act of shooting at one another'. In the first example neither *i* vowel in the suffix harmonizes, since the final vowel of the preceding stem is not one that conditions harmony for *i*; in the second example, both *i* vowels in the suffix harmonize. An example of a suffix with two unlike vowels is -*ʔin'ay*, a gerundial suffix. Compare *dos-ʔin'ay* 'reporting' with *dub-ʔun'ay* 'leading by the hand'. In these examples, *i* harmonizes after *dub-* but not after *dos-*; in neither case does the *a* harmonize, since it is never preceded by a vowel that can cause it to harmonize.

Given what has been said so far, there are some suffixes that appear not to obey the vowel harmony principle formulated in (10). The future morpheme is a case in point. Observe the following examples:

(12)   *bok'-en*   'will find'
          dub-on   'will lead by the hand'
          xat-en   'will eat'
          giy'-en   'will touch'

This suffix is an apparent anomaly in that, although it seems to contain a nonhigh vowel, it has the round variant of that nonhigh vowel when the high vowel *u* precedes, and does not have the round variant when *o* precedes. In other words, -*on* appears in the same contexts as -*hun*, and not in the contexts where -*ol* appears. The future suffix thus appears to be a systematic violation of the principle that has been claimed to govern vowel harmony in Yawelmani, namely (10). The anomalous behavior of this suffix, as well as others like it, will be reconsidered later and will be shown to be ultimately regular.

VOWEL SHORTENING

Up until this point, our attention has been restricted to alternations in the quality of suffixal vowels. Verb roots in Yawelmani show certain alternations that must now be examined before we can profitably return to a consideration of the operation of vowel harmony in a wider class of cases. One pervasive alternation in verb roots is in the length of the root vowel. In all of the previous examples, the root vowel was invariably short, whatever the nature of the following suffix. There are, however, many roots which show an alternation in vowel length. The examples in (13) are representative.

(13)

Nonfuture	Imperative	Dubitative	Future	Gloss
ṣap-hin	ṣap-k'a	ṣa:p-al	ṣa:p-en	'burn'
dos-hin	dos-k'o	do:s-ol	do:s-en	'report'
lan-hin	lan-k'a	la:n-al	la:n-en	'hear'
mek'-hin	mek'-k'a	me:k'-al	me:k'-en	'swallow'
won-hin	won-k'o	wo:n-ol	wo:n-en	'hide' (tr.)

The above examples show that whereas some roots may be invariably CV̆C-, others have a CV:C- alternant under some conditions and a CV̆C-alternant under others. What the relevant conditions are will be investigated immediately below. But first two observations need to be made, although their significance will not become clear immediately. First, there are no verb roots that have the invariable shape CeC-. Second, there are no verb roots that have the shapes Ci:C- or Cu:C- in any of their realizations.

Is there some principle that determines when a CV:C- alternant will occur as opposed to a CV̆C- alternant? Note that ṣa:p-, for example, occurs before the vowel-initial suffixes -al and -en, while ṣap- occurs before the consonant-initial suffixes -hin and -k'a. A generalization thus emerges: The long vowel alternant occurs when the vowel is in the environment ___CV (as in ṣa:p-al, ṣa:p-en), while the short vowel alternant occurs when the vowel is in the environment ___CC (as in ṣap-hin, ṣap-k'a). Examination of a variety of other languages reveals that alternations in vowel length typically revolve around differences in the consonant–vowel structure of words, with long vowels preferred in 'open syllables' (___CV) and short vowels preferred in 'closed syllables' (___CC).

Having isolated the relevant conditions for the vowel-length alternation, we must ask what the underlying representation of these alternating verb roots is. In particular, is their vowel underlyingly long or short? If it is claimed that the vowel is basically short, the representations will be /ṣap/, /dos/, /mek'/, etc. A rule such as (14) would then be required.

(14) $V \longrightarrow [+long]/\underline{\quad}CV$

/ṣap + al/ would undergo (14), yielding *ṣa:p-al*; /ṣap + hin/ would of course not be susceptible to (14). Such an account of the data runs into difficulty when we take into consideration examples such as *xat-al, dub-al, giy'-en*, etc., since (14) predicts that the root vowel in these examples should be lengthened.

Suppose that we adopt the alternative position that alternating roots such as *ṣa:p-/ṣap-* have a basic long vowel. Nonalternating roots, of course, such as *xat-*, would have a basic short vowel. A rule like (15) would then be needed.

(15) $V \longrightarrow [-long]/\underline{\quad}CC$

This rule would operate on /ṣa:p + hin/ to derive *ṣap-hin*, but would not affect /ṣa:p + al/, where the basic long vowel is not followed by a consonant cluster. There are no roots in Yawelmani that provide a counterexample to (15) since there are no roots that maintain the shape CV:C- invariably, whether a vowel-initial or a consonant-initial suffix follows. The absence of invariant CV:C- roots follows from a general principle, if we postulate the operation of (15).

Notice that (15) presupposes that the difference between alternating and nonalternating roots is that the former possess basic long vowels while the latter possess basic short ones. Let us reconsider rule (14) again. Recall that it is beset by the problem that it is too general. It will incorrectly lengthen the root vowel in *xat-al*, for example, giving **xa:t-al*. In order to maintain an analysis incorporating (14), it would be necessary to assume that /xat/ is somehow different from /ṣap/, since only the latter has a long vowel alternant. It would be possible to assign some arbitrary mark to the vowel of /ṣap/ that would differentiate it from /xat/, and then formulate (14) so that it operates only on a vowel that possesses the relevant mark. In Chapter 3 we referred to this sort of analysis as a **lexical** solution in contrast to **phonological** solutions such as the one that postulates an underlying contrast in length. The reasons for accepting the phonological solution over the lexical one in the present case are relatively clear. Roots such as *ṣa:p-/ṣap-* and *xat-* clearly must contrast somehow in the underlying representation. There is also a phonetic contrast. The former has a long vowel when prevocalic, the latter does not. There is then an actually occurring phonetic contrast associated with these morphemes which is available to distinguish them underlyingly. To prefer arbitrary marks in such a situation is gratuitous, resulting ultimately in permitting any phonetic contrast to be the result of a contrast in an arbitrary mark. Since the arbitrary mark must ultimately be 'translated' into a phonetic contrast, why not begin with the phonetic contrast and neutralize it in the relevant positions? (See Kenstowicz and Kisseberth 1977 for further discussion of this point.)

VOWEL EPENTHESIS

We have restricted the data considered so far to verb roots of the structure CVC (where V may be either short or long). Not all verb roots are of this type, though the kinds of verb roots that one encounters in Yawelmani *are* severely restricted. The data in (16) illustrate an additional type of root.

(16)
pa?ṭ-al	'might fight'	*pa?iṭ-hin*	'fights'
?ilk-al	'might sing'	*?ilik-hin*	'sings'
logw-ol	'might pulverize'	*logiw-hin*	'pulverizes'
?ugn-al	'might drink'	*?ugun-hun*	'drinks'
?ayy-al	'might pole a boat'	*?ayiy-hin*	'poles a boat'
lihm-al	'might run'	*lihim-hin*	'runs'
t'oyx-ol	'might give medicine'	*t'oyix-hin*	'gives medicine'
luk'l-al	'might bury'	*luk'ul-hun*	'buries'

Roots of this type reveal an alternation between the shape CVCC- and CVC*i*C- (the *i* being pronounced as *u* in certain cases; see below for discussion); the former alternant appears before -*al*, and other vowel-initial suffixes, while the latter occurs before -*hin*, and other consonant-initial suffixes. Confirmation of the claim that it is the initial segment of the suffix (vowel or consonant) that determines the shape of the root is provided by the examples in (17), where once again we find CVCC- in prevocalic position and CVC*i*C- in preconsonantal position.

(17)
pa?ṭ-en	'will fight'	*pa?iṭ-mi*	'having fought'
lihm-en	'will run'	*lihim-mi*	'having run'
logw-en	'will pulverize'	*logiw-mi*	'having pulverized'
?ugn-on	'will drink'	*?ugun-mu*	'having drunk'

Before analyzing the data in (16) and (17), two observations need to be made about Yawelmani phonological structure. First, words in this language neither begin nor end in a consonant cluster, and within a word the maximum number of consecutive consonants is two. Second, there are no verb roots in Yawelmani of the shape CV_1CV_2C-, where V_1 and V_2 are both short vowels, that do not have the vowel *i* in the V_2 position. And every verb root that *does* have the shape CV_1CV_2C- has this shape before consonant-initial suffixes, and has the alternant CV_1CC- before vowel-initial suffixes.

Let us turn now to the question of what basic form to assign these verb roots. If they are basically CVCiC-, then we need a rule dropping the underlying *i* vowel in case a vowel-initial suffix follows. The environment for this deletion rule might possibly be something like VC___CV (a preceding vowel must be mentioned in order to prevent /giy' + al/ from being converted to *gy' + al). In the examples given a morpheme boundary is present, the actual context being VC___C + V; but from the data inspected so far there is no evidence bearing upon whether the presence of a morpheme boundary at this point in the structure is necessary. Furthermore, given the examples cited so far, there is no evidence that the deletion would need to be restricted to just *i*. Consequently, a general rule such as (18) might be possible.

(18) $V \longrightarrow \emptyset/VC\_\_\_CV$

(18) would operate upon a representation such as /lihim + al/ to derive *lihm-al*, but would leave /lihim + hin/ unaffected, since there is no vowel in this form that meets the environment of (18).

An alternative to (18) would be to take the basic form of the roots in question to be of the shape CVCC-, with a rule that inserts the vowel *i*. The rule would presumably be that given in (19).

(19) $\emptyset \longrightarrow i/C\_\_\_CC$

Rule (19) would operate upon a representation like /lihm + hin/ to yield *lihim-hin*, but would leave /lihm + al/ unaffected since there is no three-consonant cluster present.

On what grounds can we choose between these two solutions? As formulated, both analyses will predict the correct phonetic shapes for the data considered. One significant fact is that if we decide to assign these roots the basic shape CVCiC-, they will be the only disyllabic roots in the language whose second vowel is a short vowel. In other words, we will have a curious asymmetry: CVCiC- will be a rather common shape in underlying forms, but CVCaC-, CVCuC-, CVCoC- will never occur.

Another significant fact is that if we decide that the roots in question have the basic shape CVCiC-, there will be no roots of the shape CVCC- in underlying representation. Recall also that in Yawelmani three-consonant clusters do not occur phonetically. An analysis incorporating the epenthesis rule (19) would account for the absence of three-consonant clusters, since an *i* vowel would be inserted whenever three consonants come together in the underlying form. The existence of such a rule would also account for why CVCiC- appears phonetically, but not CVCaC-, CVCuC-, etc. Disyllabic verb roots whose second vowel is short would be claimed to not exist at all in underlying form; verb roots ending in a consonant cluster would occur, however. The epenthesis rule (19) would convert CVCC- roots to CVCiC- when followed by a consonant-initial suffix.

One very general methodological principle underlies the above discussion; namely, if there is a 'pathological' phonetic pattern (i.e., a pattern that disobeys general principles of the language, as in the case under discussion, where CV_1CV_2C- is generally disallowed except if V_2 is *i*), then it is likely that this pattern is the consequence of a rule, rather than a property of the underlying form of the language. A general principle of this sort is not, of course, infallible, and one would like to find language-particular evidence as well favoring (19) over (18). One confirming piece of evidence can be mentioned briefly here. A verb root such as *xat-* 'eat' may be reduplicated to express repeated action: *xatxat-* 'eat repeatedly', as in *xatxat-al*. Before certain suffixes, the reciprocal-reflexive suffix *-iwis* for example, such reduplicated verb roots have a special shape. *xatxat-*, for example, is realized as *xatixt-*; *koykoy-* 'butt repeatedly' is realized as *koyiky-*, and so on. These forms seem to involve a zeroing of the root vowel in the second part of the reduplicated form: /xatxat/ ⟶ /xatxt/, /koykoy/ ⟶ /koyky/. The three-consonant cluster that results from this zeroing is broken up by an insertion of the vowel *i* between the first two consonants. /xatxat+iwis/ 'act of eating repeatedly' is thus realized as *xatixt-iwis*. The insertion of *i* in examples of this sort follows automatically (given the zeroing of the root vowel in the second member of the reduplicated form) if we posit rule (19); rule (18) does not make any prediction whatsoever about the shape of these forms.

Let us assume, then, the correctness of (19) and of URs such as /paʔt/, /ʔilk/, /logw/, etc. The interplay between (19)—vowel epenthesis—and the rules of vowel harmony and vowel shortening discussed in preceding sections will now be examined.

Consider first *ʔugun-hun* 'drinks', which will have the basic form /ʔugn + hin/. Since the *i* that is inserted by vowel epenthesis is pronounced as *u* in the PR, it is necessary that we construct the grammar of

Yawelmani so that the inserted *i* vowel may undergo vowel harmony just like an underlying *i* vowel. (We are assuming here that it is correct to view the fact that the inserted vowel in *ʔugun-hun* is pronounced as *u* as being due to the operation of vowel harmony. This will be discussed further below.) This can be achieved by applying the rule of vowel epenthesis before applying the rule of vowel harmony. Thus /ʔugn + hin/ will first undergo vowel epenthesis, resulting in /ʔugin + hin/; vowel harmony will then apply to this inserted vowel, deriving /ʔugun + hin/, and will then apply also to the suffixal vowel, giving the correct surface form *ʔugun-hun*.

Confirmation of this ordering of the rules can be found in such examples as *logiw-xa* 'let's pulverize', from underlying /logw + xa/. Observe that in the underlying form, the suffixal *a* meets the conditions for vowel harmony, and one would expect it to be pronounced as *o*, all other things being equal. But if vowel epenthesis does apply before vowel harmony, /logw + xa/ will be converted to /logiw + xa/ before the latter rule has a chance to apply. Once /logiw + xa/ is derived, the conditions for vowel harmony are no longer present: The presence of the epenthetic *i* means that the suffixal vowel is no longer preceded by an *o* vowel. Ordering vowel epenthesis before vowel harmony simultaneously predicts that epenthetic *i* will be rounded to *u* if preceded by *u*, and also that it will inhibit harmony when it separates *a* from a preceding *o*.

The examples in (20) provide crucial data bearing on the interplay of vowel epenthesis and vowel shortening.

(20)

	sonl-ol	'might put on the back'
	so:nil-mi	'having packed on the back'
	ʔaml-al	'might help'
	ʔa:mil-hin	'helps'
	moyn-ol	'might become tired'
	mo:yin-mi	'having become tired'
	ṣalk'-al	'might wake up'
	ṣa:lik'-hin	'wakes up'

The verb roots in (20) reveal two alternants: CV̆CC- and CV:CiC-, the former before vowel-initial suffixes and the latter before consonant-initial suffixes. Although this particular alternation pattern has not occurred elsewhere, it is clear that it is a combination of alternations we have already encountered. In particular, it consists of the V:/V̆ alternation found in examples such as *do:s-ol* 'might report', *dos-hin* 'reports' and the Ø/*i* alternation found in *ʔilk-al* 'might sing', *ʔilik-hin* 'sings'. Given that the alternation pattern in (20) appears to be a result of the alternation patterns that vowel epenthesis and vowel shortening account for, it is natural to account for the alternations in (20) by these rules as well. This can be done if we derive the *i* vowel in an alternant like *so:nil-* from vowel epenthesis, and if we derive the short vowel in *sonl-* from vowel shortening. The UR of the verb root must therefore be /so:nl/.

Postulating underlying forms such as /so:nl/, /ʔa:ml/, /mo:yn/, /ṣa:lk/ is not sufficient; we must also assume that the rules are applied in a particular sequence—namely, vowel epenthesis before vowel shortening. Consider underlying /so:nl + hin/. If vowel shortening applied first, it would give /sonl + hin/ as output; vowel epenthesis would then apply, with the result being the incorrect form **sonil-hin*. To obtain the correct results, /so:nl + hin/ must first undergo vowel epenthesis, deriving /so:nil + hin/; vowel shortening would not then be able to apply, since no long vowel is followed by a consonant cluster in this example.

It is of some interest to note that up to this point, each underlying form of a morpheme has been identical to one of the phonetic realizations of the morpheme. /giy'/ occurs in *giy'-al*; /do:s/ occurs in *do:s-ol*; /logw/ occurs in *logw-ol*. But in the case of /so:nl/, /ʔa:ml/, etc., the UR never surfaces directly in any one alternant of the morpheme. It is absolutely necessary to postulate such 'unpronounced' underlying forms if we are to account for the alternation pattern in (20) by the rules of vowel epenthesis and vowel shortening. Suppose we were to select /sonl/ as basic; we could not then account for the lengthened form of the vowel in the CV:CiC- alternant by means of vowel shortening. A separate lengthening rule would be needed. Such a lengthening rule could not be general, of course, since there are examples like *ʔilik-hin* 'sings' where the first vowel is not long. Similarly, if we were to select /so:nil/ as basic, then we would be permitting an otherwise nonoccurring type of underlying representation; in addition, a special rule deleting the *i* would be needed to obtain the alternant lacking this vowel. Only a representation like /so:nl/ permits independently motivated rules to account for the alternant pronunciations of the morphemes in question.

VOWEL HARMONY REEXAMINED

The rule of vowel harmony formulated in the first section, despite its ability to account for a wide range of facts about the pronunciation of Yawelmani suffixes, superficially appears to be unable to account for a rather significant number of examples. Table (21) illustrates some of the problematic examples.

(21)

	A		B
c'o:m-al	'might destroy'	do:s-ol	'might report'
ç'om-hun	'destroys'	dos-hin	'reports'
ṣo:g-al	'might pull out the cork'	wo:n-ol	'might hide'
ṣog-hun	'pulls out a cork'	won-hin	'hides'
wo?y-al	'might fall asleep'	sonl-ol	'might pack on the back'
wo:?uy-hun	'falls asleep'	so:nil-hin	'packs on the back'
doll-al	'might climb'	hotn-ol	'might take the scent'
do:lul-hun	'climbs'	ho:tin-hin	'takes the scent'

The examples in column B are perfectly regular with respect to our postulated rule of vowel harmony, while those in column A are systematically irregular. If the underlying form of the verb roots in column A are /c'o:m/, /ṣo:g/, /wo:?y/, /do:ll/, the following suffixal *a* vowels should round (unless separated from the root vowel by an epenthetic *i*) and following *i* vowels should not. But we find exactly the reverse. In *c'o:m-al*, suffixal *a* does not round (cf., *do:s-ol*). In *c'om-hun*, suffixal *i* is rounded (cf., *dos-hin*).

There are, initially, two reasons for hesitating to accept that the examples in A are simply exceptions to the vowel harmony rule. First, examination of a broad range of data reveals that there are, roughly speaking, as many examples like A as like B. In other words, the 'exceptions' are about as frequent as the 'regular' cases (with respect to verb roots whose root vowel appears on the surface as *o:* alternating with *o*). Second, the examples in A are bidirectionally exceptional; that is, it is not simply the case that *c'o:m-* fails to act like such verbs as *do:s-*, *logw-*, etc., in causing a following *a* to become *o*; in addition, *c'o:m-* does act like such roots as *hud-*, *dub-*, and so on, in causing a following *i* vowel to become *u*. This is a type of exceptionality rather different from the usual case, where some morpheme simply is not affected by a particular rule (cf., Chapter 10 for a discussion of exceptions to rules).

At this point we need to recall an observation made earlier—namely, just three long vowels occur in phonetic representations in Yawelmani: *e:*, *a:*, and *o:* (this is not entirely correct; the vowels *i:* and *u:* also occur phonetically as the result of certain phonological rules which will be ignored until later in the exposition). There are, on the other hand, four short vowels in underlying forms: *i*, *a*, *o*, *u* (the vowel *e* occurs only as the shortened version of *e:*). A solution to the problem is suggested by the lack of parallelism between the basic short vowels and the surface long vowels. Suppose we were to postulate that the verb roots in A have a different underlying vowel from the verb roots in B; in particular, that the

A forms have basic *u:* whereas the B forms have basic *o:*. If we then claimed that vowel harmony operates in terms of the underlying vowel quality, the data in (21) becomes perfectly regular. In *c'o:m-al*, for example, the suffixal *a* is unrounded due to the fact that it is preceded by a high round vowel *u:* in the underlying form /c'u:m + al/; in *do:s-ol* the suffixal vowel is rounded since it is preceded by a non-high round vowel *o:* in the underlying form /do:s + al/. *c'om-hun* shows the high suffixal vowel being rounded as a consequence of being preceded by a high round vowel in the underlying representation /c'u:m + hin/. *dos-hin* does not have the suffixal vowel rounded since the correct environment is not present in /do:s + hin/.

We must assume that subsequent to the operation of vowel harmony there is a rule of vowel lowering, which specifies basic *u:* as *o:*. The possibility of maintaining the existence of a rule such as vowel lowering depends upon the absence of any basic *u:* vowels that must not be lowered to *o:*. Since, as mentioned above, the only phonetic *u:* vowels in the language arise from other phonological rules, there is nothing preventing us from maintaining the existence of a vowel lowering rule. The rule obviously must be restricted to long *u:*, since the short *u* of *hud-al* and *dub-hun* does not lower to *o*.

By analyzing the A examples as containing basic *u:*, we are claiming that phonetic *o:* has two underlying sources: *u:* and *o:*. The long vowel system underlyingly is now *e:*, *a:*, *o:*, and *u:*, whereas the short vowel system is *i*, *a*, *o*, and *u*. The only difference in the vowel systems is that the front vowel is the high vowel *i* when short and the non-high vowel *e:* when long. The two systems would be more symmetrical if phonetic *e:* were analyzed as being basically *i:*, with the rule of vowel lowering being responsible for the phonetic quality of the vowel. *me:k'-al* 'might swallow' would thus be /mi:k' + al/ basically. The form of vowel lowering would be that in (22).

(22) $$\frac{V}{[+ \text{long}]} \longrightarrow [- \text{high}]$$

A rule like (22) would permit the examples in (21) to be treated as regular, and would also explain the asymmetry between the phonetic short and long vowel systems in terms of symmetrical underlying systems. But are these sufficient reasons for believing that the verb roots *c'o:m-* and *me:k'-* are in fact basically /c'u:m/ and /mi:k'/? Obviously we are achieving 'regularity' and 'symmetry' only at a certain cost: namely, setting up underlying representations with a vowel whose underlying quality is never (in the examples discussed so far at least) directly manifested in the surface. Underlying /c'u:m/ has the two alternants *c'o:m-* and *c'om-*, and in neither alternant do we find a direct manifestation of the underlying highness of the vowel. The manifestation of the highness of the vowel is its effect on a following vowel. And in the case of /mi:k'/, there is no manifestation of the basic highness of the vowel in either the realizations of the morpheme—*me:k'-* and *mek'-* —or in its effect on a following vowel. Thus we have only 'symmetry' suggesting that *e:* is basically *i:*, and both symmetry and the evidence from vowel harmony to suggest that some *o:* vowels are basically *u:*. Fortunately, there is a good deal of additional evidence that can be brought to bear upon the question of how to analyze the data in (21), and we are not forced in this case to decide whether the evidence given thus far is adequate to motivate underlying *i:* and *u:*.

We have postulated the following types of verb bases: CV̆C- (e.g., /dub/), CV:C- (e.g., /do:s/), CV̆CC- (e.g., /logw/), and CV:CC- (e.g., /ʔa:ml/). There are, in addition, two other types of verb roots to be found in Yawelmani. They are exemplified in (23) and (24).

(23)

p'axa:t'-al	'might mourn'	*p'axat'-hin*	'mourns'
hiwe:t-al	'might walk'	*hiwet-hin*	'walks'
ʔopo:t-ol	'might arise from bed'	*ʔopot-hin*	'arises from bed'
ṣudo:k'-al	'might remove'	*ṣudok'-hun*	'removes'
yawa:l-al	'might follow'	*yawal-hin*	'follows'
hibe:y-al	'might bring water'	*hibey-hin*	'brings water'
yolo:w-ol	'might assemble'	*yolow-hin*	'assembles'
t'uno:y-al	'might scorch'	*t'unoy-hun*	'scorches'

(24)

pana-l	'might arrive'	*pana:-hin*	'arrives'
ʔile-l	'might fan'	*ʔile:-hin*	'fans'
hoyo-l	'might name'	*hoyo:-hin*	'names'
c'uyo-l	'might urinate'	*c'uyo:-hun*	'urinates'
taxa-l	'might bring'	*taxa:-hin*	'brings'
nine-l	'might get quiet'	*nine:-hin*	'gets quiet'

One interesting point that can be made about the verb roots in (23) and (24) is that although they are disyllabic in all their alternants, the two vowels are not independently selectable. Verb roots of this sort have the following possible patterns, and only these:

> a. CaCa:(C)-
> b. CiCe:(C)-
> c. CoCo:(C)-
> d. CuCo:(C)-

(The long vowels in (a)–(d) are shortened, of course, when a consonant cluster follows.) In other words, if the first vowel of these disyllabic roots is *a*, then the second is *a:*; if the first vowel is *i*, the second is *e:*, etc. Examination of additional data reveals that the (c) and (d) patterns differ systematically in their vowel harmony properties: namely, in the case of verb roots of the (c) type, a following *a* vowel is rounded to *o* but a following *i* vowel is unaffected; in the case of verb roots of the (d) type, a following *i* is rounded to *u*, but a following *a* is unaffected. Thus *ʔopo:t-ol* versus *ṣudo:k'-al*, but *ʔopot-hin* versus *ṣudok'-hun*.

Notice that if we are correct in suggesting that *o:* vowels which require a following high vowel to round, and do not require a following nonhigh vowel to round, are properly represented as /u:/ in underlying form, then pattern (d) is really, at a more abstract level, C*u*C*u*:(C)-. Furthermore, if we are correct in suggesting that *e:* derives from underlying /i:/, then the pattern (b) is C*i*C*i*:(C)- at a more abstract level. We thus have the following patterns:

> a'. CaCa:(C)-
> b'. CiCi:(C)-
> c'. CoCo:(C)-
> d'. CuCu:(C)-

An obvious generalization holds for these verbs: the first vowel is a short version of the second vowel, the latter always being long (prior to the operation of vowel shortening, of course). Verb roots in Yawelmani which are invariably disyllabic always obey this constraint.

We will leave open the question of how this constraint on the selection of the vowels is to be incorporated into a systematic account of Yawelmani phonology (cf., Chapter 10). Let us simply refer to verb roots of this type as echo verbs. The important point is that only the assumption of a rule such as vowel lowering operating upon underlying /i:/ and /u:/ turning them into *e:* and *o:* makes it possible to formulate any generalization at all for the echo verbs. This analysis permits us to relate (in a non-ad hoc way) the fact that verb roots of the (d) type not only have *u* as their first vowel but also condition harmony in the same way as verb roots with an underlying high vowel. Echo verbs consequently provide an additional piece of support for the analysis proposed above for dealing with the surface exceptions to vowel harmony involving *o:*.

Before turning to some additional data that support postulating underlying /i:/ and /u:/ vowels, there are certain aspects of the pronunciation of the verb roots in (24) which we have not yet accounted for. Observe the dubitative forms *pana-l*, *ʔile-l*, *c'uyo-l*, *hoyo-l*. Although the dubitative suffix has the shape *-al* in all of the examples encountered earlier, it is simply -*l* in the case of verb roots of the form CVCV:-. Similarly, although the passive suffix generally has the shape -*it*, after the vowel-final roots of (24) it has the shape -*t*. This absence of the initial vowel of the suffix can be accounted for by postulating the rule of truncation in (25).

(25) $\qquad\qquad\qquad$ V $\longrightarrow$ ∅/V___

This rule will operate upon a representation such as /ʔili: + al/ to yield /ʔili: + l/.

However, we have not yet accounted for the final pronunciation of the dubitative and passive forms. The second vowel of the verb root is pronounced as a short vowel in these forms, even though basically a long vowel. Recall that we already have a rule of vowel shortening that operates in the environment ___CC; if we include ___C# as an additional context in which basic long vowels shorten, then the data under consideration have a straightforward explanation. In order to obtain the correct outputs from our rules, we must impose a particular sequence upon their application. Obviously, truncation must be applied prior to vowel shortening, since the rule of truncation creates the context for the latter rule to apply. In addition, it is essential that the rule of vowel lowering be applied before the vowel shortening rule; if the reverse sequencing obtained, /ʔili: + l/ would be converted to /ʔili + l/ by vowel shortening, and then vowel lowering would be inapplicable since it affects just long vowels. Incorrect *ʔili-l would result. To obtain ʔile-l, vowel lowering must be applied first, as in the following derivation:

(26) $\qquad$ /ʔili: + al/ $\qquad$ Underlying representation
$\qquad\qquad$ ʔili: + l $\qquad$ Truncation
$\qquad\qquad$ ʔile: + l $\qquad$ Vowel lowering
$\qquad\qquad$ ʔile + l $\qquad$ Vowel shortening

(In the above derivation, we showed truncation being applied prior to vowel lowering, but there is no evidence relevant to determining whether this is correct.) Shortening before two consonants also follows vowel lowering. The derivation of *ṣudok'-hun* 'removes' must be that given as follows:

(27) $\qquad$ /ṣudu:k' + hin/ $\qquad$ Underlying representation
$\qquad\qquad$ ṣudu:k' + hun $\qquad$ Vowel harmony
$\qquad\qquad$ ṣudo:k' + hun $\qquad$ Vowel lowering
$\qquad\qquad$ ṣudok' + hun $\qquad$ Vowel shortening

In order to obtain *ṣudok'-hun* from basic / ṣudu:k' + hin / it is crucial that vowel harmony be applied before vowel lowering; otherwise, the following incorrect derivation would result:

(28) /ṣudu:k' + hin/   Underlying representation
      ṣudo:k' + hin   Vowel lowering
      inapplicable   Vowel harmony
      **ṣudok'* + hin   Vowel shortening

Similarly, it is crucial that vowel lowering be applied before vowel shortening, otherwise we would have the incorrect derivation:

(29) /ṣudu:k' + hin/   Underlying representation
      ṣudu:k' + hun   Vowel harmony
      **ṣuduk' + hun*   Vowel shortening
      inapplicable   Vowel lowering

Vowel lowering would be inapplicable since it affects just long vowels.

All of the data in (23) and (24) have now been accounted for by the three rules of vowel harmony, vowel lowering, and vowel shortening, applied in that sequence. We can now return to an examination of additional data bearing on the correctness of the analysis presented here. It turns out that verb roots such as *c'uyo:-* 'urinate' and *hoyo:-* 'name' differ not only in that the former behaves, with respect to vowel harmony, as though it ends in a high vowel and the latter in a non-high vowel, but in another interesting respect as well. Verb roots of the shape CVCV:- take a future suffix that consists just of a glottal stop. Examples are cited in (30).

(30)   *pana-ʔ*   'will arrive'
          ʔili-ʔ   'will fan'
          hoyo-ʔ   'will name'
          c'uyu-ʔ   'will urinate'

Before the future suffix, the second vowel of verb roots of the shape CVCV:- appears phonetically as a short vowel. In the (a) type of verb root, this vowel is pronounced as *a*; in the (b) type, as *i*; in the (c) type, as *o*; and in the (d) type, as *u*. These examples involve a special shortening process which, examination of additional data shows, operates before word-final suffixes consisting of a glottal stop (the future suffix and a nominal case ending are the only examples). The interesting thing about these data is that the quality of the resulting short vowels in *ʔili-ʔ* and *c'uyu-ʔ* is not identical to the phonetic quality of the corresponding long vowels in *?ile :-hin* and *c'uyo :-hun*. But the quality of the short vowel is identical to that of the vowel that has been suggested as the underlying vowel: *?ili-?* would be derived from /?ili: + ?/ and *c'uyu-?* from /c'uyu: +?/. Thus if the rule that shortens a long vowel before the glottal stop of the future morpheme operates prior to the application of vowel lowering, the quality of the resulting short vowel will be an automatic consequence of the quality of the underlying vowel.

The evidence for postulating underlying /i :/ and /u :/ which (30) provides is totally independent of the evidence from vowel harmony. For verb roots of the shape CVCV :- we can find actual examples of pronunciations of the second vowel where its underlying highness is realized as phonetic highness.

One additional argument supporting underlying /i :/ and /u :/ will be given here. Certain types of verb roots in Yawelmani may be used as nouns without the addition of an overt nominalizing suffix, though certain phonological modifications are associated with this usage. Example (31) shows some of these verbal nouns; the basic form of the verb root that we suggest is indicated in parentheses.

(31)   *bok'*   'finding'   (/bok'/)
         ?ut'   'stealing'   (/?u :t'/)
         ?idil   'getting hungry'   (/?i :dl/)
         logiw   'pulverizing'   (/logw/)
         moyin   'getting tired'   (/mo :yn/)
         ?utuy   'falling'   (/?uty/)
         wu?uy   'falling asleep'   (/wu :?y/)

All of the verb roots that end in a consonant cluster in their basic representation have that consonant cluster separated by an *i* vowel (alternating with *u* by virtue of vowel harmony). Since no words in Yawelmani end in a consonant cluster, this *i* can be predicted by simply modifying the rule of vowel epenthesis so that it inserts *i* not just in the environment C____CC, but also in the environment C____C#. As was discussed earlier, the vowel epenthesis rule must be applied prior to the operation of vowel harmony. So underlying /?uty/ will first undergo vowel epenthesis, yielding /?utiy/, and then vowel harmony, with the correct *?utuy* resulting.

One other fact about the pronunciation of the verbal nouns in (31) should be noted: the first vowel is invariably short, even if it is basically a long vowel. Thus /mo :yn/ is pronounced *moyin*, and is not pronounced in this way by virtue of any general principle in the language—other than that verbal nouns of the sort under consideration always begin with a short vowel. The rule that shortens /mo:yn/ to /moyn/ is therefore a special process of very limited scope and of little general interest in itself. What is of interest is the quality of the resulting short vowel. In each case, we find the short vowel that corresponds to the suggested underlying representation. Thus /ʔu:ṭ'/, which was postulated as having a basic high vowel in order to account for its behavior with respect to vowel harmony, turns out to have a high vowel in the verbal noun *ʔuṭ'*. /mo:yn/, on the other hand, which was postulated to have a basic nonhigh vowel in order to account for its behavior with respect to vowel harmony, is pronounced with a nonhigh vowel in the verbal noun *moyin*. Similarly, basic /ʔi:dl/ is actually pronounced with a high vowel in the verbal noun *ʔidil*, even though its more common pronunciation is with a nonhigh vowel (cf., *ʔedl-al* 'might get hungry', *ʔe:dil-hin* 'gets hungry').

The pronunciation of verbal nouns like those of (31) follows automatically given the underlying representations suggested by vowel harmony considerations, provided the special shortening process associated with verbal nouns is applied prior to the operation of vowel lowering. These data provide, then, another independent source of evidence for the analysis.

At the end of the first section we noted that certain suffixes appear to violate the rule of vowel harmony. These suffixes contain low vowels that behave as though they were high vowels: The future morpheme -*en*/-*on* is a case in point. Such examples as *bok'-en* 'will find' versus *dub-on* 'will lead by the hand' appear to be anomalous until we will realize that the basic shape of the suffix must be /i:n/, since phonetic *e* in Yawelmani arises only from underlying /i:/ in our analysis. Given this underlying representation of the morpheme, the correct surface form follows from the rules we have posited:

(32)   /bok' + i:n/   /dub + i:n/
        inapplicable   *dub + u:n*   Vowel harmony
        bok' + e:n   *dub + o:n*   Vowel lowering
        bok' + en   *dub + on*   Vowel shortening

It is of some interest to note that this account of the morphophonemics of the suffix /i:n/ claims that the underlying vowel is basically long, even though in all phonetic realizations of the morpheme the vowel is pronounced short. In addition, the analysis claims that the vowel is underlyingly high, even though it is always pronounced as nonhigh. (The same is not true of the verb roots like /ʔu:t'/ or /c'uyu:/ which are, at least in some forms, pronounced with a high vowel rather than with *o:*.) These claims appear to be well-founded given the data examined here. We return to some of these points later in Chapter 6, where the issue of abstractness in phonology is discussed.

ADDITIONAL RULES

In analyzing the phonological system of Yawelmani verbs, the following rules have been developed. The lines connect those rules that require a particular sequence of application in order to obtain the correct phonetic output. If two rules are connected by a line, the rule higher in the list must be applied before the rule lower in the list.

(33)
```
    ┌──Shortening of vowels in verbal nouns
  ┌─┬─Shortening before /-?/ in final position
  │ │ ┌─Vowel epenthesis ─┐
  │ │ └─Vowel harmony ┐    │
  │ └───Vowel lowering ─┘  │
  │   ┌─Truncation          │
  └───┴─Vowel shortening ───┘
```

Certain other rules in Yawelmani phonology critically interact with the rules listed above. Consider the examples in (34).

(34)

?ile-k'	'fan!'	(cf., *giy'-k'a* 'touch!')
c'uyo-k'	'urinate!'	(cf., *dub-k'a* 'lead by the hand!')
taxa-k'	'bring!'	(cf., *xat-k'a* 'eat!')
?ile-m	'having fanned'	(cf., *giy'-mi* 'having touched')
c'uyo-m	'having urinated'	(cf., *dub-mu* 'having led by the hand')
taxa-m	'having brought'	(cf., *xat-mi* 'having eaten')

Word-final suffixes of the shape -CV have a vowelless alternant after verb roots of the structure CVCV: - (i.e., after the only vowel-final roots of the language). Thus -*k'a* has the alternant -*k'*, -*mi* has the alternant -*m*, -*xa* has the alternant -*x*. These data are readily accounted for by positing a rule of vowel drop, as in (35).

(35) $$V \longrightarrow \emptyset / V + C\_\_\_ \#$$

Evidence that a morpheme boundary must be present in the position indicated is provided by the gerundial suffix -*e:ni* basically /i:ni/) in such examples as *xat-e:ni* 'in order to eat', *?a:x-e:ni* 'in order to stay overnight', *ṣalk'-e:ni* 'waking up', where the final vowel is retained even though in the environment VC___#. A final vowel drops just in case the preceding consonant is morpheme initial.

Rule (35) operates on an underlying form like /taxa: + k'a/ to yield

/taxa: + k'/. To obtain the correct phonetic shape, vowel shortening must be applied to the output of vowel drop. There are no other rules which vowel drop must either precede or follow in the sequence of rule application.

As mentioned earlier, there are phonetic high long vowels in Yawelmani; we turn now to a brief consideration of one source of such high vowels. The reflexive/reciprocal suffix *-iwis-* is added to a verb root to form a verbal noun; the full form of the suffix shows up in the nominative case, where no suffix is added. Thus we get *wagç-iwis* 'act of dividing'. When the objective case suffix *-a* is added, the sequence *iwi* contracts to *i:*, as in *wagç-i:s-a*; similarly, there is *huwṭ-uwus* 'a shell game', but *huwṭ-u:s-a*. Although these data are limited enough to make any proposed analysis very tentative, one possible account of the facts goes as follows. The suffix has the basic shape /iws/. *wagç-iwis* arises from the operation of vowel epenthesis, which recall will insert *i* in the environment C⎯⎯C#. In *huwṭ-uwus*, vowel harmony applies to the structure /huwṭ + iwis/, which is itself the result of vowel epenthesis. Considering the objective case forms, the presence of the suffix *-a* will inhibit vowel epenthesis. A rule of contraction must be posited, such as (36).

(36)
$$\begin{Bmatrix} iw \\ uw \end{Bmatrix} \longrightarrow \begin{Bmatrix} i: \\ u: \end{Bmatrix} / \underline{\hspace{1em}} C$$

This rule must be restricted to the reflexive/reciprocal suffix, since the sequences *-iw-* and *-uw-* occur elsewhere in preconsonantal position (compare, for instance, the root *huwṭ-* above).

Rule (36) will apply to /wagç + iws + a/ to yield *wagç-i:s-a*, the correct form. Notice that it is necessary that vowel epenthesis be applied before contraction. Otherwise /wagç + iws / will become */wagç + i:s/. Furthermore, it is necessary that contraction be applied after vowel lowering, so that /wagç + i:s/ is not lowered to */wagç + e:s/. The derivation of *huwṭ-u:s-a* as follows indicates the correct order of application of the rules:

(37)   /huwṭ + iws + a/
              inapplicable   Vowel epenthesis
              huwṭ + uws + a   Vowel harmony
              inapplicable   Vowel lowering
              huwṭ + u:s + a   Contraction

Slovak

In this section we will examine the rather intricate interaction among several rules in the phonology of Slovak, a West Slavic language closely related to Czech. Since we will be citing forms in the native Slovak orthography, several remarks concerning the phonetic interpretation of the letters are in order. All of the letters employed have their usual broad phonetic interpretation, except that *y* = [i], *ä* = [æ], *ô* = [uo], and *ch* = [x]. Also the phonetic devoicing of word final obstruents is not indicated in the writing system. Finally, the acute accent sign over a vowel or a liquid indicates *length*. Thus, *á* = [a:], *ŕ* = [r:]. The acute accent sign does not indicate stress, which is always on the first vowel of the word in Slovak.

Most of the rules we shall be concerned with involve syllabic elements. The following table indicates the syllabic sounds that are to be found in phonetic representations of Slovak utterances.

(38)

Short		Long		Rising diphthongs	
i	u	í	ú		
e	o	(é)	(ó)	ie	uo
ä	a		á	ia	
l,r		í,ŕ			

The long mid vowels are placed in parentheses because they are quite rare in native Slovak words. The vowel *é* only occurs in the word *dcéra* 'daughter' and the adjectival suffix /-é/: cf. *dobr-é*, *dobr-é-ho*, the neuter nominative and genitive forms of 'good'. The vowel *ó* is limited to interjections.

If the rare *é* and *ó* are ignored, the reader will note a peculiar patterning of the long and short syllabics in (38). The short vowels *i*, *u*, and *a* and the liquids *l* and *r* can be paired with long phonetic counterparts. But *e*, *o*, and *ä* have no long phonetic counterparts. Furthermore, the diphthongs *ie*, *ô* (= [uo]), and *ia* are the only rising diphthongs in the language. A reasonable hypothesis here is that the rising diphthongs derive from underlying long *é*, *ó*, and *ä̈*. Such an analysis would regularize the pattern to a symmetrical system of eight pairs of short and long syllabic elements. Recall from our discussion of Yawelmani that asymmetrical phonetic inventories often arise from more balanced underlying ones via phonological rules that obscure the underlying pattern. This seems to be especially true with an underlying long/short contrast. In many languages long and short vowels pair up quite neatly in underlying representations, but then phonological rules obscure the pattern by modifying the quality of some of the underlying vowels (typically the long ones). Consequently, in our examination of Slovak, we might expect to find independent evidence supporting an analysis that derives the rising diphthongs *ie, ô,* and *ia* from underlying *é, ó,* and *ä̈* by a rule of diphthongization.

In fact, there is considerable evidence to indicate that this is the case. The numerous lengthening rules in the language support this interpretation of the diphthongs. In each case where an *i, u, a, l,* or *r* is lengthened, the vowels *e, o,* and *ä* are replaced by diphthongs. For example, there is a very general rule that lengthens the final vowel or liquid of a feminine or neuter noun stem in the genitive plural.

(39)

Nom. sg.	Gen. pl.	Gloss
lipa	*líp*	'linden tree'
mucha	*múch*	'fly'
lopata	*lopát*	'shovel'
srna	*sŕn*	'roe, deer'
žena	*žien*	'woman'
kazeta	*kaziet*	'box'
hora	*hôr*	'forest'
sirota	*sirôt*	'orphan'
päta	*piat*	'heel'
mäta	*miat*	'mint'

Another such rule is the one that lengthens the final vowel or syllabic liquid of a stem when the diminutive suffix *-ok* is added: *hrad, hrádok* 'castle'; *list, lístok* 'leaf'; *chlp, chĺpok* 'hair'; but *kvet, kvietok* 'flower'; *hovädo, hoviadok* (gen. pl.) 'beast'.

If the diphthongs are not derived from underlying long vowels, then each lengthening rule in Slovak would require the peculiar condition that it convert basic short *e, o,* and *ä* to the corresponding diphthongs, while simply lengthening the remaining syllabics. But why should each of these rules have this peculiar wrinkle? This is explained if we say that these rules merely assign the feature [+ long] to each syllabic element and are followed by a later rule of diphthongization:

(40) $\qquad$ [é, ó, ä̈] $\longrightarrow$ [ie, uo, ia]

This rule can also be used to derive the nonalternating diphthong in a word like *trieda* 'class' from basic /é/.

The analysis we have just proposed implies derivations like the following for forms like *lipa, líp; žena, žien;* and *trieda.*

(41) /#lip-a#/ /#lip#/ /#žen-a#/ /#žen#/ /#tréd-a#/
$\qquad$ ------- *líp* -------- *žén* -------- Lengthening
$\qquad$ ------- ----- -------- *žien* *tried-a* Diphthongization

This analysis which treats the diphthongs as derived from long vowels is also supported by the many shortening rules in Slovak. In each instance where a long vowel or liquid is shortened, a diphthong appears without its initial onglide. For example, the imperfectivizing suffix -*ova* causes a shortening of the stem final syllable.

(42)

Perfective	Imperfective	Gloss
odlísiť	*odlisovať*	'to distinguish'
kúpiť	*kupovať*	'to buy'
ohlásiť	*ohlasovať*	'to announce'
predĺžiť	*predlžovať*	'to extend'
oblietať	*obletovať*	'to fly around'
uviazať	*uväzovať*	'to bind'

To cite just one more example of this type, the root vowel of a monosyllabic adjective is shortened before the comparative suffix -*ší*: *blízky, bližší* 'near'; *úzky, užší* 'narrow'; *krátky, kratší* 'short'; but *biely, belší* 'white'; *riedky, redší* 'rare'. Once again, if the diphthongs are not derived from long vowels, there is no straightforward way to explain why they lose their initial onglide in the same contexts where other syllabics shorten. But in the analysis we have proposed, the absence of the onglide is automatically predicted. At the point where the shortening rule applies the diphthong is an underlying long vowel. When this vowel is shortened, the subsequent diphthongization rule can no longer apply. Hence, the initial onglide is not generated. This analysis implies derivations like the following.

(43) /#kúp-iť#/ / /#kúp-ovať#/ / /#uväz-ať#/ / /#uväz-ovať#/

| -------- | *kup-ovať* | ----------- | *uväz-ovať* | Shortening |
| -------- | -------------- | *uviaz-ať* | -------------- | Diphthongization |

To summarize, we have proposed an analysis for Slovak in which the rising diphthongs *ie*, *uo*, and *ia* are derived from the underlying long vowels *é*, *ó*, and *ä* regardless of whether or not they alternate with a short vowel. This permits us to regularize the underlying system of syllabics to a balanced system of eight members, each of which can contrast in length.

(44)

Long		Short	
í	ú	i	u
é	ó	e	o
ä	á	ä	a
ĺ,ŕ		l,r	

The few forms containing a long mid vowel such as *dcéra* will simply be marked as exceptions to the diphthongization rule.

The next rule to be discussed was alluded to above, namely the rule that lengthens the last syllable of a stem in the genitive plural. This rule operates in the feminine and neuter declensions.

(45)

	Sg.	Pl.	Sg.	Pl.
Nom.	*žen-a*	*žen-y*	*mest-o*	*mest-á*
Gen.	*žen-y*	*žien*	*mest-a*	*miest*
Dat.	*žen-e*	*žen-ám*	*mest-u*	*mest-ám*
Acc.	*žen-u*	*žen-y*	*mest-o*	*mest-á*
Instr.	*žen-ou*	*žen-ami*	*mest-om*	*mest-ami*
Loc.	*žen-e*	*žen-ách*	*mest-e*	*mest-ách*
Gloss	'woman'		'town'	

Examples of this rule's application in the feminine declension were cited in (39) above. To these we may add *pižama*, *pižám* 'pajama' and *nuansa*, *nuáns* 'nuance', showing that foreign borrowings also undergo the rule. Additional examples of the rule's operation in the neuter declension follow in (46).

(46)

Nom. sg.	Gen. pl.	Gloss
kopyto	*kopýt*	'hoof'
brucho	*brúch*	'belly'
blato	*blát*	'mud'
salto	*sált*	'somersault'
embargo	*embárg*	'embargo'
jablko	*jablk*	'apple'
koleso	*kolies*	'wheel'
lono	*lôn*	'lap, bosom'
hovädo	*hoviad*	'beast'

If the final syllable of the stem contains a basic long syllabic, it is unmodified in the genitive plural, as the examples in (47) show.

(47)

Nom. sg.	Gen. pl.	Gloss
vláda	*vlád*	'government'
blúza	*blúz*	'blouse'
čiara	*čiar*	'line'
trieda	*tried*	'class'
dláto	*dlát*	'chisel'
víno	*vín*	'wine'
hniezdo	*hniezd*	'nest'

This lengthening process may be formulated as follows (we use *V* here as a cover symbol to include both vowels and syllabic liquids).

(48) $\qquad$ V $\longrightarrow$ [+ long]/___C$_1$ #

Although this rule must be restricted to operate in only certain morphological contexts, we shall leave the rule in its present general state, since these restrictions are not relevant to our present purposes.

Another rule of Slovak, traditionally referred to as the "rhythmic law," shortens an underlying long vowel or liquid when the preceding syllable contains an underlying long syllabic element. The effects of this rule are most clearly seen by examination of the following partial paradigms of some neuter nouns.

(49)

Nom. sg.	Gen. sg.	Nom. pl.	Dat. pl.	Loc. pl.	Gloss
mesto	*mesta*	*mestá*	*mestám*	*mestách*	'town'
blato	*blata*	*blatá*	*blatám*	*blatách*	'mud'
hovädo	*hoväda*	*hovädá*	*hovädám*	*hovädách*	'beast'
písmeno	*písmena*	*písmená*	*písmenám*	*písmenách*	'letter'
zámeno	*zámena*	*zámená*	*zámenám*	*zámenách*	'pronoun'
dláto	*dláta*	*dláta*	*dlátam*	*dlátach*	'chisel'
víno	*vína*	*vína*	*vínam*	*vínach*	'wine'
hniezdo	*hniezda*	*hniezda*	*hniezdam*	*hniezdach*	'nest'

Comparison of the gen. sg. with the nom. pl. ending shows that the former is a constant short *a*, while the latter varies its length. It is short after a syllable containing a long vowel, and long after a syllable containing a short vowel. In order to predict this alternation in phonological terms, the long variant of the nom. pl. suffix must be selected as underlying. Otherwise there would be no way to distinguish its behavior from the gen. sg. suffix which does not alternate. Forms such as *písmená* and *zámená* show that the rhythmic law only shortens a vowel if the immediately preceding syllable is long. Finally, words like *hniezda* 'nests' show that the rhythmic law must apply before diphthongization in a derivation like the following.

(50) $\qquad$ /#hnézd-á#/

$\qquad\qquad$ *hnézd-a* $\qquad$ Rhythmic law
$\qquad\qquad$ *hniezd-a* $\qquad$ Diphthongization

If the root vowel *é* were broken to *ie* first, the rhythmic law would not apply because the root would no longer contain a long vowel.

The rhythmic law may be formulated as follows (again we use V as a cover symbol to include both the vowels and syllabic liquids).

(51) $\qquad V \longrightarrow [\ -\ \text{long}]/\acute{V}C_0\text{———}$

The interaction between vowel lengthening (VL) and the rhythmic law (RL) may be determined by inspection of disyllabic stems of the structure $C\acute{V}CVC$, that is, stems with an initial long vowel and a final short vowel. When these forms appear in the genitive plural, the final vowel will be subject to two competing principles: according to VL, the final vowel should be lengthened; but if it is lengthened, a sequence of two successive long syllables will result, contrary to RL. Therefore, one of the two mutually contradictory principles must take precedence over the other. The following data show that RL prevails, indicating that it must be ordered after VL.

(52)

Nom. sg.	Gen. pl.	Gloss
záhrada	záhrad	'garden'
nížina	nížin	'hollow, lowland'
zátoka	zátok	'inlet'
písmeno	písmen	'letter'
zámeno	zámen	'pronoun'
liečivo	liečiv	'drug'

At this point the following ordering relations have been established: VL precedes RL; VL precedes diphthongization; RL precedes diphthongization. To show how these rules work we provide derivations for the following words: *blatá* 'bogs', *čísla* 'numbers', *písmená* 'letters', *hniezda* 'nests', *žien* 'woman' (gen. pl.), and *písmen* 'letter' (gen. pl.).

(53)

/#blat-á#/	/#čísl-á#/	/#písmen-á#/	
---------	---------	------------	Vowel lengthening
---------	čísl-a	------------	Rhythmic law
---------	---------	------------	Diphthongization

/#hnézd-á#/	/#žen#/	/#písmen#/	
------------	žén	písmén	Vowel lengthening
hnézd-a	------	písmen	Rhythmic law
hniezd-a	žien	---------	Diphthongization

Before proceeding to a brief discussion of the Slovak verb, we will consider one additional alternation in the nouns, the vowel–zero alternation evident in the following data.

(54)

Nom. sg.	Gen. pl.	Gloss
ikra	*ikier*	'roe'
ihla	*ihiel*	'needle'
dogma	*dogiem*	'dogma'
sosna	*sosien*	'pine tree'
bedro	*bedier*	'hip'
radlo	*radiel*	'plough'

All of these stems end in consonant clusters whose final member is a sonorant. A similar alternation appears in stems that end in obstruent clusters (cf., *hradba*, *hradieb* 'rampart'), but appears to be less regular (cf., *doska*, *dosiek* 'board' versus *hradisko*, *hradisk* 'castle hill'). In any case, we know of no exceptions when the stem ends in a sonorant. Forms like *písmeno*, *písmen* show that this alternation must be analyzed as a case of epenthesis, if it is to be described in purely phonological terms. Finally, for the data cited so far it appears that we have two choices as to the length of the inserted vowel. We can simply insert a long *é* and have the subsequent diphthongization rule yield *ie*, or we can order the epenthesis of short *e* before VL, which will lengthen it to *é*, and the diphthongization rule will subsequently break the vowel to *ie*. There are two reasons for selecting the latter analysis. First, in most languages epenthetic vowels are short. More importantly, stems terminating in a consonant + sonorant cluster also undergo epenthesis when certain consonant initial derivational suffixes are added. Here the underlying shortness of the inserted vowel emerges on the surface, since it is not in the final syllable of the word and hence escapes VL which obscures its underlying quantity: compare, *ikra*, *ikier*, but *ikernatý* 'abounding in roe'.

We will ignore insertion in other than word final consonant + sonorant clusters. With this limitation, the rule can be formulated as follows.

(55) $\emptyset \longrightarrow e/C\underline{\hspace{1cm}}[+ \text{sonorant}] \, \#$

A form like *ikier* thus receives the following derivation.

(56) $/\#\text{ikr}\#/$

iker	Epenthesis
ikér	Vowel lengthening
—	Rhythmic law
ikier	Diphthongization

So far the discussion of epenthesis has been limited to stems containing short root vowels. In stems whose final syllabic is long, the epenthetic vowel has two alternant pronunciations.

(57)

Nom. sg.	Gen. pl.	Gloss
krídlo	*krídel ~ krídiel*	'wing'
číslo	*čísel ~ čísiel*	'number'
pásmo	*pásem ~ pásiem*	'zone, line, area'
vlákno	*vláken ~ vlákien*	'fiber'
plátno	*pláten ~ plátien*	'linen'

The variants with the short epenthetic vowel seem to show the precedence of RL over VL. *krídel* would receive the following derivation.

(58)   / # krídl # /

krídel	Epenthesis
krídél	Vowel lengthening
krídel	Rhythmic law
---------	Diphthongization

The variants with the long epenthetic vowel are the innovating pronunciation. This innovating pronunciation appears to be limited to the epenthetic vowel. The underlying root vowel /e/ in a form such as *písmeno, písmen* 'letter' is never lengthened.

The alternants in (57) with a long epenthetic vowel could be generated by simply requiring that the rhythmic law precede the vowel lengthening rule. Under this analysis, *krídiel* would be derived as in (59).

(59)   / # krídl # /

krídel	Epenthesis
—	Rhythmic law
krídél	Vowel lengthening
krídiel	Diphthongization

Note that if this analysis is accepted, the ordering relation "rhythmic law precedes vowel lengthening" would have to be limited to just forms with the epenthetic vowel (in the innovating style). In all other cases the rhythmic law follows vowel lengthening. (See Kenstowicz 1972 for further discussion of the problem posed by these data.)

We will now briefly consider how some of the rules that we have formulated for the nouns apply in the verbs. In the present tense, Slovak verbs are composed of three major constituents: a verb stem, a present tense thematic vowel, and person/number endings. The Slovak verbs are also divided into several conjugation classes depending upon what particular vowel appears as the realization of the present tense theme. Which vowel a given verb stem takes as its theme is largely unpredictable and must be provided for in the lexicon. In the following table we give several examples for the *e*-conjugation and the *i*-conjugation.

(60)

		e-conjugation		
Singular				
1	*nesiem*	*rastiem*	*leziem*	*môžem*
2	*nesieš*	*rastieš*	*lezieš*	*môžeš*
3	*nesie*	*rastie*	*lezie*	*môže*
Plural				
1	*nesieme*	*rastieme*	*lezieme*	*môžeme*
2	*nesiete*	*rastiete*	*leziete*	*môžete*
3	*nesú*	*rastú*	*lezú*	*môžu*
Gloss	'carry'	'grow'	'crawl'	'be able'

		i-conjugation		
Singular				
1	*robím*	*vidím*	*kúpim*	*hlásim*
2	*robíš*	*vidíš*	*kúpiš*	*hlásiš*
3	*robí*	*vidí*	*kúpi*	*hlási*
Plural				
1	*robíme*	*vidíme*	*kúpime*	*hlásime*
2	*robíte*	*vidíte*	*kúpite*	*hlásite*
3	*robia*	*vidia*	*kúpia*	*hlásia*
Gloss	'work'	'see'	'buy'	'announce'

Subtracting away the stem and the theme, we find the following endings: *-m, -š, -∅,* for the singular; and *-me, -te,* and *-ú* or *-ia* (from underlying /-ä̃/) for the plural. The choice of the 3 pl. ending is dependent upon the theme vowel. If the theme is /-é/, the 3 pl. is /-ú/. If the theme is /-í/, the 3 pl. is /-ä̃/.

The only new rule that we need to describe these data is one to account for the distribution of the theme vowels *-é* and *-í*. The generalization is that these vowels appear everywhere except before the 3 pl. suffix. Since the 3 pl. suffixes begin with a vowel, while all of the other endings begin with a consonant, the alternation can be accounted for by the vowel truncation (VT) rule of (61).

(61) $$V \longrightarrow \emptyset / \_\_\_V$$

This rule must apply before RL, as shown by *nesú* from /#nes-é-ú#/. If RL applied first, the /-ú/ would shorten since it is preceded by the long *é*. The /-ú/ will, however, shorten by RL if a long root vowel comes to immediately precede this suffix as a result of truncation, as in *môžu*. The following derivations show how truncation interacts with the earlier rules to explain the alternations in (60).

(62)   /#nes-é-m#/   /#nes-é-ú#/   /#móž-é-m#/   /#móž-é-ú#/

------------	*nes-ú*	------------	*móž-ú*	Vowel truncation
------------	---------	*móž-e-m*	*móž-u*	Rhythmic law
nes-ie-m	---------	*muož-e-m*	*muož-u*	Diphthongization

Turning to the *i*-conjugation forms in (60), we see that the rhythmic law shortens the theme vowel in the paradigms of *kúpim* and *hlásim*. However, the 3 pl. ending *-ia* from basic /-ǎ/ appears phonetically long (actually diphthongized via diphthongization) regardless of the length of the preceding vowel. Although one might pursue an analysis in which *-ia* is treated as some combination of the theme vowel *-i* plus either a long or short *a* or *ä*, and then somehow combine them into *ia* after the rhythmic law has applied, further research into the problem indicates that this line of analysis cannot be supported. Thus, the 3 pl. ending of the *i*-conjugation must simply be marked in the lexicon as an exception to the rhythmic law (cf., Chapter 10 for further discussion). If this is done, we have derivations like the following for the 1 sg. and 3 pl. forms of 'work' and 'buy'.

(63)   /#rob-í-m#/   /#rob-í-ǎ#/   /#kúp-í-m#/   /#kúp-í-ǎ#/

------------	*rob-ǎ*	------------	*kúp-ǎ*	Vowel truncation
------------	---------	*kúp-i-m*	---------	Rhythmic law
------------	*rob-ia*	------------	*kúp-ia*	Diphthongization

The fairly complex set of alternations exhibited by the Slovak data can thus be accounted for by five simple phonological rules. However, this is only possible if the rules are ordered in the fashion depicted in (64).

(64)
```
     ┌─Epenthesis
    ┌─┤
   ┌─┤─Vowel lengthening
  ┌─┤ ├─────────────────────────────┐
  │ └─Rhythmic law─────────────┐     ┌Vowel truncation
  └───┤                        ┴─────┘
      └─Diphthongization───────┘
```

Lardil

Lardil is an Australian language spoken on Mornington Island in the Gulf of Carpentaria. Our analysis follows closely that of Hale (1973), the only published source of data on this interesting language. The following sounds appear in Lardil.

(65)

Vowels		Consonants					
	Bilabial	Laminal dental	Apico-alveolar	Laminal ˙alveopalatal	Apicodomal	Velar
i u	p	th	t	tj	ṭ	k
e a	m	nh	n	nj	ṇ	ŋ
			l	lj	ḷ	
			r		ṛ	
	w			y		

Our analysis will be limited to the nouns. According to Hale, ''In Lardil, the object of a nonimperative verb is inflected for accusative case and, simultaneously, for tense (in agreement with the tense of the verb). The subject of a sentence, and the object of an imperative, are uninflected (as is the citation form) [p. 421].'' Thus, a noun appears inflected in an accusative nonfuture and in an accusative future form. The rules which we shall deal with here divide into two groups: those affecting different alternations in the suffixes and those that give rise to alternations in the stem. The latter are of particular interest.

As is evident from the data in (66), the nonfuture suffix is basically /-in/ and the future is /-uṛ/.

(66)

Uninflected	Nonfuture	Future	Gloss
kentapal	*kentapal-in*	*kentapal-uṛ*	'dugong'
kethar	*kethar-in*	*kethar-uṛ*	'river'
miyaṛ	*miyaṛ-in*	*miyaṛ-uṛ*	'spear'
yarput	*yarputj-in*	*yarputh-uṛ*	'snake, bird'
yaraman	*yaraman-in*	*yaraman-kuṛ*	'horse'
pirŋen	*pirŋen-in*	*pirŋen-kuṛ*	'woman'

The future suffix /-uṛ/ appears as /-kuṛ/ after nasals. Stems ending in /t/ appear as alveopalatal /tj/ and laminal dental /th/ before the /i/ and /u/ of the nonfuture and future suffixes, respectively. The rules accounting for these alternations, though quite straightforward, are of little interest, and so we shall not bother to formulate them here.

The stems of (66) end in apical consonants, a fact to which we shall return later. Examples of disyllabic vowel-final stems are given in (67).

(67)   *mela*   *mela-n*   *mela-r̪*   'sea'
       wanka   *wanka-n*   *wanka-r̪*   'arm'
       kuŋka   *kuŋka-n*   *kuŋka-r̪*   'groin'
       ŋuka   *ŋuku-n*   *ŋuku-r̪*   'water'
       kat̪a   *kat̪u-n*   *kat̪u-r̪*   'child'
       ŋawa   *ŋawu-n*   *ŋawu-r̪*   'wife'
       kent̪e   *kent̪i-n*   *kent̪i-wur̪* 'wife'
       ɲiɲe   *ɲiɲi-n*   *ɲiɲi-wur̪*   'skin'
       pape   *papi-n*   *papi-wur̪*   'father's mother'
       tjempe   *tjempe-n*   *tjempe-r̪*   'mother's father'
       wit̪e   *wit̪e-n*   *wit̪e-r̪*   'interior'

Notice that the future suffix /-ur̪/ is converted to /-wur̪/ when it is preceded by a stem ending in the vowel *i*. The rule given in (68) will account for this alternation.

(68) $\emptyset \longrightarrow w/i\_\_\_u$

The *w*-insertion prevents the vocalic sequence *iu* from appearing in phonetic representation. Other potential vocalic sequences are prohibited by virtue of a rule that deletes a vowel after a vowel.

(69) $V \longrightarrow \emptyset/V\_\_\_$

The vowel truncation rule accounts for the fact that the nonfuture suffix /-in/ loses its vowel after the vowel-final stems given in (67) above. Naturally, rule (68) must be applied before rule (69); if this were not the case, the sequence *iu* would be converted to *i* by (69) and the context for insertion of *w* would no longer exist: **papi-r̪* would be derived rather than the correct *papi-wur̪*.

As far as the stems of (67) are concerned, note that while *mela* 'sea' ends in *a* in all forms, stems like *ŋuka* 'water' appear with a final *u* in the inflected form (*ŋuku-n*, *ŋuku-r̪*). If the stem shape appearing in the uninflected form were posited as the UR, there would be no way to predict that the *a* of *mela* would remain constant while the *a* of *ŋuka* would alternate with *u*. If the inflected stem alternant /ŋuku/ were selected as the UR, then a rule that lowers underlying /u/ to /a/ in word-final position could account for the alternation. This analysis is motivated by the fact that there are no disyllabic roots that end in *u* in both the inflected and the uninflected forms. The absence of such roots is predicted by the rule changing /u/ to /a/ word-finally. Alternations such as *pape* versus *papi-n* provide additional support for a vowel lowering approach. If this root is analyzed as /papi/ underlyingly, then the uninflected alternant *pape* can be accounted for by simply extending the lowering rule so that it lowers /i/ to /e/ word-finally in addition to lowering /u/ to /a/. Such an extension is further justified by the observation that there are no disyllabic roots that are pronounced with a final /i/ in both the inflected and the uninflected forms. Furthermore, if one were to try to take the uninflected form *pape* as underlying, it would not be possible to predict why *pape* raises its final vowel when inflected but *tjempe* does not. The lowering rule that we propose is stated as (70).

(70) $V \longrightarrow [\ + \ \text{low}]/\underline{\hspace{2em}} \#$

Consider next the $V \sim \emptyset$ alternation present in (71).

(71) | | | | |
|---|---|---|---|
| *yalul* | *yalulu-n* | *yalulu-ṛ* | 'flame' |
| *mayar* | *mayara-n* | *mayara-ṛ* | 'rainbow' |
| *wiwal* | *wiwala-n* | *wiwala-ṛ* | 'bush mango' |
| *karikar* | *karikari-n* | *karikari-wuṛ* | 'butter-fish' |
| *yiliyil* | *yiliyili-n* | *yiliyili-wuṛ* | 'oyster sp.' |

These stems have the suffixal shapes that are expected after vowel-final stems. And indeed a vowel does precede the suffixes in the inflected forms. However, this vowel is absent in the uninflected form. If this vowel is considered a part of the UR of the stem, a rule to convert /yalulu/ to /yalul/ is required. Comparison of the data in (71),where the vowel $\sim \emptyset$ alternation appears,with the data in (67),where it does not,reveals that the former stems are all trisyllabic or longer in the inflected form, while those in (67) are disyllabic. The stems may thus be differentiated on the basis of their phonological shape by a rule of apocope that deletes the final vowel of a word that is preceded by at least two vowels. Rule (72) states this principle of apocope.

(72) $V \longrightarrow \emptyset/VC_1VC_1\underline{\hspace{1em}}\#$

An additional point in favor of the analysis we have suggested is that forms such as *karikar* from /karikari/ are clearly reduplications. The fact that the final /i/ is missing from the uninflected form follows from the rule of apocope.

The data in (73) require a new rule.

(73)

yukar	yukarpa-n	yukarpa-ṛ	'husband'
wulun	wulunka-n	wulunka-ṛ	'fruit sp.'
wuṭal	wuṭaltji-n	wuṭaltji-wuṛ	'meat'
kantukan	kantukantu-n	kantukantu-ṛ	'red'
karwakar	karwakarwa-n	karwakarwa-ṛ	'wattle sp.'

Once again the UR of the stem is to be indentified with the inflected alternant. Upon deletion of the final vowel by apocope, a consonant cluster is created, whose final member is absent phonetically. A rule of cluster simplification is required.

(74)   C ⟶ ∅/C___#

Once again the behavior of reduplicated stems such as /kantukantu/ support the proposed analysis. If apocope is ordered before cluster simplification, the absence of the final two sounds of the reduplicated form /kantukantu/ in the uninflected form is accounted for, as the following derivation shows.

(75)   /#kantukantu#/
          kantukant   Apocope
          kantukan   Cluster simplification

Recall that the only examples of consonant-final stems given so far—those of (66)—all ended in apical consonants. It is a general trait of Lardil phonetics that no word may end in a nonapical consonant. When a nonapical consonant appears in final position, either (a) in the UR, or (b) as a result of apocope, or (c) as a result of both apocope and cluster simplification, that nonapical consonant is deleted. The examples in (76) illustrate stems from each of these three categories.

(76)

a.
| thurara | thuraraŋ-in | thuraraŋ-kuṛ | 'shark' |
| ŋalu | ŋaluk-in | ŋaluk-uṛ | 'story' |

b.
putu	putuka-n	putuka-ṛ	'short'
murkuni	murkunima-n	murkunima-ṛ	'nullah'
ŋawuŋa	ŋawuŋawu-n	ŋawuŋawu-ṛ	'termite'
tipiti	tipitipi-n	tipitipi-wuṛ	'rock-cod sp.'
thapu	thaputji-n	thaputji-wuṛ	'older brother'

c.
| muŋkumu | muŋkumuŋku-n | muŋkumuŋku-ṛ | 'wooden axe' |
| tjumputju | tjumputjumpu-n | tjumputjumpu-ṛ | 'dragon-fly' |

Clearly a rule deleting word-final nonapical consonants is required. Rule (77) states this principle of Lardil phonology.

(77) $$C \longrightarrow \emptyset / \underline{} \#$$
[-apico]

This rule of nonapical deletion (NAD) must be ordered after vowel lowering since high vowels that come to stand at the end of a word as the result of the deletion of a nonapical consonant do not lower (cf., *ŋalu* from /ŋaluk/). It must also be ordered after apocope as shown by a form such as *putu* from /putuka/. Finally, it must be ordered after cluster simplification, as shown by *muŋkumu* from /muŋkumuŋku/. The derivations in (78) illustrate the relationship of NAD to the other rules of Lardil phonology.

(78)

/#ŋaluk#/	/#putuka#/	/#muŋkumuŋku#/	
---------	---------	muŋkumuŋka	Vowel lowering
---------	putuk	muŋkumuŋk	Apocope
---------	---------	muŋkumuŋ	Cluster simplification
ŋalu	putu	muŋkumu	Nonapical deletion

The careful reader may be wondering whether the rule of cluster simplification could be eliminated from the grammar by allowing NAD to apply twice in the derivation of *muŋkumu* from underlying /muŋkumuŋku/. That is, since both *ŋ* and *k* are nonapical sounds, cannot their deletion be attributed entirely to the principle that words do not end in nonapicals rather than invoking a separate principle of cluster simplification? Although it might be possible to dispense with cluster simplification in the case of *muŋkumu*, it is not possible to do so in the case of *kantukan* from underlying /kantukantu/. Since *t* is an apical sound, its deletion in *kantukan* cannot be attributed to the principle that words do not end in nonapical consonants. The only explanation for the loss of *t* here is the cluster simplification principle. Given that cluster simplification is independently motivated, we have allowed it to delete not only the second member of an apical cluster (such as *nt*), but also the second member of a nonapical cluster (such as *ŋk*). This simplification of final clusters is applied prior to NAD. When /nt/ is reduced to /n/ by simplification, NAD will not apply to the apical sound *n*; but when /ŋk/ is reduced to /ŋ/ by simplification, the resulting nonapical sound /ŋ/ will be deleted since it is in final position and thus subject to NAD.

We assume, then, the following rules and crucial orderings for our description of Lardil.

(79)

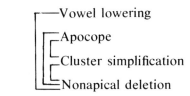

The principles of Lardil phonology discussed above have largely the effect of truncating trisyllabic and longer words. It is perhaps of some interest to note that Lardil, like most Australian languages, has a constraint that all words must be at least two syllables long phonetically. This constraint explains why the apocope rule is limited to trisyllabic or longer words. However, this prohibition against monosyllabic words does not mean that there are no monosyllabic stems in underlying representations in Lardil. Consider the data in (80).

(80)

ṛilta	*ṛil-in*	*ṛil-uṛ*	'neck'
maṛṭa	*maṛ-in*	*maṛ-uṛ*	'hand'
ṭurṭa	*ṭuṛ-in*	*ṭuṛ-uṛ*	'excrement'
wunṭa	*wun-in*	*wun-kuṛ*	'rain'
kaṇṭa	*kaṇ-in*	*kaṇ-kuṛ*	'grass'
ṭera	*ṭer-in*	*ṭer-uṛ*	'thigh'
yaka	*yak-in*	*yak-uṛ*	'fish'
ṛelka	*ṛelk-in*	*ṛelk-uṛ*	'head'

These forms have the inflectional endings that would be expected after consonant-final stems. But in the uninflected forms they are augmented by an extra syllable to render them disyllabic. The augment consists of *-a* after stems ending in an obstruent (*k* in the above examples) or *r* (phonetically a flap) and as *-Ca* if the stem ends in any sonorant but *r*. The consonant in the *-Ca* augment is a stop that is homorganic with the preceding consonant.

The augmentation process illustrated in (80) guarantees that underlying monosyllabic roots, when uninflected, will be pronounced as disyllabic and thus conform to the constraint that all words in the language be at least two syllables in length. The addition of an affix to monosyllabic roots yields a word of two syllables and thus renders the augmentation process unnecessary.

Makua (Bantu)

In this section we examine certain aspects of the tonal structure of Makua, a Bantu language spoken in southern Tanzania and in Mozambique. The analysis presented here is based on data elicited from a speaker born in the Tunduru district of Tanzania; there are no published descriptions of the tonal patterns of other dialects, thus we do not know to what extent the data presented here conform to the other dialects of Makua.

Makua, like most Bantu languages, makes a significant use of tone (i.e., the relative pitch of the voice at which a syllable is uttered) to distinguish between wordforms. For instance, the items *waápa* 'to whisper' and *wáapa* 'to whisper about him' differ just in that the former has a long vowel with rising tone and the latter has a long vowel with a falling tone. The situation in Makua can be contrasted with, say, the situation in English, where tone is used to distinguish not wordforms so much as sentences (which may happen to consist of a single word, of course). Thus English utilizes different pitch patterns to distinguish between a statement such as *There's an elephant in the backyard* and a question like *There's an elephant in the backyard?*

Before looking at the data from Makua, a few introductory remarks are required. The language contrasts long and short vowels. We will represent the long vowels as sequences of two identical short vowels. (See Chapter 9 for discussion of this treatment of vowel length.) This decision is strongly motivated by the tonal patterns that will be described below. The language permits no more than two successive vowels. Sequences of more than two vowels may occur in underlying structure, but all such sequences are affected by rules that have the result that no more than two vowels occur in succession. The language has five distinctive vowel qualities which we represent by the symbols i, e, a, o, and u. The acute mark over a vowel ($\acute{V}$) indicates a high-toned vowel, while no mark over a vowel indicates a low-toned vowel. The sequences $\acute{V}_i V_i$ and $V_i \acute{V}_i$ are to be interpreted as a long vowel with a falling tone and rising tone respectively. $\acute{V}_i \acute{V}_i$ represents a long vowel with a high level tone and $V_i V_i$ represents a long vowel with a low level tone.

We will begin our examination of Makua tonal structure by examining the infinitive form of the verb.

(81) | | | | |
|---|---|---|---|
| *u-nón-á* | 'to sharpen' | *u-th^{h}úm-á* | 'to buy' |
| *u-váh-á* | 'to give' | *u-hún-á* | 'to hurt s.o.' |
| *u-pát^h-á* | 'to get' | *u-kúš-á* | 'to carry' |

(In our Makua transcriptions *th* denotes a dental stop, while *t* is alveolar; aspiration is marked by a raised *h*. Thus, *t^h* represents an aspirated alveolar stop and *th^h* represents an aspirated dental stop. The acute accent denotes high tone and a vowel without an accent sign is low-toned. Also, the examples in (81) indicate the pronunciation that would be found when the infinitive occurs phrase-medially rather than phrase-finally; we discuss below the effect that phrase-final position has on pronunciation of words. All of the examples cited in this section represent phrase-medial pronunciation unless there is a specific statement to the contrary.)

Infinitives in Makua are characterized by the prefix *u-* and a final vowel *-a*. The verb stems in (81) are all of the structure -CVC-. Notice that in each of these examples the vowel of the verb stem bears a high tone, as does the final vowel *-a*. The infinitive prefix is low-toned. All verb stems with a -CVC- structure exhibit the same tonal pattern as the stems in (81). Clearly, then, the tonal structure of such items can be predicted by rule. In fact, it turns out that the tonal structure of all verbal forms in the language is predictable and does not need to be entered in the lexicon. Given just the data presented so far, the nature of the rule involved is naturally far from clear. Before looking at additional data, it should be noted that the pronunciation of the infinitives in (81) changes when they appear in phrase-final position. In particular, the high tone on the final vowel *-a* is replaced by a low tone. This fact suggests the possibility of a rule something like (82).

$$\text{(82)} \qquad \text{Final lowering} \qquad \overset{\text{H}}{\text{V}} \longrightarrow \overset{\text{L}}{\text{V}} /\underline{\quad}\$$$

(where H = high tone, L = low tone, \$ = phrase boundary). Consider next the following infinitive forms.

(83) | | | | |
|---|---|---|---|
| *u-lówól-a* | 'to carry' | *u-húkúl-a* | 'to sieve beer' |
| *u-páŋgác-a* | 'to make' | *u-céréw-a* | 'to be late' |
| *u-kápát-a* | 'to carry on the lap' | *u-térékʰ-a* | 'to cook' |

The verb stems in (83) have the structure -CVCVC-; all verb stems of this structure illustrate the same tonal pattern: a high tone on both vowels of the verb stem, with the infinitive prefix *u-* and the final vowel *-a* both low-toned. Furthermore, infinitives like those in (83) have the same pronunciation in phrase-final position as they do in phrase-medial position.

At this point, we would like to propose an analysis for the data in (81) and (83). The motivation behind this analysis may not be immediately obvious, though we hope in subsequent discussion to specify some of the facts leading to the proposed analysis. We assume that the infinitive prefix is basically low-toned; since it appears in these data with a low tone, this analysis is rather straightforward. We also assume that the final vowel of the infinitive form, *-a*, is basically low-toned. This vowel appears with a high tone in the data in (81), but with a low tone in (83). Thus if we take the basic tone to be low, we will need a rule to assign this vowel a high tone in (81) but not in (83). The rule that we propose is stated in (84).

(84)   Tone doubling $\overset{L}{V} \longrightarrow \overset{H\ H}{V}/VC_0\underline{\hspace{1cm}}$

The rule of tone doubling says simply that a low-toned vowel will become high-toned if the preceding vowel is high-toned. (This rule must not reapply to its own output, unlike the vowel harmony rule in Yawelmani; in other words, given a sequence of low-toned vowels after a high-toned vowel, only the first low-toned vowel will be raised to a high tone.) In order to make this rule work correctly, it is necessary to assume that the -*a* vowel is preceded by a high-toned vowel in (81) but not in (83). On the surface, the -*a* is preceded by a high tone in both sets of data. We would like to claim, however, that in an example like *u-lówól-a* the high tone that precedes -*a* is itself the result of tone doubling (and is thus not a high tone at the point in the derivation where tone doubling applies). If this claim is accepted, then we arrive at the conclusion that it is only the first vowel of the verb stem in both (81) and (83) that bears a high tone prior to tone doubling. This high tone is itself predictable, and can be assigned by the rule stated informally in (85).

(85)   TONE ASSIGNMENT: *Assign a high tone to the first vowel of a verb stem.*

(We assume that all the vowels of a verb stem are underlying low-toned.) In (86) we illustrate the derivation of *u-nón-á* 'to sharpen' and *u-lówól-a* 'to carry'.

(86)

L L L	L L L L	
u-non-a	*u-lowol-a*	Underlying representation
L H L	L H L L	Tone assignment
L H H	L H H L	Tone doubling

Recall that in phrase-final position 'to sharpen' is pronounced *u-nón-a*. If we assume a rule like final lowering, (82), then this rule must be applied after tone doubling; final lowering will have the effect of lowering the high tone on the final -*a* (which resulted from tone doubling) just in case that -*a* is in phrase-final position. An alternative to such an approach would be to constrain tone doubling so that it does not apply to a phrase-final vowel. For ease of presentation, we will continue to assume the existence of a separate rule of final lowering, rather than complicating the statement of tone doubling. We have no evidence that chooses between the two approaches.

The data in (81) and (83) can, of course, be described without invoking a rule such as tone doubling. However, it should be pointed out that an examination of Makua surface structures strongly suggests that a principle such as tone doubling is operating in the language. High tones in Makua almost always come in pairs if one disregards the effect of final lowering; where there are exceptions to this pattern on the surface, an explanation can be found in terms of the underlying structure of the utterance and the application of phonological rules. Examples of such apparent exceptions will be discussed later.

Additional motivation for tone doubling will be given later, but let us look further into the problem of tone assignment for verbs in Makua. In (87) we illustrate the tonal pattern of verb stems of the shape -CVCVCVC- and in (88) we illustrate -CVCVCVCVC- stems.

(87)	u-lókót^{h}él-á	'to pick up for'
	u-páp^{h}árúl-á	'to separate'
	u-tíkít^{h}él-á	'to rub'
	u-púkútík-á	'to drop off (leaves, hair)'
(88)	u-lókótáníh-a	'to pick up'
	u-kákámálíh-a	'to strengthen'
	u-kíríkítél-a	'to struggle for s.t.'
	u-kútíhérán-a	'to heat for one another'

Up to this point we have claimed that the final vowel -*a* will be high-toned just in case it receives a high tone as a result of tone doubling. This means that there must be a high tone not only on the first vowel of a verb stem like /lokot^{h}el/, but also on the third vowel. Furthermore, to account for the failure of the final -*a* to have a high tone in an example like *u-lókótáníh-a*, it must be the case that the fourth vowel of a verb stem like /lokotanih/ does not have a high tone. The pronunciation of *u-lókótáníh-a* is, however, consistent with the claim that the first and third vowel of all verb stems have a high tone. We propose therefore to restate the tone assignment rule for verbs as in (89).

(89) TONE ASSIGNMENT: *Assign a high tone to the first and the third (if there is one) vowel of a verb stem.*

The derivation of *u-lókót^{h}él-á* and *u-lókótáníh-a* is given in (90).

(90) L L L L L   L L L L L L
      u-lokotʰel-a   *u-lokotanih-a*   Underlying representation
      L HL H L   L H LH L L   Tone assignment
      L HH H H   L H HH H L   Tone doubling

(If *u-lókótʰél-á* appears in phrase-final position, final lowering will lower the final vowel -*a* to a low tone.)

Given the data presented so far, one might think that tone assignment would actually assign a high tone to every other vowel in the verb stem. But this is not correct. It is just the first and third vowels that are assigned a high tone. To see this, consider the following stems which are even longer than those previously cited.

(91)   u-kákámálíher-a   'to use s.t. to strengthen s.t.'
          u-kákámálíherac-a   (same meaning as above)
          u-lókótáníhac-a   'to pick up things'
          u-lókótáníherac-a   'to pick up things for'

The first four vowels of these verb stems have phonetic high tones, and all of the remaining vowels of the stem as well as the final vowel -*a* are low-toned. The analysis proposed here accounts for these pronunciations since it assumes that all the vowels of a verb stem are basically low-toned, as is the final -*a*, and that tone assignment places a high tone only on the first and the third vowel of the stem. These high tones are then doubled onto the following vowels.

So far we have restricted our attention to verb stems with short vowels. As mentioned earlier, Makua also has long vowels. In (92) we illustrate the tonal structure of verb stems containing long vowels.

(92)

Phrase-medial position	Phrase-final position	
u-lééh-a	*u-léeh-a*	'to say farewell'
u-máál-a	*u-máal-a*	'to be quiet'
u-hííh-a	*u-híih-a*	'to cause to leave'
u-máálíh-á	*u-máálíh-a*	'to make quiet'
u-lééhér-á	*u-lééhér-a*	'to order s.t.'
u-hóméér-á	*u-hóméér-a*	'to insert s.t. sharp'
u-líkáán-á	*u-líkáán-a*	'to resemble'
u-kʰúnéél-á	*u-kʰúnéél-a*	'to cover s.t.'

Let us look first of all at *u-máál-a*. This form makes it clear why we have chosen to represent long vowels as a sequence of two identical short vowels. If we considered a long vowel to be simply one vowel, then we would have expected a pronunciation such as **u-máál-á*. That is, we would have expected the final vowel *-a* to receive a high tone via tone doubling the same as it does in an example such as *u-nón-á*. By assuming the vowel sequence representation for long vowels, the pronunciation *u-máál-a* follows automatically from our rules.

(93) L LL L
       u-maal-a   Underlying representation
       L HL L   Tone assignment
       L HH L   Tone doubling

The phrase-final pronunciation *u-máal-a* is not accounted for by the analysis developed so far. The problem posed by these data is the fact that while *-máál-a* is converted to *-máal-a* when phrase-final, *-hóméér-á* is converted to *-hóméér-a* not **-hóméer-a*. The latter example shows that there is no phonetic constraint that a long level high tone cannot appear in the context ___CV\$ (where \$ indicates a phrase boundary). One description of these data would involve postulating a rule something like (94), ordered to apply before final lowering.

(94)   High fall $\dfrac{H}{V} \longrightarrow \dfrac{L\ H}{V}/V\_\_\_C_0\ \dfrac{L}{V}\ \$$

This rule says that a long level high tone will be replaced by a falling tone when it precedes a low-toned vowel that is in phrase-final position. This rule has to apply prior to final lowering, since as a result of this lowering a form such as *u-hóméér-á* will become *u-hóméér-a* and will then satisfy the conditions for (94). Example (95) shows the derivation of the phrase-final form of *u-máál-a* versus the phrase-final form of *u-hóméér-á*.

(95) L LL L   L L LL L
     u-maal-a\$ u-homeer-a\$ Underlying representation
     L HL L   L H LH L   Tone assignment
     L HHL   L H HH H   Tone doubling
     L HLL   inapplicable   High fall
     L HLL   L H HH L   Final lowering

An alternative description of the data would involve placing a constraint on tone doubling which would prevent a high tone from doubling when in the environment ___ V C_0 V\$. For convenience, we will assume the analysis that utilizes the rule stated in (94), though the analysis employing a constraint on tone doubling will work just as well.

    Examples like *u-máálíh-á* and *u-hóméér-á* both provide additional support for the claim that long vowels are structurally two short vowels and for the rule of tone assignment stated in (89). Notice that in *u-máálíh-á* the final vowel *-a* has a high tone; this high tone is the result of tone doubling, in our analysis. Consequently, there must be a high tone on the *i* vowel in the stem /maalih/. Tone assignment predicts that there will be a high tone on the *i* vowel, provided that the long *aa* vowel is counted as two vowels rather than one. Similarly, the final *-a* vowel in *u-hóméér-á* is also high-toned; in order to account for this high tone by doubling, it is necessary to assume that it is preceded by a vowel bearing a high tone (arising from tone assignment). Given a stem like /homeer/, the only way that tone assignment can assign a high tone to the last vowel of the stem is if the long /ee/ is regarded as two vowels rather than one. If the long /ee/ were regarded as a single vowel, tone assignment would place a high tone on the first vowel of the verb stem but there would be no third stem vowel to receive high tone. If long /ee/ is regarded as a sequence of two vowels, then the second of those vowels will be counted as the third stem vowel in /homeer/ and will thus be assigned high tone.

Many of the long vowels in Makua are derived by phonological rules. Some such derived long vowels can be found in infinitive forms. They arise as the result of the prefixation of the *u-* infinitive prefix to verb stems that have an initial vowel. Examples are given in (96).

(96) | | | | |
|---|---|---|---|
| *w-aáp-á* | 'to whisper' | *w-eét-á* | 'to walk' |
| *w-oóp-á* | 'to beat' | *w-uúr-á* | 'to keep' |
| *w-iíw-á* | 'to come uninvited' | | |
| *w-aáthál-a* | 'to spread out' | *w-eémél-a* | 'to stand' |
| *w-oóŋgóm-a* | 'to sit' | *w-iíhán-a* | 'to call' |
| *w-uúpúwél-a* | 'to remember' | *w-eérékél-á* | 'to cut' |

Notice that the *u-* infinitive prefix assumes the shape *w-* before vowel initial verb stems. Presumably a rule of glide formation is at work, converting the vowel /u/ to the corresponding glide /w/ in prevocalic position. The vowel that follows this glide is always a long vowel; a short vowel cannot occur in this position (unless derived from a rule not discussed here that shortens a long vowel before a consonant cluster). This long vowel appears to be the consequence of the glide formation process, since it is possible to have a short vowel after a glide if that glide does not result from glide formation. Rule (97) gives a schematic representation of the rule of glide formation.

(97)   Glide formation   u V

$$1 \quad 2 \longrightarrow \quad 1 \qquad 22$$
$$[- \text{ syll}]$$

This rule says that given a sequence of *u* plus a vowel, change *u* to a nonsyllabic sound (i.e., *w*) and make the following vowel long (remember, length is being represented as a sequence of two vowels). The long vowel that arises from glide formation is pronounced with a rising tone. Let us see how our analysis of Makua tone can account for this pronunciation. Consider an example like *w-aáp-á*. The underlying structure is /u-ap-a/. Tone assignment would be expected to convert this structure to /u-áp-a/. Tone doubling would then yield /u-áp-á/. In order to achieve the correct phonetic form, it is necessary that when glide formation converts the sequence *u-a* to *w-aa* the underlying tone contour of the input vowel sequence (namely, L-H) is retained on the derived long vowel. We will account for these facts by revising glide formation as in (97)'.

(97)' Glide formation $\begin{bmatrix} u \\ \alpha T \end{bmatrix}$ V

$$1 \qquad 2 \longrightarrow \begin{bmatrix} 1 \\ -\text{syll} \end{bmatrix} \begin{bmatrix} 2 \\ \alpha T \end{bmatrix} 2$$

This rule says that given a sequence of *u* plus a vowel, the *u* will become nonsyllabic and the following vowel will be doubled. The first element of the doubled vowel is assigned the same tone as the *u* vowel, while the second element retains the original tone. (See Chapter 7 for some discussion of an alternative way of describing cases where a tone associated with a vowel remains even though the vowel itself is either lost or devocalized.)

The principles that have been sketched up to this point account quite well for the pronunciation of infinitives having the structure *u*-verb stem-*a*. Examination of more complex infinitive structures provides additional evidence for the proposed analysis, but also requires the postulation of an additional rule, a rule of considerable importance in Makua tonology. Let us look at infinitive verbs that contain an object prefix between the *u*-prefix and the verb stem. The examples in (98) illustrate most of the object prefixes that occur in Makua (we have omitted two object prefixes that involve complexities not directly relevant to the present discussion).

(98) *u-váh-á*   'to give'
      u-kí-váh-a   'to give me s.t.'
      w-uú-váh-a   'to give you (child) s.t.'
      w-aá-váh-a   'to give him/them (adult) s.t.'
      u-ní-váh-a   'to give us s.t.'
      w-aá-váh-ac-a   'to give them (children) s.t.'

The object prefixes in (98) can be analyzed as /ki/ 1 sg., /u/ 2 sg. and pl., /a/ 3 sg. and pl., and /ni/ 1 pl. Further distinctions between singular and plural and between initiated (adult) and uninitiated (child) objects are conveyed by affixes added to the end of the verb stem (for example, the suffix *-ac-* in *w-aá-váh-ac-a* indicates a plural, uninitiated object).

The infinitive prefix remains *u-* before the object prefixes with an initial consonant (/ki/ and /ni/), but glides to *w-* before vowel-initial object prefixes (/u/ and /a/). This gliding to *w-* is accompanied by a lengthening of the following vowel. Clearly, then, the infinitive prefix undergoes the rule of glide formation (97)′ before vowel-initial object prefixes just as it does before vowel-initial verb stems.

Turning to the tone pattern exhibited by the forms in (98), it is readily apparent that the object prefixes all bear a high tone. The vowel after the object prefix is also high toned, but the following vowel is low toned. Given the analysis that we have developed to this point, it seems reasonable to assume that the high tone on the vowel after the object prefix is the consequence of tone doubling. The object prefix must itself be assumed to bear a high tone. It is not the case that object prefixes are always high toned in Makua; rather, they are high toned just in certain specifiable verbal constructions, including the infinitive. We assume therefore that the object prefixes are assigned their tone as part of the morphology; the result of the morphology will be that in infinitive constructions the object prefix is high toned.

It will be noted that when the vowel-initial prefixes /u/ and /a/ are lengthened as a consequence of glide formation, the long vowel is pronounced with a rising tone. Once again, this rising tone reflects the underlying tone sequence of a low on the infinitive prefix *u-* and a high on the vowel of the object prefix. The rising tone of *w-aá-váh-a* thus reflects the same principle as is at work in *w-aáp-á* 'to whisper'.

The forms in (98) pose a significant problem that has not yet been examined. We have formulated a tone assignment rule that places a high tone on the first and third (if there is one) vowel of a verb stem. This high tone will double onto a following vowel. Why, then, in an example such as *u-kí-váh-a* isn't there a high tone on the final vowel *-a*? We have already implicitly suggested an explanation. We noted that it was possible to regard the high tone on the root /vah/ in *u-kí-váh-a* as arising from tone doubling; if so, we would not expect such a high tone to double onto the following vowel. But in order to maintain this explanation of the tonal patterns in (98), it is necessary to explain why the root /vah/ in *u-kí-váh-a* does not have the high tone that tone assignment would predict it to have (a high tone that *would* double onto the following vowel). In other words, why does the root have just the phonetic high tone resulting from doubling and not the more fundamental high resulting from tone assignment? We offer the following explanation: A rule of tone lowering is operative in the language which has the form given in (99).

(99)   Tone lowering
$$\begin{array}{cc} H & L\,H \\ V & \longrightarrow V/VC_0\text{——} \end{array}$$

Tone lowering says that a high-toned vowel will become low-toned if it is preceded by another high-toned vowel. This rule must be applied after tone assignment but before tone doubling. Given such a rule, the derivation of *u-kí-váh-a* will be as in (100).

(100)
L H L L	
u-ki-vah-a	Underlying representation
L H H L	Tone assignment
L H L L	Tone lowering
L H H L	Tone doubling

This analysis accounts for the failure of the final vowel *-a* in *u-kí-váh-a* to receive a high tone as follows: Since the high tone on the verb stem /vah/ resulting from tone assignment is lost as a result of tone lowering, there is no high tone on the verb stem that can be doubled onto the final vowel. The tone doubling principle then places a high tone on the verb stem, since it follows the high-toned object prefix, but this phonetic high tone does not itself trigger doubling.

At first glance, the above analysis might appear to be a rather roundabout way to account for the data in (98). Nevertheless, there is considerable support for this kind of analysis. Look at the data in (101).

(101)   *u-kí-húkulél-á*   'to sieve beer for me'
       u-kí-lókotáníher-a   'to pick up for me'
       u-kí-lókotáníherac-a   'to pick up things for me'

These data will follow automatically from the analysis developed here. The derivation of *u-kí-lókotáníherac-a* is shown in (102).

(102)
L H L L L L L L L	
u-ki-lokotaniherac-a	Underlying representation
L H H L H L L L L	Tone assignment
L H L L H L L L L	Tone lowering
L H H L H H L L L	Tone doubling

Further support for the rule of tone lowering is provided by infinitive forms containing the diminutive prefix -*ši*-. This prefix parallels the object prefixes in terms of its tonal behavior, as (103) illustrates.

(103) *u-ší-pát^h-a* 'to get s.t. little or a little of s.t.'
       u-ší-lówol-a 'to carry s.t. small'
       u-ší-lókotáníh-a 'to pick up s.t. small'

In these examples, -*ši*- bears a high tone and this high tone is doubled onto the following vowel (which is the first vowel of the verb stem). The first vowel of the verb stem does not manifest the high tone that would be assigned via tone assignment, but the third vowel (if there is one) does. Thus it is just the first vowel of the verb stem that must lose the high tone assigned by tone assignment. The proposed rule of tone lowering will in fact have the effect of lowering the high tone on the first vowel of the verb stem since it is preceded by the high-toned diminutive prefix. Clearly, our analysis of the data in (98) extends naturally to the data in (103).

It happens that it is possible to have *both* the diminutive prefix and also an object prefix. There is some flexibility in the order in which they occur, but the examples cited below in (104) show the diminutive prefix before the object prefix.

(104) *u-ší-kí-pat^{h}el-a* 'to get s.t. little for me'
       u-ší-kí-pap^{h}arúlél-a 'to separate s.t. small for me'
       u-ší-kí-lokotáníher-a 'to pick up s.t. small for me'

The examples above follow automatically from our analysis as long as we make the following assumption about the way in which the tone lowering rule stated in (99) operates. This rule must operate so that in a sequence of high tones (not separated by a low tone), all but the first high tone is lowered. In other words, any number of successive high tones will be lowered after a high tone. (See Chapter 7 for some discussion of the general problem posed by examples such as this.) The derivation of *u-ší-kí-lokotáníher-a* is given in (105).

(105) L H H L L L L L L
       u-ši-ki-lokotaniher-a   Underlying representation
       L H H H L H L L L   Tone assignment
       L H L L L H L L L   Tone lowering
       L H H L L H H L L   Tone doubling

Let us now look at the combination of the object prefixes with vowel-initial verb stems:

(106)   *w-eéméš-a*   'to stand s.t. up'
         u-ké-émeš-a[1]   'to stand me up'
         u-w-éémeš-a   'to stand you (child) up'
         w-é-émeš-a   'to stand him/them (adult) up'
         u-né-émeš-a   'to stand us up'
         w-é-émeš-ác-á   'to stand them (children) up'

Taking the consonant-initial object prefixes /ki/ and /ni/ first, we see that the *i* vowel of these prefixes is absent on the surface but that the initial *e* of the verb stem /emeš/ appears in a lengthened form. There is considerable additional evidence in the language that the sequence *ie* is always replaced by *ee*. Turning to the vowel-initial object prefixes, we can readily see that the /u/ prefix glides to *-w-* before a vowel-initial verb stem and lengthens the following vowel in doing so. This gliding is of course expected, given the existence of the glide formation rule stated as (97)'. It should be pointed out, however, that there is one problem that must be worked out in a complete analysis of Makua. Given the underlying representation /u-u-emeš-a/, both the infinitive *u* and the object *u* satisfy the conditions for glide formation. It is necessary to guarantee somehow that glide formation applies first to the object prefix; when it does, it destroys the conditions for the infinitive prefix to undergo the rule.

One object prefix remains to be discussed; namely, the third person prefix /a/. Notice that in *w-é-émeš-a* 'to stand him/them up' the sequence *ae* (resulting from the juxtaposition of /a/ with the initial /e/ of the verb stem) is replaced by *ee*. The infinitive prefix *u-* glides to *w-* before this *ee* vowel. Recall that ordinarily when *u-* glides to *w-* it induces doubling of the following vowel. If this doubling occurs in the example under discussion, a form like **w-eé-émeš-a* would result. But Makua never allows more than two vowels in succession within a word. There are two approaches to preventing a form such as **w-eé-émeš-a*. The first approach would say that glide formation has the effect of doubling the following vowel only when that vowel is not followed by another vowel. The second approach would allow glide formation to induce the doubling of any following vowel, but would postulate a rule reducing a sequence of three (or more) successive vowels to two. Either of these approaches is feasible; but since there are cases in the language where a sequence of three or more successive underlying vowels must be reduced to two, we will assume that the second analysis is independently motivated and will make use of it in our discussion. We refer to this rule as vowel reduction. It is stated as (107).

---

[1] The morpheme breaks between parts of a long vowel are meant merely to indicate in a rough way the morphological structure of the word. The placement of the breaks is not meant to suggest any theoretical claim.

(107)   Vowel reduction $V_a V_a (V_a)_1^n \longrightarrow V_a V_a$
where $(V_a)_1^n$ = one or indefinitely many
successive occurrences
of V_a

Rule (107) must apply after glide formation, since (107) will eliminate the extra unit of vowel length produced by glide formation, converting /w-eé-émeš-a/ to *w-é-émeš-a*.

We have now accounted for the segmental structure of the items in (106). But what about the tone? A form like *u-k-éémeš-a* is easily derived by the analysis we have given.

(108)

L	H	L	L	L

u-ki- emeš-a   Underlying representation

L	H	H	L	L

Tone assignment

L	H	L	L	L

Tone lowering

L	H	H	L	L

Tone doubling

u-ké-émeš-a   *ie* $\longrightarrow$ *ee*

u-w-éémeš-a can also be derived easily, but requires that the high tone associated with the object prefix /u/ be transferred to the following lengthened vowel. In other words, the structure /u-ú-émeš-a/ must, following glide formation, be realized as /u-w-éémeš-a/. The tonal pattern high–high exhibited by the object prefix /u/ and the following /e/ vowel must be retained on the sequence /wee/ resulting from glide formation.

It is not, however, the case that the tone of a /u/ vowel that undergoes glide formation is always maintained on the following vowel. This can be seen from *w-éémeš-a* 'to stand him/them up'. The underlying representation of this form is /u-á-emeš-a/. Tone assignment will place a high tone on the first vowel of the verb stem, but tone lowering will in turn lower that high. Tone doubling will copy the high of the object prefix /a/ onto the following /e/ vowel. The sequence /ae/ is assimilated to /ee/. The *u-* of the infinitive prefix must glide to *w-*, but the low tone of the infinitive is lost entirely from the surface form. We would like to offer the following explanation for this fact. Recall that the rule of vowel reduction must reduce three or more identical vowels to two. In Makua, a single vowel may in general bear only one tone: high or low. Thus when a three vowel sequence is reduced to two, the three tones of these vowels must be reduced to two. We propose the following principle for how this tone reduction is to be accomplished.

(109)   HIGH TONE PRESERVATION PRINCIPLE: *When vowels undergo vowel reduction, a high tone is never deleted as long as there is a low tone available to be deleted.*

The high tone preservation principle says that if a structural tone must be lost due to the need to compress three tone-bearing elements to two, a low tone will drop out rather than a high tone. The high tone preservation principle is in effect part of the vowel reduction process, specifying the precise manner in which a sequence of vowels (and their tones) will be reduced.

The derivation of *w-é-émeš-a* 'to stand him/them up' will now be as in (110).

(110)   L HL L   L
           u- a-emeš- a   Underlying representation
           L HH L   L   Tone assignment
           L HL L   L   Tone lowering
           L HH L   L   Tone doubling
           u- e-emeš- a   ae ⟶ ee

           LH H L   L
           w-ee-emeš-a   Glide formation
           HH   L   L
           w-e-emeš- a   Vowel reduction

In this derivation, the sequence *eéé* must reduce to *éé* since the high tone preservation principle says that a low tone will be deleted in preference to a high tone.

It is not possible here to even attempt to fully justify the high tone preservation principle. We will, however, cite a variety of cases which establish that the principle as stated plays a crucial role in deriving fairly complex tonal patterns.

The prefix *-hi-* is used in various negative verbal constructions in Makua. It is used, for instance, to form a negative infinitive. The examples in (111) illustrate the behavior of *-hi-*.

(111)   *u-hí-váh-a*   'to not give'
           u-hí-hún-a   'to not hurt s.o.'
           u-hí-lókotʰel-a   'to not pick up'
           u-hí-lúpatʰ-a   'to not hunt'
           u-hé-émeš-a   'to not stand s.t. up'

It is readily apparent that the negative element *-hi-* bears a high tone in this construction and that this high tone doubles onto the following vowel. It is also apparent that the high tones assigned by tone assignment do not show up at all in these forms. The absence of the high tone assigned to the first vowel of the verb stem is expected, of course, due to the operation of tone lowering. But the absence of the high tone assigned to the third vowel of the verb stem (cf., *u-hí-lókotʰel-a*, not **u-hí-lókotʰél-á*) is unexpected. A special rule is required that lowers any stem high tone after the negative prefix *-hi-*. The derivation of *u-hí-lókotʰel-a* will be as in (112).

(112)　　　L H L L　L L
　　　　　u-hi-lokotʰel-a　　Underlying representation
　　　　　L H H L　H L　　Tone assignment
　　　　　L H L L　L L　　Tone lowering after *-hi-*
　　　　　L H H L　L L　　Tone doubling

　　With this much background, let us turn to the forms that are relevant for the high tone preservation principle. Consider the tonal behavior of negative infinitives that contain an object prefix.

(113)　　*u-hí-kí-vah-a*　　　　'to not give to me'
　　　　u-hú-ú-vah-a　　　　'to not give to you (child)'
　　　　u-hí-kí-lokotaniher-a　'to not pick up for me'
　　　　u-há-á-lokotaniher-a　'to not pick up for him'
　　　　u-hí-ké-emeš-a　　　'to not stand me up'
　　　　u-hé-é-meš-a　　　　'to not stand him up'

It is readily apparent from *u-hí-kí-vah-a* and *u-hí-kí-lokotaniher-a* that the negative prefix once again is high-toned and doubles its high tone onto the following vowel (which is part of the object prefix). There is no trace of any other high tone: not the high tone typically associated with the object prefix itself (cf., *u-kí-váh-a* 'to give to me'), not the high tones typically assigned to the first and the third vowel of the verb stem. Thus we must assume that the *-hi* morpheme triggers lowering of all these high tones. Next notice that the *i* vowel of the negative prefix assimilates the quality of the following vowel: Thus *iu* yields *uu* and *ia* yields *aa*. This presumably represents a facet of the assimilation process noted earlier that converts *ie* to *ee* and *ae* to *ee*. Finally, consider *u-hé-é-meš-a* 'to not stand him up'. This form derives from /u-hí-á-emeš-a/, apparently via a derivation something like (114).

(114)　　　L HHL　L L
　　　　　u-hi-a-emeš-a　　Underlying representation
　　　　　L HHH　L L　　　Tone assignment
　　　　　L HLL　L L　　　Tone lowering after *-hi-*
　　　　　L HHL　L L　　　Tone doubling
　　　　　u-hi-e-emeš-a　　ae ⟶ ee
　　　　　L HHL　L L
　　　　　u-he-e-emeš-a　　ie ⟶ ee
　　　　　L HH　L L
　　　　　u-he-e-meš-a　　Vowel reduction

Vowel reduction in this example reduces the sequence *ééé* to *éé*. This is just what the high tone preservation principle predicts. We have thus seen that the sequences *eéé* and *ééé* both reduce to *éé*. A low tone deletes rather than a high tone.

The long vowel *-aa-* is used in Makua as a tense/aspect marker and is placed between the subject prefix (which obligatorily appears on all finite verbs in Makua as in other Bantu languages) and the verb stem. Thus we find examples like *y-aa-lúpátʰ-a* 'he was hunting'. The *-aa-* tense/aspect marker here is low-toned. The first vowel of the verb stem is high toned (and this high tone is doubled onto the following vowel). It appears then that the tone assignment principle that operates on infinitives is also at work in this verb tense. This hypothesis is confirmed by an example such as *y-aa-lókótáníher-a* 'he was picking up', where we see that both the first and the third vowel of the verb stem bears a high tone (doubled onto the following vowel). Consider next an example like *y-aa-kí-páŋgacér-á* 'he was making s.t. for me'. As expected, the object prefix-*ki-* is high-toned, just as in the infinitive. The high tone of the object prefix induces the lowering of the high that would be assigned to the first vowel of the verb stem by tone assignment. The high tone assigned to the third vowel of the verb stem is retained, however. Consider now *y-a-á-páŋgacér-á* 'he was making s.t. for him', which results from the derivation in (115).

(115)

LLH	L	L	L	L	
y-aa-a-paŋgacer-a					Underlying representation
LLH	H	L	H	L	Tone assignment
LLH	L	L	H	L	Tone lowering
LLH	H	L	H	H	Tone doubling
LH	H	L	H	H	Vowel reduction
y-a-a-paŋgacer-a					

The vowel reduction process in this case reduces the sequence *aaá* to *aá*. Once again it is a low tone that is lost rather than a high tone. Now suppose that instead of a consonant-initial verb stem like *-paŋgacer-* we had a vowel-initial verb stem like *-etetʰel-* 'to thresh for'. The data in (116) illustrate the behavior of such verb stems in the verb tense presently under discussion.

(116)

a. *y-e-ététʰél-á*   'he was threshing for' (from: /y-aa-ététʰél-á/)
b. *y-aa-ké-étetʰél-á*   'he was threshing for me' (from: /y-aa-kí-étetʰél-á/)
c. *y-é-étetʰél-á*   'he was threshing for him' (from: /y-aa-á-étetʰél-á/)

In (116a) the sequence *aaé* is converted to *eeé* by vowel assimilation and then to *eé* by vowel reduction. In (116b) the object prefix *-ki-* comes between the tense/aspect prefix *-aa-* and the initial vowel of the verb stem, thus no vowel reduction is necessary. Example (116c) exhibits a more complex case of vowel reduction than we have yet encountered, so its derivation will be shown in full.

(117) LLHLL L L
       y-aa-a-etet^{h}el-a   Underlying representation
       LLHHL H L   Tone assignment
       LLHLL H L   Tone lowering
       LLHHL H H   Tone doubling
       y-ee-e-etet^{h}el-a   *ae* $\longrightarrow$ *ee*[2]

       HHL H H
       y-e-etet^{h}el-a   Vowel reduction

Here the sequence *eeéé* reduces to *éé*; in other words, four vowels reduce to two in such a way that both low tones are lost while the high tones are retained.

We have space only for one additional class of examples. Before turning to the relevant examples it is necessary to observe that the subject prefixes before the *-aa-* tense/aspect marker exhibit a special form. For example, *ki-* the 1 sg. prefix appears as *k-*, *mu-* the 2 p. (adult) prefix appears as *mw-*, and so on. It happens, however, that there is no overt prefix at all for a 3 sg. (child) subject. With this in mind, let us turn to examine what is often referred to by Bantu scholars as the consecutive tense. It consists of a prefix *k^{h}á-* followed by the subject prefix followed by the *-aa-* tense/aspect marker followed by the verb stem ending in *-a*. Thus we have *k^{h}á-mw-aa-t^{h}áw-á* 'and then you (adult) ran'. The tone of the *k^{h}á-* prefix is peculiar in that it does not copy onto the following vowel as expected; we have no explanation for this exceptional behavior. Now, if the subject of a verb in the consecutive tense is a 3 sg. child, no overt prefix occurs between the *k^{h}á-* prefix and the *-aa-* tense/aspect marker. We thus create a sequence of three consecutive *a* vowels. The result can be seen in *k^{h}á-a-t^{h}áw-á* 'and then he (child) ran'. Note that the sequence *áaa* reduces to *áa*. This is again just what the vowel reduction process in conjunction with the high tone preservation principle predicts.

Let us consider now what happens when the 3 sg. (adult) object prefix *-a-* occurs between the *-aa-* prefix and the verb stem. An example would

---

[2] This rule must either apply iteratively or be phrased to affect any number of *a* vowels before an *e* vowel.

be $k^há$-á-$th^húmel$-a 'and then he (child) bought it for him'. The derivation of this example is shown in (118).

(118) H LLH L L L
       k^ha-ɸ-aa-a-th^humel-a Underlying representation
       H LLH H L L   Tone assignment
       H LLH L L L   Tone lowering
       H LLH H L L   Tone doubling (note: $k^há$- must be
                                      marked as not trig-
       HH H LL   gering tone doubling)
       k^ha-a-th^humel-a Vowel reduction

It can be seen from this example that the sequence *áaaá* reduces to *áá*. Once again, this is precisely the result predicted by vowel reduction plus the high tone preservation principle.

Finally, consider the case where the verb stem is vowel initial rather than consonant initial. An example is -*etet^hel*- 'to thresh for'. Compare $k^héétét^hélá$ 'and he (child) threshed for' with $k^héétet^hélá$ 'and he (child) threshed for him'. The derivations of these forms are shown in (119) and (120).

(119) H LLLL L L
       k^ha-ɸ-aa-$etet^hel$-a Underlying representation
       H LLHL H L   Tone assignment
       inapplicable   Tone lowering
       H LLHH H H   Tone doubling (recall, $k^há$- exception-
                                       ally fails to trigger
                                       doubling)
       k^he- ee-$etet^hel$-a $ae \longrightarrow ee$
       HH H HH
       k^he-e-tet^hel-a Vowel reduction

(120)   H LLHLL L L
       k^ha-ɸ-aa-a-$etet^hel$-a Underlying representation
       H LLHHL H L   Tone assignment
       H LLHLL H L   Tone lowering
       H LLHHL H H   Tone doubling
       k^he- ee-e-$etet^hel$- a $ae \longrightarrow ee$
       HHL HH
       k^he-$etet^h$ el -a Vowel reduction

In (119), the sequence *éeeé* is reduced to *éé*, while in (120) the sequence *éeeéé* is reduced to *éé*. In the latter example five units of underlying vowel length are reduced to two on the surface. The result is again a level high tone: In other words, the two low tones from the original sequence are lost entirely.

We have shown in the latter part of this section that vowel reduction and the high tone preservation principle will account for a wide range of cases where a sequence of three or more vowels in Makua reduces to just two. These examples have also shown that the analysis of Makua tone developed earlier is applicable not just to infinitive forms of verbs, but extends to other verbal forms as well (in particular, verb tenses marked by the prefix *-aa-*). Makua, like many other Bantu languages, utilizes tone in quite complex ways, and not all aspects of the tonal structure of Makua verbs have been treated here. Nevertheless, all of the tonal principles proposed here can easily be shown to come into play in all of the verbal forms of the language, as well as in other word classes. The principles enumerated here thus help to account for a large part of the rather intricate tonal patterns of Makua.

Exercises

1. Hebrew Itpa'el pattern.

   a. Assume that all verb roots in this exercise have the URs CVCeC or CVCCeC. Formulate rules to account for the *e* ~ *a* and voicing alternations in the following data.

1 sg.	3 sg. masc.	3 sg. fem.	Gloss
itparnasti	*itparnes*	*itparnesu*	'earn'
itparsamti	*itparsem*	*itparsemu*	'become famous'
idbalbalti	*idbalbel*	*idbalbelu*	'be confused'
idgalgalti	*idgalgel*	*idgalgelu*	'revolve'

   b. Formulate a syncope rule to account for the *e* ~ ϕ alternation.

itḥamakti	*itḥamek*	*itḥamku*	'turn away'
itlabašti	*itlabeš*	*itlapšu*	'get dressed'
idbadarti	*idbader*	*idbadru*	'make fun'
idgarašti	*idgareš*	*idgaršu*	'divorce'
itpalalti	*itpalel*	*itpalelu*	'pray'
itxamamti	*itxamem*	*itxamemu*	'warm'
itmotati	*itmotet*	*itmotetu*	'quake'
it'ošašti	*it'ošeš*	*it'ošešu*	'recover consciousness'
idbodati	*idboded*	*idbodedu*	'seclude oneself'

   c. The following data require two new rules which must be ordered with earlier ones.

istaparti	istaper	istapru	'get a haircut'	(cf., *sapar* 'barber'
istarakti	istarek	istarku	'comb hair'	(cf., *ma-srek* 'comb'
ištaparti	ištaper	ištapru	'improve'	(cf., *šipur* 'improvement'
ictalamti	ictalem	ictalmu	'have one's photo taken'	(cf., *calam* 'photographer'
izdakanti	izdaken	izdaknu	'age'	(cf., *zaken* 'old'
izdarasti	izdarez	izdarzu	'hurry'	(cf., *zariz* 'alert'
itamamti	itamem	itamemu	'feign innocence'	(cf., *tamim* 'innocent'
idardarti	idarder	idarderu	'decline'	(cf., *dirdur* 'rolling'

d. The following data require three new rules ordered with earlier ones. (In the prestige dialect ʕ and ḥ do not appear phonetically. Our data reflect the nonprestige dialect.)

itmaleti	itmale	itmalʔu	'become full'
itpaleti	itpale	itpalʔu	'become surprised'
itnaseti	itnase	itnasʔu	'feel superior'
itpataḥti	itpateaḥ	itpatḥu	'develop'
idgalaḥti	idgaleaḥ	idgalḥu	'shave'
itnacaḥti	itnaceaḥ	itnacḥu	'argue'
ištagati	ištagea	ištagʕu	'become mad'
itparati	itparea	itparʕu	'cause disorder'

2. Lomongo (Hulstaert 1957).
   a. Propose an ordered set of rules to account for the phonological and tonological alternations in the following data from this Bantu language. Transcription: ę = [ε], ǫ = [ɔ], acute accent is high tone, circumflex is falling, a vowel without a tone mark is low-toned. *j* = [ǰ] is in free variation with [dz] and *ts* is in free variation with [č]. Except for the first column all forms are present tense. Assume that the final *a* of these words is a verb suffix.

Imper.	1 sg.	2 sg.	3 sg.	1 pl.	2 pl.	3 pl.	Gloss
saŋgá	ńsaŋga	ósaŋga	ásaŋga	tósaŋga	lósaŋga	básaŋga	'say'
kambá	ŋ́kamba	ókamba	ákamba	tókamba	lókamba	bákamba	'work'
jilá	ńjila	ójila	ájila	tójila	lójila	bájila	'wait'
ęna	ńjęna	węna	ęna	tswęna	jwęna	bęna	'see'
ísa	ńjísa	wísa	ísa	tswísa	jwísa	bísa	'hide'
iméjá	ńjimeja	wîmeja	îmeja	tswîmeja	jwîmeja	bîmeja	'consent'
iná	ńjina	wîna	îna	tswîna	jwîna	bína	'hate'
bína	ḿbína	óína	áína	tóína	lóína	báína	'dance'
báta	ḿbáta	óáta	ááta	tóáta	lóáta	bááta	'get'
bóta	ḿbóta	óóta	áóta	tóóta	lóóta	báóta	'beget'
męlá	ḿmęla	ómęla	ámęla	tómęla	lómęla	bámęla	'drink'
lóma	ńdǫ́ma	ólǫ́ma	álǫ́ma	tólǫ́ma	lólǫ́ma	bálǫ́ma	'kiss'
londá	ńdǫnda	ólǫnda	álǫnda	tólǫnda	lólǫnda	bálǫnda	'chase'
usá	ńjusa	wûsa	ûsa	tswûsa	jwûsa	bûsa	'throw'
asá	ńjasa	wâsa	âsa	tswâsa	jwâsa	bâsa	'search'

   b. The following data provide additional confirmation of some of the rules in a. The accent of the final vowel of the imperative obeys a polarity principle: it is always the opposite of the tone of the preceding vowel. On the other hand, the tone of certain derivational suffixes, such as the applied /-el/, is always the same as the following vowel. How must these tonological rules be ordered to account for the data in b?

Imper.	Passive imper.	Causative imper.	Applied	Applied imper.	Causative applied imper.	Gloss
báka	bákwa	bákya	-bákela	bákélá	bákéjá	'fasten'
kotá	kotswá	kotsá	-kotela	kotélá	kotéjá	'perch'
mę́ŋga	mę́ŋgwa	mę́ŋgya	-mę́ŋgęla	mę́ŋgę́lá	mę́ŋgéjá	'sway'
kondá	konjwá	konjá	-kondela	kondélá	kondéjá	'cover with sand'
kǫfá	kǫfwá	kǫfyá	-kǫfęla	kǫfélá	kǫféjá	'have an accident'
túla	tújwa	túja	-túlela	túlélá	túléjá	'forge'
bíla	bíjwa	bíja	-bílela	bílélá	bíléjá	'pull'

3. Maltese Arabic (Brame 1972).

   a. Formulate a stress insertion rule and a vowel elision rule to account for the alternations in the following perfect verb forms. Hint: order the stress rule before elision. Account for the $o \sim e$ alternation as well. (acute accent = stress).

3 sg. m.	3 sg. f.	1 2 sg.	3 pl.	2 pl.	1 pl.	Gloss
tálab	tálbet	tlábt	tálbu	tlábtu	tlábna	'ask'
ḥólom	ḥólmot	ḥlómt	ḥólmu	ḥlómtu	ḥlómna	'dream'
ḥátaf	ḥátfet	ḥṭáft	ḥátfu	ḥṭáftu	ḥṭáfna	'grab'
kórob	kórbot	króbt	kórbu	króbtu	króbna	'groan'
béza?	béz?et	bzá?t	béz?u	bzá?tu	bzá?na	'spit'

   b. The following require a new rule. How must it be ordered with the rules of (a)?

lá?at	lá?tet	il?átt	lá?tu	il?áttu	il?átna	'hit'
róḥos	róḥsot	irḥóst	róḥsu	irḥóstu	irḥósna	'become cheap'
mášat	máštet	imšátt	máštu	imšáttu	imšátna	'comb'
néfa?	néf?et	infá?t	néf?u	infá?tu	infá?na	'spend'

   c. In the imperfect nonderived roots take the underlying shape CCVC with a vowel that is generally different from that of the perfect. Do not attempt to relate the perfect and imperfect root shapes by rule. Account for the $i \sim o$ alternation in the following imperfect forms, ordering the rule correctly with the rules already in the grammar.

1 sg.	2 sg.	1 pl.	2 pl.	Gloss
nímsaḥ	tímsaḥ	nímshu	tímshu	'wipe'
nísha?	tísha?	nísh?u	tísh?u	'smash'
níkteb	tíkteb	níktbu	tíktbu	'write'
nól?ot	tól?ot	nól?tu	tól?tu	'hit'
nórbot	tórbot	nórbtu	tórbtu	'tie'
nómšot	tómšot	nómštu	tómštu	'comb'
nónfo?	tónfo?	nónf?u	tónf?u	'spend'
nískot	tískot	nísktu	tísktu	'become silent'

nízbor	*tízbor*	*nízbru*	*tízbru*	'prune'
níjbor	*tíjbor*	*níjbru*	*tíjbru*	'pick up'
nídhol	*tídhol*	*nídhlu*	*tídhlu*	'enter'
nóbzo?	*tóbzo?*	*nóbz?u*	*tóbz?u*	'spit'
nófto?	*tófto?*	*nóft?u*	*tóft?u*	'unstitch'
nó?tol	*tó?tol*	*nó?tlu*	*tó?tlu*	'kill'

d. Formulate a rule to account for the following data, ordering it correctly with the preceding rules.

ná?sam	*tá?sam*	*ná?smu*	*tá?smu*	'divide'
ná?bez	*tá?bez*	*ná?bzu*	*tá?bzu*	'jump'
náhsad	*táhsad*	*náhsdu*	*táhsdu*	'reap'
náhdem	*táhdem*	*náhdmu*	*táhdmu*	'work'

e. The following forms require a new rule. Do you encounter any problems in ordering this rule with stress and elision? How is this rule ordered with the other rules?

nišrob	*tíšrob*	*nišórbu*	*tišórbu*	'drink'
nókrob	*tókrob*	*nokórbu*	*tokórbu*	'groan'
nítlob	*títlob*	*nitólbu*	*titólbu*	'pray'
náhrab	*táhrab*	*nahárbu*	*tahárbu*	'flee'
nífrah	*tífrah*	*nifírhu*	*tifírhu*	'rejoice'
nísra?	*tísra?*	*nisír?u*	*tisír?u*	'steal'
nó?mos	*tó?mos*	*no?ómsu*	*to?ómsu*	'kick'
nídnib	*tídnib*	*nidínbu*	*tidínbu*	'sin'

5

Evidence and Motivation

In this chapter we will survey the types of reasoning and evidence that linguists typically employ in the motivation and justification of phonological descriptions. There are two broad categories of evidence. First, there is corpus-internal evidence: Here the argumentation is based on the primary body of data the linguist works with, a corpus of utterances in phonetic transcription with each utterance given at least a rudimentary grammatical and semantic analysis. This body of data may be relatively restricted in scope (in cases where the linguist does not have access to speakers of the language being studied and must rely on whatever descriptive materials are available) or open-ended (in cases where the linguist has the opportunity to work within the context of a speech community where the language is actively used).

Second, there is corpus-external evidence: Here the argumentation is based not on the language data itself, but on various types of linguistic behavior a full explanation of which seems to require appeal to the speaker's knowledge of his language. The kinds of linguistic behavior we have in mind here include foreign language acquisition, speech errors (slips of the tongue), systematic distortions of the language (language games), and so on. This particular type of evidence has only recently come to be viewed as being of great importance; thus while it is easy to find good examples of argumentation based on internal evidence, it is much more difficult to find analyses where external evidence is carefully utilized. It is for this reason that most of the argumentation in the previous (and following) chapters involves only internal evidence.

Corpus-Internal Evidence

The view of phonology espoused in this book is that all utterances (and the morphemes composing them) have an underlying representation and a phonetic representation. These representations are linked by one or more phonological rules (or no rules if the two representations happen to be identical) that express the predictable features of pronunciation found in the phonetic representation of each morpheme. Given this general conception of phonology, the analysis of any language involves determining the UR for the morphemes of the language and a statement of the rules linking this representation with the PR. In this chapter as well as the next we will discuss a number of principles and criteria that have been proposed (implicitly or explicitly) to select the most appropriate UR. The first of these may be expressed as follows:

> *Each morpheme is assumed to have a unique UR unless there is evidence to the contrary.*

As we have seen in previous chapters, a morpheme will often appear in a number (sometimes relatively large) of distinct phonetic forms depending on the context in which it is placed. Phonologists generally assume that each of the surface phonetic alternants can be derived from a single underlying phonological representation, except in the cases of suppletion like *go/went* and *good/better* in English, where the phonetic relationship between the alternants is either nonexistent or tenuous and where no general rules can be invoked to account for the alternation. In other words, morpheme alternation is viewed as a problem involving the effects that different phonological and grammatical contexts have on an UR, rather than as a problem involving the choice of which of a set of different phonological shapes to employ in a given situation. Of course, close investigation of a language may show that a phonologically unique underlying form is not a viable analysis (for instance, such a form might require implausible rules or rules that are inconsistent with other data in the language); it has been assumed, however, that such a lack of viability must be demonstrated before one accepts multiple phonological representations for one morpheme.

A second general assumption with respect to the selection of the most appropriate underlying representation can be stated as follows:

> *Unless there is evidence to the contrary, the UR of a morpheme is assumed to be identical with the phonetic representation.*

"Evidence to the contrary" would include alternations as well as nonalternating, but nevertheless predictable, noncontrastive phonetic features like the length and aspiration of *cab*, as discussed in Chapter 2. This second assumption explains why, for example, no phonologist would propose an analysis like the following. Suppose there is a language with a consonant inventory *p*, *t*, *k*, *s*, *n*, and *r*. Assume that these consonants have no defective distribution—that is, they all occur initially, medially, and finally. Lastly, assume that all words in this language begin with a consonant phonetically. In such a language we might find words like the following:

(1)

	pat	*sen*	*kustik*	*supan*
	tik	*rop*	*poster*	*rukip*
	kus	*naris*	*tarasi*	*kita*

In analyzing this language no one would propose that all occurrences of word initial *p* are to be abstracted out and inserted by a rule, so that the UR's for *pat* and *poster* are to be set up as /at/ and /oster/ and the *p*'s inserted by a rule like $\emptyset \longrightarrow p \ / \ \# \_\_\_ V$. The reason, of course, is that there is absolutely no evidence that the initial *p* in *pat* is a predictable feature of the pronunciation of this word. The *p* does not alternate with $\emptyset$, and *p* occurs freely in all other positions. Hence it has the same distribution as all of the other consonants. Why not choose one of these as predictable instead of *p*? The choice is clearly arbitrary. The general assumption that the UR of a morpheme is identical to the PR unless there is evidence to the contrary explains why no phonologist would ever propose such an absurd analysis.

To see further what evidence to the contrary means in the present context, we might usefully compare the above hypothetical language with German, where it is also the case that all words begin with a consonant phonetically.[1] In German the following stop consonants appear word-initially: *p*, *t*, *k*, *b*, *d*, *g*, *ʔ*. However, there are several reasons for

---

[1] Certain details are ignored here in the German data, but they are beside the point. For discussion, see Moulton (1947).

believing that the glottal stop is inserted by a rule of the form ∅ ⟶ ʔ/#___V. Two of the most important reasons are, first, that word-initial position is essentially the only position in which ʔ appears, and second, that the glottal stop alternates with ∅ when a morpheme becomes non-initial (for example, [ʔauf], but *hin-auf* 'up' and [ʔaus], but *her-aus* 'out'). Both this alternation and the limited distribution of the glottal stop are explained by an analysis that treats the ʔ as being inserted by a rule that prevents a word-initial vowel by adding a glottal stop in front of all such vowels. According to such an analysis, ʔ is not an underlying sound in the language and will appear phonetically only where a rule creates it. To summarize, a morpheme is assigned a more abstract representation than the phonetic representation only when the associated rule or rules explain something about the phonological behavior of the morpheme.

In addition to the two general principles just discussed, another very important corpus-internal justification is the principle of phonological predictability, which can be phrased as follows:

All other things being equal, a phonological solution is preferred over a solution that divides the lexicon into arbitrary classes (a lexical solution) or over a solution that lists the morphological/syntactic contexts in which a rule applies (a grammatical solution).

The role of this principle is most clearly seen in the analysis of alternations involving the neutralization of underlying contrasts. Thus, in situations where segment x alternates with y in some context, but there are a substantial number of xs that do not alternate with y in the same context, a general strategy is to distinguish the alternating and nonalternating xs by deriving them from different underlying sources; in particular, to derive the alternating xs from basic y and to set up the nonalternating xs as basic x. When relevant, each of the analyses in the previous two chapters adhered to this principle. For example, in the analysis of the voicing alternation in Russian obstruents we found that a large number of voiceless word-final obstruents alternated with the corresponding voiced obstruents before vowel-initial suffixes, while an approximately equal number of voiceless obstruents remained voiceless when the case suffixes were added: for example, *grop*, *grob-u* versus *trup*, *trup-u*. By the principle of phonological predictability we distinguish alternating from nonalternating obstruents by selecting the stem alternants appearing before vowel-initial suffixes as basic, for in this position the voiced-voiceless contrast appears phonetically. The alternation is then described by a general rule of final-devoicing that neutralizes that contrast in final position.

Of course, in these situations it is always possible to take the neutralized segment *x* as basic and treat *y* as derived by a rule. But this requires dividing the lexicon into arbitrary classes. If we select *grop* instead of *grob-* as the UR, in order to distinguish it from a morpheme like *trup*, which does not voice its consonant when a suffix is added, the lexicon of Russian will have to be divided into two arbitrary classes: stems that voice their final obstruent and those that do not. Such an analysis claims, falsely, that the voicing alternation is not predictable; the speaker of Russian must memorize for each stem whether or not its final obstruent is voiced when inflected.

Of course, there will be cases where this principle of phonological predictability will be inapplicable because in addition to constant *x*s, and *x*s alternating with *y*, there will be nonalternating *y*s as well, thus barring any attempt to set up the alternating *x* as *y*. In such cases it is sometimes possible to motivate some different sound *z* on the basis of which the alternating sound can be distinguished in a purely phonological way from the constant *x* and *y*. For example, in the previous chapter's analysis of Yawelmani, there were arguments for the existence of underlying /i:/ and /u:/, which were lowered to /e:/ and /o:/ in all contexts. In Yawelmani we can find nouns like the following:

(2)   Sub. case   *p'islu-ʔ*   *ʔohyo-ʔ*   *ʔutu-ʔ*
      Ind. obj. case   *p'islo:-nu*   *ʔohyo:-ni*   *ʔutu-nu*
      Gloss   'mouse'   'seeing'   'tree'

The length alternation is accounted for by the rule which shortens a vowel before a word-final glottal stop. But how is the alternation in vowel height exhibited by 'mouse' to be accounted for? To distinguish this morpheme from 'seeing', we would look at its shape in the subject case since the stem-final vowels are distinct in the latter case form. But if the stem-final vowel of 'mouse' is set up as /u/, then there would be no way to distinguish this morpheme's behavior from that of 'tree', which ends in *u* but does not alternate. As we showed in Chapter 4, a good case can be made for distinguishing this behavior in a purely phonological manner by setting up the final vowel of 'mouse' as /u:/, which will shorten to *u* before the glottal stop, and otherwise lower to *o:* by the vowel-lowering rule.

But in most cases it is impossible to motivate such an abstract phonological distinction, and the difference in morphophonemic behavior must be described in a lexical fashion by a governed rule that is sensitive to an ad hoc arbitrary division of the morphemes in the lexicon. To cite just one example here (see Chapter 10 for more discussion), the following data from Czech show that there are two sorts of *i:*s in the Standard Literary language:

(3)

	Standard	Colloquial	Gloss
	mi:st-o	*mi:st-o*	'location'
	mi:dl-o	*mejdl-o*	'soap'
	mle:k-o	*mli:k-o*	'milk'

One of these is lowered to *e:* in the colloquial language (which is then diphthongized to *ej* by a later rule we can ignore here), while the other is not. The *e:*s of the standard language are raised to *i:* in the colloquial variety. These vowel changes are implemented by a polarity rule that interchanges /e:/ and /i:/. It is clear that no matter whether the standard or the colloquial alternant is taken as basic, there will be no way to apply the principle of phonological predictability to differentiate those *i:*s that alternate from those that do not. There is an historical explanation. The alternating *i:* derives from the high, back unrounded vowel *y:* of Proto-Slavic. In colloquial Czech this vowel lowered to *e:*, while in the standard variety of the language it merged with *i:*. This difference is still reflected in the spelling *mýdlo* versus *místo*. In general, however, there is no way to motivate phonetically distinct underlying sources for the two different kinds of *i:*s as was done for the two kinds of *o:*s in Yawelmani. The morphemes 'soap' and 'location' (or 'milk' and 'location', if the colloquial alternants are selected as basic) will have to be differentiated by ad hoc information in the lexicon.

There are a number of reasons why phonological solutions, when available, are preferred over lexical solutions. First, since phonological rules frequently involve assimilating a sound to its context, there is no reason not to expect such assimilation to lead to the merger of an underlying contrast. This point can be illustrated by commonly occurring examples like the following: As we saw in Chapter 3 Russian has a voicing opposition in obstruents. This opposition is neutralized by a rule making an obstruent agree in voicing with a following obstruent. For example, the contrast between *t* and *d* is lost when the conditional particle *by* is placed after a noun ending in an underlying voiceless obstruent: compare, *rot* 'mouth', but *rod-by*. However, this voicing assimilation does not always lead to the merger of an underlying contrast. There are three obstruents that have no underlying voiced counterparts—*c*, *č*, and *x*. Voiced counterparts of these sounds do occur phonetically, but only as a result of the assimilation of *c*, *č*, and *x* to a following voiced obstruent: *otec* 'father', *otedz-by*; *reč* 'speech', *reǰ-by*; *mox* 'moss', *moγ-by*. Since the *c~dz*, *č~ǰ*, and *x~γ* alternations involve no merger of an underlying contrast, they are clearly to be handled by an assimilation rule converting *c*, *č*, and *x* to *dz*, *ǰ* and *γ*, respectively, before a voiced obstruent. But since alternations between p and b, and t and d arise under exactly the same circumstances (before voiced obstruents) and involve exactly the same feature change (from voiceless to voiced) there is no reason not to describe them by the same assimilation rule used for the $c \sim dz$, $\check{c} \sim \check{j}$, and $x \sim \gamma$ alternations. Study of numerous examples like this one reveals no general tendency on the part of language to suspend the assimilation for those cases where it would lead to the merger of an underlying contrast. Consequently, since the cases where the alternation leads to merger appear to be of exactly the same nature as those cases where no merger results, there is every reason to treat them in the same fashion by a rule of assimilation. But such a treatment presupposes giving a phonological (as opposed to a lexical) analysis for those alternations that lead to a merger of an underlying contrast. (This argument derives from Halle 1959).

Another reason for the general preference for phonological solutions is the simple fact that they permit an alternation to be accounted for by means of a general rule. In other words a phonological solution permits us to claim that the voicing alternation of obstruents in Russian is predictable and thus captures the generalization that there are no word-final voiced obstruents in Russian pronunciation. If the lexicon must be divided into arbitrary classes, we are in essence claiming that the alternation is not predictable. In general the phonologist tries to predict as much as possible about the sound pattern of a language.

In addition to preferring a phonological solution to a lexical one, most phonologists have favored purely phonological solutions, when they are available, to analyses that simply list the morphological/syntactic contexts in which a rule applies. In and of itself it is difficult to give any good reasons for this practice without regard to the particular circumstances. If the rule involves assimilating a sound or a class of sounds to its context, and if these contexts happen to correspond to a heterogeneous set of grammatical contexts, then in general one would select the phonological solution on the grounds that it gives a unitary explanation for the sound change implemented by the rule (see discussion of the final-devoicing rule of Russian in Chapter 3). On the other hand, if there is some natural grammatical context for the rule (e.g., noun plurals) while the phonological contexts do not form a particularly natural class, then the grammatically based analysis would be more appropriate, all other things being equal. Often rules require a mixture of both phonological and grammatical information in order to specify their contexts of operation completely. This point will be discussed further in Chapter 10.

In addition to the principle of phonological predictability another type of internal justification is the appeal to the phonetic plausibility and naturalness of the rules. Given two analyses A and B in which the rules of

A have a phonetic rationale and/or are found in a significant number of languages, while those of B are not, A is selected over B, other things being equal. We have given a number of examples of this kind of argument in Chapter 2. Such appeals to the phonetic plausibility of a rule make a great deal of sense, since rules reflecting the structure or dynamics of the vocal apparatus have a high degree of explanatory force. A similar explanatory power holds for a rule appearing in a significant number of languages, even if the phonetic basis for its widespread occurrence is unclear.

Symmetry and pattern congruity are additional criteria that phonologists often appeal to in motivating an analysis. We have seen how the operation of phonological rules characteristically creates gaps in the phonetic distribution of sounds. (For example, final devoicing in Russian creates the gap of no word-final voiced obstruents.) An analysis that fills in the gaps and regularizes the distribution of sounds at the underlying level and accounts for the gaps by way of a rule or rules is generally preferred over an analysis which fails to do so.

These gap-filling strategies take a number of different forms. They are most commonly employed in the analysis of a sound or group of sounds with limited distribution. If such a sound *x* can be viewed as a rule-governed variant of another sound *y*, then not only can the gap be filled and the limited distribution explained, but *x* can be eliminated from the underlying phonemic inventory. As we shall see, simplification of the underlying phonemic inventory is itself another criterion often invoked in favor of a particular analysis.

These gap-filling criteria are to be appealed to several times in the analysis of the following data from the Bukar-Sadong dialect of Land Dayak (Scott 1964).

(4)   *mālu*   'strike'   *sampɛ:*   'extending to'
        umɔ̃   'water'   *inceh*   'is'
        nābur   'sow'   *suntɔk*   'in need of'
        ənāk   'child'   *suŋkoi*   'cooked rice'
        siŋāũ   'cat'   *mpahit*   'send'

Examination of these data reveals two gaps. First, nasal vowels occur after nasal consonants; they do not occur initially or after nonnasal consonants. Second, oral vowels appear initially and after nonnasal consonants, but they do not occur after nasal consonants. Both of these gaps can be filled by analyzing the nasal vowels to be surface variants of the corresponding oral vowels after nasal consonants. In such an analysis there are only oral vowels at the underlying level, so the phonemic inventory is simplified. Furthermore, the underlying distribution of the oral vowels is completely free; they appear after all consonants (both nasal and nonnasal) as well as initially. A rule nasalizing a vowel when it stands after a nasal consonant creates the two distributional gaps noted above and, consequently, may be said to explain these gaps.

The same type of reasoning is to be employed in the analysis of the following data from Dayak:

(5)

ntakadn	'taste'	*kiñãm*	'feeling'
pəlabm	'mango'	*pimãĩn*	'a game'
kaidn	'cloth'	*pəmĩŋ*	'dizzy'
padagŋ	'field'	*tanĩn*	'story'
tu?a:dn	'open'	*nũ?ã:n*	'open'
pə?adn	'feed'	*mə̃?ãn*	'eat'

Forms like *nũ?ã:n* and *mə̃?ãn* are derived from the same bases as *tu?a:dn* and *pə?adn* by a morphological process that has the effect of changing the initial voiceless stop to the corresponding nasal. Forms like *nũ?ã:n*, *mə̃?ãn*, and *pimãĩn* show that once a nasal consonant has nasalized a following vowel, this vowel may in turn nasalize an immediately following vowel or a vowel separated from it by a glottal stop. The presence of any other consonant between the nasal vowel and a following vowel prevents the spread of nasalization. This spreading effect can be described by formulating the nasalization rule as follows and permitting it to apply to its own output.

(6) $$V \longrightarrow \tilde{V} \; /[+ \text{nasal}](?)\underline{\qquad}$$

The relevance of the above data to our present concerns consists in the status of the prestopped nasals *bm*, *dn*, and *gŋ*. These sequences have a limited distribution in Land Dayak, appearing only in final position. In addition, they only occur after an oral vowel; they never follow a nasal vowel. (Compare the alternations in *pə?adn* versus *mə̃?ãn*.) On the other hand, a plain nasal consonant without the parasitic stop does not occur in this position. These gaps can be accounted for by taking the prestopped nasals to be surface variants of underlying nasal consonants by virtue of the following rule:

(7) $$[\text{m, n, ŋ}] \longrightarrow [\text{bm, dn, gŋ}]/ \; \underset{[-\text{nasal}]}{V} \underline{\qquad} \#$$

This rule will of course be ordered after the vowel-nasalization rule. In addition to accounting for the limited distribution of the prestopped nasals, the rule also enables us to eliminate these rather suspicious sounds from the underlying inventory of phonemes. To show how these rules work we give derivations for the related forms *mə̃ʔãn* 'eat' and *pəʔadn* 'feed'. We assume that the rule turning the initial voiceless stop to a nasal in *mə̃ʔãn* has already applied.

(8)   / # məʔan # /   / # pəʔan # /

       mə̃ʔãn   ---------   Vowel-nasalization

       ---------   *pəʔadn*   Prestopping

Another gap-filling argument can be given to explain the following data, which are anomalous in terms of the analysis we have presented so far.

(9)   *əmudn*   'dew'   *banugŋ*   'tapioca'
       mə̃nabm   'sickness'   *girunugŋ*   'a small bell'
       əna:gŋ   'prawn'

These forms are problematic because they contain oral vowels following a nasal consonant. According to our analysis vowels are nasalized in this position. These data appear to indicate that nasal vowels are phonemic in Dayak after all, in spite of what we said previously. However, an explanation for these forms is suggested by the following gap in the phonetics of Land Dayak. Although voiceless stops do appear after a nasal consonant (cf., *mpahit* 'send', *ntakadn* 'taste', *suŋkoi* 'cooked rice'), voiced stops do not appear in this position. This is suspicious because otherwise voiced and voiceless stops freely contrast (*ntakadn* 'taste' versus *padagn* 'field', *banugŋ* 'tapioca' versus *pənĩŋ* 'dizzy', and *girunugŋ* 'a small bell' versus *kənãŋ* 'posterior'). We can simultaneously fill in this gap and explain the exceptions to our analysis if the forms in (9) are assigned underlying representations in which a voiced stop follows the nasal consonant. This voiced stop will then be deleted after a nasal consonant by the following rule, which will of course be ordered after vowel-nasalization:

(10)   [b, d, g] $\longrightarrow$ $\emptyset$/ C _____
                                               [+ nasal]

Furthermore, it appears that we can specify uniquely which particular voiced stop we must set up in these forms in view of the fact that a nasal consonant appears to be always homorganic with a following stop, at least in the Land Dayak data at our disposal. Thus, the URs for the problematic forms will be /əmbun/, /məndam/, /ənda:ŋ/, /banduŋ/, and /girunduŋ/. The latter form will be derived as follows:

(11)   /#girunduŋ#/
         -----------   Vowel-nasalization
         girunuŋ   Stop-deletion
         girunugŋ   Prestopping

In addition to regularizing the distribution of a sound or a class of sounds, another kind of gap-filling argument involves the regularization of a particular class of morphemes. For example, in Chapter 3 we discussed the past tense of Russian verbs showing an alternation of a dental stop with zero: *met-u*, *me-l* 'sweep'; *krad-u*, *kra-l* 'steal'. One reason for taking the dental stops as basic, of course, is that we cannot predict whether or not a stem will terminate in *t* or *d* in the present-tense form. An additional reason for not setting up the shapes *me-* and *kra-* as underlying is that to do so would create a very peculiar gap in the lexical class of verb stems: There would be stems ending in labial stops (*greb-* 'row', *skreb-* 'scrape'), in velar stops (*mog-* 'be able', *pek-* 'bake'), and in dental fricatives (*lez-* 'crawl', *nes-* 'carry'), but none in dental stops. Since dental stops appear in the same positions as the labial and velar stops and the dental fricatives in all other parts of the Russian lexicon, we expect their absence before the past-tense suffix *-l* to be due to a rule deleting a basic dental stop in this position.

Another example in which considerations of symmetry are employed to decide what is underlying and what is derived in the analysis of an alternation is the Yawelmani rule of vowel epenthesis, discussed in Chapter 4. This rule converts basic verbal roots of the form CVCC- to the shape CVC*i*C- before consonant-initial suffixes. We said that although it would be possible to take the /i/ as underlying and postulate a rule of syncope to derive the $\emptyset$ alternant, one reason for not doing so is the fact that if the alternant CVC*i*C- is selected as the basic root shape, there would be no disyllabic verb roots with a short vowel other than /i/ in the second syllable. In other words we would be creating a gap such that roots of the shape CVC*a*C-, CVC*o*C-, and CVC*u*C- would never be found in the lexicon. But if the /i/ is analyzed as epenthetic, no such gaps arise; all verbal roots would be monosyllabic, and the /i/ will have a distribution in underlying representations that parallels each of the other vowels /a/, /o/, and /u/.

In our discussion of the Dayak data we mentioned that one criterion phonologists sometimes employ is economy of phonemic inventories. If a sound or class of sounds has a limited or peculiar distribution, an analysis that eliminates this sound or sound class from the underlying inventory of segments is generally preferred over an analysis that fails to do so.

In addition to a simple reduction in the number of underlying phonemes, symmetry of underlying sound inventories is often considered criterial. An analysis that is able to reduce an asymmetric phonetic inventory to a more balanced underlying inventory is usually preferred over one that fails to do so. For example, in the Yawelmani data in Chapter 4 we argued that the asymmetric phonetic inventory of (12a) could be reduced to the more balanced system of (12b) if the vowel-lowering rule was postulated.

(12) (a) i u   (b) i u ī ū
          a o ē ā ō   a o ā ō

A similar argument was given as partial motivation for deriving the Slovak diphthongs from underlying long vowels.

Such underlying/surface disparities are usually cited in conjunction with evidence from alternations that independently motivate a rule linking the relatively more balanced underlying inventory with the asymmetric phonetic one. Thus, if it were not for the evidence provided by the vowel harmony and vowel shortening rules in Yawelmani, the claim that (12b) does indeed underlie (12a) would be considerably weaker. The same is true for Slovak, where the rule of diphthongization not only allows a symmetrical underlying vowel system but also helps to explain alternations between short vowels and diphthongs that are precisely parallel to alternations between short and long vowels.

Another important corpus-internal criterion is the notion of independent motivation. This concept is employed to justify a particular aspect of an analysis on the grounds that it accounts not just for one phenomenon, but for several unrelated phenomena. We have already appealed to this type of justification in earlier descriptions such as that of the Yawelmani vowel lowering rule (Chapter 4). We argued that this rule permits us to explain a number of separate aspects of the sound pattern of Yawelmani. First, it allows us to account for the double exceptions to the vowel harmony process. Second, the rule helps to explain the fact that some stem-final *o:* vowels and all stem-final *e:* vowels alternate with *u* and *i*, respectively, before suffixes consisting of a glottal stop. Third, the rule of vowel lowering enables us to extract the generalization that underlies the vowel-echo verb stems. In other words, we have at least four (there are in fact more) separate aspects of the phonological structure of Yawelmani that independently motivate the rule of vowel lowering. Obviously, the case for this rule and the abstract analysis it entails would be weakened considerably if it were supported on the basis of only one of these sources of evidence.

An important variant of the role of independent motivation is to be found in those cases in which the concept is used to decide between alternative treatments of a particular alternation. This arises in cases where a certain alternation can be accounted for in two different ways, but where one of them is independently needed to account for a different alternation. Recall that one of the reasons for taking the /i/ as derived rather than basic in the Yawelmani CVCC-/CVC*i*C- alternations was the fact that a rule inserting /i/ was needed independently to account for the reduplicated verbs with a zeroed stem vowel; that is, the following derivation of the verb base 'eat' is required in Yawelmani: *xat* (by reduplication) ⟶ *xatxat* (by vowel zeroing) ⟶ *xatxt* (by vowel epenthesis) ⟶ *xatixt*. Since we need a vowel epenthesis rule to account for the last step of the above derivation, this fact helps us to decide in favor of an insertion rule to account for the /i/ ~ /∅/ alternation in morphologically simple roots such as *ʔilk-/ʔilik-* 'sing'.

The concept of independent motivation is sometimes used in a rather different sense. Here, in order to simplify his description, the phonologist assigns a UR to a morpheme even though this UR is not supported by appeal to alternations or by straightforward distributional gaps. This move is justified by appealing to an independently motivated rule (one supported by alternations and/or distributional gaps) that will convert the otherwise unmotivated UR into the correct PR.

A well-known example of this kind is to be found in Leonard Bloomfield's famous paper on Menomini morphophonemics (1939). In Menomini there is a widespread process that converts *t* to *č* in certain contexts. One of these is when the *t* immediately precedes *y*. However, there are some occurrences of *ty* clusters on the phonetic surface in Menomini. Rather than treat these as exceptions to the palatalization rule, thereby complicating the description, Bloomfield sets these morphemes up with an underlying *w* between the *t* and the *y*. The *w* is then deleted by an independently motivated rule that drops a glide when it stands between a consonant and a following glide. The operation of this rule, which will be ordered after palatalization, can be seen in the derivation of *aʔsɛn-wēk* 'hard-woven cloth', which comes from /aʔsɛny-wēk/. Compare *aʔsɛny-ak* 'stones' where the stem-final glide shows up. Now in order to explain why a form like *pēhč-ekon-āhty-an* 'sacred bundles' has a *t* before a *y*, the morpheme *āhty* is assigned the otherwise unmotivated UR /āhtwy/. The *w* blocks the palatalization from applying to the *t*, and then the *w* is deleted by the independently motivated glide-deletion rule. As Bloomfield states, the *w* in such forms is set up "merely to bar" palatalization.

An alternative to this "phonological" analysis is of course simply to describe the morpheme as an exception to the palatalization rule by associating the information [−palatalization rule] in the lexical representation of this morpheme. The choice, then, is between an analysis that attributes the lack of palatalization to a phonological property of the morpheme (the /w/) versus an essentially nonphonological property (the information [− palatalization rule]). Considerations of mere simplicity fail to resolve the choice, for in general there is no way to evaluate the phonological information as being more or less simple than the nonphonological information. Unless the phonological solution can be supported by appeal to other facts (such as distributional limitations), it seems to us that the nonphonological description is to be preferred on the grounds that it is more straightforward. Evidently, in this particular case the facts are simply that the morpheme *āhty-* fails to palatalize when it should. If there are no other relevant facts about the phonological behavior of this morpheme suggesting that it should have a different UR (see the preceding text), it seems appropriate simply to state this by marking the morpheme as an exception to the palatalization rule. (We will return to the treatment of exceptions and related matters in Chapter 10.)

In addition to avoiding exceptions to phonological rules, otherwise unmotivated URs are sometimes postulated in order to simplify the inventory of sounds appearing in underlying representations. Typically, in such cases there is some phonetic segment (or class of segments) x that can be shown to be derived from y by a phonological rule that is well motivated by alternations. The rule is then extended to derive all phonetic occurrences of x in the entire language from y, even if the x is a constant, nonalternating property of some morphemes. For instance, in French there are many examples in which a nasal vowel alternates with an oral vowel + nasal consonant sequence (*genre* [žãr] 'kind', *générique* [ženerik] 'generic', *prendre* [prãdr] 'to take', *prenez* [pren-e] 'you pl. take'). Here the URs are /žen-/ and /pren-/. A general rule will convert the sequence VN to V̄ in position before a consonant. A nasalized *ē* shifts to *ā* by a subsidiary process (Schane 1968).

In some analyses of French the further move is made of deriving surface nasal vowels from underlying *VNC* clusters in morphemes that never exhibit an allomorph with an oral vowel + nasal consonant sequence. The morpheme *vend-* [vãd] 'sell' is an example; it would be set up as underlying /vend-/ even though it always surfaces in the shape *vãd-* with a nasal vowel. Given the general assumption that the UR is identical with the PR unless there is evidence to the contrary, this more abstract UR must be justified. In such cases as this two corpus-internal reasons are characteristically adduced. First, if it is possible to derive all occurrences of nasal vowels from underlying *VNC* sequences, then the underlying vowel inventory can be considerably reduced. In and of itself this is not a particularly strong reason, for why should a smaller vowel inventory be preferred at the cost of a more abstract UR? Such an appeal to a reduced phonemic inventory is usually bolstered by a gap-filling argument to the effect that the more abstract UR regularizes the underlying canonical shape of morphemes. Thus in the present instance there are no morphemes with the phonetic sequences $\tilde{V}NC$ or VNC, while other sonorants like liquids and glides may appear between a vowel and a following consonant. Since otherwise the nasal consonants have the same general distribution as the liquids and glides, this gap can be filled with the VNC sequences, which will automatically be converted to the surface $\tilde{V}C$ clusters by the independently motivated vowel-nasalization rule.

If the various corpus-internal principles discussed above are consistently followed, a general approach to phonological analysis emerges. This approach, which has been characteristic of generative grammar, at least until quite recently, has the following distinctive features: First, it is assumed that in general the phonological behavior of morphemes in the corpus can be predicted on the basis of phonetic (as opposed to arbitrary lexical) information contained in the lexical representation. The rules predicting this behavior should be natural in the sense of being either phonetically motivated and/or frequently occurring in the world's languages. Also, in addition to predicting alternations these rules should be able to account for gaps in the distribution of sounds so that the underlying inventory and/or distribution of sounds is more regular and systematic than the phonetic distribution. Finally, the rules should not have a significant number of exceptions. Generative phonologists have generally assumed that an analysis with these features provides an adequate description of the phonological structure of any language.

Generative grammarians have also claimed that a description of the phonological structure of a language is simultaneously a characterization of the linguistic knowledge of native speakers of the language. If this claim is accepted, it implies that a phonological analysis reached on corpus-internal grounds will correspond with the internalized grammar of the native speaker (i.e., that the linguistic description has "psychological reality"). But in order for this implication to be valid, we must be able to corroborate it by corpus-external evidence—that is, we must go outside the patterns in the corpus to look at other aspects of linguistic behavior, in order to determine whether the claims about the native speaker's internalized grammar reached on corpus-internal grounds are consistent with the knowledge of language revealed in other forms of linguistic behavior. If it is possible to accumulate a significant number of examples showing a correspondence between corpus-internal analyses and knowledge of language revealed corpus-externally, the linguist can legitimately assume that speakers will internalize similar analyses in cases for which, at present, no such external evidence can be provided. Unfortunately, for a number of essentially historical reasons linguists,[2] especially in the United States, have only recently begun to deal seriously with this issue. Consequently, at the moment there is not enough evidence for us to determine the psychological reality of many of the analyses in this book with a great deal of confidence.

Corpus-External Evidence

In the remainder of this chapter we shall briefly discuss some of the more important sources of corpus-external evidence that can be brought to bear upon the question of the psychological reality of phonological descriptions.

The psychological reality of a phonological regularity can often be demonstrated by the type of errors made by persons learning a foreign language. The summation of such errors is, of course, what we commonly call a foreign accent. In order to explain why most speakers of a particular language—say, French—make the same errors when learning English, while speakers of another linguistic background—say, Japanese—tend to make a different set of errors, we must assume that the errors are the result of interference from the internalized grammars of the different native languages, French and Japanese.

Frequently, the pronunciation error is due to the fact that a particular sound in the language being learned is absent in the speaker's native language. In such situations it is reasonable to assume that the person selects the sound from his native language that most closely approximates the novel sound of the target language. However, what counts as the closest sound is not always obvious. For example, both French and Serbo-Croatian lack the nonstrident dental fricatives θ and $\check{d}$ found in English "*think*" and "*these*". But French speakers substitute *s* and *z* for these sounds, while speakers of Serbo-Croatian render them as the stops *t* and *d*. Evidently, this difference must be due to some difference in the status of the dental stops and fricatives in the phonological structure of the two languages. For some discussion see Polivanov (1930).

[2] One important reason is that the primary concern of many American linguists during the first half of this century was to collect as much data as possible on the vanishing American Indian languages, rather than to develop an explicit theory of phonology. Another reason was the antimentalist bias of much of American structuralism. There was also a desire on the part of many linguists of the period, most notably Bloomfield, to make linguistics a "science" independent of all other disciplines, especially psychology.

Many times, however, the incorrect rendering of a sound cannot be attributed to the lack of this sound in the native language, but is due to constraints on where this sound may appear in the phonetic representations of the native language. Often these positional limitations are produced by phonological rules, and the error may be cited as proof of the psychological reality of the rule. For example, in Chapter 3 we cited the tendency for native speakers of Russian to devoice word-final obstruents when learning English, one of the traits of a Russian accent. We argued that this tendency corroborated the claim that native speakers of Russian possess a rule of final devoicing in their internalized grammars; otherwise there would be no reason to expect them to devoice final obstruents when learning English.

Such appeals to pronunciation errors when learning a foreign language in order to justify the psychological reality of a phonological rule or regularity are not uncommon in the literature. Jacobsen (1969) motivates, on corpus-internal grounds, a rule for Makah (a Wakashan language of the Pacific Northwest) that labializes a back consonant (velar or uvular) when preceded by an *u* vowel. He then states

> A striking feature of Makah accent in English, especially of some older speakers, is the occurrence of labialization in phrases such as *took it* and *cook it*, where the last syllable sounds like *quit* [p. 7].

To cite just one more example of this type of external evidence, this time involving an interference in the perception of a phonological feature, recall our discussion of the Slovak rhythmic law in Chapter 4. This rule shortens an underlying long vowel in position after a syllable containing a long vowel. Czech, a language very closely related to Slovak, also has a contrast between underlying long and short vowels. But in Czech there is no constraint against successive long vowel syllables appearing in phonetic representations. The underlying contrast between long and short vowels is not neutralized in Czech after a long syllable. Roman Jakobson (1931) mentions that speakers of Slovak have difficulty in making and in perceiving the difference between long and short vowels after a long syllable in a Czech word.

Another source of external evidence comes from mistakes made by people in speaking their own language—in particular, slips of the tongue, or spoonerisms. Fromkin (1971) discusses a number of these from English, showing that the types of errors found are constrained by the phonological structure of English. First, she points out that all the sounds that appear in spoonerisms occur in normal English utterances. One does not find rounding of a front vowel in anticipation of a back rounded vowel, for example. Second, the sound sequences that result from the transpositions effected by the spoonerism are constrained by what are possible sound sequences in the structure of English phonology. This is illustrated nicely by the following slip of the tongue, attributed to Rev. Spooner himself: *sphinx in moonlight* ⟶ *minx in spoonlight*. This example involves the transposition of the initial *sf-* cluster of *sphinx* with the *m-* of *moon*. But instead of finding *sfoonlight* the result is *spoonlight*. The modification of *sf* to *sp* can be explained along the following lines. An initial *sf* cluster is found in only about a dozen technical terms derived from Greek (*sphincter, sphere, sphinx*). This cluster violates a general constraint on possible morpheme-initial consonant clusters in English. If a morpheme begins with *s*, the only consonant that can appear after the *s* is a voiceless unaspirated stop (*spoon, stop, skim*) or *l* (*slim*). Consequently, when the transposition to *sfoonlight* occurs, the *sf* is changed to *sp* in order to bring it in line with this constraint on possible morpheme-initial consonant clusters. If this constraint did not constitute part of the linguistic competence of the native speaker of English, there would be no reason to expect modifications like *sf* to *sp* to occur.

Fromkin (1975) also reports a number of spoonerisms that support the relatively abstract analysis of English that derives all occurrences of phonetic [ŋ] from underlying /ng/ sequences. As pointed out by Sapir (1925) and many other linguists, this analysis is motivated on a number of corpus-internal grounds. First, [ŋ] has a more restricted distribution than *m* or *n*, since it never appears word initially (*map, nap,* but not **ŋap*) nor internal to a morpheme before a vowel (*smear, sneer,* but not **sŋeer*). Second, the sequences [nk] and [ng] do not occur in English phonetic structure, while [ŋk] and [ŋg] do (*sink, rank, finger, anger*). These distributional gaps could be accounted for by a rule assimilating /n/ to the point of articulation of a following velar. (This rule can, of course, be regarded as just one aspect of a more general nasal assimilation process.) Third, although [ŋ] occurs in final position, **[ŋg]* does not (we have *sing* [sīŋ], but not **[sīŋg]*). This distributional gap can be accounted for by deriving final [ŋ] from underlying /ng#/ by a rule that deletes *g* in the environment ŋ___#. This rule must follow the nasal assimilation rule that converts *n* to *ŋ* before *g*. The *g* deletes not only in absolute word-final position, but also before certain suffixes such as the agentive *-er (singer)*, and the verbal suffixes *-ing (singing)* and *-ed (hanged)*. Finally, there are a few alternations in English that support the rule deleting *g* word finally after [ŋ]. For example, *long* ends in a velar nasal, but the underlying /g/ surfaces phonetically in the comparative form *longer*.

The slip of the tongue [swīn] *and* [swej] for the intended *swing and sway* is one of the spoonerisms Fromkin (1975) cites in support of the analysis that derives [swĩŋ] from /swing/. The underlying /g/ seems to have been transposed to the end of *sway*, where it is no longer in position to delete. This transposition also permits the underlying /n/ in /swing/ to surface phonetically since it is no longer followed by the velar stop /g/ that gives rise to [ŋ] by nasal assimilation. Another slip of the tongue supporting underlying /g/ is [sprig]*time for* [hĩntlər] instead of the intended *Springtime for Hitler*. In this example the underlying /n/ of *Springtime* has been transposed into *Hitler*. By incorporating the /n/ into the latter word, the underlying /g/ is left behind, resulting in [sprig].

Note that the latter example also supports the position that all nasal vowels in English are derived from underlying oral vowels by a rule nasalizing vowels when they stand before nasal consonants. According to this analysis [sprĩŋ] would derive from /spring/. When the slip of the tongue removes the underlying /n/, the vowel nasalization rule can no longer apply, explaining why [sprig] results with an oral vowel. Of course, this vowel nasalization rule also explains why [hĩntler] appears with a nasal vowel.

Another source of extrasystemic evidence comes from speakers of unwritten languages who are attempting to develop a system for writing their native languages or who are attempting to learn a system that someone else has devised. In a well-known paper dealing with the problem of the psychological reality of linguistic representations (in particular, the phoneme), Sapir (1933) reported on several situations where the orthographic choices of the speaker revealed a cognizance of some part of the phonological structure of the language in question.

Several of Sapir's examples are based on his work with Alex Thomas, a native speaker of Nootka, a language of the Pacific Northwest belonging to the Wakashan family. Thomas, who was trained by Sapir in practical phonetics, transcribed a large number of Nootka texts in an orthography that Sapir refers to as "phonologic in spirit." That is, Thomas' orthographic decisions tended to be based not on phonetic identity but on phonological identity. For example, in Nootka there are, phonetically, long consonants. But not all long consonants are structurally on a par. There is apparently a rule that lengthens a consonant when preceded by a short vowel and followed by a vowel. The long consonants that come from this rule are always written as single consonants in Thomas' transcriptions; thus, orthographic *hisi:k* is normally pronounced with a long *s*. There are other phonetic long consonants, however, which Thomas transcribes as *ss* rather than just *s*. In all such cases the long consonant appears to arise from the juxtaposition of two morphologically distinct consonants: $s + s > s$: and $\check{s} + \check{s} > \check{s}$:. Thus orthographic *tsi:qšit'łassatłni* 'we went there only to speak' is morphologically *tsiqšit'ɬ-ʔas-sa-(ʔa)tɬ-ni*. Note that the combination of -*ʔas-* 'to go in order to' and -*sa-* 'just, only' is written -*assatɬ-* although it is pronounced with a long *s* that is identical to the long *s* in *hisi:k*. Sapir draws the conclusion that phonetic identity cannot be equated with phonological identity. Two occurrences of the "same" sound may have entirely different values in the phonological system of a language. Within the approach to phonology sketched in this book, the different values of the long consonants in Nootka would be characterized by deriving the long consonant in a form like *hisi:k* from a basically short consonant, whereas the long consonant in *tsi:qšit'ɬassatɬni* would derive from an underlying form containing two successive *s*s.

To cite just one more example, Sapir asked his native interpreter for Southern Paiute to syllabify the word *pa:βah* 'at the water' and to write down the sounds composing it. To Sapir's surprise the interpreter wrote *pa:pah*. Although on purely phonetic grounds the two labial consonants in *pa:βah* are quite distinct, Sapir points out that their identification by the native speaker is readily comprehensible once the phonological structure of the voiceless stops in Southern Paiute is taken into account. Underlying voiceless stops in Southern Paiute take three different surface forms when they appear in position after a stem. The bilabial stop *p*, for instance, has the form *β* when it appears after a class of stems Sapir labels "spirantizing;" it has the form *mp* in position after the nasalizing class of stems; and finally, it appears as doubled or long *p:* after geminating stems. The stem *pa:-* 'water' is a spirantizing one. Hence, when the suffix meaning 'at', which is analyzed as underlying /-pah/ by Sapir (and, unconsciously, by his interpreter as well), is appended after this stem, the combination *pa:-pah* is realized as [pa:βah] phonetically. The morpheme *pɔ:* 'trail' behaves in a parallel fashion, showing up spirantized when it follows the stem *pa:-* in the word [pa:βɔ:] 'water trail'.

What is truly interesting about this example is that since /-pah/ is a suffix, it must always follow one of the three types of stem. Hence, its underlying consonant will always appear altered in phonetic representation. But, in the words of Sapir, "its theoretical existence suddenly comes to the light of day when the problem of slowly syllabifying a word is presented to a native speaker for the first time [1933, p. 49]."

Native orthographies are not always sensitive to abstract representations from which predictable phonetic features have been eliminated. Sometimes the native informant may make orthographic decisions that respond to the phonetic form of the utterance. For instance, Stampe observes: "In my experience in teaching Soras to write their language (one of the Munda languages of India) I found to my surprise that they usually wrote [nts], [ndr], for what was clearly /ns/, /nr/ in the language, e.g. [kən] 'animal classifier' and [sim] 'chicken' = [kəntsim], these being the only triple clusters in the language [1972, p. 6]'' In other words, the *t* is a predictable off-glide in the transition from the stop to the following continuant, much like the *p* in English [warmpθ] *warmth*. Nevertheless, the Soras include this segment in their orthographic representations. Thus, it seems clear that at least in this respect the Soras are responding to the phonetic form of utterances in their orthographic policy, including information that is wholly redundant and predictable by phonological rule.

This observation on the Soras leads to an important point that must be borne in mind in all discussions of external evidence. Just because a particular feature of an internal analysis is not revealed in external linguistic behavior, it does not necessarily follow that that feature is not psychologically real. Thus, in the Sora example it can still be maintained that the *t* of [kəntsim] is epenthetic, if it is assumed that the Soras are merely representing the phonetic form of their utterances in writing this aspect of their language.

Linguists sometimes argue that the ways in which the sounds of a language are used in poetry provide insights into the phonological structure of a language. The converse thesis, that knowledge of the phonological structure of a language can help to explain deviations from or exceptions to poetic rules, is also put forth.

What counts as a rhyme is often claimed to be influenced by phonological structure rather than being purely phonetic in nature. Sapir (1925) notes that a rule in Yahi shifts *a* to *ɔ* in position after *w* or *u*. But this rule is disregarded in determining rhymes: the word *wɔwi* (from /wawi/) rhymes with such phonetic groups as *lawi* and *bawi*. Sapir argues that the rhyme pattern in this language is determined at an abstract, not a phonetic level—in particular at that level of representation that exists before the rule rounding *a* to *ɔ* is applied. If these rhymes are freely composed, it can be argued that this rule is psychologically real, for it is only by virtue of the rule that *wɔwi* can be equated with *lawi* and *bawi*. (By "freely composed" we mean that the rhyme is not something learned as part of a set of poetic conventions.)

Another example of this type is discussed by Kiparsky (1968c) in his study of the Finnish folk epic, the *Kalevala*. In Finnish poetry a long or geminate vowel may alliterate with a short vowel, as in *kulki kuusissa hakona*. Here the short *u* of the first word alliterates with the geminate *uu* in the first syllable of the second word. One also finds that (short) vowels alliterate with the initial segments of diphthongs—*e* alliterates with *ei*, *a* with *ai*, and so on. However, in some dialects of Eastern Finnish the long alliterating partner of *a* is *oa*, of *e* is *ie*, of *o* is *uo*, and of *ö* is *yö*.

Furthermore, one finds that a short vowel such as *o* does not alliterate with the *o* of the *oa* diphthong, though it does alliterate with *oi*. The explanation for this deviant alliteration pattern is to be found in the phonological structure of these dialects. All of the exceptional diphthongs may be analyzed as arising from a rule of diphthongization that raises the initial vowel of a geminate cluster: *aa* ⟶ *oa*, *ee* ⟶ *ie*, *oo* ⟶ *uo*, *öö* ⟶ *yö*. Hence, if the alliteration pattern is defined at the level of phonological structure that exists before the operation of the diphthongization rule, then the alliteration principle is quite simple: A word-initial sequence $(C_0V)_i$ alliterates with $(C_0V)_j$ only if i = j. This condition requires only that the initial consonant (cluster) and first vowel element in the word be identical. This correctly permits *Cu* to alliterate with *Cuu*; it permits *Ca* to alliterate with *Cai* as well as *Coa*, for the latter is *Caa* at this level of structure. Finally, *Co* will not alliterate with *Coa* because the latter is *Caa* at this point. Evidently, then, this complex alliteration pattern can be explained only on the assumption that the poet calls on his internalized grammar to organize the sound patterns in his verse.

The metrical structure of a poem may also be defined at a more abstract level of representation. A number of studies have shown that many metrical irregularities appearing at the phonetic level can be explained when the phonological structure of the language is taken into account. Such studies provide corpus-external evidence for the relevant aspects of phonological structure.

Zeps (1963) found in a study of Trochaic Latvian folksongs that each line is composed of two metrical units called "cola." Each colon in turn is composed of four metrical syllables. The final two syllables of each colon must belong to the same word, while the first two need not. Hence, the lines tend to have the following structure, where S = syllable (which may be long, containing a long vowel or diphthong, or short) and $\widehat{SS}$ is a bridge indicating that the two syllables must belong to the same word.

$$S \ S \ \widehat{S \ S} \qquad S \ S \ \widehat{S \ S}$$

An example of a song matching this pattern perfectly is the following:

(13) *Bēdu manu, lielu bēdu* 'O sorrow, my great sorrow
      Es par bēdu nebēdāju! I will not let thee grieve me.
      Liku bēdu zem akmena, I will put thee under a stone
      Pāri gāju dziedādama. And will singing step over it.'

There are, however, many examples of cola containing less than four syllables. For instance, *briest rudzi* 'the rye is ripening' contains only three syllables, yet occurs as a colon, as does *kuoši dzied* 'are singing beautifully' and *ruotājas* 'playing'. These examples are especially puzzling in view of the fact that there are other three- and, indeed, even some four-syllable sequences that do not constitute proper cola: *es nācu* 'I came' and *nācu es* 'came I' are not acceptable; nor is *vilks routājas* 'the wolf is playing', even though it contains four syllables.

Zeps argues that these exceptions can be explained if phonological structure is taken into account. In Latvian there is a rule that drops a final vowel under certain complex circumstances (Halle and Zeps 1966). Forms like *briest* and *dzied*, the 3rd person forms of 'ripen' and 'sing', can be analyzed as deriving from URs /briest-a/ and /dzied-a/, where the /-a/ is a present tense marker. This morpheme surfaces phonetically in verbs that permit the addition of a reflexive morpheme—*plēs* 'widen' from /plēs-a/ has the corresponding reflexive form *plēsas* from /plēs-a-si/.

Once this aspect of Latvian phonological structure has been taken into account, the cola *briest rudzi* and *kuoši dzied* are seen to be perfectly regular, provided the metrical structure is defined at the level of representation that exists before the rule of vowel elision has applied. This rule explains why *ruotājas* is metrical but *vilks ruotājas* is not, even though the latter contains four syllables. The reason is that the UR for *ruotājas* is /ruotāj-a-si/ with four syllables. Three-syllable sequences such as *es nācu* and *nācu es* are unmetrical because the UR for these words is /es/ and /nācuo/. They contain a total of only three syllables (recall that diphthongs count as one syllable).

If these songs were composed after the vowel-elision rule entered the language (Lithuanian, a closely related East Baltic language, does not possess the rule), then they would rather conclusively demonstrate the psychological reality of an abstract level of representation as well as the reality of the rule of vowel elision itself. Zeps does not state whether the composition of the songs postdates the inception of the rule, in which case it is possible to maintain that the underlying metrical pattern is a fossilized remnant of an earlier stage of the language that must be memorized when the songs are learned. However, the following point is suggestive. Zeps observes that "syllables truncated by the morphophonemic rule [vowel elision] can be reinstated during recitation or singing, although not necessarily with the same vowel [1963, p. 126].'' Thus, a colon like *agri tek* 'are bestirring themselves' may be recited as *agri teka*. Here the verb *tek* would be analyzed as deriving from /tek-a/, the elided vowel being restored. On the other hand, "such replacement is not possible, if no vowel has been truncated.'' Thus, a form like *māsinas* 'sisters' from /māsinas/ would never be recited with an extra vowel appended. This discrimination in vowel restoration suggests that the vowel elision process is still under the control of the native speaker of Latvian.

Zeps also points out that words that lose a syllable by truncation may be counted in two different ways metrically, so long as they are not the final member of a colon. Thus a word like *vilks* may function metrically as disyllabic (such as *vilks lec* 'the wolf is dancing' from /vilkas leca/) or as monosyllabic (*vilks apēda* 'the wolf ate' from /vilkas apēdā/; see Halle and Zeps 1966 for discussion of this UR for *vilks*). This kind of dual metrical behavior in which both an abstract and a more superficial form of a word are metrically acceptable is actually rather common poetic practice.

Language games and speech disguises may provide evidence about the internalized grammar of the native speaker. These games are usually based on one (or sometimes a combination) of two general principles: insertion of a sound or sound sequence at specifiable points in the word or the movement of a sound or sound sequence from one point to another. These operations often create sound combinations that do not otherwise occur in the regular, nondisguised phonetic representations of the language. Such nonoccurring combinations may then be modified in accordance with the phonological rules of the language and hence provide corpus-external evidence for the productivity and psychological reality of the phonological rules and constraints operating in the language.

One interesting example of this type is cited by Chao (1934) for the Peiping dialect of Chinese. It involves the phonological description of the following sounds:

(14)

č	č'	š	palatal
k	k'	x	velar
c	c'	s	alveolar
ç	ç'	ş	retroflex

The sounds in the first column are unaspirated, those in the second aspirated noncontinuants, while the third column is composed of continuants. The problem presented by these sounds is that the palatals are always followed by a high front vowel *i* (unrounded) or *y* (rounded), while the velars, alveolars, and retroflex consonants are never followed by a high front vowel. Hence the sounds in the first row are in complementary distribution with the sounds in the others, and can be considered assimilated variants of one of these series. The problem is to decide which one. On grounds of naturalness and phonetic plausibility the retroflex series is least likely to underlie the palatals. However, the choice between the velars and the alveolars would seem to be fairly arbitrary. (Chao points out that historically the palatals have arisen from both velars and alveolars.) In such a case one would normally look for morphophonemic alternations to try to decide the problem. However, since Chinese is a monosyllabic language, the relevant alternations do not occur.

Chao cites two pieces of external evidence that both suggest that the native speakers of this dialect consider the palatals to be variants of underlying velars. First is the fact that the velars and palatals alliterate with one another: "he [the native speaker] feels [kə, či, ku, čy] or [xə, ši, xu, šy] to be alliterative series with only different vowels [1934, p. 48]." Second, there is a secret language in this dialect that involves inserting the sequence *aik* between the initial consonant and the syllabic portion of the word: In Chao's formulation Initial + Final ⟶ Initial *ai* + *k* Final. By this rule a word such as *pei* is disguised as *pai-kei*. If this disguising rule is applied to a word whose syllabic is a high front vowel, the impermissible combination of a velar plus a high front vowel will result. In such cases *k* mutates to *č*. Thus, *mi* ⟶ *mei-ki* ⟶ *mei-či*.[3]

Chao does not say what would happen if the language game were applied to a form like *či*. Here, since the speech disguise involves splitting up the initial and the final, we might be able to determine the underlying character of the palatal *č* because it will now be before a back vowel *a*. A striking example of the way a speech disguise bears on the analysis of a sound in precisely this way comes from the language game *sorsik sunmakke* ("talking backwards") played by the Cuna Indians of the San Blas Islands in Panama (Sherzer 1970). This game provides a number of insights into the phonological structure of Cuna, the most interesting of which involves the phonological analysis of the voiceless stops. On corpus-internal grounds a fairly good case can be made for deriving the surface contrast between voiced and voiceless stops from an underlying contrast between single and geminate stops: *b* from /B/, but *p* from /BB/ (where B represents a bilabial stop which does not need to be specified for voicing); *d* from /D/, but *t* from /DD/; and so on. One fact supporting this interpretation is that the distribution of the voiceless stops parallels the distribution of a cluster of two consonants. In Cuna the maximum consonant cluster contains just two elements. Additionally, there are no word-final or word-initial consonant clusters at all. The voiceless stops have exactly the same distribution. A voiceless stop cannot occur next to another consonant (just as a consonant cluster cannot occur next to a third consonant); nor are there any examples of voiceless stops at the beginning or at the end of a word (just as there are no consonant clusters in these environments). Voiced stops, on the other hand, do not have these limitations of occurrence, as the examples in (15) illustrate.

---

[3] This may be a misprint for *mai-či*.

(15)   *obsa*   'bathed'   *dage*   'come'
         argan 'hand'   *goe*   'deer'
         neg   'house'   *biriga* 'year'

The parallel distribution of the voiceless stops and the consonant clusters can be accounted for if the voiceless stops of words such as *sapan* 'firewood', *sate* 'no', and *dake* 'see' are derived from underlying clusters of stops by a rule that reduces these clusters to a single voiceless stop.

(16)   Reduction   [BB, DD, GG] $\longrightarrow$ [p, t, k]

This interpretation of the data is also supported by two sorts of morphophonemic evidence. First, there is a rule that deletes the initial member of a three-consonant cluster. This is shown by such forms as *balimay-de* 'then, he pursued' and *balimadgu* 'having then pursued'. The latter word is basically /#balimay-de-gu#/.[4] The surface form is produced by a rule of syncope, which deletes a vowel at the end of a morpheme when a suffix is added, followed by a rule of cluster simplification which deletes the first of three consonants.

(17)   /#balimay-de-gu#/
         balimay-d-gu   Syncope
         balima-d-gu   Cluster simplification

Now, if surface voiceless stops are analyzed as coming from underlying geminate stops (unspecified for voicing), then the cluster simplification rule automatically accounts for the morphophonemic alternations between voiced and voiceless stops in examples like *dupu* 'island', but *dubdake* 'he sees the island'. Under the interpretation we are proposing (following Sherzer), these forms would be derived as follows:

(18)   /#dubbu-dagge#/   /#dubbu#/
         dubb-dagge   ----------   Syncope
         dub-dagge   ----------   Cluster simplification
         dub-dake   *dupu*   Reduction

This analysis is also supported by the fact that reduction is needed on independent grounds. When a cluster of identical voiced stops comes

---

[4] Since under the proposed analysis of Cuna, a single occurrence of a stop will be pronounced as a voiced stop, we will simplify the presentation by using the lower case symbols *b*, *d*, and *g* instead of B, D, and G in our sample derivations.

together across a morpheme boundary, the geminate is realized as the corresponding voiceless stop: *neg* 'house' + *gine* 'inside' ⟶ *nekine* 'inside the house'.

We can thus explain the distribution of the voiceless stops in Cuna if we derive the voiceless stops of *sapan*, *sate*, and *dake* as follows.

(19)   /#sabban#/   /#sadde#/   /#dagge#/
        sapan   *sate*   *dake*   Reduction

The interesting thing about this example is that the language game *sorsik sunmakke* provides some striking support for this corpus-internal analysis. The game is played by moving the initial syllable to the end of the word.

(20)

Cuna	Gloss	*Sorsik sunmakke*
ina	'medicine'	*nai*
dage	'come'	*geda*
saban	'belly'	*bansa*
obsa	'bathed'	*saob*
argan	'hand'	*ganar*
inna	'chicha'	*nain*
goe	'deer'	*ego*

Words with voiceless stops in medial position are pronounced as follows:

(21)

Cuna	Gloss	*Sorsik sunmakke*
sapan	'firewood'	*bansab*
sate	'no'	*desad*
dake	'see'	*gedag*

Such pronunciations are straightforwardly explained if we assume that these words are underlying /#sabban#/, /#sadde#/, and /#dagge#/, and that the *sorsik sunmakke* rule is defined to operate on the representations of these words that exists before the reduction rule operates. If these words are not derived from these underlying sources by reduction, then the *sorsik sunmakke* forms are completely anomalous. Why should a medial voiceless stop come out as a voiced stop in initial and final position? This is especially puzzling because voiced stops do not behave in this fashion at all: Compare *saban* ⟶ *bansa* with *sapan* ⟶ *bansab*. But if we hypothesize that in the internalized grammars of Cuna speakers voiceless stops are derived from underlying clusters of stops, as the internal evidence suggests, then the striking behavior of the voiceless stops in *sorsik sunmakke* is readily explained.

Examples of this type are significant, for they suggest that speakers may internalize, on corpus-internal grounds, relatively abstract underlying forms. If a number of examples of this type can be motivated, they will permit the phonologist to claim with some confidence that phonological analyses postulated on similar corpus-internal grounds will in general coincide with the native speaker's internalized grammar.

In this regard we must mention that *sorsik* forms with initial and final voiced stops corresponding to medial voiced stops are not the only pronunciations given in the language game. Other speakers of Cuna, called by Sherzer dialect B, pronounce the game forms for 'firewood', 'no', and 'see' as follows:

(22)

Cuna	*Sorsik*
sapan	*bansa*
sate	*desa*
dake	*geda*

In terms of the analysis for Cuna that we have proposed on internal grounds, these forms are not completely straightforward. If the URs of these words contain geminate stops, and if the *sorsik* rule is applied to representations resulting from the application of reduction, we should expect the pronunciations *pansa*, *tesa*, and *keda*, as the following derivations show:

(23) $/\#\text{sabban}\#/$ $/\#\text{sadde}\#/$ $/\#\text{dagge}\#/$

      sapan   *sate*   *dake*   Reduction

      pansa   *tesa*   *keda*   *Sorsik*

Such forms with initial voiceless stops would of course be completely anomalous in Cuna, since in normal (nondisguised) speech words never begin with a voiceless stop.

There are a number of possible interpretations for the forms in dialect B. One would be that the reduction rule plays no role in the derivation of the words with medial voiceless stops, that for these speakers the URs are $/\#\text{sapan}\#/$, $/\#\text{sate}\#/$, and $/\#\text{dake}\#/$. This analysis would differ from the one we have proposed only in that no connection would be made between the absence of word-initial voiceless stops and the absence of initial consonant clusters. These generalizations about the canonical shapes of Cuna morphemes would be described by two separate statements (or redundancy rules; see Chapter 10). The reduction rule would still be needed on morphophonemic grounds to get *neg-gine* $\longrightarrow$ *nekine* and so on. Forms like *sapan*, *sate*, and *dake* that show up with initial voiced stops in the *sorsik sunmakke* game are explained by saying that when a voiceless stop comes to stand in initial position (as the result of moving the first syllable to the end of the word in playing *sorsik sunmakke*) it is changed to the corresponding voiced stop. This change would be due to the constraint in the language that voiceless stops may not appear initially in a word.

However, this is not the only interpretation of dialect B that is possible. It could be maintained that these speakers also derive the forms *sapan*, *sate*, and *dake* from underlying forms /#sabban#/, /#sadde#/, and /#dagge#/, but that they apply the *sorsik sunmakke* rule after the reduction rule. The following derivation could then be posited.

(24)   /#sabban#/
              sapan   Reduction
              pansa   *Sorsik sunmakke* rule
              bansa   Initial voicing

The initial voicing process is, of course, the same rule required in the interpretation of dialect B given first. Further support for a process such as initial voicing might be found if Cuna speakers tend to pronounce foreign words or borrowings having initial p, t, and k with the corresponding voiced stops b, d, and g. We have no information in this connection, but this sort of behavior would be expected if initial voicing is postulated to account for a pronunciation like *bansa*.

Simply because some feature of an analysis reached on internal grounds fails to be revealed in corpus-external evidence, it does not necessarily follow that this feature is unjustified or "unreal". This point is of particular importance in the interpretation of an example like the following. Coupez (1969) reports on a language game called *kinshingelo*, which is practiced by speakers of the Bantu language Sanga. In *kinshingelo* the final two syllables of a word are permuted except for the prosodic features of length and tone, which retain their original position. (We follow Coupez' citations here in which length is indicated by a colon, acute and grave accents represent high and low pitch, an acute–grave sequence indicates a falling contour, and a grave–acute indicates a rising tone. These contour tones occur only on long vowels.)

(25) (a) /óbé múkwè꞉tù twá꞉yá꞉ kú múkólá/ $\longrightarrow$ /béó mútù꞉kwè yá꞉twá꞉ kú múlákó/
            '*Toi, mon compagnon, viens avec moi à la rivière!*' [p. 33]

(b) /bá꞉kólwè꞉ bà꞉dyá꞉ mátábá à꞉ nkà꞉mbò/ ——→ /bá꞉lwékò꞉ dyà꞉bá꞉ mábátá à꞉ mbò꞉nkà '*Les singes mangent les maïs de mon grandpère.* [p. 33]

(c) /bá꞉nábákàjì bà꞉ mú kó꞉ngò bà꞉tèmwá꞉ kúdímá/ ——→ /bá꞉mábájiká bá꞉[5] mú ngó꞉kò bà꞉mwàté꞉ kúmádí/ '*Les femmes congolaises aiment cultiver la terre.*' [p. 33]

Note that in (25a) *múkwè꞉tù* becomes *mútù꞉kwè*, where the length of the penultimate syllable and the shortness of the final syllable of the input are superimposed on the penultimate and final syllables of the output. The change of *twá꞉yá꞉* to *yá꞉twá꞉* in (25a) shows that tonal properties of the input retain their respective positions relative to one another in the output. Finally, in the change of *bá꞉kólwè꞉* to *bá꞉lwékò꞉* in (25b) we see a preservation of both length and tone.

This linguistic game is relevant to our present concern in that, as Coupez points out, the output of the *kishingelo* rule may violate a very general principle of Sanga sound structure, found in many other Bantu languages as well, according to which all vowels following a consonant plus glide cluster must be long. For instance, the transformation of *múkwè꞉tù* in (25a) to *mútù꞉kwè* produces such a violation, as does the change in (25b) of *bá꞉kólwè꞉* to *bá꞉lwékò꞉*. Clearly we cannot conclude on the basis of this external data that the rule lengthening a vowel after a consonant plus glide sequence is psychologically unreal. Rather, the correct interpretation is that, unlike in Cuna, the game rule in Sanga applies to the phonetic form of the utterance, after the lengthening rule has applied. Since the *kishingelo* rule is based on the phonetic form of the utterance, and since the length (and tone) of a vowel retains its original syllable position, violations of the lengthening rule may even be said to be expected.

The Sanga example reinforces a point made earlier in regard to the orthographic practices of the Soras. External linguistic behavior is sometimes based on the phonetic form of utterances, and very little can be concluded from such examples about the phonological structure of the language. On the other hand, linguistic behavior that presupposes more abstract representations, like the majority discussed in this chapter, can provide interesting insights into the native speaker's psychological interpretation of the sound structure of his language.

Historical changes in a language are frequently cited by phonologists in order to demonstrate the reality of a rule. Suppose that at a given point in the history of a language one is led to postulate a rule of the form X ——→ Y /____ Z on internal grounds. If, then, new instances of XZ clusters arise in the course of the language's historical development

---

[5] This may be a misprint for *bá꞉nábájikà bà꞉*.

and these are converted to YZ, the productivity and hence reality of the rule may be substantiated.

The work of Skousen (1975) on Finnish has contributed a number of examples of this type. One involves rules of stress assignment, which place primary stress on the first syllable of a word and assign secondary stress to successive odd-numbered syllables as long as they are not the final syllable of a word. Thus, *tálo* 'house' has stress on the first syllable, while *tálossàni* 'in my house' has a secondary stress on the third syllable.

Skousen cites a number of sources of external evidence for the reality of these rules. One has to do with the fact that many borrowed words are adjusted to the stress pattern called for by these rules. For example, the Swedish word *likör* 'liqueur' was borrowed into Finnish. In Swedish the stress is on the second syllable of the word, and stress causes a lengthening of a vowel so long as it is not followed by more than a single consonant. Hence the Swedish form is [likö:r]. When this word was borrowed into Finnish, the primary stress was shifted from the second to the first syllable to give *líkööri*. The assumption that there is a rule placing primary stress on the first syllable of a word in the internalized grammar of Finnish speakers explains the modification of the stress pattern in this word.

The reality of the stress rules can also be corroborated by certain sound changes that have occurred internal to the development of Finnish. One of these is a dialectal change that inserted a schwa between certain consonant clusters: *jalka* 'foot' > *jaləka*; *ilma* 'air' > *iləma*; *kylmä* 'cold' > *kyləmä*. In the Savo dialects this inserted vowel has become a full vowel taking on the quality of the preceding vowel: *jaləka* > *jalaka*; *iləma* > *ilima*; *kyləmä* > *kylymä*. The inessive form of *kylmä* appears as *kýlmässa* 'in cold' in dialects that have not undergone the vowel insertion. In this word there is only one stressed vowel (the first). But in the Savo dialects the form appears as *kýlymàssä*, with a secondary stress on the third vowel. Forms such as these testify to the productivity of the stress rules and thereby strengthen the claim that they constitute part of the Finnish speaker's internalized grammar.

Another example discussed by Skousen concerns a fairly old rule of gemination found in certain Finnish dialects. This rule lengthens a consonant when followed by a long vowel or diphthong and preceded by a short stressed syllable.

(26) $C \longrightarrow C : /CV\_\_\_V\ V$

Thus the form *téköö* 'he does' was changed to *tékköö* in these dialects. Skousen cites two pieces of evidence to demonstrate that this rule is still productive in these dialects. First, borrowings are readily modified by the rule. Swedish *polís* [poli:s] 'police' appears as *póliisi* in dialects without the rule, but as *pólliisi* in dialects that possess the gemination process. Second, some of these latter dialects have undergone a subsequent sound change whereby the sequence *Vns* has been converted into *V:s* by dropping the nasal and compensatorily lengthening the vowel. Since this change has produced new instances of long vowels, we might expect short consonants to be geminated before these new long vowels. This is indeed the case; a form like *väkensä* 'his people' in the standard language appears as *väkkees* in these dialects. The final vowel in these dialects has also been deleted. The historical development was *väkensä* ⟶ *väkens* ⟶ *väkees* ⟶ *väkkees*.

German will provide a final example of an argument for the productivity and hence psychological reality of a rule on the basis of linguistic change. In German a word-final schwa may be optionally deleted. If a voiced obstruent comes to stand in final position as a result of the loss of a schwa, it is automatically and obligatorily devoiced by the final-devoicing rule of German. All of the following citations are dative singulars:

(27)   'thief'   *Diebe*   [di:bə] ~ [di:p]
                'dog'   *Hunde*   [hundə] ~ [hunt]
                'day'   *Tage*   [tagə] ~ [tak]
        cf., 'blood'   *Blute*   [blu:tə] ~ [blu:t]
             'skirt'   *Rocke*   [ro:kə] ~ [ro:k]

This optional schwa-deletion process is a relatively recent rule of German, and the final-devoicing rule antedates it by centuries. Consequently, one may argue for the reality of final devoicing in German at the point where the schwa-deletion rule was added to the grammar. If there were no such final-devoicing rule in German, there would be no explanation for the automatic and obligatory devoicing of final *b*, *d*, and *g* to *p*, *t*, and *k*.

In the above examples we have seen how linguistic change can be employed to substantiate the psychological reality of a phonological rule. A linguistic change produces new instances of sound combinations that satisfy the input requirements to some rule; if these new combinations undergo the rule, this may be explained by the hypothesis that the rule constitutes part of the speaker's internalized grammar. It is important to realize that the opposite inference cannot in general be drawn with any confidence. That is, just because a new sound combination does not undergo a postulated rule, it does not necessarily follow that that rule is an artifact of the linguist's imagination. To make this point clear let us reconsider the example from German just discussed. Suppose, contrary to fact, that the obstruents that stand at the end of a word as a result of the dropping of the final schwa did not devoice, so that the word for 'day' would have forms like *tak* (nom. sg.), *tag-en* (dat. pl.), *tagə* ~ *tag* (nom. pl). The final-devoicing rule would still be motivated by the *tak*~*tag* alternations, and the correct surface forms could be produced by simply ordering final-devoicing before schwa dropping. Hence, if speakers of German happened to say *tagə* ~ *tag* instead of *tagə* ~ *tak*, nothing at all would follow about the reality or nonreality of the final-devoicing rule.

This is not to deny that linguistic change can be used to construct an argument for the unlikelihood of a postulated rule. It can, but it must be shown that a language changes in such a way as to make it difficult or impossible to maintain the reality of the rule. An interesting example of this type has been discussed by Hale (1973). In Proto-Polynesian a rule deleting final consonants was added to the grammar:

(28) $$C \longrightarrow \emptyset/\underline{\hspace{1cm}}\#$$

As a result of this rule all words in the various modern Polynesian languages came to end in vowels. There are numerous morphophonemic alternations showing the effects of this rule in the various daughter languages. For example, in Maori we find data like the following:

(29)

Verb	Passive	Gerundive	Gloss
awhi	*awhitia*	*awhitaŋa*	'embrace'
hopu	*hopukia*	*hopukaŋa*	'catch'
aru	*arumia*	*arumaŋa*	'follow'
tohu	*tohuŋia*	*tohuŋaŋa*	'point out'
mau	*mauria*	*mauraŋa*	'carry'
wero	*werohia*	*werohaŋa*	'stab'
patu	*patua*	*patuŋa*	'strike, kill'
kite	*kitea*	*kiteŋa*	'see, find'

If these forms constituted a representative sample of all the relevant data for a synchronic analysis of Maori, we would be led, on corpus-internal grounds, to postulate a synchronic description that essentially recapitulated the historical development. That is, we would analyze the passive suffix as being basically /-ia/ ~ /-a/ and the gerundive as /-aŋa/ ~ /-ŋa/. (The latter two alternants might be reduced to one, say /-ia/ and /-aŋa/, by postulating a vowel-deletion rule, but this point is not relevant to the following discussion). In addition, the *C*~∅ alternation would be described by setting up the consonant as basic and treating it as the final segment in the UR of the stem morphemes: /awhit-/, /hopuk-/, /arum-/, /tohuŋ-/, /maur-/, /weroh-/; versus /patu-/ and /kite-/. The zero alternants would then be produced by the consonant-deletion rule (28). That is to say, we would essentially be claiming that the Proto-Polynesian rule has remained as a phonological rule in the grammar of Maori.

This analysis for the above data is well motivated on corpus-internal grounds. If verb stems are not set up with underlying final consonants that delete by (28), but instead the consonants are analyzed as belonging to the suffix, there would be no way to predict which consonant will show up in the passive. Indeed, it would be necessary to set up a large number of unpredictable allomorphs for the passive suffix, such as /-tia/, /-kia/, and /-mia/. It would then be necessary to list which passive allomorph any given verb stem takes in the lexicon. In addition, under this lexical analysis it would be an accident that the gerundive suffix showed the same initial consonant as the passive suffix. Under this analysis there would be no connection between the stem *awhi-* taking the suffix *-tia* in the passive and *-taŋa* in the gerundive—both suffixes just happen to begin with the same consonant. Finally, such an analysis fails to hook up the $C \sim \emptyset$ alternation with the surface phonetic fact that no words end in consonants in Maori. These two facts would be separate; one could be true and the other not. In the phonological analysis, on the other hand, these two facts would be related: no words can end in a consonant in Maori because there is a phonological rule deleting word-final consonants.

The forms given above, we may reasonably assume, constitute a representative sample of all the relevant data at the point when the final-consonant-deletion rule entered the grammar of Proto-Polynesian. The importance of Hale's work is to point out a number of subsequent linguistic changes in the development of Maori (paralleled by analogous changes in other Polynesian languages) that strongly suggest that the phonological analysis of the above data is not correct for present-day Maori. At some point in the development of Maori from Proto-Polynesian the consonants that alternate with zero were reanalyzed as belonging to the suffix rather than to the preceding stems. As Hale observes, if the alternating consonant has been reanalyzed as part of the suffix, leading to a proliferation of suffixal allomorphs, one might expect a tendency to regularize the alternation by identifying one of the alternants as the regular one. "This explanation is fulfilled in Maori—the alternant /-tia/ is now regarded as the regular passive ending [Hale 1973: 417]." Hale cites six pieces of evidence supporting this interpretation. First, nominal stems used verbally in spontaneous discourse take /-tia/ in the passive. Second, derived causatives form their passive in /-tia/ even though the basic stem may take a different alternant in the noncausative. Third, certain adverbials agree in voice with the verbs they modify; these adverbials suffix /-tia/ when the verb is passive regardless of the passive ending the verb itself takes. Fourth, English loanwords, even unassimilated consonant-final ones, form their passives in /-tia/. Fifth, compound verbs formed by the incorporation of an adverbial phrase regularly form their passive in /-tia/. Sixth, /-tia/ can be used when the conventional passive suffix for a given verb is not remembered.

These six facts are very difficult to explain under the phonological analysis. Why should all verb stems in the passive regularly replace their final consonant by *t* in derived causatives? And why should the same *t* appear regularly in each of the five other cases mentioned by Hale? Under the phonological analysis these facts are completely anomalous. However, under the lexical analysis, according to which the child learning Maori must memorize a separate passive allomorph for each verb stem, these facts find a ready interpretation: the simplifying tendency for one allomorph to be generalized as the regular ending. Evidently, then, any phonologist in possession of the full range of data would be forced to provide a lexical analysis for Maori. (Hale points out that a lexical analysis for these data is characteristically found in most traditional grammars of the Polynesian languages.)

The real problem presented by this example is to explain why, once the final-consonant-deletion rule entered the grammar of Proto-Polynesian, it was later lost, yielding the present situation in Maori (as well as most of the other modern Polynesian languages). For at the point where this rule was added we would have a set of alternations for which a phonological analysis would seem to be strongly motivated on internal grounds, in particular by the principle of phonological predictability. Why, then, was the phonological solution not maintained? Hale offers a possible explanation along the following lines. Once the final-consonant-deletion rule was added to the grammar, the overwhelming fact confronting the language learner was that all words ended in vowels phonetically. Hale suggests that in language acquisition there is a tendency to analyze linguistic forms in such a way as to minimize the need to set up URs that violate universally true generalizations about the syllable shapes of surface phonetic forms. Since all words ended in vowels, this would force a tendency to set up URs with final vowels, thereby leading to a reanalysis of the consonant alternating with zero as being part of the suffix instead of as part of the stem.

Note that Hale's principle is formulated as a tendency rather than an absolute condition. This is because there is no way at present to determine whether or not a phonological (as opposed to a lexical) analysis will be given to an alternation like that of Proto-Polynesian. Perhaps we will never be able to predict, in any specific instance of this type, whether or not the next few generations of language learners will reanalyze the data in the manner that the speakers of Maori have done. It may be that the choice between continuing the phonological analysis and reanalyzing the data lexically is free to some extent. However, if the situation has remained stable in such cases, with no detectable tendency for reanalysis, for a relatively long period of time, one might argue that the phonological analysis is still in force.

In any case, Hale's example shows the need to develop additional sources of external evidence, if the linguist is to be warranted in claiming psychological reality for his analyses, be they phonological or lexical.

To summarize, generative phonologists have accepted the position that a phonological description is, simultaneously, both a description of the sound structure of a language and a description of the linguistic knowledge a native speaker has about the pronunciation of the sentences of his language. Until quite recently such descriptions were arrived at almost entirely by corpus-internal analysis. However, it would not be unreasonable to have some doubts about the psychological reality of such analyses, for they presuppose that native speakers have constructed their internalized grammars along parallel lines. Thus, in order to reasonably maintain that such analyses reflect the linguistic competence of native speakers, they must be bolstered by evidence from a different, external source.

Despite the critical nature of this issue it is only rather recently that generative phonologists have begun seriously to consider the importance of external sources of evidence. Part of the reason for this is historical. Generative phonology arose within the context of American structural linguistics, where the primary goal was to develop a set of procedures for analyzing a corpus of utterances, with very little regard for whether the resulting analysis in any way reflected the knowledge of the native speaker. In fact many linguists of the structuralist period claimed that the knowledge of the native speaker was irrelevant to linguistics. With the advent of generative grammar the empirical object of linguistic analysis radically changed: Instead of simply abstracting out surface sound patterns in the utterances composing the corpus, the linguist was to characterize the linguistic knowledge of the native speaker. But despite this drastic change in outlook, the general methodology of linguistic analysis, especially in phonology, remained much the same: discovering sound patterns in the potentially unlimited number of sentences composing the corpus. This enterprise was based on the working assumption, not unreasonable in the very early stages of generative grammar, that the child learning his language abstracted the same kinds of sound patterns in the construction of his internalized grammar. However, as long as the goal remained simply the discovery of sound patterns in the corpus, the resulting analyses became quite abstract (see the next chapter). This has naturally led many generative phonologists to question the working assumption that the kinds of corpus-internal principles discussed in the first part of this chapter parallel the principles the child follows in constructing his internalized grammar.

At the present time it is simply too early for us to be able to assert this working assumption with much confidence. One can only hope that as the various sources of external evidence are studied further, we will one day be able to delimit the general range of phonological analyses that are within the grasp of the native speaker. If a sufficient number of convincing cases can be accumulated validating the corpus-internal procedures, we can reasonably claim psychological reality for analyses of languages where no such external evidence is available.

Exercises

1. Hindi (Bhatia and Kenstowicz 1972).
   a. What are the two possible treatments of the ə ~ ∅ alternation?

Nom. sg.	Oblique pl.	Agentive	Gloss
kəmər	kəmrō:	kəmərne:	'waist'
kusum	kusumō:	kusumne:	'flower'
pəthik	pəthikō:	pəthikne:	'wayfarer'
səbək	səbkō:	səbəkne:	'lesson'
ke:sər	ke:srō:	ke:sərne:	'saffron'
ka:rək	ka:rkō:	ka:rəkne:	'case'
su:rət	su:rtō:	su:rətne:	'shape'

b. How do the following data bear on the choice in a?

qətl	qətlō:	qətlne:	'murder'
swərg	swərgō:	swərgne:	'heaven'
kəṣṭ	kəṣṭō:	kəṣṭne:	'trouble'
fikr	fikrō:	fikrne:	'worry'

c. Adjust your rule to accommodate the following.

pustək	pustəkō:	pustəkne:	'book'
ki:rtən	ki:rtənō:	ki:rtənne:	'song'
əkšər	əkšərō:	əkšərne:	'letter'
tiləsm	tiləsmō:	tiləsmne:	'magic'
surəŋg	surəŋgō:	surəŋgne:	'tunnel'
dərəxt	dərəxtō:	dərəxtne:	'tree'

d. Some of the following verbs also exhibit the ə ~ ∅ alternation. A controversial aspect of Hindi phonology is whether aspirated consonants (transcribed here as Ch) should be treated as clusters of stop + *h* or as single segments that are [+ aspirated]. Do the data below bear on this issue?

Stem	Infin.	Past	Gloss
nikəl	nikəlna	nikla	'come out'
pəkər	pəkərna	pəkṛa	'catch'
nisəns	nisənsna	nisənsa	'breathe'
səmərp	səmərpna	səmərpa	'give'
suləjh	suləjhna	suljha	'solve'
ukhər	ukhərna	ukhṛa	'be uprooted'
uchəl	uchəlna	uchla	'jump'
sihər	sihərna	sihra	'feel frigid'

e. Hindi has the following nasals phonetically: *m, n, ṇ, ŋ,* and *ɲ*. However, the latter three only appear before homorganic consonants. Furthermore, *m* and *n* are usually homorganic to a following consonant as well. The only exceptions are those occurring in words like the last three below. How might the nasal consonants be treated in Hindi?

əŋken	əŋkənō:	əŋkənne:	'mark'
pəlaŋg	pəlaŋgō:	pəlaŋgne:	'bed'
əɲcəl	əɲcəlō:	əɲcəlne:	'region'
əɲjən	əɲjənō:	əɲjənne:	'salve'
khəṇḍ	khəṇḍō:	khəṇḍne:	'part'
cəṇṭ	cəṇṭō:	cəṇṭne:	'clever'
sənək	sənkō:	sənəkne:	'craze'
kəmər	kəmrō:	kəmərne:	'waist'
cəmək	cəmka	cəməkna	'shine' (verb)

f. The following data present difficulties for the rule responsible for the *ə* ~ ∅ alternation. These data can be handled by simply embellishing the rule. However, an alternative is suggested by the following distributional facts of Hindi phonetics. First, while there is a contrast between long and short oral vowels, all nasal vowels are long. Second, within a morpheme long oral vowels do not generally appear before a cluster of nasal plus consonant. Only short oral vowels may occur here. Finally, nasal vowels do not appear before nasal consonants.

ã:gən	ã:gənō:	ã:gənne:	'courtyard'
ã:cəl	ã:cəlō:	ã:cəlne:	'corner'
ĩ:dhən	ĩ:dhənō:	ĩ:dhənne:	'fuel'
bhã:jək	bhã:jəkō:	bhã:jəkne:	'reopener'
sã:bhər	sã:bhərō:	sã:bhərne:	'refreshment'

g. Do the following data bear on the two possible analyses in f? How?

Nom. sg.	Adjectival	Agentive	Gloss
ma:nəs	ma:nsi:	ma:nəsne:	'mind'
ki:mət	ki:mti:	ki:mətne:	'price'
da:nəv	da:nvi:	da:nəvne:	'demon'
ka:nən	ka:nni:	ka:nənne:	'garden'
la:nət	la:nti:	la:nətne:	'blame'
na:nək	na:nki:	na:nəkne:	personal name

2. Bizcayan (Western Basque, de Rijk 1970). The indefinite, formed with the numeral *bat* 'one', is spoken as a closely knit phrase. Account for the alternations in the data.

If you have the correct analysis your rules will straightforwardly account for the discrepancy between the orthographic and the phonetic form of the vowels in the following words: *igaz* [iges] 'last year', *kipula* [kipule] 'onion', *ia* [iye] 'almost', *biar* [biyer] 'tomorrow', *beatz* [biac] 'toe', *bear* [biar] 'task'. Some speakers of this dialect say *semie, atie*, and *astue* instead of *semia, atia*, and *astua*. How can this be described in terms of your analysis?

Indefinite	Definite	Gloss
sagar bat	*sagara*	'apple'
gisom bat	*gisona*	'man'
buztem bat	*buztena*	'tail'
belaum bet	*belaune*	'knee'
čakur bet	*čakure*	'dog'
agim bet	*agine*	'tooth'
mutil bet	*mutile*	'boy'
alaba bat	*alabea*	'daughter'
neska bat	*neskea*	'girl'
gona bat	*gonea*	'skirt'
erri bet	*erriye*	'village'
ari bet	*ariye*	'thread'
buru bet	*buruwe*	'head'
iku bet	*ikuwe*	'fig'
seme bat	*semia*	'son'
ate bat	*atia*	'door'
asto bat	*astua*	'donkey'

3. Kekchi (Campbell 1975). These data are from the Coban dialect of Kekchi, a Mayan language of the Quichean subgroup in Guatemala.

a. How does the existence of forms such as *tu:l* 'witch', *pa:r* 'skunk', *cu:m* 'skin', *če:k* 'ripe' bear on the analysis of the alternation in vowel length below? (Note: this alternation is limited to word-final syllables.)

š-kʷar	'he slept'	*kʷa:r-k*	'to sleep'
š-aw	'he planted'	*a:w-k*	'to plant'
š-bay	'he was late'	*ba:y-k*	'to be late'
š-tam	'he joined'	*ta:m-k*	'to join'

b. In the following data the suffixes alternate unpredictably between *-Vk* and *-V:nk*. Formulate a rule to account for the alternation in stem shape.

kab	'house'	*kabl-ak*	'to make a house'
cax	'dirty'	*caxn-ok*	'to get dirty'
tiq	'hot'	*tiqkʷ-al*	'its hotness'
qes	'sharp'	*qesn-a:nk*	'to sharpen'
nax	'far'	*naxt-i:nk*	'to go far'
pox	'puss'	*poxkʷ-e:nk*	'to become infected'

c. According to Campbell the V ~ ∅ alternation in the stems of *ox* 'cough', *oxob-ak* 'to cough'; *tel* 'arm', *teleb-a:nk* 'to reach'; and *lek* 'spoon', *lekem-ak* 'to spoon out' arise from a rule inserting a copy of the root vowel between a consonant and a stem-final labial. How must this rule be ordered with those of (a) and (b)?. Campbell attempts to provide external support for this analysis by appeal to the behavior of such words in a speech disguise known as *Jerizgona*. Examine the following data and formulate the speech disguise rule. Precisely in what way do these data bear on the validity of the vowel copying process in Kekchi? How successful is Campbell's appeal to the *Jerizgona* data in support of the vowel copying process?

Kekchi		*Jerizgona*
koxob-a:nk	'to begin'	*kopoxbapa:nk/kopoxopobapa:nk*
ačab-a:nk	'to loosen'	*apačbapa:nk/apačapabapa:nk*
kulub-a:nk	'to accept'	*kupulbapa:nk/kupulupubapa:nk*
oxob-ak	'to cough'	*opoxbapak/opoxopobapak*
teleb-a:nk	'to reach'	*tepelbapa:nk/tepelepebapa:nk*

6

The Problem of Abstractness

As we have seen from previous chapters, the generative model distinguishes between systematic and idiosyncratic features of pronunciation in terms of an (ordered) set of rules that takes an underlying representation (UR), consisting of idiosyncratic, unpredictable aspects of pronunciation, and assigns to that representation all the systematic features of pronunciation. The result is a phonetic representation (PR), which includes all grammatically determined aspects of pronunciation (as opposed to aspects of pronunciation determined by physiology, for instance). Within this approach, the question naturally arises as to whether there adhere in the nature of language any constraints on the degree to which the UR of a morpheme may deviate from its associated PRs. The greater the deviation—in a sense which we will explicate in this chapter—the greater the abstractness of the UR.

Given that the linguist is attempting to formulate a grammar that represents the internalized knowledge of the native speaker, it follows that the tasks of the language learner and of the linguist resemble one another in important respects. Both are presented with a set of phonetic representations from which the distinction between systematic and idiosyncratic features must be drawn. The problem confronting the linguist is to determine what principles are to be followed in making this distinction—that is, what are the principles that the language learner utilizes in arriving at an analysis of phonetic representations? How does he decide what is to be taken as basic and what is derived? How does he choose an underlying representation and a set of rules to account for morphophonemic alternations?

In this chapter we discuss some of the important issues that revolve around the fundamental problem of the nature and choice of underlying representations. Our discussion will be quite inconclusive, reflecting the many uncertainties that the problem of "abstractness" of underlying representations engenders.

In the first section of this chapter we try to make clear exactly what is being claimed when it is said that the various phonetic realizations of a morpheme are derived from a single underlying representation. Having seen the motivation for an underlying representation, we then take up the question of the degree to which it may diverge from the PR. This issue has been approached in two different ways in the literature. First, there are writers who propose constraints for the selection of the most appropriate UR on the basis of criterial properties of its associated PRs. Within this approach one can distinguish varying degrees of divergence permitted between the UR and PR. A convenient midpoint is whether or not the UR may contain sounds which do not appear in some associated PR. In the second and third sections we examine various cases that lie on either side of this midpoint. Finally, there are writers who approach the problem of abstractness by developing constraints on the form phonological rules may assume in mapping URs into PRs. Given these constraints, only certain kinds of rules are permitted, and hence only certain kinds of URs. In the final two sections we examine a couple of the more influential constraints of this nature.

The Morpheme Alternant Theory

As we have seen, the generative model proposes to account for all systematic aspects of the pronunciation of a morpheme by letting an ordered set of rules assign such properties in the derivation of the UR. Those features which are idiosyncratic to the morpheme are listed in its lexical representation and hence appear in the UR via lexical insertion. If the morpheme happens to appear in a context which calls for the application of no phonological rules, then the PR of the morpheme in such a context is identical to the UR.

To better appreciate what is involved in the claim that the PR is derived from the UR by a set of rules, we will contrast this position with an alternative approach which we shall label the morpheme alternant theory.[1]

According to this theory, all alternants of a morpheme are to be listed in the lexicon and a set of rules is given for choosing the correct alternant for each given context in which the morpheme appears. On this view one alternant is not derived from another. Rather, the rules of selection directly state the context in which each alternant may occur. In particular, then, there is no notion of an underlying form from which all surface alternants are derived.

Although we have stated the morpheme alternant approach very imprecisely, the following example will clarify the basics of this method for dealing with alternations. Recall the alternation of the plural suffix in English. It appears as *-ɨz* after sibilants (*buses*, *brushes*, etc.), *-s* after voiceless nonsibilants (*cats*, *maps*, etc.), and as *-z* after voiced nonsibilants (*bags*, *boys*, *sofas*, etc.). Given the morpheme alternant approach, each of the alternants *-ɨz*, *-s*, and *-z* would be listed in the lexical representation of the plural suffix in the lexicon. The following rules of selection would be associated with this lexical representation to choose the correct alternant for each given noun stem.

(1)   a. *Choose -ɨz if the stem ends in a sibilant.*
      b. *Choose -s if the stem ends in a voiceless nonsibilant.*
      c. *Choose -z if the stem ends in a voiced nonsibilant.*

Note that on this approach each alternant is derived directly. No alternant is derived from any other alternant. The basic claim is thus that all alternants are on a par with one another.

The morpheme alternant approach attains an air of plausibility in this case because it is not clear which alternant is the most appropriate UR. There is a vast literature on this particular aspect of English phonology in which each of the three different alternants has been defended as basic by some linguist. The morpheme alternant theory simply avoids the issue. Since one alternant is not derived from another, the problem of which alternant is underlying does not arise. But it is precisely for this reason

---

[1] One or another version of this theory represents the basic approach to morphophonemics taken by American structuralists of the 1940s and 50s. In an important paper, Wells (1949) compares this approach with the earlier one of Sapir and Bloomfield, both of whom utilized hypothetical underlying forms to account for morpheme alternation. Bloomfield made explicit use of rule ordering as well. For further discussion, see Kenstowicz (1975).

that the morpheme alternant theory cannot be accepted as an adequate approach to phonological alternations. There are many cases in which it is quite clear that one alternant is more basic than another. Consider the following simple example from Lithuanian. In this language there are no long (geminate) consonants phonetically. If one looks at the language from the point of view of standard generative phonology, one would say that whenever a cluster of like consonants arises across morpheme boundaries degemination occurs. For purposes of the present discussion, we will assume that it is the first consonant of the cluster that deletes. As a result of this degemination process, a morpheme like /kas/ has the alternant /ka/ when followed by the future suffix /-s/ (cf., *suk-ti* 'to turn', *suk-s* 'he will turn').

(2)   *kas-ti* 'to dig'   *kas-u* 'I dig'
        kas-ki 'dig!'   *kas-i* 'you dig'
        ka-s   'he will dig'   *kas-a* 'he digs'

If we were to try to use the morpheme alternant approach to describe this alternation, the alternants /kas/ and /ka/ would both be entered in the lexical representation for 'dig' and the following rules of selection would accompany the lexical representation.

(3)   a. *Choose the alternant* /ka/ *when a morpheme follows that begins with* /s/.

        b. *Choose the alternant* /kas/ *when a morpheme follows that begins with a vowel or any consonant other than* /s/.

Since each alternant is treated as being on a par with every other one, this theory claims that there are two principles of Lithuanian phonology operating here: the use of an alternant lacking a final /s/ when /s/ follows and the use of an alternant with final /s/ when a vowel or consonant other than /s/ follows. But this is clearly absurd. The rule that /ka/ rather than /kas/ is used when a morpheme follows that begins with /s/ can be regarded as a reflection of the general constraint that two identical consonants cannot appear next to one another in Lithuanian phonetic representations. But the rule that /kas/ is chosen in the environment before vowels and consonants other than /s/ does not reflect a rule of the language. Rather, the appearance of the /s/ in these contexts is an arbitrary property of the particular morpheme 'dig'.

Practitioners of the morpheme alternant approach were of course cognizant of the fact that whereas the /ka/ alternant in the above example is the consequence somehow of the environment, the /kas/ alternant is not. In order to account for this difference, descriptions written within the morpheme alternant framework consistently replace rules of selection such as (3) with rules like (4).

(4)   a. *Choose the /ka/ alternant when a morpheme follows that begins with /s/.*
      b. *Choose the /kas/ alternant elsewhere.*

This approach says that /kas/ is used in all cases except where the /ka/ alternant is chosen. In essence, it says that the /kas/ alternant is somehow the norm, chosen without regard for context; /ka/ is a special case, selected by the environment in which the morpheme 'dig' appears.

The introduction of the notion "elsewhere" into the rules of selection renders the morpheme alternant theory largely indistinguishable (in the simplest cases) from the theory that derives alternants from a single underlying representation. For now there is a strict isomorphism between the two approaches. A rule of selection such as (4a), which chooses a particular phonetic form on the basis of the phonetic context, is comparable to a rule that modifies an UR in a particular phonetic context. The alternant that represents the "elsewhere" case is comparable to the UR (recall that phonological properties of the UR of a morpheme will be realized phonetically in all cases except where a phonological rule applies to alter the UR).

Despite the similarity between the morpheme alternant approach (as supplemented by the notion "elsewhere") and the generative approach, which utilizes a single underlying representation to account for cases of rule-governed morpheme alternation, there are significant differences. To get at some of these differences, let us begin by noting a rather obvious inadequacy of the rules of selection discussed above. Recall that these rules of selection were regarded as rules about individual morphemes. Thus (4) states when /ka/ is used as opposed to /kas/. But clearly there are situations where a large number of morphemes obey what would appear to be the same rules of selection. Consider the following example from Kinyarwanda, a Bantu language spoken in Rwanda and parts of Uganda.

In (5) we give a number of verbal forms involving the root 'cut'.

(5)   *tema*   'cut!'
          nhemera   'cut for me!'
          mutemera   'cut for him!'
          batemera   'cut for them!'

The root 'cut' ordinarily appears in the shape /tem/, but after a prefix consisting of a nasal consonant the root assumes the shape /hem/. (In some dialects, /tʰem/ may be heard rather than /hem/; the present discussion describes the speech of our consultant.) The following rule of selection might account for this alternation within the morpheme alternant approach.

(6)   a. *Choose the alternant* /hem/ *after a nasal consonant.*
      b. *Choose the alternant* /tem/ *elsewhere.*

A rule of selection like (6) is clearly inadequate. All morphemes that begin with the sound /t/ have an alternant beginning with /h/ when a nasal precedes. Thus examples like those in (7) are common.

(7)   *tuma*   'send!'   *nhuma*   'send me!'
          teeka   'cook!'   *nheekera*   'cook for me!'
          tegereza 'wait!'   *nhegereza* 'wait for me!'

    The morpheme alternant approach requires that we list in the lexicon both alternants (/tum/ and /hum/, /teek/ and /heek/, and so on). However, it is apparent that there should be just one rule of selection covering all these alternations, rather than separate rules for each example. How might such a general rule be formulated? A rule like (8) will express the generalization.

(8)   *If a morpheme has two alternants, one beginning with /t/ and the other beginning with /h/, use the alternant with /h/ after a nasal consonant and use the other alternant elsewhere.*

Given a rule such as (8), it would no longer be necessary to have a rule of selection for each morpheme exhibiting the *t ~ h* alternation. One rule would cover all such examples.

    There is an important sense in which rule (8) fails to adequately characterize the knowledge of a native speaker of Kinyarwanda. Notice that rule (8) says that *if* a morpheme has two alternants, one beginning with /t/ and the other with /h/, then the /h/ alternant will be used after a nasal. Rule (8) in no way predicts *which* morphemes will exhibit this alternation. Rule (8) does not exclude the possibility that there might be many morphemes which have a pronunciation beginning with /t/ in all environments. But this represents a significant failure; in Kinyarwanda, there are no verb roots beginning with /t/ that do not have an alternant with /h/ after a nasal. The generative approach to these data would be to say that the roots 'cut', 'send', 'cook', and 'wait' are underlyingly /tem/,

/tum/, /teek/, and /tegerez/, and that there is a rule that replaces /t/ by /h/ after a nasal. The existence of such a rule in the grammar will account for the fact that *all* roots with an initial /t/ have an alternant with /h/ after a nasal. The rule that converts /t/ to /h/ *predicts* this situation. Rule (8) does not make such a prediction. Thus the generative approach, with its use of underlying representations and associated morphophonemic rules, appears to better represent a native speaker's knowledge of his language than does the morpheme alternant approach.

The following example from the Dravidian language Pengo (Burrow 1970) provides some additional difficulties for the morpheme alternant approach. Viewed from the generative point of view, this language would be said to have a rule that neutralizes the opposition between voiced and voiceless obstruents: the rule in question assimilates the voicing of an obstruent to the voicing of a following obstruent. (9) illustrates the effects of this voicing assimilation rule.

(9)	2 sg. imperative	3 sg. past	Gerund	Gloss
	tu:b-a	*tu:p-t-an*	*tu:b-ji*	'blow'
	tog-a	*tok-t-an*	*tog-ji*	'step on'
	ṛa:k-a	*ṛa:k-t-an*	*ṛa:g-ji*	'offer worship'
	hi:p-a	*hi:p-t-an*	*hi:b-ji*	'sweep'

In the generative approach the voicing alternation would be described by taking the alternants appearing before vowels as underlying and deriving the stem alternants appearing in the 3 sg. past and gerund by a rule of voicing assimilation. How would the morpheme alternant theory handle these data? Both alternants (/tu:b/ and /tu:p/, /hi:p/ and /hi:b/, and so on) would be entered in the lexicon. The following rule of selection would account for the 3 sg. past and the gerund forms:

(10)   *If a morpheme has two alternants, one ending in a voiced obstruent and the other in a voiceless obstruent, choose the former alternant before suffixes beginning with a voiced obstruent and choose the latter alternant before suffixes beginning with a voiceless obstruent.*

Obviously, this rule of selection is very similar to the rule of voicing assimilation that the generative approach would postulate. Once again, however, this approach is inadequate because it fails to capture the significant generalization that there are no morphemes ending in an obstruent that fail to alternate when they appear in the relevant environment.

Let us turn now to the derivation of the 2 sg. imperative forms in (9). The rule of selection in (10) determines which alternant is to be used before a suffix beginning with an obstruent; it does not specify which alternant is to be used before a vowel-initial suffix. It should be obvious that there is no general rule of selection involved here. In the case of 'blow' and 'step on', the alternant ending in a voiced obstruent is used; but in the case of 'offer worship' and 'sweep', the alternant ending in a voiceless obstruent is used. Consequently, a separate selection rule will be required for each stem in the language that exhibits the voicing alternation. For the morpheme 'blow' we would need to incorporate a selection "rule" that chooses the alternant /tu:b/ before vowels, while 'sweep' would require a rule selecting /hi:p/. But clearly the appearance of a voiced versus a voiceless obstruent before a vowel is not a principle of Pengo phonology. Rather, these are idiosyncratic features of each particular morpheme. Treating them by the same device (a selection rule) as that used to select the systematic feature of voice before an obstruent is a category-mistake.

In the generative model which explicitly recognizes an underlying form, the correct distinctions are made. Predictable features of pronunciation, such as the voicing of an obstruent before another obstruent, are assigned by rule, while unpredictable features are listed in the lexicon and incorporated into the UR. The alternant that appears when no rules have applied (the prevocalic alternant in the Pengo example) is the UR—the basic alternant.

As pointed out by Wells (1949), cases of reciprocal alternation pose a serious challenge to the morpheme alternant theory. These situations involve a pair of morphemes exhibiting alternations where the choice of a particular alternant for one morpheme materially depends on the choice of a particular alternant for the other (usually adjacent) morpheme. For example, recall the alternation in the past tense of Russian verbs discussed in Chapter 3.

(11)

Stem	Masc. past	Fem. past	Neuter past	Gloss
/pisa/	*pisa-l*	*pisa-l-a*	*pisa-l-o*	'write'
/nes/	*nes*	*nes-l-a*	*nes-l-o*	'carry'
/met/	*me-l*	*me-l-a*	*me-l-o*	'sweep'
/ved/	*ve-l*	*ve-l-a*	*ve-l-o*	'lead'

The past tense suffix /-1/ has the alternant Ø when word final and preceded by a consonant, while stems ending in a dental stop have alternants
without a dental stop in the past tense. The selection rule stated as (12)
below will not be sufficient to guarantee the correct choice for the past
tense suffix.

(12)   *Choose the Ø alternant of the past tense morpheme when word-
        final and preceded by a consonant; otherwise choose the /-l/
        alternant.*

This rule will produce the correct results when the final consonant of the
preceding verb stem does not alternate with Ø, as in *nes*. But for stems
that show the dental-stop/zero alternation (12), as stated, is not sufficient.
In order to derive the forms *me-l* and *ve-l*, it must be insured that it is the
/me/ and /ve/ alternants that are used for conditioning the past tense
selection and not the consonant-final alternants /met/ and /ved/. This
might be accomplished by imposing an order on the selection rules to
insure that the stem shapes /ve/ and /me/ are first selected, and only
then spelling out the correct alternant for the past tense suffix. In order for
this to work, however, the rule selecting the /ve/ and /me/ alternants
could not take the following form: *Select the stem alternant without a
final dental stop before the past tense suffix /-l/.* This formulation is
insufficient because it presupposes that the choice between the /-l/ and Ø
alternants has already been resolved. Instead, the rule would have to be
expressed as follows: *Select the alternant without a final dental stop if the
verb is in the past tense.* Note that this formulation capitalizes on the fact
that the following morpheme has a special grammatical status as a marker
of tense; it refers to this grammatical information directly, without regard
to the phonetic shape (-*l* or Ø) of the suffix. (See Chapter 10 for discussion.)
    The morpheme alternant approach can account for the Russian data,
but it does so by introducing ordering statements—and by so doing it
moves closer to the generative approach. Furthermore, the ordering solution for the Russian data works only because it is possible to view the
selection of the /me/ and /ve/ alternants as being independent of the
particular past tense alternant chosen. In other words, for the ordering
solution to work it must be the case that the first selection rule applied is
not sensitive to the phonological make-up of the morpheme introduced by
the second selection rule. Unfortunately for the morpheme alternant
theory, such situations do arise.
    Recall the rules of vowel shortening and vowel harmony in Yawel-

mani discussed in Chapter 4. A root such as /do:s/ 'report' has a short-vowelled alternant /dos/ when preceding a consonant (due to the principle that a long vowel may not precede two consonants). This means that one must introduce the phonological shape of the suffix before one can determine correctly the alternant of the root that should be used. But recall that a suffix such as /k'a/, imperative, has an alternant /k'o/ after roots with an /o/ vowel. Thus it appears that one must introduce the phonological shape of a root before one can determine correctly the pronunciation of the suffix. Consequently, we have a problem in accounting for the pronunciation of a word such as *dos-k'o* 'report (imper.)'. We cannot choose an alternant for the root until we have chosen an alternant for the suffix, but we cannot choose an alternant for the suffix until we have chosen an alternant for the root.

In order to escape the difficulties imposed by the previous example, one might try to take advantage of the fact that the /dos/ alternant would be required by either /k'a/ or /k'o/, and the /k'o/ alternant would be required by either /do:s/ or /dos/. In other words, it is the initial consonant of the imperative suffix that is relevant to the choice of a short vowel in the root, and it is the /o/-quality of the root vowel that is relevant to the choice of /o/ in the imperative suffix. Furthermore, neither the consonant of the suffix nor the /o/ quality of the root vowel actually alternate. The above observations permit the following sort of analysis within the morpheme alternant framework.

Let us suppose that the lexical representation of the verb 'report' and the imperative suffix are as in (13).

(13)   /do $\left\{ \begin{matrix} : \\ \emptyset \end{matrix} \right\}$ s/ 'report'   k' $\left\{ \begin{matrix} a \\ o \end{matrix} \right\}$ imperative

The first step in constructing the pronunciation of the imperative of 'report' will be to combine these two representations into a single representation like (14).

(14)   / #do $\left\{ \begin{matrix} : \\ \emptyset \end{matrix} \right\}$ s + k' $\left\{ \begin{matrix} a \\ o \end{matrix} \right\}$ #/

Two rules of selection will apply to this representation. One will say that $\emptyset$ (i.e., shortness) will be chosen rather than : (i.e., length) when two successive consonants follow. The other will say that *o* rather than *a* will be used after /o/-quality vowels. This version of the morpheme alternant theory has the virtue that it no longer treats the different alternants of a morpheme as being totally unrelated in structure. Representations such as those in (13) recognize that there are certain constant features of the morphemes 'report' and the imperative suffix, as well as certain alternating features.

The above revision of the morpheme alternant theory moves it much closer to the generative approach, which utilizes a single underlying representation. Nonalternating parts of morpheme alternants have a single representation in (13); only the alternating parts have a multiple representation. It should be noted, however, that this revision of the morpheme alternant theory does not alter the fact that this theory does not predict in any way *whether* a morpheme will exhibit alternation. Thus it fails to satisfactorily account for situations where all morphemes of a particular structure exhibit alternation.

Representations such as (13) would still require ordered selection rules. For instance, the form *me-l* in Russian would derive from the representation in (15).

(15)
$$/ \# \text{me} \begin{Bmatrix} t \\ \emptyset \end{Bmatrix} + \begin{Bmatrix} l \\ \emptyset \end{Bmatrix} \# /$$

It would still be necessary to select the alternant /me-/ before determining whether to choose the /-1/ or $\emptyset$ form of the past suffix.

Notice that in the Russian example the suffixal alternant /-l/ is chosen on the basis of the stem alternant that actually appears together with the suffix in phonetic representation (/me-/) rather than on the basis of the other stem alternant (/met-/). There are, however, many examples in which the choice of a given alternant for morpheme A materially depends on an alternant for an adjacent morpheme B where the latter alternant is not, in fact, used in conjunction with morpheme A. The following example should make this observation clearer.

In many dialects of English, dental stops are deleted after a nasal when the plural suffix follows. Nevertheless, the choice of the plural allomorph depends on the deleted dental stop. The data in (16) illustrate the problem.

(16)

	Sg.	Pl.
	plant	*plan*-[s]
	hand	*han*-[z]
	plan	*plan*-[z]

A form such as *plant* has the two alternants /plant/ and /plan/ whose distribution could be specified easily enough by a selection rule (e.g., use the alternant without the final /t/ before the plural suffix, elsewhere use the alternant with final /t/). The problem is with the selection rule for the plural alternant. In order to explain why the plural of *plant* takes the voiceless fricative /s/, while the plural of *plan* takes the voiced alternant /z/, the selection rule for the plural suffix must clearly be sensitive to the alternants /plant/ and /plan/, respectively.

Under the revised morpheme alternant theory, the representations for the noun *plant* and the plural suffix would be as in (17).

(17) $$/\text{plan} \begin{Bmatrix} t \\ \emptyset \end{Bmatrix} / \quad \text{`plant'} \quad /\text{-} \begin{Bmatrix} \text{iz} \\ \text{s} \\ \text{z} \end{Bmatrix} / \quad \text{plural}$$

The representation of the plural noun *plants* would then be as in (18).

(18) $$/ \#\text{plan} \begin{Bmatrix} t \\ \emptyset \end{Bmatrix} + \begin{Bmatrix} \text{iz} \\ \text{s} \\ \text{z} \end{Bmatrix} \# /$$

In order to derive the correct phonetic form (*plan-[s]*), it is necessary to guarantee that the selection rule for the plural suffix chooses the /plant/ alternant rather than the /plan/ alternant as the appropriate environment. But how is this to be done? Ordering the selection rules is of no avail here. If we chose the stem alternant first, we would choose /plan/ (since this is the form that is used before the plural suffix). Having selected /plan/, we would then expect the /z/ form of the plural suffix to be used, since /plan/ ends in a voiced nonsibilant sound. But this is incorrect. If we try to choose the plural suffix first, then we have an ambiguous situation: The /plant/ alternant of the stem suggests a /s/ plural, but the /plan/ alternant suggests a /z/ plural. There appears to be no principled way to decide which alternant will determine the shape of the plural suffix. We must somehow specify /plant/ as being the alternant of the stem that determines the shape of the plural suffix, even though /plant/ is not the alternant that appears before the plural suffix. Obviously, this has the effect of saying that the representation /plant/ is involved in the determination of the pronunciation of *plants* even though this representation does not directly appear in the surface form of this word. Notice that this is entirely analogous to the generative claim that /plant/ is the underlying representation of the noun and that the rule determining the shape of the plural suffix applies before /plant/ is changed to /plan/.

Notice that in the generative approach a rule can be ordered so that it applies directly to the underlying structure, before any rules that alter that structure, or a rule can be ordered so that it applies only after certain other rules have had a chance to apply. The morpheme alternant approach must essentially have the same power in order to describe both the English and the Russian examples discussed above. That is, in order to derive the English plural noun *plants* the rule specifying the selection of the plural alternant must be applied in terms of the representation /plant/, even though this representation does not actually occur in the pronunciation of the plural form (*plan*-[s]). In order to derive the masculine past form *mel* in Russian, the rule selecting the past tense alternant must be applied in terms of the stem alternant /me-/, which is the alternant that actually occurs in the masculine past tense form, and not in terms of the alternant /met-/. From these examples it seems fair to conclude that an adequate theory must allow the pronunciation of one morpheme to be determined either by the actual pronunciation of an adjacent morpheme or by a different representation of that same morpheme. In the generative approach that "different" representation is either the underlying representation or some representation intermediate between the UR and the actual phonetic realization. In the morpheme alternant theory that "different" representation is presumably any alternant that the morpheme in question exhibits. This means that in order to utilize the morpheme alternant approach, one would have to identify which alternant of a morpheme is to be used to condition the choice of an alternant for a neighboring morpheme. Obviously such a specification is moving very close to the generative approach, which does much the same thing by specifying a single underlying representation for each morpheme.

In the morpheme alternant approach it would be necessary to choose the alternant for the plural suffix on the basis of the stem alternant /plant/. Notice that this is the alternant that occurs in the singular form. It is not, however, possible to claim that in English the plural alternant is **always** selected on the basis of the stem alternant that shows up in the singular. Consider examples like *knife* [nayf], *knives* [nayv-z] and *wife* [wayf], *wives* [wayv-z]. These nouns undergo a rule that applies to a restricted set of items; the rule voices the final /f/ of the noun stem in the plural. The /-z/ alternant of the plural suffix is then used; clearly, /-z/ is being chosen on the basis of the final /v/ of the noun stem, but the /v/ form of the noun occurs only in the plural and not the singular. The alternant /nayf/ is uninvolved in the selection of the plural suffix; only the alternant /nayv/ matters.

There are numerous cases where, given the morpheme alternant approach, a rule of selection must be sensitive to representations other than those that actually occur in the word in question. A particularly interesting example of this type is provided by Turkish. Turkish noun stems may end in a consonant or a vowel. A number of suffixes have two different alternants depending on whether the stem is consonant- or vowel-final. For instance, the dative suffix is *-yA* (where *A* represents a vowel that alternates between *a* and *e* due to a rule of vowel harmony that is not relevant for the present discussion) after vowel-final stems, but *-A* after stems ending in a consonant. Similarly, the 3 sg. possessive suffix is *-sI* (where *I* represents a vowel that alternates between *i, ü, ı,* and *u* by vowel harmony rules) after vowels and *-I* after consonants. These suffixes contrast with those such as the plural *-lAr* which begin with a consonant that does not alternate with ∅ and with a suffix such as the 1 sg. possessive *-Im*, which truncates its vowel after a vowel.

(19)

Abs. sg.	Abs. pl.	Dative	3 sg. poss.	1 sg. poss.	Gloss
arı	*arı-lar*	*arı-ya*	*arı-sı*	*arı-m*	'bee'
araba	*araba-lar*	*araba-ya*	*araba-sı*	*araba-m*	'wagon'
baš	*baš-lar*	*baš-a*	*baš-ı*	*baš-ım*	'head'
yel	*yel-ler*	*yel-e*	*yel-i*	*yel-im*	'wind'
kız	*kız-lar*	*kız-a*	*kız-ı*	*kız-ım*	'daughter'

Polysyllabic stems ending in *-k* exhibit a *k* ~ ∅ alternation, while most monosyllabic stems whose final consonant is *-k* do not alternate with ∅.

(20)

ok	*ok-lar*	*ok-a*	*ok-u*	*ok-um*	'arrow'
sik	*sik-ler*	*sik-e*	*sik-i*	*sik-im*	'penis'
kök	*kök-ler*	*kök-e*	*kök-ü*	*kök-üm*	'root'
ayak	*ayak-lar*	*aya-a*	*aya-ı*	*aya-ım*	'foot'
inek	*inek-ler*	*ine-e*	*ine-i*	*ine-im*	'cow'
kuyruk	*kuyruk-lar*	*kuyru-a*	*kuyru-u*	*kuyru-um*	'tail'

According to Zimmer (1975) the *k* ~ ∅ alternation is to be accounted for by a rule deleting the final *k* of a polysyllabic stem when it is intervocalic. Given a theory that permits the derivation of a phonetic form from an underlying representation, *aya-ı* 'his foot' could be derived from underlying /ayak-sı/ by ordering the rule deleting the initial *-s* of /-sI/ before the *k*-deletion rule.

(21)

    /ayak-sı/

    ayak-ı   Consonant deletion

    aya-ı   *k*-deletion

Consider the problem these data pose for the morpheme alternant theory. A rule of selection would be required for the noun stem and also for the dative and 3 sg. possessive endings. The representation for *aya-ı* 'his foot' would be as in (22).

(22) $/\#aya \left\{ \begin{matrix} k \\ \emptyset \end{matrix} \right\} + \left\{ \begin{matrix} s \\ \emptyset \end{matrix} \right\} I \#/$

In order to resolve the choice of /-sI/ versus /-I/, we must make reference to the stem alternant /ayak/ rather than /aya/, even though /aya/ is the stem alternant that is actually used in the pronunciation of this word. It is the fact that /ayak/ ends in a consonant that permits /-I/ to be chosen rather than /-sI/. Having made use of the /ayak/ alternant to derive /-I/, it is now the /-I/ form of the suffix that triggers the choice of /aya/ rather than /ayak/ (since /aya/ appears before vowels whereas /ayak/ appears before consonants). It should be obvious that this method of arriving at the surface parallels, step-by-step, the derivation given in (21) above, for in the generative approach, /ayak/ occurs in the underlying representation and permits the suffixal alternant /-I/ to be derived by the consonant-deletion rule. Once this alternant is derived, the appearance of /aya/ follows because the *k* is now intervocalic. Clearly, in order for the morpheme alternant theory to work at all in this case, we must, in effect, reintroduce the notion of a derivation, and this involves accounting for the pronunciation of a word by making appeal to a form of a morpheme that does not in fact appear directly in that word.

We will cite just one other example which shows that the morpheme alternant theory must in essence make use of an underlying form (i.e., a form that does not actually appear in the word in question, but, nevertheless, must be appealed to in order to account for the pronunciation of the word) and a derivation. The data for this example comes from Klamath, an Amerindian language spoken in Oregon (Barker 1963). Example (23) illustrates the construction of causative verbs in this language.

(23)   *ge:jïg-a*   'is tired'   *sne-ge:jïg-a*   'makes tired'
       qdo:č-a   'it rains'   *sno-qdo:č-a*   'makes it rain'
       m'a:s?-a   'is sick'   *sna-m'a:s?-a*   'makes sick'

Notice that the causative prefix in Klamath has the shape *snV-*, where the quality of V depends on the quality of the first vowel of the verb stem. In the morpheme alternant approach, the representation of the causative prefix would be as in (24).

(24) $sn \left\{ \begin{matrix} e \\ a \\ o \\ \vdots \end{matrix} \right\}$

The precise number of alternants would depend, of course, on how many different vowel qualities can be found in the first vowel of verb stems. A rule of selection like (25) would then be required to pick the appropriate alternant of the causative prefix.

(25)   *Choose the alternant of the causative prefix that has the same vowel quality as the next vowel in the word.*

This rule of selection will thus pick the alternant /sne-/ when an *e*-quality vowel follows, /sna-/ when an *a*-quality vowel follows, and so on.
   Now consider the examples in (26).

(26)   *pag-a*   'barks'   *sna-pg-a*   'makes a dog bark'
       nqot'-a   'scorches'   *sno-nqt'-a*   'scorches s.t.'
       wet-a   'laughs'   *sne-wt-a*   'makes laugh'

The verb stems in these examples each display two alternants: /pag/ and /pg/, /nqot'/ and /nqt'/, and /wet/ and /wt/. Within a generative approach we would say that the first vowel of a verb stem, if it is short, elides after the causative prefix. Long vowels do not elide, as the examples in (23) show. This rule of elision would clearly have to be applied after the rule that assigns the causative prefix its vocalic shape, since the vowel used in the causative prefix depends on the vowel of the verb stem.
   Consider now how the morpheme alternant theory would have to deal with these data from Klamath. The verb stems in (26) would have representations like (27).

(27) $/p \left\{ \begin{matrix} a \\ \emptyset \end{matrix} \right\} g/$ $/nq \left\{ \begin{matrix} o \\ \emptyset \end{matrix} \right\} t'/$ $/w \left\{ \begin{matrix} e \\ \emptyset \end{matrix} \right\} t/$

When these representations are combined with the representation of the causative prefix, the result is a representation like (28).

(28) $/\#sn \left\{ \begin{matrix} a \\ e \\ o \\ : \end{matrix} \right\} + p \left\{ \begin{matrix} a \\ \emptyset \end{matrix} \right\} g + a \# /$

The rule of selection for the stem alternant would be that the form without the vowel is chosen after the causative prefix. The rule of selection for the causative prefix (25) will assign the appropriate shape to the prefix just in case it makes reference to the stem alternant /pag/, even though /pag/ is not actually the stem alternant used in the causative form of the verb. Once again we see that the morpheme alternant theory must make use of a representation other than the one that actually occurs in the word whose pronunciation is being determined.

In Klamath one finds numerous alternations between glottalized and nonglottalized consonants. For example, the stem /sl'eq'/ 'to rust' ends in a glottalized consonant when a vowel follows (cf., *sl'eq'-a* 'it rusts') but ends in the corresponding nonglottalized consonant when an obstruent follows (*sl'eq-di:l-a* 'is rusted out underneath'). In general, glottalized consonants do not appear in front of obstruents in Klamath. Within the generative approach, we would set up underlying /sl'eq'/ and invoke a rule of deglottalization that operates when an obstruent follows. In the morpheme alternant theory, a rule of selection such as (29) would be invoked.

(29)   *If a morpheme exhibits an alternation between a glottalized and a nonglottalized consonant, choose the nonglottalized form when an obstruent follows, and choose the glottalized form elsewhere.*

Let us now consider an example such as *nt'op'-a* 'rots' and *sno-ntp'-a* 'causes to rot'. The representation for the verb stem must be $/\text{nt} \left\{ \begin{matrix} \text{'} \\ \emptyset \end{matrix} \right\} \left\{ \begin{matrix} \text{o} \\ \emptyset \end{matrix} \right\} \text{p'} /$.

When this representation is combined with the causative prefix, we get (30).

(30) $/ \# \; \text{sn} \left\{ \begin{matrix} \text{a} \\ \text{e} \\ \text{o} \\ \vdots \end{matrix} \right\} + \text{nt} \left\{ \begin{matrix} \text{'} \\ \emptyset \end{matrix} \right\} \left\{ \begin{matrix} \text{o} \\ \emptyset \end{matrix} \right\} \text{p'} \# /$

How is this representation to be assigned its correct phonetic shape? Clearly, the choice of the prefixal vowel must be made on the basis of the alternant of the stem containing the vowel /o/ rather than the alternant lacking a vowel. Of course, the alternant containing the vowel /o/ is not the one that is actually pronounced in this word. But now let us consider how we can choose the proper form of the verb stem. It is clear that in order to choose the alternant lacking glottalization we must choose the alternant that lacks the vowel /o/. It is only the absence of the stem vowel that permits the consonant exhibiting the glottalization alternation to be next to an obstruent. Recall that the rule of selection (29) chooses the nonglottalized alternant just in the event an obstruent follows immediately. It should be clear that the above process of choosing the surface form *sno-ntp'-a* precisely matches the kind of analysis that the generative approach would give; note the derivation in (31).

(31)   /snV-nt'op'-a/

        sno-nt'op'-a   Prefixal vowel harmony

        sno-nt'p'-a   Vowel elision

        sno-ntp'-a   Deglottalization

Notice that the above derivation makes use of the underlying form of the verb stem to determine the prefixal vowel, and it makes use of the form of the stem resulting from vowel elision to trigger the application of deglottalization. The morpheme alternant approach would in effect have to do exactly the same thing.

The conclusion to be drawn from the above discussion is that in order to account for the data cited, the morpheme alternant approach would have to be granted the power to choose the equivalent of an underlying representation and to impose an ordering on its rules of selection that essentially matches the derivations used in the generative approach. On the other hand, the morpheme alternant theory regards it as being totally unpredictable whether a morpheme will or will not exhibit an alternation. Since there is considerable evidence that morphemes, in fact, do alternate by rule (i.e., that all morphemes of a certain structure will predictably exhibit a certain alternation), the morpheme alternant theory cannot in fact characterize the native speaker's knowledge of his language as successfully as can the approach utilizing underlying representations plus an (ordered) set of rules modifying those underlying representations in particular contexts.

The Basic Alternant

Having given some of the motivation for the concept of an underlying representation which is converted into a phonetic representation by the application of phonological rules, we now turn to the question of possible constraints on the degree to which these two representations may diverge. The constraints examined in this section are all fairly strong in that they require a rather direct relation between the UR and its associated PRs. They all require that the UR be identical with one of its PRs. They differ in just which PR is claimed to be the UR. Some of these constraints have been explicitly proposed by one or another phonologist, while others are logical possibilities whose validity needs to be examined. We will see that none of these constraints can be accepted as absolute requirements on underlying representations if certain internally well-motivated analyses are to be maintained.

The first of these may be stated as follows:

(32)   *The UR of a morpheme is identical[2] with the phonetic alternant that appears in isolation (or as close to isolation as the grammar of the language permits).*

A principle such as this seems to be implicitly assumed in many pedagogically oriented descriptions where one often finds rules about how to construct a plural noun on the basis of the singular form of that noun, or how to construct a dative form of a noun on the basis of the nominative form, etc. This principle has also been proposed by Vennemann (1974). It seems to be motivated by the following two considerations. First, the UR of a morpheme is often obscured when it is combined with other morphemes because of the operation of phonological rules. If the morpheme can be located in isolation, this obscuring effect can be eliminated and the underlying form revealed. In addition, the unaffixed or minimally affixed form of a root morpheme often appears in a semantically more basic context (e.g., singular is more basic than plural; subject case is more basic than object case; third person is more basic than first or second), and there may be a tendency to identify the UR of a morpheme with the alternant appearing in the semantically more basic context, perhaps on the grounds that this context is more frequent—especially during the initial stages of language learning.

But we have seen that word-initial and especially word-final position often induce phonological mutations that obscure the UR of a morpheme. Recall the internally and externally motivated rule of final devoicing in Russian (Chapter 3), where in isolation the final sounds of forms such as *trup* 'corpse' and *xlep* 'bread' are identical, but contrast when a case suffix is added: *trup-u* versus *xleb-u*. Constraint (32) would require the URs of these morphemes to each end in a voiceless consonant. An arbitrary lexical division of the morphemes of Russian would then be required (one class of which would voice its final obstruent when preceding a case suffix, and another class which would not), in spite of the fact that a natural phonetic contrast (final voiced versus final voiceless obstruent) is available to differentiate the two types of stems.

The Lardil data discussed in Chapter 4 present a much more extreme

---

[2] Of course we don't mean strict identity since we wish to allow for the possibility that the UR may not contain any specification for a nonalternating redundant phonetic property (such as aspiration in English) that is entirely predictable from the phonetic context. Thus this constraint would not be violated by a UR for *cab* in which the initial consonant is unspecified for aspiration and hence not literally identical with any of its phonetic realizations. What we are concerned with here as well as in all later constraints discussed in this section is the UR for features that alternate or nonalternating features that are not predictable from phonetic context.

example of the kinds of difficulties that a principle such as (32) encounters. Recall that four rules were postulated that modify or delete the final portion of an underlying noun stem when it is not protected from word final position by a suffix: lowering of final high vowels, apocopation of final vowels from stems of three or more syllables, simplification of final consonant clusters, and the deletion of final nonapical consonants. If the uninflected form of the noun stem is selected as underlying, as (32) requires, an extremely large number of ad hoc lexical subcategorizations will be needed to derive the stem alternants appearing in the inflected forms. One such categorization will be needed to differentiate those stems such as *mela*, *mela-n* 'sea', with a final constant /a/, from stems such as *ŋuka*, *ŋuku-n* 'water', which replace final /a/ with /u/ in the inflected form. Another categorization would be needed for those stems that "add" a vowel in the inflected form: compare *miyaṛ*, *miyaṛ-in* 'spear' with *mayar*, *mayara-n* 'rainbow'. Further subcategorization would be required to identify the added vowel. The form 'rainbow' shows the addition of an /a/, while a stem such as *yalul*, *yalulu-n* shows the addition of an /u/. Vowel-final stems such as *mela* and *ŋuka* would have to be differentiated from stems such as *ŋalu*, *ŋaluk-in* 'story' and *thurara*, *thuraraŋ-in* 'shark' that add a nonapical consonant. This class would have to be broken down further into a subclass for each particular nonapical that is added. Of course, each of the classes enumerated so far would have to be differentiated from those stems such as *putu*, *putuka-n* 'short' and *muŋkumu*, *muŋkumuŋku-n* that add a consonant plus a vowel or two consonants plus a vowel. Finally, all of these many classes of stems will have to be differentiated from those that appear to subtract sounds from the uninflected stem—namely those stems such as *ṛilta*, *ṛil-in* 'neck' and *ṭera*, *ṭer-in* 'thigh' which were analyzed in Chapter 4 as taking an augment in the uninflected form. Clearly all of these subcategorizations that would be required in order to formulate the rules for building the inflected stem from the uninflected alternant are nothing but an artifact of the analysis that says that the uninflected form must be underlying.

Finally, as Hale (1973) observes, rules having the effect of apocope, cluster simplification, and nonapical deletion would be required in any case in order to give an adequate analysis of the reduplicated stems. Thus, in order to characterize *karikar*, *karikari-n* 'butter-fish' as reduplicated from the base form /kari/, a rule having the effect of apocope will be needed. Both apocope and nonapical deletion would be needed to give an adequate characterization of the reduplication involved in *tipiti*, *tipitipi-n* 'rock-cod sp.' In addition to these two rules, forms such as *muŋkumu*, *muŋkumuŋku-n* show that a rule having the effect of cluster simplification will be required. Clearly, a principle like (32) that requires such an analysis for the Lardil data must be rejected.

Having shown that the UR cannot necessarily be equated with the alternant appearing in isolation, there is another criterion which might be thought to identify the proper alternant as the UR. This is stated as (33):

(33)   *The UR of a morpheme is identical with the alternant appearing in the greatest number of contexts.*

Rule (33) is quite imprecise, due to the vagueness of the word "contexts." But for purposes of exposition we will assume that context refers to the number of different morphemes which can precede and follow the morpheme in question within the word. The limitation to within the word is a rather arbitrary restriction, but we shall see that the principle is unworkable in any case. This principle does select the alternant for Lardil that we suggested was the correct one, since the uninflected stem appears in only one context while the inflected stem occurs in at least two (and actually many more that we have ignored in our exposition of the Lardil data). It also chooses the alternant with a final voiced obstruent in the Russian *xlep*, *xleb-u* alternation, since this alternant occurs before all nonzero case suffixes, while the alternant *xlep* appears in just the nominative singular.

Nevertheless, there are many cases where the alternant that one would want to identify as the UR does not appear in the majority of contexts. The vowel reduction process in Russian offers an example. In Russian the five vowels *i*, *e*, *a*, *o*, and *u* contrast under stress, while in unstressed position only *i*, *u*, and *a* are found. When unstressed and after a palatalized or a palatal consonant underlying nonhigh vowels *e*, *o*, and *a* merge with *i*. When not preceded by a palatalized or palatal consonant, unstressed nonhigh vowels merge with *a*. We state these rules informally as follows (where C' is a cover symbol for palatals and palatalized consonants):

(34) $o,e,a \rightarrow i$ /C'___ $o,e,a \rightarrow a$ /elsewhere
         [$-$stress]   [$-$stress]

There is a large class of verbs in Russian which have the accent on the ending in the 1 sg. present and on the stem in the remaining forms of the present tense.

(35)

		Singular				
	1	*p'iš-ú*	*m'ič-ú*	*v'iž-ú*	*maš-ú*	*glaž-ú*
	2	*p'íš-iš*	*m'éč-iš*	*v'áž-iš*	*máš-iš*	*glóž-iš*
	3	*p'íš-it*	*m'éč-it*	*v'áž-it*	*máš-it*	*glóž-it*
	Plural					
	1	*p'íš-im*	*m'éč-im*	*v'áž-im*	*máš-im*	*glóž-im*
	2	*p'íš-it'i*	*m'éč-it'i*	*v'áž-it'i*	*máš-it'i*	*glóž-it'i*
	3	*p'íš-ut*	*m'éč-ut*	*v'áž-ut*	*máš-ut*	*glóž-ut*
	Gloss	'write'	'throw'	'bind'	'wave'	'gnaw'

The alternant appearing in the 1 sg. cannot be chosen as the UR for there is no way to tell what vowel will appear when the stem is stressed. Rule (33) correctly chooses the stressed alternant as underlying, since it appears in a greater number of contexts. There are, however, other stress patterns in Russian where the accent does not appear on the stem in a majority of case forms. For example, a fair number of masculine nouns have stress on the case ending except when there is a zero suffix, in which case the accent appears on the final vowel of the stem.

(36)

	Sg.	Pl.	Other examples
Nom.	*stól*	*stal-ý*	*ščít, ščit-á, ščit-ú*, etc. 'shield'
Gen.	*stal-á*	*stal-óf*	*m'éč, m'ič-á, m'ič-ú*, etc. 'sword'
Dat.	*stal-ú*	*stal-ám*	*m'áč, m'íč-á, m'ič-ú*, etc. 'ball'
Inst.	*stal-óm*	*stal-ámi*	*čoln, čiln-á, čiln-ú*, etc. 'canoe'
Loc.	*stal-é*	*stal-áx*	*vráč, vrač-á, vrač-ú*, etc. 'physician'
Gloss	'table'		

If the unstressed alternant with the reduced vowels is selected as the UR, as (33) requires, arbitrary lexical subcategorization will be needed to change the reduced vowels /i/ and /a/ into the correct vowel for the stressed alternants. Not only does (33) force us to reject a naturally available phonetic contrast to differentiate these forms, it also leads to analyzing what is patently the same alternation in one way for the verbs of (35) and in a quite different fashion for the nouns of (36).

The paradigms for many Russian verbs also present a counterexample to (33). Before the present tense endings of certain verb classes various oppositions in stem-final consonants are merged by a rule palatalizing consonants before the present tense suffixes (see Lightner 1972 for details).

(37)

	inf.	1 sg.	2 sg.	3 sg.	Gloss
k~ č	plák-at'	pláč-u	pláč-iš	pláč-it, etc.	'weep'
t~ č	pr'át-at'	pr'áč-u	pr'áč-iš	pr'áč-it, etc.	'hide'
g~ ž	dv'íg-at'	dv'íž-u	dv'íž-iš	dv'íž-it, etc.	'move'
z~ ž	l'iz-át'	l'iž-ú	l'íž-iš	l'íž-it, etc.	'lick'
x~ š	pax-át'	paš-ú	páš-iš	páš-it, etc.	'plough'
s~ š	p'is-át'	p'iš-ú	p'íš-iš	p'íš-it, etc.	'write'

The alternants with the palatal consonants appear in a large range of environments in the verb inflection, but if the alternation is to be accounted for without appeal to arbitrary lexical subcategorization, the alternant that appears before the infinitive suffix must be selected as underlying.

A third constraint for selecting the most appropriate UR might be to impose a parallelism condition on the choice of the basic alternant. This is stated as (38).

(38)   *The alternant selected as the UR must occur in the same morphological category for all morphemes of a given morphological class (verb, noun, particle, etc.)*

This constraint is not as strong as (32) and (33) in that it does not determine in advance which alternant is underlying for all morphemes, but merely requires that if, for example, the alternant appearing in the nom. sg. is selected as basic for a given noun, then the alternant appearing in the nom. sg. for all other nouns must be the UR as well. This constraint will work for the Lardil data presented earlier, since the appropriate UR always appears as the stem alternant occurring before the nonfuture suffix /-in/. Similarly, (38) will permit us to select the stem alternants appearing under stress for both the nouns (36) and the verbs (35) in the Russian data presented so far, since the nouns and verbs belong to different morphological categories and within each category we are free to choose any alternant as underlying. Thus we might choose as basic the alternant appearing in the 3 sg. for the verbs, and the alternant appearing in the gen. sg. for the nouns. In each case the vowel reduction rule (34) will account for the alternations without any appeal to lexical subcategorization.

But there is no reason to expect that the most appropriate UR will reside in the same morphological category for all alternations in the language. For example, recall again the final devoicing alternation in Russian in such nouns as *xlép*, *xléb-a* 'bread', etc. To account for this alternation properly, the alternant appearing before a case suffix must be selected as underlying, for only in this context does the voicing contrast between /p/ and /b/ appear phonetically. The contrast is neutralized in the nom. sg. where there is no case suffix. But as we have just seen, it is only in the nom. sg. that the vowel contrast between /i/, /e/, /a/, and /o/ appears phonetically for the end-stressed nouns. These contrasts are all neutralized when a case suffix follows, since the stress appears on the case suffix. To maintain the parallelism constraint of (38) we would be required to describe one of these alternations by an arbitrary lexical subcategorization, despite the clear phonetic contrasts that are available; a similar problem arises for the verbs in (37). To describe the vowel reduction of the verbs in (35) properly, a form with stress on the stem such as the 3 sg. must be selected as basic. But to describe the palatalization of (37) properly, the 3 sg. will not yield the appropriate UR. Rather the alternant appearing before the infinitive suffix must be underlying. But for end-stressed verbs of (35) the accent appears on the infinitive suffix and hence permits vowel reduction to neutralize the oppositions in the root vowels: *p'is-át', m'it-at', v'iz-át', max-át', glad-át'.* Clearly (38) is too strong a constraint.

Each of the preceding constraints, (32), (33), and (38), attempts to constrain the choice of the UR by claiming that some particular alternant will be an accurate indicator of the UR. A somewhat weaker constraint merely requires that there be a basic alternant for each morpheme. It is stated as (39).

(39)   *All of the segments appearing in the UR must occur together in at least one phonetic alternant—the basic alternant.*

Constraint (39) permits greater freedom in selecting the UR in that the basic alternant need not be any particular surface form or forms of the morpheme; nor does the decision about the UR of one morpheme force the choice of the basic alternant for any other morpheme. Nevertheless, (39) is a strong constraint on URs and seems to have been held by a number of linguists in the past (McCawley 1967). It claims that if a given morpheme exhibits two or more alternations, say x ~ y and w ~ z, choice of an underlying value for one alternation will restrict the choice for all other alternations, since all segments in the UR must appear together in some single phonetic alternant.

Constraint (39) permits the appropriate analysis of the Lardil data and all of the Russian data presented so far. It permits /xleb/ to serve as the UR for the voicing alternation exhibited by *xlep, xleb-u*; it also permits /stol/ as the UR for the vowel reduction alternation in *stól, stal-á*. But there are, nevertheless, severe problems with (39). When an underlying element *x* is changed to *y* in some context, let us refer to the context where *x* is actually pronounced as the neutral context and let us refer to the environment in which *y* is pronounced as the distorting environment. Now, when a given morpheme exhibits two separate alternations, there is no a priori reason to expect that there will be a context in which that morpheme appears which is neutral for *both* alternations. In fact, there appear to be many cases where no context occurs that is neutral for all the alternations exhibited by a morpheme. The Russian morphemes *p'irók*, *p'irag-á* 'pie' and *sapók*, *sapag-á* 'boot' represent a typical case. In the paradigm of these nouns, the accent is on the case suffix in all forms except the nom./acc. sg. (which is the only form lacking a suffix). These nouns have a final /o/ vowel under stress, but exhibit an /a/ vowel when stress is on the ending. In other words, we appear to be clearly dealing with an instance of the vowel reduction rule given in (34); these stems need to be set up with an underlying /o/ as their last vowel. But notice that these morphemes also exhibit an alternation between voiced and voiceless obstruents. We know that final obstruents are pronounced as voiceless by rule in Russian. That suggests that these morphemes should be set up with a stem-final voiced obstruent. But the voiced obstruent shows up only in those forms that are followed by suffixes, and in these forms the preceding noun stem is pronounced with the /a/ vowel rather than the /o/ vowel. Consequently, there is no form of 'pie', for instance, where both /o/ and /g/ are pronounced at the same time. This is due to the fact that while the suffixless nom./acc. sg. form is a neutral environment with respect to vowel reduction, it is a distorting environment for final devoicing; and the suffixed forms are all neutral environments for final devoicing, but distorting environments for vowel reduction. There is no form of 'pie' which is a neutral context for both vowel reduction and final devoicing. In order to account for the alternation between *p'irók* and *p'irag-á* by independently motivated rules, a representation such as /p'irog/ would be required. Final devoicing would change /g/ to /k/ when no suffix follows and thus /g/ stands at the end of a word. Vowel reduction would convert /o/ to /a/ when no stress appears on the /o/, which would be whenever a suffix follows. Constraint (39), however, would not allow such an analysis, since /p'irog/ is never a phonetic alternant. If (39) were followed, we would have to choose either /p'irók/ or /p'irag/ as basic. Whichever one we choose, we will have to formulate a new rule: either a rule voicing voiceless obstruents or a rule converting stressed /a/ to /o/. But neither of these rules would be able to apply freely, since many final voiceless obstruents would resist voicing and other stressed /a/ vowels would have to remain /a/. Thus (39) forces one to postulate a rule that is not independently needed. Furthermore, that rule would require arbitrary lexical subcategorization to distinguish alternating sounds from nonalternating sounds.

Condition (39) runs into similar problems with Russian verbs. There are hundreds of stems which participate in both the palatalization and the vowel reduction alternations: for example, *m'it-át'* 'to throw' and *méč-it* 'he throws'. To account for the palatalization without appeal to lexical subcategorization, the /t/ must be entered into the UR, while the vowel alternation requires basic /e/. But there are no alternants in the verbal paradigm where both /e/ and /t/ occur together.

So far we have dealt with counterexamples to (39) in which two separate rules are involved, but in many cases (39) can be falsified on the basis of just a single rule. This will occur in Russian when a disyllabic root exhibits a mobile stress pattern: for example, /golov/ 'head' has the alternants appearing in *galav-á* nom. sg., *gólav-u* acc. sg., and *galóf* gen. pl. Since there is no alternant in which both syllables are accented, at least one, and sometimes both, underlying /o/'s will merge with *a*. Similar facts occur in Chamorro (Chapter 3), English, and many other languages. Vowel deletion rules often exhibit this property as well. Recall from Chapter 3 that in Tonkawa one of the underlying vowels will always be deleted in three syllable verb stems, yet all of the vowels are unpredictable features of the morpheme that must be entered in the morpheme's UR. In view of numerous such counterexamples, most generative phonologists (and many other linguists not explicitly working within the generative paradigm) have rejected constraints such as (39), and a fortiori the ones discussed earlier in this section, as imposing much too restrictive a constraint on underlying representations.

Abstract Segments

All of the counterexamples to the constraints discussed in the preceding section satisfy the following condition, which we might entertain as a reasonable condition on URs:

(40)   *All of the segments appearing in the UR of a morpheme must appear in some phonetic alternant.*

Condition (40) permits the UR to be pieced together from the set of its various phonetic realizations. It does not require the UR to be identical with one of its alternants and is thus a weaker constraint than those discussed earlier. It is nevertheless a fairly strong condition in that it claims that the segments composing the UR will be a subset of the segments appearing in a morpheme's phonetic realizations.[3] It seems to us that (40) is the strongest position possible on prima facie grounds. Any of the more restrictive conditions of the preceding section would be violated by at least some URs in practically any language. Condition (40) thus represents a lower limit on the amount of abstractness that must be permitted by phonological theory. But can it serve as an upper limit as well?

The majority of underlying representations in any language will adhere to the condition imposed by (40). There are, however, many languages where internal (and sometimes external) evidence suggests incorporating a segment into the UR of some morphemes that never appears in any phonetic realization of those morphemes. Both generative and nongenerative studies have postulated such abstract segments. In general, such analyses are viewed with a healthy scepticism. Thus, in published descriptions the author will typically present as many arguments as possible in support of the abstract segment. (URs that do not involve abstract segments are usually not motivated so thoroughly, since most phonologists will accept URs that violate the conditions discussed in the preceding section.) In this section we review a few representative analyses of such abstract analyses. (See Kenstowicz and Kisseberth 1977 for more extensive discussion.)

One internally well-motivated analysis involving abstract segments was given in Chapter 4, where it was postulated that the Yawelmani underlying vowel system of (41) was converted to the phonetic system of (42) by a rule that lowers the high long vowels /i:/ and /u:/ to /e:/ and /o:/, respectively, followed by a rule shortening all vowels before two consonants or a single word-final consonant.

(41)	Yawelmani underlying	i u	i: u:
	vowel system	a o	a: o:

(42)	Yawelmani phonetic	i u	
	vowel system	e a o	e: a: o:

This analysis was motivated by a number of separate lines of evidence which we will briefly review here. First of all, postulating that /c'u:m/ 'destroy' underlies the stem alternants appearing in *c'om-hun* and *c'o:m-al* explains why this root does not display the same vowel harmony properties as a root like /do:s/ 'report'; compare *dos-hin, do:s-ol*. Recall

---

[3] Again, we wish to allow for segments in the UR to be unspecified for nonalternating features, such as aspiration in English, which are predictable from phonetic context.

that the vowel harmony rule rounds a vowel after a rounded vowel of the same height. Given that the UR of 'destroy' has a high rounded vowel, the rounding of /hin/ to *hun* and the fact that no rounding appears in /-al/ are explained. Second, the postulation of underlying long high vowels imparts a much more symmetrical underlying vowel system to the language, as comparison of (41) with (42) readily shows. Third, the long high vowels permit one to capture the generalization underlying the vowel patterns displayed by the disyllabic verb roots—namely that the vowel of the second syllable is a long vowelled version of the first vowel, as the data in (43) show.

(43)   /pana:-/   *pana:-hin*   *pana-l*   *pana-ʔ*   'arrive'
        /ʔili:-/   *ʔile:-hin*   *ʔile-l*   *ʔili-ʔ*   'fan'
        /hoyo:-/   *hoyo:-hin*   *hoyo-l*   *hoyo-ʔ*   'name'
        /cʼuyu:-/   *cʼuyo:-hun*   *cʼuyo-l*   *cʼuyu-ʔ*   'urinate'

Fourth, and particularly persuasive, was the fact that the underlying height posited for the root vowels of forms such as /ʔili:-/ and /cʼuyu:-/ actually does show up phonetically before the future suffix by virtue of the rule shortening a long vowel before a final glottal stop. The internal evidence thus strongly suggests that the UR of a root such as /cʼuyu:-/ contains the abstract segment /u:/ which never appears in any phonetic realization of this morpheme: The [+high] feature of the /u:/ appears in *cʼuyu-ʔ*, while the [+long] feature appears in *cʼuyo:-hun*. But because of the lowering rule, these two features are banned from appearing together in any phonetic realization.

Perhaps somewhat more abstract are cases in which some of the features defining the underlying segment never appear phonetically in any realization of the segment. Recall, for example, the analysis of the Yawelmani future suffix that exhibits the alternant /-on/ after stems containing an underlying /u/ or /u:/ and /-en/ elsewhere.

(44)   ṣa:p-en   'burn'
        do:s-en   'report'
        me:kʼ-en   'swallow'
        cʼo:m-on   'destroy'

This alternation pattern can be explained if the UR of the suffix is /-i:n/. The suffix will round to /-u:n/ after round high vowels; subsequent lowering yields the alternants /-e:n/ and /-o:n/, which will then shorten to /-en/ and /-on/, since the future suffix is always word final. This analysis is motivated by the fact that *e* is generally unambiguously derived from a long vowel in Yawelmani by the general shortening rule; in most cases a phonetic *e* alternates with a phonetic *e:*. Thus, *e* is not an underlying sound in the Yawelmani system, but a variant of /e:/, which itself derives from /i:/. If the future alternants *-en/-on* are not derived from a underlying long vowel, then a phonemic *e* would have to be postulated for this one morpheme, which always occurs in the context ___C #, one of the positions in which a vowel is shortened. In addition, the suffix behaves as if it had an underlying high vowel. It rounds after high round vowels and fails to round after nonhigh round vowels and is thus systematically different from a suffix like *-al* which contains a nonhigh vowel. This vowel harmony behavior is explained by deriving the suffix from an underlying /i:/—a segment that is [+high] and [+long]. But note that since this suffix is always at the end of a word, the [+long] specification is always changed to [−long]; in addition, the vowel is always realized as [−high]. Thus, in this case some of the distinctive features of the abstract segment never appear phonetically in any realization of that segment.

There is only one other kind of abstractness more extreme than this—namely, a situation in which a segment of the UR never appears in any phonetic realization of the morpheme. In fact, many generative as well as nongenerative analyses have postulated such "ghost" segments. Recall, for example, the Dayak data discussed in Chapter 5, where a rule nasalizing a vowel after a nasal consonant was postulated. A number of forms, such as *əmudn* 'dew', *banugŋ* 'tapicoa', and *girunugŋ* 'small bell', are superficial exceptions to this rule. These forms were explained by assigning a homorganic voiced stop after the nasal in the UR: /əmbun/, /banduŋ/, /girunduŋ/. These voiced stops block the vowel nasalization and are subsequently deleted by a rule zeroing voiced stops after nasals. They never appear in any phonetic realization of these morphemes. This analysis was motivated primarily on distributional grounds: Although voiced and voiceless stops freely contrast in other positions, in position after a nasal only voiceless stops are found phonetically—voiced stops may not stand in this position in Land Dayak. The distributional evidence thus suggests that it is voiced stops that block the nasalization and subsequently delete. Which voiced stop to place in the UR is decided by the preceding nasal consonant, since nasals always agree in point of articulation with a following consonant in Dayak. Thus, a /b/ is posited in the UR of *əmudn* and a /d/ in *banugŋ*.

As pointed out in the preceding chapter, generative phonologists assume that the grammar represents the native speaker's internalized knowledge about the pronunciation of sentences in his language. In order for a particular theoretical device such as abstract segments to be justified, corroborating external evidence must be found. In this regard it is significant that loanwords are modified in Dayak in a manner that accords with the abstract analysis discussed above. First, forms containing a nasal plus voiced stop are nativized by the deletion of the voiced stop and the retention of an oral vowel. Thus, Scott (1964) cites Malay *gandum* 'corn, grain' (from Persian), which appears as *ganubm* in Dayak, with deletion of the /d/, and an oral vowel following the /n/ (shown by the fact that /m/ appears as *bm*.). Similarly, a vowel appearing after a nasal is nasalized in loanword adaptation. Thus *cement* is rendered *samĩn*. If these loanwords entered Dayak after the appearance of the rule deleting post-nasal voiced stops, they could be interpreted as providing strong support for the abstract analysis.

Another example parallel to the Dayak one for which there is a modicum of external evidence involves the analysis of the velar nasal in English. As we saw in Chapter 5, many phonologists have proposed that the final *ŋ* in a morpheme such as *sing* [sĩŋ] is to be derived from /sing/, a UR in which the /g/ never appears phonetically in any realization of this morpheme. As in the Dayak case, the evidence for such an analysis is primarily distributional. Recall that Fromkin's (1975) study of speech errors provides external evidence corroborating this analysis. She observed spoonerisms such as *swing and sway* rendered as [swĩn] *and* [sweyg] and *Springtime for Hitler* rendered as [sprɨg]*time for* [hĩntlər]. Given that the URs for [swĩŋ] and [sprĩŋ] are /swing/ and /spring/, the appearance of the /g/s in these spoonerisms finds a natural interpretation: the transposition of /g/ in /swing/ to the following word *sway* and the transposition of the /n/ of /spring/ to *Hitler*. If the URs did not contain these /g/s, it would be difficult to explain their appearance in these slips of the tongue.

It thus appears that quite abstract analyses must be permitted by phonological theory. However, this does not mean that constraints on underlying representation are unnecessary. There are numerous examples in which abstract analyses that would be permitted by a completely unconstrained theory can be shown to be incorrect. To cite one well-known example, the Algonquian language Menomini possesses two kinds of surface *n*. One alternates with *s* before nonlow front vowels and *y*, while the other does not. (*t* is converted to *č* in this same environment in Menomini.)

(45) | | | | |
|---|---|---|---|
| *en-ōhnɛ-t* | 'if he walks hither' | *es-y-ā-t* | 'if he goes hither' |
| *w-ēn-owawan* | 'their heads' | *w-ēs* < /w-en-e/ | 'his head' |
| *ōn-an* | 'canoes' | *ōs* < /on-e/ | 'canoe' |

(46)   *o-tān-an*   'his daughter'   *o-tān-ew*   'he has a daughter'
        kōn   'snow'   *kōn-ēwew*   'it is snowing'
                                              kūny-ak   'lumps of snow'

Thus, in a phonological description of Menomini there must be some difference in the URs of the morphemes in (45) and (46) in order to be consistent with the fact that *n*s in the former set palatalize to *s* while those of the latter do not. In a well-known paper, Bloomfield (1939) differentiated these morphemes by representing the *n*s of (45) as /n/ underlyingly, and those of (46) with the capital letter morphophoneme /N/. The palatalization rule is then defined to operate on /n/ and ordered after it is a rule that converts the nonpalatalizing /N/s to *n*.

The artifice of capital letter morphophonemes is not available in generative phonology, where it is assumed that segments in UR should be represented the same way as in PR—as matrixes of distinctive features which specify whether or not a given segment possesses a particular phonetic property. Consequently, the two different Menomini *n*s can be distinguished in only two ways: Either they may be assigned different underlying feature matrixes (and thus differentiated in terms of an underlying phonetic contrast that is later neutralized in all positions), or the morphemes of the language can be subcategorized in terms of an arbitrary lexical classification on the basis of whether or not they undergo the palatalization rule. In effect, the latter option is equivalent to marking in the lexicon all the morphemes containing /N/s in Bloomfield's analysis as exceptions to the palatalization rule. (See Chapter 10 for discussion of exceptions.)

In contrast to our discussion of earlier examples in this section, the first option is not nearly as attractive for these data from Menomini because an underlying phonetic contrast cannot be motivated. The only difference between the two *n*s is that some undergo palatalization while others do not. In all other respects the two *n*s behave the same. Thus, if one attempts to differentiate them by an underlying phonetic contrast, the choice of which phonetic feature or features to use would be largely arbitrary. This situation can be profitably compared with that in Yawelmani where a number of separate criteria permit the underlying phonetic difference between the two kinds of *o* vowels to be pinpointed exactly.

Despite the difficulty of providing an underlying phonetic contrast in cases such as Menomini, early generative work was so biased in favor of phonological as opposed to lexical solutions that we find such analyses given even in the most implausible circumstances. This was especially true when the historical antecedents of the language were known. Thus, in his Ph.D. dissertation on Menomini, Bever (1967) differentiated the two *n*s by deriving the palatalizing one from /θ/ and the nonpalatalizing one from /n/. In Bever's analysis the palatalization rule is then defined to convert /t/ and /θ/ to *č* and *s*, respectively, before /y/, /i/, and /e/. Subsequently, another rule merges all remaining /θ/s with *n*. To some extent this analysis recapitulates the historical development, since many of the palatalizing /n/s come from Proto-Algonquian *θ*, while the non-palatalizing /n/s come from *n*. Aside from this fact, which is irrelevant in a synchronic description, Bever tries to motivate the selection of /θ/ on grounds of simplicity. To differentiate the two /n/s one needs to set up a consonant which otherwise does not occur in Menomini. This consonant must appear as *s* in the palatalizing environments and as *n* elsewhere. The choice of the underlying segment can be constrained to some extent by attempting to formulate the rules that will effect these changes to *n* and *s* as simply as possible. θ differs from *s* by just the feature of stridency (and the rule of palatalization has the effect of making a consonant strident; cf., the change of *t* to *č*). It differs from *n* by the feature of nasality. If /θ/ is selected as the underlying segment, the rules required in the analysis will be rather simple, involving minimal feature changes.

The latter argument is extremely weak because it is based on an inadequate conception of the role of simplicity in phonology. In addition, it fails to eliminate one of the two liquids, which also do not occur in Menomini, as candidates for the UR of the palatalizing *n*s. There are, besides, other relevant facts that render this analysis not only implausible, but actually incorrect. This has to do with the fact that the merger of PA *θ* to *n* was not direct, but went through an intermediate stage of *l*. In an important study, Piggott (1971) has shown that in PA *t* alternated with *č* and *θ* with *s* before front nonlow vowels and glides. In most of the Algonquian languages *θ* became *l*, merging with PA *l*. At this stage there were some *l*s (those from *θ*) that alternated with *s*; other *l*s (those from *l*) did not. If one were to follow the logic of Bever's analysis for this stage of the language, the alternating *l*s would be derived from /θ/ and the nonalternating ones from /l/, with a subsequent rule taking all /θ/s which did not palatalize to *l*. But this kind of analysis would be inconsistent with the fact that in all of the Central Algonquian languages the *l* ~ *s* alternation was generalized to the *l*s that derive from PA *l*. This is a totally unexpected change under the phonological analysis, but finds a ready interpretation under the lexical analysis which differentiates the two kinds of *l*s by means of an arbitrary lexical classification: the tendency for arbitrary, nonphonetic properties to be lost in linguistic change (cf., the fact that many of the nouns and verbs which formed their plurals or past tense by umlaut or ablaut in earlier stages of English now take the regular *-(e)s*

plural and weak past -*(e)d* endings). At some time after the merger of *θ
with *l, *l was then merged with *n to yield the present-day Menomini
situation. We thus might expect in the future development of Menomini
that either the $n \sim s$ alternation will be generalized to the ns that derive
from *n, or perhaps that the alternation will be lost from the language. In
either case, both of these changes would be comprehensible under the
lexical analysis of the $n \sim s$ alternation, but not under the phonological
analysis.

It is thus clear that linguistic theory must be constrained so that a
phonological (as opposed to a lexical) analysis of the Menomini data can
be excluded. But the constraints should not be so restrictive that they also
exclude well motivated abstract segments such as those discussed earlier
in this section. Finding a proper balance between these two extremes is a
task that still lies ahead of us.

In the next two sections we discuss two rather different constraints
that have been proposed. Though they both correctly require a lexical
analysis of the Menomini data, they are nevertheless too strong in that
they also exclude many well-motivated phonological analyses.

The Alternation Condition

In one of the first publications to raise the issue of abstractness in
generative phonology, Kiparsky (1968a) distinguished two kinds of neutralization rules: contextual and absolute. In the former, an underlying
contrast is merged in some contexts but emerges to the phonetic surface
in other contexts. The final devoicing rules of Russian and German are
contextual neutralizations. The contrast between voiced and voiceless
obstruents is neutralized at the end of a word, but appears phonetically
before a vowel. Another example would be the voicing assimilation rule of
Pengo discussed earlier in this chapter. The underlying voiced versus
voiceless opposition in obstruents is neutralized before another obstruent,
but appears phonetically before a vowel. The context giving rise to this
kind of neutralization need not be phonological but may be morphological
as well. For example, in German vowels are umlauted (fronted) in a
number of contexts which can only be defined in grammatical terms. One
such category is the nominative plural of second declension nouns, where
the ending is -*e* [ə]: for example, *Nacht* 'night', but *Nächt-e* [nɛxt-ə]
'nights'. This rule leads to neutralization because of the existence of many
nouns whose root vowel is /ɛ/, for example, *Recht, Recht-e* 'right'. Again
the neutralization is only contextual because the underlying contrast
between /a/ and /ɛ/ appears phonetically in the singular forms.

In absolute neutralization the underlying contrast is neutralized in all contexts and never appears directly on the phonetic surface. The rule in Bever's analysis of Menomini that converts /θ/ to *n* is a rule of absolute neutralization. The underlying contrast between /θ/ and /n/ is never realized directly in phonetic representation. The /θ/ appears as *s* in the palatalizing environments and as *n* elsewhere. Thus, underlying /θ/ never appears phonetically, but is always merged with some other sound in the Menomini inventory of phonemes. The Yawelmani rule lowering /i:/ and /u:/ to /e:/ and /o:/ also gives rise to absolute neutralization. Underlying /u:/ never appears directly on the phonetic surface but is always merged with some other phoneme of the language—either with /o:/ by vowel lowering or with /u/ by some of the shortening rules discussed in Chapter 4. Lowering of /i:/ to /e:/ would not be a case of absolute neutralization since /e:/ is not an independent phoneme in Yawelmani—all /e:/s may be derived from underlying /i:/.

Kiparsky claims that a study of linguistic change shows that rules of absolute neutralization have rather different properties from rules of contextual neutralization, and that after a rule of absolute neutralization has been added to a grammar in the form of a sound change, succeeding generations of language learners will tend to reanalyze their language in a lexical fashion rather than to maintain the rule of absolute neutralization. Three such properties are cited. The most important is that of "reversibility," which simply means that through further linguistic evolution an opposition that has been neutralized may reappear on the phonetic surface.

Although examples of such reversibility are not particularly common, Kiparsky cites a few. They all involve rules of contextual neutralization. For example, German has a rule of final devoicing like Russian: *Weg* [vek] 'road', but *Weg-e* [veg-ə] 'roads'. In Lithuanian Yiddish (Sapir 1915) this rule ceased to apply so that in this dialect of German *Weg* appears as [veg], with the neutralized voicing opposition restored. One of the things showing that this dialect did have the final devoicing rule and lost it is the fact that nonalternating morphemes that historically contained a final voiced obstruent retain the voiceless pronunciation in the dialect (cf., [avek] 'away', which is etymologically related to *Weg*).

Another example cited by Kiparsky concerns other dialects of German in which the umlauted *ä* [ɛ] has been shifted from a mid to a low front vowel [æ]. This linguistic change from the Standard German state of affairs, where umlauted *ä* is realized as [ɛ], only affected *ɛ*s that alternated with *a*. Original *ɛ*s like that in *Recht*, as well as historically umlauted but nonalternating *ɛ*s like that in *Bett* 'bed' (<*badi-*), are not lowered in these dialects. Thus, Standard German *Nächt-e* appears as [næcht-ə], while the

εs of *Recht* and *Bett* remain unchanged. In these dialects the neutralized opposition between /a/ and /ε/ has reemerged in the form of an /æ/ versus /ε/ opposition.
According to Kiparsky:

> The reversibility of contextual neutralization contrasts sharply with the irreversibility of the alleged cases of absolute neutralization. There is not a single case on record, to my knowledge, of analogical reversal of absolute neutralization, although given the present theory of generative phonology such a reversal is every bit as easy to express as the amply documented reversal of contextual neutralization. As far as the evidence indicates, absolute neutralization is totally irreversible [1968a: 18–19].

Thus we would not expect contemporary Menomini to undergo a linguistic change whereby the hypothetical /θ/ - /n/ opposition in Bever's analysis would reemerge on the phonetic surface.

Instead, Kiparsky claims, absolute neutralization introduces an instability into phonological structure that gives rise to a reanalysis of the rules that are sensitive to the absolutely neutralized contrast. When such reanalysis occurs, it will take one of three forms. First, the underlying phonological contrast to which the rule is sensitive may be replaced by an arbitrary lexical contrast. Earlier we argued that just this kind of reanalysis has occurred in Menomini, where the *n* ~ *s* alternation is to be accounted for by a rule converting *n* to *s* in an ad hoc set of morphemes marked in the lexicon to undergo this rule. Second, the rule may be generalized to the other member of the absolutely merged opposition. This is the response that occurred in Central Algonquian to the merger of *θ and *l—the palatalization rule was generalized to *l* < *l* as well as continuing to apply to *l* < *θ*. Finally, instead of being conditioned by the absolutely neutralized underlying contrast the rule may come to be sensitive to grammatical or morphological categories. This usually happens only when the distribution of the two terms of the absolute neutralization parallels some grammatically specifiable environment. An example is provided by German umlaut mentioned earlier. Umlaut was originally conditioned by an *i* in a following case suffix. Such *is were merged with other nonumlauting suffixes into ə so that now the umlaut rule must refer to the morphological contexts in which the *is appeared. (Of course, there has been some simplification and generalization of the contexts giving rise to umlaut so that the correspondence between the present-day morphological contexts and the former phonological one is not exact.)

In addition to reversibility and stability, Kiparsky also claims that absolute and contextual neutralizations differ with respect to productivity. New lexical items will often behave in accord with rules of contextual neutralization, but Kiparsky claimed that there were few clear cases where new lexical items were adjusted to agree with rules of absolute neutralization.

Each of these three differences between absolute and contextual neutralization led Kiparsky to hypothesize that either (i) rules of absolute neutralization do not exist in synchronic phonologies, or (ii) that they represent a linguistically complex state of affairs and are to be postulated only when the gains in linguistically significant generalization outweigh this added complexity. (i) is thus a much stronger constraint than (ii). In a later publication, Kiparsky (1971) explained that (i) was intended to prohibit absolute neutralization in those cases where the postulated underlying contrast is relevant for the statement of just a single rule or constraint in the grammar, as in the Menomini example. The weaker form of the constraint (ii) is intended to permit absolute neutralization in cases such as Yawelmani, where the underlying contrast is relevant for the statement of a number of separate rules or constraints.

While most phonologists would agree that absolute neutralization in a case such as the Menomini example is unwarranted, we believe that the historical evidence Kiparsky adduces against the existence of all rules of absolute neutralization is not particularly compelling. First of all, we are not aware of any *general* theory of what kinds of rules can or cannot be lost from a grammar. Is it the case that *any* rule of grammar could be lost? For example, could a language that reduces unstressed vowels (like Russian) lose that vowel reduction process entirely, so that all of the underlying vowel qualities return to the surface? Could a language that deletes a vowel in the environment before another vowel lose that rule, so that the underlying vowel sequence is manifested on the surface? Could a language that inserts vowels to break up three consonant clusters lose that rule, so that all underlying three consonant clusters appear phonetically? We do not know the answers to these questions, and we do not think anyone else does either. But if it is possible that there are real rules of grammar that cannot simply be dropped from the grammar (with no accompanying change of underlying representations), then we cannot be certain that the irreversibility of absolute neutralization rules shows anything about whether they are real rules of synchronic grammars.

Second, there are situations which are describable by absolute neutralization rules that give every evidence of being highly stable, contrary to Kiparsky's predictions. For instance, Newman (1944) describes several dialects of Yokuts in addition to Yawelmani, and in every one of the dialects basically the same situation can be found with respect to the behavior of surface /o:/ vowels. There is no evidence in these dialects to suggest that the situation in Yawelmani is highly unstable. Furthermore, there are many situations that are describable by fairly straightforward rules that are nevertheless unstable. For instance, the Maori example discussed in Chapter 5 involves a case of contextual neutralization that proved to be unstable and led to reanalysis. Thus even if analyses requiring absolute neutralizations were generally unstable, they are not alone in this respect. Much more work needs to be done to determine what makes a particular situation unstable. It seems clear that one thing that makes the analysis of Yawelmani with underlying high vowels so stable is that the underlying contrast between /u:/ and /o:/ is so tightly interwoven into the complex morphophonemic system of the language; a change in the underlying vowel inventory of the language would have consequences at every point in the system. If Yawelmani lost the rule lowering long high vowels, most of the words in the language would have to alter their pronunciation as a consequence. Such a wholesale restructuring of the phonemic representations of words seems unlikely to ever occur as the result of rule loss (of course, across-the-board changes in phonetic detail do occur in the course of the *addition* of rules to the grammar).

With respect to the claimed lack of productivity of absolute neutralization rules, we have little evidence available to us. Hyman (1970a) has argued that a rule of absolute neutralization applies to borrowings in Nupe, but other interpretations of his data have been given.

The constraint discussed by Kiparsky also has another aspect to it, which he calls the "alternation condition." We have seen that the prohibition against rules of absolute neutralization prevents positing an underlying opposition that is always neutralized phonetically. The alternation condition enforces a similar restriction with respect to the relationship between a given morpheme's UR and its associated phonetic realizations. Although Kiparsky never formulates this condition precisely, the following statement seems to faithfully represent the spirit of the restriction he has in mind:

(47) ALTERNATION CONDITION: *Each language has an inventory of segments appearing in underlying representations. Call these segments phonemes. The UR of a morpheme may not contain a phoneme /x/ that is always realized phonetically as identical to the realization of some other phoneme /y/.*

This constraint prevents setting up in the underlying inventory of sounds a phoneme that is always realized the same as some other phoneme. It would also require that if a morpheme contains a certain segment x that never alternates with any other segment, and if x is a phoneme in the language, then the underlying representation of this segment must be /x/. The constraint thus prevents setting up an underlying contrast in a morpheme that is never realized phonetically in one of the morpheme's alternants. The alternation condition thus prohibits rules of absolute neutralization, since they neutralize an opposition in all positions. In addition, under certain circumstances it will not allow an UR to be mapped on to a PR even if the rule relating the two has only contextual neutralization as one of its side-effects. To illustrate, consider the following data from Lithuanian. In this language there are two contrasting nasals in underlying representation: /m/ and /n/ (cf., *magas* 'magician' vs. *nagas* 'nail'). The dental nasal *n* but not the labial nasal *m* assimilates in point of articulation to a following stop.

(48)   *sen-as* 'old', *sem-bernis* 'old fellow'
         pin-a 'plaits', *pin-ti* 'to plait', *piŋ-kite* 'plait!'
         tem-o 'darkened', *tem-ti* 'to darken', *tem-kite* 'darken!'

Now consider the following forms: *tamp-yti* 'to stretch', *žemb-ti* 'to cut', *laŋg-as* 'window', *raŋk-a* 'hand'. In each of these four morphemes the nasals *m* and *n* are constant and do not alternate. The *m* of the first pair has two possible sources in the grammar of Lithuanian: /m/ and /n/, the latter via the nasal assimilation rule. The alternation condition forces us to derive the *m* in these two words from /m/. Setting it up as /n/ would violate the constraint, because the nasal in question is always realized phonetically as *m* and both /m/ and /n/ are underlying phonemes in the language. On the other hand, the nasals in *raŋka* and *laŋgas* may be derived from /n/, because even though they always appear as *ŋ* phonetically, the mapping from /n/ to *ŋ* does not involve the neutralization of an underlying contrast, since *ŋ* is not a phoneme in the language.

    The constraint enforced by the alternation condition provides an explanation for the behavior of [avek] in the Lithuanian Yiddish example discussed earlier. Etymologically this form derives from *Weg* 'road'. But in the historical evolution of German, the connection between the two words was lost; [avek] was reanalyzed as a single morpheme unrelated to *Weg*. Being an adverb, [avek] was never inflected, so that its final consonant was always in final position and hence always pronounced as the voiceless velar stop *k*. This *k* could have two underlying sources in the grammar of German: either /k/ or /g/, the latter via the final devoicing rule. The linguistic innovation in Lithuanian Yiddish, whereby the final devoicing rule was lost from the grammar, shows that, at least in this dialect, [avek] was reanalyzed as having the UR /avek/, even though historically it derives from /aveg/. The alternation condition provides an explanation for this reanalysis, because if [avek] were to be derived from /aveg/, the /g/ would always be realized as k, and both /g/ and /k/ are contrasting phonemes in German. Hence the only UR permitted by the alternation condition is /avek/, and this is precisely the form that surfaces when the obscuring effect of the final devoicing rule is removed.

While the alternation condition provides the proper account of *avek* (assuming that this is a valid example), there are, nevertheless, many internally well-motivated analyses that it would exclude. Until we are sure that such analyses are wrong, the alternation condition cannot be accepted. Consider the following example from the Bantu language Kinyarwanda. In this language the sound *h* occurs in many words: *gú-h-a* 'to give', *gu-heek-a* 'to carry on the back', *gú-hũng-a* 'to cultivate', *umu-húúngu* 'boy', *ama-hénéhene* 'goat's milk', *gu-sohok-a* 'to go out', and so on. Notice that *h* occurs both initially in a stem and also medially. The *h* in Kinyarwanda appears to derive historically from an original proto-Bantu **p* (for instance, 'to give' is *ku-p-á* in Shona and *x-p-a* in Chimwi: ni) and it still reflects this origin in part. Stems that have an initial *h* require that a preceding nasal assume the shape *m*. Since nasals ordinarily assimilate the point of articulation of a following consonant, the appearance of *m* can be seen to be a direct reflection of the original labial nature of *h*. An example illustrating this behavior of nasals is *m-h-a* 'give it to me'. While stem-initial *h* does then reflect to a certain degree its labial origin, an *h* that is interior in a morpheme and after a vowel never has an opportunity to reflect its historical origin. Thus for a verb like *gu-sohok-a* there is nothing that indicates that the *h* is anything but *h*.

From the above discussion it seems reasonable to conclude that *h* is properly regarded as a phoneme of the language. There is, of course, some uncertainty as to how to analyze stem-initial *h* in the root of a verb like 'give'. If we postulate underlying /p/, a nasal preceding such a stem would naturally assume the shape /m/ by the nasal assimilation rule. Furthermore, there is independent evidence in the language that voiceless stops are converted to *h* after a nasal (e.g., *agá-ka* 'little cow', but *iŋ-ha* 'cow'; *uru-toki* 'finger', but *in-hoki* 'fingers'). Thus the following derivation could be postulated.

(49)   N-p-a
        m-p-a   Nasal assimilation
        m-h-a   Reduction of voiceless stops to *h* after a nasal

In order to derive the *h* in *gú-h-a* 'to give' another rule would be required that converts /p/ to /h/ in all contexts. (There are some /p/ sounds in

Kinyarwanda, but they are contained in loanwords and could be regarded simply as exceptions to this rule.)

If this analysis was accepted, it would mean that an underlying /p/ is postulated that is never manifested on the surface—in other words, it would involve an abstract segment. There is, however, an alternate approach. This approach takes /h/ as basic, but assumes that it is converted to /p/ after a nasal consonant. After this *h*-to-*p* rule operates, the nasal assimilates the point of articulation of the /p/. Finally, this /p/ is converted to /h/ by the same rule that converts /t/ and /k/ to *h* after a nasal. The following derivation would be involved.

(50)   N-h-a
            N-p-a   *h*-to-*p* rule
            m-p-a   Nasal assimilation
            m-h-a   Voiceless stops to *h*

Notice that this derivation requires that a sound /p/ be introduced in the course of the derivation of *m-h-a*, and this /p/ occurs neither in the underlying structure nor in the surface structure. In a way this derivation is extremely abstract, but it is a kind of abstraction that has been largely overlooked in the discussion of abstractness in phonology.

The only alternative to the preceding two analyses is to simply say that, for some strange reason, a nasal in a prefix changes to /m/ before /h/. This approach would give up trying to account for the assimilation to *m* before *h* on phonetic grounds. This strikes us as perhaps too drastic a step to take, but it certainly is a possible approach to the difficulty.

Let us leave open what the final analysis of the above data ought to be, since the point that we are building up to does not depend on which of the above analyses is chosen. We turn now to consider some additional data from Kinyarwanda that are directly relevant to Kiparsky's alternation condition. In Kinyarwanda there are some clusters of nasal plus *h* which do not participate in any alternations. The following are representative examples:

(51)   *nhi-*   negative prefix   *ŋhána*   'on purpose'
       umuu-nhu   'person'   *ŋha*   'like'
       nhaa   'there is not'
       nhúúza   'someone'

Given the alternation condition, the *h*s in the above examples would have to be set up as underlying *h*s since they do not alternate and *h* is an underlying phoneme in the language. But such an analysis is highly suspect. First of all, /ŋ/ is not a basic sound in Kinyarwanda. In the vast majority of cases it can be shown unambiguously to be the result of assimilation of a nasal to a following velar consonant. If an underlying /h/ is postulated for examples like *ŋhána*, *ŋha*, etc., then it would be necessary to claim that a nasal becomes a velar before /h/. But the examples discussed earlier show that a nasal becomes /m/ before /h/. Furthermore, in items such as *umuu-nhu* and *nhaa* we see that the nasal does not become a velar, but rather appears as /n/. There appears to be no viable analysis of the above data, then, that assumes they have /h/ underlyingly. Instead it is necessary to assume that *nhaa* derives from a more remote structure /ntaa/ and that *ŋha* derives from a more remote structure /ŋka/ (we ignore here the question of what the underlying representation of the nasal is). The independently motivated rule changing voiceless stops to *h* after a nasal will account for the surface forms of these items. This sort of analysis violates the alternation condition (since the *h*s are nonalternating and there is a phonemic *h* in the language), but appears to us to be well-motivated.

In summary, it appears that the strong form of the alternation condition (which prevents absolute neutralization and some cases of contextual neutralization universally) is too strong, because it excludes a rather large number of well-motivated analyses. We are thus driven to accepting it in its weak form, but this is of no real help since the weak form of the condition is really just a restatement of the problem of abstractness. That is to say, in its weak form the alternation condition permits abstract URs if there is enough evidence to motivate such representations. But it says nothing about either the kinds of evidence that are relevant nor the amount of such evidence that is needed in order to accept or reject any given abstract analysis. Nevertheless, despite its inconclusive nature, Kiparsky (1968a) is a landmark study in generative phonology. It was the first paper to clarify the entire issue of abstractness and forced many linguists to reconsider some rather questionable assumptions underlying much previous work in generative phonology.

The True Generalization Condition

A much more radical approach to the problem of abstractness has recently been suggested by Hooper (1976) who proposes imposing what she calls the "True Generalization Condition" (TGC) on phonological rules. This condition requires

> that all rules express transparent surface generalizations, generalizations that are true for all surface forms and that, furthermore, [rules] express the relation between surface forms in the most direct manner possible. . . . The True Generalization Condition claims that the rules speakers formulate are based directly on surface forms and that these rules relate one surface form to another, rather than relating underlying to surface form [Hooper 1976: p. 13].

To see what is at stake here, consider Hooper's discussion of nasal vowels in French. In Schane's (1968) analysis of French all surface phonetic nasal vowels are derived from underlying sequences of oral vowel plus nasal consonant by the following two ordered rules.

(52)
$$ V \longrightarrow [+ \text{nasal}]/\underline{}C \left\{ \begin{matrix} \# \\ C \end{matrix} \right\} $$
$$ [+ \text{nasal}] $$

(53)
$$ C \longrightarrow \emptyset/ \ V \underline{} $$
$$ [+ \text{nasal}] \quad [+ \text{nasal}] $$

These rules account for the alternations displayed by masculine adjectives such as /bɔn/ 'good', which appears as [bɔ̃] before words beginning with a consonant, as in *un bon frère* [æ̃ bɔ̃ frɛr], or pause, as in *c'est bon* [se bɔ̃], but as [bɔn] in *un bon ami* [æ̃ bɔn ami]. It should be noted that Schane assumed that the # in (52) actually referred to phrase-final position and that the rule applies across word boundaries within the phrase. Given this assumption, (52) will apply in *c'est bon* since the VN sequence is phrase-final; it will block in *bon ami* because the VN sequence is followed by a vowel and the rule is assumed to apply across word boundaries. It will, however, apply in *bon frère* because the VN sequence is followed by a consonant.

According to Hooper (1976) the alternation exhibited by /bɔn/ should not be accounted for by (52) and (53), for two reasons. First, rule (52) is not true of the phonetic surface in view of the existence of feminine forms such as *une bonne sœur* [yn bɔn sœr], where an oral vowel plus nasal consonant sequence [ɔn] is followed by a consonant in PR. Schane (1968) accounted for these forms by postulating that the feminine form of the adjective contained a mute *e* (schwa), so that the UR of *bonne* would be /bɔn-ə/. In Schane's analysis this schwa is deleted by a rule ordered after the vowel nasalization rules. Such a description is not permitted by the TGC since the presence of the oral vowel plus nasal plus consonant sequence in [bɔn sœr] means that (52) does not express a generalization that is true of the surface phonetic representations of French.

There is an additional reason why the TGC would not permit the above analysis.

> An alternation is considered to be phonetically motivated only if it always takes place when the phonetic motivation is present on the surface. If an alternation fails to take place when the phonetic environment is present (as in [bɔnsœr]), or takes place when the phonetic condition is NOT present (as in [bɔ̃frer]), then it cannot be associated with a phonetic environment but must be associated with something else in the language, e.g., a particular morpheme, a syntactic category, etc. [Hooper 1976:16].

The TGC thus requires, in effect, that all phonological rules be defined to operate on the phonetic representation. The statement in (54) appears to accurately formalize the restriction Hooper has in mind.

(54)   1. *If a rule of the form X $\longrightarrow$ Y/W____Z is to be valid, then strings of the form WXZ cannot systematically occur in PR.*[4]

2. *If Y is to be derived from X by the rule X $\longrightarrow$ Y/W____Z, then Y must appear in the string WYZ in PR.*

Since strings of the form oral vowel-N-# and oral vowel-N-C (from underlying /oral vowel-N-ə-#/ and /oral vowel-N-ə-C/) systematically appear in the PRs of French, the rules of (52) and (53) would violate the first clause of the TGC stated as (54). Furthermore, the second clause is violated by the mappings of VN# and VNC to V̄# and V̄C because the nasal consonant which triggers the nasalization of the vowel does not appear in PR.

Many previous generative analyses would not be permitted by the TGC, for as we have seen, one of the basic claims of generative phonology is that phonological rules may be defined on representations which do not appear phonetically but at a more abstract level. Just how abstract is, of course, the problem we have been addressing in this chapter. It is therefore important to examine the kinds of reformulations that would be required in order to maintain the TGC. In general, this condition will require replacing rules that operate on an abstract level with rules that refer to syntactic categories or to arbitrary lexical subcategorizations.

An example in which reformulation in terms of a syntactic context is a possible analysis is to be found in the Bantu language Kirundi (Rodegem 1970; Meeussen 1959). In this language there is a contrast between long and short vowels: *gu-sib-a* 'to neglect' versus *gu-siib-a* 'to abstain',

---

[4] We say WXZ cannot occur **systematically**, in order to allow for the possibility of a few isolated lexical exceptions.

ku-gum-a 'to be firm', versus *ku-guum-a* 'to be impulsive'. However, in position before a nasal plus consonant a noninitial vowel is always pronounced long, never short: *umu-ruundi* 'a Rundi person', *ku-riind-a* 'to wait', *ku-geend-a* 'to go', *ku-roond-a* 'to look for'. Since this is a true generalization about surface PRs in Kirundi (borrowings are adjusted to conform with it), we may suppose that the grammar contains a rule specifying vowels as long when followed by a NC cluster. Rule (55) states this aspect of Kirundi structure.

(55) $V \longrightarrow [+\text{long}]/\_\_\_NC$

However, the morphological structure of the language is such that there is only one grammatical category in which a vowel length alternation occurs that could be clearly related to the principle expressed as (54). This occurs when the first person morpheme, which we represent here as a /N/, is prefixed to a verb. If that verb begins with a consonant, the /N/ will assimilate in point of articulation to the initial consonant of the verb root and a preceding vowel will be lengthened.

(56)

ku-ror-a	'to look at'	*n-tabáar-e*	'that I help'
ku-ba-ror-a	'to look at them'	*ba-tabáar-e*	'that they help'
kuu-n-dor-a	'to look at me'	*baa-n-tabáar-e*	'that they help me'

The rule in (55) will account for the lengthening of the prefixal vowels in *kuu-n-dor-a* and *baa-n-tabáar-e*. This treatment is consistent with the TGC since there are no counterexamples to the rule in phonetic representation: Vowels are always long before a NC cluster in Kirundi PRs, and, furthermore, the NC cluster that triggers the lengthening of the prefixal vowel in these examples is present on the phonetic surface.

Similar facts obtain for all other verb roots that begin with a nonnasal consonant. However, if the root begins with a nasal consonant, what we find on the surface is lengthening of the prefixal vowel but only a single nasal in phonetic representation. The data in (57) illustrate this point.

(57)

ku-meñ-a	'to know'	*ku-ñag-a*	'to rob'
ku-ba-meñ-a	'to know them'	*ku-ba-ñag-a*	'to rob them'
kuu-meñ-a	'to know me'	*kuu-ñag-a*	'to rob me'

These data could be accounted for in purely phonological terms by postulating the URs /ku-N-meñ-a/ and /ku-N-ñag-a/ and appealing to a rule that degeminates two identical consonants (there are no long consonants in Kirundi). The derivation of *kuu-meñ-a* under this analysis appears as (58).

(58)   /ku-N-meñ-a/
          ku-m-meñ-a   Nasal assimilation
          kuu-m-meñ-a   NC lengthening
          kuu-meñ-a   Degemination

Such an analysis would not be permitted by the TGC since the lengthening rule is applying in an abstract context; in particular, it is the abstract /m + m/ sequence which appears as *m* on the surface that triggers the rule. In order to maintain the TGC, the lengthening in *kuu-meñ-a* would have to be conditioned by the grammatical context. Since vowel length alternations in Kirundi only occur in the context of the first person morpheme (it being the only nasal which combines with a following consonant across morpheme boundaries to form a NC cluster preceded by a non-initial vowel), it would appear that the substitution of the grammatical context (first person) for the phonological one (____NC) does not result in the loss of any significant generalizations.[5] The phonologically based lengthening rule (55) could still be used to account for the length alternations in forms such as (56) where the first person morpheme does show up on the surface. The only difference between the two analyses is whether it is the grammatical or the abstract phonological context that is responsible for lengthening in forms such as *kuu-meñ-a*. To our knowledge, there is no evidence internal to Kirundi bearing on this matter.

There are, of course, cases where it is pretty clear that a grammatical context has been substituted for a purely phonological one. A number of these are cited in Hooper (1976) as support for the TGC. An additional example appears in Harari, a Semitic language of Ethiopia described in

[5] Actually, the details of how the grammatically based analysis is to work are far from clear, since exactly which grammatical features play a role in phonology and how they do so is largely unknown. With respect to the Kirundi data, an important question is how the category of 1 sg. object is to be represented for forms such as *kuu-meñ-a*. Note that on the surface the only feature which identifies this word as containing a 1 sg. object is the vowel length, which is what we are trying to assign by the grammatically based rule. Do we allow for a zero morph between the infinitive prefix and the verb root to condition the lengthening? Or do we say that the verb root is marked with a syntactic features such as [+1 sg. object]? Thus the appeal to grammatical conditioning is not nearly as clear a solution as might seem at first blush. It raises the fundamental question as to whether appeal to grammatical categories does not in some cases merely substitute one kind of abstractness and arbitrariness for another.

Leslau (1958). In Harari there are rigid prohibitions against medial three-consonant clusters as well as initial and final two-consonant clusters. When such impermissible clusters arise in underlying forms through the conjunction of morphemes or through the morphological modification of a root, a rule of epenthesis is activated to break up these clusters. This rule inserts *i* in the positions CC___C, CC___#, and #C___C. Its effect can be seen in the following two paradigms of the root /sbr/ 'break':

(59)

	Imperfect		Negative imperfect	
2 masc.	*tisäbri*	/t-säbr/	*zätsibär*	/zä-t-sbär/
2 fem.	*tisäbri*	/t-säbr-i/	*zätsibäri*	/zä-t-sbär-i/
3 masc.	*yisäbri*	/y-säbr/	*zäysibär*	/zä-y-sbär/
3 fem.	*tisäbri*	/t-säbr/	*zätsibär*	/zä-t-sbär/
1 pl.	*nisäbri*	/n-säbr/	*zänsibär*	/zä-n-sbär/
2 pl.	*tisäbru*	/t-säbr-u/	*zätsibäru*	/zä-t-sbär-u/
3 pl.	*yisäbru*	/y-säbr-u/	*zäysibäru*	/zä-y-sbär-u/

In the imperfect the root takes the shape /säbr/, invoking the insertion of *i* in the 2 masc., 3 masc., 3 fem. and 1 pl., where there is no suffix. Similarly, addition of the *t-*, *y-*, and *n-* prefixes creates an initial cluster that is broken by *i*. The negative imperfect is built on the jussive stem /sbär/. There is no final cluster, so inserted *i* does not appear in the 2 masc., 3 masc., 3 fem., and 1 pl., where the ending is zero. Addition of the negative morpheme /zä-/ means there is no initial cluster. However, a medial CCC arises from the combination of the prefixes *t-*, *y-*, and *n-* with the jussive root shape /sbär/. This cluster is broken by the insertion of *i* between the second and third consonants.

With these preliminaries out of the way we can now turn to the matter of current interest. Harari has a rule palatalizing a stem-final dental to a palatal when followed by a high front vowel. As it turns out, the *only* inflectional suffix beginning with *i* is the 2 feminine /-i/. Thus, the palatalization rule does not operate in any other category. In particular, the inserted *i* that occurs at the end of the 2 masc., 3 masc., 3 fem., and 1 pl. does not trigger this rule.

(60)

2 masc.	2 fem.	Gloss
ti-käft-i	*ti-käfč-i*	'open'
ti-lämd-i	*ti-lämǧ-i*	'learn'
ti-läbs-i	*ti-läbš-i*	'dress'
ti-nädl-i	*ti-nädy-i*	'make a hole'

These data could be described in purely phonological terms by formulating a rule to palatalize dentals before the vowel *i* and ordering this rule before the rule of epenthesis. Such an analysis would not be permitted by the TGC since the rule would have many counterexamples on the phonetic surface: all those dentals that stand before an inserted *i*. On the other hand, since the alternation is triggered by just the 2 fem. morpheme, an alternative would be to formulate the rule in grammatical terms: Palatalize a stem-final dental before the 2 sg. feminine suffix. In this case there is some evidence that the grammatically based analysis is correct. This evidence concerns the fact that palatalization may also (apparently optionally) affect a dental occurring earlier in the root, so long as the root appears in the 2 fem. form. Thus, beside the forms in (60) cited above, the following are also to be found.

(61)

2 masc.	2 fem.	Gloss
ti-säbr-i	*ti-šäbr-i*	'break'
ti-kätb-i	*ti-käčb-i*	'write'
ti-qädm-i	*ti-qäǧm-i*	'advance'
ti-sägd-,	*ti-šägǧ-i*	'prostrate'

Palatalization thus appears to be exploited as a sign of the 2 sg. fem. (to distinguish it from other forms of the paradigm such as the masc.) and is being extended to mark the root as a whole in this particular grammatical category. If the rule were purely phonologically based, it would be difficult to account for this (phonetically unnatural) extension of the palatalization further back in the root.

The Kirundi and Harari examples discussed above represent cases where the substitution of a grammatically based rule for a purely phonologically based one is either possible or even preferable. Cases where an arbitrary lexical subcategorization replaces a phonologically conditioned alternation are quite common. The Menomini example discussed earlier in this chapter is an example. The TGC requires that rules applying to abstract representations always be replaced by grammatical or arbitrary lexical categories. We now turn to cases where such reformulations appear to be unwarranted and where, in our opinion, the abstract analysis is distinctly better motivated.

In Chimwi:ni, a Bantu language spoken in Somalia, a perfective form of the verb is formed by suffixation of the morpheme *-i:l-* (*-e:l-* if a mid vowel precedes). However, when the verb stem ends in *s*, *z*, *sh* ([š]), or *ñ*, the liquid in the perfective suffix changes to *z*.

(62) *łum-i:ł-e* 'he bit'   *bus-i:z-e* 'he kissed'
     reb-e:ł-e 'he stopped'   *was-i:z-e* 'he made a will'
     kun-i:ł-e 'he scratched'   *uz-i:z-e* 'he sold'
     had-i:ł-e 'he said'   *yez-e:z-e* 'he filled'
     tov-e:ł-e 'he dipped'   *fañ-i:z-e* 'he did'
     łew-e:ł-e 'he got drunk'   *ush-i:z-e* 'he hid (it)'

This change of *ł* to *z* is limited to the perfective suffix. It does not, for example, affect the applied suffix whose UR is /-ił-/. It is, however, a totally general change that applies to borrowings as well as to native words. For example, *bus-i:z-e* 'he kissed', *xus-i:z-e* 'he was concerned', and *his-i:z-e* 'he felt cold' have verb roots that are Arabic loans. We formulate the rule as (63).

(63)
$$\overset{\text{ł}}{\underset{\text{[perf]}}{}} \longrightarrow z/[s,z,sh,ñ]V\_\_\_\_$$

Rule (63) interacts with another rule we shall label mutation. This rule induces the following changes on stem-final consonants that precede the perfective suffix:

   1. *Converts voiceless labial, dental, and alveolar stops to* s *and converts* k *to* sh.

   2. *Changes voiced stops to* z, *but only when preceded by a nasal.*

   3. *Shifts* ł *to* z *(but leaves other liquids unaffected).*

Some examples of mutation follow:

(64)

Infinitive	Perfective	Gloss
ku-łip-a	*łis-ił-e*	'pay'
x-kut-a	*kus-ił-e*	'fold'
ku-ło:t-a	*ło:s-eł-e*	'dream'
x-shi:k-a	*shi:sh-ił-e*	'seize'
ku-ło:mb-a	*ło:nz-eł-e*	'beg'
x-pe:nd-a	*pe:nz-eł-e*	'like'
x-shi:nd-a	*shi:nz-ił-e*	'win'
x-fu:ŋg-a	*fu:nz-ił-e*	'close'
ku-ło:mb-a	*mo:z-eł-e*	'shave'

The rule of mutation affects these changes in stem-final consonants only before the perfective suffix. It does not apply before the "applied" suffix: cf. *ku-gi:ṭ-iḷ-a* 'to pull with', not **ku-gi:s-iḷ-a*.

Comparison of a perfective form such as *bus-i:z-e* 'he kissed' from (62) with a form such as *kus-il-e* 'he folded' from (64) shows that only stems ending in *s*, *z*, *sh*, and *ñ* in the UR trigger the *ḷ*-to-*z* rule. Stems that terminate in one of these consonants as a result of mutation never do. The preceding two forms will be derived as follows.

(65)　　　/bus-i:ḷ-e/　　/kuṭ-i:ḷ-e/
　　　　　bus-i:z-e　　------------　　ḷ-to-*z*
　　　　　------------　　*kus-i:ḷ-e*　　Mutation
　　　　　------------　　*kus-iḷ-e*　　Other rules

Such an analysis is not permitted by the TGC since the *ḷ*-to-*z* rule applies in an abstract context—that is, before the rule of mutation has applied. The latter rule creates systematic counterexamples to the *ḷ*-to-*z* rule in PR. The *ḷ*-to-*z* rule thus violates the first clause of the TGC, as stated in (54) above. In order to maintain the TGC in the face of these data we cannot reformulate the rule to appeal to grammatical categories, since the category in which the rule does apply (as in *bus-i:z-e*) is exactly the same as the category in which it does not apply (as in *kus-iḷ-e*). They are both perfective forms. The only recourse is to an ad hoc division of the lexicon into one class of stems which triggers the rule and another class that does not. However, such a lexical subcategorization would be totally unwarranted in this case since it ignores the clear phonetic contrast which differentiates these two types of stems: Stems that trigger *ḷ*-to-*z* end in *s*, *z*, *sh*, and *ñ*, and stems that do not end in other consonants. The fact that borrowings from Arabic that end in these consonants systematically trigger *ḷ*-to-*z* shows that the rule is psychologically real. In this case the abstract phonological analysis is clearly the correct one.

It is not only morphologically conditioned rules such as the Chimwi:ni *ḷ*-to-*z* rule that can be defined on abstract levels of representation. Sometimes low-level phonetic rules are also sensitive to abstract levels of representation. An interesting example is to be found in Anceaux's (1965) description of Nimboran, a language of New Guinea. In this language *p* is in free variation with a voiceless bilabial fricative *ɸ* so long as it is not word final or immediately preceded by *m* or *s*. We may thus postulate an optional rule taking *p* to *ɸ* in these contexts. The language also has a rule that optionally converts /b/ to *p* when followed by a voiceless consonant.

This devoiced *b* will then alternate with *ƥ* in the same way as underlying *p* does. Examples are to be found in the following 1 sg. verb forms:

(66)

Future	Present	Past	Distal	Gloss
beka-d-u	*beka-t-u*	*beka-k-u*	*beka-sa-k-u*	'kick'
brub-d-u	*bru* {b, p, ƥ}*-t-u*	*bru* {b, p, ƥ}*-k-u*	*bru* {b, p, ƥ}*-sa-k-u*	'stab'
{p, ƥ}*yb-d-u*	{p, ƥ}*y*{b, p, ƥ}*-t-u*	{p, ƥ}*y*{b, p, ƥ}*-k-u*	{p, ƥ}*y*{b, p, ƥ}*-sa-k-u*	'fold'

In these data the suffix *-u* marks the 1 sg., while *-d*, *-t*, and *-k* are the future, present, and past morphemes. The suffix *-sa* denotes action done away from the speaker. Note that stems with an underlying final /b/ such as /brub/ and /pyb/ optionally devoice the final /b/ when followed by *-t*, *-k*, and *-sa*; this devoiced /b/ then takes on the properties of *p*; that is, it may appear as *ƥ*.

The rules implied by these data (a rule devoicing /b/ before a voiceless consonant and a rule spirantizing *p* to *ƥ*) would be permitted by the TGC. There is also a suffix beginning with /p/—the recent past. It will optionally spirantize in forms such as *beka-p-u/beka-ƥ-u* 'I kicked yesterday'. When the preceding stem ends in a /b/ the underlying /b + p/ cluster appears phonetically as *p*. But this *p* never alternates with *ƥ*: *pypu/ƥypu* 'I folded yesterday' and *brupu* 'I stabbed yesterday'.

These data could be accounted for phonologically by assuming that after the underlying /b + p/ cluster devoices to /p + p/, a rule simplifying /p + p/ to /p/ applies. The fact that /p/ from /p + p/ does not spirantize could be accounted for by ordering spirantization before degemination of /p + p/. Such an analysis would not be permitted by the TGC since the rule spirantizing /p/ to *ƥ* has systematic counterexamples in phonetic representation—all those /p/s that derive from /p + p/. But it would be incorrect to consider these /p/s from /p + p/ as arbitrary lexical exceptions, because they systematically fail to undergo spirantization. Nor would appeal to a grammatical environment be of any real help. We could not simply say that the rule does not apply in the recent past—it does when the stem ends in a vowel, as in *beka-p-u/beka-ƥ-u*. It will also apply to nonfinal /p/s within the stem in this grammatical context, as in *pypu/ƥypu*. If one were to try to specify the context in which spirantization blocks one would have to say that it does not apply at the junction between the verb stem and the recent past suffix only when the stem ends in /b/ (and presumably /p/, though Anceaux cites no examples). But clearly this is just a roundabout way of defining the abstract phonological context.

The two previous examples involve violations of the first clause of the TGC in (54), that is, where a phonological rule has systematic counterexamples in PR. We now turn to violations of the second condition, cases where phonological rules must be defined to operate in abstract phonological contexts. In a number of languages stress rules ignore inserted vowels. When such inserted vowels are phonetically identical to underlying vowels, there will be no way to position the stress correctly if the stress rule is defined on the PR. Cuna (Sherzer 1970) presents an intriguing example of this type. In Cuna stress usually falls on the penultimate syllable. There are, however, certain exceptions where an *i* appears between *r* and *g* but does not receive the accent if it is penultimate; instead, the stress appears on the antepenult: for example, *bíriga* 'year'. This word would be regular if the UR were /birga/ and the stress rule was formulated in terms of the abstract representation that exists before the application of a rule inserting *i* between *r* and *g*. As Sherzer points out, the hypothetical UR /birga/ is supported by the *sorsik sunmakke* language game. Recall from our discussion in Chapter 5 that this game involves moving the initial syllable of the word to the end of the word. The game form for the word 'year' is *gabir*, which is what would be expected if the game rule were to operate in terms of the UR /birga/. If the game were to be based on the PR /biriga/, *rigabi* would be the expected game form. But in fact according to Sherzer this pronunciation is unacceptable.

Unfortunately, Sherzer does not supply enough information to enable us to determine the exact nature or the degree of generality of the epenthesis rule implied in his discussion of *bíriga*. Hence, these data constitute only a potential counterexample to the TGC, but nevertheless a very interesting one because of the external evidence provided by the linguistic game.

We therefore turn to a parallel example for which we have more material. As in most Arabic dialects, in the Palestinian dialect stress is assigned to words by a strong cluster principle. If the final syllable of the word contains a long vowel or ends in a consonant cluster, it receives the word accent: *kamá:n* 'also', *darastí:* 'you fem. studied it', *darást* 'I studied', *barí:s* 'Paris'. If the final syllable is light (i.e., contains a short vowel followed by at most one consonant), the penultimate syllable will take the accent if it is heavy—that is, if its vowel is long or followed by two consonants: *ʔádrus* 'I study', *ʔajá:wib* 'I answer', *ʔazú:ru* 'I visit him', *darásti* 'you fem. studied', *ʔatjáwwaz* 'I marry', *baṭá:ṭa* 'potato'. If both the last and the second last syllables are light, then the accent will fall on the antepenult: *dárasat* 'she studied', *darásatu* 'she studied it', *ṣálaṭa* 'salad', *kánada* 'Canada'.

The Palestinian dialect also has a rule whereby a stem ending in the sequence *CCVC* is metathesized to *CVCC* when a vowel-initial suffix is added.

(67)

zú ʔruṭ	'bees'	*símsim*	'sesame seeds'
zú ʔurṭ-a	'a bee'	*símism-e*	'a sesame seed'
zu ʔrúṭ-na	'our bees'	*simsím-na*	'our sesame seeds'
zú ʔurt-u	'his bees'	*símism-u*	'his sesame seeds'
zú ʔurṭ-ak	'your masc. bees'	*símism-ak*	'your masc. sesame seeds'
btúdrus	'you masc. study'		
btúdurs-i	'you fem. study'	*ʔistá ʔbil*	'greet! (masc.)'
byúdrus	'he studies'	*ʔistá ʔibl-i*	'greet! (fem.)'
byúdurs-u	'they study'	*ʔistá ʔibl-u*	'greet him!'
btúdurs-u	'you. masc. study it'	*ʔista ʔbíl-na*	'greet us!'
		byistá ʔbil	'he greets'
		byistá ʔibl-u	'he greets him'
		byista ʔbíl-na	'he greets us'

Note that in all of the examples where metathesis has applied the penultimate syllable becomes heavy, but the accent is still assigned to the antepenult: *btúdurs-i*. This accentual pattern can be derived by the regular accent rules informally sketched above, if they are permitted to apply to the abstract phonological representation that exists before the rule of metathesis has applied to make the penultimate syllable heavy, as the following derivation shows.

(68)   /b-tu-drus-i/
              b-tú-drus-i   Accent
              b-tú-durs-i   Metathesis

This analysis is of course a blatant violation of the second clause of the TGC. But it will be very difficult to assign stress to the surface form of these words by any rule that fulfills the requirements of the TGC. First, we would require a long listing of a quite heterogeneous set of syntactic categories—all those in which the suffix appearing after the stem begins with a vowel. Second, lexical subcategorization would be required in order to differentiate forms which have a closed penultimate syllable in the UR, and hence which accent the penultimate syllable in the PR (e.g., *bithúbb-i* 'you fem. love'), from forms such as *btúdurs-i* where the penultimate syllable is open in the UR. Of course, this arbitrary lexical subcategorization would just happen to accidentally correlate exactly with those stems that undergo metathesis. In our opinion these data clearly show that the stress rule is applying in an abstract context. Furthermore, the stress rule is quite productive, as the accentuation of the borrowed words cited earlier indicates.

A similar problem is created by the totally general rule that degeminates consonants at the end of a word.

(69)

	2 sg. fem.	3 masc.	Gloss
	bitrínni	*byitrín*	'ring'
	bitrújji	*byitrúj*	'shake'
	bittámmi	*byitám*	'persist'

Examination of the data in (69) reveals that the stress rule must apply in terms of the abstract representation that exists prior to degemination. Otherwise we cannot explain why the 3 masc. forms in (69) have stress on the final vowel. As pointed out above, a final syllable is stressed in Palestinian Arabic just in case it has a long vowel or ends in a consonant cluster. A form like *byitrín* does not satisfy either of these conditions in phonetic structure, although the more remote representation of this item with a final geminate consonant does have the sort of structure that induces a final stress. Of course, the TGC does not allow the stress rule to apply to the representation that exists prior to degemination. If the TGC is accepted, it will be necessary to distinguish on an arbitrary basis in the lexicon between those items that end in V̄C but still take final stress from those items that have this structure but do not take final stress. But this arbitrary lexical subcategorization ignores the fact that those stems that unexpectedly take final stress always end in a geminate consonant in their underlying representation. This gemination appears in PR when the stem is followed by a vowel-initial suffix. Clearly, the TGC forces us to replace a directly observable phonetic contrast with an abstract lexical contrast. The lexical feature required by the TGC is nothing but a gratuitous device to identify morphemes that end in a geminate consonant—a device necessitated only by the assumption that phonological rules may not apply in abstract contexts.

It should be pointed out that Hooper (1976) actually does permit violations of the TGC, but only under restricted circumstances. This will occur when there are variant pronunciations of the same word in different speech styles or tempos. For example, she points out that in Brazilian

Portuguese the dental stops *t* and *d* are palatalized to *č* and *ǰ* when immediately followed by *i*. This rule applies in the slowest tempo, so that *teatrinho* 'theater' is pronounced [čiatrīɲo] from UR /tiatrīɲo/. In fast speech *i* is deleted after *č* and *ǰ* (and mid vowels are raised to high), so that *teatrinho* appears as [čatrīɲu]. Note that in this form the *i* that conditions the palatalization of underlying /t/ is absent—a violation of the second clause of the TGC.

While we certainly agree that such violations of the TGC occur in fast speech, we believe that they raise some serious questions about the logic behind the TGC for slow speech. If it is granted that, on the basis of the observation of the variants [čiatrīɲo] and [čatrīɲu], the language learner can deduce that a rule of palatalizing *t* to *č* is operative in [čatrīɲu] because the conditioning environment (i.e., the *i*) is present in the variant [čiatrīɲo], why can't the learner of Palestinian deduce from the stem variants appearing in *btúdrus* and *btúdurs-i* that the antepenultimate stress rule has applied in the latter? For the stem shape /drus/ that is needed for correct application of the antepenult rule appears phonetically in the word *btúdrus*. In short, if the language learner can deduce principles from the observation of different variants of the same word, why can't those same deductive powers be used on different variants of the same stem, especially when the different stem variants are produced by completely productive rules? Until this question is answered, it would appear that the TGC is flawed by an internal inconsistency.

We have now looked at a wide variety of possible constraints on the relationship between an UR and its associated PRs. Most of these constraints have been shown to bar some analyses that are well-motivated on internal grounds (and sometimes analyses that are well-motivated on external grounds as well). If we accept such internal evidence, then these various constraints must be rejected as absolute constraints on abstractness (they might still function as tendencies, naturally). We admit that the question of the validity of various kinds of internal evidence remains an open question, and until sufficient external evidence has been accumulated that bears upon the validity of the main types of internal evidence, the problem of abstractness will remain with us.

Exercises

1. In Standard Ukrainian there are six vowels: *i, i̇, e, a, o, u*. There is also an opposition between palatalized and nonpalatalized consonants: *luk* 'bow', *l'uk* 'trapdoor'; *lono* 'lap', *l'on-u* 'falx', gen. sg.; *lapa* 'paw', *l'apas* 'slap'; *l'id* 'ice', *m'id'* 'copper'. However, the palatalized versus nonpalatalized contrast is neutralized to non-palatalized before *i̇* and *e*: cf. *xval'-u*, 'I praise', *xval-it* 'he praises'; *or'-u* 'I plough',

or-eš 'you plough'; *umr-u* 'I die', *umr-eš* 'you die'. The opposition is also neutralized to palatal before *i*: cf. *b'il-ij* 'white', *b'il'-iti* 'become white'; *bil'* 'ache', *bol'-iti* 'to ache'. The latter has certain apparent exceptions, such as the nonpalatalized *b* in *bil'* 'ache'. Write a set of ordered rules to account for the alternations in the roots and suffixes of the following nouns. The alternation between *o* and *e* is limited to suffixes and does not occur in roots. Also for masculine nouns referring to persons the morpheme *ov/ev* is inserted between the root and the case suffix in the locative singular. The data are ambiguous as to whether or not the alternations between *o* and *i* and between *e* and *i* are to be implemented by the same rule. Consider both possibilities.

Masculine nouns

Nom. sg.	Dat. pl.	Dat. sg.	Loc. sg.	Gloss
sv'it	sv'itam	sv'itov'i	sv'it'i	'light'
z'at'	z'at'am	z'atev'i	z'atev'i	'son-in-law'
koš'il'	košel'am	košelev'i	košel'i	'basket'
kam'in'	kamen'am	kamenev'i	kamen'i	'stone'
leb'id'	lebed'am	lebedev'i	lebed'i	'swan'
l'id	ledam	ledov'i	led'i	'ice'
bil'	bol'am	bolev'i	bol'i	'ache'
riw	rovam	rovov'i	rov'i	'ditch'
stiw	stolam	stolov'i	stol'i	'table'
d'id	d'idam	d'idov'i	d'idov'i	'grandfather'
l'it	l'otam	l'otov'i	l'ot'i	'flight'
mist	mostam	mostov'i	most'i	'bridge'

Neuter nouns

Nom. sg.	Gen. sg.	Dat. sg.	Loc. sg.	Gen. pl.	Gloss
t'ilo	t'ila	t'ilu	t'il'i	t'iw	'body'
koleso	kolesa	kolesu	koles'i	kol'is	'wheel'
ozero	ozera	ozeru	ozer'i	oz'ir	'lake'
selo	sela	selu	sel'i	s'iw	'village'
pole	pol'a	pol'u	pol'i	pil'	'field'
slovo	slova	slovu	slov'i	sliw	'word'
more	mor'a	mor'u	mor'i	mir'	'sea'

Attempt to account for these data by means of the morpheme alternant approach. What difficulties do you encounter? In many nonstandard dialects of Ukrainian the statement that all consonants are palatalized before *i* is a statement that is true of the PR. Thus, in these dialects we find *b'il, st'iw, m'ist*, etc. instead of *bil', stiw, mist*. How can this dialect difference be explained? Which dialect is more likely to be the innovating one? Why?

2. Okpe (Hoffmann 1973). Like other West African languages Okpe has a contrast between two types of vowels, which we will consider here to be tense versus lax. Phonetically this contrast is operative only in Okpe mid vowels, where tense *e* and *o*

234   The Problem of Abstractness

contrast with lax ε and $\mathfrak{o}$ (transcribed here as ḍe and ḍo). In addition, any vowel can be contrastively oral or nasal (indicated by the tilde). List the UR for all the morphemes, state the rules accounting for the alternations, indicate any necessary ordering restrictions, and provide derivations for the infinitive, 1 sg. past, and 3 sg. continuative of 'buy', 'bury', 'fill', and 'eat'. Assume that all root morphemes are monosyllabic in UR and that all glides are derived by rule. You may also assume that *a* is lax.

Imperative	infinitive	3 sg. past	1 sg. past	3 sg. contin.	Gloss
da	*ẹda*	*ọ dare*	*me dare*	*ọ da*	'drink'
dẹ	*ẹdẹ*	*ọ dẹre*	*me dẹre*	*ọ dẹ*	'buy'
lọ	*ẹlọ*	*ọ lọre*	*me lọre*	*ọ lọ*	'grind'
dā	*ẹdā*	*ọ dārē*	*me dārē*	*ọ dā*	'fly'
tọ̄	*ẹtọ̄*	*ọ tọ̄rē*	*me tọ̄rē*	*ọ tọ̄*	'dig'
zẹ	*ẹzẹ*	*ọ zẹre*	*me zẹre*	*ọ zẹ*	'run'
wọ	*ẹwọ*	*ọ wọre*	*me wọre*	*ọ wọ*	'bathe'
ti	*etyo*	*o tiri*	*mi tiri*	*o tyẹ*	'pull'
ru	*erwo*	*o ruru*	*mi ruru*	*o rwẹ*	'do'
sī	*esyō*	*o sīrī*	*mi sīrī*	*o syẹ̄*	'bury'
zū	*ezwō*	*o zūrū*	*mi zūrū*	*o zwẹ̄*	'fan'
se	*ese*	*o seri*	*mi seri*	*o se*	'fill'
so	*eso*	*o sori*	*mi sori*	*o so*	'steal'
nē	*enē*	*o nērī*	*mi nērī*	*o nē*	'defecate'
gbō	*egbō*	*o gbōrī*	*mi gbōrī*	*o gbō*	'rot'
kpe	*ekpe*	*o kperi*	*mi kperi*	*o kpe*	'beat'
re	*ẹryọ*	*ọ rere*	*me rere*	*ọ rya*	'eat'
so	*ẹswọ*	*ọ soro*	*me soro*	*ọ swa*	'sing'
tē	*ẹtyọ̄*	*ọ tērē*	*me tērē*	*ọ tyā*	'refuse'
rhe	*ẹrhyọ*	*ọ rhere*	*me rhere*	*ọ rhya*	'come'

3. Ukrainian, Sadžava dialect (Popova 1972). In our transcriptions C' represents a palatalized consonant (the *k'* and *g'* are prevelar stops as in English *keep* and *geese*). Assume that all occurrences of *k'* and *g'* are derived by rule. Also assume that stress is located on the proper vowel in the UR. Write a set of ordered rules to account for the alternations in stem shape. For declensions II and III assume a rule that depalatalizes a consonant before the locative and genitive suffixes, respectively. Is your analysis permitted by Kiparsky's alternation condition?

Declension I

Nom. sg.	Gen. sg.	Loc. sg.	Gloss
plást	*plastá*	*plas'k'í*	'layer'
skorúx	*skoruxá*	*skorus'í*	'mountain ash'
γ'r'íx	*γ'r'ixá*	*γ'r'is'í*	'sin'
bék	*bəká*	*bəc'í*	'bull'
lést	*ləstá*	*ləs'k'í*	'leaf'
p'l'ít	*plóta*	*plók'i*	'wicker fence'
s'm'r'íd	*smróda*	*smróg'i*	'stench'
ʃ"íst	*fostá*	*fos'k'í*	'tail'
l'íd	*lắdu*	*lədú*	'ice'
m'íd	*mắdu*	*mədú*	'honey'

v'íl	*volá*	*vol'í*	'ox'
sér	*séra*	*sér'i*	'cottage cheese'
s'n'íp	*snopá*	*snop'í*	'sheaf'
γréb	*γrəbá*	*γrəb'í*	'mushroom'
lắb'id	*lắbəda*	*lắbəg'i*	'swan'
bắr'iγ	*bắrəγa*	*bắrəz'i*	'shore'
vór'iγ	*vóroγa*	*vóroz'i*	'enemy'
kónək	*kónəka*	*kónəc'i*	'grasshopper'
pót'ik	*potóka*	*potóc'i*	'stream'
t'ík	*tóka*	*tóc'i*	'current'
k'il	**kolá*	**kol'í*	'stake'

Declension II

Nom. sg.	Gen. sg.	Loc. sg.	Gloss
kovál'	*koval'é*	*kovalé*	'blacksmith'
učétəl'	*učétəl'ə*	*učétələ*	'teacher'
grắb'in'	*grắbən'ə*	*grắbənə*	'comb'
jač'm'ín'	*jačmắn'ə*	*jačmắnə*	'barley'
jás'in'	*jásən'ə*	*jásənə*	'ash tree'

Declension III

Nom. sg.	Gen. sg.	Gloss
más'k'	*mástə*	'fat'
s'íl'	*sólə*	'salt'
póš'is'k'	*póšəstə*	'epidemic'
zám'ik'	*zámətə*	'snowstorm'
skátər'k'	*skátərtə*	'tablecloth'
k'ís'k'	**kóstə*	'bone'

7

The Representation
of Sounds

In this chapter we take up the question of how the continuous speech stream is to be organized and represented for the purposes of phonological analysis and description. In the first section we briefly review the major arguments for representing sounds as discrete segments, each segment analyzed into a distinctive feature matrix. We then survey how the most commonly occurring speech sounds can be treated in the feature format, briefly noting some of the major issues that arise in the acceptance or rejection of a particular feature system. The next section mentions some of the evidence showing that the statement of some phonological generalizations presupposes that phonetic segments are organized into syllables. In the final section we take a brief look at some of the issues that arise in the analysis of tone. Special attention is given to the claim that tone may best be represented on a layer of structure separate from the nontonal aspects of an utterance.

The Feature Notation

In purely physical terms any utterance is a phonetic continuum. Articulatorily, it is a continuous flow of movements made by the vocal

237

apparatus. Acoustically, it is a continuously varying sound wave. All linguistic analysis presupposes that this continuum can be broken down into a sequence of discrete units which can be referred to as "phonetic segments" or "speech sounds." It is very difficult, however, to objectively divide this continuum into parts. That is, given any instrumental measurement of the speech signal it is generally not possible to say with precision where one "sound" ends and another begins. Also, if one listens to a language that one does not know, it is often not possible to isolate the number of sounds in a given utterance. For instance, what in one language might best be regarded as the sequence *ts* (cf., the last part of the English word *hats*) in another language is properly treated as a single sound *c*. Without knowing the language or its structure, one cannot objectively decide the segmentation of an utterance. Despite the difficulty of objectively dividing up this speech continuum, there are, nevertheless, good reasons for assuming that any utterance functions linguistically as if it were composed of a series of discrete segments (or perhaps more than a single series of segments layed one on top of the other; see the section on the representation of tone for some discussion of this view). We note briefly below some of the prima facie evidence for the discrete segment hypothesis.

First of all, native speakers are usually able to provide a consistent answer to the question of how many sounds comprise a given (short) utterance. Although there may be disagreement in particular cases (e.g., in complex consonant clusters, as in the word *sixths* [sɨksθs], or diphthongs), there is general agreement. Furthermore, the existence of alphabetic writing systems presupposes the analysis of the speech continuum into discrete segments. Although it may be true that the alphabetic system only arose spontaneously once in the history of mankind, while the spontaneous development of syllabic writing systems has occurred several times (suggesting that division into syllables is an easier operation than division into segments), nevertheless countless speakers have been able to develop an alphabetic orthography for their language once the alphabetic principle has been explained to them (cf., the discussion of Sapir's work in Chapter 5). Once again, this would not be possible if the native speaker did not have the ability to analyze the speech stream into discrete segments.

Further evidence for this position is provided by speech errors. As Fromkin (1971, pp. 29–30) has observed,

> What is apparent, in the analyses and conclusions of all linguists and psychologists dealing with errors in speech, is that, despite the semi-continuous nature of the speech signal, there are discrete units at some level of performance which can be substituted, omitted, transposed, or added. . . . When one finds [that it is] impossible to explain

speech production (which must include errors made) without discrete performance units, this is further substantiation of the psychological reality of such discrete units.

Among the errors Fromkin noted in her study were simple anticipatory substitution of sounds (as in *cup of coffee* —→ *cuff of coffee*, *week long race* —→ *reek long race*), and such transpositions as *keep a tape* —→ *teep a cape*, *fish grotto* —→ *frish gotto*, *brake fluid* —→ *black fruid*. Such errors indicate that, although there may be no clear delimitation into segments in the physical realization of speech, it is nevertheless articulated as if it were organized into discrete constituents.

Finally, and most importantly, many phonological operations suggest that speech is organized into discrete units. Most deletion and insertion rules apply to single segments rather than larger pieces of the utterance. The metathesis of two adjacent sounds presupposes, not only that those two sounds are distinct from one another, but also that they are distinct from the remaining portion of the utterance lying on either side. Rules which assign accent to a particular vowel in the word (e.g., the third from the last) require the utterance to be analysed into discrete consonant and vowel units.

In addition to analyzing an utterance into a string of segments, generative phonologists have assumed that each segment is represented as a matrix of phonetic features which describe the articulatory and acoustic properties of that segment. In articulatory terms each feature might be viewed as information the brain sends to the vocal apparatus to perform whatever operations are involved in the production of the sound, while acoustically a feature may be viewed as the information the brain looks for in the sound wave to identify a particular segment as an instance of a particular sound. Thus *b* and *m* will have the features bilabial, closure, voice, and so on, but differ in that the first is oral (produced with a raised velum), while the second is nasal (produced with a lowered velum). So *b* differs from *d* in that the latter has closure at the teeth, etc.

Assuming that utterances are best represented as a string of feature matrixes at the phonetic level, we can raise the question of how sounds are represented for the purpose of phonological description (i.e., in the UR and at all intermediate levels). As mentioned in Chapter 1, a fundamental tenet of generative phonology has been that sounds are most properly represented at these levels in the same way they are phonetically—namely, as feature matrixes in which each feature describes an articulatory and/or acoustic property of the sound.

Let us examine this position more carefully. Two distinct claims are involved, corresponding to two different aspects of the phonetic feature notation. As we observed in Chapter 1, the feature notation permits a formal distinction to be drawn between natural classes of segments and randomly selected sets of sounds. We have seen that phonological rules characteristically refer to natural classes. Typically a phonological rule will change x to y only in the context of certain restricted classes of sounds such as [p,t,k], [y,i,e], [p,b,m], and so forth. One will seldom, if ever, find a rule applying in the context of such random sets as [t,ŋ,e] or [r,ʔ,p]. Similarly, phonological rules usually take a particular class of sounds as input, for example, [p,t,k] in the Engiish aspiration rule. One will seldom, if ever, find a rule applying to the sounds [t,ŋ,e] and no others. Finally, rules characteristically relate sounds as input and output in a nonrandom way. [p,t,k] may be changed to [m,n,ŋ], respectively, but no rule will ever change [p,t,k] to [ŋ,m,n], respectively.

If sounds are represented by feature matrixes, natural classes may be distinguished from arbitrary sets. A natural class like [p,t,k] can be specified by the conjunction of the features voiceless and stop, [y,i,e] by front vowel and glide, and so on. On the other hand, random sets such as [t,ŋ,e] or [r,ʔ,p] could only be represented by a disjunction of features. Likewise, a natural change such as [p,t,k] to [m,n,ŋ] can be expressed by the acquisition of the features nasal and voiced, while the unnatural change of [p,t,k] to [ŋ,m,n] could not be stated as the acquisition of a common set of features.

Note, however, that if sounds were to be represented alphabetically, by the symbols of the IPA for example, the distinction between natural classes and random sets could not be formally expressed in terms of the notation. For in an alphabetic notation, each symbol is totally on a par with any other formally. In terms of the notation all sounds are equidistant, and as a result, a set [p,t,k] is equivalent to [t,ŋ,e] in that both contain three elements. Similarly, the change of [p,t,k] to [m,n,ŋ] is not formally distinguishable from the change of [p,t,k] to [m,ŋ,n].

Thus one argument for extending the feature notation to higher levels of representation in the grammar is that it permits the notion of natural class and natural sound change to be formally defined. However, this extension of the feature notation makes an additional claim—namely, that natural phonological classes and sound changes will be definable in phonetic terms. This is not a trivial claim, for language could have been organized in such a way that phonetically unrelated sets like [t,ŋ,e] or [r,ʔ,p] formed natural classes referred to by phonological rules in language after language, while such phonetically unitary sets as [p,t,k] or [y,i,e] never played any role in the statement of a phonological rule. If this were the case, the notion of natural class could still be reflected by a feature notation. The only difference would be that the phonological features grouping [t,ŋ,e] together would be arbitrarily related to the features that define their articulatory and acoustic implementation. However, since in the majority of cases natural classes and natural sound changes can be defined in terms of the features that are needed at the phonetic level, generative phonologists have viewed this as additional motivation for extending the phonetic feature notation to the UR and all intermediate levels of representation.

The claim that natural classes are definable in phonetic terms is sometimes referred to as the naturalness condition, following the terminology introduced in Postal (1968). Although the naturalness condition clearly holds in the majority of cases, there are still a number of widespread phonological processes which presuppose natural classes of sounds for which no straightforward phonetic correlates are presently known. They pose a challenge to future research and one can only hope that as phonetic science progresses, these unexplained counterexamples to the naturalness condition will eventually be resolved.

A Survey of the Features

In this section we briefly survey the features most commonly used in generative descriptions. To a large extent our discussion will focus on the features introduced in Chomsky and Halle (1968) (hereafter referred to as SPE). Although many aspects of the SPE feature system are not accepted by all generative phonologists, the notational apparatus developed in SPE is the standard repertoire of analytical devices in terms of which most generative descriptions are presented in the linguistic literature. In addition to showing how the most commonly occurring sounds are analyzed in the SPE feature system, we will, when possible, provide examples of phonological rules that refer to natural classes defined by the SPE system.

However, before discussing any particular features, it would not be inappropriate to mention the kinds of arguments that have been given in the literature to motivate a particular feature system. Four arguments are most commonly appealed to. First, an adequate feature system must permit any two sounds that contrast in any language to be represented by distinct feature matrixes. Some earlier feature systems (e.g., that of Jakobson, Fant, and Halle 1951) have proved inadequate in failing to appropriately distinguish contrasting sounds. Second, an adequate feature system should permit any natural class of sounds to be represented by the conjunction of features in a matrix. However, as we have seen, it is an empirical question whether all natural phonological classes can be defined in phonetic terms. If it should turn out that a certain natural class cannot be defined phonetically (and thus that the naturalness condition is not universally valid), one is faced with the choice of introducing a feature with no motivated phonetic correlate or having to express a natural class by a disjunction of features. Space limitations do not permit us to go into this difficult question.

Third, some writers have argued that a feature system should be able to explain why certain sound changes characteristically take place only in certain contexts. Assimilation is the notion most commonly appealed to in this kind of argument. If x changes to y in the context z and if this process is truly assimilatory, then the feature system should allow the rule to be expressed in such a way that x acquires a feature that characterizes z.

Finally, a particular feature system is sometimes argued for on the grounds that it is constructed in such a way as to formally exclude feature combinations which never describe a possible sound. In the course of our survey we shall have occasion to mention some of these kinds of arguments.

MAJOR CLASS FEATURES

The major class features define the distinctions between vowels, consonants, liquids and nasals, and glides. Since all languages distinguish between these classes of sounds, the major class features define a much more basic opposition than some of the other features that will be discussed later. It is also the case that the phonetic correlates of the major class features are much more poorly understood than most other features. Nevertheless, the sets of sounds defined by these features are repeatedly referred to by many different kinds of phonological processes.

Although there may be slight disagreement over certain details, most phonologists would accept the feature matrix in (1) as providing an adequate description of the major classes of speech sounds.

(1)

	syllabic	consonantal	sonorant
Vowels	+	−	+
Glides	−	−	+
Liquids	−	+	+
Nasals	−	+	+
Obstruents	−	+	−

[+syllabic] designates those sounds that form the nucleus of the syllable. Since the syllable has not yet been defined satisfactorily in phonetic terms, the phonetic correlates of this feature are unclear. In all languages vowels normally constitute the nucleus of the syllable and are hence [+syllabic], while glides, liquids and nasals, and obstruents are normally [−syllabic]. However, in many languages liquids and nasals may form the syllable nucleus. In such cases, the syllabic consonants are usually predictable variants of underlying nonsyllabic consonants. For example, in Czech *l* and *r* become syllabic when they are preceded by a consonant and not followed by a vowel (see Trubetzkoy 1939;172): *pr̩sti* 'fingers', *sl̩za* 'tear', *padl̩* 'he fell', *lhář* 'liar' (monosyllabic), *rváč* 'thug' (monosyllabic), *rčení* 'phrase' (disyllabic), *lžíce* 'spoon' (disyllabic). Trubetzkoy cites Serbo-Croatian *gr̩oce* (trisyllabic) 'throat, dimin.' versus *groza* (disyllabic) 'horror' as a case where "syllabicity is a distinctive property not entirely conditioned by environment [p. 172]." Although the feature syllabic is clearly phonetically contrastive in this example, it is not an underlying contrast, since *gr̩oce* derives from /grl+ce/ (cf., *grl-o* 'throat') by rules making *r* [+syllabic] between consonants and turning *l* to *o* before a consonant. However, an underlying contrast apparently occurred in Old Czech, where *l* and *r* were syllabic between two consonants in some words but nonsyllabic in others. Trubtezkoy cites *mrtvý* 'dead' and *plný* as being treated as disyllabic in verse but *krvi* 'blood' and *slza* 'tear' as monosyllabic. This rather unnatural state of affairs was replaced by the rules mentioned above, which make *krvi* and *slza* disyllabic.

Since stress predictably occurs on the first syllable in Czech, the rule of (2) will correctly stress the syllabic liquids in *pr̩sti* and *sl̩za*, but will not assign stress to the liquids in *vráč* and *kladl̩* 'he put', instead placing it on the vowel *a*. (The acute accent in Czech does not indicate stress but rather vowel length).

(2) $[+\text{syllabic}] \longrightarrow [+\text{stress}]/\#[-\text{syllabic}]_0 \underline{\quad\quad}$

The feature [+consonantal] groups together liquids, nasals, and obstruents and opposes these sounds to vowels and glides, which are [−consonantal]. According to SPE (p. 302) consonantal sounds are produced with a "radical obstruction in the midsagittal region of the vocal tract; nonconsonantal sounds are produced without such an obstruction." (See Ladefoged 1971 for critical discussion of this phonetic definition.)

A number of phonological processes depend on the contrast between vowels and glides versus consonants. For example, in many languages the feature of nasality is progressively spread from an underlying nasal consonant until a [+consonantal] segment is encountered, impeding any further spread of the feature. Thus in Malay (Onn 1976) /naik/ 'ascend' is realized as *nãĩk* (and ultimately [nãɛ̃ʔ] by other rules), with spreading of nasality through the following two vowels. The spread of nasality is blocked by an obstruent or liquid, as in /makan/ $\longrightarrow$ *mãkan* 'eat',

/məlaraŋ/ ——→ *mə́laraŋ* 'forbid'. However, the glides *w* and *y* permit nasality to pass through: /mewah/ ——→ *mẽw̃ãh̃* 'to be luxurious', /mayaŋ/ ——→ *mãỹãŋ* 'stalk'. In Malay, the laryngeals *h* and *ʔ* also do not impede the spread of nasality: /maʔap/ ——→ *mãʔãp* 'pardon', /pənəŋahan/ ——→ *pənə̃ŋãh̃ãn* 'central focus'. If we assume that, analogous to the treatment of Yawelmani vowel harmony in Chapter 4, a rule may apply to its own output, the spread of nasalization may be expressed as (3).

(3)   [−consonantal] ——→ [+nasal]/[+nasal] ＿＿＿＿

Given underlying /naik/, application of (3) yields /nãik/. But now the [−consonantal] *i* is preceded by a segment that is [+nasal] and hence may undergo the rule to give /nãĩk/. The rule may not apply to nasalize the *k* since it is [+consonantal]. Similarly, /mayaŋ/ will be converted to /mãyaŋ/, and then /mãỹaŋ/, and finally /mãỹãŋ/, since in each case a [−consonantal] segment acquires nasality from a preceding [+nasal] segment. But the spread of nasality will be blocked by the [+consonantal] *k* and *l* of *mākan* and *mə́laraŋ*.

The laryngeals *h* and *ʔ* also frequently pattern with the oral glides *y* and *w* as hiatus breakers inserted between vowels. For example, in the Kalinga dialect of Guininaag (Gieser 1970), a language of the Philippines, *y* is inserted between two vowels when the first is *i*, *w* is inserted when the first is *u*, and *ʔ* when the first is *a*: *ʔudugu* 'pity', *ʔuduguwan* 'to pity'; *daŋli* 'believing', *daŋliyan* 'to believe'; *ʔala* 'getting', *ʔalaʔan* 'to get'. This example also illustrates the affinity between the high vowels *i* and *u* and the corresponding glides *y* and *w*, on the one hand, and the affinity between the low vowel *a* and the laryngeal *ʔ* on the other hand.

Although in the preceding examples *h* and *ʔ* behaved parallel to the oral glides *y* and *w*, there are many examples where these sounds pattern with obstruents. For example, in Semitic languages *h* and *ʔ* pair up with the pharyngeals *ḥ* and *ʕ* to form the traditional class of gutterals, which condition a number of phonological rules. The oral glides *y* and *w* do not participate in these rules.

According to SPE, sonorants are produced with a vocal tract cavity configuration which permits spontaneous voicing of the vocal folds, while obstruents [−sonorant] have a cavity configuration which inhibits spontaneous voicing. (See Ladefoged 1971 for critical discussion of the SPE correlates for this feature.)

Many aspects of phonological structure are sensitive to the contrast provided by the feature sonorant. Obstruents are a natural domain for oppositions in voicing, while underlying contrasts between voiced versus voiceless sonorants are much rarer. Another reflection of this difference appears in phonological rules that can change the voicing specification of a segment. Many languages devoice final obstruents but retain voiced sonorants in this position.

Sonorants may bear pitch distinctions while obstruents do not (though they may have an effect on the pitch of adjacent sonorants). For example, in Lithuanian an accented syllable containing a long vowel or diphthong may have a rising or falling pitch: *matìːti* 'to see' versus *matíːs* 'will see'; *kàymas* 'village' versus *váykas* 'child'. If long vowels are represented as geminates, the accentual contrast may be analyzed as a contrast between high pitch (marked by the acute) versus low pitch (unmarked) on a sonorant segment: *matú̓ ti, matís, káymas, vaýkas*. Similarly, a short vowel followed by a tautosyllabic liquid or nasal may be the locus for a contrast in pitch. The initial syllables of *kártis* 'pole' and *ántis* 'duck' are falling while the initial syllables in *kařtis* 'bitterness' and *ańtis* 'breast' are rising. However, when a short vowel is followed by a tautosyllabic obstruent, there is no contrast between rising and falling pitch, since an obstruent may not bear a pitch of its own.

The class of nonsyllabic sonorants, traditionally termed resonants, appears in many phonological rules. For instance, in Lithuanian long vowels are shortened before a consonant cluster whose initial element is a sonorant, as shown by the following pairs of past tense and infinitive forms: *kuːl-eː, kul-ti* 'thresh'; *koːr-eː* (< /kaːr-eː/), *kar-ti* 'hang'; *leːm-eː, lem-ti* 'doom'; *miːn-eː, min-ti* 'trample'; *koːv-eː* (</kaːw-eː/), *kaw-ti* 'beat'. Clusters beginning with obstruents do not condition shortening: *tuːp-eː, tuːp-ti* 'perch'; *voːg-eː, voːk-ti* 'steal'.

FEATURES FOR VOWELS

For most languages the features high, low, and back are sufficient to describe the phonological behavior of vowels. In SPE these features are defined with respect to a reference point that approximates the vowel of the word *bed*. High vowels are articulated by raising the tongue body above this point, low vowels by lowering the tongue body below this point, and back vowels by retraction from this point. For a six vowel system like that of Chamarro (Chapter 3), these features define the matrix of (4).

(4)

	i	e	ä	a	o	u
high	+	−	−	−	−	+
low	−	−	+	+	−	−
back	−	−	−	+	+	+

The contrast between front and back vowels appears in many phonological rules, for example, the vowel harmony process in Turkish, whereby the plural suffix appears with the front vowel *e* after a [−back] vowel of the root (*yel-ler* 'winds', *iz-ler* 'footprints', *čöl-ler* 'deserts', *gül-ler* 'roses') and with the back vowel *a* after [+back] root vowels (*baš-lar* 'heads', *kol-lar* 'arms', *kul-lar* 'slave', *kız-lar* 'daughters'.

Many languages distinguish between just two degrees of vowel height, such as the underlying system of Yawelmani discussed in Chapter 4. Recall that the distinction between [+high] versus [−high] is also crucial for defining the vowel harmony process in Yawelmani. *i* will round to *u* only after a round vowel that is [+high] and *a* will round to *o* only after a round vowel that is [−high].

In languages that distinguish three degrees of vowel height the features of (4) are adequate to define most rules that depend on vowel height.

1. [+high] vowels: e.g., in Japanese *t* is affricated before the high vowels *i* and *u*, but not before the low vowel *a*, nor the mid vowels *e* and *o* (see exercise 4, Chapter 9).
2. [−high, −low] vowels: e.g., in Lamba (exercise 1, Chapter 3) *i* is lowered to *e* after the mid vowels *e* and *o*, but not after the high vowels *i* and *u*, nor the low vowel *a*.
3. [+low] vowels: e.g., in Chukchee (Chapter 2) *i* becomes *e* in a word containing a low vowel ε, *a*, or ɔ; the high vowels *i* and *u* and the mid vowel *e* do not trigger this rule.
4. [−high] vowels: e.g., in Russian (Chapter 6) the nonhigh vowels *e*, *o*, and *a* undergo vowel reduction in unstressed position, while the high vowels *i* and *u* do not.
5. [−low] vowels: e.g., in Chamarro (Chapter 3) unstressed high and mid vowels reduce to *ɪ* (if front) or to *ʊ* (if back), while unstressed low *ä* and *a* appear as *ə*.

Note that if the feature system of (4) is accepted, it is impossible to group high and low vowels together in a single set to the exclusion of the mid vowels. The relative rarity of such a set [as opposed to the ubiquity of sets (1)–(5) mentioned above] can be taken as support for the basic correctness of (4). (4) also makes it impossible to group front and back vowels of different heights together to the exclusion of their confreres (e.g., *e* and *u* to the exclusion of *i* and *o*). Such sets will occasionally arise, but generally they are the result of historical change obscuring an earlier more natural phonetic class. Thus, for example, in the Sadžava dialect of Ukrainian (exercise 3, Chapter 6) *ä* and *o* shift to *i* in the context ——C$_1$#, while *e* and *a* remain in this context. Originally the rule was defined on the mid vowels **e* and **o*, but in this dialect **e* became *ä* and **y* became *e*, yielding the phonetically unnatural grouping of mid back *o* and low front *ä*. (See Kenstowicz and Kisseberth 1977 for general discussion of phonetic aberration arising from historical change). Another example would be the rule of Slovak (Chapter 4) that diphthongizes *e*, *o*, and *ä*, but not *a*.

The theoretical apparatus introduced so far in this book does not permit the sound changes of the Sadžava and Slovak examples to be stated as a single rule. In Chapter 9 the device of greek letter variables will be introduced, which will make it possible to combine the sounds of the Sadžava and Slovak cases into a single set. However, one might well question the legitimacy of extending the variable notation to such cases. The issue is related to the much more difficult question of determining when two feature changes are manifestations of the same underlying phonological process. (See Chapter 9 for brief discussion).

Although the system of (4) adequately handles languages that distinguish three degrees of height, it will not provide a sufficient basis for the analysis of languages that distinguish more than three height positions. For example, in the West African language Akan vowels appear in five contrasting pairs, the first member of each pair traditionally being analyzed as a "raised" or "higher" version of the second: *i, ɪ; u, ʊ; e, ɛ; o, ɔ; ə, a*.

If the traditional analysis is correct, it would appear that one has to distinguish six degrees of vowel height (a higher and lower version for high, mid, and low vowels). However, Stewart (1967) has argued convincingly that vowel height per se is not the relevant phonetic parameter for analyzing the Akan contrast.

Phonological support for this contention derives from the vowel harmony system in the language. Within a root, vowels are either all raised or all nonraised. However, it is not possible to predict for a given root which type of vowel it will have. Thus the contrast between raised and nonraised is contrastive in roots. Affixal vowels, however, are basically nonraised; they will shift to their raised counterparts when the root contains a raised vowel. For example, the 3 sg. prefix /ɔ/ appears in its basic shape before the nonraised roots in *ɔ-bɛsi* 'he will say' and *ɔ-ɥm* 'he weaves', but as *o* before the raised roots of *o-bɛsi* 'he will build' and *o-bisa* 'he asks' (these data from Schachter and Fromkin 1968). This alternation appears to be best treated as a form of assimilation. However, if vowel height is the relevant phonetic feature, why should /ɔ/ raise to *o* before *e* and *i* but not ɪ? In terms of height the latter vowel is intermediate between *i* and *e* and thus should condition raising.

Phonetic evidence that tongue height per se is not the relevant parameter derives from Ladefoged's (1964) X-ray study of a similar vowel contrast in Igbo. Ladefoged found that there was little difference between pairs like *i* and *ɪ* or *o* and *ɔ* in terms of the position of the highest point of the tongue in the mouth. The most consistent difference is that the body of the tongue is more retracted for the nonraised vowels.

Stewart concludes that the position of the root of the tongue is the relevant phonetic contrast: The raised vowels involve an advancing of the tongue root, while the nonraised set have the root in a more retracted position. This interpretation provides a natural account of the vowel harmony: A basically [−ATR] (advanced tongue root) vowel assimilates the [+ATR] feature of a root vowel. In addition, it appears to account for the retraction of the tongue body noted by Ladefoged.

If the features of (4) are supplemented with the feature of advanced tongue root, it is possible to distinguish six different positions in the vertical dimension of the vowel space, thereby providing a means for representing the following series of front vowels found in some American English dialects: *i (beat), ɪ (bit), e, (bait), ɛ (bet), ä (bat), a* (as in the Boston pronunciation of *car*). The reader is referred to Kiparsky (1974) for discussion of such a feature system for vowels.

PLACE OF ARTICULATION IN CONSONANTS

In this section we briefly discuss the SPE features for place of articulation in consonants, noting some of the advantages and disadvantages of this system. The major consonantal points of articulation are defined by the features anterior, coronal, and high, low, and back as depicted in (5).

(5)

	p	t	č	k'	k	q	ḥ
anterior	+	+	−	−	−	−	−
coronal	−	+	+	−	−	−	−
high	−	−	+	+	+	−	−
low	−	−	−	−	−	−	+
back	−	−	−	−	+	+	+

Sounds produced with a constriction in front of the alveopalatal region are [+anterior], all other consonants being [−anterior]. We are not aware of any phonological processes that show this feature to define a natural class. It appears to only function as a way of differentiating labials and dentals from other consonants. Coronal sounds involve raising the blade of the tongue above its neutral position. This feature groups dentals and alveopalatals together as opposed to other consonants. Many phonological processes crucially depend on this distinction. To cite just one example, in Classical Arabic the *l* of the definite article *ʔal* completely assimilates to a following dental or palatal consonant, but remains unchanged before labials, velars, uvulars, pharyngeals, and laryngeals: *ʔal baab* 'the door', *ʔal faras* 'the horse', *ʔal kalb* 'the dog', *ʔal xaatam* 'the ring', *ʔal qalb* 'the heart', *ʔal ḥarb* 'the war', *ʔal ʔab* 'the father'; but *ʔat taxt* 'the bed', *ʔad daar* 'the house', *ʔas sanduuq* 'the box', *ʔaz zayt* 'the oil', *ʔar ražul* 'the man', *ʔan naas* 'the people', *ʔaš šams* 'the sun'. (The consonant represented by the letter *ǧīm* did not trigger assimilation in Classical Arabic. In some dialects, such as Egyptian, this consonant appears as *g*; more often it appears as the alveopalatal *ž* or *ǰ*, in which case it usually triggers assimilation, as in *ʔaž žaras* 'the bell'.)

SPE defines velar, uvular, and pharyngeal consonants in terms of movements of the body of the tongue from the neutral reference point (roughly where the vowel of *bed* is produced) by the features high, low, and back. This has the advantage of showing the natural affinity between particular vowel and consonantal points of articulation. The features high, low, and back are also used to describe the secondary articulations of palatalization, velarization, uvularization, and pharyngealization on labial, dental, and alveopalatal consonants.

The vowel reduction process in Russian points up the advantages of the SPE system. Recall from Chapter 6 that unstressed nonhigh vowels appear as *i* after a palatalized consonant: *n'ós* 'he carried', *n'islá* 'she carried'. In the SPE system a palatalized consonant such as *n'* is treated as [+high, −back], representing the superimposition of the *i*-like articulation on the primary dental stricture. Raising of unstressed vowels to *i* after palatalized consonants can thus be represented as an assimilatory process.

According to SPE alveopalatal consonants are also articulated with a raising of the body of the tongue and are thus (redundantly) [+high]; they are distinguished from the other points of articulation by the coronal and anterior features. However, their [+high] nature is often manifested in their raising effect on vowels. Such is the case in Russian where the alveopalatals *č*, *ž*, and *š* condition raising of unstressed nonhigh vowels: *čás* 'hour', *čisý* 'hours'; *šést'* 'six', *šistój* 'sixth'; *žóny* 'women', *žiná* 'woman'. Given that alveopalatals are [+high, −back], their raising effect on following unstressed vowels can also be viewed as an assimilatory phenomenon. Note that velars, which are [+high, +back] do not condition raising. The feature system of (5) thus permits vowel reduction in Russian to be expressed as (6).

(6)
$$
\begin{bmatrix} +\text{syll} \\ -\text{high} \\ -\text{stress} \end{bmatrix} \longrightarrow \begin{bmatrix} +\text{high} \\ -\text{low} \\ -\text{back} \\ -\text{round} \end{bmatrix} / \begin{bmatrix} -\text{syll} \\ +\text{high} \\ -\text{back} \end{bmatrix} \underline{\hspace{1cm}}
$$

The Russian data also illustrate the affinity between velarized consonants and back vowels. In Russian, palatalized (traditionally "soft") consonants are opposed to velarized (traditionally "hard") consonants. When the high front vowel *i* appears after a velarized consonant it is retracted to *y*, the high back nonround vowel: for example, *Ivan Ivanovič* is phonetically [iván yvánav'ič]. Given that velarized consonants are [+high, +back], this rule may be expressed as (7).

(7)
$$
\begin{bmatrix} +\text{syll} \\ +\text{high} \\ -\text{back} \end{bmatrix} \longrightarrow [+\text{back}] / \begin{bmatrix} -\text{syll} \\ +\text{high} \\ +\text{back} \end{bmatrix} \underline{\hspace{2em}}
$$

This rule also predicts retraction of *i* to *y* after velar consonants; but *k*, *g*, and *x* are fronted to *k'*, *g'*, and *x'* (i.e., made [−back]) before front vowels by an earlier rule and thus do not trigger the retraction rule (7).

It should be pointed out that *š* and *ž* (but not *č*) are phonetically velarized in Standard Russian. As such, they condition retraction of *i* to *y*. Thus, *žiná* /žoná/ and *šistój* /šestój/ are pronounced [žyná] and [šystój], respectively, in this variety of Russian. In terms of the analysis given above, we must assume a rule that velarizes *š* and *ž* (i.e., makes them [+back]) applied after reduction (6) but before retraction (7). This rule expresses the traditional dictum that *š* and *ž* are functionally soft but phonetically hard.

The system of (5) also allows for the expression of the lowering effect of uvulars and pharyngeals on high vowels in assimilatory terms: For example, in Greenlandic Eskimo (exercise 3, Chapter 2) *i* and *u* are realized as *e* and *o* before uvulars; in Classical Arabic (see Brame 1969:161) *i* is lowered to *a* in the environment of a pharyngeal consonant. Given that uvulars are [−high] and that pharyngeals are [+low], lowering of vowels in the environment of these consonants has a natural phonetic interpretation. However, vowels are also lowered in the context of the laryngeals *ʔ* and *h* in Arabic and many other languages. Since the tongue is presumably not involved in the production of laryngeal consonants, vowel lowering in the context of *ʔ* and *h* cannot be interpreted as an assimilatory phenomenon. In SPE laryngeals are assigned the feature [+low], but this appears to be unjustified from the phonetic point of view. One could of course still postulate a feature LOW and say that for supraglottal sounds its articulatory correlate is lowering of the tongue body while for *ʔ* and *h* it defines the laryngeal point of articulation. However, if this move is made, the feature LOW has a rather different status from most of the other features which have a unitary phonetic correlate.

A similar issue arises with respect to the relationship between lip rounding in vowels and labial stricture in consonants. In many languages consonants with a lip component naturally induce a rounding of vowels. For example, Hyman (1975) observes that Igbo verbs stems of the shape CV normally reduplicate as CiCV, but when the root consonant is a labial, the reduplication vowel *i* appears as *u*.

(8)   /le/   *o-lile*   'looks'
        /la/   *o-lila*   'returns'
        /be/   *o-bube*   'cuts'
        /ba/   *o-buba*   'enters'

Hyman observes that if labials are treated as [+anter, −coron], the rounding of *i* to *u* cannot be formally expressed as assimilation. Following Vennemann and Ladefoged (1971), he suggests introducing the "cover" feature LABIAL, which, like the SPE feature LOW, groups together two distinct articulatory gestures: rounding in vowels and some consonants (e.g., k^w) and labial stricture in other consonants (*b*, *f*, etc.). Given the feature LABIAL, the change of *i* to *u* in the context of *b* can be formally expressed as assimilatory.

Although it may be correct to view rounding of *i* to *u* in the context of a bilabial consonant as a case of assimilation (in the sense that if a vowel is to acquire a labial component and still remain a vowel, it can only take on the feature of rounding and may not acquire a labial stricture), it is not clear that appeal to a cover feature such as LABIAL is the most appropriate way of expressing the process. A possible alternative may be envisioned by virtue of the following considerations. Any adequate theory of phonology must contain postulates that will define natural sound changes. Although many of these can be expressed by appeal to the notion of assimilation defined over the features of a feature system, it is clear that not all natural sound changes fit into this mold. For example, many languages have a rule converting consonants to *ʔ* or *h* in preconsonantal and final position. Such a process is clearly not assimilatory in nature. Nevertheless phonological theory must have some apparatus for expressing the fact that neutralization to a glottal stop in these positions is a natural rule as opposed to, say, neutralization to *l*.

Given the necessity for such an apparatus, it might be more appropriate to simply postulate that rounding of vowels in the environment of labials is a natural process, instead of attempting to express this by the introduction of cover features such as LABIAL. To consider a slightly different example, in a number of languages vowels (especially when low) are nasalized in the environment of laryngeal consonants. Once again, one could attempt to express the nasalizing effect of laryngeals by introduction of some abstract cover feature that would group together the phonetic features of velum lowering and the laryngeal point of articulation. But an alternative would be to simply postulate that vowel nasalization in the context of laryngeals is a natural process (which, at least according to Ohala 1972, has a phonetic rationale). It is a task for future research to decide which of these alternative approaches to the problem is more nearly correct.

MANNER OF ARTICULATION FEATURES FOR CONSONANTS

In SPE stops, affricates, and fricatives are distinguished by the features continuant and delayed release as in (9).

(9)

	stop	affricate	fricative
Continuant	−	−	+
Delayed release	−	+	+

Stops and affricates have a stricture that impedes air-flow and hence are [−continuant], while fricatives permit air to flow through their stricture and hence are [+continuant]. The feature delayed release distinguishes the two types of consonants produced with closure. In affricates the release of the closure is gradual and hence there is a period after the release when the articulators assume the position of the cognate fricative. Since stops are abruptly released, no such fricative phase occurs during their production.

In many languages phonological rules are sensitive to the contrast between consonants produced with and without closure. For example, in Turkish the voiced stops, affricates, and fricatives *b, d, g, ǰ,* and *z* are opposed to voiceless *p, t, k, č,* and *s*. In preconsonantal and final position stops and affricates neutralize this opposition in favor of voiceless, while fricatives maintain the voicing contrast: *kap* 'lid', *kap-lar* pl., *kab-ı* 'his lid'; *kanat, kanat-lar, kanad-ı* 'wing'; *renk, renk-ler, reng-i* 'color'; *aač, aač-lar, aaǰ-ı* 'tree'; but *kız, kız-lar, kız-ı* 'daughter'. Given the system of (9), the Turkish devoicing rule may be expressed as the assignment of the feature [−voice] to [−continuant] sounds when they stand before a consonant or at the end of a word.

A sibilant harmony process found in Chumash (Beeler 1970) is sensitive to the contrast of affricates and fricatives versus stops. In Chumash all the coronal affricates and fricatives of a word must agree in the feature of apicality. This harmony is manifested as a constraint on the appearance of sounds within a root. Thus we find roots such as *osos* 'heel' and *ac'is* 'beard' containing apicals, and *šuš* 'fur' and *č'umaš* 'islanders', containing laminals (transcribed here as *š*, and *č*), but no roots combining apicals and laminals. The harmony also functions as a regressive assimilation rule in which a coronal in a root agrees with the apicality of a suffix: *k-iškín* 'I save it', but *k-iskín-us* 'I save it for him'; *k-ackáw* 'I sin', but *ačkáw-iš* 'a sin'. Since the coronal stops *t* and *t'* neither participate in nor condition the harmony, the rule must be restricted to coronal affricates and fricatives. If we assume that the feature delayed release characterizes both affricates and fricatives, the rule may be expressed as (10).

$$
(10) \quad
\begin{bmatrix} -\text{sonorant} \\ +\text{coronal} \\ +\text{del rel} \end{bmatrix}
\longrightarrow [\alpha\text{apical}]/\underline{\qquad} X
\begin{bmatrix} -\text{sonorant} \\ +\text{coronal} \\ +\text{del rel} \\ \alpha\text{apical} \end{bmatrix}
$$

However, the extension of the feature [+del rel] to fricatives is unjustified phonetically, if it is assumed that closure is required in order for a sound to have a delayed release. A number of writers have suggested that the similarity affricates bear to both stops and fricatives can better be expressed if affricates are represented as complex segments having a stop phase followed by a fricative phase. See Campbell (1974) for discussion.

The feature strident distinguishes affricates and fricatives produced with greater air turbulence from the corresponding mellow sounds. Thus, the dentals *s* and *z* and the labiodentals *f* and *v* are [+strident], while the interdentals *θ* and *ð* and the bilabials *Φ* and *β* are [−strident]. Given the feature strident, the *-ɨz* alternant of the English plural suffix (which appears after the affricates *č* and *ĵ*, and the fricatives *š*, *ž*, *s*, and *z*, but not *θ*, *ð*, *f*, or *v*) can be defined as appearing after coronal obstruents that are [+strident].

BINARY VERSUS MULTIVALUED FEATURES

While most features represent phonetic scales (and hence may be divided into more than two portions), they are characteristically organized in a binary fashion phonologically. For example, consider nasality in vowels. To our knowledge there is no language that makes more than the two-way distinction [+nasal] versus [−nasal] for this feature in UR. It is true that many languages which make this contrast also have phonological rules that assign vowels a lesser degree of nasality in the context of nasal consonants, giving rise to the three-way phonetic distinction between oral, slightly nasal, and heavily nasal vowels. However, in such languages there do not seem to be any rules whose application is sensitive to this three-way phonetic distinction in nasality (e.g., a rule that would apply to only slightly nasalized vowels but not to heavily nasalized or oral ones).

The only apparent exceptions to the binary nature of the features are those referring to height in vowels and place of articulation in consonants. Although each seems to constitute a unitary phonetic dimension, we have seen that the SPE feature system subdivides them into several subsidiary binary features. In general, this move appears to be justified. There are, nevertheless, certain aspects of phonological structure that indicate that these phonetic features are sometimes more properly regarded as single phonetic dimensions organized in a multivalued fashion. The nonbinary nature of vowel height and consonantal place of articulation is occasionally manifested in the operation of synchronic phonological rules, but more often takes the form of metaconditions on certain phonological processes or the distribution of certain other phonetic features.

Recall from Chapter 5 the Eastern Finnish rule that raises the first mora of a long nonhigh vowel: the first portion of a low vowel becomes mid (*aa* ⟶ *oa, ää* ⟶ *eä*), while the first portion of a mid vowel becomes high (*oo* ⟶ *uo, ee* ⟶ *ie*). If it is assumed that vowel height is a single multivalued dimension, the rule may be expressed as one that raises a vowel by one degree.

The only synchronic phonological rule we know of that seems to presuppose that consonantal place of articulation is organized into a single multivalued dimension is a rule characterizing possible consonant clusters in the roots of certain Caucasian languages. For example, in Circassian (Rogava and Keraševa 1966) the first member of a cluster may be a bilabial stop, a dental stop or a coronal fricative. A bilabial stop may be followed by a lateral (*ble* 'snake'), a dental, palatal, or velar fricative (*bze* 'tongue', *bže* 'bee', *px'ač'e* 'bottom', *b\gammaež* 'eagle'), or a dental or palatal affricate (*pci* 'chisel', *pčeni* 'goat'). A dental stop may be followed by a velar stop (*tk'ʷeps* 'a drop') or a velar fricative (*txen* 'be happy'). Finally, a dental fricative may be followed by a dental or velar stop (*maste* 'needle', *pske* 'a cough'), while a palatal fricative may be followed by a dental or velar stop or a velar fricative (*šten* 'to take', *mišk'ʷ* 'acorn', *šxʷel* 'udder').

Thus, if the first consonant of a cluster is a stop, the following consonant must have a point of articulation further back in the oral cavity, while if the first consonant is a fricative, the point of articulation of the second consonant may not be further forward in the oral cavity. The only exceptions to this rule are *št* and *tf*. The latter has a historical explanation in that *f* derives from **xʷ* (cf., Circassian *tfi* 'five', Kabardian *txʷi*).

Universal constraints on the operation of certain phonological processes presuppose that vowel height and consonantal place of articulation are organized into single multivalued phonetic dimensions. A number of such constraints have been discussed by Chen (1975). For example, a front vowel's ability to invoke palatalization of adjacent consonants seems to be directly correlated with its height. In many languages consonants palatalize only in the context of high front vowels. In others both high and mid front vowels will palatalize a neighboring consonant; occasionally palatalization may be extended to the low vowels. Thus, palatalization by a lower front vowel seems to imply palatalization by a higher front vowel. Similarly, a vowel's susceptibility to nasalization appears to be inversely correlated with its height. Low vowels are most easily nasalized, followed by mid, and then high vowels. Correspondingly, a higher vowel is more likely to lose the feature of nasality than a lower one.

Chen also observes that a number of processes treat consonantal place of articulation as a unitary dimension. For instance, susceptibility to palatalization seems to be inversely correlated with a consonant's distance from the lips: Velars are most easily palatalized, then dentals, and finally labials. Weakening processes (e.g., intervocalic voicing, spirantization, deletion) also tend to proceed from the back to the front of the mouth. On the other hand, processes merging the point of articulation in consonants seem to proceed in the opposite direction. In a study of the historical reflexes of final [p,t,k] and [m,n,ŋ] in the Chinese dialects, Chen found that neutralization invariably went from the front of the oral cavity backwards. Some dialects merge labials and dentals as dentals while leaving the velars unaffected, while other dialects merged both labials and dentals with velars. In no case was the point of articulation shifted forward in the oral cavity.

Finally, the distribution of the feature of glottalization in consonants is correlated with the point of articulation. Greenberg (1970), on the basis of a survey of over one hundred languages, points out that implosives favor an anterior position in the oral cavity while ejectives favor a more posterior location. If a language has just one implosive, it is invariably labial; if two implosives appear they will occupy the labial and dental positions. On the other hand, ejectives favor the velar position, then dental, and finally labial. These correlations naturally also appear in historical change. For example, in Vietnamese *b* and *d* have become implosive, while *g* remains nonimplosive.

The Syllable

It is generally accepted that at the phonetic level of representation the sounds of any utterance are organized into larger units called syllables. However, the syllable is probably the most elusive of all phonological/phonetic notions. There is a vast and inconclusive literature on the subject (see Pulgram 1970 and Allen 1973 for recent surveys). The primary reason for the great confusion surrounding the syllable is a lack of any adequate phonetic definition. At this point the only thing that can be said with any confidence is that the syllable is an abstract programming unit in terms of which speech is articulated. The chest pulse (units of musculature activity controlling the flow of air from the lungs) is the only articulatory correlate for the syllable that has been discovered. Furthermore, studies by Ladefoged (1967) indicate that the chest pulse is not always an accurate diagnostic for the syllable. Nevertheless, in many languages there are phonological generalizations whose proper statement seems to presuppose the organization of sounds into larger units. An important issue is the extent to which these generalizations cohere to provide a consistent definition of the syllable in each individual language and the level of the grammar at which such organization into syllables occurs.

Until very recently the syllable has been largely ignored in generative phonology on the assumption that, though it may make sense to talk of sounds being organized into larger units phonetically, all phonological generalizations could be satisfactorily stated in terms of the individual sounds themselves without invoking the notion of the syllable. In this section we discuss a few examples that show this assumption to be unwarranted.

Kahn (1976) has argued that a number of phonological processes in English can be adequately explained only if it is assumed that sounds are organized into syllables before the operation of these rules. Space limitations permit us to discuss only one of Kahn's examples. Recall from Chapter 2 that it was claimed that aspiration is assigned to syllable-initial voiceless stops in English. The traditional analysis of aspiration in a theory not appealing to the syllable says that voiceless stops are aspirated when followed by a stressed vowel and not preceded by *s*. Such an analysis correctly aspirates the initial *t*s in words like *tén* and *tèmpaméntal* but not the *t* of *stém*. Kahn points out that this rule fails to account for the fact that word-initial voiceless stops are also aspirated when followed by unstressed vowels, as in *Pacífic*, *tomórrow*, and *collíde*. Although the initial stops of these words are not aspirated to the extent that they are in words like *pén*, *tén*, *Kén* (where the stress strengthens the aspiration), the initial *p*, *t*, and *k* of *Pacífic*, *tomórrow*, and *collíde* nevertheless are aspirated phonetically. As Kahn observes, the phonetic facts here are confirmed by speakers of French, who are sensitive to the difference between aspirated and nonaspirated consonants, since their language lacks aspirated voiceless stops. Such speakers identify the initial *t* of *tomórrow* with that of *tén* and not that of *stém*. Thus, the presence of a following stressed vowel is not a necessary condition for a voiceless stop to be aspirated in English.

The question arises as to why a preceding *s* deprives a voiceless stop of aspiration. The answer is that *s* is the only consonant that may precede *p*, *t* or *k* in the syllable-initial clusters of English. This suggests the simple rule that voiceless stops are aspirated if syllable-initial. Such a rule accounts for the aspiration in *tén*, *tèmperaméntal*, and *tomórrow*, and the lack of aspiration in *stém*. Further support for this analysis is provided by voiceless stops in medial position. The *p* is aspirated in *suppórt* and *cápòn*, because it begins the syllable, but not in *aspáragus* and *áspen*, where *s* occupies syllable-initial position.

In Kahn's analysis there are three basic syllabication rules. The first (11a) simply makes each [+syllabic] segment the nucleus of a separate syllable. The next one (11b) syllabifies a maximal string of consonants with the following vowel provided that string is a possible syllable-initial cluster. (11c) syllabifies a maximal string of consonants with the preceding vowel provided that they have not been attached to the following vowel by (11b) and that they are a possible syllable-final cluster. It is of course assumed that each grammar will contain a listing of the possible syllable-initial and final clusters. The rules of (11) operate in terms of this list.

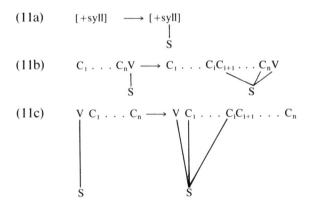

(11a) $[+syll] \longrightarrow [+syll]$
            |
            S

(11b) $C_1 \ldots C_n V \longrightarrow C_1 \ldots C_i C_{i+1} \ldots C_n V$ where $C_{i+1} \ldots n$ is a
            | member of the set of
            S   S   permissible initial clusters but $C_i C_{i+1} \ldots C_n$ is not.

(11c) $V \, C_1 \ldots C_n \longrightarrow V \, C_1 \ldots C_i C_{i+1} \ldots C_n$ where $C_1 \ldots C_i$ is a
            | member of the set of
            S   S   permissible final clusters but $C_1 \ldots C_i C_{i+1}$ is not.

These rules assign *aspen* a syllable structure as in (12) and thereby provide a formalization of the notion syllable-initial which the aspiration rule refers to.

                    (11a)   (11b)   (11c)
(12)   aspen $\longrightarrow$ aspen $\longrightarrow$ aspen $\longrightarrow$ aspen
                        | | |\ |\/
                        S S   S S   S S

The analysis of English aspiration requires a slight emendation in view of words like *happy*, where the *p* is unaspirated even though it is followed by a vowel and not preceded by *s*. Kahn's explanation is that the *p* is simultaneously a member of both syllables due to rule (13) of English that makes a syllable-initial consonant ambisyllabic when followed by an unstressed vowel.

(13)

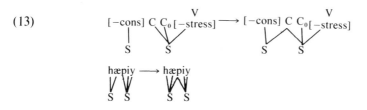

The lack of aspiration in *happy* can thus be accounted for if the rule is modified to say that *p*, *t*, and *k* are aspirated only when exclusively syllable-initial and hence not when ambisyllabic. Note that rule (13) does not apply in overly slow, precise speech; in such speech the *p* is aspirated since it remains in exclusively syllable-initial position.

Some further confirmation of this analysis is provided by another syllabication rule making a syllable-final consonant ambisyllabic when followed by an unstressed syllable.

(14)

$$\underset{\substack{| \\ S}}{C} \; \underset{S}{C}_0 \; [\; -\text{stress}] \; \underset{V}{\overset{V}{\;}} \longrightarrow \underset{S}{C} \; \underset{S}{C}_0 \; [\; -\text{stress}] \; \underset{}{\overset{V}{\;}}$$

This rule accounts for the fact that the *f* in words like *after* and *laughter* is ambisyllabic in normal rates of speech. Note that when this rule applies, the *t* is no longer syllable-initial and hence is not assigned aspiration. (In overly precise speech (14) does not apply, in which case the *t* is aspirated). Rule (14) is subject to a number of restrictions and hence does not attach all syllable-final consonants to following unstressed syllables (cf. Kahn 1976 for details). One case where the rule does not apply is in a word like *Washington*, where *ŋ* does not become ambisyllabic and there is a clear syllable break between the *ŋ* and the *t*. Note that in this case the *t* is aspirated in contrast to the *t* of *after*. Rule (14) thus assigns the syllable structures of (15) to which the aspiration rule then refers.

(15)

Thus, if phonological rules are permitted to refer to syllable structure a relatively simple account of English aspiration is possible. If reference to syllable structures is not allowed, the statement of the distribution of aspiration becomes much more complex and would have to essentially incorporate the definition of syllable-initial position into the environment of the rule. However, complexity per se is not really the issue, since one might argue that the simpler rule requires the grammar to contain more information in the form of the various syllabification rules. The analysis that appeals to syllable structure can be supported on two grounds. First, the syllabification rules that it presupposes give a consistent definition of the syllable that is required for the statement of several other phonological rules of English (see Kahn 1976). Without appeal to syllable structure each of these rules would have to incorporate some aspect of the definition of the syllable and thus a clear generalization would be missed. Second, if sounds are organized into syllables phonologically, it becomes possible to compare and identify rules of different languages as being manifestations of the same phonological process even though they may have different syllable structures. Thus, if syllable-initial position rather than the presence of a preceding *s* is the relevant factor in aspiration assignment in English, one might expect other languages with different syllable structures to have different consonants blocking the assignment of aspiration.

In addition to defining a reference point for the statement of phonological rules, the syllable may also constitute the domain of realization of a particular feature. An interesting example is provided by Cairene Arabic, where the syllable is the domain for the feature of emphasis or pharyngealization. According to Lehn,

> Emphasis never occurs as the feature of one segment only; its minimum span or domain is the sequence CV (but not VC). Within monosyllabic utterances there are no contrasts; the entire syllable is either emphatic or plain throughout: e.g. /ṛab/ 'Lord', /rab/ 'it sprouted'; /ṭiṃ/ 'mud', /tiin/ 'figs'. Within utterances of more than one syllable, there are contrasts; e.g. two-syllable utterances may have both syllables emphatic, /ṛáaʔiḍ/ (military rank), or neither emphatic, /ráaʔid/ 'sleeper', or only the first syllable emphatic, /ṛáagil/ 'man' (vs. /ráakib/ 'passenger'), or only the second emphatic, /búkṛa/ 'tomorrow' (vs. /fíkra/ 'idea') [1963, p. 32].

Numerous alternations between emphatic and nonemphatic consonants arise due to the syllabification rules in Cairene Arabic. These rules are quite simple: A consonant syllabifies with an immediately following vowel, while all other consonants syllabify with the preceding vowel. (There are no word-initial clusters and no three-consonant clusters at the point in the derivation where syllable structure is defined.) For instance, consider the following alternations (data from Lehn and Abboud 1965, with long vowels written as geminates): *ṭawiil, ṭawiil-a* and *laṭiif, laṭiif-a,* the masculine and feminine forms of 'long' and 'pleasant', respectively. In the masculine forms both syllables are emphatic. But when the feminine suffix *-a* is added, the root-final consonants syllabify with the vowel of the suffix and appear as nonemphatic. A similar alternation appears in *ḍaṛaḅ* 'he hit' versus *ḍaṛaḅ-it* 'she hit'. Since the syllabification rules apply across word boundaries in Cairene Arabic, a consonant may lose its emphasis when it syllabifies with a following vowel-initial word whose first syllable is nonemphatic. Compare *ṣ̌ạṇṭịṭ sitt* 'purse of a lady', *ṣ̌ạṇṭịt-i* 'my purse', and *ṣ̌ạṇṭịt is-sitt* 'purse of the lady'. The final *t* of 'purse' loses its emphasis when it syllabifies with the *-i* of the 1 sg. possessive suffix as well as when it syllabifies with the vowel beginning the word *is-sitt* 'the lady'. The latter is syllabified as *ṣ̌ạṇ .ṭị .t is .sitt*. Similarly, the initial consonant of a following word may acquire emphasis when it syllabifies with an emphatic syllable terminating the preceding word: compare *fid-dilta l-ṃạṭạṛ* 'in the delta [there is] rain', where the definite article /l-/ is nonemphatic, and *fil-qạḥịṛạ ḷ-ṃạṭạṛ* 'in Cairo [there is] rain', where the /ḷ-/ acquires emphasis because it attaches to the final emphatic syllable of *qạḥịṛạ*.

Since each vowel (long or short) will constitute the nucleus of a separate syllable, one might propose to analyze each vowel as distinctively emphatic or nonemphatic and then formulate rules to spread this feature to all consonants that syllabify with the vowel. On this analysis the UR for *ṭạwịịḷ* would be /tạwịịl/ and the UR for *ṭạwịịl-a* /ṭạwịịl-a/. The *l* syllabifies with the emphatic /ịị/ in the former and thus appears as *ḷ*, while in the feminine form it syllabifies with the nonemphatic vowel of the suffix and thus appears as nonemphatic.

However, such an analysis will not be able to account for examples like *ṛịxịịṣ*, *ṛịxịịṣ-ạ* 'cheap', where emphasis is spread from the root to the suffix. Furthermore, vowels in Semitic are often associated with a particular morphological category and form words by fleshing out a triconsonantal radical skeleton. In general, it is the vowels which alternate in emphasis depending on the consonantal environment rather than vice versa, as shown by the words of the structure ma + CCuuC in (16), a common adjectival pattern.

(16)	Masc. sg.	*ma-šγuul*	*ṃạ-ḅṣụụṭ*
	Fem. sg.	*ma-šγuul-a*	*ṃạ-ḅṣụụṭ-ạ*
	Pl.	*ma-šγul-iin*	*ṃạ-ḅṣụṭ-ịịṇ*
	Gloss	'busy'	'happy'

These data appear to indicate that consonants are the locus of the emphatic versus nonemphatic contrast. Emphasis is then spread to all segments that are tautosyllabic with an underlying emphatic consonant. On this analysis, we would have URs such as /ṭawīl/, /riẋiis/, /šγuul/, and /ḫṣuuṭ/.

Such an analysis does not of course preclude the possibility of other rules that may assign emphasis or nonemphasis independent of syllable structure. Rules of this type are quite clearly necessary (see Broselow 1976 for discussion), but to our knowledge have not so far been satisfactorily formulated. But regardless of the nature of such rules, the data presented above are, in our opinion, sufficient to establish that some of the rules implementing emphasis must refer to syllable structure.

Given that at least some phonological rules require sounds to be organized into syllables, a number of important questions arise, two of which will be briefly discussed here: 1. Are syllable divisions always predictable by rule or can they be distinctive? 2. At what point in the grammar will the syllable structure assignment rules apply?

Taking the latter question first, a reasonable working assumption is that the syllabification rules will be transparent in the sense that they will apply after all rules that materially affect the phonetic properties that these rules must refer to. Thus, for a language such as Arabic, where the syllabification rules merely refer to consonants and vowels, the transparency principle claims that the syllabification rules will apply after all rules that insert, delete, or rearrange consonants and vowels. For a language such as English, where the feature of stress affects the operation of the syllabification rules, the principle also requires that the syllabification rules follow all rules that stress or destress vowels. This principle could be falsified if it could be shown that, for example, a rule syncopating a vowel in open syllables could not be stated as applying simply in the context ____CV, but instead had to specifically refer to syllable-final position: For example, if the rule applied before the clusters pl, and st, but not pt and it could be shown that $VplV$, $VstV$, and $VptV$ were syllabified as $V.plV$, $V.stV$, but $Vp.tV$. Note that if, in such a case, strings like $VplV$ and $VptV$ arising from $VpVlV$ and $VpVtV$ by syncope were also syllabified as $V.plV$ and $Vp.tV$, the syllabification rules would have to apply at two separate points in the derivation. Although it has been claimed at various times in the literature that syllabification rules apply after every phonological rule, we are not aware of any convincing arguments that the more restrictive transparency principle cannot be maintained.

This principle could also be falsified if it could be shown that phonetic syllable structure must be assigned before a rule of deletion. Suppose, for example, a language has the rules VCCV ⟶ VC . CV and VCV ⟶ V . CV. Suppose further that clusters of consonant plus h are simplified by the deletion of h. If all such clusters syllabify as VC.V, then this could only be explained by assuming that syllable structure was assigned before the deletion of *h*, in violation of the transparency principle. Suppose further that the rule deleting *h* after a consonant is no longer a viable phonological rule in the language. Then the possibility arises of a given string of segments being contrastively (nonpredictably) syllabified: V.CV versus VC.V from *VChV.

A counterexample of the latter type appears to have arisen as the result of two sound changes that occurred in the dialect of Gaelic spoken on the Isle of Barra in the Outer Hebrides described by Borgstrøm (1937). According to Borgstrøm, intervocalic consonant clusters are divided by a syllable boundary, while single intervocalic consonants syllabify with the preceding vowel if it is short and with the following vowel if the preceding one is long or a diphthong.

(17)   a. V:CV ⟶ V:.CV   *mo:.ran* 'much'
        b. V:CCV ⟶ V:C.CV   *mi:l'.t'ən* 'thousands'
        c. VCV ⟶ VC.V   *ar.an* 'bread'
        d. VCCV ⟶ VC.CV   *b̥ɔt.ɔx* 'old man'

The interesting case is that of an intervocalic consonant after a short vowel. According to Borgstrøm

> The consonants in this position are not geminated; the impression of *b̥ɔt.ɔx* is different from that of the Norwegian word *at.te* 'eight'. The characteristic feature of the pronunciation is that the consonant has decreasing tension; the following vowel also has decreasing tension, but it begins with a higher tension than that with which the consonant ends; consequently there is a break in tension after the consonant . . . On the other side the type *mo:.ran* has unbroken tension; the *r* has increasing tension which begins at the point where the decreasing tension of the preceding vowel stops [p. 76].

Borgstrøm illustrates the difference between *ar.an* and *mo:.ran* by a diagram like that in (18), where the lines represent tension.

(18)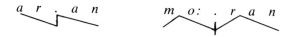

There are certain systematic exceptions to the syllabification rule (17c). In these cases a liquid or nasal syllabifies with the following vowel instead of the preceding one: e.g. *ma.rav* 'dead'. All of these cases have arisen from a sound change that inserted a vowel between a liquid or nasal and a following consonant. This inserted vowel is usually, but not always, identical with the preceding vowel. Consequently, "After short vowels there are thus two types of syllabic division, one with broken tension, the other with unbroken tension.

These two types are quite clearly distinguishable . . . Words of the type *ma.rav* sound shorter than those of the type *ar.an*, since a syllable ending in a short vowel (*ma.*) must be shorter than one ending in a consonant (*ar.*). In songs the type *ma.rav* is sung on one note, as if monosyllabic [p. 77]."

Borgstrøm goes on to say (p. 78) that "with regard to the words *fäNak* 'crow' (feannag) and *ša.Lak* 'hunting' (sealg) he [the informant] remarked: In *fäNak* there is a 'space' between the two syllables, he could pronounce *fäN. .ak*. In *ša.Lak* the *L* and the *k* are so 'close together', that such a separation is impossible; the word is nearly monosyllabic, but not quite monosyllabic."

Thus, in historical terms, what appears to have happened is that original VRVC sequences (R = liquid or nasal) have syllabified as VR . VC by (17c), while V̆RVC sequences arising from *VRC by epenthesis have syllabified as V̆.RVC, perhaps by a generalization of (17a). Some additional examples of this kind of syllabification are recorded in (19).

(19)   *a.Lapɔ*   'Scotland'   Mod. Ir.   *Alba*
       æ.r'æk'ət   'money'   Old Ir.   *arget*
       k'a.rapət   'car'   Mod. Ir.   *carbat*
       mu.ruxəγ   'Murdoch'   Mod. Ir.   *Murchad*
       du.Nuxəγ   'Duncan'   Mod. Ir.   *Donnchad*
       æ.mæšir'   'period'   Old Ir.   *aimsir*

Since in almost all cases cited by Borgstrøm the epenthesis process has occurred internal to a morpheme, there are no alternations that would motivate epenthesis as a synchronic rule. The conclusion thus appears to be that sequences of the shape C₀V̆RVC may contrast in syllable structure alone [cf., the near minimal pairs *šæ.rak* 'to fade' (searg) versus *šæR.ak* 'a glass of whisky' (searrag)].

Another contrast in syllabification occurs in vowel clusters. Between certain vowel sequences there is a syllable break, while between others of the same underlying character there is no break.

(20)   *ian*   'bird'   *N'i.an*   'girl'
       biəγ   'food'   *bi.əγ*   'let (him) be'
       Ruəγ   'red'   *Ru.əγ*   'flush in the face'
       duən   'poem'   *du.an*   'hook'

The phonetic correlates of this difference in syllabification are again primarily a matter of tension, as the diagrams in (21) illustrate (p. 149).

(21)   *ian*   N'   i   .   a   n

In addition, a slight glottal catch sometimes appears at the syllable break dividing the two vowels in the words in the righthand column of (20); also, the first vowel may be lengthened slightly. It would seem entirely appropriate to interpret these phonetic properties as a consequence of the difference in syllabification rather than vice versa.

All of these cases of vowel clusters divided by a syllable break have arisen from the deletion of an intervocalic spirant. In many cases this process still functions as a phonological rule governing alternations: compare *La:v* 'hand', *Lai.əɣ* gen.; *e.əx* 'to howl', *je:v* pret.; *L'e.əɣ* 'to read', *l'e:v* pret.

These data might be described by claiming that the syllabification rules of (17) apply before spirant deletion. A form like *L'e.əɣ* would then be derived from /L'ev + əɣ/ by first syllabifying to /L'e.vəɣ/ and then deleting the *v*. However, it is not clear that all cases where a syllable break occurs between vowels are amenable to this sort of analysis, since spirant deletion appears to have operated internal to a morpheme without leaving any synchronic alternations that would justify setting up an underlying spirant. In such cases the syllabification would have to be considered contrastive.

The Representation of Tone

As we noted in our discussion of Makua in Chapter 4, there are many languages which utilize contrasts in the relative pitch at which a syllable is pronounced to distinguish between wordforms. Furthermore, our discussion of Makua revealed that the relative pitch of the voice in such languages is subject to systematic restrictions just like any other phonetic property. It is necessary therefore to consider how tone is to be represented in tone languages: In particular, what is the nature of the tonal information contained in the lexicon and how do phonological rules apply to modify this underlying tonal information so as to produce the correct surface tonal shapes?

It is important to begin any discussion of tone by carefully distinguishing between tone and pitch. Pitch refers to our subjective perception of voiced sounds and is correlated with the frequency of vibration of the vocal cords (which itself is determined by a number of factors, some of which are under a speaker's control, others of which are physiological). The higher the frequency of vibration, the higher the pitch of the voice.

The word "tone," on the other hand, refers to the abstract entities in terms of which the pitch pattern of utterances can be understood. One might well ask, why talk about tone at all? Why not talk directly about pitch? The reason for making the distinction resides in the fact that absolute pitch is of very little linguistic interest; it is relative pitch that matters. Two vowels uttered at the same pitch level do not necessarily count linguistically as the "same" sound. Absolute pitch must be ignored and relative pitch alone taken into account.

The fact that absolute pitch is irrelevant in determining sameness and difference can be illustrated in several ways. Perhaps the most obvious piece of evidence is the simple observation that people do not have the same pitch range when talking. Consequently, the same word uttered by different speakers will be pronounced at different pitch levels. Thus a word uttered by a woman or child is generally at a higher absolute pitch than the same word uttered by a man. Rather dramatic additional evidence of the irrelevance of absolute pitch is provided by the observation that in languages exhibiting the phenomenon of **downdrift** a sound that is linguistically a high-toned sound may in some situations be pronounced at the same or even at a lower pitch level than another sound that is low-toned. To see how such an apparently contradictory situation can arise, we need to specify briefly what is meant by downdrift.

The term downdrift refers to a process found in many African tone languages whereby in a phrase any high tone that is separated from a preceding high tone by one or more low tones is pronounced at a somewhat lower pitch level than the preceding high. A high tone that is not separated from a preceding high tone by a low tone is pronounced at the same pitch height as the preceding high. In a language with downdrift, the first high tone in the phrase is phonetically the highest in pitch. No high tone that is separated from a high tone by low tones ever returns to the pitch level of the preceding high. Thus high tones step down in terms of their pitch level after each low tone (sequence). It may be the case in such languages that the low tones also drift downwards in pitch. These observations can be illustrated by examining an example from Schachter and Fromkin's (1968) description of Akan, a language where downdrift occurs. Schachter and Fromkin cite the following example: ɔbɛkɔ́ Kùmásé ánɔ́pá yí 'he will go to Kumasi this morning'. This sentence has the tone sequence LHHLHHHLHH. If we use the numeral 5 to stand for the highest pitch level and 1 to stand for the lowest pitch level, then the pitch pattern of this sentence in Akan is 3552444133. Notice that the first sequence of high tones is pronounced at the highest level (5), the next sequence at a slightly lower level (4), and the final sequence of highs at a yet lower level (3). Crucially, notice that the pitch height of the last sequence of high tones is the same as the pitch height of the initial low tone! Given a long enough sentence, it would be easy for a high tone at the end of the sentence to be lower in pitch than a low tone at the beginning of the sentence.

The above discussion has shown that sameness of pitch does not necessarily imply sameness at the phonological level. This fact has led linguists to postulate abstract entities—tones—in terms of which phonological sameness and difference can be characterized. It is only in recent years that generative phonology has attempted to deal in a serious way with these abstract entities, and the subject is an exceedingly complex one, for tone can function in surprisingly intricate ways. Consequently, there are many questions concerning the representation of tone that cannot be dealt with here in a satisfactory manner. The answers simply are not yet clear. We will of necessity limit our discussion to selected problems in the representation of tone where some answers are beginning to emerge.

First, let us mention briefly some points that must be left open pending further research. Within generative phonology, tone has most often been regarded—like other phonological features—as properly classified in terms of binary features (e.g., [±High], [±Low]). But whereas some features fall rather obviously into the category of binary contrasts, tone is similar to vowel height and point of articulation in potentially being regarded as a multivalued or scalar feature. Whereas many languages simply distinguish between two tones (generally referred to as high and low), other languages distinguish between three (high, mid, and low), and even four levels of tone is commonly found. As many as five different level tones have been reported to occur. It is of course possible to postulate a set of binary features that will allow at least five tone levels; the problem is finding data to justify either the binary approach or the scalar approach. Little substantive argumentation is available; the reader is referred to Stahlke (1975) for some discussion of the problem.

We have noted that languages have up to five contrastive level tones. Level tones, however, are not the only type of tone found. Many languages exhibit *contour* tones—that is, cases where the pitch of the voice changes in the course of pronunciation of a syllable. We will examine contour tones in some detail in the next section and show that in many cases contour tones are best analyzed as a sequence of level tones. Nevertheless, we will also see some evidence that contour tones might in some cases have to be regarded as unanalyzable units, rather than as sequences of level tones. If so, the question arises as to what the range of possible contour tones is and what feature representation is appropriate. This question cannot be satisfactorily answered until one sorts out those contour tones that are in fact sequences and those that must be regarded as units.

There is strong evidence that in many cases contour tones *develop* from underlying sequences of level tones. In such cases, then, contour tones do not need to be regarded as underlying tones. Contour tones develop from sequences of level tones in basically two ways. First, the tone of one vowel "spreads" to a neighboring vowel and creates a contour tone in doing so. Second, a vowel deletes or glides adjacent to another vowel, but the tone of the deleted or desyllabified vowel remains and associates with the adjacent vowel. We will give illustrations of both cases.

Turning now to some questions where answers are beginning to emerge, we will concentrate on the following points: 1. Are contour tones best analyzed as sequences of level tones or as unanalyzable tonological units? 2. What is the domain of tone specifications—is the domain a phonological unit (the segment, the syllable) or a grammatical unit (the morpheme, the word)? 3. Granting that tone is realized phonetically as pitch, and that pitch is a property of voiced segments, is it the case that tone is best analyzed as a part of the feature matrix of a segment or as a separate, "suprasegmental" feature independent of the segment?

THE ANALYSIS OF CONTOUR TONES

In Nupe (see George 1970), there are three level tones: high, mid, and low. The mid tones will be left unmarked in the following examples, while high tones will be indicated by an acute accent mark and low tones by a grave accent mark. These three contrasting level tones are illustrated by examples such as those in (22).

(22) *ebà* 'ground, place' *eba* 'male sexual organ' *ebá* 'husband'
     edú 'sp. of fish'   *èdù* 'Niger river'   *èdu* 'sp. of wild
     edu 'thigh'   *edù* 'deer'   yam'

There are a number of nouns of the structure V-CV, like those in (22), with a vowel prefix bearing a low tone and a high tone on the root vowel. All such examples have a consonant in root-initial position that is voiceless. Some examples follow:

(23)   *èfú* 'honey'   *èkpá* 'length'
            ètú 'parasite'   *èkó* 'shea-butter nut'

There are also a large number of nouns of the structure V-CV with a low toned prefixal vowel and a rising tone on the vowel of the noun root. All such nouns have a voiced consonant. Some examples:

(24) *ègbă* 'a border on a garment'   *ègʷă* 'name of a town'
      èbĕ 'pumpkin'   *èdză* 'sash'
      èbŭ 'cross'   *èlĕ* 'past'

Since the distribution of rising tones, as opposed to level high tones, is severely restricted in Nupe, it is possible to analyze rising tones as deriving from a level high tone by a rule such as (25) below.

(25) $$\acute{V} \longrightarrow \check{V}/\check{V}\begin{bmatrix} +\text{conson} \\ +\text{voiced} \end{bmatrix} \underline{\qquad}$$

This analysis is supported by instances of morphophonemic alternation in the verb. A verbal root may be preceded by no prefix, a mid-toned prefix, or a low-toned prefix. If the verb root is of the shape -CV, where C is voiceless, and the vowel is high-toned, then the root remains invariant in its tonal shape. But if the verb root is -CV, where C is voiced, and the vowel is basically high-toned, that high tone will be realized as a rising tone when the prefix preceding is low-toned, but not otherwise. In (26) we illustrate the case of a root with a voiceless consonant and (27) a root with a voiced consonant.

(26)   *gbìgbì tí*   'an owl hooted'
            gbìgbì ètí   'an owl is hooting'
            gbìgbì á tí   'an owl has hooted'

> Note: These forms represent a more remote structure; certain phonetic rules not relevant here operate to affect these representations. For some discussion, see George (1970)

(27) ·   *musa lá nākà̀*   'Moses took the meat'
            musa èlă nākà̀   :Moses is carrying the meat'
            u lá èdu bĕ   'he brought the yam'

The Nupe example illustrates how a contour tone can develop from a level tone through spreading: A low tone in a prefix extends itself (across a voiced consonant) to a high tone in the root to yield a rising tone on the root. Evidence that vowel deletion and vowel gliding can also lead to contour tones is provided by Lomongo, a Bantu language of Zaire (cf. Hulstaert 1961). Consider the data in (28), where we see the results of prefixing the subject prefixes *tó-* 'we' and *bá-* 'they' to verb roots.

(28) *tó-kàmb-à*   'we work'   *tó-fénd-à*   'we cross'
      bá-kàmb-à   'they work'   *bá-fénd-à*   'they cross'
      tsw-âs-à   'we search'   *tsw-ís-à*   'we hide'
      b-âs-à   'they search'   *b-ís-à*   'they hide'

The subject prefixes in the particular verb tense illustrated in (28) are high-toned. In Lomongo, as in many other Bantu languages, only the first vowel of a verb stem is tonally contrastive: It is either high-toned or low-toned. The verbs 'cross' and 'hide' are high-toned, whereas 'work' and 'search' are low-toned. Verbs are either consonant-initial or vowel-initial. 'Work' and 'cross' are consonant-initial roots, while 'search' and 'hide' are vowel-initial. Note that the vowel of the *tó-* prefix glides to *w* before a vowel. There is a rule in the language that affricates coronal consonants before the glides *w* and *y*; thus *t* affricates to *ts* before the *w* that results from the gliding of *o*. On the other hand, the vowel of *bá-* simply deletes before a vowel. But now consider the tonal shapes that result from the gliding of the vowel of *tó-* and the deletion of the vowel of *bá-*. When *tó-* glides before a verb root with an initial low-toned vowel like /às/ 'search', the result is a falling tone: *tsw-ǎs-à*, whereas when *tó-* glides before a verb root with an initial high-tone like /ís/ 'hide', the result is a simple high tone: *tsw-ís-à*. It seems then that the high tone of the prefix becomes associated with the root vowel when the vowel of the prefix glides; this produces a falling tone when the root vowel is low. Similarly, even though the vowel of *bá-* elides before a vowel, its high tone becomes associated with the following vowel, producing a falling tone when the root vowel is low-toned and a simple high level tone when the root vowel is high-toned: cf. *b-âs-à* and *b-ís-à*. This example thus very strongly indicates that contour tones in some cases develop from vowel gliding and vowel deletion.

The preceding examples show that contour tones can *originate* from representations with just level tones and thus need not be considered as distinct entities at the underlying level. Is there any evidence that, independently of origin, contour tones *behave* like sequences of level tones? Two pieces of evidence can be cited here. One is with respect to the phenomenon of downdrift mentioned earlier. Recall that in languages with downdrift, a high tone separated from a preceding high by a low tone or tones will be pronounced at a somewhat lower pitch level than the preceding high. Languages with downdrift often also have contour tones. In such languages facts about downdrift support the interpretation of contour tones as sequences of level tones.

Consider, for example, the behavior of falling tones in relationship to downdrift. In a sequence HFH, where F = falling tone, the first part of the falling tone would be pronounced at the same level as the preceding high tone. The following high tone, however, would be pronounced at a slightly lower level than the preceding high tone. These facts follow automatically if the falling tone is treated as the sequence HL, for in a sequence HHLH the second high is at the same level as the first high, but the last high is somewhat lower in pitch than the first two highs. Clearly, the facts about a falling tone with respect to downdrift exactly match the facts about a HL sequence. Further evidence of the validity of the analogy is provided by a sequence like HLF, for the first (highest) part of the falling tone is not as high as the preceding high tone. In other words, a falling tone itself downdrifts just like a high tone.

A second argument that the behavior of contour tones can best be characterized by representing them as a sequence of level tones is provided by Mandarin Chinese (cf., Cheng 1973). There are four contrastive tones in the language which are commonly referred to as tone 1 (level high), tone 2 (mid-rising), tone 3 (falling-rising), and tone 4 (high-falling). There is a rule that operates in fast speech whereby tone 2 becomes tone 1 if preceded by either tone 1 or tone 2 and followed by any tone except what is referred to as "neutral tone" (i.e., an inherently toneless syllable that is assigned tone on the basis of its environment). In this rule we see that tone 1 and tone 2 behave alike in triggering a change from tone 2 to tone 1. If tone 2 (mid-rising) is treated as a tonological unit, the rule would have to say that a mid-rising tone becomes a high tone after either a mid-rising tone or a high tone. But why should a mid-rising tone undergo a change after another mid-rising tone? And why do both mid-rising and high tones trigger the same change? Natural answers to these questions can be given if a mid-rising tone is treated as a sequence of mid tone followed by a high tone, for then the tone sandhi rule in Mandarin Chinese could be expressed as follows:

(29)   [mid] $\longrightarrow$ [high]/[high]____[high][non-neutral tone]

This rule says that the mid part of a sequence of mid followed by high will change to high just in case a high precedes. This preceding high could, of course, itself be the second part of another sequence of mid followed by high. The assimilatory nature of the tone sandhi process is clearly brought out in this formulation, as it cannot be if a mid-rising tone is treated as a unit rather than a tone sequence ending in a high tone.

We have given some evidence that contour tones originate in many cases from underlying representations containing only level tones, and we have seen that with respect to tonological processes contour tones sometimes behave as though they are sequences of level tones. The question naturally arises as to whether there is any evidence that contour tones must be regarded as tonological units rather than as sequences. We are not familiar with very many attempts to demonstrate that contour tones must *not* be sequences, but we can summarize one argument to that effect presented in Elimelech (1974).

Elimelech's argument is based upon data from Kru, a language spoken in Liberia, Ivory Coast, and Sierra Leone. Four tones occur in this language: high, low, rising, falling. Elimelech's argument centers around the rising tone. In a word such as *jŭ* 'child', the rising tone consists of a high tone that rises to a superhigh level. In slow speech, a rising tone after a rising tone starts off at the height where the previous rising tone ended and goes even higher. Thus successive rising tones get progressively higher and higher in pitch. But this is true of slow speech only. In normal speech, there is a simplification so that any number of successive rising tones will be changed to level high before a rising tone: schematically, R_0R will be converted to H_0R. In normal speech, then, a rising tone will start at the level of the final part of the preceding tone (either high, low, or falling—rising tones being excluded as a consequence of the simplification process) and go higher.

Now let us consider what the consequences would be if we attempted to represent the rising tone in Kru as a sequence of two level tones. Given that the language has just two level tones, high and low, a rising tone would have to be represented as a sequence of low followed by high. The only alternative would be to represent a rising tone as a sequence of high followed by superhigh, but that would require postulating a third underlying level tone—superhigh—which would be very limited in distribution, occurring only after a high tone on the same vowel. Assuming, then, that a rising tone is represented as a LH sequence, we would need a special phonetic rule that will say that the L in a LH sequence on a single vowel is not pronounced as low, but rather as high, and the H part of the same sequence is pronounced as superhigh, not high. A LH sequence on two separate vowels is not pronounced in analogous fashion, thus it is not the case that the behavior of level tones on separate vowels parallels the behavior of a putative sequence of level tones on a single vowel. Thus in Kru it would complicate the description of the language to represent the rising tone as a sequence of level tones. If additional evidence can be found establishing that contour tones in some languages either cannot originate as sequences of level tones or do not behave in a fashion comparable to sequences of level tones, then it will be necessary to include contour tones among the basic tonological units that a language may utilize.

THE DOMAIN OF TONE

The next question that we wish to examine can be phrased as follows: What is the domain of tonal specifications? Is it the case that tone is exclusively the property of a phonological unit (presumably either the syllabic nucleus of a syllable or the syllable itself), or can tone be a property of a grammatical unit (such as the morpheme or word)? Examination of the literature reveals that tone has been claimed in some languages to be a feature of phonological units and in other languages to be a feature of grammatical units.

The most common view of tone has been to associate it with phonological units. Consider for instance the classical definition of a tone language given by Pike: "A tone language may be defined as a language having lexically significant, contrastive, but relative pitch on each syllable [1948, p. 3]." Although it is common to view the locus of tone as being the syllable, within the framework of generative phonology tone has usually been regarded as a segmental feature associated with vowels and syllabic consonants (especially nasals). We have already seen the reason for this preference: The syllable was not until recently recognized as a possible underlying unit in generative phonology and thus could not have a role to play in terms of the representation of tone (or any other feature). But even if the syllable is recognized as a unit in underlying representations, it is not yet clear that there are generalizations about tone which can be expressed only if the syllable rather than the syllabic nucleus is taken as the domain of tone.

The motivation for regarding tone as being a property of the segment is varied. First of all, since other phonetic properties are regarded as properties of segments rather than of grammatical units, the simplest assumption is that tone is treated in parallel fashion. Of course, at various times linguists have attempted to treat phonetic features like nasalization, vowel backness, vowel rounding, and so on, as features of morphemes. These attempts have not met with general acceptance [see Kiparsky (1968a) for some discussion of the attempt to treat vowel harmony as a feature of morphemes rather than of vowels].

Even if one accepts the possibility that phonetic features may be somehow abstracted away from segments and treated as a property of morphemes, the fact remains that in many languages tone is as much an unpredictable aspect of the pronunciation of a segment as any other phonetic feature. If in underlying representations any given tone-bearing segment in a morpheme can bear any given tone it would be correct to say that tone is an idiosyncratic property of each tone-bearing segment.

Further support for the association of tones with segments in the lexicon is provided by standard Thai, for in that language there are generalizations about the distribution of tones that can be expressed only if tones are associated with segments (cf., Gandour 1974). There are five tones in Thai: high, mid, low, falling, and rising. In syllables ending in a vowel, nasal, or semivowel all five of these tones may appear. In syllables ending in a short vowel plus *p*, *t*, *k*, or *ʔ* only the low and the high tones are possible. In syllables ending in a long vowel or diphthong plus p, t, or k, only the low tone or the falling tone are allowed. If these constraints on the distribution of tone are to be expressed in the grammar of Thai, reference must be made to segments (and the environments in which these segments occur). The distribution of the tones is not independent of the segments that make up the morpheme.

Additional evidence that tone is segmental in nature is provided by the observation that in some languages the tone is affected by the segmental environment in which the tone-bearing element occurs. If tones were fundamentally separated from segments, then one would not expect tones to be affected by anything other than other tones. The fact that segments which do not inherently bear the tone may affect tone suggests that tone is located on segments.

We have already seen an example where tone is affected by neighboring segments. Recall the example from Nupe where a high tone on a CV verb root becomes rising if preceded by a low-toned prefix and if the initial consonant of the root is voiced. Another example is provided by Shona, a Bantu language spoken in Zimbabwe (cf., Fivaz 1970). In Shona, certain consonants—referred to as "depressor" consonants—affect a following high tone, causing it to be realized as a rising tone. This process, unlike the one in Nupe, is independent of the tone of the preceding vowel. The following examples illustrate some of these depressor consonant (clusters) and the rising tones they induce.

(30)   *zĭnó*   'tooth'   *kukúdzwǎ*   'to be honored'
        jĭrá   'cloth'   *mȟěpó*   'wind'
        íbwě   'it is a stone'   *dzŭngu*   'dizziness'
        izwĭ   'word'   *ȟǎmá*   'relation'

Note: Low tones are unmarked in these examples

It seems clear then that in some languages tone is inseparably linked to the segments that bear the tones. Nevertheless, a considerable body of evidence exists supporting the view that in many languages tone can best be described if it is separated from the segments that ultimately bear the tones and treated as suprasegmental (i.e., a level of representation separate from but somehow parallel to the segmental representation). One argument that tone is sometimes suprasegmental revolves around the claim that in some languages tone is a feature of a grammatical unit (the morpheme, the word) rather than of segments. The evidence for this claim is that there are generalizations about the distribution of tones in underlying representation that cannot be expressed if tone is regarded as a segmental property.

Leben (1973) claims, for example, that in Mende—a Mande language of Sierra Leone—nouns have just five tone patterns: H, L, HL, LH, and LHL. These tone patterns are independent of the number of syllables in the noun. For instance, a noun showing the H pattern has all of its syllables high-toned, while a noun belonging to the L pattern has all of its syllables low-toned. The more interesting cases are the HL, LH, and LHL patterns. Let us consider the HL and LH patterns first. If a noun possessing these patterns happens to be monosyllabic, then the noun will exhibit a contour tone; for example, *mbû* 'owl' has a HL pattern and *mbǎ* 'rice' has a LH pattern. On the other hand, if the noun has two syllables, the tone pattern will be spread over the two syllables; for example, *kényà* 'uncle' has a HL pattern and *nìká* 'cow' has a LH pattern. Consider finally the nouns exhibiting the LHL pattern. If a monosyllabic noun has this pattern, it is pronounced with a rising and then falling contour tone; Leben cites *mbã̀* 'companion' as an example. If a two-syllable noun has this pattern, it is pronounced with a low tone on the first syllable and a falling tone on the last—compare, *nyàhâ* 'woman'. Finally, if a three-syllable noun has the LHL pattern, each syllable bears one of the tones of the pattern—compare, *nìkílì* 'groundnut'.

Although Leben's claims about Mende have not been universally accepted as valid, we are interested primarily in the nature of the argument itself rather than in the ultimate correctness of the Mende example. (Similar claims have been made about a number of other tone languages; thus it seems likely that at least some languages exhibit systems comparable to that which Leben attributes to Mende.) The Mende data constitute evidence that the morpheme (a noun root in the present case) can be the domain of tone since it is only this unit that allows the generalization underlying the distribution of tone to be expressed. Suppose that we were to say that tonal information cannot be associated with the morpheme. Then, in order to account for the limitations on tonal shapes in Mende, we would have to state separate principles depending on the number of syllables in the item. For example, we would have to say that while a rising-falling contour could occur on the vowel of a CV noun root, it could not appear on the vowel of any polysyllabic root. Furthermore, falling-rising contour tones do not occur at all. Similarly, a rising tone could occur on the vowel of a CV root, but on no other vowel. A falling tone on the other hand would be allowed to occur on the vowel of a CV root or on the second vowel of a CVCV root, but nowhere else.

Although Leben cites no examples, his discussion would indicate that in three-syllable noun roots the HL pattern would be realized as high tone on the first syllable and low tone on the second and third; similarly, the LH pattern would be realized as low tone on the first syllable and high tone on the second and third. If this is in fact the case, three-syllable noun roots in Mende would exhibit the following tonal shapes: HHH, HLL, LLL, LHL, and LHH. The grammar would have to contain separate statements excluding HLH, HHL, and LLH tonal shapes for three-syllable noun roots.

It is clear that while the preceding set of statements about the distribution of tones in Mende are accurate, they fail to express the generalizations that Leben's five "tone melodies" express. The restrictions on Mende tones are not in terms of the individual syllables of a morpheme taken separately, but rather are in terms of the tonal pattern of the morpheme taken as a whole. If these restrictions are to be adequately expressed in a grammar, a tonal pattern such as LHL must be attributed to a morpheme independently of the number of syllables in that morpheme.

So far the only evidence that we have considered for a suprasegmental representation is that it allows us to express certain generalizations about the distribution of tones in the underlying representations of lexical items. We must consider now whether any additional aspects of tonal behavior lead to similar conclusions about the nature of tonal representations.

One of the points discussed earlier can, in a sense, be regarded as support for the suprasegmental representation of tone. Recall that considerable evidence was given in support of the view that in many instances contour tones are best represented as a sequence of level tones. Such contour tones may occur on short vowels. This raises an immediate problem: How can it be the case that a *sequence* of tones occurs on a single vowel? If tone is a property of the syllabic nucleus of a syllable (a vowel or a syllabic consonant), how can there be two tones but only one syllabic nucleus? Of course, one could revise the concept of a segmental feature matrix so that it may consist of ordered pairs of feature specifications like [[−High][+High]] for rising tones or ordered triplets like [[−High][+High] [−High]] for rising-falling tones. But such an approach appears to undermine the very distinction between segment and sequence of segments and thus clearly requires independent motivation. A suprasegmental representation of tone offers some hope of a way out of the dilemma. If tone is separate from segments, on a different level so to speak, then there is nothing inherently contradictory about saying that two elements at one level can be associated with one element at another level. It does not seem unreasonable to assume that two independent phonological representations, one segmental and the other tonological, might fail to line up in such a way that there is a one-to-one pairing.

Contour tones often figure in another type of argument for a suprasegmental representation of tone. This argument involves a phenomenon that has been referred to as *tone stability*. Tone stability refers to the situation where the tone of a vowel (or other tone-bearing element) is retained even though the vowel itself is deleted or converted into another element that does not bear (contrastive) tone. For example, recall our discussion of the contour tones in Lomongo, where we saw that the high tone of the subject prefix *tó-* is retained when this prefix combines with a vowel-initial verb stem like /às/ in *tsw-âs-à*. The *ó* of the prefix glides to *w* before a vowel (this *w* triggering the affrication of *t* to *ts*); if the following vowel is basically low-toned, it will be realized as a falling tone after the devocalized *tó* prefix. Thus we see that the high tone of the prefix appears as the first part of a falling tone on the root vowel. The tone of the prefix vowel is retained even though it is replaced by a glide. If tone is regarded as a property of the segment, then one would expect—all things being equal—that when a segment bearing a tone ceases to be capable of doing so, that tone would be lost. This does not happen in Lomongo, and Lomongo is by no means unique in this respect. The Makua data in Chapter 4 provide another instance of tone stability; recall that the low tone of the infinitive prefix *u-* is maintained in cases where this *u* vowel glides to *w* before a vowel.

Tone stability is not something that one is led to expect if tone is regarded as part of a segment. But a suprasegmental approach in a sense predicts the existence of tone stability. The suprasegmental approach claims that tone and segments are fundamentally separate, independent entities. If this is so, there is no reason to expect that deletion of a segment should have any effect on the tonal representation at all. And in cases of tone stability this is just what we find: segments delete, tones remain.

Another argument for the suprasegmental representation of tones involves the existence of so-called "floating tones." To gain a proper understanding of this notion, it is necessary to discuss a related (but different) phenomenon—namely, the fact that in many languages tone may be the only phonological parameter distinguishing between different morphological constructions. Welmers cites the following example from Jukun, a member of the Benue-Congo branch of the Niger-Congo language family:

> In most verbal constructions, the first and second person singular subject pronouns have low tone; all other subject pronouns have mid tone. In the hortative construction, however, all subject pronouns have the same consonants and vowels as in other constructions, but have high tone [1973:132].

Welmers cites examples like *m̀ ya* 'I went' versus *ḿ ya?* 'should I go?' and *ku ya* 'he went' versus *kú ya* 'have him go'. (´ indicates high tone,   indicates low tone, and mid tone is left unmarked in these examples.) Both the past tense and the hortative construction overtly consist of the subject pronoun plus the verb stem. But whereas the subject pronouns retain their inherent low or mid tone in the past tense, as in most other syntactic constructions in the language, the subject pronouns have a special high-toned shape in the hortative. The high tone on the subject pronouns is thus in a sense a mark of the hortative construction.

The above data from Jukun could be accounted for in a fairly straightforward fashion by a morphophonemic rule that says that the inherent (underlying) tone of subject pronouns such as *m̀* 'I' and *ku* 'he' is replaced by a high tone when a hortative verb follows (of course, this assumes that the surface syntactic structure contains the information that a verb is hortative, even though there is no overt morphology to indicate this fact). There are, however, other cases where there is considerable advantage to recognizing the possibility that a tonal alternation that occurs in a particular grammatical construction is to be accounted for not simply by a rule that changes the underlying tones in the environment of the grammatical construction in question, but rather by assuming that the construction in question contains a morpheme that has a tonal shape but no segmental shape. This tone—which is unattached to any segment, thus the term "floating tone"—is responsible for the tonal alternations that occur in the construction. Let us take an example to see how this sort of analysis works.

Goldsmith (1976) argues that in the Ọhụhụ dialect of Igbo (Nigeria) subordinate clauses are characterized by a floating high tone. Before briefly reviewing this argument, a few preliminary remarks about Igbo structure are required. Verbs ordinarily have the shape CV in Igbo; a prefix *a-* (alternating by vowel harmony with *e-*) precedes the verb root in certain tenses. There is an interconnection between the nature of the subject of the verb and the presence of the *a-* prefix. If the subject is a full noun phrase or an independent pronoun, the subject precedes the verb and the *a-* prefix is present. But when the subject is a clitic pronoun, that pronoun generally replaces the *a-* prefix. There is one situation where this replacement is blocked: namely, in relative verbal constructions, when the relative marker *na* occurs between the clitic subject pronoun and the verb. The presence of *na* between the clitic and the verb permits the *a-* prefix to be retained on the verb. The *na* relative marker is pronounced with a high tone. The *na* is not obligatory, however; it may be omitted, and when it is omitted we find the subject clitic pronoun replacing the *a-* prefix on the verb. The preceding remarks are illustrated by the following examples:

(31)

ányì á-zà-á àlà	'we swept the floor'	*ányì* = independent pronoun
ọ́ zà-á àlà	'he swept the floor'	/za/ = verb root 'sweep'
m̀gbè ọ́ ná à-zù-là ánụ́...	'whenever he buys meat'	*ọ́* = 3 sg. subject clitic
m̀gbè ọ̀ zù-là ánụ́...	'whenever he buys meat'	/zu/ = verb root 'buy'

One other point about Igbo must be noted. Like many other African tone languages, downdrift occurs in Igbo. A high tone after a low tone is somewhat lower in pitch than a preceding high tone in the phrase. But in addition to downdrift, Igbo also exhibits what is known as downstep. The term "downstep" refers to situations where a high tone is pronounced at a somewhat lower level than the preceding high tone, even though there is no low tone (on the surface at least) between these two high tones. This "step down," while not induced by a low tone (on the surface), is very similar to the tone lowering that one gets in cases of downdrift. Recall for example that in a sequence like CV́CV̀CV́CV́ where downdrift applies, the last two high tones are at the same level (which is lower than the first high tone). It is not possible within that phonological phrase to return to the level of the first high tone. Similarly, in a sequence like CV́CV̌CV́, where V̌ indicates a downstepped high tone, the last vowel in the sequence is at the same pitch level as the second vowel (which is lower than the first vowel). Again it is not possible in the same phrase to return to the pitch height of the first vowel of this sequence. While these comments do not take us very far into the intricacies of the downstep phenomenon, they should provide enough background for the following discussion of Igbo tone.

It was mentioned before that when the relative marker *na* occurs, it is high-toned. Goldsmith does not consider this high tone to be essentially a part of the *na* morpheme itself, but rather to be much more general—namely, a floating tone that is associated with all subordinate clauses, including relative clauses. This floating high tone is located in pre-verbal position, and when the relative marker *na* occurs (always in preverbal position), the floating high tone associates with—or in Goldsmith's terminology "docks" onto—the *na* morpheme. In subordinate clauses other than the relative, no marker like *na* occurs. And even in relative clauses *na* is not obligatory. Thus there are many cases where the floating high tone postulated by Goldsmith has no morpheme that it is inherently associated with. But it is just these cases where the floating high tone is most strongly supported, for the floating high tone manifests itself in a variety of ways.

For instance, consider the case where the subject of a subordinate clause is a noun that ends (in its isolation form) in a low tone. *áz̄ù* 'fish' has a high-low tonal pattern that is maintained in a relative clause such as *ázù ná réré èré* 'the fish that was rotten'; but if the *na* morpheme is omitted, we find 'fish' assuming the shape *ázù*: thus, *ázù réré èré*. In other words, when the *na* relative marker is omitted, a low tone at the end of the subject noun becomes a downstepped high. This tonal change can be readily accounted for in terms of the floating high tone that Goldsmith hypothesizes. This floating high tone is located between the subject noun and the verb. All that we need assume is that the floating high docks leftward onto the last vowel of the noun. If that vowel is low toned, the result would be a rising tone. This rising tone simplifies in Igbo to a downstepped high. (The downstep here can be seen to have its source in a low tone. In many cases, downstep can be shown to derive from a low tone that is lost on the surface. It is not necessarily the case, however, that downstep can universally be explained synchronically in terms of an underlying low tone. Synchronically unpredictable downsteps appear to occur.)

Support for the proposed analysis is provided by the observation that a subject noun that ends in a high tone exhibits no tonal change at all when the *na* relative marker is omitted—compare *àkwhá réré èré* 'the eggs that were rotten'. This is just what we would expect, since if the floating high tone docks onto a vowel that is already high, there is no reason for the tonal shape to be altered.

We have space to consider just one more argument for the floating high tone in Igbo subordinate clauses. Consider a subordinate clause like *ághù è-gbùò éghú* 'lest the leopard kill the goat'. In this construction, the verb prefix *e-* (a vowel harmony alternant of *a-*) takes on the low tone of the verb root. Now recall that if the subject of a verb is a clitic, the clitic replaces the verbal prefix. Examine closely the clause *ô gbùò éghú* 'lest he kill the goat'. Notice that the clitic appears with a falling tone. This tonal shape follows as a natural consequence of the proposed floating high tone. We have seen that this floating high is located in preverbal position. We have also seen that the prefix on the verb is low-toned in this construction; thus when the clitic replaces the prefix, we expect the clitic also to be low-toned. Since there is no subject noun in preverbal position, the floating high tone cannot dock onto the subject noun. It has only one place to which it can dock—namely, the clitic located in the prefix slot of the verb. The result is a falling tone, as can be seen from the following diagram:

(32)   ´ *ò gbùò éghú* $\longrightarrow$ *ô gbùò éghú*
                                    Docking

Although we have not had sufficient space to go through in detail Goldsmith's arguments for the floating high tone in Igbo, it is hoped that the discussion has succeeded in showing how apparently quite unrelated facts can be shown to be deeply related by means of hypothesizing floating high tones. At first glance one might think that the falling tone on a clitic pronoun subject in *ô gbùò éghú* is unrelated to the downstepped high on the subject noun in relative clauses without *na* like *áz̄ų̀ rèré èré*. The floating tone analysis has shown these two facts to follow naturally from the proposed preverbal high tone.

Now, in what way does the existence of floating tones support the suprasegmental representation of tone? The answer should be clear. If tone is always part of a segment, it is impossible for there to be tones that are not parts of segments. Consequently, floating tones should not exist. Tone cannot exist separately from segments. On the other hand, if tone is separate from segments, then it is possible for there to be tones that have no segment that they are inherently associated with. Indeed, given the suprasegmental approach, one expects tones to occur without associated segments. Floating tones are thus just what one would expect under a suprasegmental approach to tone.

A potentially important argument for the suprasegmental representation of tone would be to demonstrate that morphophonemic rules may operate directly on representations of tones independently of the number of syllables over which these tones may be distributed. For instance, Leben (1973) claims that a rule that he refers to as "tone spreading" in Maninka and Bambara (two Mande languages related to Mende, discussed earlier) operates independently of syllables. The rule says that a sequence LHH becomes LLH. Leben argues that this rule operates in terms of tones associated with morphemes rather than syllables. His argument goes as follows: In Maninka and Bambara, nouns can be analyzed as having one of two tonal melodies—H or LH. These melodies are properties of the morpheme and are independent of the number of vowels in the morpheme (cf., Leben's analysis of Mende discussed earlier). Both Maninka and Bambara also have a process of noun compounding. If the first member of a compound has the H melody, all of the vowels in the compound will be H. If the first member of the compound belongs to the LH category, then all of the vowels preceding the last word in the compound are low and the vowels of the last member of the compound are high. Compare, for example, *jírí-fínmán-nyímán* 'good black tree' with *mùsò-fìnmàn-nyímán* 'good black woman', where the noun 'tree' inherently has the H melody but 'woman' the LH melody. Leben suggests that the tonal shapes of compounds follows from a combination of the following compounding principles plus the subsequent application of tone spreading.

(33)   COMPOUND RULE: (a) *Noninitial members of compounds lose*
                                their inherent tonal specification
                            (b) *Copy the last tone of the first member of*
                                the compound (which will always be a H,
                                since nouns either have an H melody or a
                                LH melody) onto each of the noninitial
                                words of the compound

Tone spreading will operate upon the output of the compound rule.
Let us see how this analysis works. Given a compound having an
initial member with a LH pattern, the output of the compound rule will be
^{LH}x-^{H}y-^{H}z; for example, $^{LH}muso$-$^{H}finman$-$^{H}nyiman$. (We have put tonal
features associated with a morpheme in front of the morpheme in the
above example; this does not represent any sort of a claim about the
ultimate representation of suprasegmental tones.) Now, if tone spreading
operates in these languages in terms of these suprasegemtntal tones, the
rule will have the sequence LH-H-H as input. Assuming that tone spreading is applied iteratively (cf., Chapter 8 below), so that one application of
the rule can create the context for a second application, LH-H-H will
become LL-H-H by the first application of tone spreading and then
LL-L-H by a second application. As the result of this multiple application
of tone spreading, the first two members of the compound will have a L
melody associated with them while the last member will have a H melody.
Ultimately these melodies will be associated with the vowels of each
morpheme: all of the vowels in a morpheme with a L melody will have low
tones and all of the vowels in a morpheme with a H melody will have high
tones. This is just the right result in the case of examples like *mùsò-*
fìnmàn-nyímán.

In order to see more clearly the work that is done by applying tone
spreading to the suprasegmental representation of tones, let us consider
an alternative where the rule would operate entirely in terms of syllables.
Presumably in such an analysis, compounding would involve making all of
the vowels of the noninitial members of the compound high toned. In the
case of compounds where the first member has the H melody, this produces the correct result immediately. But in the case of compounds where
the initial member has the LH melody, tone spreading would have to
apply iteratively to the output of the compound rule. Given an input such
as /mùsó-fínmán-nyímán/, successive applications of tone spreading
would yield the incorrect */mùsò-fìnmàn-nyìmán/. In other words, all of
the high tones up to the last one would be lowered by tone spreading. The
last high tone escapes the rule since it is not followed by a high. In the
case where tone spreading applies to the suprasegmental representation of

tones, the last high tone in the representation escapes the rule of tone spreading since it is not followed by a high tone. But this "last" high tone will ultimately be distributed over all of the vowels of the last member of the compound, thus producing as many high tones as there are syllables in the last member. Clearly, Leben's analysis provides an interesting explanation of why the last member of a compound has all of its vowels high—an explanation that is not available if tone rules can not operate on suprasegmental representations of tone. Naturally, one hopes that many more examples can be adduced showing that rules operate in terms of tones dissociated from syllables.

THE SUPRASEGMENTAL REPRESENTATION OF TONE

We have seen that a number of tonal phenomena create difficulty for the view that tone is an inseparable part of the voiced segments that in some sense bear the tone. We turn now to consider very briefly how these difficulties might be resolved if tone were treated as constituting an independent level of representation parallel with the segmental representation but ultimately separate from it. The approach that we will summarize is developed in some detail in Goldsmith (1976).

Speech is a continuum; it is this continuum that forms the input that the language learner uses to construct a grammar. The language learner must somehow segment this continuum into the discrete, recurring elements that we have referred to as speech sounds. But suppose that the language learner does not necessarily divide this continuum up into a single sequence of discrete elements, but rather can divide it up into two or more parallel sequences of discrete elements, with some phonetic facts assigned to one level and other phonetic facts assigned to the other level(s). In particular, suppose that the tonal aspect of an utterance is relegated to one level but the more usual segmental features are allotted to a separate "segmental" level.

Under this view, the representation of a word will consist of at least two tiers: One tier will contain a partitioning of the tonal structure of the word into discrete units, while the other tier will represent a partitioning of the word into discrete segments (minus tone). Now, these tiers must be associated in some way, but it will not be the case that there is necessarily a one-to-one mapping between the parts of the two tiers. In other words, it would be possible for two units at the tonological level to be associated with a single unit at the segmental level, and vice versa. Let us indicate the association between units in different tiers by drawing a line between the associated units. Furthermore, let us assume that in any well-formed surface phonological representation, every unit in the tonological tier must be associated with at least one unit in the segmental tier. Furthermore, every segment capable of bearing contrastive tone must be associated with a unit at the tonological level. What segments are capable of bearing contrastive tone presumably is in part universal, in part language-specific. There may, of course, be other conditions on what counts as well-formed association of tiers (e.g., that association lines may not cross). Following Goldsmith, we will refer to this approach as "autosegmental"—that is, an approach that recognizes two or more autonomous but parallel segmentations of an utterance.

Let us see now how an approach like the above can account in a natural way for the kinds of data discussed earlier in support of the suprasegmental representation of tone. First, consider the case of languages such as Mende where it is claimed that it is necessary to associate a tone "melody" with each morpheme, this tone melody being independent of the number of tone-bearing elements in the morpheme. Given the autosegmental approach, this tone melody would constitute the tonological tier of the phonological representation of the morpheme. This tonological tier will be associated with the segmental tier either by means of universal conventions on how this association takes place or by means of language particular rules of association (or by a combination of both of the preceding). For instance, the underlying representation of Mende morphemes like *mbû* 'owl' and *kényà* 'uncle'—both morphemes having the HL melody—would be as in (34).

(34)   *mbu*   *kenya*
        HL   HL

In the case of *mbu* there is just one tone-bearing element (the vowel) in the representation; given the condition on representations that requires all tonological units to be associated with at least one tone-bearing element on the segmental level, it follows that both the H and the L member of the tonological tier must associated with the same segmental unit. The result is (35).

(35)   *mbu*
                 $\wedge$
                H L

In the case of *kenya* there are two tone-bearing segments and two units at the tonological level. If we assume a general principle that requires a one-to-one mapping when the tonological tier has as many units as there are segments capable of bearing contrastive tones, then the H of the melody will associate with the first vowel of *kenya* and the L will associate with the second vowel. The result is (36).

(36)
$$\underset{\text{H}\quad\text{L}}{\underset{\diagup\quad\diagdown}{kenya}}$$

Given morphemes such as *kɔ́* 'war', *pélé* 'house', and *háwámá* 'waist-line'—all instances of the H melody, the underlying representations would be the following.

(37)   kɔ   pɛlɛ   hawama
             H   H   H

In each of these cases there is only one tonological unit; given the condition on representations that every segment capable of bearing contrastive tone must be associated with a unit in the tonological tier, it follows that all the vowels in each of these words will associate with the H in the tonological tier. This yields the representations contained in (38).

(38)   kɔ   pɛlɛ   hawama
              | V   \|/
             H   H   H

The preceding discussion illustrates how the autosegmental approach can accommodate the situation where a particular tone melody is associated with a morpheme. Turning to the other kinds of evidence that were used to support suprasegmental tone representations, it should be obvious how the autosegmental approach allows contour tones to be represented as a sequence of level tones even though this sequence may be associated with a single vowel. The autosegmental approach says that units at the tonological level are not necessarily in a one-to-one relationship with the units at the segmental level. Consequently, two tonological units may be associated with a single segment, yielding a contour tone like that in *mbû* 'owl'.

Consider next how the autosegmental approach accommodates the phenomenon of tone stability discussed earlier—that is, the preservation of the tone of a segment even when the segment itself deletes or is changed to a segment type that cannot bear tone. Since the autosegmental approach regards the tonological tier and the segmental tier as autonomous, a segmental change does not of necessity imply a tonological change. And this is just what tone stability is all about. Consequently, the autosegmental approach predicts that there should be many instances of tone stability—and this appears to be correct. Within the autosegmental approach it is a more complex rule to delete both a segment and a tone than to just delete the segment.

Let us look briefly at how the example from Lomongo might be handled in the autosegmental framework. We will assume that at some point in the grammar of this language words like b-$âs$-$à$ 'they search' and b-$ís$-$à$ 'they hide' have representations like the following.

(39)
$$
\begin{array}{cc}
\textit{ba-as-a} & \textit{ba-is-a} \\
| \; | \; | & | \; | \; | \\
\text{H L L} & \text{HH L}
\end{array}
$$

These representations are submitted to the rule that elides a in prevocalic position. Deletion of a segment can be assumed to also lead to deletion of the association line connected with that segment. The result is (40).

(40)
$$
\begin{array}{cc}
\textit{b-as-a} & \textit{b-is-a} \\
| \; | & | \; | \\
\text{H L L} & \text{H H L}
\end{array}
$$

As these representations stand, they are not well-formed, since they contain tonological units that are not associated with a segment. It can be assumed that in such cases, a general principle requires that an unassociated tonological unit be associated with some segment. In the above cases, the only available such segment is the initial vowel of the root (if we accept the principle that association lines do not cross). The result of adding these association lines can be seen in (41).

(41)
$$
\begin{array}{cc}
\textit{b-as-a} & \textit{b-is-a} \\
\wedge \; | & \wedge \; | \\
\text{H L L} & \text{H H L}
\end{array}
$$

A HL sequence associated with a single vowel yields a falling tone, which is the correct pronunciation of b-$âs$-$à$. A HH sequence on a single vowel is no different from a simple H—consequently, the root vowel of b-$ís$-$à$ is pronounced as a simple high tone. It appears, then, that the autosegmental framework yields an adequate account of tone stability.

Finally, consider how the autosegmental approach deals with floating tones. Since the tonological and the segmental tiers are autonomous, there is no requirement that the underlying phonological representation of a morpheme necessarily involves two tiers. That is, a morpheme may underlyingly consist of a segmental representation without any tonological representation at all. Such morphemes have been encountered in many tone languages and are traditionally referred to as "toneless." Of course, ultimately such morphemes are associated with a tone if they contain tone-bearing elements; their tone, however, is predictable in terms of their environment. The autosegmental approach also allows the possibility that there might be morphemes that have a tonological tier, but no segmental tier. Such morphemes are in fact what we referred to earlier as floating tones. Of course, the tone of these morphemes may ultimately be associated with some segment, but the segment involved belongs to some other morpheme.

We hope that this discussion has given some idea of how the autosegmental approach might account for certain aspects of the behavior of tone. The preceding discussion was, however, only illustrative. Many issues involving this approach are unclear and require extensive investigation. Although our knowledge of tone has been increasing in recent years, much remains to be done.

Exercises

1. According to Halle (1978:33) "vowel epenthesis frequently arises as an attempt to impose the syllable structure of the rest of the words of the language on agglomerations of consonants that arise through consecutive affixation of consonantal affixes, or through the operation of vowel elision." The Harari data discussed in Chapter 6 provide a good illustration of this phenomenon. Recall that a rule was postulated to insert *i* in the contexts of CC___C (/zä+t+sbär/ ⟶ *zätsibär*), #C___C (/t+säbri/ ⟶ *tisäbri*), and CC___ #(/t+säbr/ ⟶ *tisäbri*). The syllabification rules of Harari are quite simple: a single consonant syllabifies with an immediately following vowel; a single postvocalic consonant syllabifies with the preceding vowel if it has not been syllabified to an immediately following vowel by the first rule. Given the existence of these rules in the grammar it is possible to see a generalization underlying the three contexts in which the *i* is inserted. How can the epenthesis rule be stated to reveal this generalization? What bearing does your analysis have on the transparency principle concerning syllable structure? (Hint: formulate the two syllabification rules in terms of the notation used in the discussion of English syllable structure earlier in this chapter.)

2. Shona (Bantu). The tonal shape of a word in isolation may be modified when it is juxtaposed to another word. Examine the following data and formulate rules to account for the tonological alternations. How must the rules be ordered? Assume that the isolation form is the UR. High tone is marked by the acute and low tone is unmarked.

> Isolation form: *ákaténgá* 'he bought', *ndakáténgá* 'I bought',
> *ndicábá* 'I will steal', *ákapá* 'he gave', *bhúku* 'book',
> *jírá* 'cloth', *badzá* 'hoe', *zvumá* 'beads'
>
> > *ákaténga bhúku*   'he bought a book'
> > *ndakáténga jírá*   'I bought cloth'
> > *ndicába bhúku*   'I will steal a book'
> > *ákapá bhúku*   'he gave a book'
> > *ákaténgá badzá*   'he bought a hoe'
> > *ákaténgá zvumá*   'he bought beads'

Isolation form: *ákaténgá* 'he bought', *ákapá*͙'he gave',
ndakábíka 'I cooked', *tsamba* 'letter', *cingwa* 'bread',
cirongó 'pot', *sadza* 'porridge', *badzá* 'hoe', *zvumá* 'beads'

ákaténgá tsámba	'he bought a letter'
ákaténgá cíngwa	'he bought bread'
ákaténgá círongó	'he bought a pot'
ákapá sádza	'he gave porridge'
ákaténgá badzá	'he bought a hoe'
ákaténgá zvumá	'he bought beads'
ndakábíka sadza	'I cooked porridge'

3. Tangsic (Kennedy 1953). Tangsic, a Wu dialect of Chinese, has three contrasting tones on monosyllables spoken in isolation: mid-level, rising, and falling. Following traditional practice, in which 5 denotes the highest and 1 the lowest point in the speaker's pitch range, these tones are represented as 33, 24, and 51, respectively. Propose an analysis for the following alternations. In the compounds the first syllable is stressed and the second unstressed.

kao (33)	'high'	*sae* (33)	'mountain':	*kao-sae* (33-33)	'high mountain'
tzong (33)	'middle'	*nyin* (24)	'man':	*tzong-nyin* (33-33)	'middleman'
pen (33)	'ice'	*sea* (51)	'water':	*pen-sea* (33-33)	'ice-water'
dhu (24)	'large'	*nyin* (24)	'man':	*dhu-nyin* (22-44)	'adults'
dhu (24)	'large'	*so ꞌ* (33)	'mountain':	*dhu-sae* (22-44)	'large mountain'
syao (51)	'small'	*nyin* (24)	'man':	*syao-nyin* (53-31)	'children'
ka (51)	'artificial'	*sae* (33)	'mountain':	*ka-sae* (53-31)	'rockery'
kwen (51)	'boil'	*sea* (51)	'water':	*kwen-sea* (53-31)	'boiling water'

4. Margi (Hoffmann 1963). This Northern Nigerian language has seven phonetic vowels: *i, e, a, o, u, ə*, and *u̗*. The latter two are mid and high back unrounded vowels. *u̗* is an allophone of /ə/ word-finally (and of /i/ word-finally, but only after palatal consonants). There are three surface tones (high ´, low `, and rising ˇ) and no length contrast.

a. The following forms show the definite suffix to be basically /-árì/.

Indefinite	Definite	Gloss
sál	*sálárì*	'man'
kàtsákár	*kàtsákárárì*	'sword'
àgám	*àgámárì*	'ram'
kùm	*kùmárí*	'meat'
ə́ntə̀m	*ə́ntə̀márì*	'pot'

b. Formulate rules to account for the resolution of the underlying vowel sequences formed by the addition of the definite suffix to the following vowel-final nouns.

Indefinite	Definite	Gloss	Indefinite	Definite	Gloss
kʸí	*kʸárì*	'compound'	*tóró*	*tórórì*	'threepence'
ʔímí	*ʔímyárì*	'water'	*ghàfú*	*ghàfárì*	'arrow'
kú	*kwárì*	'goat'	*látú*	*látárì*	'time'
tágú	*tágwárì*	'horse'	*mə́lá*	*mə́lárì*	'well'
kʸèkʸé	*kʸèkʸérì*	'bicycle'	*ə́ncàlá*	*ə́ncàlárì*	'calabash'
šèré	*šèrérì*	'court'			

c. Propose an analysis for the tonal alternation in the following data.

fà	fǎrì	'farm'	wù	wǎrì	'tree'
hyà	hyǎrì	'dog'	cédè	cédĕrì	'money'
tì	tyǎrì	'mourning'	pénè	pénĕrì	'halfpenny'
hù	hwǎrì	'grave'	úʔù	úʔwǎrì	'fire'

d. The following data require a tone rule.

màlà	màlárì	'woman'	màhyìdì	màhyìdyárì	'women'
làgù	làgwárì	'road'	mǝlmù	mǝlmárì	'village'
bìkù	bìkárì	'sin'			

e. Unlike with the nouns, the accentual possibilities for Margi verb roots are more restricted. The vast majority of verb roots are of one or two syllables. They fall into four accentual classes: high, low, rising, and changing. High roots have high tone, low roots low tone; rising roots have a rising accent if monosyllabic and low-high if disyllabic. Changing roots are high in some contexts and low in others. Examples, which are identical to the imperative singular of a verb, follow.

low:	dlà	'fall',	ghà	'reach',	gàrhù	'fear',	dzàʔù 'pound'
high:	tsá	'beat',	sá	'go astray',	ndábyá	'touch',	tǝdú 'fall down'
rising:	hǔ	'grow up',	vǝl	'fly',	pǝzú	'lay eggs',	ŋgùrsú 'bend'
changing:	hù	'take',	sà	'drink',	šùʔùr	'smell',	ùlù 'see'

Derivational suffixes that may be added to these roots fall into two accentual classes: high and alternating. Supplement your rules to account for the alternations in the following data.

-bá

low	ghà	'reach'	ghàbá	'reach'
high	cú	'speak'	cíbá	'tell'
changing	hù	'take'	hǝbá	'take out'
rising	hǔ	'grow up'	hǝbá	'rear'
	fì	'swell'	fìbá	'make swell'
	nú	'mould'	nǝbá	'mend'

-ŋgǝrí

low	ghà	'reach'	ghàŋgárí	'pass'
high	cú	'speak'	cíŋgárí	'tell again'
rising	pǝzú	'lay eggs'	pǝzáŋgárí	'lay eggs in addition'
changing	fà	'take many'	fáŋgárí	'take more than many'

-ari

low	gàrhù	'fear'	gàrhàrì	'frighten'
high	tsá	'beat'	tsárí	'knock'
rising	mbìdú	'blow'	mbìdárí	'blow'
changing	hù	'take'	hàrì	'lift up'

-na

low	dlà	'fall'	dlànà	'overthrow'
high	sá	'go astray'	sáná	'lead astray'
rising	bdlǔ	'forge'	bdlǝná	'forge'
changing	hù	'take'	hǝnà	'take away'

-ani

low	*nyừ*	'fill, intr'	*nyànì*	'fill, tran'
rising	*mbừ*	'be saved'	*mbàní*	'save'
changing	*mdzừ*	'spoil, intr'	*mdzànì*	'spoil, tran'

8

Rule Interaction

In an earlier discussion the notion of applying rules in sequence was introduced. In this chapter we give a more careful and detailed exposition of this notion, which has played a fundamental role in the development of generative phonology. We will examine several conceptions about how a set of phonological rules applies to relate an underlying representation (UR) to its corresponding phonetic representation (PR); we will make precise the kinds of claims these conceptions make about the nature of language; and we will evaluate these claims in the light of relevant data from a variety of languages. In particular, the consideration that led most generative phonologists to adopt partially ordered rules will be emphasized. Finally, we will examine the question of the interaction of different applications of the same rule.

The Direct Mapping Hypothesis

The first view we shall examine may be referred to as the direct mapping hypothesis (DMH), which claims that the set of phonological

291

rules is applied directly to the UR to give as output the corresponding PR, as depicted in (1).

(1)

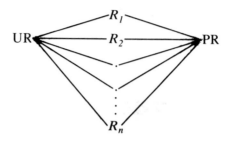

The essential claim of the DMH is that the input structure to each of the phonological rules is the underlying representation. The applicability of a rule is entirely a function of whether the underlying form meets the input requirements of that rule. The phonetic representation is then the result of applying the changes called for by the rule to the UR. The effects of a rule are necessarily irrelevant to the applicability of any other rule, since only the underlying form determines whether a rule applies or not. This view claims, then, that URs can be mapped into PRs without postulating intermediate levels of representation. Consequently, we refer to it as the direct-mapping hypothesis. It is often referred to as simultaneous application of the rules.

The claims of the DMH are supported by data where indeed it is the UR that governs whether a rule applies, regardless of the effects of other rules in the grammar. In Tunica (Haas 1940) there is evidence that the vowel /a/ assimilates the backness and roundness of a preceding vowel when just a glottal stop (or nothing) separates the two vowels.

(2)

	'to Verb'	'he Verbs'	'she Verbs'	'she is V-ing'	Gloss
	pó	*pó ʔuhki*	*pó ʔɔki*	*póhk ʔaki*	'look'
	pí	*pí ʔuhki*	*pí ʔɛki*	*píhk ʔaki*	'emerge'
	yá	*yá ʔuhki*	*yá ʔaki*	*yáhk ʔaki*	'do'
	čú	*čú ʔuhki*	*čú ʔɔki*	*čúhk ʔaki*	'take'

The morpheme /ʔaki/ has the alternant [ʔɔki] when a round back vowel precedes, and [ʔɛki] when a nonround nonback vowel precedes. It remains [ʔaki] when a nonround back vowel precedes. The following rule of vowel assimilation characterizes this alternation.

(3)

$$\begin{bmatrix} +\text{syll} \\ +\text{low} \end{bmatrix} \rightarrow \begin{bmatrix} \alpha\text{back} \\ \beta\text{round} \end{bmatrix} / \begin{bmatrix} +\text{syll} \\ \alpha\text{back} \\ \beta\text{round} \end{bmatrix} \text{?} \underline{\quad\quad}$$

In this rule α and β are variables that can take the value of + or −. The rule thus says that a low vowel takes on the values for back and round, be they plus or minus, of the preceding vowel when a glottal stop intervenes. (See Chapter 9 for further discussion of this variable notation.)

Another rule in Tunica drops unstressed vowels before a glottal stop. In the examples of (2) /ʔaki/ and /ʔuhki/ are preceded by stressed vowels, which are retained. Compare the examples in (4), where the vowel has been syncopated.

(4)

hára	*hár ʔuhki*	*hár ʔaki*	*hárahk ʔáki*	'sing'
hípu	*híp ʔuhki*	*híp ʔɔki*	*hípuhk ʔáki*	'dance'
náši	*náš ʔuhki*	*náš ʔɛki*	*nášihk ʔáki*	'lead s. o.'

Examples such as *hár ʔuhki* (cf., *hára*) and *híp ʔuhki* (cf., *hípu*) reveal the operation of syncope; *hárahk ʔáki* and *hípuhk ʔáki* reveal that the presence of other consonants between an unstressed vowel and a glottal stop inhibits syncope. The rule can be stated as follows:

(5)

$$\begin{bmatrix} +\text{syll} \\ -\text{stress} \end{bmatrix} \longrightarrow \emptyset / \underline{\quad\quad} \text{?}$$

Note now examples such as *híp ʔɔki* and *náš ʔɛki*. The vowel of /ʔaki/ is assimilated, but the vowel that causes the assimilation is not present in the phonetic surface, having been dropped by the rule of syncope. The fact that syncope drops the final /u/ of /hipu/ and the final /i/ of /naši/ in no way interferes with the fact that the /a/ of /ʔaki/ assimilates the quality of these vowels. The DMH predicts that this is the case, because the URs /hipu-ʔaki/ and /naši-ʔaki/ satisfy the input requirements of both vowel assimilation and syncope. Consequently, both rules must apply.

(6)

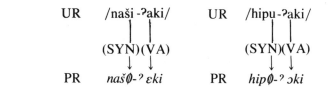

(We will briefly take up the stress alternations—note *hár ʔaki*, but *hárahk ʔáki*—later in this chapter). In the above example syncope has the effect of removing the conditions for vowel assimilation, but this effect is ignored. Both rules are applied as a consequence of the fact that the UR satisfies the input requirements of both rules.

A similar example was given in Chapter 4 in our discussion of Yawelmani. Recall the rule of vowel lowering (VL), which lowers long high vowels, and the rule of vowel shortening (VS), which shortens vowels before a consonant cluster. We motivated URs like /mi:k'/ 'swallow', which is realized as [me:k'] in *me:k'-al* and as [mek'] in *mek'-hin*. The DMH predicts just these outputs. Given /mi:k'-al/, just VL will be able to apply, deriving *me:k'-al*. But given /mi:k'-hin/, the input requirements of both VL and VS are met, so both rules apply, giving *mek'-hin*.

(7)   UR   /mi:k'-hin/

                    |

         (VS) and (VL)

                    |
                    ↓

         PR   *mek'-hin*

Once again the vowel of the verb root becomes short as a consequence of VS, but this in no way interferes with the rule of VL, which lowers this same vowel on the basis of its underlying length. The failure of one rule to interfere with the application of some other rule is just what we expect, given the direct-mapping hypothesis.

Ki-Rundi (Meeussen 1959) provides a third example supporting the DMH. In this language the vowels *i* and *e* are pronounced as *y*, and the vowels *u* and *o* are pronounced as *w* when in prevocalic position. A wide variety of examples provide evidence for such a rule of glide formation. Consider the data in (8) first.

(8)   *ku-bóh-a*   'to tie'   *ku-dáh-a*   'to make vomit'   *ku-rég-a*   'to accuse'
      kw-íí-boh-a   (reflex.)   *kw-íí-dah-a*   (reflex.)   *kw-íí-reg-a*   (reflex.)

The infinitive prefix has the shape *ku-* before the consonant-intitial verb roots /bóh/, /dáh/, /rég/, but assumes the shape *kw-* when the reflexive prefix intervenes between it and the verb root. This alternation is due, we claim, to glide formation.

(9)   *ibi-raato*   'shoes'   *ivy-oobo*   'pits'
      ibi-baánza   'places'   *ivy-aakirizo*   'wooden milk jugs'
      ibi-tabu   'books'   *ivy-uúmba*   'rooms'

In (9) the prefix *ibi-* retains this shape when a consonant-initial root follows; but when a vowel-initial root follows, the alternant *ivy-* occurs. The shift of *b* and *v* will not concern us here. The shift of the final *i* of the prefix to *y* is thus another instance of the operation of glide formation.

So far we have seen instances of *u* and *i* gliding. The data in (10) reveal additional examples of the gliding of these vowels and of mid vowels gliding.

(10) | | | | |
|---|---|---|---|
| *ku-ry-á* | 'to eat' | cf., *-ri-iye* | (perfect stem) |
| *ku-gw-a* | 'to fall' | cf., *-gu-uye* | (perfect stem) |
| *gu-sy-a* | 'to grind' | cf., *-se-eye* | (perfect stem) |
| *ku-mw-a* | 'to shave' | cf., *-mo-oye* | (perfect stem) |

Observe that a verb root of the form *Cw-* in the infinitive may be either *Cu-* or *Co-* in the perfect stem (where a suffix *-ye* is added, which appears to lengthen the preceding vowel); similarly, a verb root of the form *Cy-* in the infinitive may correspond to either *Ci-* or *Ce-* in the perfect stem. If the form of the root that appears in the perfect stem is taken as basic, we can predict the shape of the infinitive form by the rule of glide formation.

Notice that in the ultimate formulation of glide formation it will be necessary to block the rule from affecting the first part of a long vowel, since long vowels in Ki-Rundi have been represented here as a sequence of two identical short vowels (*ii*, *uu*, *ee*). This point is not particularly relevant here, so we give glide formation in somewhat simplified form, as follows:

(11)
$$\begin{bmatrix} -\text{cons} \\ -\text{low} \end{bmatrix} \longrightarrow [-\text{syll}]/\underline{\quad}[+\text{syll}]$$

This formulation assumes that a general principle of the language will interact with this rule so as to assign the resulting glide the feature [+high]. (See Chapter 10 for a discussion of this point.)

In Ki-Rundi there are a number of derivational suffixes that show an alternation between *i* and *e*. The high vowel alternant occurs when either a high or low vowel precedes. The mid alternant occurs when a mid vowel precedes. Some examples are given in (12).

(12) | | | |
|---|---|---|
| *gu-kúbit-ir-a* | *gu-kúbit-iish-a* | (root: /kúbit/'strike') |
| *gu-sek-er-a* | *gu-sek-eesh-a* | (root: /sek/'laugh') |
| *ku-rim-ir-a* | *ku-rim-iish-a* | (root: /rim/'cultivate') |
| *gu-som-er-a* | *gu-som-eesh-a* | (root: /som/'read') |
| *ku-ruh-ir-a* | *ku-ruh-iish-a* | (root: /ruh/'be tired') |
| *ku-rak-ir-a* | *ku-rak-iish-a* | (root: /rak/'be angry') |

-ir/-er- is referred to as the applicative suffix in many grammatical descriptions of Bantu languages, and has meanings approximating 'to' or 'for'; *-iish-/-eesh-* is a causative suffix. We will assume that the underlying form of these suffixes has a high vowel (though nothing that follows crucially depends on this assumption), and that a rule of harmony (H) is operative.

(13)

$$\begin{bmatrix} +\text{syll} \\ +\text{high} \end{bmatrix} \longrightarrow [-\text{high}]/ \begin{bmatrix} +\text{syll} \\ -\text{high} \\ -\text{low} \end{bmatrix} C_0 \underline{\qquad}$$

Harmony says that a high vowel becomes mid if preceded by a mid vowel; any number of consonants, including zero, may intervene between the two vowels in question. Our formulation here ignores the fact that the rule is restricted to a certain morphological class of suffixes.

Having motivated the rules of glide formation and harmony, we can turn to some examples that support the direct-mapping hypothesis. Consider the two paradigms in (14).

(14)

ku-nyw-á	*-nyó-oye* (perfect stem)	
ku-nyw-éer-a	*ku-nyw-éesh-a*	(root: /nyó/'drink')
ku-mw-a	*-mo-oye* (perfect stem)	
ku-mw-eer-a	*ku-mw-eesh-a*	(root: /mo/ 'shave')

(*ny* represents a palatal nasal.) According to the analysis suggested in the previous discussion, the form of the root that occurs in the perfect stem is to be taken as underlying—/nyó/ and /mo/. The infinitive form is then derived by glide formation. Thus, /ku-nyó-a/ is realized as *kunywá*. But now consider the forms with the applicative and causative suffixes; these are basically /ku-nyó-ir-a/ and /ku-nyó-iish-a/. Glide formation will of course be applicable to such examples; it will convert the underlying /o/ to *w*. Notice, however, that the vowel of the applicative and of the causative suffix must be affected by harmony. Given the DMH, these suffixes will in fact undergo harmony, even though the mid vowel of the root, which is responsible for the lowering of the suffixal vowel, is pronounced as a high glide. (It should be mentioned that the vowel of the applicative suffix is lengthened in the phonetic output, but this is the consequence of a general rule not discussed here.)

(15) /ku - nyó - ir - a/

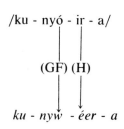

ku - nyẅ - éer - a

Contrast the examples of (14) with those in (16).

(16)
ku-v-a	*-vu-uye* (perfect stem)	(root: /vu/ 'leave
ku-v-iir-a	*ku-v-iish-a*	from')
gu-pf-á	*-pfú-uye* (perfect stem)	(root: /pfú/ 'die')
gu-pf-íir-a	*gu-pf-íish-a*	
ku-gw-a	*-gu-uye* (perfect stem)	(root: /gu/ 'fall')
ku-gw-iir-a	*ku-gw-iish-a*	

Consider the root /gu/. The infinitive form /ku-gu-a/ simply undergoes glide formation; /ku-gu-ir-a/ likewise undergoes glide formation. The applicative suffix is not affected by harmony, since the preceding vowel is not a mid vowel. Consequently, /ku-gu-ir-a/ is pronounced *ku-gw-iir-a*, whereas /ku-mo-ir-a/ is pronounced ku-mw-eer-a. The examples *ku-v-iir-a* and *gu-pf-íir-a* are parallel except that they show the effects of another principle of Ki-Rundi phonology, which disallows *w* after labial nonstops.

Ki-Rundi thus presents an additional example where it is the underlying form (/gu/, /mo/, e.g.) that determines the applicability of a rule (harmony, in this case), rather than the form derived by rule (e.g., [gw], [mw]). In other words, the application of glide formation does not have any effect on the application of harmony, even though glide formation eliminates the basic conditions that determine whether harmony applies.

The three examples discussed so far in support of the DMH are of the same general character. They represent cases where the application of one rule R$_i$ would remove or destroy structures relevant for the application of some other rule R$_j$. This is commonly referred to as a **potentially bleeding** interaction between the two rules. In cases such as the three examined above, where the destruction of the relevant environment has no effect on the application of R$_j$, the interaction between the rules is referred to as **counterbleeding**. Thus, in the Ki-Rundi example, glide formation is said to counterbleed vowel lowering. The DMH is generally consistent with counterbleeding interactions.

Further support for the DMH is provided by cases where some rule R_i derives a structure identical in essential character to underlying structures that undergo some other rule R_j. In such situations, rule R_i is said to **potentially feed** rule R_j. The DMH will be supported in those cases where the structures derived from R_i do not in fact undergo R_j. Here rule R_i is said to **counterfeed** R_j.

Our first example of this sort comes from Sea Dayak (Scott 1957), closely related to the Dayak dialect known as Land Dayak, which was briefly discussed in Chapter 5. In both dialects there is a general principle whereby a nasal consonant induces the nasalization of an immediately following vowel (and any subsequent vowel up to the first consonant other than *w* or *y*). Some examples are *māta* 'an eye', *gonē* 'a sack', *mõā* 'the face', *māyā* 'a season'. A true consonant between a nasal and a following vowel inhibits the nasalization of that vowel. Sea Dayak also has the rule that deletes a voiced stop or affricate after a nasal, but it is an optional instead of an obligatory rule. Let us call this rule nasal-cluster simplification (NCS):

(17)
$$\begin{bmatrix} -\text{contin} \\ +\text{voice} \end{bmatrix} \longrightarrow \emptyset / \begin{bmatrix} +\text{nasal} \\ +\text{cons} \end{bmatrix} \underline{\qquad}$$

As a result of NCS a vowel that formerly was separated from a nasal by a true consonant will come to follow that nasal immediately. The conditions for vowel nasalization thus are created by the application of NCS. The vowel in question is always pronounced oral, however. We consequently have surface contrasts like [nāŋaʔ] 'set up a ladder' versus [nāŋãʔ] 'straighten', where the former derives from /naŋga/ and the latter derives from /naŋa/.

The DMH accounts for these data automatically, since, given the UR /naŋga/, only the first vowel meets the conditions for nasalization, while in /naŋa/ both vowels meet the conditions. Application of NCS to /naŋga/ will of course give a phonetic output where the second vowel is immediately preceded by a nasal; but the DMH correctly claims that this surface sequence of a nasal consonant followed by a vowel is of no relevance, since all rules apply just in terms of the underlying sequence of segments.

A second example of a structure derived by one rule that fails to undergo some other rule that affects underlying structures is provided by the Mecayapan, Veracruz dialect of Isthmus Nahuat (Law 1958). Short unstressed vowels are optionally deleted in the environment VR____#, where R stands for voiced sonorants. The data in (18) exemplify this alternation.

(18)   *šikakíli* ~ *šikakíl*   'put it in it'
         kítaya ~ *kítay*   'he already sees it'
         kikówa ~ *kików*   'he buys it'
         támi ~ *tám*   'it ends'

Let us call this rule apocope.

Another rule in Isthmus Nahuat specifies syllable-final *l*, *w*, and *y* as voiceless under somewhat varying conditions: *l* is always voiceless when syllable-final; *y* in this environment is voiceless unless followed by a voiced consonant; *w* is syllable-final only when it is word final, and it is optionally voiceless.

(19)   *táyo:L*   'shelled corn'   *čaYča:yi*   'centipede'
        e:Lwatoȼ   'a skinny person'   *kišaygamáka*   'he turns a cheek to him'
        só:tkuY   'elbow'   *čoów~čoóW*   'boy!'

Observe that forms resulting from apocope do not undergo devoicing, even though they may contain syllable-final sonorants. Thus, *šikakíl*, not **šikakíL*; only *kików*, not **kikóW*. Although apocope creates structures of a form just like those that undergo devoicing, the latter rule does not apply. This failure to apply follows directly from the DMH, which does not permit derived structures to undergo rules by virtue of the fact that they are derived structures.

A third example is derivable from the English dialects where such words as *writer* and *rider*, *latter* and *ladder*, *bitter* and *bidder*, *matter* and *madder*, differ phonetically just in that the stressed vowel of the former is shorter than the stressed vowel of the latter, the medial consonant in all cases being a voiced flap we write as [D]. The phonetic difference in the length of the stressed vowel is due to the general rule of English whereby a vowel is longer if the following consonant is a voiced sound than if it is voiceless. This rule of lengthening is given as follows:

(20)
$$V \longrightarrow [+long]/\underline{\quad\quad}(\left\{ \begin{array}{c} y \\ w \end{array} \right\}) \begin{bmatrix} +cons \\ +voice \end{bmatrix}$$

Lengthening will account for the occurring data if the URs are /rayt-r/ versus /rayd-r/, /læt-r/ versus /læd-r/, and so on, and if this rule applies in terms of the underlying form. In actual pronunciation the contrast between /t/ and /d/ is neutralized as the voiced flap [D] in the environment V̇___ (glide) V, where V̇ is a stressed vowel. As a result of the flapping rule the stressed vowel in both *writer* and *rider* is in the environment for lengthening, but the latter rule does not apply to the output of flapping. It applies to the preflapping level of representation, which can be equated with the UR in the examples considered here. The DMH once again predicts just this state of affairs. It claims that a rule such as lengthening could not apply by virtue of the existence of a structure resulting from some other rule's application.

Although the DMH does account for a significant range of data, there is considerable evidence that its basic premise—that the effects of phonological rules are irrelevant to the operation of other phonological rules—is misguided. In particular, there is much evidence that phonological rules may create structures that then undergo other phonological rules—a so-called **feeding** interaction. The Lardil data discussed in Chapter 4 provide a good example. Recall that the following rules were claimed to operate in Lardil:

(21) Apocope (AP): $V \longrightarrow \emptyset / V\ C_1\ V\ C_1$ ___ #

(22) Cluster simplification (CS): $C \longrightarrow \emptyset / C$ ___ #

(23) Non-apical deletion (NAD): $\begin{bmatrix} -\text{syll} \\ -\text{apic} \end{bmatrix} \longrightarrow \emptyset /$ ___ #

AP accounts for the fact that the stem of *mayara-n* 'rainbow' is realized as *mayar*, not **mayara*, when no suffix follows. CS is involved in accounting for the fact that the stem of *kantukantu-n* 'red' is realized as *kantukan*, not **kantukant*, when uninflected. NAD is the rule that converts the stem of *pereŋ-in* 'vagina' to *pere* when no suffix follows.

The above formulations cannot be maintained if we adopt the DMH. To see that this is so let us begin by considering NAD. The rule is claimed to be that a nonapical consonant drops in final position. This formulation works adequately for *pere*, derived from /pereŋ/, and for *ŋalu* 'story', derived from /ŋaluk/ (cf., the affixed for *ŋaluk-in*). But consider the examples in (24):

(24)
puṭuka-n	*puṭu*	'short'
ŋawuŋawu-n	*ŋawuŋa*	'termite'
murkunima-n	*murkuni*	'nullah'

The URs of the stems are quite clearly /puṭuka/, /ŋawuŋawu/, and /murkunima/. They are vowel-final. As a consequence the above formulation of NAD will **not** apply, given the DMH, since the UR in each case does not meet the input requirements of the rule. The UR in each case **does** satisfy the requirements of apocope (Ap). Thus, the DMH predicts a derivation like the following.

(25)   UR   / # puṭuka # /

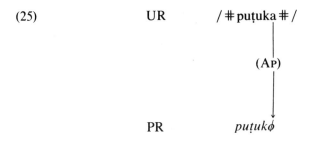

          PR   puṭukɸ

The output is the incorrect **puṭuk*. In order to derive the correct PR the final *k* must be dropped. The crucial observation is that once Ap has applied to the forms in question, the consonant that was nonfinal in the UR becomes final—and we see that if the consonant is nonapical in these cases, it does not appear in the PR. (Cf., *mayar* from /mayara/, where an apical consonant that is word-final as a result of Ap is retained.) Thus, if NAD were permitted to apply not just to URs, but also to representations derived by Ap, no additional rule would be required to explain *puṭu*, *ŋawuŋa*, *murkuni*.

Of course, the DMH does not permit the structure that results from Ap to condition the application of NAD. In order to preserve the DMH it is necessary to add a second nonapical deletion rule so that the nonfinal nonapicals in question may be deleted. What would this new rule look like? The only nonapicals that drop, besides those that are underlyingly final, are those that are followed by a vowel that will undergo Ap. Thus, the new rule would have to be something like NAD II.

(26)   NAD II $\begin{bmatrix} -\text{syll} \\ -\text{apic} \end{bmatrix} \longrightarrow \emptyset / \text{VC}_1\text{V} \underline{\quad\quad} \text{V} \#$

NAD II must identify a nonapical consonant that is followed by a word-final vowel that undergoes Ap; to do this the rule must incorporate the environment of Ap as part of its own environment. Whereas the first rule of nonapical deletion has a natural environment (since truncation of word-final elements occurs in many languages), NAD II has a totally unnatural environment. Although consonants will sometimes drop intervocalically, with various additional restrictions, the additional restrictions do not ordinarily involve requirements that the following vowel be word final and the preceding vowel be itself preceded by at least one vowel. On the other hand, rules that drop final vowels are often restricted to applying to words of some minimum length. For example, monosyllabic words often resist apocope processes, especially if stressed.

One major objection to the DMH, then, is that it forces one to claim that there are wildly unnatural rules operative in a given language. Although languages do sometimes have unnatural rules, in general rules can be shown to have a much more plausible form if we grant that the output of one rule may be subject to another rule.

Observe that NAD II and Ap are totally unconnected phenomena in the analysis the DMH leads to. In other words an implicit claim is involved: A rule such as NAD II might exist even if Ap did not. There is no necessary connection between the existence of the two rules. But the claim that NAD II is unnatural is just the claim that such a rule cannot in general be motivated except if a language also has a rule like Ap. Thus, the implicit claim of the DMH (namely, that deletion of nonapicals in the environment $VC_1V\_\_\_V \#$ has nothing to do with the existence of a rule of apocope that drops a vowel in the environment $VC_1VC_1\_\_\_\#$) is falsified if we consistently find no evidence that the rules the DMH forces us to postulate ever occur independently in grammars.

Some additional examples from Lardil will further illustrate this point. Consider the example *kantukantu-n*, whose stem appears as *kantukan* when unsuffixed. The UR must be /kantukantu/. Given the DMH, the rule of cluster simplification (CS) is inapplicable, if formulated as (22), since the rule is written to drop a word-final consonant preceded by a consonant. There is no element in /kantukantu/ satisfying this structural description. But once Ap applies to /kantukantu/, the resulting structure would satisfy CS. By requiring that rules apply to URs, the DMH forces adoption of a new principle of cluster simplification (whether the original formulation would also have to be maintained as a rule depends on whether any URs ending basically in a consonant cluster must be postulated). The principle must, evidently, be CS II:

(27) $\qquad$ CS II $\qquad$ C $\longrightarrow \emptyset / VC_1VC \_\_\_ V \#$

In other words the second member of a consonant cluster deletes just in case the following vowel is an environment where it will undergo apocope.

The previous formulation of CS characterized the process as an instance of an extremely frequent phenomenon (reduction of clusters word-finally), but the revised formulation of the rule is totally unnatural. There is nothing about the environment $VC_1VC\_\_\_V \#$ that, in itself, is conducive to the simplification of consonant clusters. We see, consequently, that the DMH requires not only the unnatural rule of NAD II, but also the equally unnatural rule of CS II.

In addition to both being unnatural, CS II and NAD II are similar in another way. CS II likewise repeats the entire environment of AP as part of its own environment. Thus, the DMH leads us again to claim that it is totally accidental that cluster simplification applies to nonfinal consonant clusters followed by a word-final vowel that itself deletes by another rule of the language. According to the required analysis, the fact that CS II operates in the environment $VC_1VC\underline{\quad}\#$ has nothing to do with the fact that the following vowel is deleted by AP. It could just as well be the case that the following vowel is always retained in the PR. We know of no actual cases where cluster-simplification processes operate in an environment like $VC_1VC\underline{\quad}V\#$ and the following vowel is present in the PR. The failure to find such examples argues against the basic claim that CS II makes, and thus against the DMH that leads to the formulation of rules like CS II.

To phrase the general point somewhat differently, insofar as such repetitions of the environment of one rule as part of the environment of some other rule are a common consequence of the DMH, that hypothesis is seriously defective, since it offers no explanation of why the repetition of environments should consistently occur. The hypothesis cannot account for an apparently very general property of language. Taking a significant number of cases where such repetitions of environments occur, if it can be shown that the repetition can be eliminated by allowing some rules to apply to the structures created by other rules, then we have strong grounds for rejecting the DMH. Furthermore, if the resulting rules are in most cases of a sort that occur in many languages and are reflective of natural phonological processes, we have additional grounds for accepting the proposition that the applicability of rules may be a function not just of the UR, but also of the UR as it has been modified by yet other phonological rules.

Consider next the following examples from Lardil. The inflected form of the noun meaning 'wooden ax' is *muŋkumuŋku-n*, while the uninflected form is *muŋkumu*. Similarly, the inflected form of 'dragonfly' is *tjumputjumpu-n*, while the uninflected form is *tjumputju*. In order to derive the uninflected form from the UR (which is overtly manifested in the inflected form), it seems that all three of the rules we have discussed must apply, since the entire sequence . . . *ŋku* . . . must be dropped in the first example and . . . *mpu* . . . in the second. But the rules, even as modified above, cannot yield the correct outputs, given the DMH. The reason is that given a UR like /tjumputjumpu/, AP can delete the final vowel and CS II can delete the preceding p, but none of the rules will delete the m that precedes the p. Recall in particular that NAD II deletes nonapicals in the environment VC_1V___$V\#$. Clearly, the last m of /tjumputjumpu/ does not meet the conditions for the operation of the rule. In order to delete this m we must further revise NAD II so that it deletes a nonapical that is followed either directly by a word-final vowel subject to apocope or by a consonant that is followed by a word-final vowel subject to apocope. The rule would have to be NAD III:

(28)   NAD III $\begin{bmatrix} -\text{syll} \\ -\text{apic} \end{bmatrix} \longrightarrow \emptyset \ / \ VC_1V \ \underline{\hspace{1cm}} \ (C)V \ \#$

Here the parentheses enclose optionally intervening material. The consonant mentioned in the parentheses is of course just the consonant that is deleted by cluster simplification. In other words, when NAD III applies in the environment VC_1V___$CV\#$, it is always the case that the following CV sequence is absent in the surface form as a consequence of the combined effects of Ap and CS II. The structural description of NAD III now includes the environment of CS II as well as the environment of Ap.

Repetition of environments is not required, however, if we permit the output of one rule to be the input to another rule. Suppose NAD (as originally formulated) is permitted to apply to the output of CS (as originally formulated), which in turn is permitted to apply to the output of Ap. Then an example such as *tjumputju* from /tjumputjumpu/ can be predicted. The derivation of the surface form would involve the following steps:

(28)   /#tjumputjumpu#/
         tjumputjump   Apocope
         tjumputjum   Cluster simplification
         tjumputju   Nonapical deletion

(Observe that the output of NAD must not be allowed to be an input to Ap, otherwise, /tjumputju/ would become */tjumputj/. We return to this point later.) In the above derivation application of Ap creates the context for CS. CS applies and, in so doing, creates the context for NAD, which then applies to yield *tjumputju*. By permitting rules to apply to the output of other rules, we can explain why the last m in /tjumputjumpu/ deletes, even though Lardil has no rule that would delete it in the position where it occurs in the UR. By maintaining that Lardil has just a rule that deletes nonapicals in word-final position, we predict that the m in /tjumputjumpu/ could not delete except if there are other rules in the language that would cause *m* to become word-final. Consequently, in such an analysis the fact that the final *m* of /tjumputjumpu/ is absent in PR is totally dependent on the existence of apocope and cluster simplification in the grammar of Lardil. In the absence of such rules the *m* could not delete. The loss of *m* is thus nonaccidentally related to the existence of these other two rules in the grammar.

Earlier in this chapter some examples were given where a phonological rule R_i creates a structure S_i, which is identical in basic character to other structures that are subject to some rule R_j, but S_i remains unaffected by R_j. Although such cases exist, Lardil is more typical, for here S_i does undergo R_j. Additional examples are readily available. Recall the rules of final devoicing (FD) and *l*-drop in Russian. The former devoices final obstruents, while the latter deletes the past-tense suffix *l* if it is preceded by a consonant in final position. In an example like *greb-l-a* 'she rowed' neither rule is applicable. But in *grep* 'he rowed' from /greb-l/, both the loss of *l* and devoicing occur. Given the DMH, FD could not affect the underlying /b/ of /greb-l/, since it is not word-final. Just *l*-drop would apply, giving **greb*. To preserve DMH it would be necessary to revise FD so that it would affect /greb-l/. Since the rule must affect just obstruents at the end of a word and those that are followed by final *-l*, the modified rule would have to appear as FD II rather than FD I.

(29)   FD I $[-sonor] \longrightarrow [-voice] / \underline{\hspace{1em}} \#$

   FD II $[-sonor] \longrightarrow [-voice] / \underline{\hspace{1em}}(-l) \#$

FD II says that an obstruent is devoiced either word-finally or before word-final *l*. FD II is subject to precisely the same objections as the various reformulations of the Lardil rules to which direct mapping leads. FD II claims that the fact that *l* may intervene between the devoiced obstruent and the word boundary is only accidentally connected to the fact that there is a rule of *l*-drop in the language. FD II will apply to /greb-l/ whether or not there is any rule in the language that deletes the final *l*. But we know of no examples where a rule like FD II would be required independent of the existence of some other rule in the language which has the effect of deleting the segment following the obstruent that is devoiced. The DMH thus forces us to adopt rules that are apparently never required in language on grounds independent of a particular assumption about rule interaction.

Another example where the application of one rule is made possible by the application of another rule is provided by Tunica. Recall the rule of syncope:

(30)

$$\begin{bmatrix} +\text{syll} \\ -\text{stress} \end{bmatrix} \longrightarrow \emptyset \ / \ \underline{\quad}\ ?$$

The location of stress in Tunica is predictable. The fundamental principle is that the first vowel of each nonaffixal morpheme is stressed. Thus, all monomorphemic words have initial stress: *hípu* 'to dance', *nára* 'snake', *méli* 'black', *pánu* 'very'. In compounds both elements have initial stress (with systematic exceptions, which will be discussed momentarily): *nára-méli* 'congo snake' (lit., 'black snake'), *wíši-rúwina* 'whiskey' (lit., 'hot liquid'). In verbal constructions consisting of a verb root and an auxiliary verb both elements have initial stress (again with systematic exceptions): *hára-hk-ʔáki* 'she is singing', *hára-hk-ʔúhki* 'he is singing'. In order to simplify the discussion we will assume this basic stress is assigned in the lexicon itself, and is thus present in the UR that is submitted to the phonological rules.

There is evidence for a rule in Tunica that destresses a vowel if the preceding vowel in the word is stressed. Call this right destressing (RS):

(31) $\acute{V} \longrightarrow V/\acute{V}C_1\underline{\quad}$

This rule accounts for the fact that if a monosyllabic root combines with another root to form a compound, only the first is realized with surface stress. Thus, contrast *yá-nami* 'goat' (lit., 'stinking deer') with *nára-méli*. Stress is retained on *méli* 'black' in *nára-méli* since it is preceded by an unstressed vowel, while *námi* 'stinking' loses it stress in *yá-nami*, since a stressed vowel precedes. But now consider the examples in (32).

(32)   *pó-ʔuhki*   'he looks'   cf., *pó-hk-ʔuhki*
      hár-ʔaki   'she sings'   cf., *hára-hk-ʔáki*
      híp-ʔuhki   'he sings'   cf., *hípu-hk-ʔúkhi*

The auxiliary verbs *ʔáki* and *ʔúhki* are always unstressed after monosyllabic roots like *pó*, but are unstressed after disyllabic roots like *hára* and *hípu*, just in case these roots are realized as monosyllabic on the phonetic surface through the operation of syncope.

Let us consider how the grammar must be constructed in order to obtain these surface forms. Suppose that we adopted the direct-mapping hypothesis. Then, given a UR like /hára-ʔáki/, only the rule of syncope would be applicable; RD is not applicable, since there are not two adjacent stressed vowels in the UR. Direct mapping consequently predicts the incorrect output *hár-ʔáki*. In order to get RD to apply to the UR we would need to modify it so that it will apply not just to a stressed vowel where the preceding vowel in the word is stressed, but also to a vowel in the environment $\acute{V}C_1V\text{?}\_\_$. But to claim that there is a rule that destresses a vowel in such a context is, it seems to us, absurd. The fact that /ʔáki/ is unstressed in *hár-ʔaki* but stressed in *hára-hk-ʔáki* is surely because in the former there is no vowel separating /ʔáki/ from the stressed vowel of the root, whereas in the latter there is an intervening vowel. But this contrast is not present in the underlying forms /hára-ʔáki/ versus /hára-hk-ʔáki/. It is thus a contrast to which the DMH cannot, in principle, appeal.

The Free Reapplication Hypothesis

A possible modification of the DMH, designed to accommodate the observation that phonological rules must be able to operate on structures resulting from the application of other rules, would be the following, which we shall refer to as the free-reapplication hypothesis (FRH):

> *The set of phonological rules are applied (simultaneously) to the UR, yielding a structure S_1; S_1 is then submitted as input to the set of rules, and they are applied (simultaneously), deriving as output S_2; and so on, until a structure S_n is reached, to which none of the rules is applicable.*

This proposal does not require that the UR be directly related to the PR, but instead permits there to be a series of intermediate levels of representation serving as input to the set of rules. It makes allowance for the observation that one application of a rule may create structures that then serve as input to another rule. To see how this accommodation is made, consider again the rules of vowel assimilation, syncope, and right destressing in Tunica. The derivation of *náš-ʔɛki* would be as follows:

(33)   /#náši-ʔáki#/
     S_1 *náš-ʔéki*   Syncope and Vowel assimilation
     S_2 *náš-ʔɛki*   Right destressing

Both syncope and vowel assimilation will apply directly to the UR, giving S_1; when the rules are applied to S_1, just right destressing is applicable. Similarly, the derivation of *híp-ʔɔki* will be:

(34)   /#hípu-ʔáki#/
     S_1 *híp-ʔóki*   Syncope and Vowel assimilation
     S_2 *híp-ʔɔki*   Right destressing

In examples like *pó-ʔɔki* vowel assimilation and right destressing apply on the first application of the rules, and syncope is inapplicable:

(35)   / # pó-ʔáki # /
   S₁   *pó-ʔɔki*   Vowel assimilation and Right destressing

What claims does the free-reapplication hypothesis make? Like the DMH, it claims that if the UR (or any subsequent structure) satisfies the structural requirements of a rule, then that rule necessarily applies—even though some other rule may have the effect of changing the UR in such a way that it no longer (on the surface) meets the input requirements of the rule in question. For example, vowel assimilation in Tunica operates on /hípu-ʔáki/, even though syncope eliminates the *u* vowel that is the conditioning factor, yielding *híp-ʔɔki*. Unlike the DMH, however, FRH permits structures created by rule to be subject to the phonological rules of the language.

In attempting to accommodate the observation that in Tunica, for example, the output of syncope must be able to undergo right destressing, the FRH no longer accounts for some of the examples that appeared to motivate the DMH. We have seen that examples like *náš-ʔɛki* from /náši-ʔáki/ present no difficulty for the FRH; this kind of example involves a situation where a rule's applicability depends on some property of the UR, even though that property is not present in the surface form. But consider cases where a rule creates some structure that meets the input requirements of some other rule, which fails to apply. Recall the example from Sea Dayak, where /naŋga/ 'set up a ladder' is pronounced [nãŋaʔ], while /naŋa/ 'straighten' is pronounced [nãŋãʔ]. The FRH predicts that the two forms should be pronounced identically, namely [nãŋãʔ]. The predicted derivation of [nãŋaʔ] is:

(36)   /naŋga/
    nãŋaʔ   Vowel nasalization; Nasal cluster simplifica-
                 tion; Insertion of a glottal stop
    nãŋãʔ   Vowel nasalization

The FRH predicts that even though vowel nasalization is inapplicable to the second vowel of /naŋga/, since it is not immediately preceded by a nasal sound, it will be applicable once the nasal cluster simplification rule has applied. Free reapplication claims that a rule applies if the conditions for its application are met either in the UR or in any structure that results from applying the rules of the language to the UR. But Sea Dayak contradicts this claim.

The Isthmus Nahuat example discussed above likewise contradicts the FRH. Recall that although syllable-final *l*, *w*, and *y* are devoiced under varying conditions, the optional rule of apocope in this language creates syllable-final *l*, *w*, and *y* elements which do not devoice even though they are in the proper environment. Thus /šikakíli/ may be optionally pronounced [šikakíl], even though /táyo:l/ is obligatorily pronounced [táyo:L]. The FRH requires that if /šikakíli/ drops its final vowel, the syllable-final *l* will be voiceless *[šikakíL], since this approach permits all rules to apply whenever they have the opportunity.

From the above discussion it is apparent that if the DMH cannot naturally account for the fact that sometimes the output of one rule is subject to another rule, the FRH cannot account for the fact that sometimes the output of a rule is not subject to other rules. That is, for both principles it is an all-or-nothing proposition; either structures derived by rule are never subject to other rules, or are always subject to other rules. The evidence seems to be against either of these extremes.

Additional evidence against both direct mapping and free reapplication can be brought forth. Both of these approaches to the problem of rule interaction claim that if the structural description of a rule is satisfied at any point in the UR, then the rule must apply. Free reapplication goes even further, claiming that if the structural description of a rule is satisfied at any point, then it must apply. There is considerable evidence that these claims are false. We have already seen cases where derived structures fail to undergo a rule whose structural description they satisfy. But underlying representations as well may fail to undergo rules. A typical example was discussed in the analysis of Yawelmani in Chapter 4. The relevant rules are vowel epenthesis, which inserts *i* in the context C___CC, and vowel shortening, which shortens a long vowel in the context ___CC. In order to account for the alternations like *ʔaml-al* 'might help' and *ʔa:mil-hin* 'helps' by these rules, it is necessary to postulate the UR's /ʔa:ml-al/ and /ʔa:ml-hin/. But given either the DMH or the FRH the predicted derivations are as follows:

(37)   /ʔa:ml-al/   /ʔa:ml-hin/
    S_1 ʔaml-al   (VS)   ʔamil-hin   (VS) and (VE)
        [ʔaml-al]   [ʔamil-hin]

But *ʔamil-hin in incorrect. Both principles of rule application require VS to apply, since its environment is met in the UR.

In order to preserve either DMH or FRH in the face of an example such as this it would be necessary to revise VS so as to inhibit its operation in the case of /ʔa:ml-hin/ but not in the case of /ʔa:ml-al/. Clearly, the difference is that the former example meets the structural description of VE while the latter does not. VS would have to be revised to something like VS II:

(38) VS II V ⟶ [-long]/___CCV

This formulation would prevent /ʔa:ml-hin/ from being affected, as is required. But the same objections can be made against VS II as were made against the various reformulations of the Lardil rules required in order to permit DMH to account for the instances in that language where the output of one rule apparently undergoes another rule. By mentioning the context ___CCV we are specifically trying to exclude ___CCC, which is just the environment where VE applies. The environment of VS II does not, then, repeat the environment of VE (as the revised rules in Lardil repeated the other rules), but rather gives its complement (in part). Rule (38) claims that the restriction of VS II to the environment ___CCV has nothing to do with the existence of the VE rule in the grammar of Yawelmani. They are independent rules. Thus VS II is claimed to be a rule that could exist in a grammar where VE is lacking. Once again, we know of no such cases.

The Yawelmani example represents a case where the application of one rule (in this case VE) **bleeds** or removes inputs to another rule (VS). Another example of this kind of interaction is to be found in Modern Hebrew where a rule assimilates the voicing of an obstruent to the voicing of a following obstruent.

(39)

šavar	'he broke'	*yi-žbor*	'he will break'
taval	'he immersed'	*ti-dbol*	'you will immerse'
pazal	'he squirted'	*yi-vzol*	'he will squirt'
	(cf., *bzil-a* 'squirting')		
yi-dafes	'it will be printed'	*(h)i-tpis*	'he printed'
sagur	'closed (sg.)'	*zgur-im*	'closed (pl.)'
bicea	'he operated'	*mi-fca*	'an operation'
batuax	'confident (sg.)'	*ptux-im*	'confident (pl.)'

In the above examples we see the effects of another rule that spirantizes *p*, *b*, and *k* in postvocalic position (cf. šavar, but yi-žbor; mi-fca, but bicea). The operation of this rule will not be relevant to the present discussion and hence will be ignored.

From an example like šavar /yi-žbor we see that a voiceless obstruent is voiced when followed by a voiced obstruent; and from one like *yi-*

*d*afes/(*h*)*i-tpis* we see that the reverse is also true: a voiced obstruent becomes voiceless before a voiceless obstruent. Thus, the rule seems to be that an obstruent has the same voicing as a following obstruent. (There are systematic exceptions: *x* does not voice—(h)i*x*bid 'he made hard'.)

In Modern Hebrew there are several suffixes indicating person and number that begin with *-t*. They are added to imperfective verb stems. If the stem ends in *t* or *d*, the suffixes may be optionally separated from the stem by an epenthetic *e*.

(40) *kišat-eti*   ~ *kišat-ti*   'I decorated'
       kišat-et   ~ *kišat-t*   'you (f. sg.) decorated'
       kišat-etem ~ *kišat-tem*   'you (pl.) decorated'

       yarad-eti   ~ *yarat-ti*   'I descended'
       yarad-et   ~ *yarat-t*   'you (f. sg.) descended'
       yarad-etem ~ *yarat-tem*   'you (pl.) descended'

(The resulting geminate *tt* may be degeminated in fast speech.) From (40) we see that if the *e* is inserted, the stem-final consonant retains its basic voicing, but if *e* is not inserted, the stem-final consonant assimilates the voicing of the suffixal consonant. Given a representation such as /yarad-ti/, both the DMH and the FRH require that voicing assimilation apply, since it is an obligatory rule and the UR satisfies its structural description. Thus, the incorrect **yarat-eti* is predicted as an optional variant of *yarat-ti*, rather than the correct *yarad-eti*. There is no way to revise the voicing-assimilation rule so that it will fail to apply in just the right cases. It fails to apply just in case an epenthetic vowel separates the stem-final *d* from the suffixal *t*. But whether an epenthetic vowel will appear in this context is optional. Thus, it is impossible to determine whether voicing assimilation should be applied on the basis of just the UR /yarad-ti/. This example reveals that not only do the DMH and the FRH force one to postulate rules that make incorrect claims about the nature of the process involved, but there are situations that these hypotheses cannot describe at all.

The Russian rules of *l*-drop and dental-stop deletion (DSD) stand in a mutual bleeding relationship and provide another instance of the failure of both the DMH and the FRH. Recall that the former rule drops the past tense suffix *-l* in the environment C____#, while the latter deletes a dental stop before the past tense suffix. Thus, /nes-l/, /pek-l/, and /greb-l/ are realized as *nes, pek,* and *grep* as a consequence of *l*-drop; /plet-l/, /bred-l/, and /krad-l/ are realized as *ple-l, bre-l,* and *kra-l* as a consequence of DSD. Given a UR /plet-l/, both DMH and FRH predict **ple*, because this representation satisfies the structural description of both rules and thus both will apply.

To avoid the incorrect outputs one of the rules requires modification. Since it is the operation of *l*-drop that must be blocked, we could revise the rule to delete *l* after all consonants except dental stops. But even this reformulation will fail to account for a verb stem like /rost/ 'grow', which appears as *ros* in the masculine past. To the UR /rost-l/ *l*-drop must still apply, even though a dental stop precedes. The reason that *l*-drop still applies seems to be clear. Even when root-final *t* deletes, the *l* is still preceded by a consonant, and thus drops. To take this observation into account a revision of *l*-drop would have to say that *l* drops after a consonant that is not a dental stop, or after a dental stop, provided the latter is itself preceded by a consonant. Obviously, the mention of the preceding dental stop involves repeating the environment for DSD. And mentioning the consonant preceding the dental stop really repeats the information that *l* drops after a consonant. Thus, in this formulation of the rule the information that word-final *l* is dropped after a consonant is mentioned twice.

Ukrainian provides additional data bearing on the correctness of the DMH and the FRH. In addition to the rules of *l*-drop and DSD, this language has a general rule that shifts syllable-final *l* to *w*. Thus, the past-tense marker /-l/ is realized as a glide in some of the following examples:

(41)

1 sg. pres.	Masc. past.	Fem. past.	Neut. past.	Pl. past	Gloss
piš-u	*pisa-w*	*pisa-l-a*	*pisa-l-o*	*pisa-l-i*	'write'
liz-u	*liz*	*liz-l-a*	*liz-l-o*	*liz-l-i*	'crawl'
nes-u	*nis*	*nes-l-a*	*nes-l-o*	*nes-l-i*	'carry'
hreb-u	*hrib*	*hreb-l-a*	*hreb-l-o*	*hreb-l-i*	'rake'
peč-u	*pik*	*pek-l-a*	*pek-l-o*	*pek-l-i*	'bake'
paš-u	*pax*	*pax-l-a*	*pax-l-o*	*pax-l-i*	'smell'

pisa-w vs. *pisa-l-a* shows that the past-tense suffix /-l/ remains *l* when it is between vowels, but changes to *w* in syllable-final position. *Nis* shows that /-l/ deletes when in the environment C____# (Ukrainian is just like Russian in this respect). Also, to the UR of this form—namely, /nes-l/—another rule applies that shifts *e* to *i* if no vowel follows. Finally, the last two examples display a velar~palatal alternation that will not concern us here. The basic point is that the data in (41) show that Ukrainian also has the rule of *l*-drop.

The data in (42) show that the language also has the rule of DSD. An example like *kla-l-i* from /klad-l-i/ shows that DSD is operative in Ukrainian. The form *kla-w* shows that *l*-drop does not apply to the UR

(42)

klad-u	*kla-w*	*kla-l-a*	*kla-l-o*	*kla-l-i*	'put'
ved-u	*vi-w*	*ve-l-a*	*ve-l-o*	*ve-l-i*	'lead'
met-u	*mi-w*	*me-l-a*	*me-l-o*	*me-l-i*	'sweep'
plet-u	*pli-w*	*ple-l-a*	*ple-l-o*	*ple-l-i*	'twist'

/klad-l/; rather, DSD does. The resulting output is then subject to the rule that shifts /l/ to *w* syllable-finally.

So far all of the facts cited from Ukrainian parallel those from Russian cited earlier. What makes Ukrainian particularly relevant for the DMH and the FRH is the fact that there are at least two verbs in Ukrainian that exceptionally fail to undergo DSD:

(43)

zblid-u	*zblid*	*zblid-l-a*	*zblid-l-o*	*zblid-l-i*	'turn pale'
obrid-u	*obrid*	*obrid-l-a*	*obrid-l-o*	*obrid-l-i*	'disgust'

These examples are crucial, for they show clearly that if a dental stop fails to delete before *l*, that *l* will drop when word-final after a consonant. But if *l*-drop is formulated so that it drops *l* only after consonants other than dental stops, it will be unable to delete the *l* in /zblid-l/ and /obrid-l/, since a dental stop precedes.

Thus, given URs like /klad-l/ and /zblid-l/, whether *l*-drop applies is dependent on whether DSD applies. The latter rule has priority, so to speak. When it applies, as in the case of /klad-l/, it creates the structure *kla-l*, which no longer satisfies the structural description of *l*-drop. If, however, DSD happens not to apply, as in an exceptional case like /zblid-l/, the context for *l*-drop is present and the rule does apply. This example thus motivates an approach to the problem of rule interaction where one rule may be granted priority over another rule, in the sense that the former has first opportunity to apply and the latter applies just in case the conditions for its application are present subsequent to the application of the former rule. Neither direct mapping nor free reapplication allow for rule priority.

The Ordered-Rule Hypothesis

Thus, there are grounds for rejecting both the direct-mapping hypothesis and the free-reapplication hypothesis. A third alternative, the ordered-rule hypothesis, maintains that the phonological rules of the language are applied in sequence. The first rule operates on the UR. Each subsequently applied rule operates on the structure resulting from the application of the preceding rule. Furthermore, it maintains that the choice of what sequence to apply the rules in is not free. The sequencing of rules is at least partially determined by ordering statements of the form "R_i precedes R_j," which are interpreted as meaning that before R_j may be applied in the sequencing of the rules, R_i must be tried. If no ordering statement exists for a pair of rules, the rules may be applied in either sequence. Furthermore, it has generally been assumed that a rule may be applied at just one point in the sequence of rule applications (though sometimes rules must be permitted to reapply to their own output; if so, the constraint would be that a rule may apply more than once in a sequence, but all applications of a single rule must be adjacent; see below for further discussion of this point). Finally, it has usually been held that in the normal case the rules apply in the same sequence for all URs.

Unlike direct mapping the ordered-rule hypothesis does not require that URs be mapped directly into PRs. It permits intermediate stages, so that the applicability of some rules can be determined by the applicability of other rules. Unlike free reapplication, the ordered-rule hypothesis does not require all rules to apply whenever their structural descriptions are satisfied. The applicability of some rules may prevent the application of other rules. To see that this hypothesis deals adequately with all of the data presented so far, we will illustrate briefly one example of each type of rule interaction.

Consider the kind of examples that seemed to motivate direct mapping. Recall the Tunica UR /náši-ʔáki/, which must be realized as *náš-ʔɛki*. The *a* vowel in -*ʔáki* must assimilate to the preceding *i*, even though the latter is not present in PR. Ordered rules will predict this result as well as direct mapping, as long as vowel assimilation is ordered to apply before syncope.

(44)   /náši-ʔáki/
         náši-ʔéki   Vowel assimilation
         náš-ʔéki   Syncope
         náš-ʔɛki   Right destressing

(We return below to the sequencing of right destressing.) In general, if a rule R_i applies even though some other rule R_j has (or would have) the effect of removing the conditions for the application of R_i—so-called counterbleeding—then R_i must be ordered to precede R_j.

The second type of situation that was cited to motivate the DMH is represented by Sea Dayak, where an oral vowel is generally nasalized when a nasal consonant immediately precedes. But when a cluster of nasal consonant plus voiced stop is optionally reduced to a simple nasal consonant, the following vowel is still pronounced oral. This kind of rule interaction is also describable in terms of ordered rules. All that is required is that vowel nasalization be ordered before nasal cluster simplification. The required derivation of *naŋa?* 'set up a ladder' will be as follows:

(45) /naŋga/
        nãŋga   Vowel nasalization
        nãŋa   Nasal cluster simplification
        nãŋa?   Other rules

In general, if some rule R_i creates a structure that meets the input requirements of some rule R_j, but the latter rule does not apply—so-called counterfeeding—then R_j must be ordered to apply before R_i.

An example of a case that argues against direct mapping is the interaction of syncope and right destressing in Tunica. The application of the former makes possible the application of the latter. For example, /náši-?áki/, is subject to right destressing just because syncope drops the final vowel of /náši/. The above derivation of *náš-?ɛki* shows clearly that ordered rules can predict such a rule interaction. In general, if the application of some rule R_i makes it possible for another rule R_j to apply—so-called feeding—then R_i must be ordered before R_j.

Or consider the Lardil examples; *puṭu* can be derived from /puṭuka/ provided apocope is ordered before nonapical deletion:

(46) /puṭuka/
        puṭuk   Apocope
        puṭu   Nonapical deletion

And *tjumputju* can be derived from /tjumputjumpu/ provided apocope is ordered before cluster simplification, and the latter rule is ordered before nonapical deletion:

(47) /tjumputjumpu/
        tjumputjump   Apocope
        tjumputjum   Cluster simplification
        tjumputju   Nonapical deletion

Apocope may not apply to /tjumputju/, since apocope must precede nonapical deletion, not follow it.

We now come to the type of rule interaction that argues not only against direct mapping, but also against free reapplication. Consider first the interaction of vowel epenthesis and vowel shortening in Yawelmani, where underlying /ʔa:ml-hin/ must be realized as *ʔa:mil-hin*. This can be achieved as long as VE is ordered to apply before VS:

(48)   /ʔa:ml-hin/
                         ʔa:mil-hin   VE
                         inapplicable   VS

In general, if a given structure fails to undergo a rule R_i as a consequence of the application of some other rule R_j—so-called bleeding—then R_j must be ordered before R_i.

In Ukrainian *l*-drop and dental-stop deletion provide a second example. As we saw above, DSD has priority. When phrased in terms of rule ordering, DSD precedes *l*-drop. The derivation of *klaw* is thus:

(49)   /klad-l/
                         kla-l   DSD
                         inapplicable   l-drop
                         kla-w   Other rules

It is necessary to order DSD before *l*-drop so that the latter rule does not apply to /klad-l/ to give */klad/. It is presumably also necessary to order DSD before the *l*-to-*w* rule so that the latter rule does not change /klad-l/ to /klad-w/, thus deriving a structure to which DSD would not be able to apply.

Ordered rules, then, are able to describe all of the kinds of rule interaction that we have cited in this chapter. Furthermore, all of the examples discussed here are consistent with the widely accepted constraints on ordering mentioned above: namely, that (*a*) it is not necessary to apply a rule both before and after some other rule in a derivation and (*b*) it is not necessary to have two rules apply in different orders in different derivations. It will perhaps be useful to briefly consider what kinds of data would falsify the particular version of the ordered-rule hypothesis presented above. The Lardil example just cited suggests a kind of interaction that this hypothesis would exclude. Suppose that an example like *tjumputju* from underlying /tjumputjumpu/ were actually pronounced **tjumputj*. This pronunciation could be described if apocope were permitted to apply before cluster-simplification and nonapical-deletion and also after these rules, as the derivation in (50) illustrates.

(50)   /tjumputjumpu/
            tjumputjump   Apocope
            tjumputjum   Cluster-simplification
            tjumputju   Nonapical-deletion
            tjumputj   Apocope

The derivation in (50) would not be possible given the particular version of the ordered-rule hypothesis being considered here; in order to derive *tjumputj* a second apocope rule would be required, but such a rule would obviously be a duplication of the independently needed apocope rule that deletes the last vowel of the underlying representation /tjumputjumpu/. Consequently, if derivations like (50) are required in order to describe natural languages, the ordered-rule hypothesis sketched above would have to be modified to permit rules to apply more than once in a derivation (at least in some cases).

A second, related type of interaction that would be evidence against the ordered-rule hypothesis formulated above would be a situation where for one range of cases the rule R_i must be applied before R_j, but for another range of cases R_j must be applied before R_i. For instance, suppose that a language has a rule that palatalizes k to $\check{c}$ before the vowel i and also a rule that drops a vowel before a vowel. Furthermore, suppose that an underlying sequence k-i-a is pronounced $\check{c}$-a while an underlying sequence k-a-i is also pronounced $\check{c}$-a. To describe these data, the derivations in (51) would be required.

(51)   /k-i-a/   /k-a-i/
        č-i-a Palatalization   *k-i*   Vowel truncation
        č-a   Vowel truncation   *č-i*   Palatalization

Such derivations are not allowed by the ordered-rule hypothesis described above; thus if such derivations are required by any data from natural languages it may be necessary to modify the ordered-rule hypothesis to accommodate such data.

A third kind of interaction that the ordered-rule hypothesis would not be able to account for would be if, in Ukrainian, /kład-l/ were pronounced **kla* by virtue of the rules of dental-stop deletion and *l*-drop. Since each of these rules destroys the conditions that would permit the other to apply, there is no way that they can be applied in sequence so that both apply. Sequencing DSD first gives the correct PR *kla-l*. If *l*-drop applied first, **klad* would result. No ordering of the rules will yield **kla*. Thus if forms like *kla* had to be derived in any natural language, the ordered-rule hypothesis would be unable to achieve this result. Some form of simultaneous application of rules would be necessary, so that /kład-l/ could undergo both DSD and *l*-drop.

It seems fair to say that in the great majority of cases so far examined in the generative framework the ordered-rule hypothesis (as formulated above) makes the correct claims. We know of no examples of the third type, where simultaneous application would be required. Possible instances of the first two types of counterexamples have been discussed in recent years, but they are in general either not straightforward or are explicable in terms of auxiliary principles that leave the ordered-rule hypothesis basically in tact. (See Anderson 1974 for an extended effort to support the existence of counterexamples to the ordered rule hypothesis formulated in this chapter.) A rather different approach to rule interactions of the counterfeeding and counterbleeding type is discussed in Kenstowicz and Kisseberth (1977). Finally, there are phonologists such as Hooper (1976) who attempted to do away with all interactions except the feeding type by reanalyzing the data in terms of more concrete URs; as briefly discussed in Chapter 6, we believe this approach to be fundamentally misguided.

The Multiple Application Problem

In the preceding sections of this chapter we outlined three approaches to the problem of the interaction of rules in the conversion of the underlying representation to the phonetic representation. In this section we briefly discuss the closely related problem of how different applications of the same rule interact to convert a given input string into the correct output string. Not surprisingly, there have been three approaches to this issue that closely parallel the direct mapping, free reapplication, and ordered-rule hypotheses. Corresponding to the direct mapping principle is the simultaneous application principle (SA). This is the approach to the multiple application problem that is advocated in Chomsky and Halle (1968).

(52) To apply a rule, the entire string is first scanned for segments that satisfy the environmental constraints of the rule. After all such segments have been identified in the string, the changes required by the rule are applied simultaneously [p. 344].

According to this principle all applications of a rule to a string are defined on the orginal input string. Application of the rule at any point in the string may not prevent (bleed) application at any other point, nor may one application of a rule create the conditions that make possible the application of the rule at some other point. Thus a feeding interaction between applications of a rule is prohibited.

The counterfeeding corollary of the simultaneous application principle is consistent with the input-output relations of many rules. To cite just one example here, in Hidatsa (Harris 1942) there is a rule apocopating the final mora of a word-final vowel, as evidenced by the data in (53).

(53)

Past	Imperative	Gloss
cixi-c	*cix*	'jump'
kikua-c	*kiku*	'set a trap'
ikaa-c	*ika*	'look'

If long vowels are represented as geminates, the shortenings that occur in the imperative can be described by the following rule:

(54) $$V \longrightarrow \emptyset / \underline{\quad} \#$$

Application of this rule to the URs /#cixi#/, /#kikua#/, and /#ikaa#/ yields the correct surface forms *cix*, *kiku*, and *ika*. Note that the latter two representations also contain word-final vowels and hence satisfy the input requirements of (54). But it is only underlying word final vowels that delete. Those that come to stand at the end of a word by one application of apocope do not. If all applications of a rule are defined on the original input string, as SA requires, the correct results are achieved. Even though *kiku* and *ika* satisfy the input requirements to (54), they will not undergo the rule if phonological rules are applied in terms of the simultaneous application principle.

The simultaneous application principle also requires multiple applications that interact in a counterbleeding fashion. That is, application of the rule at one point in the input string may not inhibit application at another point. The rhythmic law of Slovak illustrates this pattern. In Chapter 4 we cited examples where the conjugation vowels /i:/ and /e:/ appear long after short root vowels and as short after underlying long root vowels. The verbs in (55) come from another conjugation of Slovak, marked by the suffix /a:/. This suffix exhibits the same length alternation.

(55)

1 sg.	3 sg.	1 pl.	Gloss
vol-a:-m	*vol-a:*	*vol-a:-me*	'call'
či:t-a-m	*či:t-a*	*či:t-a-me*	'read'

The rhythmic law, restated here as (56), accounts for the shortening of the /a:/ after the root /či:t/.

(56) $$V \longrightarrow [-\text{long}]/V:C_0 \underline{\quad}$$

Underlying forms with three successive long vowels occur when the frequentative suffix /a:v/ is appended to the verb root. Stems formed with this suffix require the /a:/ conjugation vowel. Observe that when the root vowel of the frequentative verb is long, the long vowels of both the frequentative morpheme /a:v/ and of the conjugation vowel /a:/ are shortened.

(57)

	1 sg.	3 sg.	1 pl.	Gloss
	čes-a:v-a-m	*čes-a:v-a*	*čes-a:v-a-me*	'comb'
	vol-a:v-a-m	*vol-a:v-a*	*vol-a:v-a-me*	'call'
	či:t-av-a-m	*či:t-av-a*	*či:t-av-a-me*	'read'
	pi:s-av-a-m	*pi:s-av-a*	*pi:s-av-a-me*	'write'

If the rhythmic law is applied simultaneously to a UR such as /pi:s-a:v-a:/, the correct output *pi:s-av-a* is obtained. The long vowel in /a:v/ is preceded by the long vowel of the root, and the long vowel of the conjugation marker /a:/ is preceded by the long vowel in /a:v/. Note that as a result of the shortening of the vowel in /a:v/, the conjugation marker is no longer preceded by a long vowel. If the shortening of /a:/ were to take place after shortening of /a:v/ the wrong output **pi:s-av-a:* would be obtained. Since simultaneous application does not permit a bleeding interaction, such an incorrect output could not be derived.

But it is precisely for this reason that the simultaneous application principle cannot be accepted as a universally valid method for applying a rule to a string. In some cases one application of a rule must be permitted to bleed another application of the rule. An interesting example appears in the Australian language Gidabal (Geytenbeek 1971). This language has a rule of exactly the same form as the Slovak rhythmic law, but it must be applied in a bleeding fashion. In order to keep this rule distinct from the rhythmic law we will refer to it as vowel shortening. In fact, the rules are identical; they are just applied differently.

There are many suffixes in Gidabal with an underlying long vowel that is realized phonetically as a short vowel just in case the preceding vowel is long. Compare, for instance, the subjunctive suffix /-ya:/ with the potential suffix /-ye/:

(58)   *badi-ya:*   'should hit'   *badi-ye*   'may hit'
        yaga:-ya   'should fix'   *yaga:-ye*   'may fix'
        ga:da-ya: 'should chase'   *ga:da-ye*   'may chase'

Clearly, the potential suffix has a basic short vowel (it is never pronounced long). The subjective suffix has a basic long vowel, which shows up when the preceding vowel is short. If the preceding vowel is long, the vowel of /-ya:/ shortens.

Other examples of suffixes with an underlying long vowel include the intensifiers /-da:ŋ/ and /-be:/ and the locational suffix /-ya:/. The initial consonant of the latter, if preceded by a nasal, becomes an oral stop homorganic with that nasal.

(59)

njule-da:ŋ	'he' (emphatic)	*gadi-be:*	'right here'
nu:n-daŋ	'too hot'	*bugal-be:*	'very good'
yu:-daŋ	'much later'	*buřu:ř-be*	'only two'
bala-ya:	'is under'		
ba:m-ba	'is halfway'		
gila:-ya	'that'		
djubunj-dja:	'is night'		

Now consider some examples where these suffixes are combined with one another. *babař-a:-daŋ* 'straight above' from /babař-ya:-da:ŋ/ has two successive long vowels in the UR, the second of which shortens. In *djalum-ba:-daŋ-be:* 'is certainly right on the fish' from /djalum-ba:-da:ŋ-be:/ there are three successive long vowels in the input string. Only the middle one shortens. SA would predict the form **djalum-ba:-daŋ-be*, with shortening of the long vowel in /-be:/, since this vowel is preceded by a long vowel in the input string. *gunu:m-ba-da:ŋ-be* 'is certainly right on the stump' has four successive long vowels in the input string. Only the second and fourth shorten. SA incorrectly predicts **gunu:m-ba-daŋ-be* with a shortening of all the long vowels that appear after long vowels in the input string.

In order for SA to be consistent with the data from Gidabal it is necessary to suppose that the rule of vowel shortening has a rather different form from that attributed to it in the preceding discussion. In order for this rule to shorten alternate long vowels, it would have to have the following form, where $\check{V}$ is a cover symbol for a short vowel:

(60)
$$V: \rightarrow \check{V} \ / \ \left\{ \begin{matrix} \# \\ \check{V} \end{matrix} \right\} \ C_1 V: (C_1 V: C_1 V:)^* C_1 \underline{\quad}$$

The material inside the braces is necessary in order to identify the following long vowel as being the first in a sequence of long vowels. The remainder of the environment identifies the vowel undergoing the rule as being the second, the fourth, the sixth, etc., in a sequence of long vowels. This rule has recourse to the "infinite schema" notation introduced in SPE (p. 344). The notation ( )* abbreviates an infinite set of rules. One of the rules contains no occurrence of the material inside the parentheses, thereby denoting a string of two successive long vowels. The next contains one occurrence of the material in parentheses, denoting a string of four consecutive long vowels. The next one contains two occurrences of the parenthesized material, identifying a string of six long vowels, etc.

This formulation of vowel shortening that one is driven to in order to maintain SA is objectionable for the very same reasons as the rules required by the direct mapping hypothesis. We showed that to apply two or more phonological rules simultaneously to the UR often leads to the repetition of the structural description of one rule (or its complement) in the structural description of another rule. Similarly, in order to apply vowel shortening in Gidabal simultaneously, the SD of the rule must be repeated in its own SD. For the material in parentheses, with its reference to two successive long vowels, repeats the remainder of the SD, which also mentions two successive long vowels. With the infinite schema notation, this repetition of material is treated as entirely accidental. The material inside the parentheses could just as well have been totally different from the material outside of the parentheses. But, in fact, every case we know of in which phonologists have appealed to the infinite schema notation has involved mentioning material inside the parentheses that also occurs outside the parentheses. This fact demonstrates that the relationship between the material inside and outside of the parentheses is not accidental at all.

In addition, only one of the rules abbreviated by the infinite schema given above can be shown to be a real rule of grammar: namely, the sub-rule that results when there is no material inside the parentheses (and also when the material inside of the braces is omitted, for this information is present merely to identify the first vowel in a sequence of long vowels, and is not really part of the rule at all). We have seen, for example, that Slovak possesses this rule. The remaining rules abbreviated by the infinite schema, continuing to ignore the braces are as follows:

(61) $V: \longrightarrow \breve{V}/V: C_1\ V: C_1\ V: C_1$ ____
         $V: \longrightarrow \breve{V}/V: C_1\ V: C_1\ V: C_1\ V: C_1\ V: C_1$ ____
         etc.

Clearly, none of these rules has independent justification, in the sense that there is probably no language where just one of these rules and not the others would have to be assumed to be operative. That is to say, there is no language which shortens the final vowel in a string of six successive long vowels, unless that language also shortens the final member of a string of four, and of two. A similar objection can be made to many of the rules one is forced to write if one does not permit separate rules to apply in sequential fashion rather than simultaneously. Consequently, it appears that many of the same reasons which lead to a rejection of simultaneous application of separate rules also force the rejection of a principle that requires that a single rule must be applied simultaneously to all points in the input string that satisfy the input requirements of the rule.

Let us now turn to the counterfeeding corollary of the simultaneous application principle. If all applications of a rule are defined on the original input string, a feeding application between individual applications of the same rule is prohibited. Surely the most important phenomenon calling this into question is vowel harmony. Recall the vowel harmony process of Yawelmani (Chapter 4). Given our earlier analysis of this language, the underlying vowel system contains eight members: *i*, *u*, *a*, and *o* (a low back vowel), each of which can be long or short. In words containing two syllables (a root and a suffix), the harmony process will transform suffixal *i* to *u* if the preceding root contains *u* and suffixal *a* to *o* if the preceding root contains *o*.

(62) | *xil-it* | *xil-hin* | *xil-al* | *xil-k'a* | 'tangle' |
       | *gop-it* | *gop-hin* | *gop-ol* | *gop-k'o* | 'care for an infant' |
       | *dub-ut* | *dub-hun* | *dub-al* | *dub-k'a* | 'lead by the hand' |
       | *max-it* | *max-hin* | *max-al* | *max-k'a* | 'procure' |

The suffixal alternations in these data can be accounted for by the following rule which states that a vowel becomes round (and back) if the preceding vowel is round and of the same tongue height.

(63)
$$\begin{bmatrix} +\text{syll} \\ \alpha\text{high} \end{bmatrix} \longrightarrow \begin{bmatrix} +\text{round} \\ +\text{back} \end{bmatrix} \Big/ \begin{bmatrix} +\text{syll} \\ +\text{round} \\ \alpha\text{high} \end{bmatrix} C_0 \underline{\hspace{1cm}}$$

Now let us consider verbal roots with the basic shape *CVCC-*. When a consonant-initial suffix follows, these roots are subject to the rule of epenthesis that inserts *i* in the context C___CC.

(64) | *ʔilkit* | *ʔilikhin* | *ʔilkal* | *ʔilikk'a* | 'sing' |
       | *logwit* | *logiwhin* | *logwol* | *logiwk'a* | 'pulverize' |
       | *ʔutyut* | *ʔutuyhun* | *ʔutyal* | *ʔutuyk'a* | 'fall' |
       | *paʔṭit* | *paʔiṭhin* | *paʔṭal* | *paʔiṭk'a* | 'fight' |

Let us focus on the derivation of *ʔutuyhun* from /ʔuty-hin/. After epenthesis we will have the structure /ʔutiy-hin/. Since the inserted *i* is preceded by *u*, harmony is applicable and would give as output /ʔutuy-hin/. But now the suffixal *i* is in the proper context for the rule to operate. If one application of a rule can feed another application, we will be able to obtain the correct output *ʔutuyhun* by simply reapplying the rule. But if the simultaneous application principle is accepted, then we must revise the rule by making it an infinite schema. It could not, however, simply be the following:

(65)

$$\begin{bmatrix} +\text{syll} \\ \alpha\text{high} \end{bmatrix} \longrightarrow \begin{bmatrix} +\text{round} \\ +\text{back} \end{bmatrix} \Big/ \begin{bmatrix} +\text{syll} \\ +\text{round} \\ \alpha\text{high} \end{bmatrix} (C_0 V)^* C_0\text{—}$$

To see why such a rule would not work, consider *logiwk'a* from /logw-k'a/. Epenthesis gives /logiw-k'a/. If harmony were formulated as immediately above, the suffixal vowel in /logiw-k'a/ would round since it meets the SD of the rule. It is separated from a round vowel of the same height by one vowel, and the infinite schema permits any number of vowels to intervene. Given the harmony rule in its original formulation, however, the suffixal vowel in /logiw-k'a/ could not be affected, since the presence of the epenthetic vowel means that the suffixal vowel is not immediately preceded by a round vowel of the same height. In order for the infinite schema approach to achieve the same results, it would have to be reformulated as follows:

(66)

$$\begin{bmatrix} +\text{syll} \\ \alpha\text{high} \end{bmatrix} \longrightarrow \begin{bmatrix} +\text{round} \\ +\text{back} \end{bmatrix} \Big/ \begin{bmatrix} +\text{syll} \\ +\text{round} \\ \alpha\text{high} \end{bmatrix} (C_0 \begin{bmatrix} +\text{syll} \\ \alpha\text{high} \end{bmatrix})^* C_0\text{—}$$

The above rule requires that between the vowel being harmonized and the conditioning vowel there may occur only vowels that are themselves eligible to undergo harmony and would, once affected by the SC of the rule, be able to condition harmony. This requirement means that whether any vowel in the word is subject to harmony depends upon whether the preceding vowel itself harmonizes. Actually, the rule does not require that the intervening vowel undergo harmony, only that it be eligible to do so. However, in all cases that we know of, the intervening vowel does in fact undergo the rule. We know of no cases where harmony exceptionally skips over a vowel and continues to operate even though the vowel that is skipped could not itself condition harmony.

In the face of the examples discussed above, it appears that the simultaneous application principle formulated in SPE cannot be maintained. A rule must be permitted to apply to its own output. This effect could be achieved by modifying the principle in the following fashion:

(67)   ITERATIVE APPLICATION PRINCIPLE: *To apply a rule to a string, identify all segments in the string which meet the structural description (SD) of the rule. Carry out the structural change (SC) of the rule simultaneously to all segments so identified to obtain a derived string S_1. Then identify all segments in S_1 that meet the SD of the rule and carry out the SC on these segments to obtain a derived string S_2. Repeat this process until a derived string S_n has been obtained to which the rule can no longer apply non-vacuously. When such a string has been obtained, the derivation moves on to the next rule in the ordered set.*

This iterative principle is quite analogous to the free reapplication principle discussed earlier. It permits a feeding interaction between applications of a rule and hence is able to overcome the objections raised against simultaneous application with respect to the Yawelmani example discussed above. The iterative application principle will permit the most optimal formulation of harmony in Yawelmani. A form like *ʔutuyhun* from /ʔuty-hin/ will now be derived as follows. Epenthesis yields /ʔutiy-hin/. This structure is now submitted to the harmony rule. Only the inserted *i* meets the structural description of the rule, since only it is immediately preceded by an *u*. Application of the rule produces the derived string /ʔutuy-hin/. The suffixal *i* now meets the SD of the rule, because the immediately preceding syllable now contains an *u*. Consequently, the harmony rule must be applied again, producing the correct surface from *ʔutuyhun*. Since a rule may apply to its own output under the iterative principle, the harmony process does not have to be triggered necessarily by the first vowel of the word, as in the simultaneous approach. Thus, a form like *logiwk'a* from /logw-k'a/ causes no problem. After epenthesis of the *i*, the suffixal *a* is not immediately preceded by a low round vowel. Hence, it will not round.

The iterative principle is also consistent with counterbleeding interactions. In a Slovak word like *písava* from /pi:s-a:v-a:/, both long *a:*s in the UR meet the SD of the rhythmic law. This rule is then applied simultaneously to both of these vowels, shortening each to produce the correct surface form. The iterative principle always produces a counterbleeding as opposed to a bleeding interaction, since whenever a structure satisfies the SD of a rule at two or more points, the rule will apply simultaneously at all those points. Application of the rule at one point cannot affect the application of the rule at some other point.

But it is for exactly this reason that the iterative application principle must be rejected. It cannot produce the bleeding multiple applications required by the Gidabal example. A Gidabal form containing more than two successive long vowels will always be converted into the wrong output by shortening of all vowels but the first. The correct output, in which only the second, fourth, and so on, vowels in a string of successive long vowels is shortened, can only be obtained if the SD of the rule is repeated inside the asterisked parentheses. Hence, all of the arguments against simultaneous application in examples like this apply to the iterative principle as well.

In addition, the iterative principle cannot deal effectively with the counterfeeding interaction found in languages like Hidatsa. If the Hidatasa apocope rule is applied iteratively, / ⧧ kikua ⧧ / will be converted to / ⧧ kiku ⧧ / by one application of the rule. But this derived string also meets the SD of the apocope rule. According to the iterative principle, the rule must be applied again. But this produces the incorrect output *kil.

In permitting a rule to apply to its own output, the iterative principle is a step in the right direction. However, like free reapplication, it is too strong in that it claims that a rule must always be reapplied whenever its SD is met. Evidently, then, some device must be developed which will permit control over when reapplication will occur. A number of generative phonologists (e.g., Anderson 1969; Johnson 1971; Morin and Friedman 1971) have suggested the following principle to control the reapplication of a rule.

(68)   DIRECTIONAL ITERATIVE APPLICATION: *A rule may be applied to a string in one of two ways: iteratively left-to-right or iteratively right-to-left. In left-to-right iterative application, the left-most segment in the string is examined first to see if it meets the SD of the rule. If it does, the rule is applied to obtain a derived string S_1. One then moves on to examine the next segment in the string (the derived string S_1 if the rule has applied, or the original string S_0 if it has not) and applies the rule to this segment if it meets the SD of the rule. This procedure is repeated segment by segment until the right-most segment in the string has been processed. At this point the derivation moves on to the next rule in the ordered set. In right-to-left iterative application, the same procedure obtains except that the right-most segment is the one checked first and the application of the rule to the string ceases after the left-most segment has been processed.*

Under this mode of application, the reapplication of a rule is possible. However, reapplication can (always?) be prevented by reversing the direction of iteration. This is made possible by the fact that once a segment x has been checked (and modified by the rule if the SD has been satisfied), one may not go back and reapply the rule to x even though subsequent applications of the rule may have modified the string so that x does come to meet the SD of the rule. For example, consider the Hidatsa case. If a left-to-right application is imposed on the rule of apocope, a form like *kiku* from /#kikua#/ will be derived as follows. The first, second, third, and fourth segments of the UR will be checked successively. The rule will not apply to any of them since they are not in final position. When the fifth segment is examined, it will be deleted since it satisfies the SD of the rule, deriving the string /#kiku#/. Since the apocopated *a* was the final segment of the string, we must move on to the next rule in the ordered set. In particular, apocope cannot apply to the *u* in/#kiku#/ even though it meets the SD of the rule. This is because the *u* has already been checked. Under the directional iterative mode of application, once a segment has been checked, we cannot go back and reapply the rule to that segment.

In the Yawelmani example the required feeding application pattern can be achieved by employing a left-to-right direction of iteration. For instance, Yawelmani /ʔutiy-hin/ will be converted into /ʔutuy-hin/ when the first *i* is checked. And when the suffixal vowel is checked, it will also be rounded because in the derived string it is immediately preceded by a high round vowel.

Turning to bleeding and counterbleeding multiple applications, we argued earlier that both Slovak and Gidabal have essentially the same rule which shortens a vowel in the context $V:C_0$___. In Slovak the rule must shorten all but the first vowel in a string of consecutive long vowels: For example, $V:CV:CV:CV:$, etc. $\longrightarrow V:CVCVCV$. This pattern can be obtained by imposing a right-to-left direction on the application of the rule. Gidabal, on the other hand, requires an alternating pattern: $V:CV:CV:CV: \longrightarrow V:CVCV:CV$. If the same shortening rule is applied in a left-to-right direction this pattern is readily achieved.

In essence, the directional iterative mode of application permits the applications of a single rule to interact with one another in just the same ways that rule ordering permits separate rules to interact with one another. The data presently available to us suggests that it is indeed the case that all of the types of rule interaction sketched above—feeding, counterfeeding, bleeding, and counterbleeding—are required both for the application of separate rules and also for the multiple applications of a single rule. For extensive discussion of matters related to rule ordering, see Kenstowicz and Kisseberth (1977, pp. 155–229).

Exercises

1. Catalan. Account for the alternations in the following adjectives and nouns, paying particular attention to the ordering relations between the rules. Characterize each ordering relation in terms of the notions of feeding, counterfeeding, bleeding, and counterbleeding.

Masc. sg.	Masc. pl.	Fem. sg.	Fem. pl.	Gloss
ultim	ultims	ultimə	ultimes	'last'
bo	bons	bonə	bones	'good'
ple	plens	plenə	plenes	'full'
sa	sans	sanə	sanes	'sane'
kla	klas	klarə	klares	'plain'
du	dus	durə	dures	'hard'
seɣu	seɣus	seɣurə	seɣures	'safe'
profun	profuns	profundə	profundes	'deep'
for	fors	fortə	fortes	'strong'
al	als	altə	altes	'tall'
blaŋ	blaŋs	blaŋkə	blaŋkes	'white'
kam	kams			'field' (cf. *kamp-amen* 'camp'
kork	korks			'termite'
kalk	kalks			'copy'
serp	serps			'snake'
petit	petits	petitə	petites	'small'
kazat	kazats	kazaðə	kazaðes	'married'
sek	seks	sekə	sekes	'dry'
sek	seks	seɣə	seɣes	'blind'
gros	grosos	grosᴢ	groses	'big'
gris	grizos	grizə	grizes	'grey'
ʎeč	ʎejos	ʎejə	ʎejes	'ugly'
boč	božos	božə	božes	'crazy'
roč	rožos	rožə	rožes	'red'
desič	desijos			'wish'
despač	despačos			'office'
kalaš	kalašos			'drawer'

2. Javanese (Dudas 1976). Account for the alternations in the following data, paying particular attention to the ordering relations between the rules. Characterize each ordering relation in terms of the notions feeding, counterfeeding, bleeding, and counterbleeding. The vowels [ı, ʊ, ɛ, ɔ] are the lax counterparts of tense [i,e,u,o]. Assume that all lax vowels are derived by rule from underlying tense vowels.

Noun	'My' noun	'This' noun	Gloss
babi	babiku	babine	'pig'
ibu	ibuku	ibune	'mother'
ḍeje	ḍejeku	ḍejene	'insect'
peso	pesoku	pesone	'knife'
čaŋklɪr	čaŋklɪrku	čaŋkire	'cup'
čukUr	čukUrku	čukure	'haircut'
kečap	kečapku	kečape	'soy sauce'
səbap	səbapku	səbabe	'reason'
kulɪt	kulɪtku	kulite	'skin'

murIt	murItku	muride	'student'
beḍUk	beḍUkku	beḍuge	'mosque drum'
aḍI?	aḍI?ku	aḍi?e	'little brother'
omah	omahku	omae	'house'
butUh	butUhku	butue	'need'
sisIh	sisIhku	sisie	'side'
mejɔ	mejaku	mejane	'table'
darmɔ	darmaku	darmane	'duty'
jarwɔ	jarwaku	jarwane	'meaning'
kɔjɔ	kajaku	kajane	'wealth'
ɔṇḍɔ	aṇḍaku	aṇḍane	'ladder'
kɔňčɔ	kaňčaku	kaňčane	'friend'
ɔŋkɔ	aŋkaku	aŋkane	'number'
agɔmɔ	agamaku	agamane	'religion'
antɔkɔ	antakaku	antakane	'death'

Adjective	Demonstrative	Causative	Gloss
risi	risine	ŋrisɛ?ake	'uncomfortable'
jəro	jərone	ňjərɔ?ake	'deep'
seje	sejene	nɛjɛ?ake	'different'
geḍe	gedene	ŋgɛḍɛ?ake	'big'
boḍo	boḍone	mbɔḍɔ?ake	'stupid'
lɔrɔ	larane	ŋlara?ake	'sick'
ɔmbɔ	ambane	ŋamba?ake	'broad'
rosɔ	rosane	ŋrosa?ake	'strong'
garIŋ	gariŋe	ŋgarIŋake	'dry'
apI?	api?e	ŋapI?ake	'nice'
lirIh	lirie	ŋlirIhake	'soft sounding'

3. Keley-i (Hohulin and Kenstowicz 1976). As in most Philippine languages the verb in Keley-i is inflected for past, present, and future tenses. Verbs also agree with the NP that is the "topic" or "focus" of the sentence. In Keley-i, verbs will agree with focused subjects, direct objects, instrumentals, locatives, or beneficiaries. This problem centers upon the underlying forms for certain affixes and the proper ordering of the associated rules.

a. Segment these verbs into their constituent morphemes and list the underlying form for each of the affixes. In particular, what are the possible underlying forms for the instrumental prefix? Assume a rule that geminates the second consonant of a CVCVC root in the future tense.

Subj. foc. future	Dir. obj. foc. past	Instr. foc. past	Gloss
?umbayyu?	binayu?	?imbayu?	'pound rice'
?umdillag	dinilag	?indilag	'light'
?umgubbat	ginubat	?iŋgubat	'fight'
?umbuŋŋet	binuŋet	?imbuŋet	'scold'
?umduntuk	dinuntuk	?induntuk	'punch'
?umgalgal	ginalgal	?iŋgalgal	'chew'
?um?agtu?	?inagtu?	?in?agtu?	'head carry'
?umhullat	hinulat	?inhulat	'cover'
?um?ehneŋ	?inehneŋ	?in?ehneŋ	'stand'

b. Supplement your analysis to account for the alternations in the following data set. Do these data bear upon the underlying form for the instrumental prefix? How must the rules be ordered? Assume a rule that reduplicates the first syllable of a CeCVC root in the future tense.

Subj. foc. future	Dir. Obj. foc. past	Instr. foc. past	Gloss
ʔumbebhat	binhat	ʔimbehat	'cut rattan'
ʔumdedʔek	dinʔek	ʔindeʔek	'accuse'
ʔumtetpen	simpen	ʔintepen	'measure'
ʔumpeptut	pintut	ʔimpetut	'dam'
ʔumtetkuk	siŋkuk	ʔintekuk	'shout'
ʔumkekbet	kimbet	ʔiŋkebet	'scratch'
ʔumbebdad	bindad	ʔimbedad	'untie'
ʔumdedgeh	diŋgeh	ʔindegeh	'hurt'

c. The second and third columns contain the contrastive identification prefixes. These give the verb the force of the English expressions *It was John who Verbed* or *John was the one who Verbed*. What are the possible underlying representations for these prefixes? What reasons can be given for or against each possibility? Supplement your analysis to account for these data. Give derivations for *neŋbet* and *nembaʔ*.

Instr. foc. past	Contr. id. fut.	Contr. id. past	Gloss
ʔinduntuk	menuntuk	nenuntuk	'punch'
ʔimbayuʔ	memayyuʔ	nemayuʔ	'pound rice'
ʔiŋgubat	meŋubbat	neŋubat	'fight'
ʔinhulat	menullat	nenulat	'cover'
ʔimpedug	memdug	nemdug	'chase'
ʔimbedad	memdad	nemdad	'untie'
ʔiŋkebet	meŋbet	neŋbet	'scratch'
ʔimbekaʔ	memkaʔ	nemkaʔ	'dig'
ʔintepen	mempen	nempen	'measure'
ʔintebaʔ	membaʔ	nembaʔ	'kill pig'
ʔintekuk	meŋkuk	neŋkuk	'shout'
ʔindegeh	meŋgeh	neŋgeh	'hurt'
ʔinhepaw	mempaw	nempaw	'possess'

d. Do the following data bear upon the analysis? In what way? Modify your analysis to account for these forms.

Instr. foc. past	Contr. id. fut.	Contr. id. past	Gloss
ʔindeʔek	menʔek	nenʔek	'accuse'
ʔinʔebaʔ	meŋbaʔ	neŋbaʔ	'carry on back'
ʔinʔinum	meŋinnum	neŋinum	'drink'

4. Moroccan Arabic (Harrell 1962). Formulate rules to account for the vowel~zero alternations and the placement of stress in the following perfect verb forms. How must the rules be ordered? How can the multiple applications of the rule for the vowel~zero alternation be described?

1 sg.	2 sg. f.	3 sg. m.	3 sg. f.	1 pl.	3 pl.	Gloss
qeddémt	qeddémti	qéddem	qéddmet	qeddémna	qéddmu	'presented'
gerbélt	gerbélti	gérbel	gérblet	gerbélna	gérblu	'sifted'
ktébt	ktébti	ktéb	kétbet	ktébna	kétbu	'wrote'
texlért	texlérti	téxler	txélret	texlérna	txélru	'got scared'

9

Notation

The task of the present chapter is to develop a systematic way of formulating phonological rules such that, first, any rule expressed in terms of this system will have a precise, totally unambiguous interpretation, and second, this system will provide a way of stating rules that is appropriate to the data. What we mean by "appropriate to the data" is not well defined at this point, and much of this chapter's discussion will try to make this concept clear.

The most extensive discussion of the notation and conventions governing the formulation and the application of phonological rules is to be found in Chomsky and Halle's *The Sound Pattern of English* (SPE). Hence, a large portion of our discussion will center on the notational devices developed in SPE. We shall also take into account some of the modifications and emendations to the SPE system that have been proposed in the literature.

There are two chief motivations for constructing an explicit formalism for the formulation of phonological rules. First, when we formulate a rule for a given language, we are (if the viewpoint espoused in this book is accepted) making a claim about the speaker's tacit knowledge of his language, which is at the same time a prediction about the sound structure of the sentences the speaker creates. In order to determine the sufficiency of a postulated rule, we must be able to determine what predictions it makes about the pronunciation of sentences. But to make such a determination we must know precisely what the rule is supposed to do in any situation that arises—whether or not that situation was expressly considered by the linguist in arriving at the formulation of the rule. A rule makes a verifiable claim about the structure of the language, and ultimately about the speaker's knowledge of that structure, only to the extent that it can be falsified. But it is falsifiable only to the extent that it is explicit.

In addition to explicitness, however, generative phonologists have often required that the system of rule formulation be constructed in such a way as to permit the distinction between possible and impossible (or more versus less natural) phonological rules to be formally expressible in terms of the notation. We saw in Chapter 7 that this requirement was the chief argument for adopting a feature notation (as opposed to an alphabetic one) for the representation of sounds in general, and also for the acceptance or rejection of a particular set of features. A similar requirement has been placed on the conventions for the formulation and the application of phonological rules. Given this requirement, there are two general grounds on which a proposed set of notational apparatus has been evaluated. First, the apparatus should permit natural rules to be expressed simply and easily. If there is some phenomenon judged to be typical and characteristic of phonological structure that cannot be easily expressed in the theory, then we have evidence against the theory. Second, this requirement has sometimes been interpreted to mean that if some phenomenon judged to be atypical and uncharacteristic of phonological structure can also be easily expressed in terms of the notational apparatus, then we also have evidence against the theory. However, one may legitimately question the validity of these kinds of objections. As we observed in Chapter 7, any satisfactory theory of phonology must have postulates about what are natural and unnatural rules. Some of these postulates may be derivative from the particular set of notational apparatus used for representing sounds and formulating phonological rules. But it is far from obvious that all such postulates must be expressed in this way. (The reader is referred to McCawley 1972 for further discussion of this point.)

Convention on Rule Application

In this section we develop the conventions which determine whether or not a given phonological rule applies to any utterance and what the result of a rule application is. Toward this end we follow SPE (pp. 336–337) in defining a concept of distinctness and, on the basis of this notion, a convention on the application of rules.

The concept of distinctness is defined as follows (by unit we mean either a segment, partially or fully specified for the set of phonetic features, or a boundary).[1]

(1)   *A unit X is distinct from another unit Y if and only if either there is some feature F such that one unit is specified + and the other − for that feature, or if the units have different integral values.*

Thus, /p/ and /b/ will be distinct, because the former is − and the latter + for the feature voice: /á/ and /à/ (where the acute and grave represent primary and secondary stress, respectively) are distinct, since the former would have the value 1 for the feature of stress and the latter the value 2. Furthermore, two strings of units are distinct if they are of different lengths or if the *i*th unit of one is distinct from the *i*th unit of the other. Thus the strings /ab/ and /ba/ are distinct since although they contain exactly the same units, the linear order of the units is different; the strings /ab/ and /aba/ are distinct since they differ in length.

Given the definition of (1) the convention on rule application may be expressed as (2).

(2)   *A rule of the form A* $\longrightarrow$ *B/X___Y applies to a string Z =* *. . . X'A'Y'. . . , just in case the string X'A'Y' is not distinct from XAY.*

Another way we will sometimes refer to this convention is that a rule applies to a string if that string meets or matches the structural description (SD) of the rule. The SD of any rule is determined by forming a string of units consisting of the material to the right of the slant bar in the rule and by placing the unit to the left of the arrow within the space occupied by the environmental dash. Thus, the SD of the above rule is the string XAY; the SD of the rule M $\longrightarrow$ N/___O is the string MO; the SD of the rule P $\longrightarrow$ Q is simply P.[2]

---

[1] In SPE boundaries are formalized in terms of features like [+/−word boundary], [+/−morpheme boundary], etc.

[2] We assume that if a rule is a word-level rule then a morpheme boundary + may freely occur in a string without making that string distinct from the SD of the rule and that if a rule is a phrase-level rule then a word boundary # may freely occur in a string without making that string distinct from the SD of the rule. See Chapter 10 for further discussion of boundaries.

To see how this part of the convention works recall the vowel-reduction rule of Russian (Chapter 7), which raises unstressed nonhigh vowels to *i* in position after a consonant that is [+high].

(3)

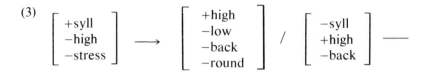

By the above convention this rule is applicable to the second segment in the feature representations of each of the following words: /l'esá/ 'forests', /n'osú/ 'I carry', /p'atá/ 'heel'. This is because first, these segments contain the feature specifications [+syll, −high, −stress], and second, the segments immediately preceding them contain the specifications [−syll, +high, −back]. In other words the string composed of the first two segments of these words is not distinct from the SD of the rule. On the other hand, the rule is not applicable to /l'isá/ 'fox' because the second segment is [+high], not to /nosí/ 'noses' because the first segment is [−high] (not a palatalized consonant); nor, finally, to /p'áti/ 'heels' because the second segment is [+stress].

The second clause in this convention specifies what happens as a result of applying the rule. (We shall sometimes refer to this as the structural change (SC) implemented by the rule.)

(4)   *The rule A $\longrightarrow$ B/X____Y converts Z to Z', where Z = . . . X'A'Y' and where Z' = . . . X'B'Y', and where B' contains all of the feature specifications in B in addition to all of the feature specifications in A' that are not specified in B.*

Thus, the result of applying a rule to a segment is a segment that has all of the feature specifications mentioned to the right of the arrow (B in the preceding case). The segment retains the same specifications it had prior to the application of the rule for all of those features not mentioned in B. In other words, the segment remains exactly as it was before the application of the rule except for those features specifically mentioned in B. The effects of this convention can be seen by comparing the feature representations for the second segments of 'forests', 'I carry', and 'heel' before and after applying the vowel reduction rule in accord with the convention:

(5)

	Before /l'esá/	After /l'isá/	Before /n'osú/	After /n'isú/	Before /p'atá/	After /p'itá/
Syll	+	+	+	+	+	+
Sonor	+	+	+	+	+	+
Cons	−	−	−	−	−	−
High	−	+	−	+	−	+
Low	−	−	−	−	+	−
Back	−	−	+	−	+	−
Round	−	−	+	−	−	−
Nasal	−	−	−	−	−	−
Voice	+	+	+	+	+	+
Stress	−	−	−	−	−	−

The conventions of (2) and (4) actually play a more fundamental role than merely ensuring that the phonological rules apply correctly to utterances, which is essentially a technical matter. Perhaps the best way to illustrate this is to pose a problem. Recall the final-devoicing alternation in Russian discussed in Chapter 3. On the basis of internal and external evidence we claimed that rule (6) was the appropriate description of the alternation.

(6) $\begin{bmatrix} -\text{sonorant} \\ +\text{voice} \end{bmatrix} \longrightarrow [-\text{voice}]/\underline{\quad}\#$

But another possible description exists. Instead of having a single rule to handle the alternations, we could formulate a whole series of rules, one to devoice each underlying voiced obstruent. (The rules given below are, of course, abbreviations for rules expressed in terms of phonetic features.)

(7) $b \longrightarrow p/\underline{\quad}\#$ $v \longrightarrow f/\underline{\quad}\#$
$d \longrightarrow t/\underline{\quad}\#$ $z \longrightarrow s/\underline{\quad}\#$
$g \longrightarrow k/\underline{\quad}\#$ $ž \longrightarrow š/\underline{\quad}\#$

We argued that (6) was the correct description because it treated all the alternations as being manifestations of a single underlying process, while the description in (7) claims in effect that the rules of (7) do not bear any special relationship to each other. The various pieces of evidence we cited all pointed to the underlying unity of the $b\sim p$, $d\sim t$, etc. alternations and hence to the correctness of (6) versus (7).

As we have explicated the theory of phonology to this point, however, both descriptions (6) and (7) are possible; there is nothing in the theory of grammar that would force us to choose (6) and reject (7) as the appropriate description of the voicing alternation in Russian. The problem is somehow to amend the theory so that it follows as a consequence of the theory that (6) and not (7) is the correct solution.

Initially, there seem to be two possible approaches to the problem. One would be to constrain the theory of phonology in such a way that only certain rules could be formulated in constructing grammars for individual languages. In the present instance this does not seem too promising, since it would require claiming that a rule that devoiced just *b* in final position is not a possible rule. But this claim is probably incorrect. In many dialects of Byelorussian and Ukrainian the gradual spread of the final-devoicing process, which reached completion long ago in most of the other Slavic languages, has been observed in progress for over a century. According to Andersen (1972:16), "in some localities, /b/ is subject to devoicing earlier than /d/, while in others the reverse is true." Since many of these dialects have no *g*, and since the data appear to indicate that stops tend to devoice earlier than fricatives, it is entirely possible that there could be a dialect where only *b* devoices. Hence it would appear that we cannot rule out the description of (7) by constraining the theory of phonology so that the rules of (7) are excluded as possible rules of grammar.

Early in the development of generative phonology a rather different approach to the problem was taken. Instead of attempting to exclude certain rules altogether, a criterion of appropriateness was proposed to evaluate alternative analyses of the same body of data. The criterion developed was brevity or conciseness, measured by the number of feature specifications contained in the alternative grammars. If phonological theory incorporates condition (8) on grammars, the analysis embodied in (6) will be selected since it contains fewer feature specifications than that in (7).

(8)   CONCISENESS CONDITION: *If there is more than one possible grammar that can be constructed for a given body of data, choose the grammar that is most concise in terms of the number of feature specifications.*

We are now in a position to see why the definition of distinctness and the condition on rule application developed above play more than a mere technical role. It is by virtue of these that we can specify uniquely the class of segments undergoing the final-devoicing process by just mentioning the features [−sonorant] and [+voice], and therefore do not have to say anything about whether the segment is a dental, a stop, or whatever. Also, the second clause of the rule-application convention permits us just to mention [−voice] in the structural change of the rule. In other words these conventions make it possible to formulate a rule that generalizes to all voiced obstruents, rather than having to write separate rules for each sound that obeys the rule. Given the conciseness condition, it is this formulation of the rule that must be selected instead of a set of rules like (7).

The conciseness condition actually has the effect of requiring that the final-devoicing rule be expressed as in (9).

(9) $\qquad$ [−sonorant] $\longrightarrow$ [−voice]/_____ #

That is, it is not necessary to specify the segments that undergo the rule as [+voice], since even if the rule applies to voiceless obstruents the correct phonetic shapes will result (voiceless obstruents will simply remain voiceless in final position).

When rules are formulated as concisely as possible, they will frequently make claims that go beyond the data on which they are originally based. For example, the underlying obstruent system of Russian lacks voiced counterparts to the voiceless affricates /c/ and /č/ and to the voiceless fricative /x/.

(10)

Stops	p,b	t,d		k,g
Affr.		c	č	
Fric.	f,v	s,z	š,ž	x

The final-devoicing rule formulated in (9) claims, in effect, that if the segments /ǰ/ and /dz/ did appear in the Russian obstruent system, they would devoice word-finally just as /b/, /d/, etc., do. Notice that the final-devoicing rule would have to be complicated considerably if it were to be written so as to specifically exclude /ǰ/ and /dz/. Sometimes it is possible to verify such claims. Recall from our discussion in Chapter 3 that Russian speakers tend to devoice word final obstruents when learning English, one of the characteristics of a Russian accent. Such speakers not only tend to pronounce *Bob* as [bɔp] but also render words like *badge* and *judge* with a final *č* even after they have learned to pronounce *ǰ* in nonfinal position. This suggests that the final devoicing rule applies to the class of obstruents as a whole and that the Russian speaker will apply this rule to any sound that possesses the feature [−sonorant].

Although the conciseness condition makes the correct predictions in many cases, there are numerous other circumstances in which it makes the wrong claims if it is followed literally. For example, one can often take illegitimate advantage of gaps in the sound inventory of a language to generalize a rule vacuously. Consider a hypothetical language having the consonant system of (11).

(11) $\qquad\qquad\qquad$ t $\quad$ k
$\qquad\qquad\qquad\quad$ f $\quad$ s
$\qquad\qquad\qquad$ m $\quad$ n
$\qquad\qquad\qquad\qquad$ l

Assume this language has a rule palatalizing *t* to *č* before *i*. This process can be formulated as (12).

(12) $\quad \begin{bmatrix} -\text{contin} \\ -\text{voice} \\ +\text{coron} \\ +\text{anter} \end{bmatrix} \longrightarrow \begin{bmatrix} -\text{anter} \\ +\text{del rel} \end{bmatrix} / \underline{\qquad} \begin{bmatrix} +\text{syll} \\ +\text{high} \\ -\text{back} \end{bmatrix}$

However, since the language lacks /p/ (12) could be simplified by eliminating the [+coronal] specification. If the conciseness condition is followed literally this is the formulation that must be given. However, in this case such simplification of the rule is a mere trick made possible by the fortuitous gap in the sound inventory of the language. Furthermore, this analysis claims that if the language were to acquire a /p/ it would shift to *č* just as /t/ does. But this is very unlikely. Many languages possessing (12) have /p/ in their consonant inventory. To our knowledge none of these languages shift /p/ to the palatal point of articulation. Since the tongue is not involved in the production of /p/ there is no reason to expect a following high front vowel to alter this consonant's basic point of articulation. Note that /d/ is also missing from the inventory of (11). Thus, (12) could also be simplified by not mentioning [−voice]. This simplification of the rule is much more reasonable. Most languages that palatalize *t* to *č* will also change *d* to *ǰ* if the voiced dental stop appears in their segmental inventory. The tendency for a change of *d* to *ǰ* to accompany the change of *t* to *č* has a clear phonetic motivation: dental stops assimilating the point of articulation of the following vowel.

Reflection on these two different examples of rule generalization suggest that it is not conciseness per se that is involved in giving the correct formulation of a phonological rule. Rather, it is a complex and little-understood set of considerations commonly referred to as rule naturalness or optimality. Many phonological rules belong to sets or families that have an optimal, or most natural, form. It is this optimal form that occurs most frequently in the languages of the world, that languages tend to gravitate toward in historical evolution, that is sometimes revealed in loanword adaptation. In many cases the optimal form of a rule will also be rather concise formally, for the simple reason that optimal rules refer to natural classes of sounds. However, it must be emphasized that the size of the class and the members composing it are strictly relative to particular rules and processes. Thus rules of final devoicing characteristically refer to the rather large class of obstruents, while rules shifting consonants to the palatal point of articulation before *i* characteristically refer to the smaller class that includes dentals (and often velars) but excludes labials. If it is true that the most appropriate description (consistent with the data of the language) is the most natural one, then it will not be sufficient simply to require phonological theory to select the most concise rule. Rather, the concept of naturalness must be made explicit and somehow employed in the selection of the most appropriate description. However, for purposes of the present chapter we will ignore this problem, since most of the notational devices discussed here were developed before the distinction between conciseness and naturalness was made explicit.

Abbreviatory Devices—An Overview

In the previous section we showed that the feature notation, in conjunction with the convention on rule application, permitted the various manifestations of final devoicing in Russian to be implemented by the same basic rule. Generative phonology has claimed that there are a number of other circumstances in which different feature changes must be viewed as manifestations of a unitary process, but where the feature notation alone does not permit this unity to be reflected in the grammar. In order to reflect this underlying unity, various notational conventions have been developed to permit different manifestations of the same underlying process to be expressed as a single rule or rule schema. Before reviewing these conventions in more detail it would be profitable to briefly consider the motivations lying behind this general approach. An excellent example was brought up by Kiparsky (1968b). In Old English vowels were shortened before three or more consonants: *go:dspell* ⟶ *godspell* 'gospel', *brä:mblas* ⟶ *brämblas* 'brambles'. In addition, Old English vowels were shortened when they stood in the antepenultimate syllable, provided they were followed by two consonants: *ble:dsian* ⟶ *bledsian* 'bless'. The rules responsible for these shortenings would be (13) and (14).

(13) $V \longrightarrow [-\text{long}] / \underline{\quad} CCC$

(14) $V \longrightarrow [-\text{long}] / \underline{\quad} CCVC_0VC_0\#$

In Early Middle English long vowels were shortened when they stood before two consonants (*hu:sband* ⟶ *husband*) or when they appeared before a single consonant in the third syllable from the end of the word (*sti:ropes* ⟶ stiropes 'stirrups', *divi:nity* ⟶ *divinity*). Examples (15) and (16) express these two shortening rules.

(15) $V \longrightarrow [-long]/\underline{\quad}CC$

(16) $V \longrightarrow [-long]/\underline{\quad}CVC_0VC_0 \#$

Kiparsky observed that rule (15) can be considered a simplification of rule (13), shortening a long vowel before two consonants rather than requiring three. The only difference between (13) and (15) is that the former requires one additional consonant to follow the vowel being shortened. Notice that rule (14) is related to (16) in the same way: the former rule requires one more consonant to follow the long vowel than does the latter rule. Evidently, then, the linguistic change from Old English to Middle English consists of the simplification of the Old English rules (13) and (14) by deletion of one of the members of the consonant cluster in their environment.

Kiparsky also pointed out that these linguistic changes occurred at exactly the same point in the historical development of English. This strongly suggests that there is some linguistically significant connection between rules (13) and (14). Otherwise, it would have to be claimed to be a complete accident that both rules changed in exactly the same way (by loss of a consonant from their environments) at the same time.

As Kiparsky (1968b) points out, the relationship between (13) and (14) could be expressed in terms of the abbreviatory device of braces, which collapses two rules into one schema by factoring out common features and enclosing the differences inside braces. The brace notation would permit these rules to be expressed as (17).

(17) $V \longrightarrow [-long]/\underline{\quad}C\ C \begin{Bmatrix} C \\ VC_0\ V\ C_0\ \# \end{Bmatrix}$

Given the brace notation, the conciseness condition would force the selection of the grammar containing (17) over a grammar that contains (13) and (14) stated as separate rules. A principled explanation is now available for why shortening before two consonants occurred at the same time as shortening before a single consonant in the antepenultimate syllable, if we say that the diachronic change was defined over the abbreviated schema (17). Loss of the initial consonant from the SD of (17) means that both shortening rules will be changed simultaneously. The resultant schema (18) abbreviates the Middle English rules (15) and (16).

(18) $\qquad V \longrightarrow [-\text{long}]/\underline{\hspace{1em}}C \left\{ \begin{array}{l} C \\ V C_0 \ V \ C_0 \ \# \end{array} \right\}$

The preceding example indicates that two rules may differ in certain significant respects but still represent phenomena that the native speaker tacitly knows to be in some sense the same. Although (13) and (14) are obviously distinct rules, still it appears that speakers of English regarded them as sufficiently the same to be altered in precisely the same way at the same point in time. This being the case, it is appropriate to seek notational conventions that will allow us to characterize such cases.

Before discussing the major notational conventions that have been employed in generative phonology, let us briefly sketch the general position taken by SPE on this matter, since many of these conventions were originally developed in this work and most subsequent emendations have remained within the general framework outlined in SPE. First, as we have seen, the purpose of these notational conventions is to express linguistically significant relationships between phonological rules which cannot be captured by the feature notation alone. (The difficult and important question of how it can be determined whether a relationship is linguistically significant will be discussed in more detail later. Obviously, evidence from linguistic change, such as the Old English example just discussed, is one important source.) Second, these devices are viewed as a means for collapsing two or more rules into a single schema on the basis of formal properties shared by the rules. Third, in order for two rules to be collapsed together they must be adjacently ordered—they must have the same ordering relations with all the other rules of the grammar. Presumably, if two rules have different ordering relations, according to SPE this would constitute evidence that they are not part of an underlying unitary process.

Finally, SPE makes a distinction between elementary rules and schemata. Elementary rules are simple context-sensitive phonological rules of the form $A \longrightarrow B/C \underline{\hspace{1em}} D$. They do not contain any auxiliary notations such as braces, parentheses, C_0, etc. According to SPE all feature changes in the grammar are implemented by elementary rules. Schemata, which expresses linguistically significant relations between elementary rules, are obtained by employing the various notational conventions that collapse together elementary rules. It is assumed that there is a unique way to break down each schema into its constituent elementary rules and to determine the ordering relations among these subrules.

Likewise, it is hypothesized that there is a completely formal and unique way to collapse adjacent elementary rules into schemata.

In the remaining sections of this chapter we will explicate the most important notational devices that have been employed by generative phonologists. Our major point of reference will be the interpretations of these devices given in SPE, which represents the standard theory of generative phonology. Where appropriate, we shall discuss interpretations given by other linguists that are different from the standard interpretation.

The Parenthesis Notation

Earlier a formalism was introduced for rules in which the segment(s) triggering the rule were adjacent to the segment undergoing the rule. There are, however, many cases in which the triggering segment may be separated from the element undergoing the rule by intervening material. For example, the following data from Karok (Bright 1957) evidence a rule palatalizing /s/ to *š* when *i* precedes.

(19)

3 sg.	1 sg.	Gloss
ʔu-skak	*ni-škak*	'jump'
ʔu-suprih	*ni-šuprih*	'measure'
ʔu-si:tva	*ni-ši:tva*	'steal'

'His' noun	'My' noun	Gloss
mu-sipnu:kiθ	*nani-šipnu:kiθ*	'money basket'
mu-sara	*nani-šara*	'bread'
mu-sva:k	*nani-šva:k*	'chin'

These data could be handled by the rule in (20).

(20)   s ⟶ š/i___

However, this rule will not account for the following forms.

(21)   *ʔu-ksah*   *ni-kšah*   'laugh'
             ʔu-ksup   *ni-kšup*   'point'
             mu-psi:h   *nani-pši:h*   'leg'

The preceding data could be accounted for by postulating a new rule (22).

(22) $s \longrightarrow \check{s}/iC\_\_\_$

According to (22) basic /s/ palatalizes to /š/ if preceded by a consonant that is in turn preceded by *i*. But to formulate (20) and (22) as separate processes misses the point that all of the data considered are instances of the same generalization: /s/ palatalizes after *i* whether or not a consonant intervenes. If we accept the claim that one requirement of an adequate theory of phonology is that it provide a formal characterization of unitary phenomena, some expansion of the theoretical apparatus is required so that (20) and (22) can be characterized as a single process.

  Before introducing the required extension of phonological theory, we will briefly consider one kind of evidence that helps to establish that a single process underlies a given range of data. The similarities between (20) and (22)—in terms of the structures on which they operate and the changes they implement—are so great that there is little room for doubting that a single unitary process is involved. There are, however, cases where the similarities are less striking and the basic unity less obvious.

  Sameness of restrictions on the operation of rules, especially idiosyncratic restrictions, provides prima facie evidence of underlying unity. For example, some speakers of Karok do not apply rule (20) across the boundary separating possessive prefixes from a following noun stem. Thus, where some speakers use *mu-sipnūkiθ* 'his money basket', but *nani-šipnūkiθ* 'my money basket', other speakers retain /s/ in both forms. If rule (22) is actually the same as rule (20), we would expect speakers who fail to palatalize /s/ when it immediately follows the possessive prefixes also to fail to palatalize /s/ when a consonant intervenes between the /s/ and the /i/ of the prefix. And this is just what we find; such speakers say *nani-psih* rather than *nani-pših* 'my leg.'

  Dissimilar processes are sometimes restricted similarly (e.g., a certain syntactic class of affixes like the possessive prefixes in Karok may behave exceptionally with respect to a large number of varied rules). But given a certain degree of structural similarity, along with similar restrictions on the scope of their application, we have some reason to believe that the rules are manifestations of the same process.

  Returning to the question of how to characterize (20) and (22) as part of the same process, observe that the basic requirement is that the vowel *i* precede /s/; a consonant may or may not intervene. Thus, what is required is some way to express optionally intervening material. In generative phonology this has been done by enclosing such material within parentheses. This notation permits palatalization in Karok to be expressed as (23).

(23) $s \longrightarrow \check{s}/i(C)\_\_\_$

This rule will be interpreted as operating on two classes of structures: one where /s/ is immediately preceded by *i*, the other where a consonant intervenes. More generally, we stipulate that a rule of the form A ⟶ B/___(C)D will be interpreted as operating on strings of the form AD and ACD, and a rule of the form A ⟶ B/C(D)___ is interpreted as operating on strings of the form CA and CDA.

The process of syncope in the Mecayapan, Veracruz dialect of Isthmus Nahuat (Law 1958) is a rather different case that also illustrates the need for a device to represent intervening material. In this language short unstressed vowels are optionally dropped in the environment VR___#, where R is a cover symbol for the class of resonants (nasals, liquids, and glides). The operation of this process is illustrated in (24).

(24)

šikakíli ∼ šikakíl	'put it in it'
kítaya ∼ kítay	'he already sees it'
kikówa ∼ kików	'he buys it'
támi ∼ tám	'it ends'

The unstressed vowel that syncopates is not, however, always in word-final position; a glottal stop or /h/ may intervene between the vowel and the word boundary:

(25)

kikówaʔ ∼ kikówʔ	'he bought it'
támiʔ ∼ támʔ	'it ended'
ḍayá:niʔ ∼ cayá:nʔ	'it split'
tómaʔ ∼ tómʔ	'tomato'
nikakílih ∼ nikakị̄	'I put it in it'
kikówah ∼ kikóW	'they buy it'
kámoh ∼ káM	'sweet potato'
akánah ∼ akáN	'nowhere'

Note that an *R-h* sequence resulting from syncope is realized as a voiceless resonant.

Once again, without a device to handle intervening material the two contexts of syncope would have to be described by different rules (in the informal statement of these rules V̌ is a cover symbol for short unstressed vowels and R represents the class of resonants).

(26)   V̌ ⟶ ∅/VR___ #

(27)   V̌ ⟶ ∅/VR ___ [ʔ,h]#

But the formal similarity, as well as the fact that both rules are optional, forces us to recognize a linguistically significant relationship between the two. With the parenthesis notation both instances of syncope can be formulated as following from the same underlying rule.

(28) $\qquad \check{V} \longrightarrow \emptyset/VR \underline{\qquad} ([?,h]) \ \#$

Within the SPE framework the parenthesis notation is given a rather different interpretation from that developed here. As noted earlier, SPE hypothesizes that all feature changes in the grammar are implemented by elementary context-sensitive rules of the form $A \longrightarrow B/C\underline{\qquad}D$ containing no auxiliary notation such as parentheses or braces. Linguistically significant relations between elementary rules are expressed by abbreviating the elementary rules into schemata. Thus, for SPE the Karok palatalization rule (29) is interpreted as a schema that abbreviates the elementary subrules (30) and (31).

(29) $\qquad s \longrightarrow \check{s}/i(C)\underline{\qquad}$

(30) $\qquad s \longrightarrow \check{s}/iC \underline{\qquad}$

(31) $\qquad s \longrightarrow \check{s}/ i \underline{\qquad}$

On the other hand, under the interpretation of the parenthesis notation developed in this book, (29) does not abbreviate (30) and (31). There is just one rule that is interpreted as applying to the strings *iCs* and *is*.

Secondly, according to SPE the subrules abbreviated by a schema containing parentheses are to be applied in a special manner which only makes sense in the light of the data that it was originally introduced to handle—the stress patterns of English words. Hence, we will turn to a brief discussion of the SPE analysis of English stress, showing how it leads to this particular interpretation of the parenthesis notation.[3]

The analysis begins with an examination of the stress patterns found in the following groups of English nouns.

(32)

A	B	C	D
América	balaláika	agénda	capríce
génesis	muséum	ellípsis	regíme
alúminum	arthrítis	amálgam	cocáine
cínnamon	propósal	galáctin	paróle

[3] We follow the exposition given in Halle and Keyser (1971) rather than that given in SPE, simply because the former is somewhat simpler. Materially the two analyses are the same.

The stress placements in each of these groups are manifestations of the following regularities that characterize the stress position for many English nouns:

(33)   a. *If the ultima is lax, stress goes on the antepenult if the penult is lax and followed by no more than one consonant.*
       b. *If the ultima is lax, stress goes on the penult if the penult is tense.*
       c. *If the ultima is lax, stress goes on the penult if the penult is followed by two or more consonants.*
       d. *If the ultima is tense, it is stressed.*

In these expressions ultima refers to the final vowel of the word, penult to the prefinal vowel, and antepenult to the pre-prefinal vowel.

Each of these regularities can be expressed in the form of the following stress-placement rules.

(34)

$$\text{A.} \quad V \longrightarrow \acute{V}/\underline{\quad} C_0 \ \breve{V} \ C_0^1 \breve{V} \ C_0 \#$$

$$\text{B.} \quad V \longrightarrow \acute{V}/ \underset{[+\text{tense}]}{\underline{\quad\quad}} C_0 \breve{V} \ C_0 \#$$

$$\text{C.} \quad V \longrightarrow \acute{V}/\underline{\quad} C_2 \breve{V} \ C_0 \#$$

$$\text{D.} \quad V \longrightarrow \acute{V}/ \underset{[+\text{tense}]}{\underline{\quad\quad}} C_0 \#$$

In these rules $\breve{V}$ is used as a cover symbol for a lax vowel. In addition, the expression C_0^1 stands for zero or one consonant, C_2 for two or more consonants, and so on.

Chomsky, Halle, and Keyser observe that a more concise statement of the rules is possible if the concept signified by the English words *elsewhere* or *otherwise* is used. Given this notion the regularities in (33) can be simplified to read as follows:

(35)   a'. *If the ultima is lax, stress goes on the antepenult if the penult is lax and followed by no more than one consonant.*
       b'. ***Otherwise***, *if the ultima is lax, stress goes on the penultimate vowel.*
       c'. ***Otherwise***, *stress goes on the ultima.*

The simplifications achieved by this statement of the regularities are as follows: First, (a) and (a') are identical. Second, (b) and (c) have been combined into (b'); in addition, mention of the condition that the penult is lax or that it be followed by two or more consonants has been eliminated. Finally, (d) has been simplified to (c') by elimination of the condition that the ultima be tense. Just as the regularities of (a)–(d) can be expressed in the form of rules of stress placement, so too (a')–(c') find their analogs in the following rules.

(36)   A'. $V \longrightarrow \acute{V}/\_\_\_C_0 \breve{V} C_0^1 \breve{V} C_0 \#$
         B'. $V \longrightarrow \acute{V}/\_\_\_C_0 \breve{V} C_0 \#$
         C'. $V \longrightarrow \acute{V}/\_\_\_C_0 \#$

In order for the rules of (36) to assign the correct stress patterns, however, two conditions must be met. First, the rules must be applied in the order (A'), (B'), (C'). For if rule (B') preceded (A') it would assign penultimate stress to a form like *America* to give /Amerîca/. Similarly, (B') must precede (C'), since the opposite order would have rule (C') assign a final stress to all words. Second, only one of the rules can apply to a given word. To see this consider once again the form *America*. Application of the first rule (A') yields the correct stress pattern *América*. But notice that, as formulated, both (B') and (C') are applicable. If applied, they would give the incorrect *Américá*. Similarly, the derivation of a form like *agenda* would proceed as follows: (A') would be inapplicable; (B') would give penultimate stress *agénda*; but (C') could then apply to yield the incorrect *agéndá*. Hence, in order to maintain the more concise statement of the rules found in (A')–(C') and still guarantee that the correct phonetic representations are generated, a way must be found to prevent rule (B') from applying if (A') has, and to prevent (C') from applying if (B') or (A') has applied.

One's first reaction to this problem might be to propose a general convention that would prevent a rule from assigning the feature [+stress] to a word that already bears a stress. However, many English words contain more than a single accented vowel. For example, three-syllable nouns with a final tense vowel generally exhibit accent on both the initial and final syllables: *húrricàne*, *báritòne*, *párachùte*. In *SPE* these words are assigned final stress by rule (C') of (36) and a subsequent rule stresses the initial syllable of three-syllable words having a final accent to give *húrricáne*. Subsidiary principles will then reduce the final accent to give *húrricàne* (see Schane 1976). If this analysis is correct, a convention barring the assignment of stress to a word that already bears a stress cannot be maintained.

In the face of these difficulties the authors simply propose that a new type of rule interaction be allowed by phonological theory—one that prevents a rule from being applied even though its SD is satisfied, so long as some other rule has applied. This kind of rule interaction is termed disjunctive ordering, in the sense that although a given word may be subject to more than one rule in a disjunctively ordered set, it will undergo just one of them.

So far in the exposition the only motivation cited for the introduction of disjunctive ordering is that it permits a simpler statement of the stress rules. But unless this simplification has some consequences, it is of no particular significance. However, the authors go on to observe that the more concise set of rules permitted by disjunctive ordering makes valid predictions about the stress patterns of words not yet considered. Two such word classes are cited. First, according to the authors, there is no necessary reason why monosyllabic nouns with a lax vowel (such as *pig*, *pen, monk, list, hut*, etc.) should bear a stress, since English has monosyllabic prepositions and auxiliaries that do not normally receive a stress. If we were providing an analysis in the style of (34), where there is a rule for every regularity, an additional rule would be required for these nouns. But they will automatically be assigned stress by the more concise analysis. Being monosyllabic, they will escape rules (36A′) and (36B′), and hence will be subject to (36C′), which places stress on the final and, in this case, only vowel of the word.

The second type of stress pattern validly predicted by these rules involves disyllabic nouns containing lax vowels and having a weak penultimate cluster: *vénom, cábin, sýrup, cólor, vómit*. Once again an analysis in the style of (34) would require another rule.

(37) $$V \longrightarrow \acute{V}/\#C_0 \underline{\hspace{1cm}} C_0 \breve{V} C_0 \#$$

But the stress pattern of these nouns is correctly assigned by the more concise analysis (36); since *vénom, cábin*, etc., do not contain three syllables and do have a lax ultima, they will go by rule (36B′).

Given the analysis embodied in the rules of (36), it appears that disjunctive ordering must be incorporated into phonological theory. It would, of course, be desirable if this type of rule interaction could be predicted on the basis of the formal properties displayed by the rules. In this regard, Chomsky, Halle, and Keyser pointed out the following relationship between the rules of (36): It is possible to obtain a later rule in the set from an earlier rule by blocking out a portion of the earlier rule. Thus, (B′) can be derived from (A′) by deleting the expression $\breve{V}C_0^1$ and (C′) can be derived from (B′) by deletion of $\breve{V}C_0$. SPE thus hypothesized that any two adjacently ordered rules displaying this formal property will be disjunctively ordered. In accord with the general SPE program for the expression of linguistically significant relationships between elementary rules, an abbreviatory notation must be devised to permit such rules to be collapsed into a single schema. The notation adopted was parentheses. Thus, two elementary rules related by this formal property are collapsed together by enclosing in parentheses the material that yields the later (shorter) rule. Thus, (A') and (B') will be collapsed into the schema of (38) by parenthesizing the expression $\breve{V}C_0^1$.

(38) $\qquad V \longrightarrow \acute{V}/\underline{\quad}C_0\ (\breve{V}C_0^1)\breve{V}C_0\#$

Similarly, (38) will be collapsed with (C') by enclosing $(\breve{V}C_0^1)\breve{V}C$ in parentheses to yield (39).

(39) $\qquad V \longrightarrow \acute{V}/\underline{\quad}C_0\ ((\breve{V}C_0^1)\breve{V}C_0)\#$

The SPE position is thus that any two adjacently ordered elementary rules that can be abbreviated by the parentheses notation will be disjunctively ordered, so that if a given sequence of sounds undergoes the "longer" rule in a disjunctively ordered set it will be barred from undergoing the "shorter" rule. Subsequent research has shown that this claim is too strong. First of all, not all rules abbreviable by parentheses can be disjunctively ordered. Recall, for example, the Karok rule palatalizing *s* to *š* in the context i(C)____. According to the SPE position, this rule would be interpreted as abbreviating two disjunctively ordered elementary rules: one palatalizing *s* to *š* in the context iC____ and the other in the context i____. If a string of sounds happened to meet the SD of both rules, the second would have to be skipped. This prediction is falsified by examples like *ʔiššaha* 'water'. Recall that *s* and *š* do not contrast in underlying representation. All occurrences of *š* can be derived from *s* by the palatalization rule. If the input to the palatalization rules in the derivation of *ʔiššaha* is /ʔissaha/, application of the first subrule in the context iC____ will yield /ʔisšaha/. However, since the subrules are disjunctively ordered, the second rule applying in the context i____ would have to be skipped and the incorrect **ʔisšaha* would be derived.

It should be pointed out that this example could be made consistent with the SPE position by taking advantage of the fact that geminate consonants are predictable in Karok: They occur intervocalically after a short accented vowel. Disjunctive ordering of palatalization could be retained by simply ordering gemination after palatalization. However, we see no reason why the palatalization rule should not affect both *s*'s. If the input to the rule is /iss/ the SPE position would make the phonetically implausible prediction that palatalization would only affect the *s* that is furthest removed from the high front vowel. But in general such assimilation rules will affect consonants that are closer to the vowel. Thus, while this example is not as strong as one would like, it does point up the difficulties that can arise with the claim that all rules abbreviable by parentheses are disjunctively ordered.

There are also difficulties with the claim that the parenthesis notation will adequately define the cases where disjunctive ordering is required. For example, in colloquial Egyptian Arabic (Mitchell 1956) stress is assigned in accord with the following principles. If the last syllable is heavy (contains a long vowel or ends in a consonant cluster), it takes the stress. If the last syllable is light and the penult is heavy, the penult takes the accent. If the last two syllables are light and the antepenult is also light, stress is placed on the antepenult if it is the first syllable of the word or if it is preceded by a heavy syllable. But if the last two syllables are light and either the antepenult is heavy or the antepenult is preceded by a light syllable, then the penult is stressed.

(40)
i) mafhúum 'understood', fanagíin 'cups', ḍarábt 'I/you hit'
ii) qáabil 'he met', muʕállim 'teacher', fihmúuha 'they understood her', dáawa 'he cured', qaahíra 'Cairo', ʕaadátan 'usually'
iii) kátabit 'she wrote', ʔinkásarit 'it f. was broken'
iv) maknása 'broom', mahiyyíti 'my pay', ḍarabítu(h) 'she hit him'

The following set of rules will assign the stress correctly, if they are applied disjunctively.

(41) A. $V \longrightarrow \acute{V} / \left\{ \begin{matrix} \#C_0 \\ VCC \end{matrix} \right\} \underline{\hspace{1cm}} [-long] \; C_0 \check{V} C_0^1 \check{V} C_0^1 \#$

B. $V \longrightarrow \acute{V} / \underline{\hspace{1cm}} C_0 \check{V} C_0^1 \#$

C. $V \longrightarrow \acute{V} / \underline{\hspace{1cm}} C_0 \#$

However, observe that while (B) and (C) can be collapsed together by parenthesization of $\check{V}C_0^1$, neither (B) nor (C) can be collapsed with (A). (A) allows just a single consonant after the stressed vowel, while (B) and (C) require C_0. Furthermore, while (B) and (C) will assign stress to a vowel regardless of its length, case (A) requires the vowel to be short if it is to be stressed. In sum, later rules in the set cannot be derived from earlier ones by enclosing material in parentheses. Nevertheless disjunctive ordering is clearly required since only one of the rules may apply to any given word.

In Kiparsky (1973) an alternative approach to the prediction of disjunctive ordering is proposed. Instead of abbreviability by parentheses, Kiparsky suggests that a pair of rules will exhibit disjunctive ordering if the set of strings that meet the SD of the earlier rule is a subset of the set of strings that meet the SD of the later rule. This inclusion relationship clearly obtains among the subrules of (36) that assign stress to English nouns. Case (36C′) denotes the set of all nouns and thus includes case (36B′) which defines the set of nouns whose final syllable contains a lax vowel. Similarly, the set denoted by case (36B′) includes the set defined by case (36A′)—the set of nouns whose final syllable contains a lax vowel and whose penult is light. A similar inclusion relationship obtains among the stress rules of (41) for Colloquial Egyptian Arabic. Case (41C) obviously includes (41B). And case (41B), the set of words whose final syllable is light, includes case (41A)—the set of words whose last three syllables are light and preceded by a word boundary or a heavy syllable. The subset principle adduced by Kiparsky also correctly fails to predict disjunctive ordering in the Karok example. The set of strings that satisfy the expression *iCs* is not included in the set denoted by *is*.

It appears to us, then, that Kiparsky's approach to the problem of characterizing which rules in a grammar will be disjunctively ordered with respect to one another has a better chance of being correct (or of leading us closer to the correct answer) than the purely formal approach of Chomsky, Halle, and Keyser. Thus we will continue to use the parentheses notation to cover situations where certain material is optionally present (as in the Karok and Isthmus Nahuat examples earlier in this section) but not necessarily present for a rule's application. Furthermore, it seems to us invalid to consider rule (29) a schema abbreviating two elementary rules (30) and (31). Our objection to this is that rule (30)—which says that *s* is palatalized just in case it is preceded by the sequence *iC*—is not a rule in its own right. That is to say, we seriously doubt that one would find a language that palatalized *s* after *iC* but did not palatalize *s* when immediately preceded by *i*. We believe that the concept of "elementary" rule ought to be reserved for a rule that has some independent status as a possible rule of grammar.

It should be observed, however, that the stress rules of (36)—which can be collapsed into rule (39) by the use of parentheses—do appear to represent a case of several distinct elementary rules. For example, (36C′) would be the stress rule for a language that uniformly assigns stress to the last vowel of a word. Although (36B′) would not very likely be the only stress rule in a language (since it would fail to assign stress to monosyllables and to words whose last vowel is long), it could be one of a set of stress rules whose character would not necessarily be at all related to (36A′) and (36C′). In other words, it is not the case that one of the stress rules of (36) necessarily implies the other, the way that (30) implies (31). The function of the parentheses in (39) thus seems to us rather different from the function of the parentheses in the Karok rule (29).

Given this difference in function, perhaps the simplest step to take would be to introduce a distinct notation for collapsing the stress rules of (36) into (39). If, however, parentheses are to continue to be used to characterize both palatalization in Karok and the stress rules of English, it will be necessary to characterize precisely under what conditions parentheses are to be regarded as a means of indicating irrelevant intervening material and when they are a device for abbreviating a set of elementary rules. Perhaps the determination is simply made on the following basis: In order for parentheses to represent an abbreviated set of elementary rules, this set must be of a character that requires disjunctive ordering. (Assuming that some such principle as that proposed by Kiparsky can provide an exhaustive characterization of what rules are disjunctively ordered.) Given this principle, the rule of palatalization in Karok given as (29) could not be viewed as an abbreviation for the two rules (30) and (31), since the latter pair of rules are not of the type that requires disjunctive ordering.

Since most linguists use the parentheses notation in the double function sketched above, we will continue this practice here.

Angled Brackets

In this section we examine the uses of the angled bracket notation. One essential use of this notation is to express certain dependencies between noncontiguous parts of the SD of a rule. It was originally introduced in SPE to state the relationship between the stress rule for nouns and that for verbs and adjectives. The data in (42) suggest that penultimate stress is assigned to a verb or adjective if the final syllable is light (contains a lax vowel and ends in a single consonant). Otherwise final stress occurs.

(42)

astónish	*maintáin*	*eléct*
édit	*caréen*	*lamént*
detérmine	*devóte*	*usúrp*
cáncel	*surmíse*	*collápse*
elícit	*pursúe*	*convínce*
frántic	*ináne*	*diréct*
vúlgar	*supréme*	*succínct*
cómmon	*remóte*	*absúrd*
hándsome	*secúre*	*corrúpt*
sólid	*discréet*	*imménse*

Employing the parenthesis notation with disjunctive ordering, these stress patterns can be assigned by the following schema:

(43) $\qquad$ $V \longrightarrow \acute{V}/\underline{\quad}C_0(\breve{V}C_0^1)\#]$

$\qquad\qquad\qquad\qquad$ V, Adj

This schema is quite similar to the one assigning stress in nouns, which we repeat here as (44).

(44)
$$V \longrightarrow \acute{V}/\underline{\quad} C_0((\check{V}C_0^1)\check{V}C_0)\#]_N$$

If we ignore for the moment the references in (43) and (44) to the word categories noun, verb, and adjective, then it is obvious that (43) can be derived from (44) by the omission of the $\check{V}C_0$ appearing at the end of (44). Thus, there is a correlation between the material $\check{V}C_0$ and the information that the constituent undergoing the rule is a noun. Now notice that rule (44) is longer than (43); if the two rules were disjunctively ordered, any form that undergoes (44) would be barred from undergoing (43). Thus there would be no need to restrict (43) so as to apply just to verbs and adjectives; the rule could be generalized so that no reference to syntactic category is required. We can then replace (43) by (45).

(45)
$$V \longrightarrow \acute{V}/\underline{\quad} C_0 (\check{V}C_0^1)\#$$

Now we can collapse (44) and (45) by means of the angled bracket notation, where angled brackets are used to enclose the two discontinuous parts of (44) that differ from (45), namely, the $\check{V}C_0$ at the end of the word and the syntactic category noun. The abbreviated rule is given below as (46).

(46)
$$V \longrightarrow \acute{V}/\underline{\quad} C_0((\check{V}C_0^1) \langle\check{V}C_0\rangle)\#]_{\langle N\rangle}$$

SPE interprets any schema with angled brackets as abbreviating a pair of disjunctively ordered elementary rules, the first of which includes the material inside the angled brackets while the second lacks this material. If the longer rule applies to a string, the shorter rule may not. The disjunctive ordering associated with angled brackets is quite natural from the point of view of the general theory of SPE, since angled brackets are in effect a special type of parenthesis notation, which, as we have seen, SPE interprets as imposing disjunctive ordering. But notice that Kiparsky's principle for determining what rules are disjunctively ordered will likewise predict that (44) and (45) are disjunctively ordered. For any string that meets the conditions for (44) will also meet the conditions for (45), but not vice versa (since any word that is an adjective or a verb would not satisfy the condition on (44) that it applies only to nouns).

Angled brackets function like paired parentheses in symbolic logic to express discontinuous dependencies (i.e., some material is included in an expression if and only if some nonadjacent material is also present). If there is such a dependency relation between two contiguous pieces of information, both are included in parentheses (rather than angled brackets). In the English stress example, the two dependent parts of the expression were a sequence of sounds on the one hand and membership in a certain syntactic category on the other hand. The dependent parts may, of course, both be sequences of sounds or even feature specifications of sounds. Furthermore, it is not always the case that both dependent parts are in the structural description of the rule. It may be the case that a certain aspect of the structural change of a rule will be dependent upon certain other material occurring in the structural description. For example, in Old High German vowels were fronted when the following syllable contained an /i/: *wurmi* ⟶ *wörmi* 'worms'; *ta:ti* ⟶ *tä:ti* 'deeds'; *noti* ⟶ *nöti* 'needs'. But when a short *a* was fronted it was specified [−low] in addition to [−back]. Thus *slagi* ⟶ *slegi* 'strokes'; *gasti* ⟶ *gesti* 'guests'. Hence, all vowels were fronted, but only short (and not long) *a* was raised to a mid vowel.

Without a device like the angled-bracket notation, there are two ways these data can be described. First, a general umlaut rule can be formulated to specify all vowels as [−back] when an *i* follows in the next syllable. This fronts short *a* to short *ä*. A subsequent rule will then raise short *ä* to *e*. However, this latter rule is possible only if one can formulate the raising rule so that it applies to just those *ä*s that result from the umlaut rule. If *ä*s from a source other than the umlaut rule occur in the umlauting environment and do not raise to *e*, it would not be possible to adopt this treatment in which we send *a* to *ä* and then later raise the *ä* to *e*.

Under the second analysis, we would have to break down the umlauting process into two rules: one that applies to the short *a* and then a later more general rule to handle the umlauting of the remaining vowels. This implies an analysis with two rules:

(47)
$$\begin{bmatrix} +\text{syll} \\ +\text{low} \\ +\text{back} \\ -\text{long} \end{bmatrix} \longrightarrow \begin{bmatrix} -\text{back} \\ -\text{low} \end{bmatrix} \quad /\underline{\quad}C_1 i$$

(48)
$$[\ +\text{syll}] \longrightarrow [-\text{back}] \quad /\underline{\quad}C_1 i$$

These two rules are connected with one another in a linguistically significant way: Both front a vowel in the same context. The only difference is that (47) also specifies its vowel as [−low], while (48) does not. Hence, we have prima facie evidence for collapsing these two rules together into one schema expressing the connection between them. Notice that the angled-bracket notation can be employed here, since formally (47) differs from (48) in that the former contains two discontinuous pieces of information (the specifications [+low, +back, −long] and [−low]) that are lacking in the latter. Hence, with the help of this notation (47) and (48) can be collapsed into a single schema by enclosing inside paired angled brackets the information present in (47) that is lacking in (48).

(49)
$$
\begin{bmatrix} +\text{syll} \\ \left\langle \begin{matrix} +\text{low} \\ +\text{back} \end{matrix} \right\rangle \\ -\text{long} \end{bmatrix}
\longrightarrow
\begin{bmatrix} -\text{back} \\ \langle -\text{low} \rangle \end{bmatrix} / \underline{\quad} C_1 i
$$

Given the SPE conventions for the expansion of schemata abbreviated with the angled-brackets notation, (49) abbreviates the disjunctively ordered set of rules (47) and (48). Notice that the motivation for disjunctive ordering of (47) and (48) is not as strong as in the case of the English stress rules. It is necessary that the longer rule (47) applies first so that it can convert /a/ to /e/; if (48) were applied first, it would convert /a/ to /ä/ and this /ä/ would then be unable to undergo (47), since the latter rule applies only to back vowels. Thus the ordering of (48) before (47) results incorrectly in /ä/ rather than /e/. Notice, however, that once (47) has applied to change /a/ to /e/, there is no possibility that (48) can now apply. Even if it did apply, it would just redundantly specify /e/ as a nonback vowel. The situation is thus quite different from the English stress rules, where if there were no disjunctive ordering, both the longer and the shorter stress rules would apply (incorrectly).

The crucial factor, then, is that the longer rule be applied before the shorter rule in the case of rules like (47) and (48). Disjunctive ordering achieves that result. Although SPE attributes this method of applying (47) and (48) to the fact that they can be abbreviated by the angled-brackets notation, it should be pointed out that Kiparsky's suggested principle will also make the same prediction. Clearly, the SD of (47) designates a set of strings that is properly included within the set of strings designated by (48). Thus Kiparsky's proposal will require (47) to apply first; and once it applies, (48) will be barred from applying. It is not clear, of course, that preventing (48) from trying to apply has any significance, since the structure resulting from (47) will not meet the SD of (48) in any case.

Let us return now to the problem of motivating a rule such as (49), with its angled brackets, as opposed to an analysis like the one suggested earlier which would postulate a general vowel fronting rule and then a second rule that raises /ä/ to /e/. The facts at our disposal about Old High German do not permit us to determine whether the problem arises of distinguishing *ä*s formed by the umlaut process from other sources. An example from Polish shows, however, that this difficulty can occur.

In Polish there is a palatalization rule operating in certain morphological contexts that converts the underlying velar consonants *k, g,* and *x* into *c, dz,* and *š,* respectively; here *c* and *dz* represent voiceless and voiced dental affricates, while *š* is a voiceless alveo-palatal fricative.

(50)

Nom. sg.	Loc. sg.	Gloss
reŋka	*rence*	'hand'
noga	*nodze*	'leg'
muxa	*muše*	'fly'

The problem here is that the velar stops become dental [+anterior], while the velar fricative shows up as a palatal [−anterior]. In the analysis of these data it would not be possible to palatalize all of the velars to strident dentals first (that is, take *k, g,* and *x* to *c, dz,* and *s*) and then follow this up with a rule taking *s* to *š*, because there are underlying *s*s that occur in this context, and they do not show up as *š* (*kosa, kose*[4] 'scythe'); only underlying *x* appears as *š*. Nor could we palatalize velars to the alveopalatal series *č, ǰ,* and *š* and then later shift *č* and *ǰ* to their [+anterior] counterparts *c* and *dz,* since *č* and *ǰ* also appear as underlying phonemes in Polish. If recourse is made to the angled bracket notation, the palatalization process can be broken down into two subrules: The first (51) will shift *k* and *g* to *c* and *dz,* while the second (52) will take the remaining velar fricative *x* to *š*.

(51)

$$\begin{bmatrix} +\text{cons} \\ +\text{back} \\ -\text{contin} \end{bmatrix} \longrightarrow \begin{bmatrix} -\text{back} \\ +\text{coron} \\ +\text{anter} \\ +\text{del rel} \end{bmatrix} / \underline{\quad} + e \\ [\text{loc sg}]$$

(52)

$$\begin{bmatrix} +\text{cons} \\ +\text{back} \end{bmatrix} \longrightarrow \begin{bmatrix} -\text{back} \\ +\text{coron} \end{bmatrix} / \underline{\quad} + e \\ [\text{loc sg}]$$

Note that (51) differs from (52) in that the former contains two discontinuous pieces of information (the [−contin] and the [+anter] specifications) lacking in the latter. Hence these two rules can be collapsed into the schema (53) by enclosing these two pieces of information inside angled brackets.

---

[4] The *s* of *kose* becomes palatalized [+high] but remains dental (i.e., does not shift to the alveopalatal point of articulation) by a later rule.

(53)
$$\begin{bmatrix} +\text{cons} \\ +\text{back} \\ \langle -\text{contin}\rangle \end{bmatrix} \longrightarrow \begin{bmatrix} -\text{back} \\ +\text{coron} \\ \langle +\text{anter}\rangle \\ +\text{del rel} \end{bmatrix} / \underline{\hspace{1cm}} + \begin{matrix} e \\ [\text{loc sg}] \end{matrix}$$

It is necessary, of course, that the subrule (51) apply first to take k and g to c and dz, respectively. If (52) were applied first, k and g would be specified as [−back, +coron]; as a result of having been assigned the property [−back], these sounds would then fail to undergo rule (51). The result is that we fail to derive the correct sounds c and dz. The correct ordering of (51) and (52) can be obtained as a consequence of the principle of disjunctive ordering, since disjunctive ordering requires that the longer rule (51) apply before the shorter rule (52). Of course, disjunctive ordering also says that once (51) applies, (52) cannot be tried. In the present instance, this aspect of disjunctive ordering is irrelevant, since by its very nature application of (51) precludes the application of (52). Also it should be noted that the disjunctive ordering relationship of (51) and (52) is consistent both with SPE's claim that all rules abbreviated by the angled-bracket notation are disjunctively ordered and also with Kiparsky's principle.

Although the angled-bracket notation seems to us a necessary device for expressing the unity of certain phonological processes, there are still problems related to its actual implementation in grammar writing. We have space here to consider just one problematical example. In Chi-Mwi:ni, prefixes of the shape CV-, where V is a high vowel, are subject to vowel deletion. The conditions for deletion vary, however, depending on the nature of the consonant of the prefix and also on the nature of the consonant that follows the prefix. If the prefix consists of a sonorant plus high vowel, that high vowel drops before any consonant-initial morpheme (except in a few well-defined contexts not relevant to the present discussion). Thus the noun class prefix /mu/ lacks its high vowel in most of the examples listed in (54).

(54)

m-baðiri	'squanderer'	wa-baðiri	'squanderers'
m-pokezi	'midwife'	wa-pokezi	'midwives'
m-darisa	'teacher'	wa-darisa	'teachers'
m-to:ro	'thief'	wa-to:ro	'thieves'
m-ge:ni	'stranger'	wa-ge:ni	'strangers'
m-ke:zi	'one who visits for the day'	wa-ke:zi	'visitors'

cf.,

mu-ke	'woman'	wa-ke	'women'
mu-bli	'man'	wa-bli	'men'

Prefixes that consist of an obstruent plus a high vowel delete that vowel just in case the following morpheme begins with a voiceless obstruent. The infinitive prefix /ku/ can be used to illustrate this phenomenon. Notice that when /ku/ elides its vowel, the /k/ is converted to /x/ in pre-obstruent position. This fact can be attributed to a separate rule.

(55)   *ku-bo:ɬ-a*   'to steal'   *x-pik-a*   'to cook'
         ku-ɖuguw-a   'to limp'   *x-ʈek-a*   'to laugh'
         ku-ji:b-a   'to answer'   *x-chi:mbiɬ-a*   'to flee'
         ku-gaf-a   'to make a mistake'   *x-kos-a*   'to make a mistake'

A rule something like (56) is required to account for the behavior of prefixes such as /mu/, whereas a rule like (57) is required for prefixes such as /ku/.

(56) $$\text{V} \longrightarrow \emptyset / + \quad \text{C} \quad \underline{\quad\quad} + \text{C V C}_0 \text{ V}$$
$$[+\text{high}] \qquad\qquad [+\text{sonor}]$$

(57) $$\text{V} \longrightarrow \emptyset / + \quad \text{C} \quad \underline{\quad\quad} + \quad \text{C} \quad \text{V C}_0 \text{ V}$$
$$[+\text{high}] \qquad\quad [-\text{sonor}] \qquad [-\text{voiced}]$$

(We have not given all of the relevant evidence to show that the prefixal vowel deletes just in case it is followed by at most one consonant and there are at least two vowels following in the word.) It is obvious that (56) and (57) are very similar to one another. If we could simply omit the requirement in (56) that the prefixal consonant be [+sonorant], then the only difference between the two rules would be that (57) contains two noncontiguous pieces of information not in (56): namely, the constraint that the prefixal consonant be [−sonorant] and that the consonant following the prefixal vowel be voiceless. The angled-brackets notation would then allow us to abbreviate (56), minus the specification [+sonorant], and (57) as (58).

(58) $$\text{V} \longrightarrow \emptyset / + \quad \text{C} \quad \underline{\quad\quad} + \quad \text{C} \quad \text{V C}_0 \text{ V}$$
$$[+\text{high}] \qquad \langle -\text{sonor}]\rangle \qquad \langle [-\text{voiced}]\rangle$$

Unfortunately, (58) will not produce the correct results if it is interpreted in the same manner as the previous examples of the angled-bracket notation. Let us see why (58) does not work. The principle of disjunctive ordering should be applicable to (58), according to Kiparsky's principle as well as SPE's. Disjunctive ordering requires that the longer rule be applied before the shorter rule; if the longer one applies, the shorter one cannot. But if the longer rule is inapplicable, then the shorter rule does apply. Now consider an infinitive form such as *ku-bo:ɬ-a* 'to steal'. If one tries to apply the longer rule (57) to this item, it will be inapplicable, since the consonant after the prefix is not voiceless. But now we can try to apply (56). Recall, however, that (56) is no longer restricted to prefixes that have a [+sonorant] consonant—that specification was omitted from the rule so that we could collapse (56) and (57) together as (58). But this means that (56) will now delete the high vowel from *all* prefixes, regardless of whether the consonant after the prefixal vowel is voiced or voiceless. This is incorrect; *ku-bo:ɬ-a* must retain its vowel.

In order to prevent (56) from applying incorrectly to *ku-bo:ɬ-a*, we might attempt to reintroduce the constraint on (56) that the prefixal consonant be a sonorant. But if we do so, (56) and (57) can no longer be abbreviated by the angled-brackets notation; and we thus fail to express the underlying unity of the two processes. The evidence for this unity resides in the fact that they share largely the same restrictions, and in addition there is some evidence that an item that behaves exceptionally with respect to one of them also behaves exceptionally with respect to the other. For relevant discussion, see Kisseberth and Abasheikh (1976).

A rule such as (58) will yield the correct results only if it is given the following interpretation: If a string S_i satisfies the [−sonorant] condition of (57), then S_i will undergo (57) if the remaining conditions are satisfied, but S_i cannot be submitted to (56) for processing. In other words, the shorter rule (56) cannot be applied at all to a string that satisfies the [−sonorant] condition of the longer rule (57). Notice, incidentally, that if a string S_i meets the [−voiced] condition on (57) it can still undergo (56). Thus a representation like /mu-ʈo:ro/ meets the [−voiced] condition on (57), but does not meet the [−sonorant] condition; nevertheless, /mu-ʈo:ro/ is still able to undergo (56) and delete its prefixal vowel. Thus there is an asymmetry between the conditions [−sonor] and [−voiced]; it is only if a string meets the former condition that it is barred from undergoing (56).

It is not clear to us at present whether such an interpretation of (58) is supported by parallel examples from other languages. But this example from Chimwi:ni does strike us as a case where two rules appear to be reflections of the same underlying process, and where the angled-bracket notation would appear to represent the appropriate notation. If so, then a solution must be found to explain why (58) is not disjunctively ordered in the same way that the previous rules discussed in this section were.

The Brace Notation

Sometimes the same underlying phonological process manifests itself in what appear to be two (or more) distinct contexts. One common example is provided by rules that apply in preconsonantal and word-final positions: for example, vowel nasalization, neutralizations of various consonantal oppositions, and epenthesis. For example, recall that Yawelmani epenthesis inserts an *i* between two consonants followed by a third or followed by a word boundary (see Chapter 4). Given the notation we have explicitly developed to this point, these two manifestations of vowel epenthesis would have to be implemented by separate rules:

(59) VE 1 $\emptyset \longrightarrow i/C\rule{1cm}{0.4pt}C\#$

(60) VE 2 $\emptyset \longrightarrow i/C\rule{1cm}{0.4pt}CC$

However, there are reasons for believing that these two rules are not totally unconnected with one another (which is what we would in effect be claiming if the process were to be described by two separate rules in the grammar), but rather are instances of the same unitary process. First, the two rules are virtually identical formally: both insert an *i* between two consonants. Second, they both serve the same function of breaking up syllable-final consonant clusters. Finally, both rules are ordered exactly the same with respect to all other rules in Yawelmani.

The relationship between these two manifestations of epenthesis could be captured by appealing to the brace notation introduced in SPE. This notation permits adjacently ordered elementary rules whose SD or SC refer to partially identical strings to be collapsed into a single schema by factoring out the identities and enclosing the differences in braces. Given this notation, the Yawelmani epenthesis process would be expressed as (61).

(61) $\emptyset \longrightarrow i/C\rule{1cm}{0.4pt}C\left\{ \begin{array}{c} \# \\ C \end{array} \right\}$

Schemata abbreviated by braces are expanded into their constituent elementary rules from top to bottom. Furthermore, the subrules are interpreted as conjunctively ordered. Thus, the schema (61) abbreviates the subrules (59) and (60) with (59) ordered to apply before (60). In many cases the ordering of the subrules is immaterial. This, for example, is true with the subrules of the Old English vowel shortening process discussed earlier. But in other cases the ordering will be necessary. For example, if the /i/ appearing in the Yawelmani passive aorist suffix /-it/ is interpreted as epenthetic, then in the derivation of *logw-it* from /#logw-t#/, subrule (59) must break up the final cluster first and thereby bleed application of (60). If the schema of (61) were written with the C above instead of below the #, the wrong result would be obtained for this derivation. For such a schema would imply that subrule (60) applies before (59). With this expansion of (61) /#logw-t#/ would first be converted to /#logiw-t#/ and then /#logiw-it#/. But *logiwit* is ungrammatical.

It has often been observed that if only a partial formal identity is required for the abbreviation of adjacently ordered rules, the brace notation will collapse together rules that are manifestly not instances of a unitary underlying process, simply by virtue of the fact that in any grammar there is a high probability that some successively ordered rules will accidentally share a few properties in common. For example, recall from Chapter 3 that Tonkawa has rules of apocope and vowel truncation that delete vowels in the contexts ____# and ____V, respectively. In purely formal terms these rules are quite similar; in fact, there is no more difference between them than there is between VE 1 and VE 2 of Yawelmani. Hence, they could be collapsed into schema (62).

$$(62) \qquad V \longrightarrow \emptyset / \underline{\quad} \left\{ \begin{array}{c} \# \\ V \end{array} \right\}$$

However, unlike the two instances of vowel epenthesis, the presence of apocope in a grammar has little if any relationship to the presence of a rule of vowel truncation. Many languages possess one without the other. Furthermore, they can arise and drop out of grammars quite independently. Finally, there is very little tendency for them to be adjacently ordered, while this is typically not the case with rules applying in preconsonantal and final position. In fact, the reader will recall that the vowel elision process of Tonkawa had to be ordered between apocope and truncation. Needless to say, we could still employ the brace notation to abbreviate all three rules by devising a schema of the following form.

$$(63) \qquad V \longrightarrow \emptyset / \left\{ \begin{array}{c} \underline{\quad} \# \\ \# \; C_0 \; V \; C_0 \underline{\quad} C_0 \; V \; C_0] \\ \underline{\quad} V \qquad \text{stem} \end{array} \right\}$$

However, now the vacuity of the unlimited use of the brace notation is clearly evident, for each of these rules has nothing in common except that they drop a vowel.

It would seem that the use of the brace notation, like any of the other devices discussed in this chapter, must be restricted. Indeed, one of the most pressing tasks in phonological theory is to define the set of circumstances in which each piece of notation is to be properly employed. In the case of the brace notation McCawley (1972) has claimed that all known uses of this device can be dispensed with because either the abbreviated rules are only accidentally related or the underlying relationships between the rules can be expressed more properly in some other fashion. For example, it has been claimed that the use of braces to express the frequent conjunction of C and # in phonological rules can be dispensed with if rules are permitted to refer to syllable structure. Normally a segment that appears before a consonant in such rules terminates the syllable. And of course the final segment of a word is also the final segment of a syllable, at least when the word is spoken in isolation. Thus, if a dot is used to represent the syllable boundary, the Yawelmani epenthesis rule can be formulated as (64).

(64) $\emptyset \longrightarrow i/C\underline{\hspace{1cm}}C.$

The fact that a string CCC# appears as CCiC# rather than CiCiC# could be handled by imposing a right-to-left iteration of the rule. Note that if this analysis is accepted the syllable structure assignment rules will have to apply both before and after (64) since insertion of *i* creates a new syllable nucleus.

It is not entirely clear, however, that the conjunction $\{^{\#}_{C}\}$ can universally be replaced by a reference to syllable boundary. Consider, for example, Newman's description of Bella Coola phonology (1947). Bella Coola, like other Salish languages of the Northwest coast, is remarkable for its "almost unlimited toleration . . . for consonant clusters . . . Bella Coola words made up entirely of consonants are frequent [p. 132]." Newman cites examples such as *pɫt* 'thick', *ɫmk'mɫp* 'jack-pine tree', *sk'lxlxc* 'I'm getting cold', *ti ɫq'ʷlxc'ntx* 'that which is fading out', *k'xɫc* 'I looked', *ɫk' ʷtxʷ* 'make it big!', and *ɫxʷtɫc* 'I went through an opening'. Of course, some of these words have phonetic vowels, but they are predictable in terms of the nature and positioning of the consonants. Newman concludes that in Bella Coola, the notion syllable is irrelevant at the phonemic level; while there are phonetic syllables, such syllables are determined by the underlying configuration of structural units in a word, where vowels may or may not be present.

Even though the notion syllable appears to be irrelevant for Bella Coola underlying representations, nevertheless the conjunction $\{^{\#}_{C}\}$ is critical for the operation of several rules in the language. One such rule specifies the sonorant consonants *m*, *n*, and *l* as syllabic in the environment between consonants or between a consonant and a word boundary; that is, in the environment $\{^{\#}_{C}\}$ ___ $\{^{\#}_{C}\}$. Newman states that these syllabic consonants are "preceded by a brief vowel of variable quality. Most commonly, this nonphonemic element is a central mid vowel with the quality of [ə] [p. 130]." By virtue of this syllabification process, then, *mtm* 'sea egg' is pronounced [əmtəm] and *plsti* 'diminutive fish scale' is pronounced [pəlsti].

Nonglottalized stops and affricates in Bella Coola are pronounced either with or without aspiration according to the context in which they occur. Newman formulates the rule as follows: "These consonants are aspirated before consonants (except syllabic m, n, l) or before word junctures. In prevocalic position and before syllabic m, n, l they occur as intermediates, that is, voiceless unaspirated consonants [p. 129]." As a consequence of this rule, *pɫt* 'thick' is pronounced with an aspirated *p* and an aspirated *t*, whereas *plsti* 'diminutive fish scale' is pronounced with an unaspirated *p* and *t*. The *p* in the latter example is unaspirated due to the fact that it is followed by a syllabic *l* (which phonetically involves the pronunciation of a [ə] vowel before the *l*). The voiceless lateral spirant *ɫ* in *pɫt* is not syllabic, and thus the *p* is realized as aspirated.

A third rule in Bella Coola that is sensitive to the conjunction $\{^{\#}_{C}\}$ has to do with the pronunciation of the prepalatal consonants *k*, *k'*, and *x* (which contrast with the velar consonants *q*, *q'*, and *x̣*) and with the pronunciation of both the labiopalatals *k*ʷ, *k'*ʷ, and *x*ʷ and the labiovelars *q*ʷ, *q'*ʷ, and *x̣*ʷ. If we take *k* as being representative of the prepalatals and *k*ʷ as being representative of both the labiopalatals and the labiovelars, then the rules for the pronunciation of these sounds is as follows. Before a vowel, *k* is realized as [ky] and *k*ʷ is realized as [kw]. Before consonants (other than *m*, *n*, and *l*) and before word boundary, *k* is realized as [kⁱ] and *k*ʷ as [kᵘ], where the raised vowel indicates a voiceless vowel. (The pronunciation of *k* and *k*ʷ before *m*, *n*, and *l* varies due to the fact that *m*, *n*, and *l* may be syllabic; the variations involved are not relevant to the present discussion). We thus have another case of a rule that is operative both before a consonant and also before a word boundary.

One last example can be cited. Although we have already noted that there is great freedom in consonant clustering in Bella Coola, nevertheless there is one notable constraint on clustering: "w, y, and ʔ do not occur between consonants or between a consonant and a word juncture. They are found only before, after, or between vowels [pp. 131–132]." If this particular distributional gap is properly accounted for in terms of a rule about morpheme structure, then that rule apparently makes reference to the disjunction $\{^{\#}_{C}\}$.

Given evidence such as that from Bella Coola, it appears to us to be premature to claim that all instances of the brace notation represent either false generalizations or else can be reformulated in a more insightful way. As matters stand, the brace notation seems justified, but (like most of the other notational devices sketched in this chapter) capable of being misused. One approach to the problem would be to allow only certain expressions to be conjoined by the brace notation: that is, to set up a universal inventory of conjoined expressions. This inventory would include $\{ {}^*_C \}$ but not, presumably, $\{ {}^*_V \}$. It is unclear at this stage whether such an approach to restricting the use of braces is viable.

Variable Feature Values

So far we have developed only one way of referring to the feature specification of a segment: The segment is either plus or minus for that feature. However, there are numerous cases where the value for a certain feature F_i depends on the value for another feature F_j, where F_j may be plus or minus. For instance, recall from Chapter 6 that in Pengo an obstruent assimilates the voicedness of a following obstruent: *tu:b-a*, *tu:p-tan*, *tu:b-ji* 'blow' versus *hi:p-a*, *hi:p-tan*, *hi:b-ji* 'sweep'. Such cases have been treated in generative phonology by the introduction of a variable specification (designated by the early letters of the Greek alphabet) ranging over the values plus and minus. With this notation, the Pengo voicing assimilation rule may be expressed as (65).

(65) $[-\text{sonorant}] \longrightarrow [\alpha\text{voice}] / \_\_\_\_ \begin{bmatrix} -\text{sonorant} \\ \alpha\text{voice} \end{bmatrix}$

This rule is interpreted as saying: specify an obstruent with the same value (plus or minus) for the feature [voice] as the value for [voice] of the following obstruent.

In other cases a segment must be assigned a specification that is the opposite of the specification for some (other) feature. For example, in Huamelultec Chontal (Waterhouse 1949) the imperative morpheme *-laʔ* has an initial voiced *l* after voiceless segments and a voiceless allophone, *ɬ* after voiced ones. (The palatal variants are assigned by a rule of palatalization operating after high vowels and *y*).

(66) | | | | |
|---|---|---|---|
| *koɬaʔ* | 'say it!' | *kanɬaʔ* | 'leave it!' |
| *miiɬʸaʔ* | 'tell him!' | *panxlaʔ* | 'sit down!' |
| *puɬʸʔ* | 'dig it!' | *fušlʸaʔ* | 'blow it!' |

These data can be accounted for by the rule in (67), which says that a lateral has a value for [voice] that is the opposite of the value for this feature in the preceding segment.

(67) $l \longrightarrow [-\alpha\text{voice}]/[\alpha\text{voice}]\_\_\_\_$ (where if $\alpha = +$, then $-\alpha = -$;
                                                   and if $\alpha = -$, then $-\alpha = +$)

In some cases more than a single variable specification can appear in a rule. A frequent example of this type involves rules of nasal assimilation where a nasal acquires the point of articulation of a following consonant. For example, in Guininaang (Gieser 1970) the verbalizing prefix /man-/ exhibits this behavior: *mam-ba?al* 'wear a loincloth', *mam-muma* 'chew muma', *man-tadam* 'be sharp', *man-sagana* 'prepare', *maŋ-kapi* 'drink coffee', *maŋ-ŋina* 'buy'. The varying realizations of this prefix can be accounted for by the rule in (68).

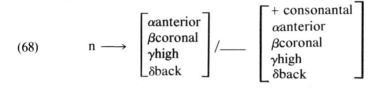

(68)   n ⟶
$$\begin{bmatrix} \alpha\text{anterior} \\ \beta\text{coronal} \\ \gamma\text{high} \\ \delta\text{back} \end{bmatrix} / \underline{\quad} \begin{bmatrix} + \text{consonantal} \\ \alpha\text{anterior} \\ \beta\text{coronal} \\ \gamma\text{high} \\ \delta\text{back} \end{bmatrix}$$

The variable relation may hold not only between a feature of the structural change and a feature of the context, but also between features contained solely in the SD of a rule. For example, recall the vowel harmony rule of Yawelmani which rounds and backs a vowel in assimilation to a preceding vowel, provided they are of the same height. This rule was formulated as (63) in the previous chapter, with the alphas expressing the height restriction.

In the examples discussed so far the specification for a given feature of one segment has been the same or the opposite as the value for that same feature in another segment. There are, however, cases where the variable relation holds between different features. For example, in a language like Chamarro (Chapter 3), which has the underlying vowel system of [i,e,ä,u,o,a], specification for the feature [round] is redundant and may be predicted from the values for high, low, and back. Low vowels are [−round] and the value for [round] in nonlow vowels agrees with the value for [back]. Thus lexical entries may be unspecified for [round] and the proper values for this feature may be assigned by morpheme structure rules. The rule assigning nonlow vowels their [round] specifications may be expressed as (69).

(69)
$$\begin{bmatrix} +\text{syll} \\ -\text{low} \\ \alpha\text{back} \end{bmatrix} \longrightarrow [\alpha\text{round}]$$

The most intriguing examples of the variable relation are polarity rules, where two segments exchange places in the phonemic pattern. For example, where /e:/ and some /i:/s appear in Literary Czech, the colloquial language has /i:/ and /ej/, respectively. As explained in Chapter 5, the /i:/s that switch to /ej/ derive historically from /y:/, a high, back nonround vowel that has merged with /i:/ in the Literary language. The historical difference between the two /i:/s is preserved in the orthography. Thus, Literary *mýdlo* 'soap' and *mléko* 'milk' are realized as *mejdlo* and *mlíko* in colloquial Czech. If the vocalism of the Literary language is assumed to be basic, the colloquial forms can be derived by a polarity rule interchanging /i:/ and /e:/, followed by a rule diphthongizing /e:/ to /ej/. The polarity rule may be stated as (70).

(70)
$$
\begin{bmatrix}
+\text{syll} \\
-\text{back} \\
+\text{long} \\
\alpha\text{high}
\end{bmatrix}
\longrightarrow [-\alpha\text{high}]
$$

In Dinka (Gleason 1955), a language of the Sudan, the plural of a certain class of nouns is formed by length polarization. If the singular has a short vowel, the plural has a long vowel, and vice versa. Thus, the plurals of *pal* 'knife', *bit* 'spear', *čiin* 'hand', and *leec* 'tooth', are *paal*, *biit*, *čin*, and *lec*. Assuming the singular form to be basic, the polarity rule would take the form (71).

(71)
$$
\begin{bmatrix}
+\text{syll} \\
+\text{plural} \\
\alpha\text{long}
\end{bmatrix}
\longrightarrow [-\alpha\text{long}]
$$

(The use of the feature [+plural] is simply an ad hoc device to indicate that in order to undergo this rule, a vowel must be part of a root that is functioning as a plural noun.)

Within the SPE framework, rules containing variables are viewed as schemata, each subrule in the schema being formed by uniformly interpreting each variable as plus and minus. Given this interpretation, the subrules must be disjunctively ordered, at least in the case of polarity rules. (71) would thus abbreviate two rules: one making short vowels long and the other making long vowels short. If they were not disjunctive, the second rule would always cancel the effects of the first.

Anderson (1974) has claimed that all polarity rules are either morphologically or lexically restricted. Although only about a half dozen polarity rules have been reported in the literature, all seem to corroborate this generalization.

Mirror-Image Rules

Sometimes phonological rules must be formulated to change x to y when adjacent to some sound *z*. For example, in Lithuanian the underlying sequences /s + š/ and /š + s/ are both realized as š phonetically. A compound noun like *saušala* 'bitter cold', composed of the roots *saus-* 'dry' and *šalt-* 'cold', illustrates the first. The second may be exemplified by addition of the future suffix *-si* to a root ending in *š*. Thus, /neš-si/ 'you will carry' appears as *neši* phonetically (cf., *neš-a* 'he carries', and *sek-si* 'you will watch'). Thus, it would appear that we need rules to delete *s* when it is preceded or followed by *š*. (Further study of Lithuanian actually reveals that a rule taking *s* to *š* when adjacent to a palatal followed by degemination of long consonants is the better analysis, but we may retain the analysis which deletes *s* adjacent to *š* for purposes of discussion; see Kenstowicz 1972 for details.) If the changes of /s + š/ and /š + s/ to *s* are implemented as separate rules, they bear a strong resemblance to one another; the SD of one is the mirror-image of the other.

Bach (1968) was the first generative phonologist to study such rules. He proposed that the formal similarity of mirror-image rules be captured by collapsing them together into a single schema by simple elimination of the environmental dash. Bach's proposal would permit the Lithuanian rule to be expressed as (72).

(72)   s ⟶ ∅/š

The schema in (72) is interpreted as abbreviating two subrules: one deleting *s* before *š* and the other deleting *s* after *š*.

Bach noted that in some cases the order of expansion of the schema makes a difference. This is not true for the Lithuanian example, but does hold for the allophonic rule of English that assigns varying points of articulation to velar stops depending on adjacent vowels. Bach noted that velars are relatively front when preceded or followed by a front vowel (*peak*, *keep*) and relatively backed when preceded or followed by a back vowel (*spook*, *cool*). But when velars appear between vowels that differ in backness, the following vowel determines the point of articulation of the velar: in *kabuki* the k is frontal, while in *Miku* it is relatively back. Bach proposed that the velar assimilation rule be expressed as (73) and that any such schema be interpreted as abbreviating two conjunctively ordered rules: the first with the environmental dash after the material to the right of the slash (i) and the second with the dash preceding (ii).

(73)

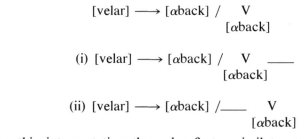

$$[\text{velar}] \longrightarrow [\alpha\text{back}] / \quad \begin{matrix} V \\ [\alpha\text{back}] \end{matrix}$$

$$\text{(i) } [\text{velar}] \longrightarrow [\alpha\text{back}] / \quad \begin{matrix} V \\ [\alpha\text{back}] \end{matrix} \underline{\quad}$$

$$\text{(ii) } [\text{velar}] \longrightarrow [\alpha\text{back}] / \underline{\quad} \begin{matrix} V \\ [\alpha\text{back}] \end{matrix}$$

Under this interpretation the velar first assimilates to the preceding vowel; but the effects of this assimilation are then wiped out by assimilation to the following vowel. (One could also account for these data by assuming that the subrules are disjunctive, with (ii) ordered before (i); but as we shall see, Bach's proposal is unworkable in any case.)

Subsequent investigation has shown that mirror-image rules cannot be satisfactorily accounted for by Bach's proposal. For example, Anderson (1974) discusses an example from Icelandic where the subrules are ordered the opposite from that in the English example. In Icelandic high vowels glide when adjacent to another vowel: /ai/ $\longrightarrow aj$, /ia/ $\longrightarrow ja$, /au/ $\longrightarrow aw$, /ua/ $\longrightarrow wa$. But the sequence /iu/ is realized as *ju* not *iw*, which would be the output required if mirror-image rules were always to be expanded in the order proposed by Bach. Thus, although not many crucial examples are available, it appears that the ordering of the subrules of mirror-image schemata cannot be predicted universally.

Another defect of Bach's proposal for expressing mirror-image rules is that it claims that the segment undergoing the rule will always be located at the end of the string forming the SD of the rule. Anderson (1974) has shown that this condition is not always satisfied. For instance, in Faroese, when two vowels come together at a morpheme boundary, a glide is inserted if one of the vowels is high. If the first vowel is high, the glide agrees in backness with the first vowel: $i + a \longrightarrow ija$, $u + a \longrightarrow uwa$; $i + u \longrightarrow iju$; $u + i \longrightarrow uwi$. If the first vowel is not high, the glide will agree in backness with the following high vowel: $a + i \longrightarrow aji$, $a + u \longrightarrow awu$. If neither vowel is high, no glide is inserted. The two ordered subrules involved are stated in (74).

(74) A.

$$\emptyset \longrightarrow \begin{bmatrix} -\text{syll} \\ -\text{cons} \\ \alpha\text{back} \end{bmatrix} / \begin{bmatrix} +\text{syll} \\ +\text{high} \\ \alpha\text{back} \end{bmatrix} \underline{\quad} [+\text{syll}]$$

B.

$$\emptyset \longrightarrow \begin{bmatrix} -\text{syll} \\ -\text{cons} \\ \alpha\text{back} \end{bmatrix} / [+\text{syll}] \underline{\quad} \begin{bmatrix} +\text{syll} \\ +\text{high} \\ \alpha\text{back} \end{bmatrix}$$

If we apply Bach's convention, the following schema is obtained.

(75)
$$\emptyset \longrightarrow \begin{bmatrix} -\text{syll} \\ -\text{cons} \\ \alpha\text{back} \end{bmatrix} \Big/ \begin{bmatrix} +\text{syll} \\ +\text{high} \\ \alpha\text{back} \end{bmatrix} [+\text{syll}]$$

But now the glide will be inserted at the end of the string of vowels instead of the middle. Thus, a completely new notation is required for the expression of mirror-image rules. The reader is referred to Anderson (1974) for details of one approach to the problem. As is the case with all problems of notation, it is crucial that many more relevant examples be unearthed so that decisions about notation can be made on a solidly established basis.

Transformational Rules in Phonology

The majority of phonological rules found in any grammar have a rather restricted formal nature: they specify some segment for one or more features in some context (which may be null). The essential format that we have chosen for stating rules reflects these paradigm cases of phonological rules. We have assumed that in an expression of the form $x \longrightarrow y \big/ \underline{\quad} z$, the specifications to the left of the arrow refer to a single sound unit, and that the specifications to the right of the arrow determine changes in the specification of that single sound unit. In other words, this format does not allow x or y to refer to a sequence of sounds.

There are, however, processes that differ to a certain extent from the paradigm case sketched above. Such processes include deletion, insertion, metathesis, copying, and contraction. Some of these processes may require a more powerful rule of grammar (so-called "transformational rules") than allowed for by expressions like $x \longrightarrow y \big/ \underline{\quad} z$. This section briefly surveys the general problem of formulating rules of the sort cited above.

We have already encountered numerous instances of deletion and insertion in the course of this book, so there is little need to illustrate them further here. It should be apparent that the rule format $x \longrightarrow y \big/ \underline{\quad} z$ can be used for simple cases of deletion and insertion. In the case of deletion, all that is involved is that the symbol $\emptyset$ can occur in the position to the right of the arrow. This symbol is interpreted as meaning that the segment identified by the features to the left of the arrow is simply deleted from the string. In the case of insertion, the symbol $\emptyset$ is placed to the left of the arrow. This is interpreted to mean that in place of nothing at all, a segment bearing the features specified to the right of the arrow will appear, if the conditions z are met.

The type of rule that is most difficult to treat by means of the format x $\longrightarrow y$ / ___z is metathesis, for metathesis differs from most of the processes described in this book in that it affects more than a single segment. Hence, such rules appear to motivate a rather different format for expressing rules. To illustrate, examine the following data from Hanunoo, a language of the Philippines (Gleason 1955).

(76)

ʔusa	'one'	*kasʔa*	'once'
duwa	'two'	*kadwa*	'twice'
tulu	'three'	*katlu*	'thrice'
ʔupat	'four'	*kapʔat*	'four times'
lima	'five'	*kalima*	'five times'
ʔunum	'six'	*kanʔum*	'six times'
pitu	'seven'	*kapitu*	'seven times'

The data in (76) show that Hanunoo has a rule that metathesizes a ʔ with a following consonant. This rule applies to the output of another rule that syncopates u after a vowel-final prefix so long as a three-consonant cluster does not arise. The UR of 'once' is thus /ka-ʔusa/. Syncope yields /ka-ʔsa/ which is then metathesized to /ka-sʔa/.

Let us now consider the problem of formulating the metathesis rule. The SD of the rule is clearly ʔC. The structural change is that these two segments reverse the order in which they occur. But there is no way to express such a change in relative ordering directly by the rule format x $\longrightarrow y$ / ___z. One could of course achieve the effect of metathesis by formulating two rules (both expressible in the standard format): one rule would convert the sequence ʔC_i to C_iʔC_i by a rule inserting a consonant immediately before a ʔC sequence, where the inserted consonant would be identical to the consonant that follows the glottal stop. The second rule would then delete the original post-ʔ consonant. While such an analysis might "work," it has very little to recommend it. In particular, the rule that inserts the consonant completely lacks plausibility. We doubt that such a rule can be found to occur as an independently motivated rule of grammar. If no support for this two step approach can be amassed (and we know of none), then the alternative transformational format of rule formulation is required.

A rule written in the transformational format consists of two parts, just like any other phonological rule: a structural description and a structural change. It is customary to index each of the relevant parts of the structural description with integers. The structural change of the rule is then defined over this structural index. Hence, the Hanunoo rule that interchanges a ʔ and a following consonant is formalized as follows:

(77)   Structural description   ʔ   [+conson]
                        Structural index   1   2
                        Structural change   2   1

The structural change of this rule says that the segment indexed as 2 (namely, the consonant) precedes the segment indexed as 1 (namely, the glottal stop) in the output, even though in the original structure the order was the reverse.

The transformational format seems particularly appropriate for rules of metathesis. But once this format is accepted, the question arises as to whether or not it is appropriate in other situations as well. One kind of rule that can be expressed very simply in the transformational format is copying. By "copying" we mean the insertion of some element that is identical to another element in the string. For example, in Kolami, a Dravidian language described in Emeneau (1955), stems that end underlyingly in a consonant cluster undergo a process that inserts a vowel within the cluster when the stem is word final or followed by a consonant. The inserted vowel is identical to the vowel that precedes the consonant cluster.

(78)

Nom.	Acc.	Loc.	Gloss
cilum	*cilum-un*	*cilum-t*	'pipe'
popos	*popos-un*	*popos-t*	'lung'
ayak	*ayk-un*	*ayak-t*	'rubbish'
mitik	*mitk-un*	*mitik-t*	'brain'
tupuk	*tupk-un*	*tupuk-t*	'gun'
teḍep	*teḍp-un*	*teḍep-t*	'cloth'

The first two forms show that we are dealing with an insertion as opposed to a deletion rule. The copying process can be easily expressed in the transformational format.

(79)   SD   V C C]$\left\{\begin{matrix} \# \\ C \end{matrix}\right\}$

                  SI   1 2 3   4
                  SC   1 2 1 3   4

The bracket in the above rule represents the stem boundary; reference to this boundary is required since it is only stem-final consonant clusters that are broken up by vowel copy. Clusters that arise across morpheme boundaries, such as that in *cilum-t,* are not subject to vowel copy.

Although the transformational format provides a simple method of describing a copying process, it is not the case that the standard format is unable to express the same phenomenon. It can, as (80) shows.

(80)
$$\emptyset \longrightarrow \begin{bmatrix} +\text{syll} \\ \alpha\text{back} \\ \beta\text{high} \\ \gamma\text{low} \\ \cdot \\ \cdot \end{bmatrix} / \begin{bmatrix} V \\ \alpha\text{back} \\ \beta\text{high} \\ \gamma\text{low} \\ \cdot \\ \cdot \end{bmatrix} C \underline{\quad} C] \begin{Bmatrix} \# \\ C \end{Bmatrix}$$

Furthermore, if one permited the introduction of some cover symbol such as F (where F stands for the entire set of distinctive phonetic features), (80) could be replaced by the much simpler (81).

(81)
$$\emptyset \longrightarrow \begin{bmatrix} +\text{syll} \\ \alpha F \end{bmatrix} / \begin{bmatrix} V \\ \alpha F \end{bmatrix} C \underline{\quad} C] \begin{Bmatrix} \# \\ C \end{Bmatrix}$$

Consequently, copy rules do not provide evidence for the necessity of transformational rules; they simply represent a kind of rule that can be expressed simply within the transformational notation.

There are a variety of rules that affect two segments in a string; some of these provide possible motivation for the transformational framework. Let us consider first of all cases where a sound drops out, but in doing so affects the neighboring sound in some manner. A typical example would be languages where a sequence of vowel plus nasal is pronounced simply as a (possibly long) nasalized vowel when in position before a consonant or word boundary. Within the standard format, this process could be described in terms of the following two (ordered) rules:

(82)
$$V \longrightarrow \tilde{V} / \underline{\quad} N \begin{Bmatrix} C \\ \# \end{Bmatrix}$$

(83)
$$N \longrightarrow \emptyset / \tilde{V} \underline{\quad}$$

This analysis says that first a vowel becomes nasalized in the environment ____ NC or ____ N #, and then the nasal deletes after a nasalized vowel. The transformational format offers the following alternative to (82) and (83).

(84)

	SD	V	N	$\begin{Bmatrix} C \\ \# \end{Bmatrix}$
	SI	1	2	3
	SC	$\begin{bmatrix} 1 \\ +\text{nasal} \end{bmatrix}$	$\begin{bmatrix} 2 \\ \emptyset \end{bmatrix}$	3

One objection that might be made to rules (82) and (83) is that it is just the nasalized vowels that are the output of (82) that cause the deletion of the nasal in (83). Thus even though these are being regarded as separate processes, they are not clearly so. Consequently, an analysis such as (82) and (83) could be strengthened by showing that, for instance, underlying nasalized vowels also trigger the loss of a nasal. Or by showing that some of the nasalized vowels created by (82) undergo some additional process that allows the nasal consonant to be retained. In other words, (82) and (83) would be strengthened if it can be shown that first, not all of the nasalized vowels created by (82) trigger loss of the nasal and second, some nasal vowels in addition to those created by (82) cause a following nasal to delete. On the other hand, an analysis such as (82) and (83) could not be maintained in the face of clear data that contradict the rule (83) that deletes a nasal after a nasalized vowel.

In the languages familiar to us, we do not know of any data crucial to choosing between rules (82)–(83) and rule (84). But there are phenomena somewhat comparable in nature where the two-step approach runs into problems. For instance, in a number of languages (e.g., Klamath) one can find a process whereby the sequence V? is realized as a long vowel in the environment before a consonant or word-boundary. How might this change be expressed in the standard format? One possibility would be as in (85) and (86).

$$(85) \qquad \text{V} \longrightarrow \text{V:} / \underline{\quad} ? \left\{ \begin{matrix} \text{C} \\ \# \end{matrix} \right\}$$

$$(86) \qquad ? \longrightarrow \emptyset / \text{V} \underline{\quad} \left\{ \begin{matrix} \text{C} \\ \# \end{matrix} \right\}$$

There are at least two reasons for objecting to this analysis. First, rule (85) does not represent the sort of phonological process that can be motivated on independent grounds. That is, vowels do not typically lengthen before the sequences ?C and ?#. Second, the environment in (86) obviously repeats the environment of (85). It is just the glottal stops that induce lengthening before them that also drop out. (We are assuming that glottal stops are retained in position between two vowels, thus (86) could not be simplified to say that a glottal stop deletes after a vowel.)

Since it is a common phonological process for glottal stops to delete before a consonant or word-boundary, one might try to postulate a rule such as (87).

$$(87) \qquad ? \longrightarrow \emptyset / \underline{\quad} \left\{ \begin{matrix} \text{C} \\ \# \end{matrix} \right\}$$

While such a rule would indeed be plausible, a difficulty immediately arises. How can we account for the lengthening of the preceding vowel? Once the glottal stop has been lost, we simply have a vowel standing next to a consonant or word-boundary. It is not possible to say that all vowels are lengthened in the environment ____C and ____#. In other words, once the glottal stop is lost, we have no way to identify which vowels must be lengthened. (But see Kisseberth (1973) for an alternative approach to this problem, involving the use of global rules.)

It should be clear that the transformational format provides a simple means for the description of the change of V$\mathrm{?}$ to a long vowel.

$$(88) \quad \mathrm{SD} \quad V \quad \mathrm{?} \quad \begin{Bmatrix} C \\ \# \end{Bmatrix}$$

$$\mathrm{SI} \quad 1 \quad 2 \quad 3$$

$$\mathrm{SC} \quad \begin{bmatrix} 1 \\ +\mathrm{long} \end{bmatrix} \quad \begin{bmatrix} 2 \\ \emptyset \end{bmatrix} \quad 3$$

Processes like that just described are sometimes referred to as "compensatory lengthening." In general, this class of rules necessitates the transformational format for writing rules (unless one allows for other changes in the theory of rule application—see the reference above to global rules).

One additional type of example requires mentioning. It is quite common to find languages where a sequence of two vowels is pronounced as one vowel, but where the vowel that appears on the surface is not identical to either of the original vowels but is instead a kind of compromise vowel. For instance, one might find the sequence *ia* being realized phonetically as *e*. Call this vowel coalescence. The standard format for writing rules requires that this coalescence be regarded as a two-step affair. First, one of the vowels must be converted to *e*. Then the other vowel must be deleted. (89) and (90) illustrate such a description.

$$(89) \quad a \longrightarrow e/i\text{____}$$

$$(90) \quad V \longrightarrow \emptyset/\text{____}V$$

This kind of approach could be motivated if it were possible to show that the vowel assimilation phenomenon is somehow independently motivated (i.e., *a* is replaced by *e* due to a preceding *i* even when the *i* does not delete) and that the vowel truncation rule is independently motivated (i.e., the first of two vowels always deletes, even in cases where the quality of the second vowel is not modified at all).

On the other hand, (91) and (92) could also account for the change of *ia* to *e*.

(91) $\qquad$ i $\longrightarrow$ e/____ a

(92) $\qquad$ V $\longrightarrow$ $\emptyset$/V____

Again, this two-step approach could be motivated by showing that the two rules involved are more general. If neither of the two steps can be independently motivated, one might well look in the direction of a transformational rule. (93) and (94) are both possible formalizations.

(93)

SD

$$
\text{V} \quad \begin{bmatrix} +\text{high} \\ -\text{back} \end{bmatrix} \qquad \text{V} \quad \begin{bmatrix} +\text{low} \\ +\text{back} \end{bmatrix}
$$

SI $\qquad$ 1 $\qquad$ 2

SC

$$
\begin{bmatrix} 1 \\ \emptyset \end{bmatrix} \qquad \begin{bmatrix} 2 \\ -\text{low} \\ -\text{back} \end{bmatrix}
$$

(94)

SD

$$
\text{V} \quad \begin{bmatrix} +\text{high} \\ -\text{back} \end{bmatrix} \qquad \text{V} \quad \begin{bmatrix} +\text{low} \\ +\text{back} \end{bmatrix}
$$

SI $\qquad$ 1 $\qquad$ 2

SC

$$
\begin{bmatrix} 1 \\ -\text{high} \end{bmatrix} \qquad \begin{bmatrix} 2 \\ \emptyset \end{bmatrix}
$$

According to (93), the sequence *ia* is changed to *e* by simultaneously converting *a* to *e* and dropping *i*. According to (94), *ia* changes to *e* by simultaneously converting *i* to *e* and dropping *a*. Actually, if one takes the position that the change of *ia* to *e* represents a coalescence of two separate vowels into one vowel, none of the descriptions above characterize the process in just that way. It is conceivable, however, that the transformational format might be modified so as to unambiguously interpret the process as one of coalescence. Consider the rule given in (95).

(95)

SD

$$
\text{V} \quad \begin{bmatrix} +\text{high} \\ -\text{back} \end{bmatrix} \qquad \text{V} \quad \begin{bmatrix} +\text{low} \\ +\text{back} \end{bmatrix}
$$

SI $\qquad$ 1 $\qquad$ 2

SC

$$
\begin{bmatrix} 1,\ 2 \\ -\text{high} \\ -\text{low} \\ -\text{back} \end{bmatrix}
$$

If we interpret the structural change in (95) as follows: take the item indexed 1 and the item indexed 2 and merge them into one sound unit; this unit then has whatever phonetic properties 1 and 2 share in common plus the properties [−high, −low, −back]. The formalism in (95) thus treats the change as being a merger of two vowels into one, the resulting vowel being a compromise between *i* and *a*.

It is very common in the literature on generative phonology to find vowel coalescence processes formulated in transformational terms. Considerable work remains to be done to establish that this approach is not only intuitively appropriate, but that it is necessary in some cases—that is, we need to find instances where a two-step approach is simply not possible. But even if we are able to eventually establish that transformational rules should be available for the description of vowel coalescence phenomena, the question still remains whether the two-step approach might not also be valid in some cases. We would like to sketch briefly one example that seems to support the two-step approach.

In her description of Tunica, Haas (1940) points out that the sequence *ia* is realized as *ɛ* and *ua* is realized as *ɔ*. For instance, there is a quotative postfix -*ani* which can be attached to *mili* 'red' to yield *milɛni* 'it is red' and to *niku* 'he says' to yield *nikɔni*. Indeed, any of the front vowels *i*, *e*, and *ɛ* will coalesce with *a* to yield *ɛ*, and the round back vowels *u* and *ɔ* will coalesce with *a* to form *ɔ* (the sequence *oa* does not arise apparently). The sequence *aa* simplifies to *a*.

There is some independent evidence that the coalescences described above should be described in terms of two rules: The first rule assimilates *a* to the backness and roundness of a preceding vowel, and the second deletes a vowel that stands before another vowel. Consider first of all the rule that drops a vowel before a vowel. Such a rule is required anyhow to account for the fact that any vowel before *i* simply drops out. (Haas cites no examples of vowels occurring before *u* or *o*, and only a couple *Ve* sequences; the latter sequence can probably be analyzed as paralleling the *Va* sequences in behavior.) Turning to the rule that would assimilate *a* to the backness and roundness of a preceding vowel, we saw in Chapter 8 that this rule also has independent motivation. Recall that *a* will assimilate to *ɔ* when separated from a preceding *u* or *o* by a glottal stop and that *a* will assimilate to *ɛ* when separated from a preceding *i* or *e* by a glottal stop: /pó + ʔaki/ 'she looks' and /pí + ʔaki/ 'she emerges' are realized phonetically as *pó ʔɔki* and *pí ʔɛki*. It therefore seems that the coalescence of a front vowel plus *a* to *ɛ* and of a round back vowel plus *a* to *ɔ* can reasonably be regarded as the result of two independent steps: assimilation of *a* to the preceding vowel and deletion of the preceding vowel.

The Tunica example thus raises the possibility that even if some instances of coalescence can be accounted for by transformational rules, yet others are properly described in other terms.

The Representation of Length

In both traditional as well as generative descriptions long vowels and consonants have been represented in two different ways: either as a single segment specified [+long] or as a sequence of two identical segments. The latter is sometimes referred to as the geminate notation. It is fairly clear that both kinds of representation are necessary for the proper statement of phonological rules. A clear example requiring the geminate representation occurs in Lithuanian (Kenstowicz 1970). In this language there is a rule that deletes the final half of a diphthong with falling tone (represented here by an acute accent [=high pitch] on the first half) in word-final position. Long vowels with a falling tone become short in final position. These alternations are evident from the following indefinite and definite forms of the adjective *ger-as* 'good':

(96)

	Indef.	Def.
Masc. instr. sg.	*ger-ú*	*ger-úo-ju*
Masc. nom. pl.	*ger-í*	*ger-íe-ji*
Fem. instr. sg.	*ger-á*	*ger-áa-ja*

The URs for the case suffixes are /úo/, /íe/, and /áa/. These appear phonetically when protected by the definite suffixes *ju*, *ji*, and *ja* (themselves derived from /j-úo/, /j-íe/, and /j-áa/). If long vowels are represented as geminates, then the shortening of the /áa/ to *á* can be accounted for by the same rule that deletes the final half of a diphthong.

(97) $\qquad$ $V \longrightarrow \emptyset / \acute{V} \underline{\qquad} \#$

As Pyle (1971) has pointed out, a compelling argument for the feature notation for length derives from the possibility of finding polarity rules defined over this feature. Recall the earlier discussion of the Dinka rule that reverses the length of a vowel in the formation of the plural for nouns. If long vowels were to be represented as geminates, this pluralization process would have to be formulated as two separate and quite different rules: The first rule would lengthen a short root vowel by inserting an identical vowel; the second rule would shorten a long (=geminate) root vowel by deleting one of the vowels. Such a treatment is subject to a number of criticisms. First, it is unexplained why the insertion and deletion processes both are stated in terms of vowel identity. Second, there is no presently available notation that would permit the two radically different processes of insertion and deletion to be collapsed together into a single rule or rule schema. If the long vowels are represented in the feature notation, the two processes can be collapsed together as a polarity rule. Finally, it automatically follows from this treatment that the lengthening and shortening processes are disjunctively ordered. If they were to be formulated as two separate rules of insertion and deletion, there would be no motivated way to impose disjunctive ordering.

The Lithuanian and Dinka data show that both the geminate and the feature notation for length must be allowed for. Furthermore, Kenstowicz (1970) and Pyle (1970, 1971) have shown that there are cases where both notations are required in the analysis of a single language.

Cuna provides an interesting example showing the necessity for both representations of length. Recall from Chapter 6 that stress is regularly placed on the penultimate vowel: *gammái* 'sleeping', *gomnáe* 'go to drink', *dáge* 'come', *sában* 'belly'. In Cuna long vowels only appear in final position. According to Sherzer, speakers of Cuna divide into two dialects with respect to the interaction of stress and length. In dialect A stress falls on a word-final long vowel: *gʷalludíi* 'kerosene', *andíi* 'my water'. In dialect B stress appears on the penult in such words: *gʷallúdii*, *ándii*. (We follow Sherzer's transcription of long vowels as geminates.) Suppose that these two dialects differ solely in the representation for vowel length, such that in dialect A the sequence notation is used, while in dialect B long vowels are represented as [+long]. Then the penultimate stress rule, which is independently needed in both dialects for words with no long vowels, will account for the stress differences in both dialects for long vowelled words. Given the UR /#andii#/ for A, the first mora of the long vowel will be the penultimate vowel and hence take stress. Given the UR /#andi:#/ for B, where the final vowel is treated as [+long], the *a* will occupy penultimate position and hence take the stress.

The *sorsik sunmakke* language game provides external evidence supporting this interpretation of length. Recall from Chapter 5 that this game is played by moving the initial syllable to the end of the word: *dage* 'come', *osi* 'pineapple', and *goe* 'deer' are disguised as *geda*, *sio*, and *ego*, respectively. Sherzer points out that speakers of dialect A disguise the words *muu* 'grandmother' and *dii* 'water' as *umu* and *idi*. Given that these speakers treat long vowels as geminates, this rendering of these words in the game is explained. On the other hand, B speakers do not change these words at all in *sorsik sunmakke*. In this dialect they are pronounced as *muu* and *dii* in both disguised and nondisguised speech.

Given that the long vowels are represented as single segments marked [+long], the rule moving the first syllable to the end of the word will naturally fail to apply to these words.

The Cuna example shows how corpus-external evidence may bear upon the justification of a particular notational device. We now turn to an explicit discussion of this difficult question.

Sources of Evidence for the Underlying Unity of Phonological Processes

Throughout this chapter we have been concerned with developing a notational apparatus for the formulation of phonological rules that will permit the expression of the underlying unity of a set of separate feature changes. The question naturally arises as to the empirical evidence for the postulated unity. In the past most of the abbreviatory devices developed in generative phonology have been based on two types of evidence: formal similarity and adjacent ordering. If two or more (sub)rules share a significant number of features and have the same ordering relation to all other rules in the grammar, it has been assumed that the rules should be collapsed together as manifestations of a single underlying process. However, if we accept the idea that the rules of a grammar are simultaneously a statement of the structure of a given language and a description of the native speaker's knowledge of that language, then the claim that two phenomena are reflections of an underlying unitary process must be bolstered by corpus-external evidence, at least in a modicum of cases. If this can be done, it is reasonable to assume that speakers have internalized a unitary process in analogous cases, even when no direct external evidence is available.

Some of the sources of external evidence were discussed in Chapter 5. In general, each of these can potentially bear on the question of underlying unity. We have just seen how the Cuna language game provides an argument for the two different representations for vowel length. The language game also supports the contention that the rule reducing the voiced geminate stops *bb*, *dd*, *gg* to *p*, *t*, and *k* is a unitary process. If these feature changes were each described by separate rules, there would be no explanation for why *bb*, *dd*, and *gg* behave in exactly the same way with respect to the *sorsik sunmakke* rule moving the initial syllable to the end of the word. But if each of these feature changes is implemented by the process formalized as (98), the parallel behavior follows automatically.

(98)
$$\begin{array}{lll} \text{SD} & [-\text{cont}]_i & [-\text{cont}]_j \quad \text{where } i = j \\ \text{SI} & 1 & 2 \\ \text{SC} & \left[\begin{array}{c} 1,2 \\ -\text{voice} \end{array}\right] \end{array}$$

(Notice, incidentally, that the change of *bb* to *p*, *dd* to *t*, and so on, is quite naturally expressed in the transformational format discussed in the previous section.)

Also relevant to the present discussion is the fact that the *l* of Cuna patterns as if it were derived from /rr/. When *l* comes into contact with a following consonant it reduces to *r*: *mila* 'tarpon', but *mir-sate* 'no tarpon'; *yala* 'mountain', but *yar-dake* 'see the mountain'. Recall from Chapter 5 that voiceless stops alternate with corresponding voiced stops preconsonantly (i.e., a morpheme that ends in *p* when a vowel follows will end in *b* when a consonant follows) and that there is a general rule deleting the first member of a three consonant cluster. Given that *p* derives from /bb/, the alternation between prevocalic *p* and preconsonantal *b* can be accounted for by this rule. So, too, if *l* is represented as underlying /rr/, the shift of *l* to *r* preconsonantally will follow automatically from the independently needed rule deleting the first of three consonants: /#mirra-sadde#/ becomes /#mirr-sadde#/ by a syncope rule, and the latter is converted to /#mir-sadde#/ by the cluster simplification process. Finally, the rule reducing a geminate stop to a simple voiceless stop will derive /#mir-sate#/. If *l* is derived from /rr/ underlyingly, then we require a rule that will convert /rr/ to *l*. The question arises as to whether this rule should be considered an instance of the same rule as takes /bb/ to /p/ and so on.

When we turn to the *sorsik sunmakke* game, we find that, unlike the case of reduction of voiced stops to voiceless stops, the *rr* ⟶ *l* process is not revealed in the game. This is shown by the following data.

(99)

Cuna	Underlying	Sorsik	Gloss
mila	/mirra/	*lami*	'tarpon'
mola	/morra/	*lamo*	'cloth'
yala	/yarra/	*laya*	'mountain'

If the *rr* ⟶ *l* process behaved the same as the *bb* ⟶ *p*, etc., process, we would expect the *sorsik* variant of a form like 'tarpon' to be *ramir*. But this pronunciation is never heard in the *sorsik* game. Although this does not necessarily argue against the validity of the *rr* ⟶ *l* rule, it does show that this rule does not form a completely unitary underlying process with the reduction of voiceless stops, since the latter may be split up in the *sorsik* game (cf., *sapan* ⟶ *bansab*). Consequently, if the *rr* ⟶ *l* process is part of the grammar of Cuna, it must be a separate rule that cannot be collapsed with (98).

Historical change is another important source of external evidence bearing on the question of an underlying unity. If two similar rules are generalized in the same fashion at roughly the same point in the historical development of a language, there is prima facie evidence that the two rules are manifestations of an underlying unitary process. As we have seen from earlier discussion in this chapter, Kiparsky (1968b) argued for the underlying unity of the Old English shortening rules on just this basis. Similarly, two rules that behave in tandem with respect to diachronic rule reorderings also support an underlying unity. On the other hand, if some rule is inserted between two other rules by historical change, generative phonologists have generally assumed that this constitutes evidence against the postulated unity.

An interesting example is discussed in Piggott (1971). By internal reconstruction Piggott shows that Proto-Algonquian *t* palatalized to *č* and *θ* palatalized to *š* before high front vowels and glides. In the development of the Algonquian languages **θ* merged with **l* into *l*. In most of the Central languages this *l* then further merged with PA **n* to present-day *n*. In modern Ojibwa languages one finds that *n* (<**θ*) still alternates with *š* and *t* with *č*: /ki-nān-i-min/ 'you fetch us' and /kēttimit-ik/ 'they who are lazy' are realized as *kināšimi* and *kēttimičik*. Thus, it is necessary to assume rules palatalizing *θ* ⟶ *š* and *t* ⟶ *č* before *i* and *y* in PA. Because of their formal similarity and adjacent ordering, they can be collapsed as (100).

(100) $\begin{bmatrix} +\text{coronal} \\ -\text{sonorant} \\ -\text{strident} \end{bmatrix} \longrightarrow \begin{bmatrix} +\text{high} \\ -\text{anterior} \end{bmatrix} /\!\!\!\underline{} \begin{bmatrix} -\text{cons} \\ +\text{high} \\ -\text{back} \end{bmatrix}$

In the historical development of Ojibwa an apocope rule was added. As (101) shows, apocope was ordered between palatalization of *n* (<**θ*) and palatalization of *t*.

(101) /ki-nān-i/ ⟶ [kināš]   'you fetch me'
       /kēttimit-i/ ⟶ [kēttimit]   'he who is lazy'

Piggott argues that since the two instances of palatalization were split apart in the historical development of Ojibwa, they were never manifestations of a single underlying process in Proto-Algonquian, as the rule in (100) claims. This argument is somewhat vitiated by Piggott's failure to establish the relative chronology of the addition of the apocope rule to the grammar and the merger of *θ with *l, and subsequently of *l with *n. For if apocope was added to the grammar only after the completion of these mergers, one might argue that a rule taking t to $\check{c}$ and another rule taking n to $\check{s}$ are not sufficiently identical formally to be collapsed together into a single underlying process. In other words, this analysis would say that while there was a unitary rule like (100) prior to the mergers in question, once those mergers occurred the language learner no longer had sufficient evidence to lead him to construct a grammar with the single rule (100). In any case, whether or not Piggott's argument can be ultimately maintained, his work is a good illustration of the kind of evidence that linguistic change can bring to bear on the question of whether or not two rules are part of an underlying unitary phenomenon.

A diachronically based argument for the unity of a phonological process has been presented by Davis (1970). In a study of the dissimilative jakan'e process in Southern Russian dialects, Davis found that this rule has been reordered with another rule that diphthongizes stressed e and o to ie and uo, respectively. Dissimilative jakan'e refers to the pronunciation of pretonic nonhigh vowels after a palatalized consonant, that is, in the environment C'___C_0 $\acute{V}$. In all of these dialects a nonhigh vowel is pronounced as i or a in this position. Which option is selected depends on the quality of the following stressed vowel, of which there are seven: $i, u,$ $e, o, \varepsilon, \mathfrak{o},$ and a. In the Don dialect nonhigh vowels are realized as a when the following stressed vowel is high (i or u); they appear as i when the stressed vowel is nonhigh. On the other hand, in the Obojansk dialect the pretonic vowel is realized as a not only before i, u (as in the Don dialect) but also before e, and o. If the stressed vowel is low $\varepsilon, \mathfrak{o},$ or a, then nonhigh vowels are pronounced as i. If it is recalled that in both dialects stressed /é/ and /ó/ are realized phonetically as the diphthongs /ie/ and /uo/, then the differences between the two dialects can be described in terms of a different ordering of the dissimilation and diphthongization rules. In the Obojansk dialect, where underlying /e/ and /o/ behave like high vowels, the dissimilation rule will be ordered after diphthongization. In the Don dialect /e/ and /o/ behave like the nonhigh vowels. Accordingly, in this dialect dissimilation is ordered before diphthongization. The dissimilation rule itself will be formulated as follows:

(102)
$$\begin{bmatrix} +\text{syll} \\ -\text{high} \end{bmatrix} \longrightarrow \begin{bmatrix} -\text{round} \\ \alpha\text{low} \\ -\alpha\text{high} \end{bmatrix} / \text{C'}\underline{\hspace{1em}}C_0 \begin{bmatrix} +\text{syll} \\ +\text{stress} \\ \alpha\text{high} \end{bmatrix}$$

It seems evident that the historical difference between these dialects is that one of them has changed the original order of the rules. Presently available information does not permit us to determine which dialect reflects the historically earlier state of affairs. But in any case, the fact that all of the changes summarized by rule (102) were reordered as a group supports the claim that (102) reflects a unitary process. To the extent that (102) is a unitary phenomenon, the notation that allows it to be expressed as a unitary process (namely, the alpha notation and the use of phonetic features) finds support.

Sameness of restrictions on the operation of rules, especially if they are idiosyncratic, is prima facie evidence for an underlying unity. Recall that we argued for uniting the two contexts in which Karok palatalizes *s* to *š* on these grounds. The converse argument is also possible. If the distribution of exceptions or other idiosyncratic restrictions in the parts of a rule are radically different, it is reasonable to conclude, other things being equal, that they are not parts of the same underlying process. An argument along these lines is to be found in Zwicky's (1970) discussion of the Sanskrit *ruki* rule. According to this rule, *s* is retroflexed to *ṣ* when preceded by an underlying *r*, *u*, *k*, or *i*. In addition to the fact that [r, u, k, i] is an unnatural grouping of sounds, the unity of this process is suspect on the grounds that, while there are no exceptions to the rule when the conditioning sound is *k*, there are many examples where *s* fails to retroflex when preceded by *r*, *u*, or *i*. This marked difference in the distribution of exceptions suggests that retroflexion after *k* is separate from retroflexion after *u*, *i*, and *r*.

In this section we have surveyed some of the kinds of evidence that can be used in support of the claim that a particular set of rules represents an essentially unitary phenomenon. In order to decide just what notational apparatus is necessary in grammars and what conventions govern its application to phonological representations, it is not sufficient to merely show that a particular notation or convention can give a unified description of a certain body of data; in addition, we must be able to show that there is external evidence in favor of the claim that this body of data does in fact reflect a unified process. Thus it is imperative that we continue to look painstakingly for external evidence that bears on the problem of the unity of various phonological processes.

Exercises

1. Kera (Chad) (Ebert 1974). Propose a set of ordered rules to account for the alternations in the following data. You may assume that vowels are represented in terms of the following feature matrix and that *h* and *ʔ* are [+low], as in SPE.

	i	e	a	ə	o	u
high	+	−	−	+	−	+
back	−	−	+	+	+	+
round	−	−	−	−	+	+
low	−	−	+	−	−	−

Formulate your rules explicitly in terms of feature matrixes.

hama-n	'eat me'	*se:ne-n*	'my brother'	*kolo-n*	'change me'
hama-m	'eat you m.'	*se:ne-m*	'your masc. brother'	*kolo-m*	'change you masc.'
həm-i	'eat you f.'	*si:n-i*	'your fem. brother'	*kul-i*	'change you fem.'
həm-u	'eat him'	*si:n-u*	'his brother'	*kul-u*	'change him'
ham-a	'eat her'	*se:n-a*	'her brother'	*kol-a*	'change her'
hama-ŋ	'eat you pl.'	*se:ne-ŋ*	'your pl. brother'	*kolo-ŋ*	'change you pl.'

cə:rə-n	'my head'	*gunu-n*	'wake me'	*gi:di-n*	'my belly'
cə:rə-m	'your m. head'	*gunu-m*	'wake you masc.'	*gi:di-m*	'your masc. belly'
ci:r-i	'your f. head'	*gun-i*	'wake you fem.'	*gi:d-i*	'your fem. belly'
cu:r-u	'his head'	*gun-u*	'wake him'	*gi:d-u*	'his belly'
cə:r-ə	'her head'	*gun-ə*	'wake her'	*gi:d-ə*	'her belly'
cə:rə-ŋ	'your pl. head'	*gunu-ŋ*	'wake you pl.'	*gi:di-ŋ*	'your pl. belly'

bəla-n	'want me'	*ŋəfa-n*	'meet me'	*hara-n*	'give me back'
bəla-m	'want you m.'	*ŋəfa-m*	'meet you masc.'	*hara-m*	'give you masc. back'
bəl-i	'want you f.'	*ŋəf-i*	'meet you fem.'	*hər-i*	'give you fem. back'
bəl-u	'want him'	*ŋəf-u*	'meet him'	*hər-u*	'give him back'
bəl-a	'want her'	*ŋəf-a*	'meet her'	*har-a*	'give her back'
bəla-ŋ	'want you pl.'	*ŋəfa-ŋ*	'meet you pl.'	*hara-ŋ*	'give you pl. back'

ʔasa-n	'know me'	*ʔapa-n*	'find me'	*ba*	'not'
ʔasa-m	'know you m.'	*ʔapa-m*	'find you masc.'	*pa*	'again'
ʔəs-i	'know you f.'	*ʔəp-i*	'find you fem.'	*bə-pa*	'no more'
ʔəs-u	'know him'	*ʔəp-u*	'find him'	*koroŋ*	'left'
ʔas-a	'know her'	*ʔap-a*	'find her'	*da*	'to here'
ʔasa-ŋ	'know you pl.'	*ʔapa-ŋ*	'find you pl.'	*fadi*	'quickly'
				koroŋ-də-fadi	'came here quickly'

balna-n	'wanted me'	*ŋafna-n*	'met me'
balna-m	'wanted you m.'	*ŋafna-m*	'met you masc.'
bəln-i	'wanted you f.'	*ŋəfn-i*	'met you fem.'
bəln-u	'wanted him'	*ŋəfn-u*	'met him'
baln-a	'wanted her'	*ŋafn-a*	'met her'
balna-ŋ	'wanted you pl.'	*ŋafna-ŋ*	'met you pl.'
bal-l-a	'you must want!'	*ŋaf-l-a*	'you must meet'

2. Macedonian. Account for the placement of stress in these data. Express the stress rule in terms of the SPE parenthesis notation.

	Nondefinite	Definite	Gloss
Masculine	*grát*	*grádot*	'city'
	gróp	*gróbot*	'grave'
	vózdux	*vózduxot*	'air'
	jázik	*jázikot*	'tongue'
	žéludnik	*želúdnikot*	'stomach'
	sínovi	*sinóvite*	'sons'
Feminine	*gláva*	*glávata*	'head'
	nóga	*nógata*	'leg'
	plánina	*planínata*	'mountain'
	svékṛva	*svekṛ́vata*	'mother-in-law'
	vodénica	*vodenícata*	'mill'
Neuter	*sélo*	*séloto*	'village'
	gṛ́lo	*gṛ́loto*	'throat'
	ézero	*ezéroto*	'lake'
	kóleno	*kolénoto*	'knee'
	kolíčestvo	*količéstvoto*	'quantity'

3. Classical Arabic (Brame 1971). Account for the placement of stress. Express the rule in terms of the SPE parenthesis notation.

lán	'not'	*kássarat*	'she smashed'
fáqaṭ	'only'	*kasártu*	'I broke'
málikun	'a king'	*kassártuhu*	'I smashed it'
malíkatun	'a queen'	*kasártuhu*	'I broke it'
malikátuhu	'his queen'	*sa :fártu*	'I traveled'
maktábatun	'a library'	*qábla*	'before'
maktabátuhu	'his library'	*kitá :bun*	'a book'
yastaqbíluhu	'he receives him	*ká :tibun*	'a writer'
	(as a guest)'	*kassarú :hu*	'they smashed it'
ja :wárahu	'it bordered it'	*kasarná :hu*	'we broke it'
yuja :wíruhu	'it borders it'	*sá :fara*	'he traveled'
		ka :tibí :na	'writers'

4. Japanese (Bach and Harms 1972). In Japanese the high vowels *i* and *u* have the effects on preceding dental obstruents that are depicted below. Formulate rules for the changes produced by each vowel and then try to collapse these rules together into a single schema by the appropriate notational apparatus. Assume that the consonants are represented in terms of the feature matrix given below.

						t	d	s	z	c	č	ǰ	š
ti $\longrightarrow$ *či*		*tu* $\longrightarrow$ *cu*			coronal	+	+	+	+	+	+	+	+
si $\longrightarrow$ *ši*		*su* $\longrightarrow$ *su*			anterior	+	+	+	+	−	−	−	−
di $\longrightarrow$ *ǰi*		*du* $\longrightarrow$ *zu*			del.rel.	−	−	+	+	+	+	+	+
zi $\longrightarrow$ *ǰi*		*zu* $\longrightarrow$ *zu*			voice	−	+	−	+	−	−	+	−
					contin.	−	−	+	+	−	−	−	+

5. Modern Greek (Newton 1972). When vowel clusters result from attaching a vowel final clitic to a following vowel initial word, they are resolved in a manner known as Chatzidakis' rule. What are the basic patterns of deletion? Try to express them in rules employing the notational devices discussed in this chapter. What difficulties are encountered?

$$
\begin{array}{llllll}
i + i \longrightarrow i & e + i \longrightarrow e & u + i \longrightarrow u & o + i \longrightarrow o & a + i \longrightarrow a \\
i + e \longrightarrow e & e + e \longrightarrow e & u + e \longrightarrow u & o + e \longrightarrow o & a + e \longrightarrow a \\
i + u \longrightarrow u & e + u \longrightarrow u & u + u \longrightarrow u & o + u \longrightarrow o & a + u \longrightarrow a \\
i + o \longrightarrow o & e + o \longrightarrow o & u + o \longrightarrow o & o + o \longrightarrow o & a + o \longrightarrow a \\
i + a \longrightarrow a & e + a \longrightarrow a & u + a \longrightarrow a & o + a \longrightarrow a & a + a \longrightarrow a
\end{array}
$$

6. Turkish has eight phonetic vowels: front [i,ü,e,ö] and back [u,ı,o,a]. Ignoring exceptions due to loanwords, all the vowels of a word agree in backness. Since Turkish is exclusively suffixing, alternations only arise in suffixes. Since suffixes never appear in isolation, their backness is always determined by the preceding root and hence may be left unspecified (i.e., [0back]) in the lexicon. For purposes of this exercise, also assume that all noninitial roots vowels are [0back] in UR, to be filled in by the backness harmony rule. Turkish also has a labial harmony rule whereby all high vowels agree in rounding with the preceding vowel. Again only suffixes alternate and you may assume that the feature round is unspecified for all but the first vowel of a root. Finally, *o* and *ö* only appear in initial syllables. Thus, noninitial vowels only contrast in height. We shall let the symbols I and A stand for high and nonhigh vowels, respectively, that are unspecified for the features back and round. Examine the following data and formulate the two harmony rules.

Abs. sg.	Abs. pl.	Gen. sg.	Gen. pl.	Gloss
iz	*izler*	*izin*	*izlerin*	'footprint'
gül	*güller*	*gülün*	*güllerin*	'rose'
yel	*yeller*	*yelin*	*yellerin*	'wind'
čöl	*čöller*	*čölün*	*čöllerin*	'desert'
kul	*kullar*	*kulun*	*kulların*	'slave'
kız	*kızlar*	*kızın*	*kızların*	'daughter'
kol	*kollar*	*kolun*	*kolların*	'arm'
baš	*bašlar*	*bašın*	*bašların*	'head'

There are a number of phonological contexts in which apparent exceptions to the harmony rules occur. One of these involves disyllabic roots whose first vowel is *a* followed by a labial consonant. In these cases the second vowel is *u* instead of the expected *ı*: *avlu* 'courtyard', *armud* 'pear', *sabun* 'soap', *čaput* 'raid'. Since there are no alternations and since this rule does not hold across morpheme boundaries (cf., *yap-ıl* 'be made'), it is perhaps best described in terms of the following morpheme structure rule.

$$
\begin{bmatrix} +\text{syll} \\ +\text{high} \end{bmatrix} \longrightarrow [+\text{round}]/a \; C_0 \; [\text{labial}] \; C_0\_\_\_
$$

Suffixal vowels harmonize to the *u*: *sabun-u* 'the soap', *armud-u-dur* 'it is his pear'. According to Lightner (1972) a problem arises when one tries to order this rule with rounding harmony, as can be seen from the following derivations.

/armId-I-dIr/		/armId-I-dIr/	
armUd-I-dIr	labial assim.	armud-ı-dır	round (and back) harmony
armud-ı-dır	round (and back) harmony	armud-ı-dır	labial assim.

In the first derivation labial assimilation has applied, but its effect is wiped out by the round harmony rule that, recall, assimilates vowels to the first vowel of the word. Switching the order of the rules is of no avail, as the second derivation shows.

A similar problem arises with a rule that fronts a vowel after the palatal lateral λ: *ka*λ*b* 'heart', *ka*λ*b-im* 'my heart', *ka*λ*b-ler-den* 'from the hearts'; *usu*λ 'system', *usu*λ*-üm, usu*λ*-ler-den*. If lateral assimilation applies first, its effect will be wiped out by backness harmony. But if harmony applies first we would derive **ka*λ*b-ler-dan* and **usu*λ*-ler-dan*. Finally, in the Istanbul dialect noninitial vowels are raised and unrounded before the palatal consonants [y,š,ĵ], as evidenced by the following infinitive and imperative forms: *ye-mek, yi-yin* 'eat'; *üšü-mek, üši-yin* 'be cold'; *oku-mak, okı-yın* 'read'; *sakla-mak, saklı-yın* 'hide'. Again an ordering paradox appears to result in the derivation of forms like *üši-yin*. If unrounding applies first, its effect is cancelled by rounding harmony. If harmony is first and then unrounding, we derive *üši-yün. How can these ordering paradoxes be resolved?

10

The Role of Syntax and the Lexicon in Phonology

To this point in our exposition of generative phonology we have explicitly discussed two factors which may control the application of a phonological rule: the phonetic properties comprising the feature matrixes of segments and the derivational source of a segment (underlying or derived by rule). There are, however, other, essentially nonphonetic factors that may govern the application of a rule and thus play a significant role in forming the phonological structure of a language. Considerably less is known about the role that these factors play in phonology. As a result, the discussion of this chapter will be more discursive, reflecting our tentative understanding of these matters.

The nonphonetic factors influencing the application of a phonological rule fall into two broad categories. First, there are what we will refer to as extra-grammatical factors—"extragrammatical" because they fall outside of "grammar" as this term has been normally understood in generative as well as in most other theories of linguistics. Although most linguists have acknowledged the importance of these factors, they have been studied least of all. The second nonphonetic factor influencing the application of phonological rules is grammatical information, which can be divided into two broad categories: syntactic/morphological versus lexical. The former represents information that is independently needed in the grammar in order to describe the syntactic or morphological structure of morphemes and words, while the latter represents information that, while not independently motivated, is nevertheless required in order to provide a full description of the phonological behavior of a morpheme.

The present chapter is organized as follows. First we illustrate how various extragrammatical factors affect the operation of phonological rules. Then we examine various types of lexical determinants that control rule application. Next we take up the role of syntax and morphology. The discussion here focuses on three topics: a survey of the kinds of morphosyntactic categories and features that seem relevant to phonology, the role of boundaries, and the role of phrase structure in imposing a cyclic application of phonological rules. In the final section we take another look at the lexicon, developing the notion of "morpheme-structure rules." At first glance such rules might appear tangential to the concerns of the present chapter, but we conclude by suggesting that they too play a role (either directly or indirectly) in determining the applicability of phonological rules.

Extragrammatical Information

Perhaps the most frequently cited extragrammatical factor controlling the application of a phonological rule is the rate or style of speech. In many languages "fast" speech provides the context for the application of rules which do not operate in "slow" speech. For instance, in English fast speech (Zwicky 1972) schwa may be deleted from a pretonic syllable, giving rise to clusters that otherwise do not occur in initial position: *b(e)come*, *p(e)dantic*, *d(e)posit*, *b(e)side*, *d(i)scover*, *C(a)nadian*, *m(i)raculous*.

In addition to providing the context for new rules, fast speech frequently exhibits the extension of slow speech rules to new and wider contexts. One of the most common extensions is across word boundaries. Thus, in slow speech in Spanish (Harris 1969), nasals assimilate the point of articulation of a following obstruent within a word but not across word boundaries:[1] /con + padre/ ⟶ *compadre* 'friend', /con + ducir/ ⟶ *conducir* 'to lead', /con-currir/ ⟶ *coŋcurrir* 'to concur'. In fast speech we find /con#padre/ ⟶ *com#padre* 'with father', /cantan#bien/ ⟶ *cantam#bien* 'they sing well', and /Juan#canta/ ⟶ *Juaŋ#canta*

---

[1] Except for the effects of nasal assimilation, these forms are cited in the Spanish orthography and thus *c* represents a velar when it stands before a back vowel letter.

'John sings'; in slow speech these word-final nasals would fail to assimilate.

Though often correlated with rate of speech, another apparently independent extragrammatical factor is what we can vaguely label ''style of speech.'' In most languages there is a contrast between colloquial speech and other more formal styles, which are frequently learned later in life as part of the initiation to the social levels or settings where that style is used. Typically the more formal styles are conservative in the sense that the phonetic output of the colloquial style can be derived from that of the formal by further application of rules.

The phenomenon of liaison in French is a well-known example of a phonological rule that is controlled by stylistic levels. In French word final obstruents are generally deleted. In certain well defined cases this process is blocked when the following word begins with a vowel, in which case the final obstruent generally syllabifies with the following vowel. The retention of such final consonants is referred to as *liaison* 'linking'.

Selkirk (1972) has shown that liaison is governed by both grammatical and stylistic factors. In the most colloquial style of French a final obstruent will delete unless it terminates a monosyllabic 'function' word that modifies a following vowel-initial head. Thus, the final consonants of such quantifiers as *très* 'very' and *trop* 'too' will escape deletion (indicated by the ligature) when immediately followed by a vowel-initial adjective: *très‿incommode* 'very inconvenient', *trop‿élégant* 'too elegant'. On the other hand, polysyllabic modifiers fail to link in this colloquial style. Thus, the final consonants of *assez* and *extrêmement* are deleted in *assez intime* 'rather intimate' and *extrêmement amusant* 'extremely amusing'. Similarly, monosyllabic auxiliaries will link with a following verb while polysyllabic ones will not: *Ils sont‿entrés* 'they entered' versus *Vous avez étonné* 'you surprised'. Prepositions exhibit the same contrast. There is linking in *chez‿elle* 'at hers' but not in *depuis un an* 'since a year'. On the other hand, both mono- and polysyllabic words, whether lexical or nonlexical, link with a following vowel initial noun: *mes‿oignons* 'my onions', *un long‿hiver* 'a long winter', *plusieurs‿écrits* 'several writings', *les aimables‿italiens* 'the amiable Italians'.

On the other hand, in more guarded speech (a style Selkirk labels *conversation soignée*) polysyllabic modifiers will link with their following vowel-initial heads. Thus, in this style linking will occur in *assez‿intime*, *extrêmement‿amusant*, *vous avez‿étonné*, and *depuis‿un an*.

Finally, in the most formal style of *lecture et discours* the final consonant of the head of a phrase will link with a following vowel-initial modifier if that consonant constitutes an inflectional morpheme. Thus, the final *s* in *les marchands‿anglais* 'the English merchants' will link since it marks the plural, while the final *d* will not link in *un marchand anglais* since it does not realize an inflectional suffix.

It should be noted that all of the liaison contexts appearing in the colloquial style are carried over into the two more formal styles. Similarly, all of the liaisons made in *conversation soignée* are carried over into *lecture*. The rule of final-obstruent deletion thus displays a characteristic property of stylistically governed rules: It is extended to more contexts as speech becomes less formal. As we have seen, the transition from slower to faster rates of speech is associated with the same kind of extension of a rule. In fact, in many cases rate of speech is directly correlated with style of speech, the slowest rate being the most formal. However, there are other cases, as in French liaison, where a stylistic parameter distinct from rate of speech must be recognized.

In addition to rate and style of speech, factors which more or less affect all speakers of a language in the same way, the age, social class, or sex of the speaker may play a role in determining the phonological structure of his speech. For example, according to V. Jochelson (Trubetzkoy 1939:17) the underlying alveolar stops of Yukaghir, a language of Northeastern Siberia, are realized as palatalized *t'* and *d'* by adult males of hunting age, as alveolar affricates *c* and *dz* by children and women of child-bearing age, and as palatalized affricates *č'* and *j'* by old people.

There are many other examples like this scattered through the literature. According to Sapir, the great majority of words in Yana, an Amerindian language of Northern California, have two distinct forms: a full or "male" form and a reduced or "female" form. Male forms are used only when one male is speaking to another male. When a female is speaking, either to a male or female, or when a male is speaking to a female, the reduced, female forms are employed. However, as Sapir notes, the male forms are not tabooed to the females, "for a female uses the male forms without hesitation when she quotes the words of a male speaking to a male, as in relating a myth in which one male character speaks to another [1929, p. 206]."

The differences between the male and female forms involve two types of reduction of the basic male form, one morphological and the other phonological. The latter involves the devoicing of a word final vowel in the male form accompanied by an aspiration of a preceding lenis stop, if there is one. Thus, male *i:si* 'man', *imamba* 'deer liver', and *ga:gi* 'crow' are realized as female *i:sI*, *imampA*, and *ga:kI*.

Studies by Labov (1970) have shown that the phonetic realizations of the initial consonants in the English words *this*, *that*, *these*, *the*, *them*, and *they* are systematically correlated with social class. The lower the social status of the speaker, the more likely these words are to be realized with initial *d*, although speakers from any social class might on a given occasion pronounce these words with either *d* or *ð*. The choice between the stop versus the fricative pronunciation is also correlated with the social setting of the speech act. Setting up a parameter labeled "attention paid to speech" (reading lists of words, reading passages, careful speech, casual speech), Labov found that the percentage of stop pronunciations systematically increased as the speaker moved in the direction of casual speech. This systematic variation occurred in all social classes investigated.

Such detailed and careful studies as those by Labov show that extragrammatical factors can influence phonological structure in a nonrandom fashion and hold great promise for further study of this hitherto neglected aspect of linguistics.

Lexical Information

Perhaps the simplest kind of situation in which an ad hoc lexical specification is required involves lexical exceptions. In such cases the overwhelming majority of morphemes that satisfy the SD of the rule do undergo or condition the rule but there nevertheless remain a small number that unpredictably fail to do so. These are most properly handled by marking such morphemes in the lexicon as exceptions to the rule. A simple example of each type will be mentioned here. Recall from Chapter 4 the rhythmic law of Slovak that shortens a vowel after a syllable containing a long vowel. All inflectional suffixes containing a long vowel undergo this rule except for the 3 pl. ending of the second conjugation. This suffix is underlyingly /-ä:/. It appears phonetically as *-ia* by the diphthongization rule regardless of whether the preceding stem ends in a long or a short vowel: *rob-ia* 'they work', *vid-ia* 'they see', *ku:p-ia* 'they buy', *hla:s-ia* 'they announce'. This morpheme thus contrasts with the perfectly regular behavior exhibited by the theme vowel /-e:/. The latter appears as the diphthong *ie* after short vowels but is shortened after long vowels: *nes-ie* 'he carries', but *muož-e* from /mo:ž-e:/ 'he can'.

In SPE a formalism has been developed for the treatment of exceptions. Each morpheme in the lexicon is assigned a rule-feature [αrule n], where α may be + or −, for each of the phonological rules in the grammar. If a given morpheme is an exception to a rule *n*, the rule-feature [−rule n] will be listed ad hoc in the morpheme's lexical representation. All morphemes that behave regularly with respect to the rule will be unmarked for the corresponding rule-feature. Instead, their specification [+rule n] will be assigned by a general convention. In this way the lexical entries of exceptions will be more complex than the entries of morphemes that behave regularly.

SPE also assumes another general convention that incorporates these rule-features into the feature matrix of each segment contained in the morpheme. It is then proposed that any phonological rule of the form A $\longrightarrow$ B/C____D will apply to an A′ just in case A′ contains the specification [+rule n.] If a segment has acquired the specification [−rule n] by virtue of appearing in a morpheme which has been marked in the lexicon as an exception to rule *n*, then rule *n* will not apply to that segment even though that segment may otherwise satisfy the structural description of the rule. Thus, in the case of the 3 pl. morpheme in Slovak, it will be marked [−rhythmic law] in the lexicon. By general convention, this feature specification will be assigned to the feature matrix of each (in this case, the only) segment of the morpheme. When, in the course of the derivation of a form such as /ku:p-ä:/, the rhythmic law scans the /-ä:/, the rule will fail to apply since this segment is [−rhythmic law].

A morpheme may also be exceptional in failing to condition the application of a rule. Recall from Chapter 6 the rule of Chimwi:ni that converts the liquid of the perfective suffix /i:ł/ to *z* if the preceding stem ends in *s*, *sh* (= [š]), *z*, or *ñ:* compare *jib-i:ł-e* 'he answered' with *fiłis-i:z-e* he went bankrupt', *anz-i:z-e* 'he began'. Although the vast majority of stems ending in *s*, *sh*, *z*, or *ñ* trigger this rule, there are a handful that do not: *bariz-i:ł-e* 'he appeared', *asis-i:ł-e* 'he founded'. Even though the liquid does not undergo the expected change to *z* in these forms, it is not the perfective suffix that is exceptional; rather these roots are exceptional in failing to trigger the rule.

There are various ways in which exceptions such as *bariz-i:ł-e* could be accounted for in a formal grammar. One treatment would involve extending the SPE formalism to permit a rule A $\longrightarrow$ B/C____D to apply to the string C′A′D′ just in case each segment in the string is specified [+rule n]. Given this treatment, /bariz/ would be specified [−ł-to-z] ad hoc in its lexical representation. When the ł-to-z rule scans the structure /bariz-i:ł-e/, it will fail to apply to the ł in the suffix since the preceding *z* will bear the feature [−ł-to-z]. This sort of analysis would be inadequate if a given morpheme turned out to be regular in that it undergoes rule *n* but irregular in failing to condition that same rule, or if a given morpheme turned out to be irregular in failing to undergo rule *n* but regular in that it does trigger that same rule. Below we will cite examples that suggest that such cases exist.

A second treatment of *bariz-i:ł-e* would be to say that the suffix *-i:ł-* is assigned the rule-feature [−ł-to-z] when it occurs after the verb root

/barɨz/. This analysis characterizes the exceptionality of /bariz/ not by associating with this morpheme an exceptional value for a rule-feature, but rather by making this item the environment for the assignment of an exceptional rule-feature.

A third possible treatment involves recognizing two types of rule-features: one feature that characterizes whether an item is a possible *target* for a rule (i.e., whether it can undergo the rule) and a second feature that characterizes whether an item is a possible *environment* for a rule (i.e., whether it can condition or trigger the rule's application). In this approach, a rule of the form A ⟶ B/C____D would, by convention, apply to a string C′A′D′ just in case A′ is [+target of rule n] and C′ and D′ are both [+env of rule n]. Thus /bariz/ in Chimwi:ni would be specified as [−env of ɨ-to-z] while the suffix -i:ɨ- would be [+target of ɨ-to-z]. A structure such as /bariz-i:ɨ-e/ would fail to undergo the ɨ-to-z rule since the *z* of /bariz/ is not capable of triggering the rule since it carries a negative value for the rule-feature [environment of ɨ-to-z].

Although we tend to favor an approach involving the recognition of two sets of rule features, much more data needs to be assembled to work out the details of such a treatment of the problem and to justify it.

The Slovak and Chimwi:ni examples discussed above represent cases where the number of morphemes not undergoing or triggering the rule is small compared to the number of morphemes that do undergo or condition the rule. In acquiring these languages the language learner must memorize the exceptional morphemes. The descriptive analogue of this memorization is the negative rule-feature that must be listed ad hoc in the lexical representation of these morphemes. There are, however, cases where the vast majority of morphemes fail to undergo or condition a rule. Only a small number of morphemes behave positively with respect to the rule. In this case the language learner must memorize the morphemes which do undergo or condition the rule.

Russian provides a couple of examples of these minor rules. In Russian there is a pair of underlying vowels *ĭ* and *ŭ*, traditionally called yers, which exhibit the following behavior in verbs. In the derived imperfective of prefixed verbs, *ĭ* and *ŭ* appear as *i* and *y*, respectively, when they occur in the root. Outside of this grammatical context, the yers are regularly realized in the following fashion: *ĭ* and *ŭ* merge with underlying *e* and *o*, respectively, when the following syllable contains a yer, and delete otherwise. Examples where the yers "vocalize" to *e* and *o* before another yer will be given later in this chapter. At this point we are concerned with cases where this context does not arise. Examine the data in (1).

(1)

Root	Inf.	1 sg.	3 sg.	Past	Derived imp.	Gloss
/žĭd/	žd-at'	žd-u	žd-et	žd-al	vy-žid-at'	'wait'
/rŭv/	rv-at'	rv-u	rv-et	rv-al	u-ryv-at'	'tear'
/bĭr/	br-at'	ber-u	ber-et	br-al	po-bir-at'	'take'
/zŭv/	zv-at'	zov-u	zov-et	zv-al	na-zyv-at'	'call'

The roots *žĭd-* and *rŭv-* behave prefectly regularly with respect to the yer rules. Their root vowels appear as *i* and *y* in the derived imperfectives and delete in the remaining forms cited, since they are followed by a vowel that is not a yer. On the other hand the roots *bĭr-* and *rŭv-* are exceptional in that their vowels are vocalized to *e* and *o* in the present tense. The vocalization in the present tense cannot come from the regular rule vocalizing yers before another yer since the following syllables in the present tense do not contain yers. Rather, a special rule to vocalize yers in the present tense is required. However, the vast majority of roots with yers do not undergo this rule but rather follow the regular rule that deletes yers before another non-yer syllable. Only a couple other roots behave like *bĭr-* and *rŭv-*. Thus, the language learner must memorize those few yer roots that exceptionally vocalize their vowel in the present tense.

The behavior of the Russian comparative suffix illustrates a case where a small number of morphemes trigger the application of a rule. After the overwhelming majority of adjectival roots, the comparative suffix appears as *-eje*. After a relatively small number of roots the initial vowel of the suffix is deleted and the resultant C + j merges into a palatal consonant: *zdorov-eje* 'healthier', *cenn-eje* 'more valuable', but *molož-e* from /molod-je/ 'younger', *suš-e* from /sux-je/ 'drier'. The language learner thus must memorize the relatively small number of roots like /molod/ that trigger the rule deleting the vowel of the comparative suffix.

In order to achieve the state of affairs where a minus rule feature is considered exceptional for examples like the Slovak and Chimwi : ni ones, but where a plus rule-feature is exceptional for examples like the ones in Russian, it has been customary to make a distinction between major versus minor rules. In a major rule the vast majority of items that meet the SD of the rule undergo it or condition it, while in the case of a minor rule only a small percentage of morphemes satisfying the SD undergo or condition the rule. Given that each rule in the grammar is marked as being major or minor, exceptions will be handled as follows. Exceptions to a major rule will be marked minus in the lexicon and a general convention will mark all other morphemes as plus. Morphemes that undergo or condition a minor rule will be marked plus for that rule in the lexicon and a general convention will mark all other morphemes as minus for the minor rule. In this way the lexical entries for exceptional morphemes (those that fail to trigger or undergo major rules and those that do trigger or undergo minor rules) will be more complex than the entries of regular morphemes.

In some cases the number of morphemes that satisfy the SD of a rule but nevertheless fail to undergo or condition its application is approximately equal to the number of morphemes that do condition or undergo the rule. In such cases it is not clear which behavior is regular and which exceptional. These situations must also be handled by ad hoc lexical marking, but the plus/minus specification must be mentioned in the lexical representation of each relevant morpheme. A simple example appears in Spanish, where *e* and *o* diphthongize under stress to *ye* and *we* in a large number of verb roots. There are, however, an approximately equal number of roots with mid vowels (at least in everyday vocabulary) that fail to diphthongize when stressed. Thus, compare *dormír, dúermo* 'sleep' and *perdér, píerdo* 'lose', where the rule applies, with *cosér, cóso* 'sew' and *bebér, bébo* 'drink', where the rule blocks. In this case a root such as /dorm/ will be marked [+diphthongization] while /cos/ will be marked [−diphthongization]. No general convention will assign either [+diphthongization] or [−diphthongization] since, for any given root, there is no way to predict whether its mid vowel will be susceptible to the rule.

It should be pointed out that there is an historical explanation for the different behavior of the mid vowels with respect to diphthongization. Those that undergo the rule can be traced back to short vowels, while most mid vowels that fail to diphthongize derive from historical long vowels. In the history of Spanish short *e* and *o* diphthongized and vowel length was subsequently lost, resulting in the present state of affairs. Since an underlying length contrast cannot be motivated in a synchronic discription of contemporary Spanish, the alternation must be accounted for by lexical marking. (See Harris 1969 for why the diphthongs cannot be taken as underlying the alternation.)

A more complex example requiring lexical specification is provided by the Arawakan language Piro spoken in Peru (Matteson 1965). Piro has a rule that elides a morpheme-final vowel in the context VC____ + CV. Among the suffixes triggering application of this rule are the nominalizer *-lu* and the possessive *-ne*, the latter used in combination with a pronominal prefix.

(2)

yimaka	'teach'	*yimak-lu*	'teaching'
kama	'make'	*kam-lu*	'handicraft'
xipalu	'sweet potato'	*n-xipal-ne*	'my sweet potato'
čalu	'fish net'	*n-čal-ne*	'my fish net'
kahli	'clay'	*n-kahli-ne*	'my clay'

Although the number of suffixes that trigger elision is large there are approximately an equal number that fail to condition the rule. One such suffix is *-ta*, a verbal theme formative. It occurs in the word *hata-ta* 'to illuminate'. The final vowel of the root /hata/ meets the SD for elision but the rule fails to apply. This cannot be explained by simply marking the root as exceptionally failing to undergo elision, for it will lose its vowel when followed by other suffixes: for example, *hat-nu* 'light, shining' from /hata-nu/, where *-nu* is a suffix used to form abstract nouns. Another suffix that fails to condition elision is the anticipatory suffix *-nu: heta-nu* 'going to see' from *heta* 'to see' (cf., *het-lu* 'to see it').

Although the morphemes *-ta* and *-nu* fail to elicit the elision of a preceding vowel, they nevertheless regularly undergo elision. This is shown by a word such as *yono-t-na-wa* 'to paint oneself'. This word is composed of the root /yono/ 'to paint', followed by /ta/, followed in turn by the reflexive elements /na-wa/. Elision of the vowel of anticipatory /nu/ appears in *heta-n-ru* 'going to see him', from /heta-nu-lu/ by elision and a rule turning *l* to *r* after a nasal.

The Piro data indicate that a morpheme may be exceptional with respect to the environment of a rule but regularly undergo the structural change of that rule. Assuming the existence of two sets of rule-features, [±target of rule n] and [±env of rule n], then suffixes such as /ta/ and /nu/ would be specified as [+target of vowel elision] but [−env of vowel elision]. They contrast with a suffix like the causative /kaka/ which is + for both of the above rule features. /kaka/ triggers vowel elision, as shown by comparing *čokoruha* 'to harpoon' with *čokoruh-kaka* 'to cause to harpoon', and it undergoes vowel elision, as can be seen from *salwa-kak-lu* 'cause to visit him' (which consists of the verb *salwa* 'to visit' plus /kaka/ plus the 3 sg. pronominal suffix /lu/).

Piro also has a suffix that both fails to condition and fails to undergo elision. This is the suffix *-wa* meaning 'yet, still'. Forms like *heta-wa* 'still see' show that it fails to elicit elision (cf., *het-lu* 'see it' and *het-ya* 'see there' showing that *heta* cannot be considered an exception to elision). Forms such as *heta-wa-lu* 'to see him yet' and *hišinka-wa-lu* 'to still be thinking about it' demonstrate that *wa* also fails to undergo elision, for the pronominal suffix *-lu* normally does condition the rule, as shown by *het-lu* 'see it'.

The Piro data available to us are not sufficient for us to be able to determine whether morphemes such as *kaka* and *wa*, which have the same value for both types of rule feature, represent the normal situation. A similar example of a lexically restricted rule from French discussed by Dell and Selkirk (1976) suggests that this may indeed be true. In French the front mid vowels *ɛ* and *œ* are backed to *a* and *o*, respectively, before an arbitrary group of morphemes. Some of the suffixes that trigger this rule are recorded in (3).

(3) *-isme*

naturel [ɛ] 'natural'	*natural-isme*	'naturalism'
terreur [œ] 'terror'	*terror-isme*	'terrorism'

    -ité

pair [ɛ] 'even'	*par-ité*	'parity'
supérieur [œ] 'superior'	*supérior-ité*	'superiority'

    -at

notaire [ɛ] 'notary public'	*notari-at*	'profession of notary public'
professeur [œ] 'professor'	*professor-at*	'professorship'

    -aire

heure [œ] 'hour'	*hor-aire*	'hourly'
honneur [œ] 'honor'	*honor-aire*	'honorary'

    -eux

vapeur [œ] 'vapor'	*vapor-eux*	'vaporous'

    -ien

agraire [ɛ] 'agrarian'	*agrar-ien*	'agrarian'

A few of the suffixes that fail to condition backing are cited in (4).

(4) *-et/ette*

clair [ɛ] 'light, clear'	*clair-et*	'pale'	(cf., *clar-ité* 'clarity')
fleur [œ] 'flower'	*fleur-ette*	'little flower'	(cf., *flor-al* 'floral')

    -ement

clair [ɛ] 'light, clear'	*clair-ement*	'clearly'	
seule [œ] 'alone'	*seul-ement*	'only'	(cf., *sol-itaire* 'lonely')

To account for these data the suffixes of (3) will have to be marked as [+env of backing] while those in (4) will be [−env of backing]. Similarly, root morphemes with underlying /ɛ/ or /œ/ must be lexically subcategorized for whether or not they undergo the rule. Dell and Selkirk cite about 30 roots that undergo the rule and about 40 that do not. A few of the latter are given in (5).

(5)

moderne	'modern'	*modern-isme*	'modernism'
complexe	'complex'	*complex-ité*	'complexity'
peur	'fear'	*peur-eux*	'easily frightened'
pierre	'stone'	*pierr-eux*	'stony'
grammaire	'grammar'	*grammair-ien*	'grammarian'

The natural question to ask at this point is what happens to suffixes having the feature [+env of backing] if they themselves contain an underlying /ɛ/ or /œ/ and are followed by a suffix that is capable of triggering backing?

Dell and Selkirk point out that such suffixes consistently undergo the rule. For example, we have seen that /-ien/ is [+env of backing] by virtue of *agrar-ien* (cf., *agraire*). This suffix undergoes backing when followed by a suffix that induces backing: *hégél-ien* 'Hegelian', *hégél-ian-isme* 'Hegelianism'. Similarly, /-aire/ triggers backing and is itself susceptible to undergoing the rule: *ovaire* 'ovary', *ovar-ien* 'ovarian'; *volontaire* 'voluntary', *volontar-iat* 'status of an enlisted man'; *complémentaire* 'complementary', *complémentar-ité* 'complementarity'. To cite just one more example, /-eux/ triggers backing in *vapor-eux* 'vaporous' (cf., *vapeur* 'vapor') and may also undergo the rule: *nerv-eux* 'nervous', *nerv-os-ité* 'nervousness'. Thus, in French there is a strong correlation between a morpheme's specification in triggering the lexically governed rule of backing and its specification in undergoing the rule. Only further study will reveal if this kind of a correlation represents the normal situation.

It should also be pointed out that while in the Spanish, Piro, and French examples just discussed the number of morphemes having a positive lexical marking for the relevant rule is approximately equal to the number that must be specified negatively, in the French and Spanish cases at least, a positive specification is not productive. Newly coined words that meet the SD of backing in French and diphthongization in Spanish consistently fail to undergo the rule. One might infer from this fact that the backing and diphthongization rules will eventually be lost and the alternations they produce eliminated. Again, much further study is required before such predictions can be advanced with any confidence.

There are a number of other questions about lexical rule features that cannot be answered at this point. Two will be mentioned here. According to the theory advocated in SPE, a lexical feature is the property of an entire morpheme that is spread to each segment of the morpheme by general convention. This predicts that, at least in the normal case, all of the segments composing a morpheme will behave the same with respect to a governed rule. However, it is quite conceivable that such lexical specifications are really just a property of the segment rather than the entire morpheme. Most examples we know of do not bear on this issue because one cannot find morphemes containing two (or more) segments that each meet the SD of a lexically governed rule. A hypothetical example would be if Spanish had polysyllabic morphemes with mid vowels such that the stress alternated between each vowel. The theory that lexical markings are a property of the entire morpheme would predict that one vowel of such a morpheme could not diphthongize under stress unless the other did, while the theory that takes such rule features as properties of individual segments would be consistent with such a situation. The choice between these two theories is a task for future research.

Another complex question concerns the extent to which lexical specification for one rule correlates with lexical specification for other rules. This issue arises most often in the nativization of loanwords. A borrowed lexical item will often be exceptional with respect to several phonological rules. Although we have not studied the matter in any detail, it is our impression that such morphemes are often not nativized in one fell swoop, but may gradually be regularized with respect to some rules and remain exceptions to others. An interesting question is whether or not there are any consistent implicational relations such that regularization with respect to one rule implies regularization with respect to another rule. This is also a poorly understood matter that requires further study.

Grammatical Categories and Features

Generative phonology has assumed that the surface syntactic structure of a sentence constitutes the input to the phonological component of the grammar. Hence, phonological rules may potentially refer to any of the information that is present in surface structure. An important task facing phonological theory is to determine just what aspects of syntactic structure are relevant to the application of a phonological rule. At present, very little is known about this question. One reason is that it is often unclear what the precise surface syntactic structure of a given sentence is. A further obstacle is the lack of any adequate theory of the morphological structure of words. Finally, the role of grammar in phonology is a subject that, until recently, has been largely ignored in generative studies and even more so in structuralist linguistics. Thus, just what aspects of grammar are relevant to phonology is one of the most poorly understood areas of linguistics.

In this section we shall have to content ourselves with just a few illustrations of the kinds of grammatical information that seem to control the application of a phonological rule. No attempt will be made to determine exactly how the rules refer to this information.

At the outset, we wish to observe that in many cases it is not clear that appeal to a grammatical category is the appropriate description. To cite a typical example, recall the rule of Russian (Chapter 3) that deletes *t* and *d* before the past tense suffix *-l* and the rule that deletes this suffix in the context C____#. Given the notion of minor rules, a possible formulation of these rules would be to simply mark the suffix *-l* in the lexicon as triggering dental stop deletion and undergoing the rule of *l*-drop. The past tense morpheme would be the only morpheme in the language bearing either of these rule features. An alternative would be to capitalize on the fact that this morpheme has a special grammatical status in Russian, namely as the morphological marker of the past tense of verbs. Assuming that the suffix bears a feature like [+past], these rules could be formulated as in (6).

(6)   [t,d] $\longrightarrow$ $\emptyset$/___   l   l $\longrightarrow$ $\emptyset$/C ___ #
                              [+past]   [+past]

Although either analysis will account for the facts,[2] they do make different claims. If the grammatical status of the suffix is really a relevant feature, one might expect the rule to generalize along grammatical lines in the further evolution of the language. For instance, if Russian were to develop a distinction between a simple and a perfect past tense, the analysis in (6) would be consistent with a generalization of the rules to this new category.[3] On the other hand, if dental stop deletion were generalized along phonological lines to apply before other suffixes beginning with -*l*, such as the adjectival suffix in *svet-l-oj* 'bright' and *pod-l-oj* 'mean', the minor rule analysis would be supported.

Thus, just because a rule is limited to apply in the context of a

---

[2] Another possible account of these data can be excluded. This analysis would attempt to retain a purely phonological statement of the context for the rules by trying to capitalize on the fact that the past tense suffix consists of just the one sound *l* and state the environment of the rules as +*l* +. This analysis is precluded by the existence of an adjectival suffix that has the same shape. The latter does not condition dental stop deletion or undergo *l*-drop: compare *pod-l-oj* 'mean, vile' and the short form predicate adjective *pod-l*. As Lightner (1972) has observed, there are minimal pairs in which the same root appears before each suffix. The past tense suffix undergoes *l*-drop while the adjectival suffix does not: compare *xrip-l-a* 'she became hoarse' and *xrip* from /xrip-l/ 'he became hoarse' versus *ona xrip-l-a* 'she is hoarse' and *on xrip-l* 'he is hoarse'.

[3] Note that the rules stated in (6) refer to both the grammatical status of the suffix and the phonological information that it is a lateral consonant. An alternative would be to claim that only the grammatical information is relevant and reformulate dental stop deletion to drop *t* and *d* at the end of a stem in the past tense (or before the past tense suffix without mentioning its phonological character). There are, however, cases where the phonological character of an affix triggering a grammatically restricted rule is relevant. For example, in Czech *k* is palatalized to *c* before the loc.sg.m. suffix -*e* (as well as in a few other grammatically definable contexts). However, there is a growing tendency to replace this suffix by -*u* and whenever this happens palatalization is blocked: cf. the alternants *potok-u/potoc-e* 'brook' and *jazyk-u/jazyc-e* 'tongue'. If the phonological nature of the suffix were irrelevant, one might expect the rule to continue to apply when the suffix is given a different phonetic shape.

morpheme having a particular grammatical status does not automatically warrant the conclusion that that grammatical feature is relevant to the rule's application. There are two situations in which one can be reasonably sure that grammatical information is the relevant factor. First, when such grammatical information captures a clear generalization about the context in which a rule applies that could not be captured by simply marking an arbitrary list of morphemes as conditioning a minor rule. A second such situation would be one where a rule applies in a particular grammatical context which is not marked by some affix that could be interpreted as triggering a minor rule.

A rather striking example of the first type has been pointed out by Kiparsky and Halle (1977) in a study of the accent of Russian nouns. Russian morphemes fall into two basic accentual types: accented and unaccented. If a morpheme is accented, and has more than a single syllable, one cannot in general predict which syllable will bear the accent. This suggests that the accent of all morphemes in the accented class be included in their lexical representation, while unaccented morphemes will not bear an accent in underlying representation. Given this system, there are four possible types of underlying forms for monomorphemic roots + case suffixes in the inflection of nouns. If the root is accented and the suffix unaccented, the phonetic accent appears on the root, while accent appears on the suffix when an accented suffix is combined with an unaccented root. When both the root and the suffix are accented, a general rule deleting all but the leftmost accent in a word makes the root accent predominate. Finally, a rule accenting the first syllable of unaccented words takes care of nouns composed of unaccented roots plus unaccented suffixes.

Of interest to us here are nouns composed of unaccented roots. Suffixes that always bear the accent when combined with such roots are identified as accented morphemes. In the masculine inflectional class these are all the suffixes of the plural except for the nom.-acc. -*y*. In neuter nouns they are all the suffixes of the plural. In feminine nouns they are all suffixes except for the accusative sg. and the nom.-acc. pl. -*y*. Kiparsky and Halle identify all other suffixes as unaccented. When these unaccented suffixes are combined with unaccented roots, accent is assigned to the initial syllable of the word. Examples from each gender appear in (7).[4] This accentual type is traditionally called mobile, since the stress alternates between the initial and final syllable.

Within the class of unaccented stems there is another set, traditionally called oxytone, that triggers a lexically governed rule that

---

[4] When a final yer -*ŭ* is accented, the stress is retracted to the preceding syllable by a general rule that is of no concern here. Thus the gen. pl. of 'head' is [galóf].

(7)

	Singular		
Nom.	*vólos-ŭ*	*zérkal-o*	*golov-á*
Gen.	*vólos-a*	*zérkal-a*	*golov-ý*
Dat.	*vólos-u*	*zérkal-u*	*golov-é*
Acc.	*vólos-ŭ*	*zérkal-o*	*gólov-u*
Instr.	*vólos-om*	*zérkal-om*	*golov-ój*
Loc.	*vólos-e*	*zérkal-e*	*golov-é*
	Plural		
Nom.	*vólos-y*	*zerkal-á*	*gólov-y*
Gen.	*volos-ŭ*	*zerkal-ŭ*	*golov-ŭ*
Dat.	*volos-ám*	*zerkal-ám*	*golov-ám*
Acc.	*vólos-y*	*zerkal-á*	*gólov-y*
Instr.	*volos-ámi*	*zerkal-ámi*	*golov-ámi*
Loc.	*volos-áx*	*zerkal-áx*	*golov-áx*
Gloss	'hair' masc.	'mirror' neut.	'head' fem.

accents the case ending in all forms. Nouns belonging to this class include *sapog-ŭ* 'boot', *koles-ó* 'wheel', and *kočerg-á* 'poker'.

As documented in Kiparsky (1962), a rule entered Russian in the early 19th century that retracts accent from the plural suffixes onto the last vowel of the stem. When one examines the nouns that are subject to this retraction, it is clear that the rule serves the function of increasing the accentual opposition between the singular and plural.

First, in the neuter nouns retraction now applies to all nouns that formerly belonged to the oxytone (end-stressed) class. Thus 'wheel' has suffixal accent in the singular (*koles-ó*, *koles-á*, etc.), but has replaced suffixal stress with retracted stress in the plural (*kolés-a*, *kolés-am*, etc.). Particularly significant is the fact that, with one exception, retraction has not applied to neuter nouns that belonged to the mobile pattern. Thus, *zérkal-o*, *zérkal-a* 'mirror' still retains suffixal accent in the plural (*zerkal-á*, *zerkal-ám*, etc.). Retraction thus will supply stem stress to a plural noun only if that noun has suffixal stress in the singular.

In the feminine declension the picture is slightly different. Here a fair number of oxytone nouns still retain final stress in the plural (e.g., *kočerg-á* 'poker' is not subject to retraction: *kočerg-í*, *kočerg-ám*, etc.). Formerly oxytone nouns that have fallen under the sway of retraction include *kolbas-á* (*kolbás-y*, *kolbás-am*) 'sausage', and *strekoz-á* (*strekóz-y*, *strekóz-am*) 'dragonfly'. A few nouns, such as *vin-á* 'fault' and *karg-á* 'crow', vacillate between suffixal and presuffixal stress in the plural. Finally, unlike in the neuter nouns, many formerly mobile nouns have undergone retraction in the feminine declension: for example, *vesn-á* (*vésn-y*, *vésn-am*) 'spring'. The reason why feminine mobiles are freely subject to retraction while neuters are not presumably resides in the fact that for the feminine type the majority of case endings in the singular are stressed. Retraction in the plural once again sharpens the contrast between singular and plural.[5]

Finally, in masculine nouns no retraction has occurred. This is to be expected for mobiles, since, like the neuters, the stem is accented in the singular by the rule that assigns initial stress to unaccented words. However, we have no explanation for why masculine oxytones like *sapog-ú* 'boot' retain suffixal stress in the plural.

In contrast to the past tense suffix of Russian discussed above, it is clear that the grammatical information of [+plural] controls the application of the retraction rule. Marking each plural suffix in the lexicon as arbitrarily triggering a minor rule of retraction would clearly fail to reveal the underlying generalization that all such suffixes are plural. In addition, the retraction rule will have to refer to the inflectional category of the noun stem, for, as we have seen, only feminine and neuter nouns undergo retraction. Masculines must be excluded from the domain of this rule.

English stress rules provide an example where the option of a minor rule triggered by grammatical affixes is not available and direct reference to the grammatical category of a word is required. Although Ross (1972) has shown that the contrast between verbs and adjectives versus nouns is not a valid distinction for the assigment of main stress, as was claimed in the SPE rules discussed in Chapter 9, this grammatical contrast is still relevant for a stress retraction rule. In Ross's reanalysis of English stress, all words ending in clusters like *st* and *kt* are subject to final stress. In three-syllable words ending in such clusters stress is placed on the initial syllable by a retraction rule to give forms such as *mánifést, flábbergást, ánapést* and *dériléct, récolléct,* and *díaléct.* A subsequent rule reduces the final stress to a secondary stress. The grammatical contrast emerges in disyllabic words. Nouns may or may not retract the final stress onto their initial syllables: compare *gýmnàst* and *ínsèct*, which undergo the rule, with *behést* and *respéct*, which do not. However, disyllabic verbs and adjectives rarely exhibit initial stress: *divést, diréct, robúst, succínct.* Failure of the retraction rule to apply to verbs and adjectives accounts for the following well-known oppositions: *cóntràst* (noun) versus *contrást* (verb), *ábstràct* (noun) versus *abstráct* (adjective). Since no grammatical affix differentiating a noun from a verb or adjective occurs, the retraction rule for disyllables must refer directly to the feature [+noun].

Other stress rules of English are grammatically conditioned as well. The principles that subordinate one stress to another within a phrase are

---

[5] Interestingly, retraction has been generalized to all feminine nouns (both mobile and oxytone) in Byelorussian.

crucially dependent on the contrast between the lexical categories of noun, verb, adjective versus the phrasal categories noun phrase, verb phrase, adjective phrase. If two words are combined into a compound noun, verb, or adjective, the stress of the first will predominate, while if the two words are members of a phrasal category, the stress of the second word predominates. This grammatical contrast explains the differing stress patterns of the well-known pair *the Whíte Hòuse* (a noun) versus *the whìte hóuse* (a noun phrase). Similarly, contrast the compounds *to áir-condìtion* (verb) and *héart-bròken* (adjective) with *rùn hóme* (verb phrase) and *èasy to réad* (adjective phrase).

Another stress subordination rule of English that operates at the level of the phrase depends on the slightly different contrast between lexical versus nonlexical categories. Nouns, verbs, and adjectives—parts of speech representing open classes—will normally retain some degree of stress in the phrase, while the nonlexical class of function words will, if monosyllabic, normally lose their inherent stress in the phrase. Upon the deletion of their inherent stress, the nonlexical items may undergo a number of largely idiosyncratic reduction processes. Selkirk (1972) has shown that monosyllabic articles, prepositions, quantifiers, pronouns, conjunctions, and auxiliaries will lose their stress when they are followed by the lexical items they "modify." Reduction will normally fail to take place if such lexical items are deleted or moved to another position in the sentence.

The following examples, taken from Selkirk (1972), illustrate the strong (stressed) versus weak (unstressed) form of a selected sample of nonlexical items.

(8)   a. Forms of BE both as auxiliary and main verb:

Strong	Weak
Indeed I am.	*I'm ready. Why am* [əm] *I going?*
I think she is.	*Joan's here.*
And there he was.	*He was* [wəz] *there. John was going.*

b. Other auxiliaries and modals:

While they had eight.	*Before we had* $\begin{Bmatrix} \text{[wiy'd]} \\ \text{[wiyəd]} \end{Bmatrix}$ *finished.*
No more than you will.	*That'll do.*
If you really must.	*We must* [məst] *go now.*

c. Prepositions:

Who were you thinking of?	*A blade of* [əv] *grass.*
The one we were talking to.	*They're going to* [tə] *Spain.*

d. Pronouns:

You and Harry.	*Do you* [yə] *like it?*

e. Determiners:
And they say it's their job.   *We saw their* [ðər] *pictures.*
They won SOME money, but not much.   *I want some* [sm̩] *tea.*

f. Conjunctions:
But, she said, it'll soon be over.   *They came, but* [bət] *said nothing.*

Boundaries

Probably the most common situation in which grammatical structure determines the applicability of a phonological rule has to do with the location of the sounds appearing in the structural description of the rule relative to the beginning or end of a grammatical unit. Let us refer to the beginning and end of such units as the boundaries of such units. Thus we can speak of morpheme boundaries, word boundaries, phrase boundaries, and so on.

Boundaries appear to play two different roles in the application of a rule: an inhibiting function and a conditioning function. A boundary will inhibit the application of a rule A $\longrightarrow$ B/C___D to the string C'A'D' if the occurrence of the boundary in question between C' and A' or between A' and D' prevents the application of the rule. A boundary conditions the application of a rule if the rule is restricted to apply only when C', A', or D' is located at a particular kind of boundary.

The word boundary is the one that most frequently affects the application of a rule. Concerning its inhibiting function, most rules affecting the string C'A'D' will only apply if this sound sequence is located within the same word. Phonological rules tend to apply within words, not across words; the word is the most common domain for phonological rules. Vowel harmony, for instance, is usually a word-level phenomenon. Thus, in Yawelmani /a/ rounds to *o* if an /o/ occurs in the immediately preceding syllable. This rule applies only within words. In a sentence such as *wonxo na?* 'let me hide (it)', the vowel of the 1 sg. subject pronoun remains unrounded. The word boundary appearing between *wonxo* and *na?* inhibits the spread of the harmony.

With regard to the conditioning function of the word boundary, a great variety of phonological rules are formulated with reference to the beginning and the end of the word: for example, stress assignment in Czech (where the first vowel of the word is accented), glottal prothesis in German (where a glottal stop is inserted before underlying vowel-initial words), final-devoicing in Russian, stress assignment in English.

The Quicha language Puyo Pongo of Eastern Ecuador (Orr 1962)

provides an example of the conditioning role that a morpheme boundary
may assume. In this language voiced and voiceless stops contrast after
nasals when the nasal and the stop belong to the same morpheme.

(9) | *šiŋki* | 'soot' | *čuntina* | 'to stir the fire' |
        |---------|--------|-----------|--------------------|
        | *čuŋga* | 'ten' | *indi* | 'sun' |
        | *pampalʸina* | 'skirt' | *ñukanči* | 'we' |
        | *hambi* | 'poison' | *punja* | 'day' |

However, when a suffix which underlyingly begins with a voiceless occlusive is added to a morpheme ending in a nasal, the suffix initial occlusive
is voiced. (Also, basic /n/ assimilates to /m/ before a bilabial.) The
genitive suffix is/-pa/; it appears in this shape in *sinik-pa* 'porcupine's'
and *čilis-pa* 'streamless region's', but shows the allomorph /-ba/ in
kam-ba 'yours' (cf., *kan* you) and *hatum-ba* 'the big one's' (cf., *hatun*
'big'). The locative affix /-pi/ shows the same behavior: *sača-pi* 'in the
jungle', *punja-pi* 'in the daytime', but *hatum-bi* 'in big one's' and *atam-bi*
'on the frog' (cf., *atan* 'frog'). The objective suffix /-ta/ and the question
suffix /-ču/ have a similar distribution:

(10) | *wasi-ta* | 'house' | cf., *kan-da* | 'you' |
        |-----------|---------|---------------|-------|
        | *ayča-ta* | 'meat' | *atan-da* | 'the frog' |
        | *puru-ta* | 'gourd' | *wakin-da* | 'others' |
        | *ali-ču* | 'is it good?' | *kan-ju* | 'you?' |
        | *lumu-ču* | 'manioc?' | *tiyan-ju* | 'is there?' |
        | *mana-ču* | 'isn't it?' | *čarin-ju* | 'does he have?' |

These data show that a voiceless occlusive will become voiced after a
nasal just in case the nasal and the occlusive belong to different morphemes. If they belong to the same morpheme no voicing takes place.

While the morpheme boundary may trigger the application of a rule it
does not normally constitute the domain in which a phonological rule (as
opposed to a morpheme structure rule—see section on morpheme structure constraints later in this chapter) applies. If a rule applies to a certain
sound sequence that occurs within a single morpheme, the rule will
generally also apply to that same sound sequence if it arises across
morpheme boundaries. For example, in Russian an obstruent assimilates
the voicing of a following obstruent. This rule applies to a pair of
obstruents contained within a single morpheme (cf., *voš* 'louse', *fš-i* 'lice')
as well as to a pair of obstruents separated by a morpheme boundary (cf.,
lez-u 'I crawl', *les-t* 'to crawl'). In SPE this implicational relationship
(rules applying within a morpheme will also apply across morpheme
boundaries) has been raised to the status of a constraint on the way in
which rules may be formulated to refer to boundaries. A rule that applies

only across morpheme boundaries is formulated by mentioning the boundary in the statement of the rule. Thus, the Puyo-Pongo rule voicing occlusives after morpheme-final nasals would be formulated as (11).

(11) $[-\text{contin}] \longrightarrow [+\text{voice}]/[+\text{nasal}] +\underline{\quad}$

On the other hand, a rule of the form A $\longrightarrow$ B/___C is interpreted as applying to the strings A' + C' as well as to A'C', thereby making it impossible to formulate a rule to apply to A'C' only when A' and C' are contained within the same morpheme. The Russian voicing assimilation rule will thus be formulated as (12).

(12) $[-\text{sonorant}] \longrightarrow [\alpha\text{voice}]/\underline{\quad} \begin{bmatrix} -\text{sonorant} \\ \alpha\text{voice} \end{bmatrix}$

Since no boundary is explicitly mentioned in the rule, (12) will apply to any pair of obstruents contained within a word regardless of whether a morpheme boundary separates them or not.

While it is generally true that rules applying within a morpheme also apply across morpheme boundaries, there are exceptions. Kenstowicz and Kisseberth (1977) discuss a couple of examples where rules appear to be constrained to apply to a string of segments that are contained wholly within a morpheme. If these examples are correct, then the SPE constraint discussed above concerning the reference to morpheme boundaries in the statement of a rule cannot be maintained. A simple alternative is to just mark each particular rule for the type of domain in which it applies. On this view there will be morpheme-level rules, word-level rules, phrase-level rules, and so on. Each such rule will only apply to strings contained within the relevant grammatical unit. Thus, a morpheme-level rule will apply to the string XY but not to X+Y or X#Y; a word-level rule will apply to XY and X+Y, but not to X#Y; and a phrase-level rule will apply to XY, X+Y, and X#Y. Of course rules may still be restricted to apply at a particular boundary by mentioning that boundary in the structural description of the rule.

In many languages a fairly clear distinction can be made between derivational and inflectional affixes. Inflectional affixes tend to mark such categories as person, number, case, and tense, while derivational affixes are typically associated with such categories as causative, benefactive, reciprocal, as well as marking the derivation of one part of speech from another (e.g., a noun from a verb, a verb from a noun, a noun from an adjective, etc.). Semantically, the meaning of a root plus inflectional affix is compositional, while the meaning of a root plus derivational affix often cannot be predicted entirely from the meaning of its parts. Also, in most cases a given root can be combined with all the inflectional affixes of a particular part of speech to form a paradigm of words, while it is normally not the case that derivational affixes can be grouped into sets so that an acceptable word will always result from the combination of a root with members of the set. The list of words resulting from the combination of a set of roots with a set of derivational affixes usually contains many gaps. Finally, affixes from these two different categories are not normally interspersed in the composition of a word. When both types appear in the same position (left or right) relative to the root, derivational affixes are usually placed between the root and the inflectional affixes.

In such languages it is often useful to introduce the notion of a stem, defined as the word minus its inflectional affixes. The root plus derivational affixes (or, in the case where there are no derivational affixes, the root alone) thus constitutes the stem. Given that the stem can be defined as a unit on grammatical/morphological grounds, it is not surprising that the stem may constitute the domain for the operation of phonological rules.

An interesting example is provided by the development of the lax high vowels *$\breve{\imath}$ and *$\breve{u}$ from Common Slavic into Russian (Isačenko 1970). As mentioned earlier, these vowels (traditionally known as the yers) either deleted or were merged ("vocalized") with the corresponding mid vowels *e* and *o*. Vocalization occurred when the following syllable contained a yer and deletion took place in all other positions. When a word contained a series of consecutive yers, the original development was that, counting from the end of this series, even numbered yers vocalized and odd numbered ones deleted. This alternating pattern of vocalization is preserved to some extent in Ukrainian, where we find examples such as *švec'* < *$\breve{s}\breve{\imath}v\breve{\imath}c\text{-}\breve{\imath}$* 'shoemaker', but *ševc'-a* < *$\breve{s}\breve{\imath}v\breve{\imath}c\text{-}a$* gen. sg. In Russian a different pattern of vocalization has been adopted. The final yer of a stem will delete or vocalize depending on whether it occupied odd or even position in a sequence of yers, as the following examples show.

(13) | | | | |
|---|---|---|---|
| *voš* | <*$v\breve{u}\breve{s}\text{-}\breve{\imath}$* | 'louse', | nom. sg. |
| *fš-i* | <*$v\breve{u}\breve{s}\text{-}\breve{\imath}$* | | gen. sg. |
| *voš-ju* | <*$v\breve{u}\breve{s}\text{-}\breve{\imath}ju$* | | instr. sg. |
| *fš-ej* | <*$v\breve{u}\breve{s}\text{-}\breve{\imath}j\breve{\imath}$* | | gen. pl. |

Thus, across the stem boundary a stem-final yer will delete or vocalize depending on whether or not the following yer deletes or vocalizes. On the other hand, within the stem a yer will always vocalize if it is followed by another yer. This can be shown by the addition of diminutive suffixes containing yers to a root such as /dĭn'/ 'day', which also contains a yer.

(14)
Nom. sg.	*den'*	<*[dĭn']ĭ	'day'
Gen. sg.	*dn'-a*	<*[dĭn']a	
Nom. sg.	*den'-ok*	<*[dĭn'-ŭk]ŭ	'day' dimin.
Gen. sg.	*den'-k-a*	<*[dĭn'-ŭk]a	
Nom. sg.	*den'-oč-ek*	<*[dĭn'-ŭk-ĭk]ŭ	'day' affectionate dimin.
Gen. sg.	*den'-oč-k-a*	<*[dĭn'-ŭk-ĭk]a	

We have enclosed the stem within brackets in (14) for ease of exposition. It is easy to see that within the stem a nonalternating pattern of vocalization has arisen. The different patterns of vocalization of the yers could be described in terms of the apparatus introduced in Chapter 8 by having (15) apply in a left-to-right direction within the stem followed by a right-to-left iteration from the end of the word for stem-final yers and yers in inflectional suffixes.

(15) $\qquad$ $[ĭ, ŭ] \longrightarrow [e,o]/\underline{\hspace{1cm}}C_0 [ĭ, ŭ]$

In many cases a phonological rule refers to material that belongs to two or more separate words. Such phrase-level rules may be divided into two types: those that apply only between words versus those that apply both between as well as within words. An example of the former type occurs in western dialects of Polish where a word-final obstruent is voiced if followed by a sonorant consonant or a vowel: *brat* 'brother', but *bra[d] mówił* 'brother spoke', *bra[d] opowiadał* 'brother reported'. This rule does not apply within words, as shown by the *p* in *opowiadał*. Given that the symbol # appears between words, the Polish sandhi rule may be stated as (16).

(16) $\qquad$ $[-\text{sonorant}] \longrightarrow [+\text{voice}]/\underline{\hspace{1cm}} \# \ [+\text{sonorant}]$

Cairene Arabic (Mitchell 1956) provides an example of a phrase-level rule that also applies within the word. In this dialect of Arabic short unstressed high vowels are deleted in the context VC___CV. Examples of this rule applying within a word appear in (17).

(17)
kátab	'he wrote'	*fíhim*	'he understood'
kátab-it	'she wrote'	*fíhm-it*	'she understood'
kátab-u	'they wrote'	*fíhm-u*	'they understood'
katáb-ti	'you f. wrote'	*fihím-ti*	'you fem. understood'
yíktib	'he writes'	*yáaxud*	'he takes'
tiktíb-i	'you f. write'	*táaxd-i*	'you f. take'
yiktíb-u	'they write'	*yáaxd-u*	'they take'

Addition of vowel-initial suffixes to the roots /fihim/ and /axud/ place the final vowels in these roots in the context for the syncope rule to operate.

Since /katab/ has a low vowel in its second syllable, the addition of a vowel-initial suffix does not lead to deletion. The imperfect root form /ktib/ remains unaltered when a vowel-initial suffix is added due to the fact that the vowel of this root is stressed and also preceded by two consonants.

An unstressed short high vowel that is in an open syllable will also syncopate from the initial syllable of a word when the preceding word provides the appropriate context. Phrase-level syncopation operates in a variety of syntactic contexts. A few examples are cited in (18).

(18)   Verb + noun

	ḍárab Ḥuséen	'he struck Huseen'
	ḍarábti Ḥséen	'you fem. struck Huseen'

Noun + noun

	Faríid mudárris	'Farid is a teacher'
	ána mdárris	'I am a teacher'

Noun + verb

	húwwa fíhim	'he understood'
	ána fhím-t	'I understood'

Noun + adjective

	kitáab gidíid	'a new book'
	kúrsi gdíid	'a new chair'

Noun + preposition

	híyya fi lmáktab	'she is in the office'
	híyya f maktábha	'she is in her office'

Verb + article

	ḍárab il wálad	'he struck the boy'
	ḍárab l afándi	'he struck the gentleman'

When the righthand (C)V portion of the rule is provided by a following word the rule sometimes applies and sometimes does not.

(19)

	fíhim Faríid	'he understood Farid'
	fíhm iddárs	'he understood the lesson'
but	*dáras-it iddárs*	'she studied the lesson'
	ḍárab-u Faríid	'they struck Farid'
	tiktíb-i gawáab	'you fem. write a letter'

There are two possible explanations for the failure of syncope to apply in (19). In cases where the rule blocks, the high vowel forms part of the inflectional ending. The rule could thus be formulated to apply to short *i* and *u* so long as they do not appear in an inflectional suffix. (Note that if the rule were to apply in these cases, ambiguity would result, since *daras-t* is the form for 'I studied', *ḍarab* is 'he struck', and *tiktib* is you masc. write'). Alternatively, one could appeal to the fact that short high vowels are phonetically tense in final position, lax otherwise. Since a rule tensing *i* and *u* in final position is needed anyway, if this rule is ordered before syncope and the latter is restricted to lax high vowels, as in (20), the failure of the final vowels in *ḍárab-u* and *tiktíb-i* to syncopate can be explained on phonological grounds.

(20)
$$\begin{bmatrix} +\text{syll} \\ +\text{high} \\ -\text{stress} \\ -\text{tense} \end{bmatrix} \longrightarrow \emptyset/\text{VC}\_\_\_\text{CV}$$

However, this analysis still fails to explain why the 3 f. suffix /-it/ does not lose its vowel. If (20) is adopted, this suffix would have to be marked as an exception to the rule.

In the Cairene Arabic example discussed above, a short unstressed high vowel will delete from the second of two adjacent words in a variety of syntactic configurations. The only constraint is that there may not be a pause between the two words. In other languages, however, phrase-level rules often will only apply between words that bear a close syntactic relationship. For example, recall our earlier discussion of liaison in French. Selkirk (1972, 1974) has pointed out a number of examples that show that two words must belong to the same phrasal category in order for linking to occur. In the most informal style of French the final consonant of the word *naïvement* will not be pronounced in a sentence such as *Il a naïvement exprimé ses sentiments* and, as a result, the sentence will be ambiguous depending on whether *naïvement* is given a sentential or an adverbial reading. But in the more guarded style of speech where a polysyllabic adverb will link with a following verb, the sentence may be disambiguated. If the final consonant of *naïvement* is pronounced it must have the adverbial interpretation ('he expressed his feelings in a naive fashion') while if no linking occurs it can also have the sentential reading ('it was naive of him to express his feelings'). It is reasonable to assume that these two different interpretations correspond to two different surface structures: one in which *naïvement* modifies the following verb and hence is its left sister, and the other where it does not and hence is not included in the same phrasal category as the verb.

A similar minimal pair appears in *un marchand de draps anglais*. In the most formal style of French an inflectional ending may link with a following vowel-initial modifier. If the final consonant of *draps* is pronounced the phrase has the reading 'a merchant of English cloth'. If no linking occurs, it could also mean 'an English cloth merchant'. It is reasonable to assume that the latter has a surface structure approximating (21b) while the former derives from (21a).

(21)   a.   b.

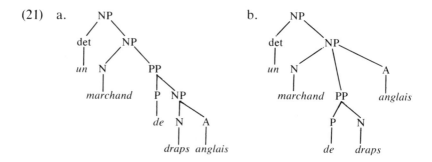

If we say that linking only occurs between sisters (elements immediately dominated by the same phrasal category), the different interpretations of the phrase can be accounted for.

Although the contrast between whether or not two successive words belong to the same phrasal category is apparently all the syntactic information that is required to describe liaison properly, there are other cases where a phrase level rule must have access to the type of constituents involved. We have already seen that the stress subordination rules in English materially depend on the contrast between a compound lexical versus phrasal category. Data discussed by Kaisse (1977) suggest that more elaborate syntactic information is required to describe the resolution of vowel clusters arising across word boundaries in Modern Greek. According to Kaisse there are four separate rules of vowel deletion. First, between a subject and a following verb, a prevocalic unstressed nonhigh vowel deletes. Second, between an adjective and a following noun, unstressed *a* will delete before another vowel, but *o* will not. Third, between a verb and following adverb unstressed *a* will delete before *o* but not before any other vowel and unstressed *o* never deletes. Finally, between a pronominal clitic and a following verb, *e* will delete after *a* and *o*, with transfer of stress to the preceding vowel. In this case from Greek the phrase-level rules of elision must evidently refer to the part of speech of the adjacent words.

(22)   Subject + verb
     tá áloɣa érxonde 'the horses are coming' ⟶   *á* #*e*
     tá áloɣ érxonde
     tó áloɣo érxete 'the horse is coming' ⟶   *ø* #*e*
     tó áloɣ érxete

   Adjective + noun
     tá meɣála eláfya 'the big deer (pl)' ⟶   *á* #*e*
     tá meɣál eláfya
     tó meɣálo eláfi 'the big deer (sg.)' ⟶   *o* #*e* (no deletion)
     tó meɣálo eláfi

Verb + adverb
    ðiávaza oloéna 'I was reading continually' —→   *a̗ #o*
    ðiávaz oloéna
    ðiávasa éfkola 'I read easily' —→   *a #e* (no deletion)
    ðiavázo éfkola
    ðiavázo éfkola 'I read (pres.) easily' —→   *o #e* (no deletion)
    ðiavázo éfkola

Clitic + verb
    ta éxo 'them I have' —→ *tá xo*   *a #e̗*
    to éxo 'it I have' —→ *tó xo*   *o #e̗*

In each of the examples presented so far the boundaries have had a clear syntactic motivation. It is obvious that phonological theory must place strong constraints on the appeal to boundaries as being the relevant factor in conditioning a rule. As Chomsky, Halle, and Lukoff (1956) have noted, in the absence of such constraints it would be possible to provide such trivial analyses as the one which would claim that English has only one underlying nasal consonant /n/. With the help of a special boundary =, *m* could be derived from /=n/ and *ŋ* from /n=/ by rules that would labialize and velarize /n/ when they stand next to this special boundary. An adequate theory of boundaries would delimit the number of distinct boundary types (e.g., morpheme boundary, stem boundary, word boundary, and phrase boundary) and the positions in the string of sounds which these boundaries occupy. Such a theory would preclude this absurd analysis for the nasals of English.

In addition to being syntactically motivated, another reasonable boundary constraint would be a requirement of grammatical consistency. If two elements displaying a particular morphological or syntactic relationship to one another are separated by a particular boundary, then all other elements displaying this relationship would also be separated by the same boundary.

The following data from Cairene Arabic illustrate the role that the requirement of grammatical consistency plays in the appeal to boundaries in the formulation of phonological rules. Roots with the underlying shape /CayaC/ or /CawaC/, traditionally referred to as hollow roots, exhibit two different phonetic shapes in the perfect tense: /CiC/ and /CuC/, respectively, before consonant-initial suffixes marking the subject of the sentence, and /CaaC/ before vowel-initial or zero suffixes.

	Singular	
(23)	1 *šil-t*	*šuf-t*
	2 *šil-ti*	*šuf-ti*
	3 masc. *šaal*	*šaaf*
	3 fem. *šaal-it*	*šaaf-it*

Plural

1 *šil-na*	*šuf-na*	
2 *šil-tu*	*šuf-tu*	
3 *šaal-u*	*šaaf-u*	
Root /šayal/	'carry'	/šawaf/ 'see'

A full discussion of the root alternations exhibited by hollow verbs would require more space than is available here. We only wish to observe that the difference in root shape can be correlated with the phonological character of the following suffix: one root shape appears before consonant-initial suffixes and the other before vowel-initial or zero suffixes.

When the object of a transitive verb in Arabic is a pronoun, it appears to be marked in the same fashion as the subject markers, that is, as a suffix on the verb. Since the 3 sg. masculine form of a verb consists of just the root without any subject marker, the morphological structure of such a verb with a pronominal object appears to be the same as that of a verb with an overt subject marker: root + suffix. However, there is a consistent difference in the vocalism exhibited by hollow roots before subject suffixes and object suffixes. Before consonant-initial subject suffixes the hollow roots take the shape /CiC/ and /CuC/. But before consonant-initial object markers the root has the shape /CaaC/.

(24)

šaal-ni	'he carried me'		*šaaf-ni*	'he saw me'
šaal-ak		you masc.'	*šaaf-ak*	you masc.'
šaal-ik		you fem.'	*šaaf-ik*	you fem.'
šaal-u		him'	*šaaf-u*	him'
šaal-ha		her'	*šaaf-ha*	her'
šaal-na		us'	*šaaf-na*	us"
šaal-kum		you pl.'	*šaaf-kum*	you pl.'
šaal-hum		them'	*šaaf-hum*	them'

If it is assumed that the rules producing the vocalism for hollow roots refer to the phonological character of the following suffix, then there must be a difference in the type of boundary that intervenes between a root and a subject suffix versus that which intervenes between the root and an object suffix: Compare the minimal pair *šil-na* 'we carried' with *šaal-na* 'he carried us'. But can a boundary difference be motivated here on grammatical grounds in order to satisfy the requirement of grammatical consistency in the placement of boundaries? An argument supporting a boundary difference could be made on the following grounds. First of all, when the object is a pronoun it must appear as a suffix on the verb and cannot appear as an independent word: *šaal-ni* 'he carried me', but **šaal ana*, where the independent first person pronouns *ana* is used. Second, the object suffix will only appear when the object of the verb is a pronoun.

If the object is a full noun phrase, no pronoun suffix may appear on the verb: compare, *šaal il kitaab*, but **šaal-u il kitaab* 'he carried the book'. Subject suffixes differ in these two respects. They obligatorily occur with both pronominal and lexical NP subjects: *ana šil-t il kitaab*, 'I carried the book', *Maryam šaal-it il kitaab* 'Mary carried the book'. Finally, in addition to the subject-verb-object word order, Arabic also permits verb-subject-object order. But if the object is a pronoun, it must be expressed as a suffix on the verb: *šaal Fariid il kitaab* 'Farid carried the book', *šaal-u Fariid* 'Farid carried it'. A natural account of these data would be to claim that the subject suffixes arise from an agreement transformation, while object suffixes arise from a transformation that cliticizes a pronominal object to the verb.

Given such a difference in syntactic origin it would not be unreasonable to claim that object suffixes are separated from the root by a stronger boundary than subject suffixes. Following SPE, we can make a distinction between a single word boundary # versus a double word boundary # #. In SPE it is assumed that a # is placed at the beginning and end of every lexical word. On this view, *šaal Fariid* 'he carried Farid' would be represented as /#šaal# #Fariid#/. Rules that apply across a word boundary would then have to be reformulated to allow for two occurrences of #. (It should also be noted that if a nonlexical item is followed by a lexical item, only one word boundary will intervene between the two words. Thus, 'the book' will be represented as /il#kitaab#/. In the SPE approach, the contrast between a lexical versus a nonlexical word is thus partially translated into a boundary difference. See Selkirk [1972, 1974] for discussion.)

Given the SPE distinction between a single versus double word boundary, we could claim that whenever a clitic is attached to a word, it will be separated from that word by a single #. In this way the contrast between *šil-na* 'we carried' versus *šaal-na* 'he carried us' can be accounted for in a natural way. The former will be represented as /#šayal+na#/ and the latter as /#šayal#na#/. The rules that spell out the root vocalism for hollow verbs will now be able to treat /#šayal#na#/ in the same way as /#šayal#/ to give the root shape /šaal/, in contradistinction to /#šayal+na#/, which will result in the root shape /šil/.

To complete this discussion we must show that when object clitics are attached to the verb the resulting unit still forms a word, justifying the three-way boundary distinction + versus # versus # #. This is easily shown by the stress rule (Chapter 9) which counts both types of suffixes in its domain. Recall that if the second syllable from the end of the word is closed, it will take stress. Addition of consonant-initial subject or object suffixes to the root /daras/ both result in penultimate stress: *darás-ti* 'you fem. studied', *darás* #*hom* 'he studied them'. Similarly, addition of vowel-initial suffixes of either type result in equivalent stress: *dáras-u* 'they studied', *dáras* #*u* 'he studied it'. Thus, the rule assigning word stress treats subject suffixes and object suffixes the same. This means that the rule assigning stress will have to be formulated to measure from # # and to ignore the single word boundary intervening between the object suffix and the preceding stem.

The Cairene Arabic data show how the postulation of an internal word boundary can be motivated to satisfy the requirements of grammatical significance and grammatical consistency. There are, however, cases where the appeal to such a boundary appears appropriate, but where no such grammatical motivation can be given. An example is provided by the voicing sandhi that occurs in the imperative of Polish verbs. In Polish an obstruent assimilates the voicing of a following obstruent within the word: *grub-i* 'thick', *grup-ši* 'thicker'; *obraz-ek* 'image', *obras-k-a* gen. sg.; *pros'-i* 'requests', *proz'-ba* 'request', *lič-i* 'counts', *liǰ-ba* 'number'. Before sonorants, obstruents retain the voicing contrast: *znak* 'sign', *s'n'ek* 'snow', *s'm'et-nik* 'dustbin', *s'red-nik* 'semicolon', *n'es'-l'i* 'they carried', *v'ez'-l'i* 'they transported'.

At the end of a word obstruents are devoiced. However, if the following word begins with an obstruent, voicing assimilation will take place. Thus, /s'n'eg/ 'snow' appears with its underlying voiced obstruent in tact before the genitive suffix in *s'n'eg-a*, but as *s'n'ek* in isolation. Assimilation to a following obstruent appears in *s'n'ek taje* 'snow melts' and *s'n'eg z'imova* 'snow of winter'. An underlying voiceless obstruent exhibits the same behavior in these positions: *noč* 'night', *noč-i* gen. sg., *noč xod'-i* 'night goes', *noǰ z'imova* 'night of winter'. Thus we have the following rules, assuming the SPE distinction between single and double word boundaries.

(25) $[-\text{sonorant}] \longrightarrow [-\text{voice}]/\underline{\hphantom{xx}} \#$

(26) $[-\text{sonorant}] \longrightarrow [\alpha\text{voice}]/\underline{\hphantom{xx}} \#_0 \begin{bmatrix} -\text{sonorant} \\ \alpha\text{voice} \end{bmatrix}$

Whether final devoicing applies first and then voicing assimilation (so that underlying *g* # #*z* is converted to *k* # #*z* and then to *g* # #*z*) or instead Kiparsky's elsewhere condition is invoked (so that voicing assimilation is disjunctive with final devoicing) is not relevant to the present discussion.

When the following word begins with a sonorant, Polish splits into two dialects. In the standard dialect of Warsaw, obstruents are devoiced in this position, while in the western dialect of Cracow obstruents are voiced by the sandhi rule stated earlier as (16) and repeated here as (28) (Schenker 1966).

(27)

	Warsaw	Cracow	
kup'-i 'buys'	*kup owuvek*	*kub owuvek*	'buy a pencil!'
lud-ovi 'people's'	*lut rosyjski*	*lud rosyjski*	'Russian people'
zrob'-i 'does'	*zrup mi to*	*zrub mi to*	'do it for me!'

(28) $[-\text{sonorant}] \longrightarrow [+\text{voice}]/\_\_\_\#_1 [+\text{sonorant}]$

With these rules as background we can now turn to the imperative, which occurs in three inflectional forms: 2 sg., 2 pl., 1 pl.—the latter having an exhortative meaning. The imperative is marked by the suffix *-ij* followed by the inflectional affixes $\emptyset$ for 2 sg., *-t'e* for 2 pl., and *-mi* for 1 pl. The latter two suffixes also mark second and first person in the present tense of verbs. The imperative morpheme *-ij* is subject to a special rule deleting it unless the preceding root either contains no vowel or ends in the sequence C + *n*. However, the underlying presence of the *-ij* can be detected in the palatalizing effect it has on preceding consonants.

(29)

		Warsaw	Cracow	
vy-tš-ij	*vy-tš-ij-t'e*	*vy-tš-ij-mi*	ibid.	'wipe!'
za-pomn'-ij	*za-pomn'-ij-t'e*	*za-pomn'-ij-mi*	ibid.	'remember!'
v'es'	*v'es'-t'e*	*v'es'-mi*	*v'ez'-mi*	'transport!'
vut'	*vut'-t'e*	*vut'-mi*	*vud'-mi*	'lead'
n'es'	*n'es'-t'e*	*n'es'-mi*	*n'ez'-mi*	'carry!'

The 1 pl. forms are the items of interest. Note that in the Warsaw dialect the final obstruents of /v'ez/, /vod/, and /n'es/ are devoiced, while in Cracow they appear as voiced. As we have seen both dialects permit an underlying voice contrast to appear phonetically before sonorants within the word, but neutralize this opposition before the initial sonorant of the following word—to voiceless in Warsaw and to voiced in Cracow. Thus, in the imperative we find that stem final obstruents follow the voicing neutralization characteristic of that which applies between words rather than that which applies within words.

A natural account of these facts would be to postulate an internal word boundary between the imperative suffix and the inflectional endings. Such an analysis accounts immediately for the voicing sandhi and is further motivated by the rule (Chapter 3, exercise 3) that converts /o/ to

/u/ before underlying voiced nonnasal consonants in final position. Thus, /vod/ 'lead' appears with an /u/ not only in the singular of the imperative but also before the suffixes /#t'e/ and /#mi/. This analysis yields the following representations and derivations in the two dialects.

(30)

Warsaw:

/#‡vod+ij#t'e#‡/ vod'‡t'e	/#‡vod+ij#mi#‡/ vod'‡mi	/#‡n'es+ij#mi#‡/ n'es'‡mi	Palatalization and imperative deletion
vud'‡t'e	vud'‡mi	inapplicable	o ⟶ u
vut'‡t'e	inapplicable	inapplicable	(26)
inapplicable	vut'‡mi	vacuous	(25)

Cracow:

/#‡vod+ij#t'e#‡/ vod'‡t'e	/#‡vod+ij#mi#‡/ vod'‡mi	/#‡n'es+ij#mi#‡/ n'es'‡mi	Palatalization and imperative deletion
vud'‡t'e	vud'‡mi	inapplicable	o ⟶ u
vut'‡t'e	inapplicable	inapplicable	(26)
inapplicable	· vacuous	n'ez'‡mi	(28)
inapplicable	inapplicable	inapplicable	(25)

(In these derivations we have assumed that (25) does not apply if (26) or (28) applies—that is, these rules are disjunctively ordered).

While the postulation of the internal word boundary seems to be well motivated on phonological grounds, we are not aware of any morphological or syntactic considerations that would warrant assigning Polish imperatives this structure. In particular, there is no evidence that the suffixes *-t'e* and *-mi* arise from a cliticization process analogous to the Arabic material discussed earlier. In this case the internal word boundary would have to be assigned by an ad hoc rule or else perhaps included directly in the lexical representation of these affixes.

As in the Cairene Arabic material discussed earlier, the stress rule of Polish counts the suffixes *-t'e* and *-mi* as part of the word for purposes of accent assignment. In Polish stress is regularly assigned to the penultimate syllable; we have *vý-tš-ij*, *vy-tš-íj#t'e*, and *vy-tš-íj#mi* for the imperative forms of 'wipe'. Thus, the stress rule must be formulated to measure from the double word boundary #‡ and to ignore the single internal word boundary in these forms. These data also appear to support the SPE distinction between +, #, and #‡. However, the facts are actually more complex than our discussion so far would indicate. Polish has a set of clitics that mark first and second person in the past tense of verbs. In colloquial speech these may be "detached" from the verb and cliticized to the first stressed word of the clause. Thus, the 3 pl. masc. past of 'write' is *p'isál'i* and the 1 pl. masc. past is *p'isál'i-s'mi*. When an adverb such as *tróxe* 'awhile' precedes the verb, *-s'mi* may be cliticized to it: *tróxe-s'mi p'isál'i* 'we were writing for awhile'. Note that in all cases *-s'mi* does not count for stress and thus must be ignored by the penultimate accent rule. A natural account of these data would be to consider *-s'mi* as separated from the preceding word by an internal word boundary (compare our treatment of the object suffixes in Cairene Arabic). But this analysis is not possible, since we have already appropriated the single internal word boundary for the imperative, which, it will be recalled, does count for stress. If the assignment of boundaries is the appropriate mechanism to appeal to in the analysis of these data then it appears that we need to recognize at least three boundaries intermediate in strength between the morpheme boundary and the phrase boundary: a weak internal word boundary (separating the inflectional endings from the imperative suffix), which permits the material after it to be counted in the assignment of word stress; a strong internal word boundary (separating the first and second person clitics from the word they attach to), which blocks the following material from being counted in stress assignment; and the external word boundary, which separates phonologically independent words.

Such an analysis raises a number of difficult questions, however. Is there any limit to the number of boundaries that could conceivably be motivated if argumentation like the preceding is accepted? On what basis can one justify attributing the phonological behavior of a certain item to the boundary that precedes or follows it rather than to the morphosyntactic identity of the items in question? Obviously, boundaries are another aspect of the relationship between grammar and phonology that requires much additional study.

Cyclic Rules

In some cases it appears necessary to require phonological rules to apply cyclically. According to this mode of application, a given rule or set of rules is applied to a certain (grammatically defined) domain to obtain an output. This rule or set of rules is then reapplied to a larger domain that includes within it the smaller domain processed on the first cycle. A key feature of the cyclic mode of application is that it permits a given rule to be applied before as well as after another rule. This situation will arise if rule X applies before Y on the first cycle, but then rule X reapplies on the second cycle to give the series of applications X-Y-X.

Limitations of space will permit us to cite just one simple example. Brame (1974) has shown that the stress assignment rule of Palestinian Arabic must be applied cyclically. Recall from Chapter 6 that stress is assigned in this dialect of Arabic according to the following principles: if one of the last three syllables of the word is heavy, stress the rightmost one. In all remaining words stress the antepenult (or first syllable in mono- and disyllabic words). The stress rule interacts with a syncope rule that deletes unstressed short high vowels in the context ____CV. Syncope is ordered after the stress rule and will derive the various allomorphs of the underlying root /fihim/ 'understand' depicted in the following perfect verb paradigms.

(31)				
	1sg., 2sg. masc.	*darás-t*	*fhím-t*	/fihim+t/
	2sg. fem.	*darás-ti*	*fhím-ti*	/fihim+ti/
	3sg. masc.	*dáras*	*fíhim*	/fihim/
	3sg. fem.	*dáras-at*	*fíhm-at*	/fihim+at/
	1pl.	*darás-na*	*fhím-na*	/fihim+na/
	2pl.	*darás-tu*	*fhím-tu*	/fihim+tu/
	3pl.	*dáras-u*	*fíhm-u*	/fihim+u/
	Gloss	'study'	'understand'	

Certain problems arise in the analysis of verb stems with high vowels when they are inflected with object suffixes. A representative sample is cited in the paradigms of (32) where *fíhim* 'he understood', *fíhm-at* 'she understood', and *fhím-t* 'I/you masc. understood' are followed by object markers.

(32)	Object	*fíhim*	*fíhm-at*	*fhím-t*
	Singular			
	1	*fihím-ni*	*fihm-át-ni*	*fhím-t-ni*
	2 masc.	*fíhm-ak*	*fíhm-at-ak*	*fhím-t-ak*
	2 fem.	*fíhm-ik*	*fíhm-at-ik*	*fhím-t-ik*
	3 masc.	*fíhm-u*	*fíhm-at-u*	*fhím-t-u*
	3 fem.	*fihím-ha*	*fihm-át-ha*	*fhím-t-ha*
	Plural			
	1	*fihím-na*	*fihm-át-na*	*fhím-t-na*
	2	*fihím-kum*	*fihm-át-kum*	*fhím-t-kum*
	3	*fihím-hum*	*fihm-át-hum*	*fhím-t-hum*

These data present two problems: First, we must explain why the first vowel of *fihim* 'he understood' is not deleted when it is unstressed. Such forms arise when the object suffix begins with a consonant, closing the second root syllable, which then takes the stress. Contrast the minimal pair *fihím-na* 'he understood us' with *fhím-na* 'we understood'—both from underlying /fihim-na/. Second, we must explain why stress appears on the fourth last vowel in the UR of 3sg. fem. forms when the suffix begins with a vowel, as in *fíhm-at-u* 'she understood him'. The stress rules are formulated so that they will never assign stress to the left of the antepenult (cf., *darás-at-u* 'she studied it'). It is of course true that stress appears on the phonetic antepenult in *fíhm-at-u*. This could be derived if the stress rule were to apply after syncope. However, stress must be assigned before syncope because the latter rule is materially dependent upon the plus/minus stress contrast introduced by the stress rule.

Brame showed that these data can be adequately explained if the rules are applied cyclically, with the root plus subject markers constituting the first domain of application and inclusion of object markers only occurring on the second cycle. Given this mode of application, the following derivations obtain:

(33)	UR	/ #fihim+na# /	/ # fihim # na # /	
First cycle		/fihim+na/	/fihim/	
		fihím +na	fíhim	Stress
		fhím +na	inapplicable	Syncope
Second cycle			/fíhim # na/	
			fíhim # na	Stress
			inapplicable	Syncope
			fihím # na	Stress deletion
Output		fhím +na	fihím # na	
Gloss		'we understood'	'he understood us'	

The derivation of *fhím + na* is straightforward and requires no comment. In *fihím + na* the root alone constitutes the domain of the first cycle. Stress is assigned to the first vowel and syncope is not applicable since the unstressed second vowel is not followed by CV. The output of the first cycle is thus /fíhim/. The input to the second cycle is /fíhim/ plus the object suffix -*na*. The same two rules are reapplied in the same order. Stress is now assigned to the second root vowel. Syncope may not apply to the first root vowel since it bears a stress, assigned on the first cycle. For some speakers of Palestinian Arabic that we have polled, a secondary stress appears to remain on the first vowel of 'he understood us', so that phonetically the word appears as *fihímna*, while other speakers appear to delete the stress entirely. An experimental phonetic study is required to verify these subjective impressions. If the first vowel is indeed unstressed, then a late rule deleting all but the final stress of a word will be required.

Cyclic application of the rules also provides an explanation for the stress placement in *fíhm-at-u* 'she understood him'. The root plus subject suffix /fihim + at/ will constitute the domain of the first cycle. Stress assignment and syncope yield /fíhm + at/ as output. The input to the second cycle is thus /fíhm + at # u/. Stress will be vacuously assigned to the first vowel and syncope is inapplicable.

In this example the domain of cyclic application has a natural grammatical basis for, as in the Cairene dialect, object suffixes are clitics in Palestinian Arabic and thus have their syntactic origin outside of the verbal word. An important theoretical issue with respect to the cycle is whether or not the domains of application always have a grammatical basis. As with all questions concerning the relation of phonology and grammar, much further study is required before an adequate answer can be given. For some discussion of this matter, the reader is referred to Brame (1974).

Morpheme Structure Constraints

In generative studies phonological rules have characteristically been motivated by alternations. Nevertheless, in all languages there are numerous aspects of phonological structure that are not (directly) involved in alternations. For example, in English the features [+round] and [−round] co-occur with [+back] and [−back], respectively, for the vowels *u* and *i*. While the opposite combinations [+round, −back] and [−round, +back] are impossible in English, they do occur in many other languages (e.g., Turkish). Although this is unrelated to any alternations in English, it must nevertheless be expressed in any adequate grammar. Similarly, the fact that no English word begins with two successive stops is unrelated to any alternations but must be expressed in any adequate grammar of English.

In this section we briefly consider how generative phonology has treated such constraints on possible feature combinations within a segment and on possible sequences of segments that are not directly involved in alternations. A number of difficult problems are tied up with this issue, only some of which will be dealt with here. See Kenstowicz and Kisseberth (1977) for more extensive discussion.

In any language only certain features of pronunciation are distinctive—that is, unpredictable and hence capable of distinguishing between lexical items in URs. The remaining features are nondistinctive—that is, predictable and hence incapable of distinguishing one underlying form from another. Of course, such nondistinctive features may in some instances distinguish words in PR even though never doing so in the lexicon itself. For example, vowel length in English is predictable in terms of the voicing of a following consonant; but in fast speech final stops may become nonreleased and effectively merge the underlying voicing contrast so that the preceding vowel length may be the only distinguishing factor (compare [kʰæp˺] *cap* and [kʰæːp˺] *cab*). The present discussion is concerned with features that are nondistinctive in UR. Whether these features sometimes acquire a distinctive function phonetically is beside the point at issue.

Given that nondistinctive features are predictable and can in many cases be shown by external evidence to be rule governed, generative phonologists have generally assumed that the lexicon will omit any plus/minus specification for such features. They will instead be marked 0 in the lexicon, where 0 means unspecified. Rules must then be formulated to map this 0 onto a + or − value. It is generally assumed that such rules (called morpheme structure rules or redundancy rules) apply within the lexicon to convert the 0 specifications into a plus/minus specification. By expressing the possible feature combinations that may occur within a segment, such MSRs express constraints on what possible sounds may occur in the underlying structure of a given language.

To take a specific example, recall from Chapter 2 that voicing is not a distinctive feature in Zoque. All sonorants are voiced and all obstruents are voiceless, except that stops and affricates are voiced after nasals by a phonological rule. Thus, all sounds will be represented as [0voice] in their lexical representations. A MSR such as (34) will then apply in the lexicon to convert [0voice] to [+voice] for sonorants and [−voice] for obstruents.

(34) $\qquad$ [αsonorant] $\longrightarrow$ [αvoice]

All obstruents will thus be [−voice] in underlying representation. They will acquire the specification [+voice] by the phonological rule of (35).

(35) $\qquad$ [−sonorant] $\longrightarrow$ [+voice]/[+nasal]____

Rule (35) applies only in a specific context and hence is like other phonological rules based on alternations. A rule such as (34), on the other hand, is context-free and may be regarded as supplying the basic value (unmodified by context) for the nondistinctive feature of voicing in Zoque sounds. By permitting the MSR of (34) to apply in the lexicon, it is guaranteed that all sonorants will be [+voice] in UR and all obstruents will be [−voice], thereby capturing the fact that voiceless sonorants and voiced obstruents do not appear in the underlying inventory of Zoque sounds.

This approach thus assumes that each nondistinctive feature has a normal or basic value ([+voice] for sonorants and [−voice] for obstruents in the Zoque example). This normal value is assigned by a set of MSRs that apply directly to the lexical representation before the morpheme is inserted into syntactic structures. These MSRs simply replace 0 specifications by plus/minus ones. In so doing they express limitations on what particular sounds may appear in the underlying inventory of a language. After the MSRs have applied each segment in the morpheme is thus specified plus/minus for all features. This underlying representation is then input to the phonological rules which adjust the pronunciation of each segment as required by the context in which it occurs in the utterance.

The contrast between distinctive and nondistinctive features is more complex than we have indicated in that many features are distinctive in only some contexts, but not in others. For example, in the Bantu language Ki-Rundi vowel length is distinctive, as shown by such minimal pairs as *gu-sib-a* 'to neglect' versus *gu-siib-a* 'to abstain' and *ku-gum-a* 'to be solid' versus *ku-guum-a* 'to be impulsive'. However, the vowel in a morpheme-internal VNC sequence is always long phonetically (ignoring word-initial position where all vowels are regularly shortened). Furthermore, to our knowledge there is no evidence for an underlying contrast between VNC and VVNC. Thus, while vowel length is generally distinctive in Ki-Rundi, this contrast is inoperative in the context ____NC. Hence, the length of the vowel in a root such as *ku-riind-a* 'to wait' is nondistinctive and therefore would be represented as [0long] in the lexicon. The [+long] specification could be assigned by a MSR such as (36).

(36) $[+syll] \longrightarrow [+long]/\text{____}NC$

Rule (36) would apply in the lexicon to convert the [0long] to [+long] for a morpheme such as /riind/. This rule expresses the constraint that only long vowels may appear before a NC cluster in Rundi morphemes. It thus expresses a limitation on the possible sequences of sounds that may occur in Rundi. Morpheme structure rules that convert a nondistinctive 0 into a + or − only in a specific context are commonly referred to as sequence-structure MSRs. They are to be distinguished from segment-structure MSRs such as the one in Zoque that replaces [0voice] by [+voice] for sonorants and [−voice] for obstruents. The latter apply wholly within a segment and make no reference to adjacent segments of the morpheme.

Nevertheless, the function of both sequence-structure and segment-structure MSRs is to specify the normal value for nondistinctive features.

The approach to nondistinctive features that we have just outlined claims that MSRs are totally distinct from phonological rules in three ways. First, MSRs have the morpheme in isolation as their domain, whereas a phonological rule applies to a morpheme as it is situated in a particular string of words. Second, MSRs simply supply predictable feature values that have been omitted from lexical representations, while phonological rules alter plus/minus feature values. Third, all MSRs apply prior to the application of any phonological rule.

Very early it was realized that within such an approach the MSRs will often duplicate phonological rules. What appears to be a single generalization must be stated twice—once by a MSR and again by a phonological rule. For example, recall from Chapter 3 that Chamorro has six underlying vowels: ($i, u, e, o, \ddot{a}$, and a) distinguished in terms of the features high, low, and back. The feature round in this system is nondistinctive. All vowels will thus be [0round] in the lexicon and the proper basic values can be assigned by the following two segment-structure rules.

(37)
$$\begin{bmatrix} +\text{syll} \\ +\text{low} \end{bmatrix} \longrightarrow [-\text{round}]$$

(38)
$$\begin{bmatrix} +\text{syll} \\ -\text{low} \\ \alpha\text{back} \end{bmatrix} \longrightarrow [\alpha\text{round}]$$

Low vowels are unrounded while nonlow vowels have the same value for round as for back. These rules will apply in the lexicon. Recall that Chamorro also has a vowel fronting process that converts [u,o,a] to [i,e,ä] in the first syllable of a root if a front vowel precedes. Given that this is a rule of assimilation, it would appear to be appropriate to express the fronting rule as follows (ignoring the limitation to first root syllable).

(39)
$$[+\text{syll}] \longrightarrow [-\text{back}] / \begin{bmatrix} +\text{syll} \\ -\text{back} \end{bmatrix} C_0 \underline{\hspace{1cm}}$$

The above formulation does not, however, yield the correct results. It simply fronts a vowel; it does not account for the fact that when u and o are fronted they appear as nonround i and e, rather than $\ddot{u}$ and $\ddot{o}$. To achieve the correct results the rule could be modified to say that a fronted vowel is also assigned the feature [−round]. However, one might legitimately ask whether the inclusion of this information in the vowel fronting rule does not ignore the fact that all front vowels are unrounded in

Chamorro. That is to say, is the fact that *u* and *o* appear as unrounded *i* and *e* totally unrelated to the fact that the MSR (38) attempts to capture? If there are rules in the grammar that require front vowels to be unrounded, should not those rules be capable of accounting for the fact that when a rounded vowel is fronted, it appears as nonround? If MSRs apply in the lexicon it appears that the same fact (that front vowels are predictably nonround) must be stated twice: once in the MSR and once in the fronting rule.

Sequence-structure MSRs lead to the same problem. Recall from Chapter 6 that when a VNC cluster arises across morpheme boundaries in Ki-Rundi an underlying short vowel is lengthened: *ku-ror-a* 'to look', *kuu-n-dor-a* 'to look at me'; *ba-tabáar-e* 'that they help', *baa-n-tabáar-e* 'that they help me'. Is the lengthening that occurs here across morpheme boundaries totally different from the length that appears in a morpheme such as /riind/? That is what is claimed if MSRs apply within the lexicon before the application of phonological rules that change feature values. Once again it appears that the same fact is being stated twice.

Given the existence of numerous examples such as those discussed above, some method must be found for dealing with the duplication problem. One solution that has been attempted is to permit MSRs to be taken out of the lexicon and to be ordered within the set of phonological rules. Let us refer to this proposal as the ordering solution. For example, if the MSR (38) expressing the fact that front vowels are unrounded in Chamorro is taken out of the lexicon and ordered after the fronting process, the latter may retain the formulation of (39) that simply fronts a vowel. Both before and after the application of vowel fronting all vowels will be [0round]. Hence, a fronted /u/ and an underlying /i/ will both be [0round]. The subsequent MSR will now assign both the value [−round]. The duplication is eliminated, since the nonroundedness of front vowels is now stated just once in the grammar.

Permitting MSRs to apply within the block of phonological rules now provides a way to avoid the duplication of the Ki-Rundi example as well. If (36) is not applied directly to the lexicon but instead placed with the phonological rules, there will be no need to invoke a second lengthening rule for alternations. Rule (36) would be sufficient, since it specifies a vowel as [+long] in the context ____NC. The rule would now be performing a double function: it would be specifying the nondistinctive [0long] of the morpheme /riind/ as [+long] and it would change the underlying distinctive specification [−long] of a morpheme such as /ku/ to [+long] when it appears in a word such as *kuu-n-dor-a* 'to look at me'. Once again lengthening does not have to be stated twice in the grammar.

The Ki-Rundi example is by no means an isolated case. It is common to find that a constraint that determines how sounds are pronounced next to other sounds in adjoining morphemes will also constrain the kinds of sequences of sounds that occur in the URs of single morphemes. Thus, recall that Russian requires an obstruent at the end of one morpheme to assimilate the voicing of the obstruent that begins the next morpheme (*lez-u* 'I crawl', *les-ti* 'to crawl'). Similarly, in lexical representation all obstruent clusters agree in voicing: there are clusters such as *st* (as in /most/ 'bridge') and *zd* (as in /borozd/ 'furrow') but no clusters *sd* or *zt*. Given the ordering solution, the dental fricatives in /most/ and /borozd/ would be unspecified for voicing. The voicing assimilation rule that applies to change an underlying [+voice] to [−voice] in *les-ti* from /lez-ti/ would also supply the *s* of /most/ with the value [−voice] and the *z* of /borozd/ with the value [+voice].

Thus, with the ordering solution, a sequence-structure rule will in many cases not apply to the lexicon, but rather will be ordered among the phonological rules. However, in this situation the sequence-structure rule is indistinguishable from an ordinary phonological rule. It differs only in that it has a double function: Besides altering a plus or minus specification for a particular feature (the function of an ordinary phonological rule), it will also convert a 0 specification into a plus or minus value (the function of an ordinary MSR). Within such an approach one can tell if a rule expresses a constraint on sound sequences in UR only by determining if that rule ever functions to convert a 0 into a plus or minus. If a given rule performs this function, then one would have to infer that it expresses a sequence-structure constraint.

Although the ordering solution to the duplication problem seems fairly attractive, we nevertheless believe that it is inadequate. One argument against the ordering solution is based on the fact that its attendant double function rules (filling in zeros and changing pluses and minuses) will often fail to correctly state the constraints on underlying morpheme shapes. For example, in Klamath (Barker 1963) phonetic representations, voiceless aspirated stops (transcribed here as *p, t, č, k, q*) contrast with voiced unaspirated ones (*b, d, ǰ, g, g̣*) prevocalically. Except before voiced nonglottalized sonorants, there is no phonetic contrast in aspiration preconsonantally. In this position, the intermediate voiceless unaspirated stops (represented here as *P, T, Č, K,* and *Q*) appear. In order to account for numerous alternations, it is necessary to recognize the existence of a rule converting all stops to *P, T, Č,* etc. before a consonant. Thus *skod-a* 'puts a blanket on', but *ho-sKd-a* 'puts a blanket on someone', where the addition of the causative prefix *hV-* elicits deletion of the short root vowel, as mentioned in Chapter 6. Contrast *sdig-a* 'smells', *hi-sTg-a* 'makes someone smell'.

Thus there is clear evidence that an aspirated versus nonaspirated contrast exists prevocalically in UR. The existence of such a contrast in preconsonantal position is shown by forms such as *mboTy'-a* 'wrinkles', but *mbodi:-Tk* 'wrinkled up'. The root is /mbody'-/. An underlying /d/ is required to explain why *d* appears phonetically when /y'/ vocalizes to /i:/ in the context C____C. In *mboTy'-a* the /y'/ is not vocalized and the /d/ thus appears as *T*. Compare the alternation in *lo:Čw'-a* 'covets', but *lo:čo-t* 'can covet'. The root here is /lo:čw'-/. The root must contain an underlying aspirated stop /č/ to account for the fact that when /w'/ vocalizes to /o:/ (ultimately /o/ by virtue of another rule not discussed here) in the context C____C, a /č/ appears. When the glide fails to vocalize, the underlying stop loses its aspiration and thus /Č/ appears in *lo:Čw'-a*.

Further evidence for an underlying preconsonantal aspiration contrast is provided by a rule of epenthesis that inserts a schwa (transcribed here as *a*) to break up various consonant clusters. The UR /t'abk'-/ 'mash up something sticky' is motivated by the alternation *n-t'aPk'-a* 'mashes up something sticky with a round instrument', but *n-t'abaK-t-a* 'mashes up something sticky with a round instrument against something'. Insertion of the epenthetic schwa permits the underlying /b/ to appear phonetically. Compare the root /t'apq'/ 'leaf'. When unsuffixed, the root appears as *t'apaq*, with epenthetic schwa breaking the final consonant cluster. The underlying aspirated /p/ appears in this context, but is neutralized to /P/ in examples like *t'aPq'-al-a* 'leafs out (as a tree in spring)'.

We have seen that while there is a phonological rule neutralizing the aspirated/unaspirated contrast preconsonantally, it is nevertheless necessary to set up URs where both types of stops appear before a consonant. However, there are many morphemes containing an internal obstruent cluster that never undergo any phonological rule that would place the initial member of the cluster in an environment that would reveal whether it is underlyingly aspirated or unaspirated: for example, *jigaČg-is* 'grasshopper', *paPg-as* 'board', *m'oTč'oč'o:y'-a* 'grins'. Since a vowel never separates these clusters, it is impossible to determine whether the initial member is aspirated or unaspirated in UR. It would be quite reasonable, therefore, to simply leave these stops unspecified for aspiration in the lexicon and allow the phonological rule to supply the correct feature specifications. This solution would avoid having to arbitraily choose between, for example, /p/ and /b/ as the UR of the /P/ in *paPg-as* and would characterize the fact that the UR of such preconsonantal stops is indeterminate.

The consequence of such an analysis is that there would be many stops unspecified for aspiration in underlying forms, and these stops would be assigned their correct phonetic shape by the phonological rule that neutralizes the aspirated/unspirated contrast in preconsonantal position. This rule would thus have a double function: filling in zeros and changing underlying pluses and minuses. But in this case it would be incorrect to infer that the language does not have a contrast between aspirated and unaspirated stops in preconsonantal position underlyingly. Klamath does have such a contrast. Thus, a rule that has a double function does not necessarily express a constraint on the underlying shape of morphemes.

Perhaps the strongest reason for rejecting the ordering solution to the duplication problem is that this problem is really just a special subcase of the more general problem of conspiracies. It is reasonable to suppose that any adequate theory of conspiracies will naturally extend itself to the duplication problem as a special subcase. On the other hand, there is simply no way in which the ordering solution can be generalized to handle conspiracies. The term conspiracy (due to J. R. Ross) refers to a situation in which several formally distinct rules or conditions seem to work towards achieving the same target structure. A rather striking example appears in Tonkawa. Recall from Chapter 3 that the rule of elision deletes the first or second vowel of a verb stem. The first stem vowel is lost when a CV- prefix precedes the stem while the second is lost when no such prefix precedes. Further examination of Tonkawa reveals that if the first stem vowel is long, it will shorten when a CV- prefix precedes; if it is short, it will simply delete.

(40) *netle-n-o?*   *we-ntale-n-o?*   'he is licking it/them'   (root /netale/)
      picna-n-o?   *we-pcena-n-o?*   'he is cutting it/them'   (root /picena/)
      na:t-o?   *we-nat-o?*   'he steps on it/them'   (root /na:t/)
      ya:c-o?   *we-yac-o?*   'he sees it/them'   (root /ya:c/)

If long vowels are represented as geminates, then the shortening of a long vowel and the deletion of a short vowel may both be expressed as following from the rule of elision.

Although elision is a quite general rule of Tonkawa phonology, there are many cases where it fails to apply. But in each case an explanation for its failure to apply can be given on the basis of the fact that, if it were to apply, the resultant structure would contain a sound sequence that is not permitted in the UR of morphemes.

For example, there are no three-consonant clusters in the UR of Tonkawa morphemes. Furthermore, a root such as /salke/ 'pull sinew from meat' does not delete its first vowel when the 3 sg. prefix is attached: *we-salk-o?*. If elision were to apply, the resultant *we-slk-o?* would violate the constraint against three-consonant clusters that governs the UR of morphemes. Similarly, a root such as /nepaxke/ may not delete its second vowel. Thus, we have *nepaxke-n-o?* 'he is smoking', not **nepxke-n-o?*. The first root vowel may be elided (*we-npaxk-o?* 'he smokes them'), but in this case no three-consonant cluster arises.

The failure of elision to apply in these cases is closely related to the fact that three-consonant clusters are not permitted in the UR of morphemes. But there is no way in which this connection can be expressed by the ordering solution. The prohibition against CCC in the UR of a morpheme might be expressed by a MSR like (41).

(41)   [   ] ⟶ [+syll]/___ CC
                                              CC___

Rule (41) specifies a segment that is either before or after a consonant cluster as predictably [+syll]. But there is no way in which this MSR can directly account for the fact that elision is blocked in the context C___CC. The relation between these two aspects of Tonkawa phonological structure is a functional one, not a formal one.

In our opinion the proper way to account for these data is to express the elision rule as follows: delete a vowel (= a single short vowel or one mora of a long vowel) from the second syllable of the word so long as it is not in the final syllable of the stem (the necessity for the latter restriction was discussed in Chapter 3). Notice that this statement of the rule says nothing about the consonantal structure surrounding the vowel to be elided. Failure of the rule to apply in the context C___CC is not to be stated as part of the rule itself but should follow from the constraint that three successive consonants are not tolerated in Tonkawa. This constraint thus does two things: First, it expresses a limitation on possible sequences of sounds in the UR of morphemes (thus barring CCC from occurring in the UR of any morpheme) and second, it controls the application of the elision rule by blocking it if a CCC sequence were to arise from the loss of a vowel.

A perhaps more striking example of the connection between a constraint on UR and the application of a phonological rule derives from the fact that a glottalized consonant never appears before another consonant in the UR of Tonkawa morphemes. This could be expressed by a MSR such as (42).

(42)   [-syll] ⟶ [-glottalized]/___C

The constraint barring sequences of C'C also governs the application of the elision rule. The root /s'ako/ 'scrape' does not elide its first vowel after a CV- prefix, as in *we-s'ak-oʔ* 'he scrapes them'. However, the root /s'eːt/ 'cut' does shorten its vowel in this context: *ke-s'et-oʔ* 'he cuts me'. Thus, elision in Tonkawa may apply so long as a cluster of glottalized consonant plus consonant does not arise.

Compare the Tonkawa facts with those from Russian discussed earlier. Obstruent clusters must agree in voicing in the UR of Russian morphemes. When a vowel is deleted to give rise to a sequence of obstruents that disagree in voicing, the first assimilates to the second by the voicing assimilation rule: compare, *voš* 'louse', *fš-i* 'lice'. In this case a constraint on the UR of morphemes carries over to adjust the output of vowel deletion. On the other hand, in Tonkawa the constraint barring C'C functions to block vowel deletion. In both cases a constraint on UR affects the application of a phonological rule—by adjusting the output of the rule in one case and by preventing application of the rule in the other. An ordering solution works for the former but not the latter. Thus, the ordering solution cannot be accepted as a totally general solution to the duplication problem. It would seem that once a way is found to express the conspiratorial relation between MSRs and the application of phonological rules in examples such as the Tonkawa one, the duplication involved in examples such as Russian should fall out as a special subcase.

Given that the ordering solution to the duplication problem is not viable, we can return to the original position sketched at the beginning of this section, which claims that all MSRs apply to the lexicon. Another problem associated with MSRs is the question of whether such rules always take the form of filling in zeros. The assumption that this is true has given rise to the alternative labeling of such rules as redundancy rules. There is, of course, a deep connection between the observation that certain features of pronunciation are redundant, being predictable from other features either within the same segment or in a neighboring segment, and the observation that there are limitations on the sounds and the sequences of sounds that may occur within a morpheme. Features of pronunciation are redundant (predictable) by virtue of such limitations. Thus the specification [−voice] will be redundant for stops in a language if that language does not have voiced stops in its repertoire of underlying sounds. The point of articulation of a nasal will be redundant in the context before an obstruent if a language does not allow nonhomorganic clusters of nasal plus obstruent within the same morpheme. Given this deep connection between redundancy and limitations on morphemes, it might be natural to propose that the postulation of rules that predict redundant feature values will at the same time express the limitations on morpheme shapes that occur in a language. This was in fact the position expressed in Halle (1964), where it was argued that a morpheme-structure rule is motivated only if the postulation of such a rule would result in a simplification of the grammar (in particular, simplification of the lexicon as a consequence of eliminating feature specifications).

There are significant problems with the claim that constraints on the shapes of morphemes are to be expressed by rules assigning redundant features. The prediction of all the redundant features in a language will not necessarily lead to the expression of all the significant limitations on morpheme shapes in the language. Comparison of the following two examples will make this point clear. In Russian (and more generally, in all Slavic languages) root morphemes always end in a consonant. As such, the value for the feature syllabic in the last segment of a root is redundant and may be left unspecified in the lexicon. A rule specifying the last segment of a root as [−syllabic] will predict this redundant feature and at the same time express the constraint that no root may end in a vowel. Contrast this constraint on root shapes with the one that exists in Classical Arabic, where all underlying verb roots are required to be of the shape /CVCVC/[6]. In this case the specifications for the feature syllabic are redundant for all segments in the morpheme. Consequently, each segment in a verbal root can be entered as [0syllabic] in the lexicon. MSRs that would specify the first, third, and fifth segments of a verbal root as [−syllabic] and the second and fourth as [+syllabic] would fill in all redundant features. But notice that these rules do not in themselves express the generalization that all verbal roots have the underlying shape /CVCVC/. They in no way prevent roots of the shape /CVC/ or /CVCVCVC/, for example. In order to bar morphemes of this shape from the lexicon, we would require a principle that says that all verbal roots must consist of five segments. But a principle of this sort does not predict redundant feature values. Thus, it is not true that the prediction of redundant features will automatically express the significant limitations or morpheme shapes.

A distinction can thus be made between if-then and positive MSRs. If-then rules say that if x occurs, then y also occurs (e.g., in Zoque if a segment is [αsonorant] then it is [αvoice]). They do not, however, require that x occur; they simply express the fact that y always appears if x does. Since a rule that assigns redundant features also says that if x occurs, then y also (predictably) occurs, it is clear that such rules will in general be able to express if-then constraints on morpheme shapes. Positive MSRs, on the other hand, require that x appears. Morphemes not possessing the property x (e.g., Arabic verbal roots of less or more than five segments)

[6] Our discussion ignores /CVCCVC/ roots; however, the same points hold, *mutatis mutandis*, for this root class.

are simply disallowed. As we have seen, rules assigning redundant features do not succeed in expressing positive constraints on morpheme shapes.

Although redundancy rules can in general express if-then constraints, there are problems that arise involving directionality. A rule assigning redundant feature values assumes that certain feature values are given in the lexicon and that other feature values are predicted on the basis of those that are already given. There is consequently a direction in which the prediction works: given x, y can be predicted. It turns out that in many cases the direction of the prediction is ambiguous. Given x, y can be predicted; but given y, x can be predicted.

For example, recall from Chapter 4 that all disyllabic roots in Yawelmani must have identical vowels in UR. There are roots with the underlying shape /CaCa:C/ and /CiCi:C/, but none with the shapes /CaCi:C/ or /CiCa:C/. In view of this constraint the quality of the first vowel is predictable from that of the second and vice versa. If this constraint were to be expressed by a MSR filling in zeros the choice of which vowel to consider as unspecified would appear to be arbitrary. Although the Yawelmani constraint is a type of if-then constraint (if one of the vowels is of a certain quality then the other has the same quality), it is not a directional one. Rules that assign redundant features are directional by nature and thus do not seem to be the appropriate devices to express such constraints.

Thus there is some evidence that at least some of the limitations on morpheme shapes should be expressed by means of conditions on underlying representations, rather than by rules that assign redundant feature values. Whether all limitations on morpheme shape should be expressed in this fashion is an issue we shall not go into here. Our discussion of morpheme structure rules/constraints has also ignored the question of whether the morpheme is in fact only domain for such rules/constraints and also the question of whether lexical representation is the only level at which such rules apply. For some discussion of these issues see Kenstowicz and Kisseberth (1977).

To summarize, both generative as well as earlier approaches to phonology have focused chiefly on the mutations a sound experiences when it is situated in a phonetic or phonological context. Given this focus, a great deal has been learned about how the phonetic properties of a sound and its context determine the sound patterns of language. Considerably less attention has been given to the role of the essentially non-phonetic factors we have surveyed in this chapter. One can only hope that as these factors are studied further, our understanding of their contribution to phonological structure will begin to approach the degree of sophistication with which our knowledge of phonetics permits us to predict the phonological behavior of sounds.

Exercises

1. Gilyak (Krejnovich 1937)

	labial	dental	palatal	velar	uvular
voiceless aspirated stop	pʻ	tʻ	ṭʻ	kʻ	qʻ
voiceless unaspirated stop	p	t	ṭ	k	q
voiceless fricative	f	ř	s	x	x̱
voiced fricative	v	r	z	γ	γ̱
voiced stop	b	d	ḍ	g	g̱
nasal	m	n	ṇ	ŋ	

This problem concerns the alternation of initial obstruents. Almost all obstruent-initial nouns and verbs begin with voiceless (aspirated or unaspirated) stops in isolation. In certain contexts these initial stops appear as the corresponding fricatives or voiced stops. Examine the following data to determine the phonological and grammatical context in which the alternation occurs.

a. noun + noun

pəŋx	'soup'	tʻom	'fat'
amsp vəŋx	'seal sp. soup'	ət řom	'duck fat'
pe vəŋx	'bird sp. soup'	maṭŋa řom	'seal sp. fat'
kʻəŋraj vəŋx	'duck soup'	kʻəŋraj řom	'duck sp. fat'
ṭxəf pəŋx	'bear sp. soup'	laŋř tʻom	'seal sp. fat'
vaqs pəŋx	'whitefish soup'	ṭxəf tʻom	'bear sp. fat'
ṭoŋř	'head'	qʻos	'neck'
həjk zoŋř	'rabbit head'	ṭopip xos	'bird sp. neck'
pe zoŋř	'bird sp. head'	ṭʻolqi xos	'reindeer neck'
kʻəŋraj zoŋř	'duck head'	ŋə xos	'otter neck'
qʻotř ṭoŋř	'bear sp. head'	laqř qʻos	'squirrel neck'
kəxkəx ṭoŋř	'swan head'	ves qʻos	'crow neck'

b. adjective + noun

pos 'material', *təf* 'house', *qan* 'dog'

Amur dialect		Saxalin dialect
pila dəf	'big house'	*pilan dəf*
urla gan	'good dog'	*urlan gan*
piula bos	'black material'	*piulan bos*

c. pronoun + noun. In isolation pronouns appear as follows: *ŋi* 'I', *ṭʻi* 'you', *if* (*jaŋ* Saxalin dialect) 'he', *ŋəŋ* 'we'. Formulate rules to account for the following possessive constructions.

'N'	pəx	pʻuf	tux	tʻu	ṭaqo
'my N'	ŋ-vəx	ŋ-fuf	ŋ-rux	ŋ-řu	ŋ-zaqo
'your N'	ṭʻ-fəx	ṭʻ-fuf	ṭʻ-řux	ṭʻ-řu	ṭʻ-saqo

'his N'	i-bəx	i-p'uf	i-dux	i-t'u	i-ɖaqo
'our N'	ŋəŋ-bəx	ŋəŋ-p'uf	ŋəŋ-dux	ŋəŋ-t'u	ŋəŋ-ɖaqo
	'paint'	'saw'	'axe'	'sledge'	'knife'

'N'	t'amrx	ki	k'u	qan	q'ax
'my N'	ŋ-samrx	ŋ-ɣi	ŋ-xu	ŋ-ɣan	ŋ-xax
'your N'	t'-samrx	t'-xi	t'-xu	t'-xan	t'-xax
'his N'	i-t'amrx	i-gi	i-k'u	i-gan	i-q'ax
'our N'	ŋəŋ-t'amrx	ŋəŋ-gi	ŋəŋ-k'u	ŋəŋ-gan	ŋəŋ-q'ax
	'harpoon'	'shoe'	'bullet'	'dog'	'spear'

d. direct object + verb. In isolation obstruent-initial transitive verbs begin with a fricative. You may assume a special rule to account for these forms (see Jakobson 1971 for discussion).

vəkz-ɖ	'throw away'	zosq-t̥	'break'
mot vəkz-ɖ	't.a. pillow'	mlət̥ zosq-t̥	'break boat seat'
ləq vəkz-ɖ	't.a. ski'	laq zosq-t̥	'b. ski'
ki vəkz-ɖ	't.a. shoe'	mu zosq-t̥	'b. boat'
taj vəkz-ɖ	't.a. pipe'	taj zosq-t̥	'b. pipe'
q'ax pəkz-ɖ	't.a. spear'	ŋax t̥osq-t̥	'b. cage'
ŋas pəkz-ɖ	't.a. belt'	p'ax t̥osq-t̥	'b. glass'

řo-ɖ	'carry'	ɣe-ɖ	'take, buy'
lep řo-ɖ	'c. bread'	mot ɣe-ɖ	't. pillow'
puŋd řo-ɖ	'c. bow'	kəp ɣe-ɖ	't. tree'
t̥'o řo-ɖ	'c. fish'	ki ɣe-ɖ	't. shoe'
kəj řo-ɖ	'c. sail'	kəj ɣe-ɖ	't. sail'
t̥af t'o-ɖ	'c. whetstone'	pəx ke-ɖ	't. paint'
tux t'o-ɖ	'c. axe'	pos ke-ɖ	't. material'

Note the following examples: ŋir ɖosqt̥ 'break cup' (cf. ŋirŋ 'cup', Saxalin), q'axku t'oɖ 'carry spears' (cf. q'axkun Saxalin).

The above four constructions appear to exhaust the grammatical contexts in which the alternation occurs. Note the following constructions where the alternation does not take place: subject + intransitive verb, where the initial obstruent of the verb does not appear as a fricative: t̥aqo pəkzɖ 'the knife disappeared', ŋo t̥osqt̥ 'the barn broke'. In a subject + direct object + indirect object + verb structure the initial obstruent of the direct object and the initial obstruent of the indirect object are not spirantized: ŋi t̥aqo p'əkən k'im ɖ 'I gave brother a knife'. Other data not cited here suggest that the initial obstruent of a verb will spirantize after an indirect object. What is to be explained is why the initial obstruents of the direct and indirect object do not spirantize in this construction.

2. Mandarin Chinese (Cheng 1973). Mandarin Chinese has four contrastive tones: high level (55), mā 'mother'; rising (35), má 'hemp'; falling-rising (315), mǎ 'horse'; and falling (51), mà 'to scold'. The falling-rising tone (315) is replaced by the rising tone (35) when it is followed by a falling-rising tone: compare hǎo shū 'good book', hǎo rén 'good man', hǎo kàn 'good looking', but háo jiǔ 'good wine'. When there are more than two successive falling-rising tones, two pronunciations are generally possible— one for slow speech and one for a normal rate. Examine the following data to determine precisely how the tone sandhi rule produces each pronunciation. Is the grammatical structure relevant? How? Is the rule cyclic? If not, how does it apply?

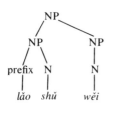

'rat'   'tail'

slow: *láo shŭ wĕi*
normal: *láo shú wĕi*
gloss: 'tail of rat'

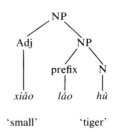

'small'   'tiger'

slow: *xĭao láo hŭ*
normal: *xíao láo hŭ*
gloss: 'small tiger'

Note: the morpheme *lăo* is a prefix that optionally appears with certain nouns; thus *shŭ* 'rat' and *hŭ* 'tiger' may stand alone. The prefix appears in its basic shape before nouns whose tone is not (315), such as *níu* 'cow': compare *lăo níu.*

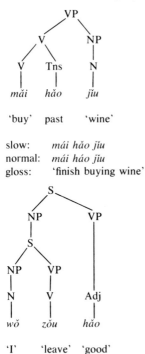

'buy'   past   'wine'

slow: *mái hăo jĭu*
normal: *mái háo jĭu*
gloss: 'finish buying wine'

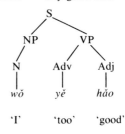

'buy'   'good'   'wine'

slow: *măi háo jĭu*
normal: *mái háo jĭu*
gloss: 'buy good wine'

'I'   'leave'   'good'

slow: *wó zŏu hăo*
normal: *wó zóu hăo*
gloss: 'it is best if I leave'

'I'   'too'   'good'

slow: *wŏ yé hăo*
normal: *wó yé hăo*
gloss: 'I also am fine'

3. Old Russian possessed the following system of obstruents in underlying representation.

Voiceless stops	p	t	k
Voiced stops	b	d	g
Voiceless fricatives	f	s	š	x
Voiced fricatives	v	z	ž
Voiceless affricates		c	č

The same system of sounds comprised the obstruent set in phonetic representation, except that *x, c,* and *č* had voiced allophones when they stood before voiced obstruents. In Old Russian there were three separate palatalization rules. The first palatalized the velars [k,g,x] to [č,ž,š] before front vowels: for example, *volk* 'wolf', *volč-e* 'vocative'; *bog-u* 'god, dat. sg.', *bož-e* 'vocative'; *pastux* 'shepherd', *pastuš-e* 'vocative'. The second palatalization shifted the velars [k,g,x] to [c,z,s] before certain morphologically defined suffixes beginning with a front vowel, such as the dative sg. *-e* of feminine nouns: *ruk-a, ruc-e* 'hand'; *nog-a, noz-e* 'leg'; *mux-a, mus-e* 'fly'. The third rule shifted the dentals [t,d,s,z] to [č,ž,š,ž] before jod: *bogat* 'rich', *bogač-je* 'richer'; *molod* 'young', *molož-je* 'younger'; *uz* 'narrow', *už-je* 'narrower' (the *j* deleted after a palatal by a later rule). Formulate the three palatalization rules in distinctive features. Does the inventory of underlying obstruents control the outputs of these rules in any way? How could this be expressed in terms of the "ordering solution"?

References

Allen, W. S. (1973). *Accent and rhythm*. Cambridge: University Press.

Anceaux, J. C. (1965). *The Nimboran language*. Verhandelingen van het Koninklijk Instituut voor Taal-. Land- en Volkenkunde 44.

Andersen, Henning (1972). Diphthongization. *Language, 48*, 11–51.

Anderson, Stephen (1969). *West Scandinavian vowel systems and the ordering of phonological rules*. Bloomington: Indiana University Linguistics Club.

Anderson, Stephen (1974). *The organization of phonology*. New York: Academic Press.

Bach, Emmon (1968). Two proposals concerning the simplicity metric in phonology. *Glossa, 2*, 128–149.

Bach, Emmon and Robert Harms (1972). How do languages get crazy rules? In R. Stockwell and R. Macaulay (Eds.), *Linguistic change and generative theory*. Bloomington: Indiana University Press. Pp. 1–21.

Barker, M. A. R. (1963). *Klamath dictionary*. University of California Publications in Linguistics, 31, Berkeley and Los Angeles: University of California Press.

Beeler, M. S. (1970). Sibilant harmony in Chumash. *International Journal of American Linguistics, 36*, 14–17.

Bever, Thomas (1967). *Leonard Bloomfield and the phonology of the Menomini language*. Unpublished Ph.D. dissertation, Massachusetts Institute of Technology.

Bhatia, Tej, and Michael Kenstowicz (1972). Nasalization in Hindi: A reconsideration. *Papers in Linguistics, 5*, 202–212.

Bloomfield, Leonard (1939). Menomini morphophonemics. *Travaux du Cercle Linguistique de Prague, 8*, 105–115. Reprinted in V. Makkai (Ed.), *Phonological theory*. New York: Holt, 1972. Pp. 58–64.

441

Borgstrøm, Carl (1937). The dialect of Barra in the Outer Hebredes. *Norsk Tidsskrift for Sprogvidenskap*, *8*, 71–242.

Brame, Michael (1969). *Arabic phonology*. Unpublished Ph.D. dissertation, Massachusetts Institute of Technology.

Brame, Michael (1971). Stress in Arabic and generative phonology. *Foundations of Language*, *7*, 556–591.

Brame, Michael (1972). On the abstractness of phonology: Maltese ʕ. In Michael Brame (Ed.), *Contributions to generative phonology*. Austin: University of Texas Press. Pp. 22–61.

Brame, Michael (1974). The cycle in phonology: Stress in Palestinian, Maltese, and Spanish. *Linguistic Inquiry*, *5*, 39–60.

Bright, William (1957). *The Karok language*. University of California Publications in Linguistics, 13. Berkeley and Los Angeles: University of California Press.

Broselow, Ellen (1976). The phonology of Egyptian Arabic. Unpublished Ph.D. dissertation, University of Massachusetts.

Burrow, T. (1970). *The Pengo language*. Oxford: The Clarendon Press.

Campbell, Lyle (1974). Phonological features: Problems and proposals. *Language*, *50*, 52–65.

Campbell, Lyle (1975). Theoretical implications of Kekchi phonology. *International Journal of American Linguistics*, *40*, 269–278.

Chao, Y-R. (1934). The non-uniqueness of phonemic solutions of phonetic systems. In M. Joos (Ed.), *Readings in linguistics I*. Chicago: University of Chicago Press, 1957. Pp. 38–54.

Chen, Matthew (1975). Metarules and universal constraints in phonological theory. *Proceedings of the 11th International Congress of Linguists*. The Hague: Mouton. Pp. 1152–1167.

Cheng, Chin-Chuan (1973). *A synchronic phonology of Mandarin Chinese*. Monographs on Linguistic Analysis 4. The Hague: Mouton.

Chomsky, Noam (1965). *Aspects of the theory of syntax*. Cambridge, Massachusetts: MIT Press.

Chomsky, Noam and Morris Halle (1968). *The sound pattern of English*. New York: Harper and Row.

Chomsky, Noam, Morris Halle, and Fred Lukoff (1956). On accent and juncture in English. In Morris Halle (Ed.), *For Roman Jakobson*. The Hague: Mouton. Pp. 68–80.

Coupez, A. (1969). Une leçon de linguistique. *Africa-Tervuren*, *15*, 33–37. Musée Royal de l'Afrique Centrale.

Davis, Phillip (1970). A classification of the dissimilative jakan'e dialects of Russian. *Orbis*, *19*, 360–376.

Dell, François and Elisabeth Selkirk (1976). On morphologically governed vowel alternations in French. To appear in *Recent transformational studies in European languages*. Linguistic Inquiry Monograph Series, Vol. 3.

de Rijk, Rudolf (1970). Vowel interaction in Bizcayan Basque. *Fontes Linguae Vasconum*, *2*:5, 149–167.

Doke, C. (1938). *Textbook of Lamba grammar*. Johannesburg: Witwaterstrand Press.

Dudas, Karen (1976). *The phonology and morphology of modern Javanese*. Unpublished Ph.D. dissertation, University of Illinois.

Ebert, Karen (1974). Partial vowel harmony in Kera. *Studies in African Linguistics*, Supplement 5, 75–80.

Elimelech, Baruch (1974). On the reality of underlying contour tones. In Ian Maddieson

(Ed.), *The tone tome: Studies on tone from the UCLA tone project.* Working Papers in Phonetics, 27. University of California, Los Angeles.

Elson, Ben (1947). Sierra Popoluca syllable structure. *International Journal of American Linguistics*, *13*, 13–17.

Emeneau, M. (1955). *Kolami, a Dravidian language.* University of California Publications in Linguistics, 12. Berkeley and Los Angeles: The University of California Press.

Fivaz, Derek (1970). *Shona morphophonemics and morphosyntax.* Johannesburg: University of Witwatersrand Press.

Freeland, L. (1951). *Language of the Sierra Miwok.* Indiana University Publications in Anthropology and Linguistics.

Fromkin, Victoria (1971). The non-anomalous nature of anomalous utterances. *Language*, *47*, 27–54.

Fromkin, Victoria (1975). When does a test test a hypothesis, or, What counts as evidence? In D. Cohen and J. Wirth (Eds.), *Testing linguistic hypotheses.* New York: Wiley. Pp. 43–64.

Gandour, Jack (1974). On the representation of tone in Siamese. In Ian Maddieson (Ed.), *The tone tome: Studies in tone from the UCLA tone project.* Working Papers in Phonetics 27, 118–146. University of California, Los Angeles.

George, Isaac (1970). Nupe tonology. *Studies in African Linguistics*, *1*, 100–122.

Geytenbeek, Brian and Helen Geytenbeek (1971). *Gidabal grammar and dictionary.* Australian Institute of Aboriginal Studies, no. 43. Canberra.

Gieser, C. (1970). The morphophonemic system of Guininaang (Kalinga). *Philippine Journal of Linguistics*, *1*, 52–68.

Gleason, Henry (1955). *Workbook in descriptive linguistics.* New York: Holt.

Goldsmith, John (1976). *Autosegmental phonology.* Unpublished Ph.D. dissertation, Massachusetts Institute of Technology. Reproduced by Indiana University Linguistics Club.

Greenberg, Joseph (1970). Some generalizations concerning glottalic consonants, especially implosives. *International Journal of American Linguistics*, *36*, 123–143.

Haas, Mary (1940). Tunica. *Handbook of American Indian Languages*, Vol. 4. Smithsonian Institution, Bureau of American Ethnography. Washington, D.C.

Hale, Kenneth (1973). Deep-surface canonical disparities in relation to analysis and change: An Australian example. *Current Trends in Linguistics*, *11*, 401–458.

Halle, Morris (1964). Phonology in generative grammar. In J. Fodor and J. Katz (Eds.), *The structure of language.* Englewood Cliffs, New Jersey: Prentice-Hall. Pp. 334–352.

Halle, Morris (1978). Metrical structure in phonology. Unpublished manuscript.

Halle, Morris and Samuel Keyser (1971). *English stress.* New York: Harper and Row.

Halle, Morris and V. Zeps (1966). A survey of Latvian morphophonemics. Quarterly Progress Report 83, 105–113. Research Laboratory of Electronics, Massachusetts Institute of Technology.

Harrell, Richard (1962). *A short reference grammar of Moroccan Arabic.* Washington, D.C.: Georgetown University Press.

Harris, James (1969). *Spanish phonology.* Cambridge, Massachusetts: The MIT Press.

Harris, Zellig (1942). Morpheme alternants in linguistic analysis. *Language*, *18*, 169–180.

Hoffmann, Carl (1963). *A grammar of the Margi language.* London: Oxford University Press.

Hoffmann, Carl (1973). The vowel system of the Okpe monosyllabic verb. Research Notes 6 (nos. 1–3), 79–112. Department of Linguistics, University of Ibadan, Nigeria.

Hohulin, Lou, and Michael Kenstowicz (1976). Keley-i phonology and morphophonemics. Unpublished manuscript.

Hoijer, Harry (1933). *Tonkawa: An Indian language of Texas*. Handbook of American Indian Languages 3. New York.

Hoijer, Harry (1949). *An analytical dictionary of the Tonkawa language*. University of California Publications in Linguistics 5. Berkeley and Los Angeles: University of California Press.

Hooper, Joan (1976). *An introduction to natural generative phonology*. New York: Academic Press.

Hulstaert, G. (1957). *Dictionnaire Lomóngo-Français*. Annales du Musée Royal du Congo Belge. Tervuren. Linguistique 16.

Hulstaert, G. (1961). *Grammaire du Lomóngo. Première partie*. Annales Linguistique, Tervuren.

Hyman, Larry (1969). How concrete is phonology? *Language, 46*, 58–76.

Hyman, Larry (1970). The role of borrowing in the justification of phonological grammars. *Studies in African Linguistics, 1*, 1–48.

Hyman, Larry (1975). *Phonology: Theory and analysis*. New York: Holt.

Isačenko, A. V. (1970). East Slavic morphophonemics and the treatment of the jers in Russian: A revision of Havlik's Law. *International Journal of Slavic Linguistics and Poetics, 13*, 73–124.

Jacobsen, William (1969). Labialization in Nootkan. Paper presented at the 4th International Conference on Salish Languages, University of Victoria, B.C.

Jakobson, Roman (1931). Phonemic notes on Standard Slovak. Reprinted in R. Jakobson, *Selected Writings I*. The Hague: Mouton, 1962. Pp. 221–230.

Jakobson, Roman (1972). Notes on Gilyak. In R. Jakobson, *Selected Writings II*. The Hague: Mouton, 1972. Pp. 72–97.

Jakobson, Roman, Gunnar Fant, and Morris Halle (1951). *Preliminaries to speech analysis*. Cambridge, Massachusetts: MIT Press.

Johnson, C. D. (1971). Unbounded expressions in rules of stress and accent. *Glossa, 4*, 185–196.

Kahn, Daniel (1976). Syllable-based generalizations in English phonology. Bloomington: Indiana University Linguistics Club.

Kaisse, Ellen (1977). On the syntactic environment of a phonological rule. In W. Beach et al. (Eds.), *Papers from the 13th regional meeting*. Chicago: Chicago Linguistics Society. Pp. 173–185.

Kennedy, George (1953). Two tone patterns in Tangsic. *Language, 29*, 367–373.

Kenstowicz, Michael (1970). On the notation of vowel length in Lithuanian. *Papers in Linguistics, 3*, 73–114.

Kenstowicz, Michael (1971). Lithuanian phonology. *Studies in the Linguistic Sciences* 2, no. 2, 1–85. Department of Linguistics, University of Illinois.

Kenstowicz, Michael (1972). The morphophonemics of the Slovak noun. *Papers in Linguistics, 5*, 550–567.

Kenstowicz, Michael (1975). Rule application in pregenerative American phonology. In A. Koutsoudas (Ed.), *The application and ordering of grammatical rules*. The Hague: Mouton. Pp. 259–282.

Kenstowicz, Michael and Charles Kisseberth (1977). *Topics in phonological theory*. New York: Academic Press.

Kiparsky, Paul (1968a). How abstract is phonology? Bloomington: Indiana University Linguistics Club. Also in O. Fujimura (Ed.), *Three dimensions of linguistic theory*. Tokyo: TEC. Pp. 5–56.

Kiparsky, Paul (1968b). Linguistic universals and linguistic change. In E. Bach and R. Harms (Eds.), *Universals in linguistic theory*. New York: Holt.

Kiparsky, Paul (1968c). Metrics and morphophonemics in the Kalevala. In C. Gribble (Ed.), *Studies presented to Professor Roman Jakobson by his students.* Cambridge, Massachusetts: Slavica Publishers. Pp. 137–148.

Kiparsky, Paul (1971). Historical linguistics. In W. Dingwall (Ed.), *A survey of linguistic science.* Linguistics Program, University of Maryland. Pp. 577–642.

Kiparsky, Paul (1973). "Elsewhere" in phonology. In S. Anderson and P. Kiparsky (Eds.), *A Festschrift for Morris Halle.* New York: Holt. Pp. 93–106.

Kiparsky, Paul (1974). A note on the vowel features. *Papers from the 5th Annual Meeting.* Northeastern Linguistic Society, Harvard University. Pp. 162–171.

Kiparsky, Paul and Morris Halle (1977). Towards a reconstruction of the Indo–European accent. In L. Hyman (Ed.), *Studies in stress and accent.* Southern California Occasional Papers in Linguistics, 4, University of Southern California.

Kiparsky, V. (1962). *Russische historische Grammatik.* Heidelberg.

Kisseberth, Charles (1969). On the abstractness of phonology: The evidence from Yawelmani. *Papers in Linguistics, 1*, 248–282.

Kisseberth, Charles (1970). On the functional unity of phonological rules. *Linguistic Inquiry, 1*, 291–306.

Kisseberth, Charles (1973). On the alternation of vowel length in Klamath: A global rule. In M. Kenstowicz and C. Kisseberth (Eds.), *Issues and phonological theory.* The Hague: Mouton. Pp. 9–26.

Kisseberth, Charles and Mohammad Abasheikh (1976). Chimwi:ni prefix morphophonemics. *Studies in the Linguistic Sciences, 6:2*, 142–173. Department of Linguistics, University of Illinois.

Krejnovich, E. (1937). *Fonetika nivxskogo jazyka.* Leningrad.

Kuroda, S-Y. (1967). *Yawelmani phonology.* Cambridge, Massachusetts: MIT Press.

Labov, William (1970). The study of language in its social context. *Studium Generale, 23*, 30–87.

Ladefoged, Peter (1964). *A phonetic study of West African languages.* Cambridge: The University Press.

Ladefoged, Peter (1967). *Three areas of experimental phonetics.* London: Oxford University Press.

Ladefoged, Peter (1971). *Preliminaries to linguistic phonetics.* Chicago: University of Chicago Press.

Law, Howard (1958). Morphological structure of Isthmus Nahuat. *International Journal of American Linguistics, 24*, 108–129.

Leben, William (1973). *Suprasegmental phonology.* Unpublished Ph.D. dissertation, Massachusetts Institute of Technology.

Lehiste, Ilse (1970). *Suprasegmentals.* Cambridge, Massachusetts: MIT Press.

Lehn, Walter (1963). Emphasis in Cairo Arabic. *Language, 39*, 29–39.

Lehn, Walter and Peter Abboud (1965). *Beginning Cairo Arabic.* Austin: University of Texas Press.

Leslau, W. (1958). *The verb in Harari.* University of California Publications in Semitic Philology 21. Berkeley.

Lightner, Theodore (1972). *Problems in the theory of phonology: Russian phonology and Turkish phonology.* Linguistic Research, Inc.: Edmonton, Alberta.

Makkai, Valerie (1972). *Phonological theory.* New York: Holt.

Mandelbaum, David (1949). *Selected writings of Edward Sapir.* Berkeley: University of California Press.

McCawley, James (1967). Sapir's phonological representation. *International Journal of American Linguistics, 33*, 106–111.

McCawley, James (1968). *The phonological component of a grammar of Japanese*. The Hague: Mouton.

McCawley, James (1972). The role of notation in generative phonology. In M. Gross et al. (Eds.), *The formal analysis of natural languages*. The Hague: Mouton. Pp. 51–62.

Matteson, Esther (1965). *The Piro (Arawakan) language*. University of California Publications in Linguistics 42. Berkeley and Los Angeles: University of California Press.

Meeussen, Achiel (1959). *Essai de grammaire rundi*. Tervuren, Musée Royal du Congo Belge.

Mitchell, T. F. (1956). *An introduction to Egyptian Colloquial Arabic*. London: Oxford University Press.

Morin, Yves and Joyce Friedman (1971). *Phonological grammar tester. Underlying theory.* Natural Language Studies 10. University of Michigan Phonetics Laboratory, Ann Arbor.

Moulton, William (1947). Juncture in Modern Standard German. *Language, 23*, 212–226. Reprinted in Martin Joos (Ed.), *Readings in linguistics I*. Chicago: University of Chicago Press, 1957. Pp. 208–214.

Newman, Stanley (1944). *Yokuts language of California*. Viking Fund Publications in Anthropology 2. New York.

Newman, Stanley (1947). Bella Coola I: Phonology. *International Journal of American Linguistics, 13*, 129–134.

Newton, B. (1972). *The generative interpretation of dialect: A study of modern Greek phonology*. London: Cambridge University Press.

Ohala, John (1972). Physical models in phonology. *Proceedings of the 7th International Congress of Phonetic Sciences*. The Hague: Mouton. Pp. 1166–1171.

Onn, Farid (1976). *Aspects of Malay phonology and morphology*. Unpublished Ph.D. dissertation, University of Illinois.

Orr, Carolyn (1962). Ecuador Quichua phonology. In B. Elson (Ed.), *Studies in Ecuadorian Indian languages I*. Norman, Oklahoma: Summer Institute of Linguistics. Pp. 60–77.

Piggot, G. (1971). Some implications of Algonquian palatalization. *Odawa Language Project*, Anthropological Series 9. University of Toronto, Department of Anthropology. Also in E. Cook and J. Kaye (Eds.), *Linguistic studies of native Canada*. Vancouver, University of British Columbia Press, 1978.

Pike, Kenneth (1948). *Tone languages*. Ann Arbor: University of Michigan Press.

Polivanov, E. (1930). La perception des sons d'une langue étrangère. *Travaux du Cercle Linguistique de Prague, 4*, 79–96.

Popova, T. V. (1972). Paradigmatičeskije konsonantyje rjady čeredovany v jugo-zapadnyx ukrainskix dialektax (na materiale govora s. sadžava). In G. Klepikova (Ed.), *Karpatskaja dialektologia i onomastika*. Moscow. Pp. 179–239.

Postal, Paul (1968). *Aspects of phonological theory*. New York: Harper and Row.

Powlison, Paul (1962). Palatalization portmanteaus in Yagua. *Word, 18*, 280–299.

Pulgram, Ernst (1970). *Syllable, word, nexus, cursus*. The Hague: Mouton.

Pyle, Charles (1970). West Greenlandic Eskimo and the representation of vowel length. *Papers in Linguistics, 3*, 115–146.

Pyle, Charles (1971). *The treatment of length in generative phonology*. Unpublished Ph.D. dissertation, University of Illinois.

Robins, R. H. and Natalie Waterson (1952). Notes on the phonetics of the Georgian word. *Bulletin of the School of Oriental and African Studies, 14*, 55–72. University of London.

Rodegem, F. M. (1970). *Dictionnaire Rundi-français*. Tervuren, Musée Royal de l'Afrique Centrale.

Rogava, G. and Z. Keraseva (1966). *Grammatika adygejskogo jazyka*. Krasnodar, Majkop.

Ross, John (1972). A reanalysis of English word stress. In M. Brame (Ed.), *Contributions to generative phonology*. Austin: University of Texas Press. Pp. 229–323.

Sapir, Edward (1915). Notes on Judeo–German phonology. In D. Mandelbaum (Ed.), *Selected writings of Edward Sapir*. Berkeley: University of California Press. Pp. 252–272.

Sapir, Edward (1925). Sound patterns in language. *Language 1*, 37–51. Reprinted in Joos (1957), 19–25; and Makkai (1972), 13–21.

Sapir, Edward (1929). Male and female forms of speech in Yana. In D. Mandelbaum (Ed.), *Selected writings of Edward Sapir*. Berkeley: University of California Press. Pp. 206–212.

Sapir, Edward (1933). The psychological reality of phonemes. In Mandelbaum (1949), 46–60; and in Makkai (1972), 22–31.

Saxton, Dean and Lucille Saxton (1969). *Papago and Pima to English Dictionary*. Tucson: University of Arizona Press.

Schachter, Paul and Victoria Fromkin (1968). *A phonology of Akan*. Working Papers in Phonetics 9. University of California, Los Angeles.

Schane, Sanford (1968). *French phonology and morphology*. Cambridge, Massachusetts: The MIT Press.

Schane, Sanford (1976). Noncyclic English word stress. In D. Goyvaerts and G. Pullum (Eds.), *Essays on the sound pattern of English*. Ghent: E. Story Scientia.

Schenker, Alexander (1966). *Beginning Polish, Vol. 1*. New Haven: Yale University Press.

Schultz-Lorentzen, C. W. (1945). *A grammar of the West Greenlandic language*. Meddelelser om Grønland 129.

Scott, N. C. (1957). Notes on the pronunciation of Sea Dayak. *Bulletin of the School of Oriental and African Studies*, *20*, 509–512. University of London.

Scott, N. C. (1964). Nasal consonants in Land Dayak (Bukar-Sadong). In D. Abercrombie (Ed.), *In honour of Daniel Jones*. London:Longmans.

Selkirk, Elisabeth (1972). *The phrase phonology of English and French*. Unpublished Ph.D. dissertation, Massachusetts Institute of Technology.

Selkirk, Elisabeth (1974). French liaison and the X̄ notation. *Linguistic Inquiry*, *5*, 573–590.

Sherzer, Joel (1970). Talking backwards in Cuna: The sociological reality of phonological descriptions. *Southwestern Journal of Anthropology*, *26*, 343–353.

Skousen, Royal (1975). *Substantive evidence in phonology*. The Hague: Mouton.

Skorik, P. (1961). *Grammatika chukotskogo jazyka*. Moscow: Akademia Nauk.

Stahlke, Herbert (1975). Some problems with binary features for tone. In R. Herbert (Ed.), *Proceedings of the 6th Conference on African Linguistics*, 210–226.

Stampe, David (1972). How I spent my summer vacation. Unpublished manuscript.

Stewart, J. (1967). Tongue root position in Akan vowel harmony. *Phonetica*, *16*, 185–205.

Topping, Donald (1968). Chamorro vowel harmony. *Oceanic Linguistics*, *7*, 67–79.

Trubetzkoy, N. S. (1939). *Grundzuge der Phonologie. Travaux du Cercle Linguistique de Prague*. English translation by C. Baltaxe, Los Angeles: University of California Press, 1969.

Vennemann, Theo (1974). Words and syllables in natural generative grammar. In T. Bruck et al. (Eds.), *Papers from the parasession on natural phonology*. Chicago: Chicago Linguistics Society. Pp. 346–374.

Vennemann, Theo and Peter Ladefoged (1971). Phonetic features and phonological features. *Working Papers in Phonetics 21*, 13–24. University of California, Los Angeles.

Waterhouse, V. (1949). Learning a second language first. *International Journal of American Linguistics*, *15*, 106–109.

Wells, Rulon (1949). Automatic alternation. *Language*, *25*, 99–116.

Welmers, William (1973). *African language structures*. Los Angeles: University of California Press.

Wonderly, W. (1951). Zoque I, II, III, IV. *International Journal of American Linguistics*, *17*, 1–9, 105–123, 137–162, 235–251.

Zeps, V. (1963). The meter of the so-called trochaic Latvian folksongs. *International Journal of Slavic Linguistics and Poetics, 7,* 123–128.

Zimmer, Karl (1975). Some thoughts on likely phonologies for non-ideal speakers. In R. Grossman et al. (Eds.), *Papers from the parasession on functionalism.* Chicago: Chicago Linguistics Society. Pp. 556–567.

Zwicky, Arnold (1970). Greek letter variables and the Sanskrit *ruki* class. *Linguistic Inquiry*, *1*, 549–555.

Zwicky, Arnold (1972). Note on a hierarchy in English. In R. Stockwell and R. Macaulay (Eds.), *Linguistic change and generative theory.* Bloomington: Indiana University Press. Pp. 295–301.

Zwicky, Arnold (1973). The strategy of generative phonology. In W. Dressler and F. Mareš (Eds.), *Phonologica 1972.* München: Wilhelm Fink Verlag.

Language Index

449

Subject Index

453